Fine Handmade

TABLE GLASSWARE

by

1949-1953

The Cambridge Glass Company

Cambridge, Ohio, U. S. A.

The current values in this book should be used only as a guide. They are not intended to set prices, which vary from one section of the country to another. Auction prices as well as dealer prices vary greatly and are affected by condition as well as demand. Neither the Author nor the Publisher assumes responsibility for any losses that might be incurred as a result of consulting this guide.

FOREWORD

This study aid for Cambridge glass represents the combined efforts of a large group of dedicated, hard working and generous members of the National Cambridge Collectors, Inc.

National Cambridge Collectors, Inc., was incorporated in 1973 as a non-profit educational organization, dedicated to the preservation and collection of the products of the Cambridge Glass Co., of Cambridge, Ohio. The objective of the organization is to establish a permanent museum in or near Cambridge for the purpose of display and study of this fine hand-made glassware.

The Cambridge Glass Co. did not issue a new catalog of their products each year. Instead, their method was to issue a complete catalog occasionally and then to keep their customers current with production additions, changes or deletions by the issuance of Circular Letters. If a product addition was involved, the Circular Letter would be supplemented by additional catalog pages which the customer could insert into their original catalog.

The catalog that has been reprinted in this volume is an example of the foregoing methods. The following is a listing of the sequence of additions that we have been able to reconstruct for this catalog.

June, 1949	- Original catalog consisting of pages 1 through 148.
August, 1949	- 8A-F, 149-152, 153A-B.

Additions came quite frequently during the last half of 1949 and early 1950. By September of 1950 a major revision was made to the catalog Index. This Index included the following additional pages:

2A, 40A-D, 50A-D, 90A-E, 106A, 108A-B, 114A-B, 116A, 142A-L, 148A-D, 152C-D, 153, 154, 154A, 155, 156, 157, 157A-E, 158 through 167.

Month (?), 1951	- 100A, 114C-D.
May, 1952	- 36A-D, 100B.
August, 1952	- 157F-G.
October, 1952	- 36H (36E through G had been added between May and October).

In October, 1953, a new Price List was issued which included prices for the items and patterns which are shown on pages:

2B, 90F-I, 98A-B, 148E-F, 154B-D, and 168 through 192.

After exhaustive search of all available material such as the Price Lists, Circular Letters, and advertising materials, we believe this catalog to be complete for the period of June, 1949 through 1953.

If you, the reader, are using this reprint to date specific items of Cambridge glass, we would remind you that items appearing on the original pages could have been introduced at any time prior to June, 1949. The items appearing on any of the subsequent pages could possibly be only a new color or decorative treatment. With these guidelines, it is still possible to very closely date many of the lines and variations such as Pristine (page 8A), Cambridge Rose (page 100A) or Rondo (page 189).

We are hopeful that you enjoy using this catalog reprint as much as we have enjoyed bringing it to you. If you should desire more information and knowledge of this beautiful glassware, we encourage you to seek membership in

National Cambridge Collectors, Inc.

P. O. Box 416,   CAMBRIDGE, OHIO   43725

The Cambridge Glass Company

INDEX

NOTE
This index is not an original Cambridge Glass Co. document. It is a compilation of information from various items of Cambridge Glass origin.

Cambridge, Ohio - - - U.S.A.

STEMWARE

GOLD DECORATION

ROCK CRYSTAL

ROCK CRYSTAL (Cont.)

CAPRICE

300—9 oz.
Goblet

300—6 oz. Tall
Sherbet

300—6 oz.
Low Sherbet

300—3 oz.
Cocktail

300—4½ oz.
Claret

300—1 oz.
Cordial

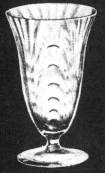

300 2—12 oz.
Ftd. Tumbler o

300—2½ oz.
Wine

300—4½ oz. Oyster
Cocktail

300—5 oz. Ftd.
Tumbler

21—6½ in. B & B Plate
22—8½ in. Salad Plate
23—7½ in. Salad Plate
24—9½ in. Dinner Plate

13—3½ in. Coaster

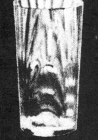

310—12 oz. Ice Tea

40—Ind. Sugar & Cream

129—6½ in. 3 pc.
Mayonnaise Set

17—Cup & Saucer

38—Sugar & Cream

39—3 pc. Sugar & Cream Set

CAPRICE

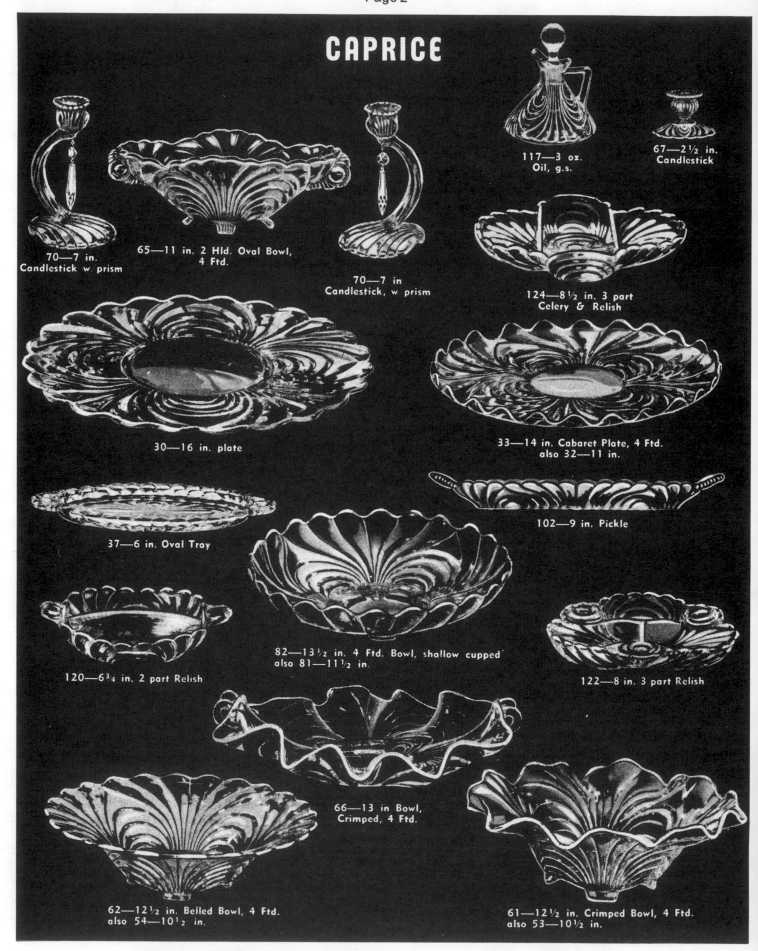

70—7 in. Candlestick w prism

65—11 in. 2 Hld. Oval Bowl, 4 Ftd.

70—7 in Candlestick, w prism

117—3 oz. Oil, g.s.

67—2½ in. Candlestick

124—8½ in. 3 part Celery & Relish

30—16 in. plate

33—14 in. Cabaret Plate, 4 Ftd. also 32—11 in.

37—6 in. Oval Tray

102—9 in. Pickle

120—6¾ in. 2 part Relish

82—13½ in. 4 Ftd. Bowl, shallow cupped also 81—11½ in.

122—8 in. 3 part Relish

66—13 in Bowl, Crimped, 4 Ftd.

62—12½ in. Beiled Bowl, 4 Ftd. also 54—10½ in.

61—12½ in. Crimped Bowl, 4 Ftd. also 53—10½ in.

Caprice

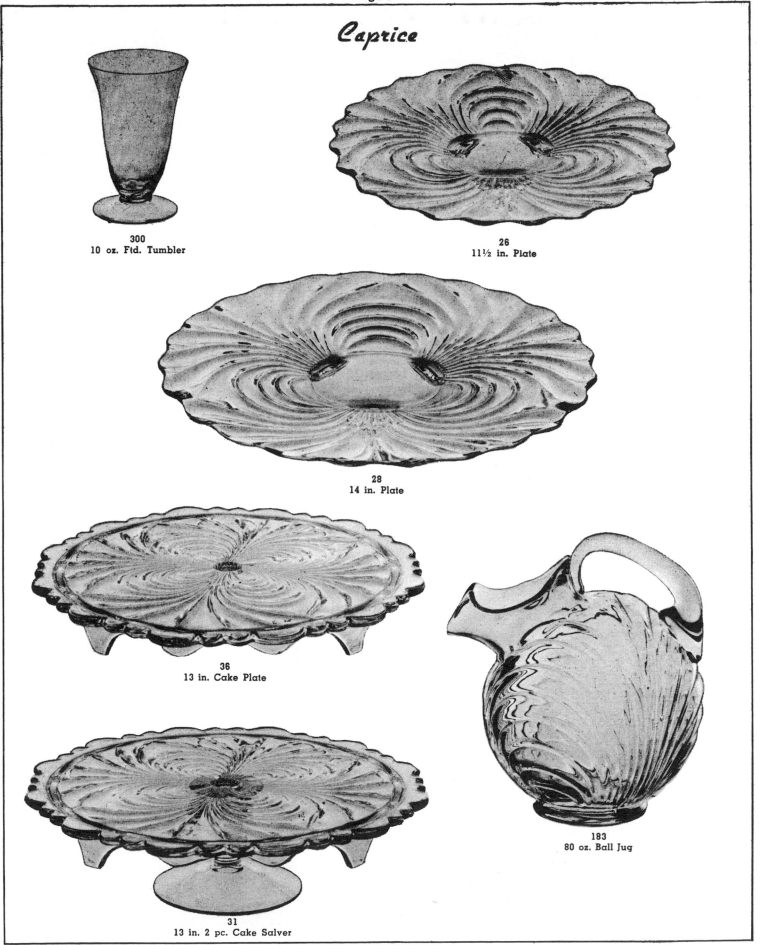

300
10 oz. Ftd. Tumbler

26
11½ in. Plate

28
14 in. Plate

36
13 in. Cake Plate

183
80 oz. Ball Jug

31
13 in. 2 pc. Cake Salver

CAPRICE

301
Goblet

301
Sherbet

301
Cocktail

301
Claret

301
Cordial

301
Wine

301
Low Cocktail

301
Juice

301
Ice Tea

CAPRICE

214 215 216 3 pc.
Ash Tray Set

216—5 in. Ash Tray

215—4 in. Ash Tray

214—3 in. Ash Tray

213—2¾ in.
3 Ftd. Ash Tray

646—5 in. Candlestick

165—6 in. 3 Ftd.
Candy Box & Cover

208—Cigarette Box &
Cov. 4½ x 3½ in.
also 207—3½ in. x 2¼ in.

152—6 in. 2 Hld. Lemon Plate

96—Salt & Pepper Shaker

131—8 in. Low Ftd. Plate

130—7 in. Low Ftd. Comport

154—6 in. 2 Hld. Bonbon,
Square

133—6 in. Low Ftd.
Bonbon, Square

151—5 in. 2 Hld. Jelly

136—7 in. Tall Comport

647—2 lite Candlestick

1338—3 lite Candlestick

MOUNT VERNON

1—10 oz. Goblet

2—6½ oz. Tall Sherbet

26—3½ oz. Cocktail

27—3 oz. Wine

87—1 oz. Ftd. Cordial

20—12 oz. Ftd. Tumbler

3—10 oz. Ftd. Tumbler

21—5 oz. Ftd. Tumbler

22—3 oz. Ftd. Tumbler

31—4½ in. Fruit Saucer

5—8½ in. Salad Plate
also 19—6⅜ in. B & B Plate

9 Covered Urn

23—Fingerbowl
23—Fingerbowl Plate (19)

7—Cup & Saucer

PRISTINE

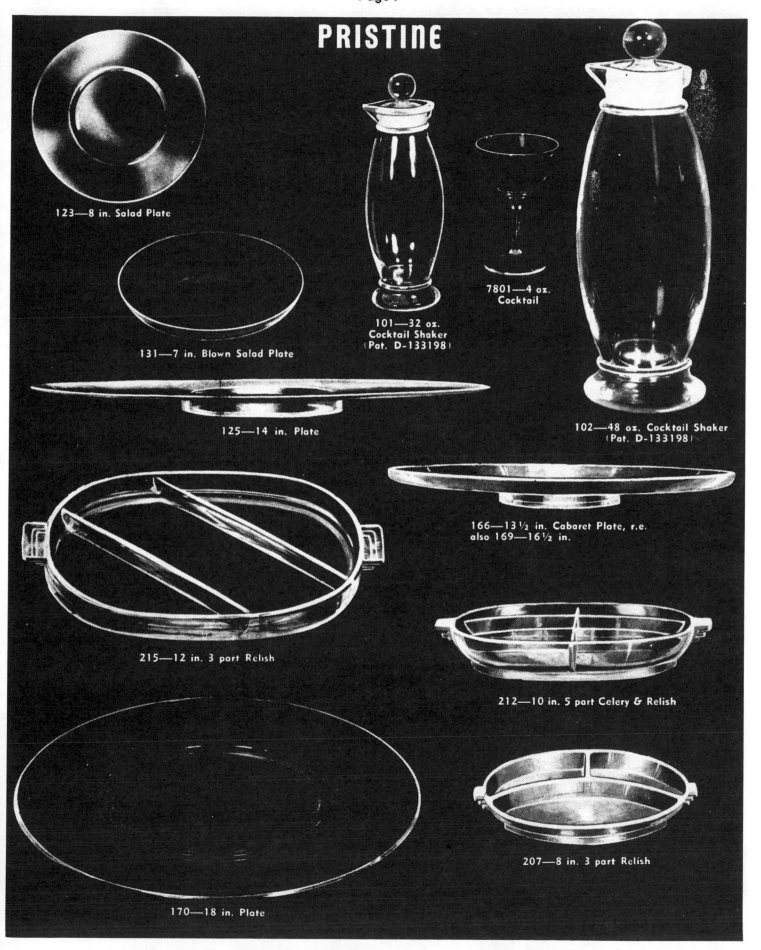

123—8 in. Salad Plate

131—7 in. Blown Salad Plate

101—32 oz. Cocktail Shaker (Pat. D-133198)

7801—4 oz. Cocktail

102—48 oz. Cocktail Shaker (Pat. D-133198)

125—14 in. Plate

166—13½ in. Cabaret Plate, r.e. also 169—16½ in.

215—12 in. 3 part Relish

212—10 in. 5 part Celery & Relish

207—8 in. 3 part Relish

170—18 in. Plate

PRISTINE

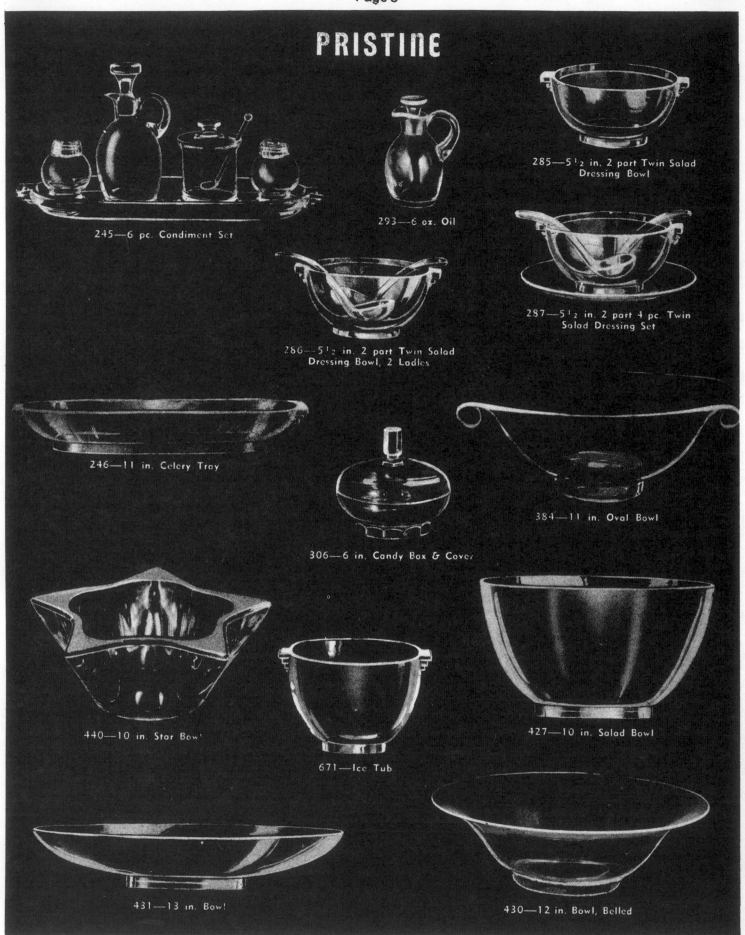

245—6 pc. Condiment Set

293—6 oz. Oil

285—5½ in. 2 part Twin Salad Dressing Bowl

287—5½ in. 2 part 4 pc. Twin Salad Dressing Set

286—5½ in. 2 part Twin Salad Dressing Bowl, 2 Ladles

246—11 in. Celery Tray

306—6 in. Candy Box & Cover

384—11 in. Oval Bowl

440—10 in. Star Bowl

671—Ice Tub

427—10 in. Salad Bowl

431—13 in. Bowl

430—12 in. Bowl, Belled

PRISTINE

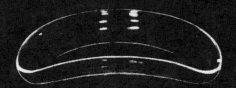

454—8 in. Crescent Salad Plate

103—7 in. 3 part Candy Box & Cover

300—6 in. 3 Ftd. Candy Box & Cover

477—9½ in. Corn Dish or Fickle

151—3 oz. Mustard & Cover

531—7 in. Tall Comport

533—5½ in. Low Comport

147—8 oz. Marmalade & Cover

532—6 in. Tall Comport

533—3 pc. Mayonnaise Set

PRISTINE

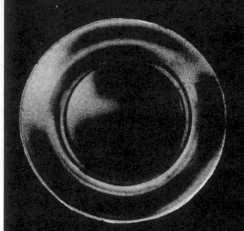

555—7½ in. Salad Plate

298—7 oz. Marmalade & Cover
also
295—3 oz. Mustard & Cover

1534—5 in. Blown Nappy

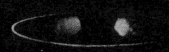

1535—6½ in. Blown Nappy

556—8 in. Salad Plate
668—6 in. B & B Plate
810—9½ in. Dinner Plate

922—Cream Soup and Saucer

1491—5½ in. 4 pc.
Twin Salad Dressing Set

933—Cup and Saucer

1532—3 pc. Mayonnaise Set

253—Individual Sugar and Cream

138—Sugar and Cream

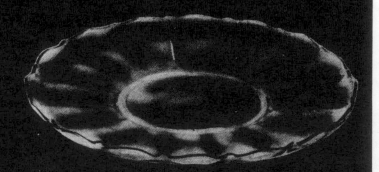

1397—13½ in. Plate, Cabaret

PRISTINE

41
2 pc. Frappe Set

506
4 in. Candelabrum

454
8 in. Crescent Salad Plate
(revised)

426
8 in. Salad Bowl

747
Cigarette Box and Cover
(4½ x 3½ in.)

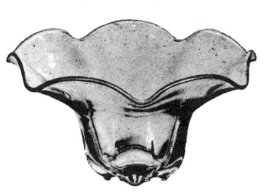

569
9 in. Crimped Vase

1359
10½ in. Bowl

1496
11½ in. Cheese and Cracker

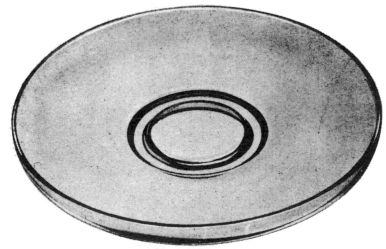

126
13½ in. Gardenia Bowl

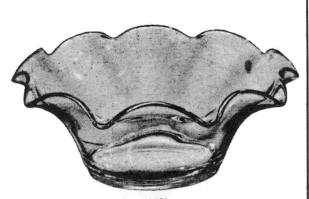

1351
10½ in. Bowl, Crimped

PRISTINE

254
Sugar and Cream

925
A D Cup & Saucer

604
8 in. Ftd. Bud Vase

466
6½ in. Baked Apple

381
8½ in. Rim Soup

248
11 in. Celery

306
6 in. Candy Box and Cover
Cut knob

281
5½ in. 3 pc. Mayonnaise Set

223
10 in. 3 part Bowl

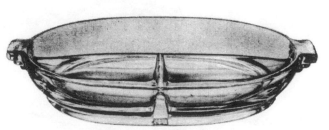

214
10 in. 3 part Relish

PRISTINE

11 oz. Goblet

6 oz. Tall Sherbet

6 oz. Low Sherbet

1 oz. Cordial

5 oz. Oyster Cocktail

3½ oz. Cocktail

4½ oz. Claret

3 oz. Wine

12 oz. Ftd. Ice Tea

5 oz. Ftd. Tumbler

5 in. Blown Comport
(3700)

Finger Bowl & Plate

Pristine

436
13 in. 2 pc. Sea Food Server

437
13 in. 2 pc. Flower Center

361
3 pc. Salt & Pepper Set
(Chrome Tops)

425
11½ in. 3 pc. Relish

424
13½ in. 2 pc. Sandwich Set

Pristine

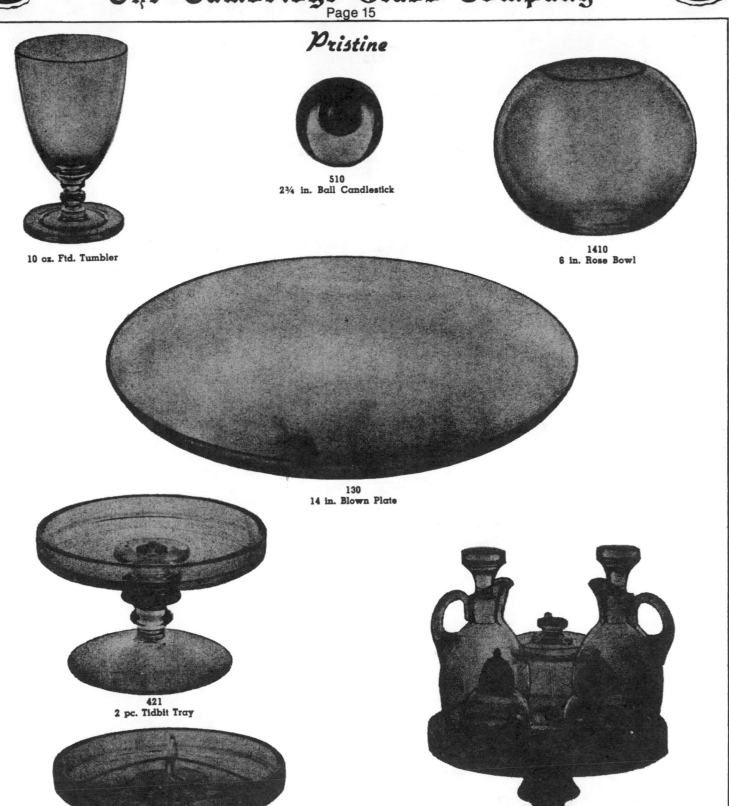

10 oz. Ftd. Tumbler

510
2¾ in. Ball Candlestick

1410
6 in. Rose Bowl

130
14 in. Blown Plate

421
2 pc. Tidbit Tray

432
9 pc. Caster Set

428
7 in. 2 pc. Relish

Pristine

442
3 pc. Tidbit Set

436/1902
8 pc. Shrimp Server

443
3 pc. Tidbit Set

Pristine

1497
6 in. 2 Part Relish

208
8 in. Oval Dish

247
11½ in. Celery

461
10½ in. Shallow
Cupped Bowl

1498
8 in. 3 Part Relish

P: 418—12 in.
5 Part Celery & Relish

419—12 in. 2 Pc. Relish
also
419—12 in. 6 Part Relish
(no center cup)

435
7½ in. 2 Hdl. Bowl

1495
11½ in. 2 Hdl.
Cake Plate

Cambridge Circle

3796
Goblet

3796
16 oz. Ice Tea

3796
Sherbet

3796
Cocktail

3796
5 oz. Ftd. Tumbler

3796
7 in. Salad Plate

3796
1 oz. Cordial

3400

3400 4—12 in. 4 Ftd. Bowl, Flared

3400/52—5½ in. Butter and Cover

3400/35—11 in. 2 Hld. Plate

3400/62—8½ in. Salad Plate
3400/176—7½ in. Salad Plate

3400 45—11 in. 4 Ftd. Bowl, fancy edge

3400/90—6 in. 2 Hdl. 2 part Relish

3400/48—13 in. Bowl, 4 Ftd.
crimped, shallow

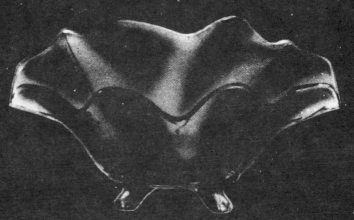

3400 160—12 in. 4 Ftd. Bowl,
oblong, fancy edge

3500

3500/54—6½ in. 2 Hld.
Low Ftd. Comport

3500/5—8½ in. Salad Plate
also
3500/167—7½ in. Salad Plate

3500/69—6½ in. Relish,
no handle, 3 part

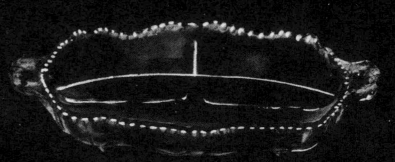

3500/64—10 in. Relish, 2 Hdl., 3 part, 4 Ftd.

3500 148—6 in. Comport

3500 101—5⅜ in. Comport,
Blown

3500 161—8 in. Ftd. Plate

MATCHED BARSEMBLE
Lattice
(1)

497
14 oz. Hiball

497
12 oz. Hiball

321
12 oz. O.F. Cocktail

321
9 oz. O.F. Cocktail

7801
4 oz. Cocktail

7801
5 oz. Whiskey Sour

7801
1 oz. Pousse Cafe

321
1½ oz. Whiskey

26 oz. Decanter
(Polished-in Stopper)

P. 101
Cocktail Shaker

3900/114
32 oz. Martini Mixer

P. 671
Ice Tub

MATCHED BARSEMBLE
Swirl
(23)

497
14 oz. Hiball

497
12 oz. Hiball

321
12 oz. O.F. Cocktail

321
9 oz. O.F. Cocktail

7801
4 oz. Cocktail

7801
5 oz. Whiskey Sour

7801
1 oz. Pousse Cafe

321
1½ oz. Whiskey

P. 92
26 oz. Decanter
(Polished-in Stopper)

P. 101
Cocktail Shaker

3900/114
32 oz. Martini Mixer

P. 671
Ice Tub

MATCHED BARSEMBLE
Star
(4)

497
14 oz. Hiball

497
12 oz. Hiball

321
12 oz. O.F. Cocktail

321
9 oz. O.F. Cocktail

7801
4 oz. Cocktail

7801
5 oz. Whiskey Sour

7801
1 oz. Pousse Cafe

321
1½ oz. Whiskey

P. 92
26 oz. Decanter
(Polished-in Stopper)

P. 101
Cocktail Shaker

3900/114
32 oz. Martini Mixer

P. 671
Ice Tub

MATCHED BARSEMBLE
Fleur-De-Lis
(6)

497
14 oz. Hiball

497
12 oz. Hiball

321
12 oz. O.F. Cocktail

321
9 oz. O.F. Cocktail

7801
4 oz. Cocktail

7801
5 oz. Whiskey Sour

7801
1 oz. Pousse Cafe

321
1½ oz. Whiskey

P. 92
26 oz. Decanter
(Polished-in Stopper)

P. 101
Cocktail Shaker

3900/114
32 oz. Martini Mixer

P. 671
Ice Tub

MATCHED BARSEMBLE
ETCHED VICHY

497
14 oz. Hiball

497
12 oz. Hiball

321
12 oz. O.F. Cocktail

321
9 oz. O.F. Cocktail

7801
4 oz. Cocktail

7801
5 oz. Whiskey Sour

7801
1 oz. Pousse Cafe

321
1½ oz. Whiskey

P. 92
26 oz. Decanter
(Polished-in Stopper)

P. 101
Cocktail Shaker

3900/114
32 oz. Martini Mixer

P. 671
Ice Tub

CANDLESTICKS

2—4 in. Star

646—5 in.

647—6 in. 2 lite

628—3½ in.

1338—6 in. 3 lite

1357—6 in. 3 lite

1307—5 in. 3 lite

Caprice 67—2½ in.

Marthc 494—4 in.

Martha 495—5½ in.—2 lite

1457—6½ in.—3 lite

P.492—1¾ in.
Square

P.493—2¾ in.
Square

P.495—3¾ in.
Square

P.499—6½ in.
Calla Lilly

P.500—6½ in (Leaf)

CANDELABRA

648—6 in.

3121—7½ in.

C.70—7 in.

1440—9 in.

1356—7 in. 2 lite

1268—6 in. 2 lite

M.496—6½ in. 2 lite

CANDELABRA

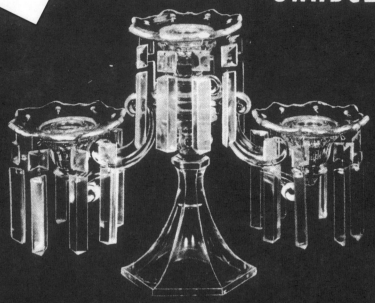

652—10 in. 3 lite
Pat. No. 1,977,816

1568—11 in. 5 lite

1545—5½ in. 3 lite

1358—7 in. 3 lite

1458—7½ in. 3 lite

1569—8½ in. 5 lite

EPERGNES

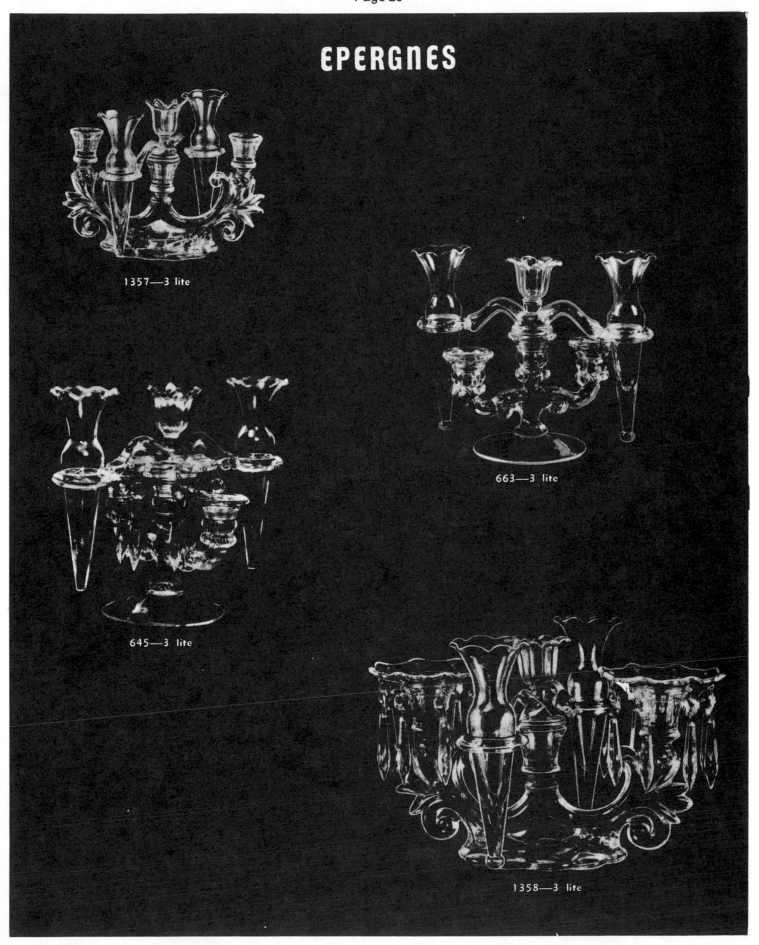

1357—3 lite

663—3 lite

645—3 lite

1358—3 lite

HURRICANE LAMPS

1603—10 in.

1617—9 in.

1613—17 in.

DECANTERS

3400 92—32 oz. g.s.

3400 119—12 oz. g.s.

Mt. V. 47—
11 oz. g.s.

Mt. V. 52—40 oz. g.s.

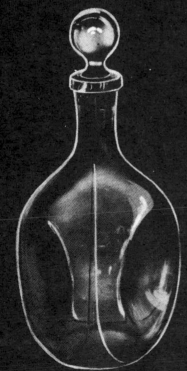

1070—36 oz. Pinch, g.s.

1379—26 oz. Colonial, g.s.

1321—28 oz. Ftd., g.s.

FLOWER ARRANGERS

2899—2¼ in. Flower Block

2899—3 in. Flower Block

2899—3½ in. Flower Block

518—8½ in. Figure Flower Holder

1114—6 in. Figure Flower Holder

1136—9 in. Figure Flower Holder
(Heron)

1138—8½ in. Figure Flower Holder
(Sea-Gull)

PUNCH SETS

Martha—15 pc. Punch Set
1—478 15 in. Bowl (10 qts.)
12—488 5 oz. Cups
1—111 ladle
1—129 18 in. Tray

Pristine—15 pc. Punch Set
1—476 11½ in. Bowl (5 qts.)
12—486 5 oz. Cups
1—485 ladle
1—169 16½ in. Tray

PUNCH SETS

3200—15 pc. Punch Set
1—3200 12½ in. Bowl & Foot (6 qts.)
12—3200 5 oz. Cup
1—111 Ladle

1221—15 pc. Swan Punch Set
1—1221 16 in. Bowl and Base (5 qts.)
12—1221 5 oz. Cup
1—485 Ladle

SALT AND PEPPER SHAKERS

Caprice 96

1203—Individual

1177

1465—Cut Flower

1476

Mt. V. 89

1258

1262

1525—Open Salt

P. 360—Regular
also P. 358—Individual

SMOKERS' ITEMS

P.731—6½ in. Star Ash Tray

P.726—5 in. Star Ash Tray

1040—3 in.
Swan Ash Tray

P.721—2½ in.
Ash Tray, Square

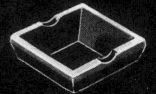

P.725—3½ in.
Ash Tray, Square

P.732—3½ in.
Ash Tray, Square

P.728—5 pc.
Ash Tray Set

C.214—3 in.
Ash Tray

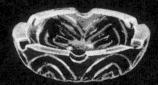

C.215—4 in.
Ash Tray

C.216—5 in.
Ash Tray

C. 214 215 216—3 pc.
Ash Tray Set

390—6 in. Ash Tray

C.213—2¾ in. 3 Ftd.
Ash Tray w placecard holder

C.207—3½x2½ in.
Cigarette Box & Cover

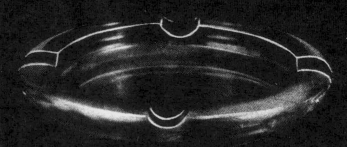

391—6 in. Ash Tray

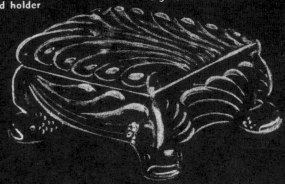

C.208—4½x3½ in. Cigarette Box & Cover

SMOKERS' ITEMS

Sea Shell 33—4 in. 3 Ftd.
Ash Tray

Sea Shell 34—4 in. 3 Ftd.
Ash Tray

P.733—3 in. Ash Tray

P.734—4½ in. Ash Tray

P.735—6 in. Ash Tray

C.207 213—5 pc.
Cigarette Set in
White Display Box

P.733 4 5—3 pc. Ash Tray Set

SS34—8 pc.
Ash Tray Set in
White Display Box

"Stackaway" Ash Tray Set

SWANS

1040—3 in.

1042—6½ in.

1041—4½ in.

1043—8½ in.

1044—10 in.

TUMBLERS

321—1½ oz.

321—7 oz. O.F. Cocktail

497—14 oz.

497—12 oz.

497—10 oz.

498—5 oz.

498—10 oz.

498—12 oz.

498—14 oz.

1206—12 oz.

3143/50—13 oz.
Gyro Optic

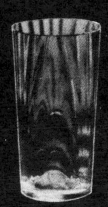

Caprice 310—12 oz.

3143/51—12 oz.
Gyro Optic

TUMBLERS

400—14 oz.

400—12 oz.

400—9 oz.

400—5 oz.

400—3 oz. Cocktail

400—6 oz. Fruit Salad

(THESE NUMBER 400 ITEMS HAVE SOLID BALL BOTTOM)

400—1 oz. Cordial

1341—1 oz.

3400 92—2½ oz.

1070—2 oz. Pinch

319—9 oz. Georgian

Mt.V.59—14 oz.

Mt.V.58—10 oz. Tall

Mt.V.51—10 oz. Table

Mt.V.57—7 oz. O.F. Cocktail

Mt.V.56—5 oz.

Mt.V.55—2 oz.

VASES

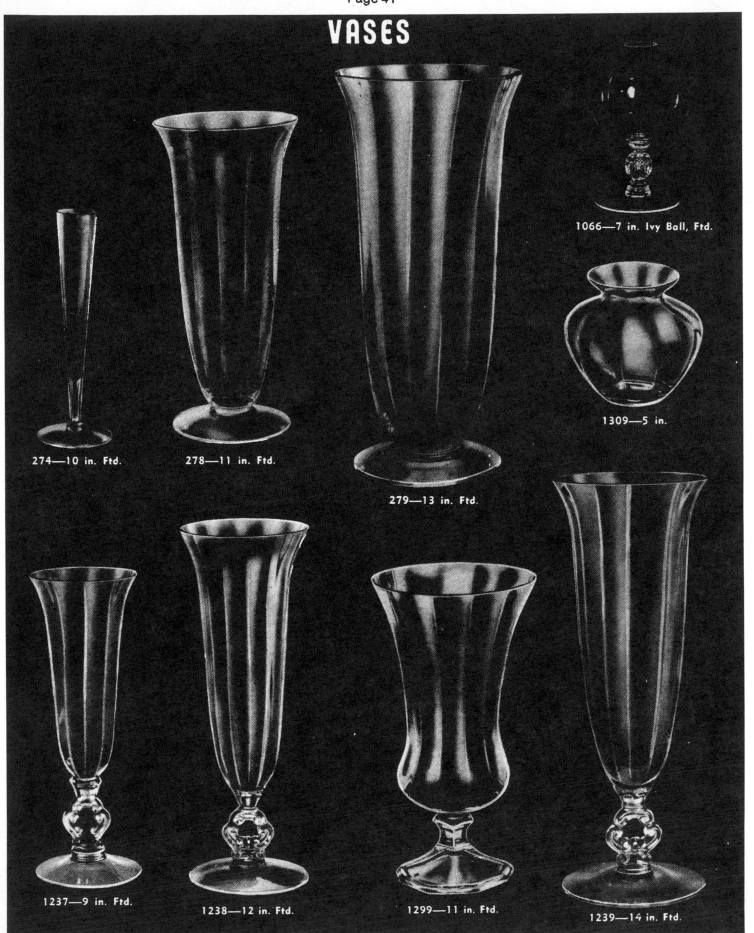

1066—7 in. Ivy Ball, Ftd.

274—10 in. Ftd.

278—11 in. Ftd.

279—13 in. Ftd.

1309—5 in.

1237—9 in. Ftd.

1238—12 in. Ftd.

1299—11 in. Ftd.

1239—14 in. Ftd.

Cambridge, Ohio - - - U. S. A.

VASES

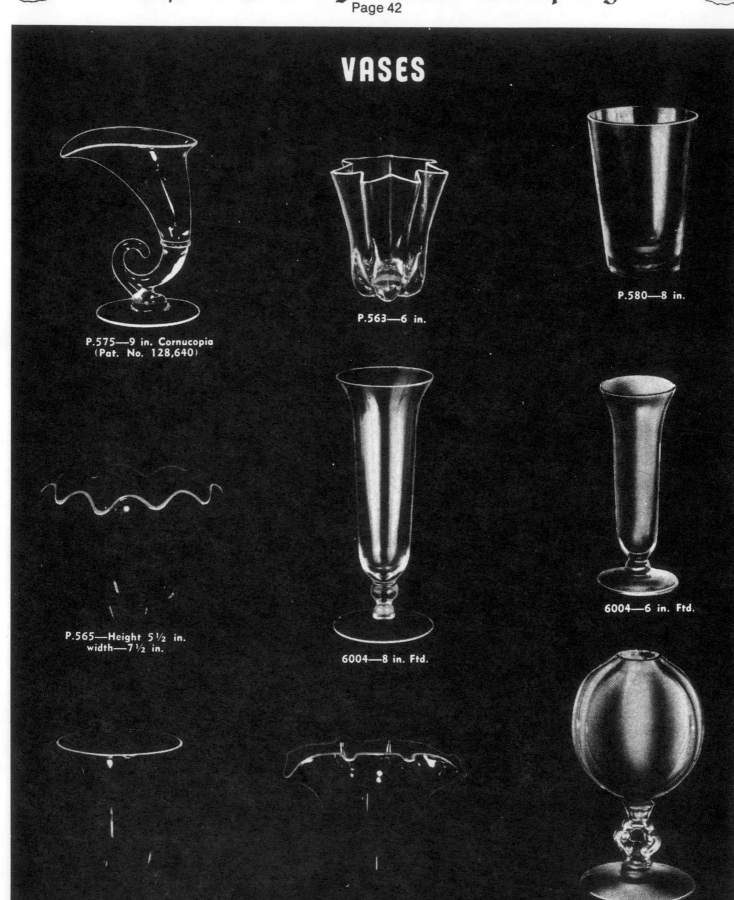

P.575—9 in. Cornucopia
(Pat. No. 128,640)

P.563—6 in.

P.580—8 in.

P.565—Height 5½ in.
width—7½ in.

6004—8 in. Ftd.

6004—6 in. Ftd.

P.572—6 in.

P.568—Height 6 in.
Width—7 in.

1236—7½ in. Ivy Ball
Ftd.

MISCELLANEOUS

M.157—Deviled Egg Plate

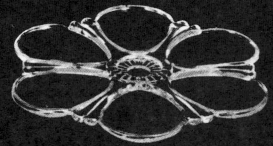

M.156—Oyster Plate

1570—Cheese Preserver Jar & Cover

M.156/69—Oyster Plate & Sauce Cup

V.134—10½ in. Cake Salver

1571—Cheese Preserver Jar & Cover

MISCELLANEOUS

Caprice 13—3½ in. Coaster

604—5¼ in. Coaster

Mt. V. 70—3 in. Coaster

968—2 pc. Cocktail Icer

3121—5⅜ in.
Tall Comport (Blown)

1263—French Dressing
Bottle

Oil

Vinegar

Martha 250—Individual
Sugar and Cream

1—4½ in. Muddler

Martha 123—8½ in. Salad Plate
Martha 122—7½ in. Salad Plate

7966—2 oz
Sherry

3700—9 oz.
Goblet

Regency 10 oz.
Goblet

CROWN TUSCAN

SS 31—8 in. Oval Dish, 4 Ftd.

SS 18—10 in. 3 Ftd. Bowl

SS 11—7 in. Comport, Ftd.

SS 21—6 in. Ftd. Candy
Box & Cover

3011—9 in. Candlestick

SS 40—10 in. Flower or Fruit Center

SS 15—6 in. Comport, footed

CROWN TUSCAN

SS 10—5 in. Comport

SS 35—Cigarette Box & Cover
4½x3½ in.

647—6 in. 2 lite Candlestick

SS 33—4 in. 3 Ftd. Ash Tray

3400 91—8 in. 3 part Relish Tray

3400 4—12 in. Bowl, 4 Ftd

3500 57—8 in. 3 part
Candy Box & Cover

1040—3 in. Swan

1043—8½ in. Swan

CROWN TUSCAN

6004—6 in. Ftd.

6004—8 in. Ftd.

1237—9 in. Ftd.

1238—12 in. Ftd.

274—10 in. Ftd.

278—11 in. Ftd.

1236—7½ in. Ftd. Ivy Ball

Pristine 575—9 in. Cornucopia

1309—5 in.

ETCHINGS

3111—Goblet
E Candlelight

3775—Goblet
E Chantilly

3600—Goblet
E Chantilly

3625—Goblet
E Chantiliy

3121—Goblet
E Portia

3130—Goblet
E Portia

3500—Goblet
E Elaine

3121—Goblet
E Elaine

3122—Goblet
E Diane

3121—Goblet
E Rose Point

3500—Goblet
E Rose Point

3121—Goblet
E Wildflower

ROCK CRYSTAL

3121—Goblet
Achilles (698)

3500—Goblet
Adonis (720)

3700—Goblet
Ardsley (1005)

3750—Goblet
Bexley (1014)

3725—Goblet
Bijou (1011)

3725—Goblet
Cadet

3130—Goblet
Cordelia (812)

3500—Goblet
Croesus (722)

3778—Goblet
Deerfield (1033)

3750—Goblet
Euclid (1017)

3750—Goblet
Fuchsia (1019)

3130—Goblet
Glendale (1028)

Cambridge, Ohio - - - U. S. A.

ROCK CRYSTAL

3750—Goblet
Hanover (1015)

3139—Goblet
Juliana (997)

3700—Goblet
King Edward (821)

King George image

3139—Goblet
King George (1027)

3778—Goblet
Larchmont (1036)

3139—Goblet
Laurel Wreath

3700—Goblet
Laurel Wreath

7966—Goblet
Lexington (758)

3116—Goblet
Lucia (824)

3700—Goblet
Manor (1003)

3776—Goblet
Maryland (985)

3776—Goblet
Minuet (990)

ROCK CRYSTAL

3750—Goblet
Minton Wreath (1012)

3700—Goblet
Montrose (1004)

3725—Goblet
Plaza (1018)

3775—Goblet
Roxbury (1030)

3725—Goblet
Star (1016)

3700—Goblet
Tempo (1029)

3130—Goblet
Wedding Rose (9981)

P.101—32 oz. Cocktail
Shaker, Chesterfield
(952)

Windsor (500)

Celestial (600)

P.92—Decanter (1049)

P.92—Decanter (1043)

1379—Decanter (1041)

CAMBRIDGE SQUARE
PATENT PENDING

3797
Goblet

3797
Sherbet

3797
Cocktail

3797
Cordial

3797
Wine

3797
14 oz. Ice Tea

3797
5 oz. Juice

3798
Goblet

3798
Sherbet

3798
Cocktail

3798
Cordial

3798
Wine

3798
12 oz. Ice Tea

3798
5 oz. Juice

CAMBRIDGE SQUARE
PATENT PENDING

3797/16
4½ in. Dessert

3797/18
2 pc. Cocktail Icer

3797/22
7 in. Salad Plate

3797/24
9½ in. Tidbit Plate

3797/27
6½ in. Ind. Salad Bowl

3797/28
13½ in. Plate

3797/26
11½ in. Plate

3797/29
4 pc. Buffet Set

3797/34
7½ in. Ice Tub

3797/35
7½ in. Rose Bowl

3797/36
9½ in. Rose Bowl

CAMBRIDGE SQUARE

PATENT PENDING

3797/37
8 in. Oval Tray

3797/40
Ind. Sugar & Cream

3797/41
Sugar & Cream

3797/42
3 pc. Sugar & Cream Set
(Individual)

3797/47
8 in. Bon Bon

3797/48
10 in. Oval Dish

3797/49
9 in. Salad Bowl

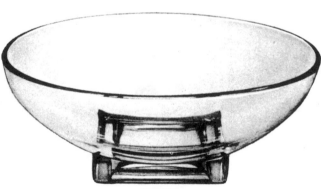

3797/57
11 in. Salad Bowl

3797/76
Salt & Pepper
w/chrome top

3797/67
Cupped Candlestick

3797/65
12 in. Oval Dish

CAMBRIDGE SQUARE
PATENT PENDING

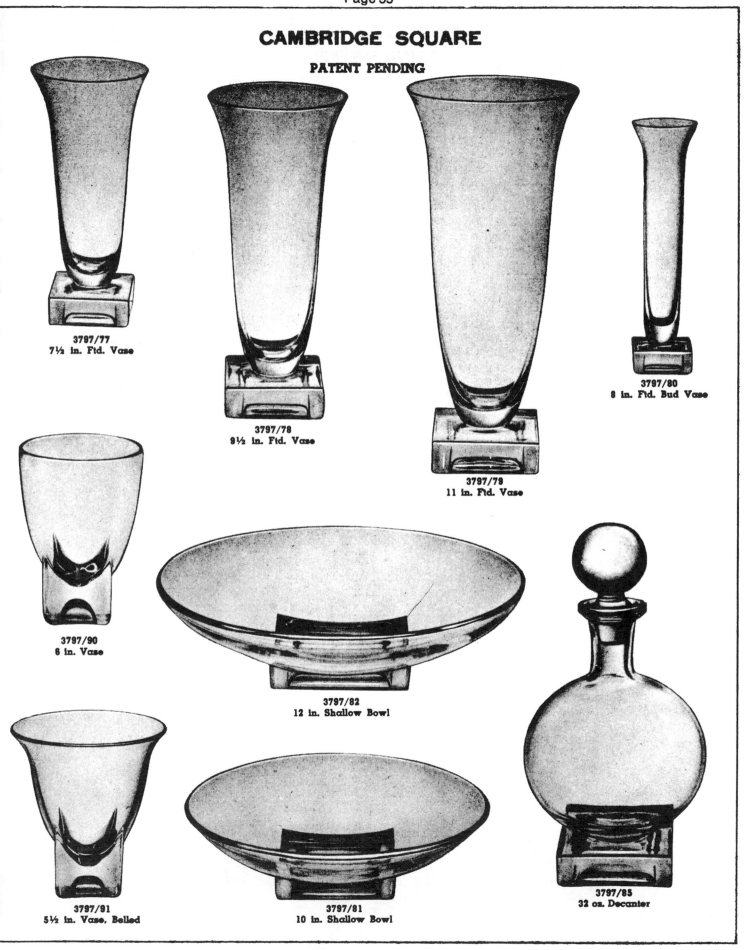

3797/77
7½ in. Ftd. Vase

3797/78
9½ in. Ftd. Vase

3797/79
11 in. Ftd. Vase

3797/80
8 in. Ftd. Bud Vase

3797/90
6 in. Vase

3797/82
12 in. Shallow Bowl

3797/85
32 oz. Decanter

3797/91
5½ in. Vase, Belled

3797/81
10 in. Shallow Bowl

CAMBRIDGE SQUARE
PATENT PENDING

Cordial Set
3797/87—7 Pc. Cordial Set

Wine Set
3797/88—7 Pc. Wine Set

CAMBRIDGE SQUARE
PATENT PENDING

3797/100
4½ oz. Oil

3797/104
4 pc. Condiment Set
(37/100/76)

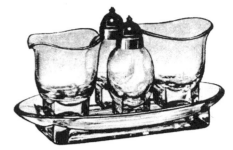

3797/105
5 pc. Condiment Set
(37/40/76)

3797/120
6½ in. 2 Part Relish

3797/125
8 in. 3 Part Relish

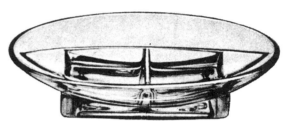

3797/126
10 in. 3 Part Celery & Relish

3797/127
Mayonnaise Bowl

3797/127/445
Mayonnaise & Ladle

3797/129
3 pc. Mayonnaise Set

3797/150
6½ in. Ash Tray

3797/151
3½ in. Ash Tray

3797/164
7 in. Bon Bon

3797/165
Candy Box & Cover

CAMBRIDGE SQUARE
PATENT PENDING

3797/35/493
3 Pc. Table Centerpiece

3797/35
7½ in. Rose Bowl

3797/493
2¾ in. Candlestick

3797/47/492
3 Pc. Table Center Piece

3797/47
8 in. Bowl

3797/492
1¾ in. Candlestick

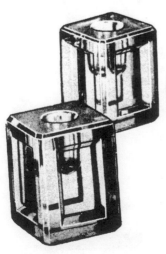

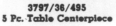

3797/36/495
5 Pc. Table Centerpiece

3797/36
9½ in. Rose Bowl

3797/495
3¾ in. Candlestick

Cambridge Square
Designed for Present Day Living
PATENT PENDING

3797/15
Tea Cup & Saucer

3797/15
Tea Cups, Stacked

3797/92
5 in. Vase, belled

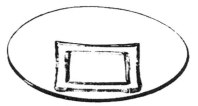

3797/54
6 in. Comport

3797/17
Coffee Cup & Saucer

3797/17
Coffee Cups, Stacked

3797/20
6 in. Bread & Butter Plate

3797/23
7 in. Dessert or Salad Plate

3797/25
9½ in. Dinner or Luncheon Plate

3797/103
11 in. Celery

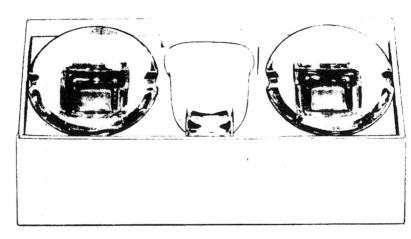

3797/152
3 Pc. Smoker Set in Display Box

3797/68
2 Pc. Hurricane Lamp

3900 LINE—CORINTH

17
Cup & Saucer

20
6½ in. Bread & Butter Plate

22
8 in. Salad Plate

19
2 pc. Mayonnaise Set

24
10½ in. Dinner Plate

26
12 in. 4 Ftd. Plate

28
11½ in. Ftd. Bowl

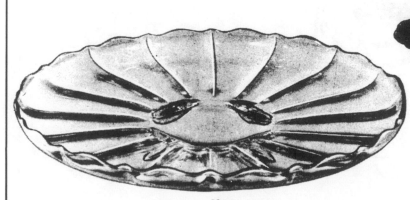

33
13 in. 4 Ftd. Torte Plate, r.e.

34
11 in. 2 Handled Bowl

3900 LINE—CORINTH

35
13½ in. 2 Handled Cake Plate

40
Ind. Sugar & Cream

41
Sugar & Cream

54
10 in. 4 Ftd. Bowl, flared

62
12 in. 4 Ftd. Bowl, flared

65
12 in. 4 Ftd. Oval Bowl

67
5 in. Candlestick

72
6 in. 2 lite Candlestick

74
6 in. 3 lite Candlestick

3900 LINE—CORINTH

75
Epergne

99
4 oz. Bitter Bottle with tube

100
6 oz. Oil, g. s.

111
4 pc. Mayonnaise Set

114
32 oz. Martini Jug

115
76 oz. Jug

115
13 oz. Tumbler

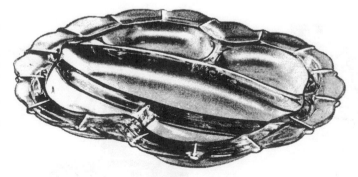

120
12 in. 5 part Celery & Relish

123
7 in. Relish or Pickle

124
7 in. 2 part Relish

3900 LINE—CORINTH

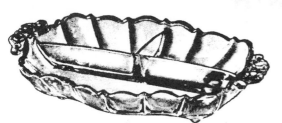

125
9 in. 3 part Celery & Relish

129
3 pc. Mayonnaise Set

126
12 in. 3 part Celery & Relish

130
7 in. 2 handled Ftd. Bonbon

131
8 in. 2 handled Ftd. Bonbon Plate

136
5½ in. Comport

165
Candy Box & Cover

1177
Salt & Pepper Shaker

671
Ice Bucket with Chrome Handle
Chrome Ice Tongs (long)

166
14 in. Plate, r.e.

3900 LINE CORINTH

| 9 oz. Goblet | 6 oz. Tall Sherbet | 6 oz. Low Sherbet | 3 oz. Cocktail |

| 2½ oz. Wine | 4½ oz. Claret | 4½ oz. Oyster Cocktail | 1 oz. Cordial |

| 5 oz. Ftd. Tumbler | 5 in. Blown Comport | 10 oz. Ftd. Tumbler | 12 oz. Ftd. Ice Tea |

Cambridge, Ohio - - - U. S. A.

40-A

3900 LINE CORINTH

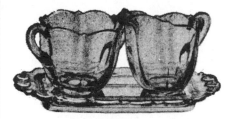

39
3 pc. Sugar and Cream Set

37
Sugar and Cream Tray

38
3 pc. Sugar and Cream Set
(Individual)

135
5 in. Comport

135
13½ in. Cheese and Cracker

18
2 pc. Cocktail Icer

68
5 in. Candlestick

124
7 in. 2 part Relish
(Revised)

244
7 pc. Condiment Set

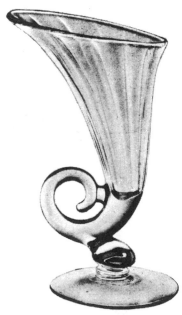

575
10 in. Cornucopia Vase

245
6 pc. Condiment Set

3900 LINE—CORINTH
JUGS AND TUMBLERS

3900/114
32 oz. Martini

3900/117
20 oz. Gyro Optic

3900/117
5 oz. Gyro Optic

3900/117
20 oz. Optic

3900/117
5 oz. Optic

3900/118
32 oz. Optic

3900/118
5 oz. Optic

3900/118
32 oz. Gyro Optic

3900/118
5 oz. Gyro Optic

3900 LINE—CORINTH
JUGS AND TUMBLERS

3900/115
76 oz. Optic

3900/115
13 oz. Optic

3900/116
80 oz., Ball
Optic

3900/116
13 oz. Optic

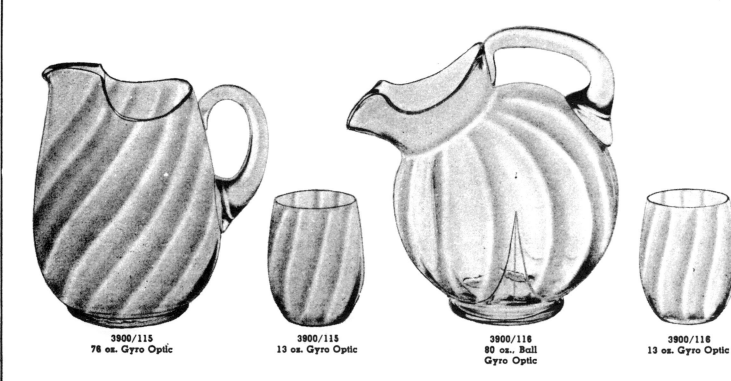

3900/115
76 oz. Gyro Optic

3900/115
13 oz. Gyro Optic

3900/116
80 oz., Ball
Gyro Optic

3900/116
13 oz. Gyro Optic

4000 LINE - CASCADE

Patent Nos. Des. 140826-141034

1
Goblet

2
Sherbet

3
Cocktail

9
12 oz. Ftd. Tumbler

11
5 oz. Ftd. Tumbler

14
12 oz. Tumbler

15
5 oz. Tumbler

16
4½ in. Fruit Saucer

17
Cup & Saucer

21
6½ in. Bread & Butter Plate

26
11½ in. 4 Ftd. Plate

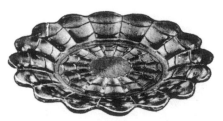

22
8½ in. Salad Plate

41
Sugar & Cream

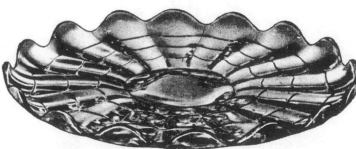

33
14 in. 4 Ftd. Torte Plate, r.e.

4000 LINE - CASCADE
Patent Nos. Des. 140826-141034

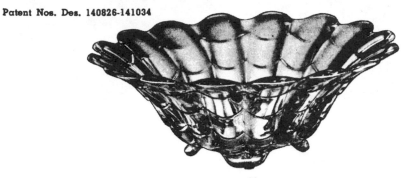

54
10 in. 4 Ftd. Bowl, flared

62
12½ in. 4 Ftd. Bowl, flared

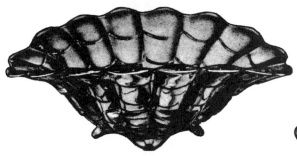

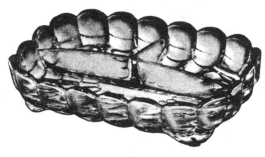

65
12 in. 4 Ftd. Oval Bowl

67
5 in. Candlestick

64
10 in. 3 part Celery & Relish

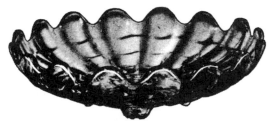

81
10½ in. 4 Ftd. Bowl, shallow

72
6 in. 2 lite Candlestick

96
Salt & Pepper Shaker

89
6½ in. Relish or Pickle

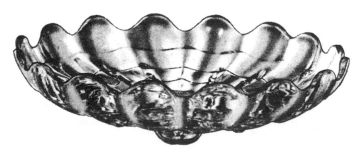

90
6½ in. 2 part Relish

82
13 in. 4 Ftd. Bowl, shallow

4000 LINE - CASCADE
Patent Nos. Des. 140826-141034

129
3 pc. Mayonnaise Set

130
7 in. 2 Handled Ftd. Bonbon

131
8 in. 2 Handled Ftd. Bonbon Plate

165
Candy Box & Cover

136
5½ in. Comport

214
4½ in. Ash Tray

164
6 in. Bonbon

215
6 in. Ash Tray

574
9½ in. Vase, oval

216
8 in. Ash Tray

214/215/216
3 pc. Ash Tray Set

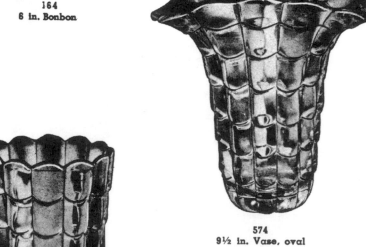

573
9½ in. Vase

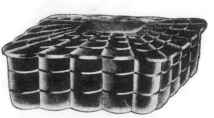

616
Cigarette Box & Cover

671
Ice Tub
Chrome Ice Tongs

4000 LINE - CASCADE

Patent Nos. Des. 140826-141034

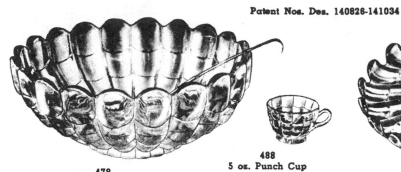

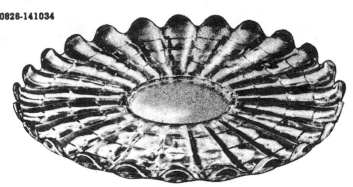

478
15 in. Punch Bowl (10 qts.)
Chrome Punch Ladle

488
5 oz. Punch Cup

479
21 in. Plate

216
Base for Punch Bowl

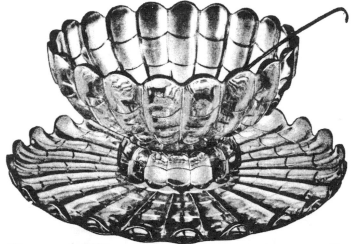

478/479/488/216
16 Pc. Punch Set With Chrome Ladle

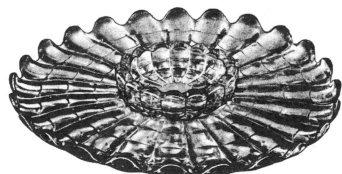

479/216
21 in. 2 Pc. Sunday Evening
or Buffet Supper Set

478/488/216
15 pc. Punch Set With Chrome Ladle

Rose Point

3900/17
Cup & Saucer

3900/20
6½ in. Bread & Butter Plate

3900/22
8 in. Salad Plate

3900/19
2 pc. Mayonnaise Set

3900/24
10½ in. Dinner Plate

3900/26
12 in. 4 Ftd. Plate

3900/28
11½ in. Ftd. Bowl

3900/33
13 in. 4 Ftd. Torte Plate, R. E.

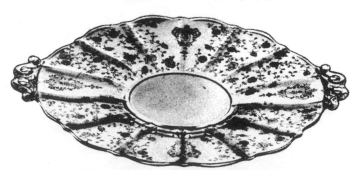

3900/34
11 in. 2 Handled Bowl

3900/35
13½ in. 2 Handled Cake Plate

3900/40
Ind. Sugar & Cream

3900/41
Sugar & Cream

Cambridge, Ohio - - - U. S. A.

Rose Point

3900/54
10 in. 4 Ftd. Bowl, flared

3900/67
5 in. Candlestick

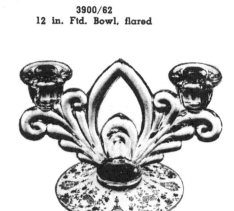

3900/62
12 in. Ftd. Bowl, flared

3900/65
12 in. 4 Ftd. Oval Bowl

3900/72
6 in. 2 lite Candlestick

3900/111
4 pc. Mayonnaise Set.

3900/74
6 in. 3 lite Candlestick

3900/100
6 oz. Oil, g. s.

3900/115
13 oz. Tumbler

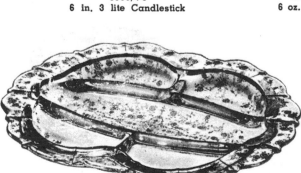

3900/120
12 in. 5 part Celery & Relish

3900/123
7 in. Relish or Pickle

3900/124
7 in. 2 part Relish

Rose Point

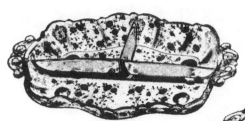

3900/125
9 in. 3 part Celery & Relish

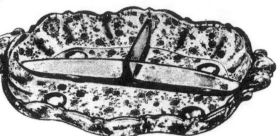

3900/126
12 in. 3 part Celery & Relish

3900/129
3 pc. Mayonnaise Set

3900/130
7 in. 2 handled Ftd. Bonbon

3900/131
8 in. 2 handled Ftd. Bonbon Plate

3900/136
5½ in. Comport

3900/165
Candy Box & Cover

3900/166
14 in Plate, r. e.

3900/671
Ice Bucket with Chrome Handle

3900/1177
Salt & Pepper Shaker (doz. pr.)

968
2 pc. Cocktail Icer

3121
5⅜ in. Blown Comport

Rose Point

274
10 in. Bud Flower Holder

278
11 in Ftd. Flower Holder

279
13 in. Ftd. Flower Holder

1238
12 in. Ftd. Flower Holder

1309
5 in. Globe Flower Holder

1237
9 in. Ftd. Flower Holder

1299
11 in Ftd. Flower Holder

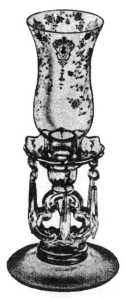

1603
Hurricane Lamp

1617
Hurricane Lamp

6004
6 in. Ftd. Flower Holder

6004
8 in. Ftd. Flower Holder

Rose Point

3121
10 oz. Goblet

3121
6 oz. Tall Sherbet

3121
3 oz. Cocktail

3121
10 oz. Ftd. Tumbler

3121
12 oz. Ftd. Ice Tea

3121
6 oz. Low Sherbet

3121
4½ oz. Oyster Cocktail

3121
4½ oz. Claret

3121
5 oz. Ftd. Tumbler

3121
3½ oz. Wine

3121
1 oz. Cordial

3121
5 oz. Cafe Parfait

3121
5⅜ in. Blown Comport

Rose Point

3500
10 oz. Goblet

3500
7 oz. Tall Sherbet

3500
3 oz. Cocktail

3500
12 oz. Ftd. Ice Tea

3500
10 oz. Ftd. Tumbler

3500
7 oz. Low Sherbet

3500
4½ oz. Oyster Cocktail

3500
4½ oz. Claret

3500
5 oz. Ftd. Tumbler

3500
2½ oz. Wine

3500
1 oz. Cordial

3500
5 oz. Cafe Parfait

3500/101
5⅜ in. Blown Comport

Rose Point

3400/52
5 in. Butter & Cover

3400/71
3 in. 4 Ftd. Nut Cup

3400/91
8 in. 3 part Relish

3900/1177
Salt & Pepper Shaker
with Chrome Top

3900/38
3 pc. Sugar & Cream Set, Ind.

3900/39
3 pc. Sugar & Cream Set

3900/135
5 in. Comport

3900/135
13½ in. Cheese & Cracker

3900/575
10 in. Cornucopia Vase

3900/75
Epergne

Rose Point

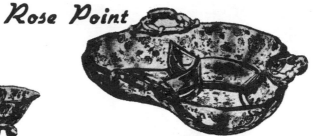

3400/52
5 in. Butter & Cover

3400/71
3 in. 4 Ftd. Nut Cup

3400/91
8 in. 3 part Relish

3900/1177
Salt & Pepper Shaker
with Chrome Top

3900/38
3 pc. Sugar & Cream Set, Ind.

3900/39
3 pc. Sugar & Cream Set

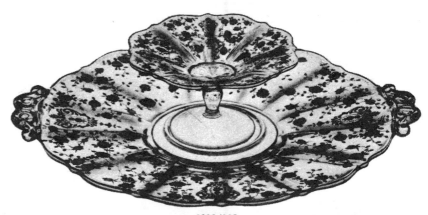

3900/135
5 in. Comport

3900/135
13½ in. Cheese & Cracker

3900/575
10 in. Cornucopia Vase

3900/75
Epergne

Rose Point

3500
10 oz. Goblet

3500
7 oz. Tall Sherbet

3500
3 oz. Cocktail

3500
12 oz. Ftd. Ice Tea

3500
10 oz. Ftd. Tumbler

3500
7 oz. Low Sherbet

3500
4½ oz. Oyster Cocktail

3500
4½ oz. Claret

3500
5 oz. Ftd. Tumbler

3500
2½ oz. Wine

3500
1 oz. Cordial

3500
5 oz. Cafe Parfait

3500/101
5⅜ in. Blown Comport

Rose Point

3900/68
5 in. Candlestick

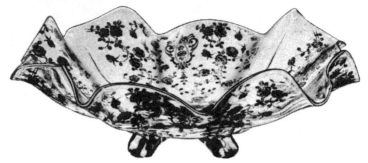

3400/48
11 in. 4 Ftd. Bowl,
Fancy edge

646
5 in. Candlestick

647
6 in. 2 lite Candlestick

3400/160
12 in. 4 Ftd. Bowl, Oblong

1338
6 in. 3 Lite Candlestick

3400/4
12 in. 4 Ftd. Bowl, Flared

Rose Point

3900/117
20 oz. Jug

3900/118
32 oz. Jug

3900/114
32 oz. Martini Jug

P.101
32 oz. Cocktail Shaker
Pat. D-133,198

3900/117
5 oz. Tumbler

7801
4 oz. Cocktail

3900/115
76 oz. Jug

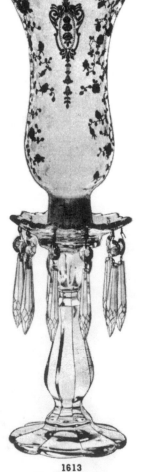

3900/116
80 oz. Ball Jug

1321
.28 oz. Ftd. Decanter

7966
2 oz. Sherry

1613
Hurricane Lamp

Rose Point

P. 721
2½ in. Ash Tray

P. 747
Cigarette Box & Cover

P. 728
5 pc. Ash Tray Set

3900/167
14 in. Plate

103
2 pc. Nite Set

3400/141
80 oz. Jug (not Optic)

1066
5⅜ in. Blown Candy Box & Cover

1066
5⅜ in. Blown Comport

Rose Point
No. 1948—9 Item Assortment

477
9½ in. Pickle

3500/15
Ind. Sugar & Cream

3400/1181
6 in. 2 Hdl. Plate

3400/90
6 in. 2 Part Relish

3500/55
6 in. 2 Hdl. Ftd. Basket

3500/69
6½ in. 3 part Relish

3400/1180
5¼ in. 2 Hdl. Bonbon

3500/54
6 in. 2 Hdl. Ftd. Bonbon

3500/161
8 in. 2 Hdl. Ftd. Plate

P.101
32 oz. Cocktail Shaker
(Pat. D-133,198)

3400/91
8 in. 3 part Relish

3500/57
8 in. 3 part Candy Box & Cover

Candlelight

3111
10 oz. Goblet

3111
7 oz. Tall Sherbet

3111
7 oz. Low Sherbet

3111
2½ oz. Wine

3111
3 oz. Cocktail

3111
4½ oz. Oyster Cocktail

3111
12 oz. Ftd. Ice Tea

3111
5 oz. Ftd. Tumbler

Candlelight

3776
9 oz. Goblet

3776
7 oz. Tall Sherbet

3776
7 oz. Low Sherbet

3776
2½ oz. Wine

3776
3 oz. Cocktail

3776
4½ oz. Oyster Cocktail

3776
12 oz. Ftd. Ice Tea

3776
5 oz. Ftd. Tumbler

3776
4½ oz. Claret

3776
1 oz. Cordial

3121
5⅜" Blown Comport

Candlelight

3900/19
2 pc. Mayonnaise Set

3900/17
Cup & Saucer

3900/20
6½ in. Bread & Butter Plate

3900/22
8 in. Salad Plate

3900/24
10½ in. Dinner Plate

3900/26
12 in. 4 Ftd. Plate

3900/33
13 in. 4 Ftd. Torte Plate, R. E.

3900/28
11½ in. Ftd. Bowl

3900/34
11 in. 2 Handled Bowl

3900/35
13½ in. 2 Handled Cake Plate

3900/40
Ind. Sugar & Cream

3900/41
Sugar & Cream

Candlelight

3900/54
10 in. 4 Ftd. Bowl, flared

3900/67
5 in. Candlestick

3900/62
12 in. Ftd. Bowl, flared

3900/65
12 in. 4 Ftd. Oval Bowl

3900/72
6 in. 2 lite Candlestick

3900/74
6 in. 3 lite Candlestick

3900/100
6 oz. Oil, g. s.

3900/111
4 pc. Mayonnaise Set

3900/115
13 oz. Tumbler

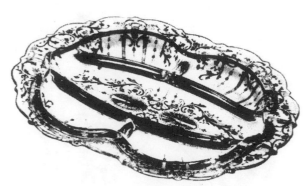

3900/120
12 in. 5 part Celery & Relish

3900/123
7 in. Relish or Pickle

3900/124
7 in. 2 part Relish

Candlelight

3900/125
9 in. 3 part Celery & Relish

3900/126
12 in. 3 part Celery & Relish

3900/129
3 pc. Mayonnaise Set

3900/130
7 in. 2 handled Ftd. Bonbon

3900/131
8 in. 2 handled Ftd. Bonbon Plate

3900/136
5½ in. Comport

3900/165
Candy Box & Cover

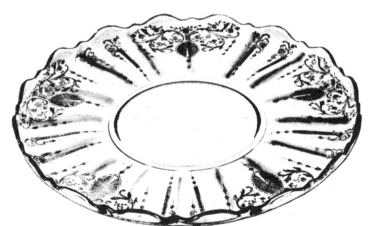

3900/166
14 in. Plate, r. e.

3900/1177
Salt & Pepper Shaker (doz. pr.)

3900/671
Ice Bucket with Chrome Handle

968
2 pc. Cocktail Icer

3121
5⅜ in. Blown Comport

274
10 in. Bud Flower Holder

Candlelight

278
11 in. Ftd. Flower Holder

279
13 in. Ftd. Flower Holder

1299
11 in. Ftd. Flower Holder

1309
5 in. Globe Flower Holder

1237
9 in. Ftd. Flower Holder

1238
12 in. Ftd. Flower Holder

6004
5 in. Ftd. Flower Holder

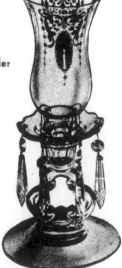

1603
Hurricane Lamp

1617
Hurricane Lamp

6004
8 in. Ftd. Flower Holder

1613
Hurricane Lamp

Chantilly

3779
9 oz. Goblet

3779
6 oz. Tall Sherbet

3779
6 oz. Low Sherbet

3779
3 oz. Cocktail

3779
2½ oz. Wine

3779
1 oz. Cordial

3799
4½ oz. Oyster Cocktail

3779
12 oz. Ftd. Ice Tea

3779
5 oz. Ftd. Tumbler

3779
4½ oz. Claret

Chantilly

3600
10 oz. Goblet

3600
7 oz. Tall Sherbet

3600
7 oz. Low Sherbet

3600
2½ oz. Cocktail

3600
2½ oz. Wine

3600
4½ oz. Claret

3600
4½ oz. Oyster Cocktail

3600
1 oz. Cordial

3600
12 oz. Ftd. Ice Tea

3600
5 oz. Ftd. Tumbler

Chantilly

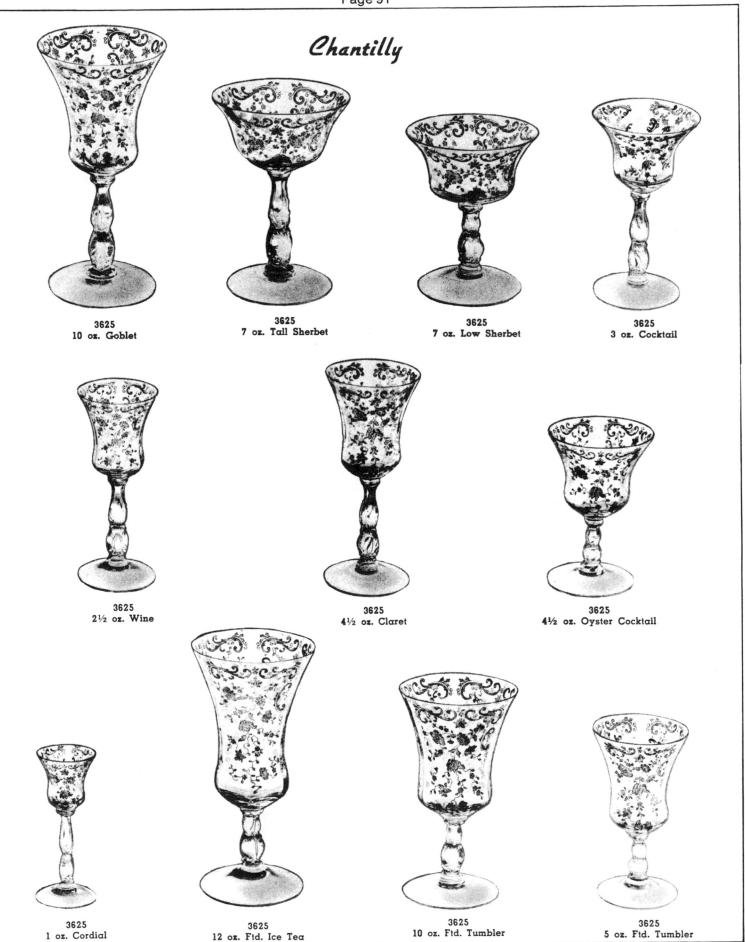

3625
10 oz. Goblet

3625
7 oz. Tall Sherbet

3625
7 oz. Low Sherbet

3625
3 oz. Cocktail

3625
2½ oz. Wine

3625
4½ oz. Claret

3625
4½ oz. Oyster Cocktail

3625
1 oz. Cordial

3625
12 oz. Ftd. Ice Tea

3625
10 oz. Ftd. Tumbler

3625
5 oz. Ftd. Tumbler

Chantilly

3775
10 oz. Goblet

3775
6 oz. Tall Sherbet

3775
6 oz. Low Sherbet

3775
3 oz. Cocktail

3775
2½ oz. Wine

3775
4½ oz. Claret

3775
4½ oz. Oyster Cocktail

3775
1 oz. Cordial

3775
12 oz. Ftd. Ice Tea

3775
10 oz. Ftd. Tumbler

3775
5 oz. Ftd. Tumbler

Chantilly

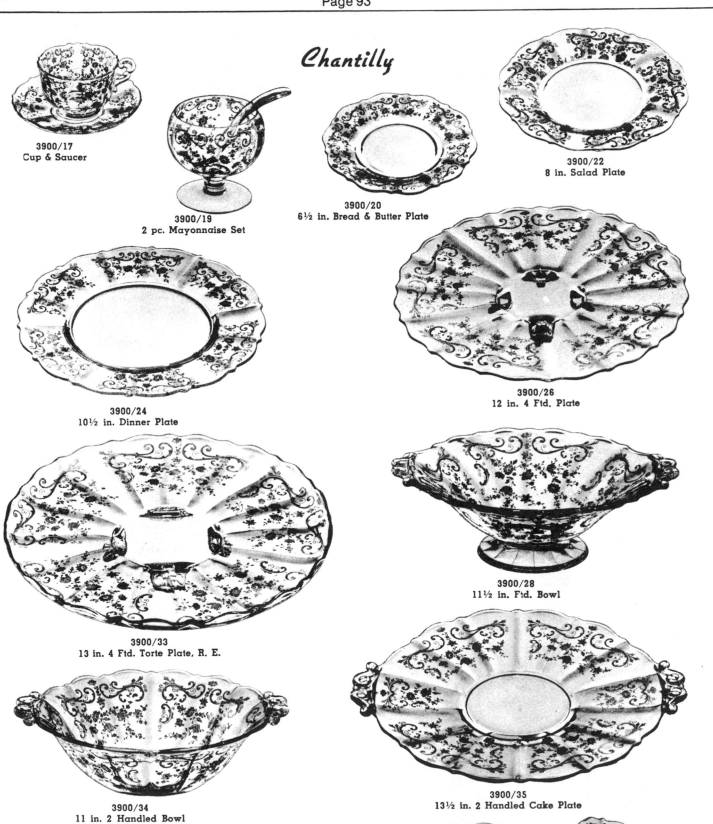

3900/17
Cup & Saucer

3900/19
2 pc. Mayonnaise Set

3900/20
6½ in. Bread & Butter Plate

3900/22
8 in. Salad Plate

3900/24
10½ in. Dinner Plate

3900/26
12 in. 4 Ftd. Plate

3900/33
13 in. 4 Ftd. Torte Plate, R. E.

3900/28
11½ in. Ftd. Bowl

3900/34
11 in. 2 Handled Bowl

3900/35
13½ in. 2 Handled Cake Plate

3900/40
Ind. Sugar & Cream

3900/41
Sugar & Cream

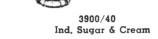

Chantilly

3900/54
10 in. 4 Ftd. Bowl, flared

3900/67
5 in. Candlestick

3900/62
12 in. Ftd. Bowl, flared

3900/65
12 in. 4 Ftd. Oval Bowl

3900/72
6 in. 2 lite Candlestick

3900/74
6 in. 3 lite Candlestick

3900/100
6 oz. Oil, g. s.

3900/111
4 pc. Mayonnaise Set

3900/115
13 oz. Tumbler

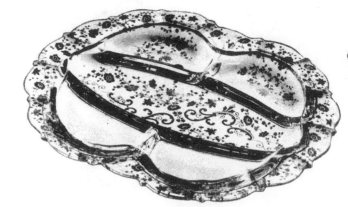

3900/120
12 in. 5 part Celery & Relish

3900/123
7 in. Relish or Pickle

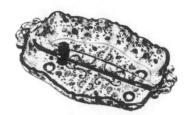

3900/124
7 in. 2 part Relish

Chantilly

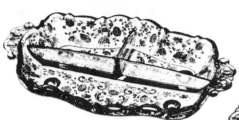

3900/125
9 in. 3 part Celery & Relish

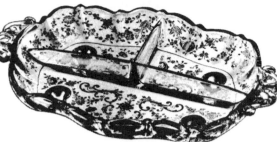

3900/126
12 in. 3 part Celery & Relish

3900/129
3 pc. Mayonnaise Set

3900/130
7 in. 2 handled Ftd. Bonbon

3900/131
8 in. 2 handled Ftd. Bonbon Plate

3900/136
5½ in. Comport

3900/165
Candy Box & Cover

3900/166
14 in. Plate, r. e.

3900/671
Ice Bucket with Chrome Handle

3900/1177
Salt & Pepper Shaker (doz. pr.)

968
2 pc. Cocktail Icer

3121
5⅜ in. Blown Comport

Chantilly

274
10 in. Bud Flower Holder

278
11 in. Ftd. Flower Holder

279
13 in. Ftd. Flower Holder

1237
9 in. Ftd. Flower Holder

1238
12 in. Ftd. Flower Holder

1309
5 in. Globe Flower Holder

1299
11 in. Ftd. Flower Holder

1603
Hurricane Lamp

1617
Hurricane Lamp

6004
8 in. Ftd. Flower Holder

6004
6 in. Ftd. Flower Holder

Diane

3122
9 oz. Goblet

3122
7 oz. Tall Sherbet

3122
7 oz. Low Sherbet

3122
3 oz. Cocktail

3122
2½ oz. Wine

3122
4½ oz. Claret

3122
4½ oz. Oyster Cocktail

3122
1 oz. Cordial

3122
12 oz. Ftd. Ice Tea

3122
9 oz. Ftd. Tumbler

3122
5 oz. Ftd. Tumbler

Diane

3900/17
Cup & Saucer

3900/19
2 pc. Mayonnaise Set

3900/20
6½ in. Bread & Butter Plate

3900/22
8 in. Salad Plate

3900/24
10½ in. Dinner Plate

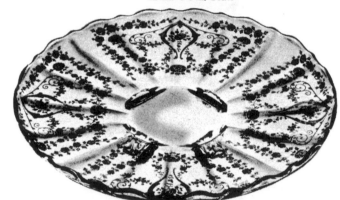

3900/26
12 in. 4 Ftd. Plate

3900/28
11½ in. Ftd. Bowl

3900/33
13 in. 4 Ftd. Torte Plate, R. E.

3900/34
11 in. 2 Handled Bowl

3900/35
13½ in. 2 Handled Cake Plate

3900/40
Ind. Sugar & Cream

3900/41
Sugar & Cream

Diane

3900/54
10 in. 4 Ftd. Bowl, flared

3900/67
5 in. Candlestick

3900/62
12 in. Ftd. Bowl, flared

3900/65
12 in. 4 Ftd. Oval Bowl

3900/100
6 oz. Oil, g. s.

3900/72
6 in. 2 lite Candlestick

3900/74
6 in. 3 lite Candlestick

3900/115
13 oz. Tumbler

3900/111
4 pc. Mayonnaise Set

3900/120
12 in. 5 part Celery & Relish

3900/123
7 in. Relish or Pickle

3900/124
7 in. 2 part Relish

Diane

3900/125
9 in. 3 part Celery & Relish

3900/126
12 in. 3 part Celery & Relish

3900/129
3 pc. Mayonnaise Set

3900/130
7 in. 2 handled Ftd. Bonbon

3900/131
8 in. 2 handled Ftd. Bonbon Plate

3900/136
5½ in. Comport

3900/165
Candy Box & Cover

3900/166
14 in. Plate, r. e.

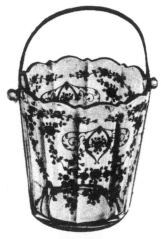

3900/671
Ice Bucket with Chrome Handle

3900/1177
Salt & Pepper Shaker (doz. pr.)

968
2 pc. Cocktail Icer

3121
5⅜ in. Blown Comport

Diane

274
10 in. Bud Flower Holder

278
11 in. Ftd. Flower Holder

279
13 in. Ftd. Flower Holder

1237
9 in. Ftd. Flower Holder

1238
12 in. Ftd. Flower Holder

1309
5 in. Globe Flower Holder

1299
11 in. Ftd. Flower Holder

1603
Hurricane Lamp

1617
Hurricane Lamp

6004
6 in. Ftd. Flower Holder

6004
8 in. Ftd. Flower Holder

Diane
No. 1948—9 Item Assortment

3400/1180
5¼ in. 2 Hdl. Bonbon

477
9½ in. Pickle

3400/1181
6 in. 2 Hdl. Plate

3500/15
Ind. Sugar & Cream

3400/90
6 in. 2 part Relish

3500/54
6 in. 2 Hdl. Ftd. Bonbon

3500/69
6½ in. 3 part Relish

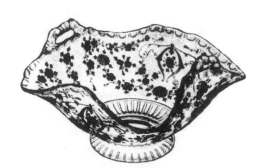

3500/55
6 in. 2 Hdl. Ftd. Basket

3500/161
8 in. 2 Hdl. Ftd. Plate

Elaine

3121
10 oz. Goblet

3121
6 oz. Tall Sherbet

3121
6 oz. Low Sherbet

3121
3 oz. Cocktail

3121
3½ oz. Wine

3121
4½ oz. Claret

3121
4½ oz. Oyster Cocktail

3121
1 oz. Cordial

3121
5 oz. Cafe Parfait

3121
12 oz. Ftd. Ice Tea

3121
10 oz. Ftd. Tumbler

3121
5 oz. Ftd. Tumbler

Elaine

3500/1
10 oz. Goblet

3500
7 oz. Tall Sherbet

3500
7 oz. Low Sherbet

3500
3 oz. Cocktail

3500
2½ oz. Wine

3500
4½ oz. Claret

3500
4½ oz. Oyster Cocktail

3500
1 oz. Cordial

3500
5 oz. Parfait

3500
12 oz. Ftd. Ice Tea

3500
10 oz. Ftd. Tumbler

3500
5 oz. Ftd. Tumbler

3500/101
5⅜ in. Tall Comport

Elaine

3900/17
Cup & Saucer

3900/19
2 pc. Mayonnaise Set

3900/20
6½ in. Bread & Butter Plate

3900/22
8 in. Salad Plate

3900/26
12 in. 4 Ftd. Plate

3900/24
10½ in. Dinner Plate

3900/33
13 in. 4 Ftd. Torte Plate, R. E.

3900/28
11½ in. Ftd. Bowl

3900/34
11 in. 2 Handled Bowl

3900/35
13½ in. 2 Handled Cake Plate

3900/40
Ind. Sugar & Cream

3900/41
Sugar & Cream

Elaine

3900/54
10 in. 4 Ftd. Bowl, flared

3900/67
5 in. Candlestick

3900/62
12 in. Ftd. Bowl, flared

3900/65
12 in. 4 Ftd. Oval Bowl

3900/72
6 in. 2 lite Candlestick

3900/74
6 in. 3 lite Candlestick

3900/100
6 oz. Oil, g. s.

3900/111
4 pc. Mayonnaise Set

3900/115
13 oz. Tumbler

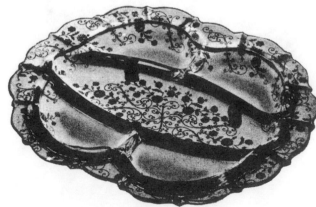

3900/120
12 in. 5 part Celery & Relish

3900/123
7 in. Relish or Pickle

3900/124
7 in. 2 part Relish

Cambridge, Ohio - - - U. S. A.

Elaine

3900/125
9 in. 3 part Celery & Relish

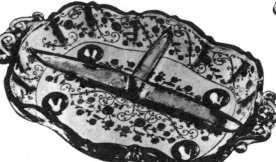

3900/126
12 in. 3 part Celery & Relish

3900/129
3 pc. Mayonnaise Set

3900/130
7 in. 2 handled Ftd. Bonbon

3900/131
8 in. 2 handled Ftd. Bonbon Plate

3900/136
5½ in. Comport

3900/165
Candy Box & Cover

3900/166
14 in. Plate, r. e.

3900/671
Ice Bucket with Chrome Handle

3900/1177
Salt & Pepper Shaker (doz. pr.)

968
2 pc. Cocktail Icer

3121
5⅜ in. Blown Comport

Elaine

274
10 in. Bud Flower Holder

278
11 in. Ftd. Flower Holder

279
13 in. Ftd. Flower Holder

1237
9 in. Ftd. Flower Holder

1238
12 in. Ftd. Flower Holder

1309
5 in. Globe Flower Holder

1299
11 in. Ftd. Flower Holder

1603
Hurricane Lamp

1617
Hurricane Lamp

6004
6 in. Ftd. Flower Holder

6004
8 in. Ftd. Flower Holder

Elaine
No. 1948—9 Item Assortment

3400/1180
5¼ in. 2 Hdl. Bonbon

477
9½ in. Pickle

3400/1181
6 in. 2 Hdl. Plate

3500/15
Ind. Sugar & Cream

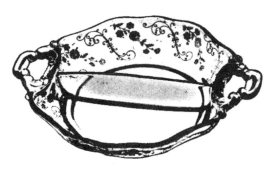

3400/90
6 in. 2 part Relish

3500/54
6 in. 2 Hdl. Ftd. Bonbon

3500/69
6½ in. 3 part Relish

3500/55
6 in. 2 Hdl. Ftd. Basket

3500/161
8 in. 2 Hdl. Ftd. Plate

Portia

3121
10 oz. Goblet

3121
6 oz. Tall Sherbet

3121
6 oz. Low Sherbet

3121
3 oz. Cocktail

3121
3½ oz. Wine

3121
4½ oz. Oyster Cocktail

3121
1 oz. Cordial

3121
5 oz. Cafe Parfait

3121
12 oz. Ftd. Ice Tea

3121
10 oz. Ftd. Tumbler

3121
5 oz. Ftd. Tumbler

Portia

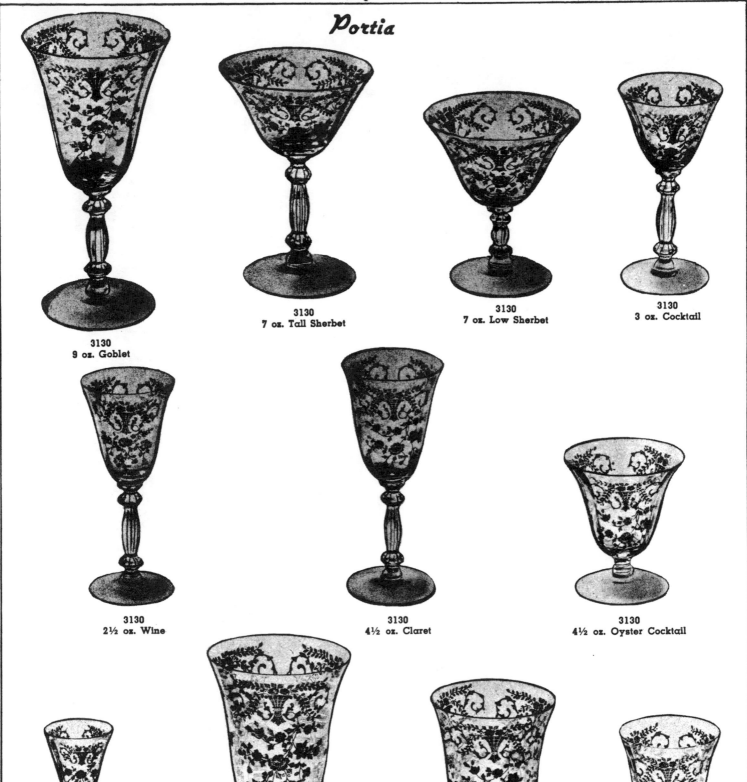

3130
9 oz. Goblet

3130
7 oz. Tall Sherbet

3130
7 oz. Low Sherbet

3130
3 oz. Cocktail

3130
2½ oz. Wine

3130
4½ oz. Claret

3130
4½ oz. Oyster Cocktail

3130
1 oz. Cordial

3130
12 oz. Ftd. Ice Tea

3130
10 oz. Ftd. Tumbler

3130
5 oz. Ftd. Tumbler

Cambridge, Ohio - - - U. S. A.

Portia

3900/17
Cup & Saucer

3900/19
2 pc. Mayonnaise Set

3900/20
6½ in. Bread & Butter Plate

3900/22
8 in. Salad Plate

3900/24
10½ in. Dinner Plate

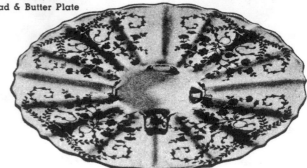

3900/26
12 in. 4 Ftd. Plate

3900/28
11½ in. Ftd. Bowl

3900/33
13 in. 4 Ftd. Torte Plate, R. E.

3900/34
11 in. 2 Handled Bowl

3900/35
13½ in. 2 Handled Cake Plate

3900/40
Ind. Sugar & Cream

3900/41
Sugar & Cream

Portia

3900/54
10 in. 4 Ftd. Bowl, flared

3900/67
5 in. Candlestick

3900/62
12 in. Ftd. Bowl, flared

3900/65
12 in. 4 Ftd. Oval Bowl

3900/72
6 in. 2 lite Candlestick

3900/74
6 in. 3 lite Candlestick

3900/100
6 oz. Oil, g. s.

3900/111
4 pc. Mayonnaise Set

3900/123
7 in. Relish or Pickle

3900/115
13 oz. Tumbler

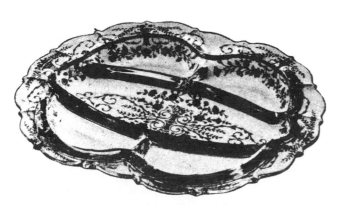

3900/120
12 in. 5 part Celery & Relish

3900/124
7 in. 2 part Relish

Portia

3900/125
9 in. 3 part Celery & Relish

3900/126
12 in. 3 part Celery & Relish

3900/129
3 pc. Mayonnaise Set

3900/130
7 in. 2 handled Ftd. Bonbon

3900/131
8 in. 2 handled Ftd. Bonbon Plate

3900/136
5½ in. Comport

3900/165
Candy Box & Cover

3900/166
14 in. Plate, r. e.

3900/671
Ice Bucket with Chrome Handle

3900/1177
Salt & Pepper Shaker (doz. pr.)

968
2 pc. Cocktail Icer

3121
5⅜ in. Blown Comport

Portia

274
10 in. Bud Flower Holder

278
11 in. Ftd. Flower Holder

279
13 in. Ftd. Flower Holder

1237
9 in. Ftd. Flower Holder

1238
12 in. Ftd. Flower Holder

1309
5 in. Globe Flower Holder

1299
11 in. Ftd. Flower Holder

1603
Hurricane Lamp

1617
Hurricane Lamp

6004
8 in. Ftd. Flower Holder

6004
6 in. Ftd. Flower Holder

Portia

1321/7966—7 pc. Sherry Set
1321—28 oz. Ftd. Decanter
7966—2 oz. Sherry

P.101/7801—7 Pc. Cocktail Set
P.101—32 oz. Cocktail Shaker
(Pat. No. D-133,198)
7801—4 oz. Cocktail

Portia
No. 1948—9 Item Assortment

3400/1180
5¼ in. 2 Hdl. Bonbon

477
9½ in. Pickle

3400/1181
6 in. 2 Hdl. Plate

3500/15
Ind. Sugar & Cream

3400/90
6 in. 2 part Relish

3500/54
6 in. 2 Hdl. Ftd. Bonbon

3500/69
6½ in. 3 part Relish

3500/55
6 in. 2 Hdl. Ftd. Basket

3500/161
8 in. 2 Hdl. Ftd. Plate

Wildflower

3121
10 oz. Goblet

3121
6 oz. Tall Sherbet

3121
6 oz. Low Sherbet

3121
3 oz. Cocktail

3121
3½ oz. Wine

3121
4½ oz. Claret

3121
4½ oz. Oyster Cocktail

3121
1 oz. Cordial

3121
5 oz. Cafe Parfait

3121
12 oz. Ftd. Ice Tea

3121
10 oz. Ftd. Tumbler

3121
5 oz. Ftd. Tumbler

Wildflower

3900/17
Cup & Saucer

3900/19
2 pc. Mayonnaise Set

3900/20
6½ in. Bread & Butter Plate

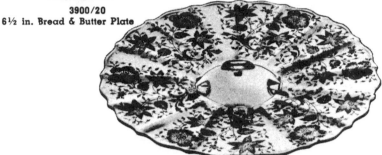

3900/22
8 in. Salad Plate

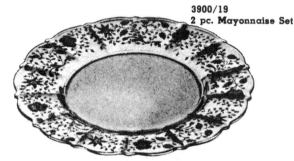

3900/24
10½ in. Dinner Plate

3900/26
12 in. 4 Ftd. Plate

3900/28
11½ in. Ftd. Bowl

3900/33
13 in. 4 Ftd. Torte Plate, R. E.

3900/34
11 in. 2 Handled Bowl

3900/35
13½ in. 2 Handled Cake Plate

3900/40
Ind. Sugar & Cream

3900/41
Sugar & Cream

Wildflower

3900/54
10 in. 4 Ftd. Bowl, flared

3900/67
5 in. Candlestick

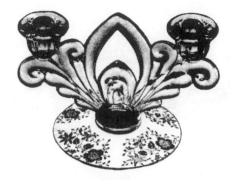

3900/72
6 in. 2 lite Candlestick

3900/65
12 in. 4 Ftd. Oval Bowl

3900/62
12 in. Ftd. Bowl, flared

3900/74
6 in. 3 lite Candlestick

3900/100
6 oz. Oil, g. s.

3900/111
4 pc. Mayonnaise Set

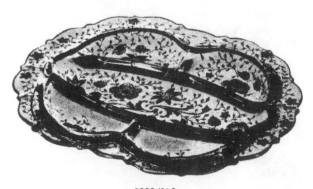

3900/120
12 in. 5 part Celery & Relish

3900/123
7 in. Relish or Pickle

3900/115
13 oz. Tumbler

3900/124
7 in. 2 part Relish

Wildflower

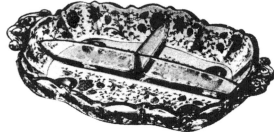

3900/125
9 in. 3 part Celery & Relish

3900/129
3 pc. Mayonnaise Set

3900/126
12 in. 3 part Celery & Relish

3900/130
7 in. 2 handled Ftd. Bonbon

3900/131
8 in. 2 handled Ftd. Bonbon Plate

3900/136
5½ in. Comport

3900/165
Candy Box & Cover

3900/166
14 in. Plate, r. e.

3900/671
Ice Bucket with Chrome Handle

3900/1177
Salt & Pepper Shaker (doz. pr.)

968
2 pc. Cocktail Icer

3121
5⅜ in. Blown Comport

Wildflower

274
10 in. Bud Flower Holder

278
11 in. Ftd. Flower Holder

279
13 in. Ftd. Flower Holder

1237
9 in. Ftd. Flower Holder

1238
12 in. Ftd. Flower Holder

1309
5 in. Globe Flower Holder

1299
11 in. Ftd. Flower Holder

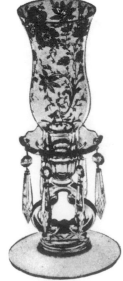

1603
Hurricane Lamp

1617
Hurricane Lamp

6004
6 in. Ftd. Flower Holder

6004
8 in. Ftd. Flower Holder

WILDFLOWER
No. 1948—9 Item Assortment

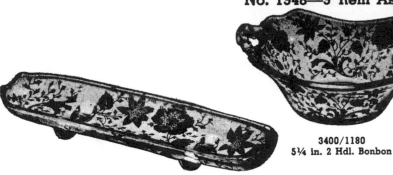

3400/1180
5¼ in. 2 Hdl. Bonbon

477
9½ in. Pickle

3400/1181
6 in. 2 Hdl. Plate

3400/90
6 in. 2 part Relish

3500/54
6 in. 2 Hdl. Ftd. Bonbon

3500/15
Ind. Sugar & Cream

3500/55
6 in. 2 Hdl. Ftd. Basket

3500/69
6½ in. 3 part Relish

3500/161
8 in. 2 Hdl. Ftd. Plate

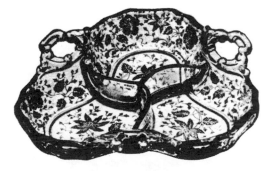

3400/91
8 in. 3 part Relish

3500/57
8 in. 3 part Candy Box & Cover

Roselyn

90-A

3779
9 oz. Tall Goblet

3779
6 oz. Tall Sherbet

3779
9 oz. Low Goblet

3779
6 oz. Low Sherbet

3779
3 oz. Cocktail

3779
2½ oz. Wine

3779
4½ oz. Oyster Cocktail

3779
4½ oz. Claret

1174
6 in. B & B Plate, Square

3779
1 oz. Cordial

3779
12 oz. Ftd. Ice Tea

3779
5 oz. Ftd. Tumbler

1176
8½ in. Salad Plate, Square

Roselyn

3400/35
11 in. 2 Hdl. Plate

3900/41
Sugar & Cream

3400/90
6 in. 2 part Relish

3900/166
14 in. Plate, r.e.

3900/125
9 in. 3 part Celery & Relish

3400/91
8 in. 3 part Relish

3900/126
12 in. 3 part Celery & Relish

3900/120
12 in. 5 part Celery & Relish

P. 248
11 in. Celery Tray

Roselyn

646
5 in. Candlestick

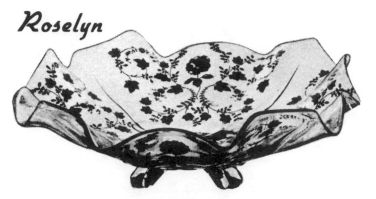

3400/48
11 in. 4 Ftd. Bowl, Fancy Edge

647
6 in. 2 lite Candlestick

3400/160
12 in. 4 Ftd. Bowl, oblong

1338
6 in. 3 lite Candlestick

3400/4
12 in. 4 Ftd. Bowl, flared

P. 533
3 pc. Mayonnaise Set

P. 1491
4 pc. Twin Salad Dressing Set

Roselyn

3500/57
3 part Candy Box & Cover

P. 306
6 in. Candy Box & Cover
(cut knob)

P. 293
6 oz. Oil

3400/52
5 in. Butter & Cover

P. 360
Salt & Pepper
w/Chrome Top

3121
5⅜ in. Blown Comport

3500/69
6½ in. 3 part Relish

3500/55
6 in. 2 Hdl. Ftd. Basket

3400/1181
6 in. 2 Hdl. Bonbon Plate

3400/1180
5½ in. 2 Hdl. Bonbon

3500/54
6 in. 2 Hdl. Ftd. Bonbon

Roselyn

3900/118
32 oz. Jug

3900/116
80 oz. Ball Jug

P. 101
32 oz. Cocktail Shaker

3900/115
76 oz. Jug

3900/671
Ice Pail w/Hdl. & Tong

274
10 in. Ftd. Bud Vase

278
11 in. Ftd. Vase

1238
12 in. Ftd. Vase

1237
9 in. Ftd. Vase

DAFFODIL

3779
9 oz. Tall Goblet

3779
6 oz. Tall Sherbet

3779
6 oz. Low Sherbet

3779
9 oz. Low Goblet

3779
3 oz. Cocktail

3779
2½ oz. Wine

3779
4½ oz. Claret

3779
1 oz. Cordial

3779
4½ oz. Oyster Cocktail

3779
12 oz. Ftd. Ice Tea

3779
5 oz. Ftd. Tumbler

1176
8½ in. Salad Plate

DAFFODIL

P. 54
6½ in. 2 Hdl. Low Ftd. Comport

P. 293
6 oz. Oil

P. 55
6 in. 2 Hdl. Low Ftd. Basket

P. 248
11 in. Celery

P. 214
10 in. 3 part Relish

P. 253
Individual Sugar & Cream

P. 254
Sugar & Cream

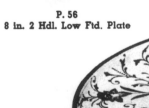

P. 56
8 in. 2 Hdl. Low Ftd. Plate

P. 166
13½ in. Cabaret Plate, r.e.

DAFFODIL

P. 306
6 in. Candy Box & Cover, cut knob

P. 360
Salt & Pepper w/Chrome tops

P. 384
11 in. Oval Bowl

628
3½ in. Candlestick

3900/72
6 in. 2 lite Candlestick

P. 430
12 in. Bowl, belled

P. 1491
4 pc. Twin Salad Dressing Set

3400/141
76 oz. Jug

DAFFODIL

3400/1180
5¼ in. Bonbon, 2 Hdl.

P. 533/445
2 pc. Mayonnaise Set

1495—11½ in. 2 Hdl.
Cake Plate

P. 533
3 pc. Mayonnaise Set

3400/1181
6 in. 2 Hdl. Bonbon Plate

P. 533
5½ in. Comport

6004
8 in. Ftd. Vase

278
11 in. Vase, Ftd.

532
6 in. Tall Comport

ROCK CRYSTAL
Achilles
(698)

3121
10 oz. Goblet

3121
6 oz. Tall Sherbet

3121
3 oz. Cocktail

3121
12 oz. Ftd. Ice Tea

3121
10 oz. Ftd. Tumbler

3121
6 oz. Low Sherbet

3121
4½ oz. Oyster Cocktail

3121
4½ oz. Claret

3121
5 oz. Ftd. Tumbler

3121
3½ oz. Wine

3121
1 oz. Cordial

3121
5⅜ in. Blown Comport

ROCK CRYSTAL
Achilles
(698)

3900/22
8 in. Salad Plate

3900/41
Sugar & Cream

3900/35
13½ in. 2 Handled Cake Plate

3900/62
12 in. 4 Ftd. Bowl, flared

3900/72
6 in. 2 lite Candlestick

3900/111
4 pc. Mayonnaise Set

3900/125
8 in. 3 part Celery & Relish

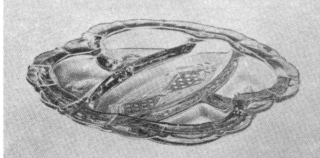

3900/120
12 in. 5 part Celery & Relish

3900/126
12 in. 3 part Celery & Relish

ROCK CRYSTAL
Achilles
(698)

3900/129
3 pc. Mayonnaise Set

968
2 pc. Cocktail Icer

3900/130
7 in. 2 handled Ftd. Bonbon

3900/131
8 in. 2 handled Ftd. Bonbon Plate

3900/136
5½ in. Comport

3900/165
Candy Box & Cover

3900/166
14 in. Plate. r. c.

278
11 in. Ftd. Vase

ROCK CRYSTAL
Adonis
(720)

3500
10 oz. Goblet

3500
7 oz. Tall Sherbet

3500
7 oz. Low Sherbet

3500
3 oz. Cocktail

3500
2½ oz. Wine

3500
4½ oz. Claret

3500
4½ oz. Oyster Cocktail

3500
1 oz. Cordial

3500
5 oz. Cafe Parfait

3500
12 oz. Ftd. Ice Tea

3500
10 oz. Ftd. Tumbler

3500
5 oz. Ftd. Tumbler

ROCK CRYSTAL
Adonis
(720)

3500/101
5⅜ in. Blown Comport

3900/22
8 in. Salad Plate

968
2 pc. Cocktail Icer

3900/35
13½ in. 2 Handled Cake Plate

3900/41
Sugar & Cream

3900/72
6 in. 2 lite Candlestick

3900/62
12 in. 4 Ftd. Bowl, flared

ROCK CRYSTAL
Adonis
(720)

3900/111
4 pc. Mayonnaise Set

3900/129
3 pc. Mayonnaise Set

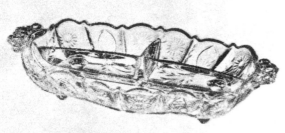

3900/125
8 in. 3 part Celery & Relish

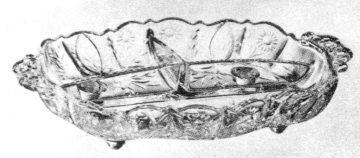

3900/126
12 in. 3 part Celery & Relish

3900/130
7 in. 2 handled Ftd. Bonbon

3900/131
8 in. 2 handled Ftd. Bonbon Plate

3900/120
12 in. 5 part Celery & Relish

ROCK CRYSTAL
Adonis
(720)

3900/136
5½ in. Comport

3900/165
Candy Box & Cover

3900/166
14 in. Plate, r. e.

274
10 in. Ftd. Bud Vase

278
11 in. Ftd. Vase

7966
2 oz. Sherry

1321
28 oz. Ftd. Decanter

ROCK CRYSTAL
Ardsley
(1005)

3700
9 oz. Goblet

3700
6 oz. Tall Sherbet

3700
6 oz. Low Sherbet

3700
3 oz. Cocktail

3700
2½ oz. Wine

3700
4½ oz. Claret

3700
4½ oz. Oyster Cocktail

3700
1 oz. Cordial

3700
12 oz. Ftd. Ice Tea

3700
10 oz. Ftd. Tumbler

3700
5 oz. Ftd. Tumbler

555
7½ in. Salad Plate

ROCK CRYSTAL
Bexley
(1072)

P. 427
10 in. Salad Bowl

P. 360
Salt & Pepper w/chrome top

3121
Blown Comport

647
6 in. 2 lite Candlestick

P. 384
11 in. Bowl

3900/41
Sugar & Cream

3900/115
76 oz. Jug (Not Optic)

ROCK CRYSTAL

Bexley

(1072)

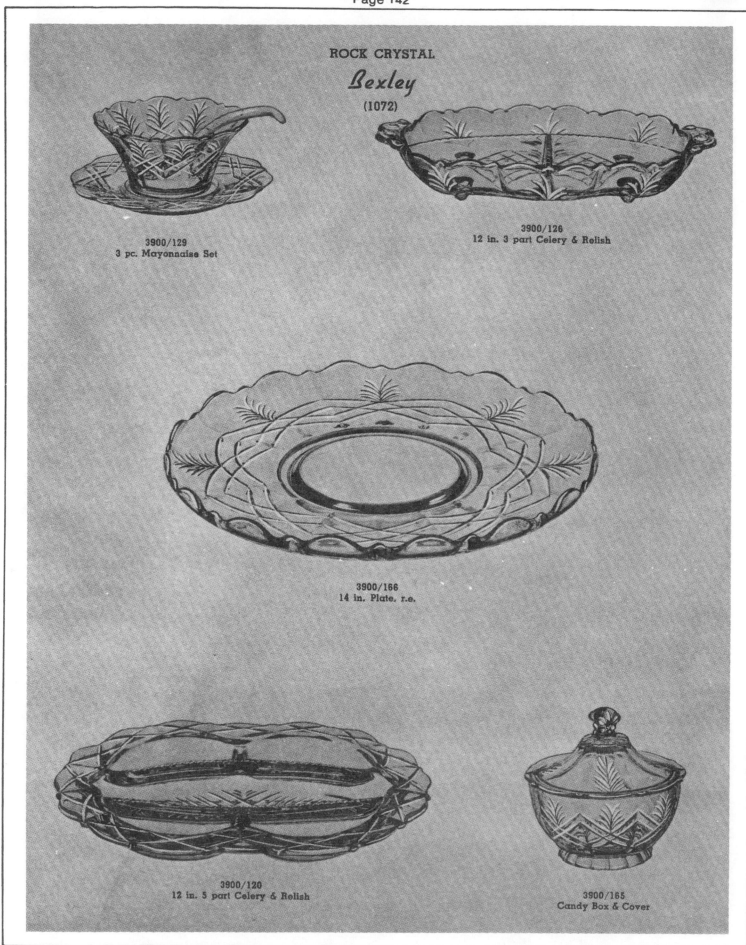

3900/129
3 pc. Mayonnaise Set

3900/126
12 in. 3 part Celery & Relish

3900/166
14 in. Plate, r.e.

3900/120
12 in. 5 part Celery & Relish

3900/165
Candy Box & Cover

ROCK CRYSTAL
Bexley
(1014)

3750
10 oz. Goblet

3750
6 oz. Tall Sherbet

3750
6 oz. Low Sherbet

3750
3½ oz. Cocktail

3750
3 oz. Wine

3750
4½ oz. Claret

3750
5 oz. Oyster Cocktail

3750
1 oz. Cordial

3750
12 oz. Ftd. Ice Tea

3750
5 oz. Ftd. Tumbler

555
7½ in. Salad Plate

ROCK CRYSTAL
Bijou
(1011)

3725
9 oz. Goblet

3725
7 oz. Tall Sherbet

3725
7 oz. Low Sherbet

3725
2½ oz. Cocktail

3725
2½ oz. Wine

3725
4½ oz. Claret

3725
4½ oz. Oyster Cocktail

3725
1 oz. Cordial

3725
12 oz. Ftd. Ice Tea

3725
5 oz. Ftd. Tumbler

497
14 oz. Tumbler

497
12 oz. Tumbler

321
7 oz. O. F. Cocktail

321
1½ oz. Tumbler

555
7½ in. Salad Plate

ROCK CRYSTAL
Cambridge Rose
(1074)

3700
9 oz. Goblet

3700
6 oz. Tall Sherbet

3700
6 oz. Low Sherbet

3700
3 oz. Cocktail

3700
2½ oz. Wine

3700
4½ oz. Claret

3700
4½ oz. Oyster Cocktail

3700
1 oz. Cordial

3700
12 oz. Ftd. Ice Tea

3700
5 oz. Ftd. Tumbler

555
7½ in. Salad Plate

ROCK CRYSTAL ENGRAVED

Cambridge Rose

(1074)

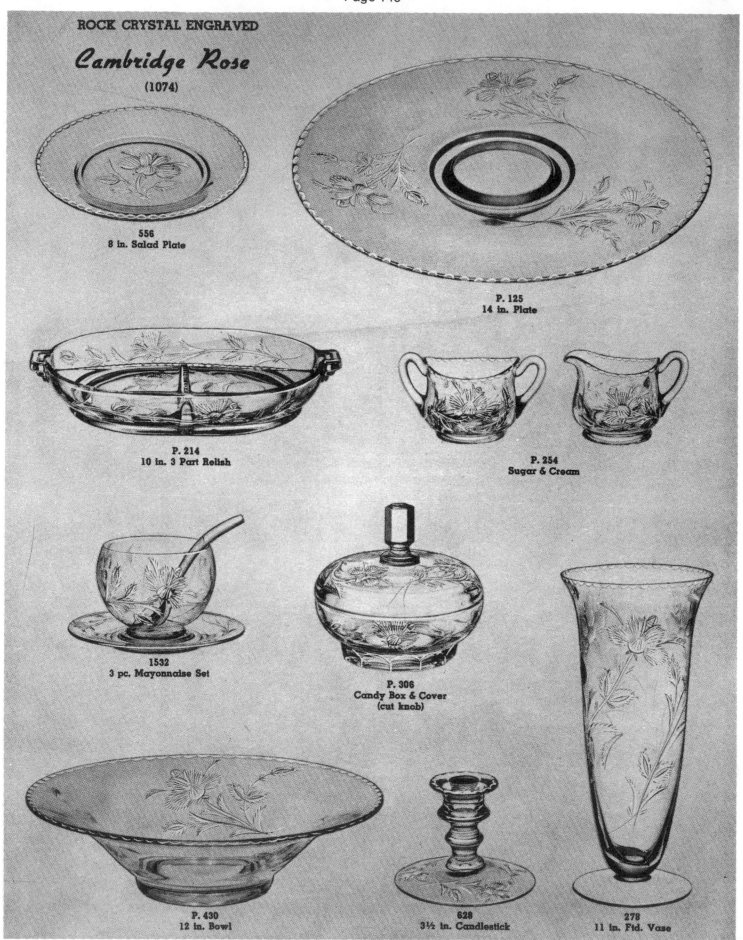

556
8 in. Salad Plate

P. 125
14 in. Plate

P. 214
10 in. 3 Part Relish

P. 254
Sugar & Cream

1532
3 pc. Mayonnaise Set

P. 306
Candy Box & Cover
(cut knob)

P. 430
12 in. Bowl

628
3½ in. Candlestick

278
11 in. Ftd. Vase

ROCK CRYSTAL
Cadet

3725
9 oz. Goblet

3725
7 oz. Tall Sherbet

3725
7 oz. Low Sherbet

3725
2½ oz. Cocktail

3725
2½ oz. Wine

3725
4½ oz. Claret

3725
4½ oz. Oyster Cocktail

3725
1 oz. Cordial

555
7½ in. Salad Plate

3725
12 oz. Ftd. Ice Tea

3725
5 oz. Ftd. Tumbler

556
8 in. Salad Plate

ROCK CRYSTAL
Cordelia
(812)

3130
9 oz. Goblet

3130
7 oz. Tall Sherbet

3130
7 oz. Low Sherbet

3130
3 oz. Cocktail

3130
2½ oz. Wine

3130
4½ oz. Claret

3130
4½ oz. Oyster Cocktail

3130
1 oz. Cordial

3130
12 oz. Ftd. Ice Tea

3130
10 oz. Ftd. Tumbler

3400/62
8½ in. Salad Plate

3130
5 oz. Ftd. Tumbler

3400/176
7½ in. Salad Plate

968
2 pc. Cocktail Icer, Ftd.

555
7½ in. Salad Plate

ROCK CRYSTAL ENGRAVED
Corsage
(1075)

3116
10 oz. Goblet

3116
6 oz. Tall Sherbet

3116
6 oz. Low Sherbet

3116
3 oz. Cocktail

3116
3 oz. Wine

- 3116
4½ oz. Oyster Cocktail

3116
4½ oz. Claret

3116
1 oz. Cordial

3116
12 oz. Ftd. Ice Tea

3116
10 oz. Ftd. Tumbler

3116
5 oz. Ftd. Tumbler

555
8 in. Salad Plate

ROCK CRYSTAL
Croesus
(722)

3500
10 oz. Goblet

3500
7 oz. Tall Sherbet

3500
7 oz. Low Sherbet

3500
3 oz. Cocktail

3500
2½ oz. Wine

3500
4½ oz. Claret

3500
4½ oz. Oyster Cocktail

3500
1 oz. Cordial

3500
5 oz. Cafe Parfait

968
2 pc. Cocktail Icer

3500
12 oz. Ftd. Ice Tea

3500
10 oz. Ftd. Tumbler

3500
5 oz. Ftd. Tumbler

3500/5
8½ in. Salad Plate

3500/167
7½ in. Salad Plate

ROCK CRYSTAL
Deerfield
(1033)

3778
10 oz. Goblet

3778
7 oz. Tall Sherbet

3778
7 oz. Low Sherbet

3778
2½ oz. Cocktail

3778
2½ oz. Wine

3778
4½ cz. Claret

3778
4½ oz. Oyster Cocktail

3778
1 oz. Cordial

3778
12 oz. Ftd. Ice Tea

3778
5 oz. Ftd. Tumbler

968
2 pc. Cocktail Icer

555
7½ in. Salad Plate

ROCK CRYSTAL
Euclid
(1017)

3750
10 oz. Goblet

3750
6 oz. Tall Sherbet

3750
6 oz. Low Sherbet

3750
3½ oz. Cocktail

3750
3 oz. Wine

3750
4½ oz. Claret

3750
5 oz. Oyster Cocktail

3750
1 oz. Cordial

3750
12 oz. Ftd. Ice Tea

3750
5 oz. Ftd. Tumbler

555
7½ in. Salad Plate

Cambridge, Ohio - - - U. S. A.

ROCK CRYSTAL
Fuchsia
(1019)

3750
10 oz. Goblet

3750
6 oz. Tall Sherbet

3750
6 oz. Low Sherbet

3750
3½ oz. Cocktail

3750
3 oz. Wine

3750
4½ oz. Claret

3750
5 oz. Oyster Cocktail

3750
1 oz. Cordial

3750
12 oz. Ftd. Ice Tea

3750
5 oz. Ftd. Tumbler

555
7½ in. Salad Plate

ROCK CRYSTAL
Festoon
1071

3790
Goblet

3790
Low Sherbet

3790
Cocktail

3790
Wine

3790
Claret

3790
Oyster Cocktail

3790
Cordial

3790
12 oz. Ftd. Ice Tea

3790
5 oz. Ftd. Tumbler

555
7½ in. Salad Plate

ROCK CRYSTAL
Glendale
(1028)

3130
9 oz. Goblet

3130
7 oz. Tall Sherbet

3130
7 oz. Low Sherbet

3130
3 oz. Cocktail

3130
2½ oz. Wine

3130
4½ oz. Claret

3130
4½ oz. Oyster Cocktail

3130
1 oz. Cordial

3130
12 oz. Ftd. Tumbler

3130
5 oz. Ftd. Tumbler

968
2 pc. Cocktail Icer. Ftd.

555
7½ in. Salad Plate

ROCK CRYSTAL
Hanover
(1015)

3750
10 oz. Goblet

3750
6 oz. Tall Sherbet

3750
6 oz. Low Sherbet

3750
3½ oz. Cocktail

3750
3 oz. Wine

3750
4½ oz. Claret

3750
5 oz. Oyster Cocktail

3750
1 oz. Cordial

3750
12 oz. Ftd. Ice Tea

3750
5 oz. Ftd. Tumbler

555
7½ in. Salad Plate

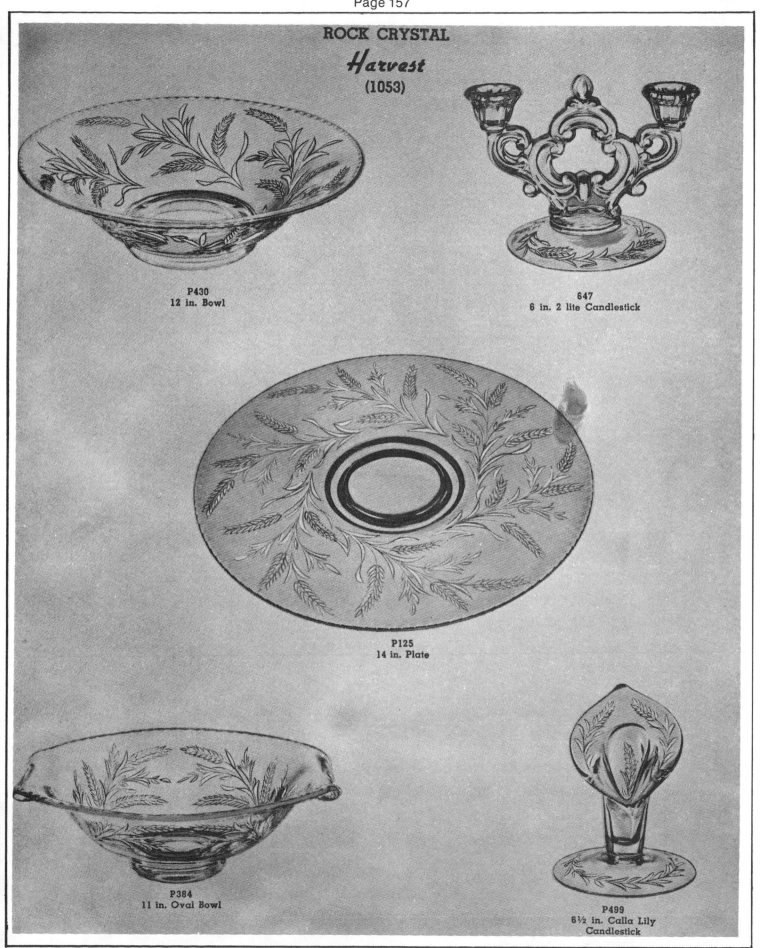

ROCK CRYSTAL
Harvest
(1053)

P430
12 in. Bowl

647
6 in. 2 lite Candlestick

P125
14 in. Plate

P384
11 in. Oval Bowl

P499
6½ in. Calla Lily
Candlestick

ROCK CRYSTAL

Harvest

(1053)

P254
Sugar & Cream

532
6 in. Tall Comport

P306
6 in. Candy Box and Cover

103
7 in. 3 part Candy Box and Cover

P212
10 in. 5 part Celery and Relish

1491
4 pc. Twin Salad Dressing Set

278
11 in. Ftd. Vase

P427
10 in. Salad Bowl

ROCK CRYSTAL
Harvest
(1053)

3750
10 oz. Goblet

3750
S oz. Tall Sherbet

3750
6 oz. Low Sherbet

3750
3½ oz. Cocktail

3750
3 oz. Wine

3750
4½ oz. Claret

3750
5 oz. Oyster Cocktail

3750
1 oz. Cordial

532
6 in. Tall Comport

3750
12 oz. Ftd. Ice Tea

3750
5 oz. Ftd. Tumbler

P. 125
14 in. Plate

555
7½ in. Salad Plate

ROCK CRYSTAL
Juliana
(997)

3139
10 oz. Goblet

3139
7 oz. Tall Sherbet

3139
4½ oz. Oyster Cocktail

3139
2½ oz. Cocktail

3139
2½ oz. Sherry Wine

3139
4½ oz. Claret

3139
1 oz. Cordial

3139
12 oz. Ftd. Ice Tea

3139
5 oz. Ftd. Tumbler

555
7½ in. Salad Plate

968
2 pc. Cocktail Icer

Cambridge, Ohio - - - U. S. A.

ROCK CRYSTAL
King Edward
(821)

3700 9 oz. Goblet	3700 6 oz. Tall Sherbet	3700 6 oz. Low Sherbet	3700 3 oz. Cocktail
3700 2½ oz. Wine	3700 4½ oz. Claret	3700 4½ oz. Oyster Cocktail	3700 1 oz. Cordial
3700 12 oz. Ftd. Ice Tea	3700 10 oz. Ftd. Tumbler	3700 5 oz. Ftd. Tumbler	

ROCK CRYSTAL
King Edward
(821)

555
7½ in. Salad Plate

533
6 in. Footed Comport

556
8 in. Salad Plate

138
Sugar & Cream

P. 293
6 oz. Oil

532
6 in. Tall Comport. Footed

647
6 in. 2 lite Candlestick

628
3½ in. Candlestick

1491
4 pc. Twin Salad Dressing Set

533
3 pc. Mayonnaise Set

321
7 oz. O. F. Cocktail

321
1½ oz. Whiskey

497
12 oz. Tumbler

ROCK CRYSTAL
King Edward
(821)

P. 430
12 in. Bowl, flared

1321
28 oz. Ftd. Decanter

P. 101
32 oz. Cocktail Shaker (Pat. D-133, 198)

P. 427
10 in. Bowl

103
7 in. 3 part Candy Box & Cover

P. 212
10 in. 5 part Celery & Relish Tray

1397
13½ in. Plate

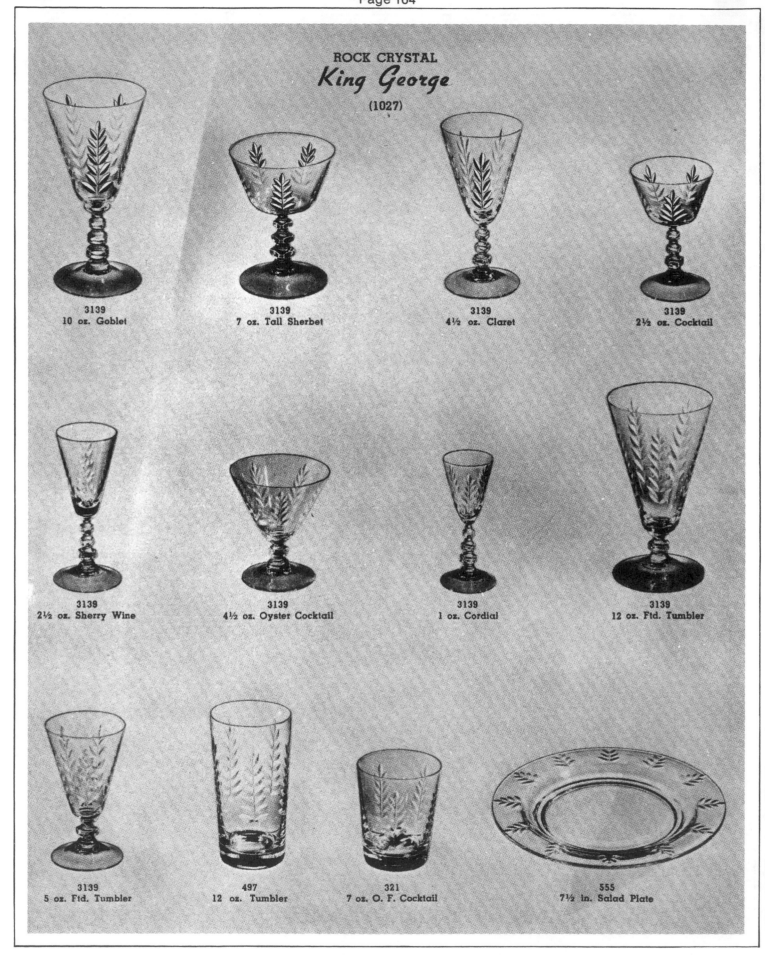

ROCK CRYSTAL
King George
(1027)

3139
10 oz. Goblet

3139
7 oz. Tall Sherbet

3139
4½ oz. Claret

3139
2½ oz. Cocktail

3139
2½ oz. Sherry Wine

3139
4½ oz. Oyster Cocktail

3139
1 oz. Cordial

3139
12 oz. Ftd. Tumbler

3139
5 oz. Ftd. Tumbler

497
12 oz. Tumbler

321
7 oz. O. F. Cocktail

555
7½ in. Salad Plate

ROCK CRYSTAL
Lily of the Valley
1069

3790
Goblet

3790
Low Sherbet

3790
Cocktail

3790
Wine

3790
Claret

3790
Oyster Cocktail

3790
Cordial

3790
12 oz. Ftd. Ice Tea

3790
5 oz. Ftd. Tumbler

555
7½ in. Salad Plate

ROCK CRYSTAL
Lynbrook
1070

3790
Goblet

3790
Low Sherbet

3790
Cocktail

3790
Wine

3790
Claret

3790
Oyster Cocktail

3790
Cordial

3790
12 oz. Ftd. Ice Tea

3790
5 oz. Ftd. Tumbler

555
7½ in. Salad Plate

ROCK CRYSTAL
Lynbrook
(1070)

628
3½ in. Candlestick

M. 495
6 in. 2 lite Candle

P. 430
12 in. Bowl

P. 306
Candy Box & Cover

1532
3 pc. Mayonnaise Set

P. 214
10 in. 3 part Relish

533
6 in. Comport

ROCK CRYSTAL
Lynbrook
(1070)

P. 293
6 oz. Oil

3900/115
76 oz. Jug

P. 298
Marmalade & Cover & Spoon

P. 360
Salt & Pepper

3700
5 in. Blown Comport

P. 254
Sugar & Cream

P. 166
13½ in. Plate

ROCK CRYSTAL
Larchmont
(1036)

3778
10 oz. Goblet

3778
7 oz. Tall Sherbet

3778
7 oz. Low Sherbet

3778
2½ oz. Cocktail

3778
2½ oz. Wine

3778
4½ oz. Claret

3778
4½ oz. Oyster Cocktail

3778
1 oz. Cordial

3778
12 oz. Ftd. Ice Tea

3778
5 oz. Ftd. Tumbler

968
2 pc. Cocktail Icer

555
7½ in. Salad Plate

Cambridge, Ohio - - - U. S. A.

ROCK CRYSTAL
Laurel Wreath

3700
9 oz. Goblet

3700
6 oz. Tall Sherbet

3700
6 oz. Low Sherbet

3700
3 oz. Cocktail

3700
2½ oz. Wine

3700
4½ oz. Claret

3700
4½ oz. Oyster Cocktail

3700
1 oz. Cordial

3700
12 oz. Ftd. Ice Tea

3700
10 oz. Ftd. Tumbler

3700
5 oz. Ftd. Tumbler

968
2 pc. Cocktail Icer

Cambridge, Ohio - - - U. S. A.

ROCK CRYSTAL
Laurel Wreath

P.430
12 in. Bowl, Flared

3900/72
6 in. 2 lite Candlestick

P.306
Candy Box & Cover
(Cut Knob)

533
6 in. Comport

P.293
6 oz. Oil
(Polished in Stopper)

P.298
Marmalade & Cover & Spoon

P.254
Sugar & Cream

3700
5 in. Blown Comport

P.360
Salt & Pepper

1532
3 pc. Mayonnaise Set

P.214
10 in. 3 part Relish

P.166
13½ in. Plate, r.e.

ROCK CRYSTAL
Laurel Wreath

3139
10 oz. Goblet

3139
7 oz. Tall Sherbet

3139
2½ oz. Cocktail

3139
2½ oz. Sherry Wine

3139
4½ oz. Claret

3139
4½ oz. Oyster Cocktail

3139
1 oz. Cordial

3139
5 oz. Ftd. Tumbler

3139
12 oz. Ftd. Ice Tea

555
7½ in. Salad Plate

556
8 in. Salad Plate

497
14 oz. Tumbler

497
12 oz. Tumbler

321
7 oz. O. F. Cocktail

321
1½ oz. Whiskey

Cambridge, Ohio - - - U. S. A.

ROCK CRYSTAL
Lexington
(758)

7966
9 oz. Goblet

7966
6 oz. Tall Sherbet

7966
3½ oz. Cocktail

7966
3 oz. Wine

7966
4 oz. Claret

7966
2 oz. Sherry

7966
1 oz. Cordial

7966
12 oz. Ftd. Ice Tea

968
2 pc. Cocktail Icer

556
8 in. Salad Plate

555
7½ in. Salad Plate

1321
28 oz. Ftd. Decanter

P. 101
32 oz. Cocktail Shaker (Pat. D-133, 198)

Cambridge, Ohio - - - U. S. A.

ROCK CRYSTAL
Lucia
(824)

3116
10 oz. Goblet

3116
6 oz. Tall Sherbet

3116
6 oz. Low Sherbet

3116
3 oz. Cocktail

3116
3 oz. Wine

3116
4½ oz. Oyster Cocktail

3116
12 oz. Ftd. Ice Tea

3116
10 oz. Ftd. Tumbler

3116
5 oz. Ftd. Tumbler

3121
5⅜ in. Blown Comport

ROCK CRYSTAL
Lucia
(824)

3900/22
8 in. Salad Plate

3900/131
8 in. 2 handled Ftd. Bonbon Plate

3900/41
Sugar & Cream

3900/111
4 pc. Mayonnaise Set

3900/72
6 in. 2 lite Candlestick

3900/62
12 in. 4 Ftd. Bowl, flared

3900/125
8 in. 3 part Celery & Relish

3900/120
12 in. 5 part Celery & Relish

3900/126
12 in. 3 part Celery Relish

ROCK CRYSTAL
Lucia
(824)

3900/129
3 pc. Mayonnaise Set

3900/35
13½ in. 2 Handled Cake Plate

3900/130
7 in. 2 handled Ftd. Bonbon

3900/136
5½ in. Comport

3900/165
Candy Box & Cover

278
11 in. Ftd. Vase

3900/166
14 in. Plate, r. e.

968
2 pc. Cocktail Icer

ROCK CRYSTAL
Manor
(1003)

3700
9 oz. Goblet

3700
6 oz. Tall Sherbet

3700
6 oz. Low Sherbet

3700
3 oz. Cocktail

3700
2½ oz. Wine

3700
4½ oz. Claret

3700
4½ oz. Oyster Cocktail

3700
1 oz. Cordial

3700
12 oz. Ftd. Ice Tea

3700
10 oz. Ftd. Tumbler

3700
5 oz. Ftd. Tumbler

3121
5⅜ in. Blown Comport

ROCK CRYSTAL
Manor
(1003)

968
2 pc. Cocktail Icer

3900/35
13½ in. 2 Handled Cake Plate

3900/22
8 in. Salad Plate

3900/62
12 in. 4 Ftd. Bowl, flared

3900/165
Candy Box & Cover

3900/111
4 pc. Mayonnaise Set

3900/129
3 pc. Mayonnaise Set

3900/72
6 in. 2 lite Candlestick

3900/136
5½ in. Comport

3900/41
Sugar & Cream

ROCK CRYSTAL
Manor
(1003)

3900/125
8 in. 3 part Celery & Relish

3900/131
8 in. 2 handled Ftd. Bonbon Plate

3900/120
12 in. 5 part Celery & Relish

3900/130
7 in. 2 handled Ftd. Bonbon

3900/166
14 in. Plate, r. e.

3900/126
12 in. 3 part Celery & Relish

278
11 in. Ftd. Vase

1613
17 in. Hurricane Lamp

ROCK CRYSTAL
Maryland
(985)

3776
9 oz. Goblet

3776
7 oz. Tall Sherbet

3776
7 oz. Low Sherbet

3776
3 oz. Cocktail

3776
2½ oz. Wine

3776
4½ oz. Claret

3776
1 oz. Cordial

3776
12 oz. Ftd. Ice Tea

3776
5 oz. Ftd. Tumbler

3121
5⅜ in. Blown Comport

968
2 pc. Cocktail Icer

ROCK CRYSTAL
Maryland
(985)

3900/22
8 in. Salad Plate

3900/35
13½ in. 2 Handled Cake Plate

3900/62
12 in. 4 Ftd. Bowl, flared

3900/41
Sugar & Cream

3900/120
12 in. 5 part Celery & Relish

3900/72
6 in. 2 lite Candlestick

3900/126
12 in. 3 part Celery & Relish

3900/125
8 in. 3 part Celery & Relish

ROCK CRYSTAL
Maryland
(985)

3900/129
3 pc. Mayonnaise Set

3900/130
7 in. 2 handled Ftd. Bonbon

3900/111
4 pc. Mayonnaise Set

3900/136
5½ in. Comport

3900/165
Candy Box & Cover

274
10 in. Ftd. Bud Vase

3900/131
8 in. 2 handled Ftd. Bonbon Plate

3900/166
14 in. Plate, r. e.

278
11 in. Ftd. Vase

Cambridge, Ohio - - - U. S. A.

ROCK CRYSTAL
Minton Wreath
(1012)

3750
10 oz. Goblet

3750
6 oz. Tall Sherbet

3750
6 oz. Low Sherbet

3750
3½ oz. Cocktail

3750
3 oz. Wine

3750
4½ oz. Claret

3750
5 oz. Oyster Cocktail

3750
1 oz. Cordial

3750
12 oz. Ftd. Ice Tea

3750
5 oz. Ftd. Tumbler

555
7½ in. Salad Plate

The Cambridge Glass Company

ROCK CRYSTAL
Minuet
(990)

3776
9 oz. Goblet

3776
7 oz. Tall Sherbet

3776
7 oz. Low Sherbet

3776
3 oz. Cocktail

3776
2½ oz. Wine

3776
4½ oz. Claret

3776
1 oz. Cordial

3776
12 oz. Ftd. Ice Tea

3776
5 oz. Ftd. Tumbler

555
7½ in. Salad Plate

556
8 in. Salad Plate

Cambridge, Ohio - - - U. S. A.

ROCK CRYSTAL
Montrose
(1004)

3700
9 oz. Goblet

3700
6 oz. Tall Sherbet

3700
6 oz. Low Sherbet

3700
3 oz. Cocktail

3700
2½ oz. Wine

3700
4½ oz. Claret

3700
4½ oz. Oyster Cocktail

3700
1 oz. Cordial

3700
12 oz. Ftd. Ice Tea

3700
10 oz. Ftd. Tumbler

3700
5 oz. Ftd. Tumbler

555
7½ in. Salad Plate

ROCK CRYSTAL
Plaza
(1018)

3725
9 oz. Goblet

3725
7 oz. Tall Sherbet

3725
7 oz. Low Sherbet

3725
2½ oz. Cocktail

3725
2½ oz. Wine

3725
4½ oz. Claret

3725
4½ oz. Oyster Cocktail

3725
1 oz. Cordial

3725
12 oz. Ftd. Ice Tea

3725
5 oz. Ftd. Tumbler

555
7½ in. Salad Plate

ROCK CRYSTAL
Roxbury
(1030)

3775 10 oz. Goblet	3775 6 oz. Tall Sherbet	3775 6 oz. Low Sherbet	3775 3 oz. Cocktail
3775 2½ oz. Wine	3775 4½ oz. Claret	3775 4½ oz. Oyster Cocktail	3775 1 oz. Cordial
3775 12 oz. Ftd. Ice Tea	3775 5 oz. Ftd. Tumbler	555 7½ in. Salad Plate	968 2 pc. Cocktail Icer

ROCK CRYSTAL
Star
(1016)

3725
9 oz. Goblet

3725
7 oz. Tall Sherbet

3725
7 oz. Low Sherbet

3725
2½ oz. Cocktail

3725
2½ oz. Wine

3725
4½ oz. Claret

3725
4½ oz. Oyster Cocktail

3725
1 oz. Cordial

3725
12 oz. Ftd. Ice Tea

3725
5 oz. Ftd. Tumbler

555
7½ in. Salad Plate

ROCK CRYSTAL

Tempo

(1029)

3700
9 oz. Goblet

3700
6 oz. Tall Sherbet

3700
6 oz. Low Sherbet

3700
3 oz. Cocktail

3700
2½ oz. Wine

3700
4½ oz. Claret

3700
1 oz. Cordial

3700
4½ oz. Oyster Cocktail

3700
12 oz. Ftd. Ice Tea

3700
5 oz. Ftd. Tumbler

555
7½ in. Salad Plate

968
2 pc. Cocktail Icer

ROCK CRYSTAL
Wedding Rose
(998)

3130	3130	3130	3130
9 oz. Goblet	7 oz. Tall Sherbet	7 oz. Low Sherbet	3 oz. Cocktail

3130	3130	3130	3130
2½ oz. Wine	4½ oz. Claret	4½ oz. Oyster Cocktail	1 oz. Cordial

3130	3130	3130	555
12 oz. Ftd. Ice Tea	10 oz. Ftd. Tumbler	5 oz. Ftd. Tumbler	7½ in. Salad Plate

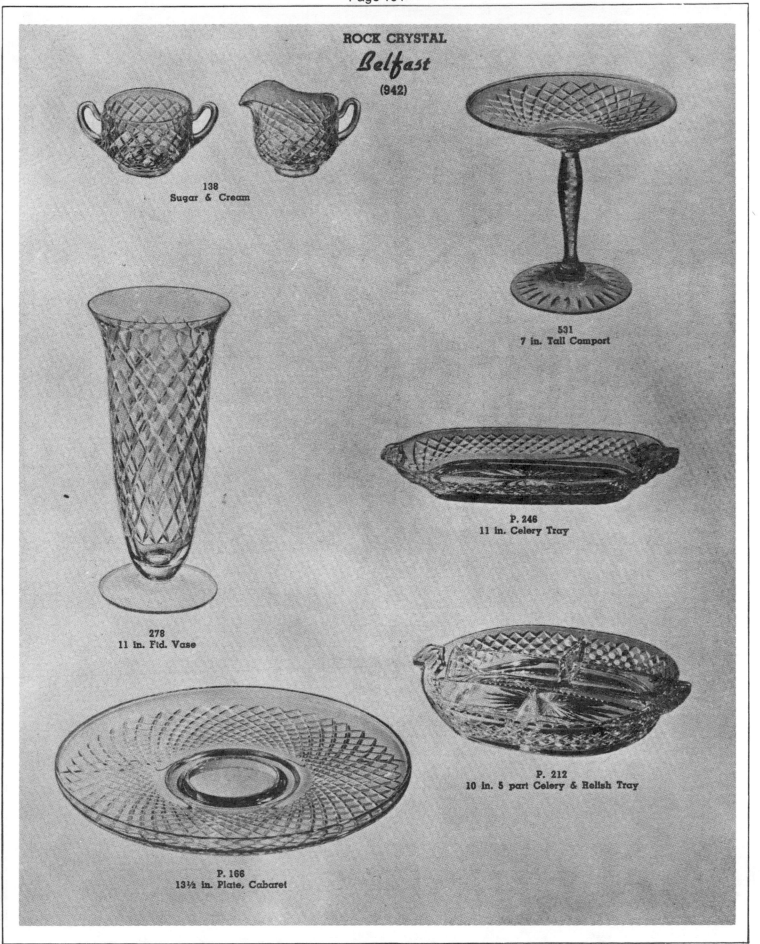

ROCK CRYSTAL
Belfast
(942)

138
Sugar & Cream

531
7 in. Tall Comport

278
11 in. F'td. Vase

P. 246
11 in. Celery Tray

P. 212
10 in. 5 part Celery & Relish Tray

P. 166
13½ in. Plate, Cabaret

ROCK CRYSTAL
Belfast
(942)

P. 430
12 in. Bowl flared

628
3½ in. Candlestick

647
6 in. 2 lite Candlestick

P. 427
10 in. Bowl

P. 671
6 in. Ice Tub

P. 287
4 pc. Twin Salad Dressing Set

P. 101
32 oz. Cocktail Shaker (Pat. D-133, 198)

ROCK CRYSTAL
Carnation
(732)

3900/35
13½ in. 2 Handled Cake Plate

3900/41
Sugar & Cream

3900/62
12 in. 4 Ftd. Bowl, flared

3900/72
6 in. 2 lite Candlestick

3900/111
4 pc. Mayonnaise Set

3900/120
12 in. 5 part Celery & Relish

3900/165
Candy Box & Cover

278
11 in. Ftd. Vase

3900/166
14 in. Plate, r. e.

3900/136
5½ in. Comport

ROCK CRYSTAL
Celestial
(600)

600/25
7 in. Candy Box & Cover.
3 Footed

600/9
7 in. Tall Comport

600/628
3½ in. Candlestick

600/2
8 in. Flip Flower Holder

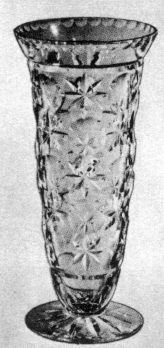

600/5
11 in. Ftd. Flower Holder

600/17
10 in. 5 part Relish Tray

ROCK CRYSTAL
Celestial
(600)

600/647
6 in. 2 lite Candlestick

600/11
12 in. Bowl

600/10
10 in. Bowl

600/6
11 in. Ftd. Flower Holder

600/8
14 in. Plate

ROCK CRYSTAL
Windsor
(500)

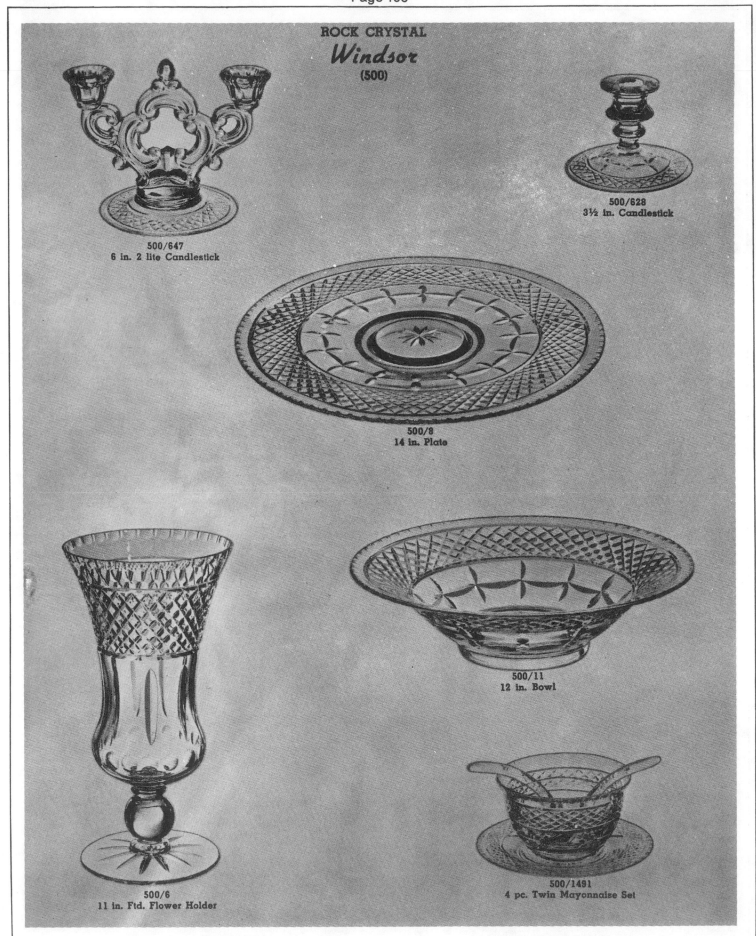

500/647
6 in. 2 lite Candlestick

500/628
3½ in. Candlestick

500/8
14 in. Plate

500/11
12 in. Bowl

500/6
11 in. Ftd. Flower Holder

500/1491
4 pc. Twin Mayonnaise Set

ROCK CRYSTAL
Windsor
(500)

500/14
7 in. Candy Box & Cover,
3 part

500/25
7 in. Candy Box & Cover,
3 Footed

500/9
7 in. Tall Comport

500/17
10 in. 5 part Relish Tray

500/5
11 in. Ftd. Flower Holder

500/10
10 in. Bowl

ROCK CRYSTAL
Ivy
(1059)

3750
10 oz. Goblet

3750
6 oz. Tall Sherbet

3750
6 oz. Low Sherbet

3750
3½ oz. Cocktail

3750
3 oz. Wine

3750
4½ oz. Claret

3750
5 oz. Oyster Cocktail

3750
1 oz. Cordial

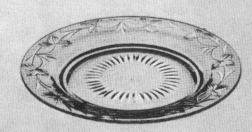

3750
12 oz. Ftd. Ice Tea

3750
5 oz. Ftd. Tumbler

555
7½ in. Salad Plate

ROCK CRYSTAL
Ivy
(1059)

138
Sugar & Cream

P.306
6 in. Candy Box & Cover

1491
4 pc. Twin Salad Dressing Set

103
7 in. 3 part Candy Box & Cover

532
6 in. Tall Comport

P.212
10 in. 5 part Celery & Relish

P.427
10 in. Deep Salad Bowl

647
6 in. 2 lite Candlestick

278
11 in. Ftd. Vase

P.125
14 in. Plate

P.430
12 in. Flower Bowl

ROCK CRYSTAL
Maywood
(1058)
8 Item Small Assortment

3400/1180
5¼ in. 2 Hdl. Bonbon

3400/1181
6 in, 2 Hdl. Plate

3400/90
6 in. 2 Part Relish

3500/15
Ind. Sugar & Cream

3500/54
6 in. Ftd. Bonbon

3500/55
6 in. Ftd. Basket

3500/161
8 in. Ftd. Plate

3500/69
6½ in. 3 part Relish

HIGH BALL TUMBLERS
Engraved

497—12 oz.
Engraved Star (1060)

497—12 oz.
Engraved Classic (1061)

497—12 oz.
Engraved Jewel (1062)

497—12 oz.
Engraved Fern (1063)

ROCK CRYSTAL
Miscellaneous

Kimberley
(1043)

321
1½ oz. Whiskey

P. 92
26 oz. Decanter

P. 671
Ice Tub
Chrome Ice Tongs (short)

497
12 oz. Hiball

321
7 oz. O. F. Cocktail

Lansdowne
(1049)

321
1½ oz. Whiskey

P. 92
26 oz. Decanter

P. 671
Ice Tub
Chrome Ice Tongs (short)

497
12 oz. Hiball

321
7 oz. O. F. Cocktail

ROCK CRYSTAL
Miscellaneous

1379
26 oz. Decanter (Manhattan)

1379
26 oz. Decanter-Norwood (1041)

P. 101
32 oz. Cocktail Shaker
(Pat. D-133, 198)
Chesterfield (952)

3700
3 oz. Cocktail-Chesterfield (952)

Norwood
(1041)

P. 92
26 oz. Decanter

P. 671
Ice Tub
Chrome Ice Tongs (short)

497
12 oz. Hiball

321
1½ oz. Whiskey

321
7 oz. O. F. Cocktail

ROCK CRYSTAL
1064

3900/35
13½ in. 2 Hdld. Cake Plate

3900/62
12 in. 4 Ftd. Bowl, flared

3900/72
6 in. 2 lite Candlestick

3900/41
Sugar & Cream

3900/111
4 pc. Mayonnaise Set

3900/129
3 pc. Mayonnaise Set

3900/125
8 in. 3 part Celery & Relish

3900/126
12 in. 3 part Celery & Relish

3900/120
12 in. 5 part Celery & Relish

ROCK CRYSTAL
1064

3900/130
7 in. 2 handled Ftd. Bonbon

3900/131
8 in. 2 handled Ftd. Bonbon Plate

3900/165
Candy Box & Cover

3900/136
5½ in. Comport

3900/166
14 in. Plate, r.e.

274
10 in. Ftd. Bud Vase

278
11 in. Ftd. Vase

3121
5⅜ in. Blown Comport

ROCK CRYSTAL
1065

3900/35
13½ in. 2 Hdld. Cake Plate

3900/62
12 in. 4 Ftd. Bowl, flared

3900/72
6 in. 2 lite Candlestick

3900/41
Sugar & Cream

3900/111
4 pc. Mayonnaise Set

3900/129
3 pc. Mayonnaise Set

3900/125
8 in. 3 part Celery & Relish

3900/126
12 in. 3 part Celery & Relish

3900/120
12 in. 5 part Celery & Relish

Cambridge, Ohio - - - U. S. A.

ROCK CRYSTAL
1065

3900/130
7 in. 2 handled Ftd. Bonbon

3900/131
8 in. 2 handled Ftd. Bonbon Plate

3900/165
Candy Box & Cover

3900/136
5½ in. Comport

3900/166
14 in. Plate, r.e.

274
10 in. Ftd. Bud Vase

278
11 in. Ftd. Vase

3121
5⅜ in. Blown Comport

ROCK CRYSTAL
Thistle
(1066)

P.254
Sugar & Cream

P.1491
4 pc. Twin Salad Dressing Set

P.532
6 in. Tall Comport

P.306
6 in. Candy Box & Cover

P.533
3 Pc. Mayonnaise Set

P.125
14 in. Plate

278
11 in. Ftd. Vase

P.126
13½ in. Gardenia Bowl

ROCK CRYSTAL
Thistle
(1066)

P.499
Calla Lily Candlestick

3900/72
6 in. 2 Lite Candlestick

P.384
11 in. Oval Bowl

P.430
12 in. Belled Bowl

P.214
10 in. 3 part Relish

P.426
8 in. Salad Bowl

P.427
10 in. Salad Bowl

ROCK CRYSTAL
Silver Maple
(1067)

P.254
Sugar & Cream

P.1491
4 Pc. Twin Salad Dressing Set

P.532
6 in. Tall Comport

P.306
6 in. Candy Box & Cover

P.533
3 Pc. Mayonnaise Set

P.125
14 in. Plate

278
11 in. Ftd. Vase

P.126
13½ in. Gardenia Bowl

ROCK CRYSTAL
Silver Maple
(1067)

P.499
Calla Lily Candlestick

3900/72
6 in. 2 lite Candlestick

P.384
11 in. Oval Bowl

P.430
12 in. Belled Bowl

P.214
10 in. 3 Part Relish

P.426
8 in. Salad Bowl

P.427
10 in. Salad Bowl

ROCK CRYSTAL
Miscellaneous Items

3900/117
20 oz. Jug
King Edward (821)

3900/114
32 oz. Martini Jug
King Edward (821)

3900/115
76 oz. Jug
King Edward (821)

P. 437
13 in. 2 pc. Flower Center
Harvest (1053)

29
Cambridge Arms Unit
Harvest (1053)

ROCK CRYSTAL
Miscellaneous Items

3900/115
76 oz. Jug
Engraved 1064

3900/115
76 oz. Jug
Engraved Laurel Wreath

3900/115
76 oz. Jug
Engraved 1065

3900/115
76 oz. Jug
Engraved Bexley

ROCK CRYSTAL
Granada
(1068)

3900/35
13½ in. 2 Hdl. Cake Plate

3900/68
5 in. Candlestick

3900/166
14 in. Torte Plate

278
11 in. Ftd. Vase

3121
5⅜ in. Comport

3900/41
Sugar & Cream

647
2 lite Candlestick

3900/62
12 ir. 4 Ftd. Bowl

ROCK CRYSTAL
Granada
(1068)

3900/125
9 in. 3 part Celery & Relish

3900/126
12 in. 3 part Celery & Relish

3900/120
12 in. 5 part Celery & Relish

3900/131
8 in. 2 Hdl. Ftd. Bonbon Plate

3900/111
4 pc. Mayonnaise Set

3900/34
11 in. 2 Hdl. Bowl

3900/129
3 pc. Mayonnaise Set

274
10 in. Ftd. Vase

3900/165
Candy Box & Cover

3900/130
7 in. 2 Hdl. Ftd. Bon Bon

Cambridge, Ohio - - - U. S. A.

146-L

ROCK CRYSTAL
Granada
(1068)

3139
10 oz. Goblet

3139
7 oz. Sherbet

3139
2½ oz. Cocktail

3139
2½ oz. Sherry Wine

3139
4½ oz. Claret

3139
4½ oz. Oyster Cocktail

3139
1 oz. Cordial

3139
12 oz. Ftd. Ice Tea

3139
5 oz. Ftd. Tumbler

555
7½ in. Salad Plate

Rock Crystal Engraved Miscellaneous

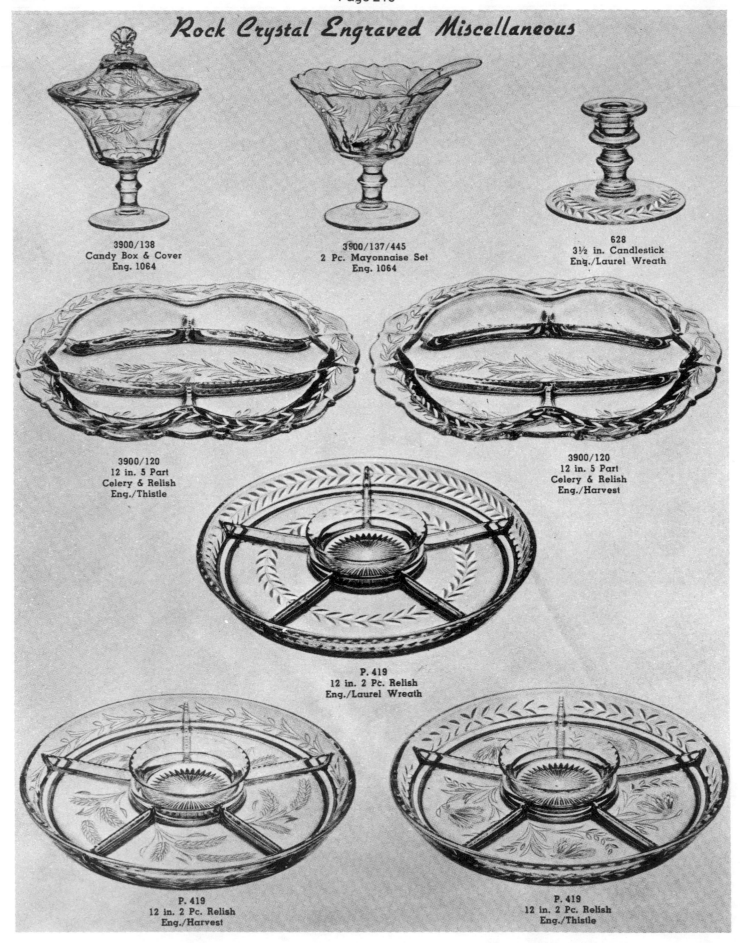

3900/138
Candy Box & Cover
Eng. 1064

3900/137/445
2 Pc. Mayonnaise Set
Eng. 1064

628
3½ in. Candlestick
Eng./Laurel Wreath

3900/120
12 in. 5 Part
Celery & Relish
Eng./Thistle

3900/120
12 in. 5 Part
Celery & Relish
Eng./Harvest

P. 419
12 in. 2 Pc. Relish
Eng./Laurel Wreath

P. 419
12 in. 2 Pc. Relish
Eng./Harvest

P. 419
12 in. 2 Pc. Relish
Eng./Thistle

Cambridge, Ohio - - - U. S. A.

ROCK CRYSTAL ENGRAVED

Rondo
(1081)

Delhi
(1078)

7966
Low Goblet
Rondo

7966
Low Sherbet
Rondo

7966
Low Cocktail
Rondo

7966
Low Wine
Rondo

7966
Low Cordial
Rondo

555
7½ in. Salad Plate
Rondo

555
7½ in. Salad Plate
Delhi

7966
Low Cordial
Delhi

7966
Low Goblet
Delhi

7966
Low Sherbet
Delhi

7966
Low Cocktail
Delhi

7966
Low Wine
Delhi

Miscellaneous

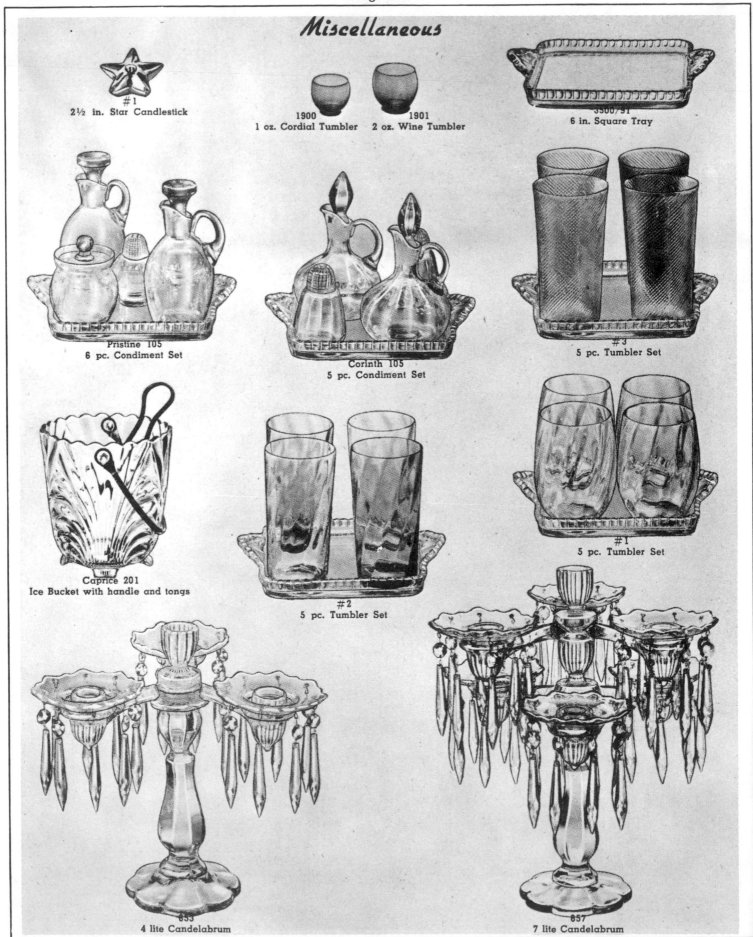

#1
2½ in. Star Candlestick

1900
1 oz. Cordial Tumbler

1901
2 oz. Wine Tumbler

3500/91
6 in. Square Tray

Pristine 105
6 pc. Condiment Set

Corinth 105
5 pc. Condiment Set

#3
5 pc. Tumbler Set

Caprice 201
Ice Bucket with handle and tongs

#2
5 pc. Tumbler Set

#1
5 pc. Tumbler Set

653
4 lite Candelabrum

657
7 lite Candelabrum

Miscellaneous
15 ITEM ASSORTMENT

3400/90
6 in. 2 part Relish

3400/1180
5¼ in. 2 Handle Bonbon

3400/1181
6 in. 2 Handle Plate

3900/1177
Salt & Pepper Shaker

3500/15
Ind. Sugar & Cream

3500/54
6½ in. Ftd. Bonbon

3500/55
6 in. Ftd. Basket

3500/69
6½ in. 3 part Relish

3500/139
5½ in. Square Honey Dish

3900/124
7 in. 2 part Relish

3500/161
8 in. Ftd. Plate

P.477
9½ in. Pickle

3900/153
7¼ in. Shallow cupped Bonbon

3900/151
5 in. Low Cupped Bonbon

3900/152
6½ in. Shallow Crimped Bonbon

MISCELLANEOUS

92
Mount Vernon
Ice Bucket with Handle and Tongs

68
Mount Vernon
4 in. Ash Tray

63
Mount Vernon
3½ in. Ash Tray

3011
3 oz. Cocktail

43
Martha Washington
7 in. 3 part Candy Box and Cover

235
Cascade
5 in. Rose Bowl

| 1203 | Caprice 96 | P.358 | P.360 | 1258 | Cascade 96 |

(with chrome tops)

209
Caprice Cigarette Box and Cover
(4½ x 3½)

| 1465 (Cut) | 3900/1177 | 1262 | Mt. V. 89 (Tall) | 1476 (Tall) |

(with chrome tops)

1596
6½ in. Candlestick

3400/71
3 in. 4 ftd. Nut Cup

39
Cascade
3 pc. Sugar and Cream Set

Miscellaneous

3400/142
3 pc. Oil Set

1401
8⅜ in. Salad Plate

496
12 oz. Tall Joe

496
1 oz. Little Joe

3011
1 oz. Cordial

3011
3 oz. Cocktail

COLORED GLASSWARE
Ebony

1713
4 pc. Smoker Set

P.733
3 in. Ash Tray

P.734
4½ in. Ash Tray

P.735
6 in. Ash Tray

P.747
Cigarette Box & Cover

390
6 in. Ash Tray

1711
2¼" x 3½" Ash Tray

391
8 in. Ash Tray

P.360
Salt & Pepper
(Chrome Tops)

P.361
3 pc. Salt & Pepper Set
(Chrome Tops)

1237
9 in. Ftd. Vase

1066
7 in. Ftd. Ivy Ball

3011
3 oz. Cocktail

3900/575
10 in. Cornucopia Vase

COLORED GLASSWARE
Ebony

3400/48
13 in. 4 Ftd. Bowl, Crimped

3400/4
12 in. Ftd. Bowl, Flared

P.499
Calla Lily Candlestick

P.492
1¾ in. Candlestick

P.493
2¾ in. Candlestick

P.495
3¾ in. Candlestick

3500/55
6 in. 2 Hdl. Basket

P.384
11 in. Oval Bowl

P.569
9 in. Crimped Vase

P.300
6 in. 3 Ftd. Candy Box & Cover

P.532
6 in. Tall Comport

1176
8, in. Salad Plate
also

1174
6 in. Bread & Butter Plate

Miscellaneous

3500/87
12 in. 7 Pc.
Peg Relish Set

7801—5 oz.
Whiskey Sour

321—9 oz.
Old Fashioned Cocktail

321—12 oz.
Old Fashioned Cocktail

7801
1 oz. Pousse Cafe

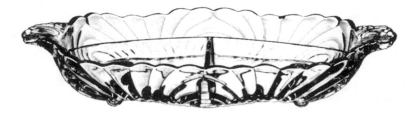

Caprice
125—12 in. 3 Part
Celery & Relish

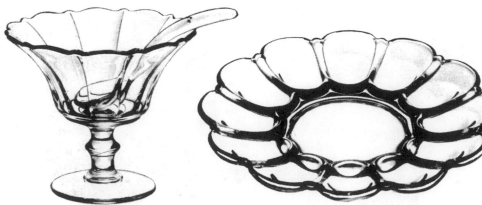

3900/137/445
2 Pc. Mayonnaise Set
also
3900/137
6 in. Comport (no ladle)

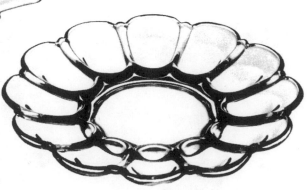

3600/157
Deviled Egg Plate

3900/138
Candy Box & Cover

Miscellaneous

MV 102
Miniature Urn
Coral

P. 578
Miniature
Cornucopia
Coral

702
Miniature
Cornucopia
Coral

1040
3 in. Swan
Coral

1715
4 pc. Stackaway
Ash Tray Set

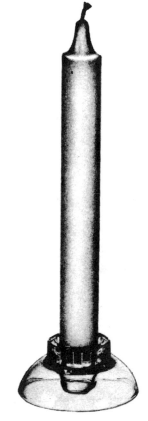

1715
Candleholder

1715
Ash Tray

55
Hurricane Lamp

1539
6 in. Peg Nappy
Blown

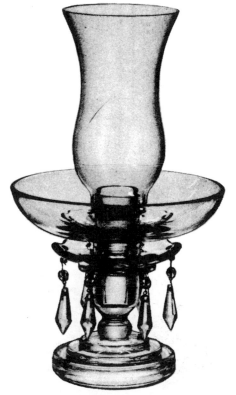

54
Hurricane Lamp

COLORED GLASSWARE
Emerald
Mandarin Gold

1401
Goblet

1401
Sherbet

1401
Cocktail

1401
12 oz. Ftd. Tumbler

1401
5 oz. Ftd. Tumbler

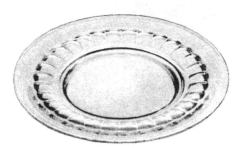

1401
8⅜ in. Salad Plate

Cascade 129
3 pc. Mayonnaise Set
(Crystal Ladle)

Cascade 165
Candy Box & Cover

Cascade 573
9½ in. Vase

Cambridge, Ohio - - - U. S. A.

COLORED GLASSWARE
Emerald
Mandarin Gold

Cascade 39
3 pc. Sugar & Cream Set

Cascade 41
Sugar & Cream

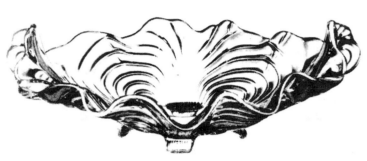

Caprice 66
13 in. Bowl, crimped, 4 Ftd.

Caprice 151
5 in. 2 Handle Jelly

Caprice 133
6 in. Low Ftd. Bonbon, Square

Caprice 1338
3 lite Candlestick

3900/37
Sugar & Cream Tray

3900/125
9 in. 3 part Celery & Relish

COLORED GLASSWARE
Emerald
Mandarin Gold

3900/135
5 in. Comport

3900/136
5½ in. Comport

M.250
Individual Sugar & Cream

P.499
Cally Lily Candlestick

3900/37/M.250
3 pc. Sugar & Cream Set

1138
Sea Gull (Crystal)

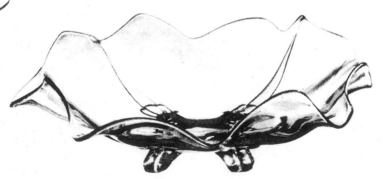

3400/48
13 in. Bowl, 4 Ftd.
Crimped Shaliow

SS 33
4 in. 3 Ftd. Ash Tray

SS 31
8 in. Oval Dish, 4 Ftd.

SS 35
Cigarette Box & Cover,
4½″ x 3½″

COLORED GLASSWARE
Emerald
Mandarin Gold

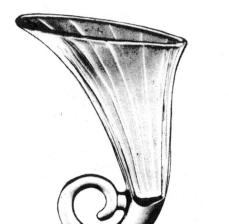

3900/575
10 in. Cornucopia

1040
3 in. Swan

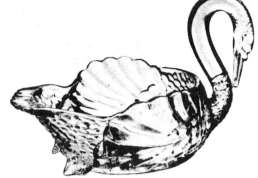

1043
8½ in. Swan

6004
6 in. Ftd. Vase

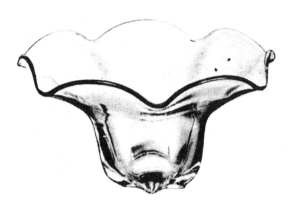

P.569
4 x 9 in. Crimped Vase

3400/71
3 in. 4 Ftd. Nut Cup

319
9 oz. Georgian Tumbler

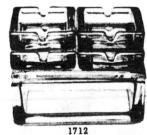

1712
6 pc. Stowaway Set—Crys. Box & Cover
This set can be furnished with Crys. Box
& Cover and 4 Ash Trays of either color
or 2 Ash Trays of each color.

1713
4 pc. Smoker Set
1—S.S.35 Bottom—Mandarin Gold or Emerald
1—1712 Cover—Crystal
2—1712 Ash Trays—Mandarin Gold or Emerald

COLORED GLASSWARE
Emerald
Madarian Gold

P.384
11 in. Oval Bowl

3900/166
14 in. Plate, r.e.

P.360
Salt & Pepper
(Chrome Tops)

P.361
3 pc. Salt & Pepper Set
(Chrome Tops)

1711
2¼" x 3½"
Ash Tray

1237
9 in. Ftd. Vase

1238
12 in. Ftd. Vase

SS-11
7 in. Comport

6004
8 in. Ftd. Vase

1066
7 in. Ftd. Ivy Ball

COLORED GLASSWARE
Emerald
MANDARIN GOLD

1337
Cigarette Holder

1714
3 pc. Smoker Set

1066
5⅜ in. Comport, Blown

1066
5⅜ in. Cov'd Candy Box

P. 572
6 in. Vase

1042
6½ in. Swan

4000/67
5 in. Candlestick

306
3 in. Vase

307
3 in. Vase Crimped

309
4½ in. Vase

310
3½ in. Vase

3400/1181
6 in. 2 Hdl. Plate

3400/1180
5¼ in. 2 Hdl. Bonbon

3500/161
8 in. 2 Hdl. Ftd. Plate

3500/55
6 in. 2 Hdl. Ftd. Basket

3400/90
6 in. 2 part Relish

3500/54
6 in. 2 Hdl. Ftd. Bonbon

3500/69
6½ in. 3 part Relish

COLORED GLASSWARE
Carmen

3103
10 oz. Goblet

3103
6 oz. Low Sherbet

3103
3½ oz. Cocktail

3103
3 oz. Wine

3103
4½ oz. Claret

3103
5 oz. Oyster Cocktail

3103
1 oz. Cordial

3103
12 oz. Ftd. Ice Tea

3103
5 oz. Ftd. Tumbler

555
7½ in. Salad Plate

COLORED GLASSWARE
Carmen

319
9 oz. Georgian Tumbler

3011
Cocktail

1066
7 in. Ftd. Ivy Ball

1066
5½ in. Blown Comport

1066
Ftd. Candy Box & Cover

P.569
9 in. Crimped Vase or Bowl

6004
6 in. Ftd. Vase

1237
9 in. Ftd. Vase

1040
3 in. Swan

1042
6½ in. Swan

1043
8½ in. Swan

1901
2 oz. Tumbler

3400/92
32 oz. Ball Decanter

3400/48
13 in. 4 Ftd. Crimped Bowl

1066 Line
Stemware

11 oz. Goblet

7 oz. Tall Sherbet

3½ oz. Cocktail

3 oz. Wire

4½ oz. Claret

1 oz. Cordial

12 oz. Ftd. Ice Tea

5 oz. Ftd. Tumbler

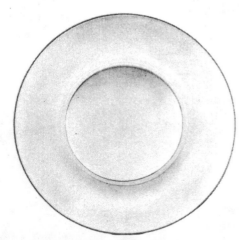

556
8 in. Salad Plate

Regency Stemware

10 oz. Goblet

7 oz. Tall Sherbet

7 oz. Low Sherbet

3½ oz. Cocktail

3 oz. Wine

4½ oz. Claret

4½ oz. Oyster Cocktail

1 oz. Cordial

12 oz. Ftd. Ice Tea

10 oz. Ftd. Tumbler

5 oz. Ftd. Tumbler

3790 LINE
Stemware
"SIMPLICITY"

Goblet

Low Sherbet

Cocktail

Wine

Claret

Oyster Cocktail

Cordial

12 oz. Ftd. Ice Tea

5 oz. Ftd. Tumbler

555
7½ in. Salad Plate

3795 LINE
STEMWARE
Sweetheart

Goblet

Low Sherbet

Cocktail

Wine

Claret

Oyster Cocktail

Cordial

12 oz. Ftd. Ice Tea

5 oz. Ftd. Tumbler

(7967) *(Melody)* STEMWARE

Low Goblet

Low Sherbet

Low Cocktail

7967
7 in. Salad Plate

(3796)

Low Wine

Low Cordial

3109 Line
Stemware

9 oz. Goblet

6 oz. Tall Sherbet

6 oz. Low Sherbet

4 oz. Claret

3 oz. Wine

3½ oz. Cocktail

1 oz. Cordial

4½ oz. Oyster Cocktail

12 oz. Ftd. Ice Tea

5 oz. Ftd. Tumbler

556
8 in. Salad Plate

7966 Line
Stemware

9 oz. Goblet

6 oz. Tall Sherbet

6 oz. Low Sherbet

3½ oz. Cocktail

2 oz. Sherry

1 oz. Cordial

4 oz. Claret

4½ oz. Oyster Cocktail (3109)

12 oz. Ftd. Ice Tea

556
8 in. Salad Plate

Tuxedo
(Patent Pending)

1
10 oz. Goblet

2
7 oz. Sherbet

3
2½ oz. Cocktail

4
2½ oz. Wine

5
4½ oz. Claret

6
1 oz. Cordial

10
14 oz. Ftd. Ice Tea

7
12 oz. Ftd. Tumbler

8
8 oz. Ftd. Tumbler

9
5 oz. Ftd. Tumbler

1401 LINE
Stemware

1401
10 oz. Tall Goblet

1401
6 oz. Tall Sherbet

1401
10 oz. Low Goblet

1401
6 oz. Low Sherbet

1401
3½ oz. Cocktail or Wine

1401
1 oz. Cordial

1401
4½ oz. Claret

1401
12 oz. Ftd. Ice Tea

1401
5 oz. Ftd. Tumbler

1401
8⅜ in. Salad Plate

Cambridge 4 pc. Game Set

10 oz. Ftd. Tumbler
Heart and Diamond foot in Carmen
Spade and Club Foot in Ebony

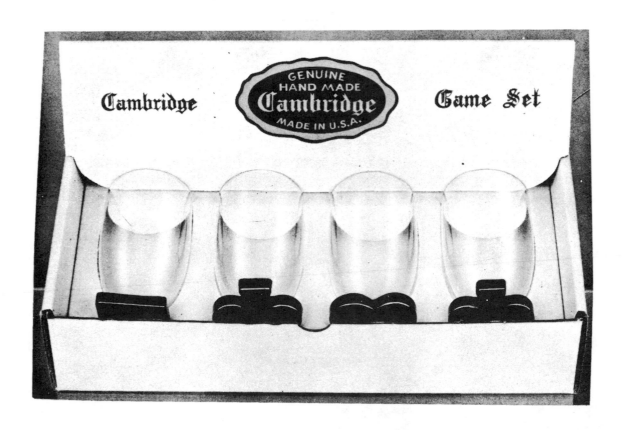

Cambridge   GENUINE HAND MADE Cambridge MADE IN U.S.A.   Game Set

Miscellaneous

7966
4½ oz. Oyster Cocktail

7966
10 oz. Ftd. Tumbler

103
2 pc. Nite Set

3400/141
80 oz. Jug

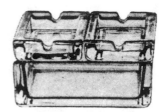

1714
3 pc. Smoker Set

1066
5⅜ in. Comport

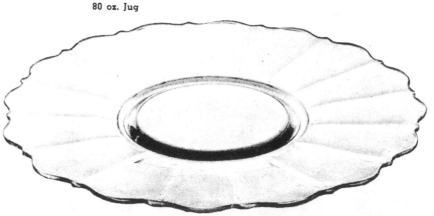

3900/167
14 in. Plate

1066
5⅜ in. Candy Box & Cover

M.V. 102
2 Hdl. Miniature Vase
Coral

SS66
Candlestick
Coral

GOLD DECORATION
D/1063 (Talisman Rose)

7966
9 oz. Goblet

7966
6 oz. Tall Sherbet

7966
6 oz. Low Sherbet

7966
4½ oz. Oyster Cocktail

7966
4 oz. Claret

7966
3½ oz. Cocktail

7966
2 oz. Sherry

7966
1 oz. Cordial

7966
12 oz. Ftd. Ice Tea

7966
10 oz. Ftd. Tumbler

556
8 in. Salad Plate

GOLD DECORATED
D/1063 (Talisman Rose)

628
3½ in. Candlestick

P. 430
12 in. Bowl, Belled

274
10 in. Ftd. Vase

532
6 in. Tall Comport

306
6 in. Candy Box & Cover
(Cut Knob)

721
2½ in. Ash Tray Square
(D/450)

747
Cigarette Box & Cover

278
11 in. Ftd. Vase

P. 125
14 in. Plate

GOLD DECORATED
D/Woodlily

7966
Low Goblet

7966
Low Sherbet

7966
Low Cocktail

1176
8½ in. Salad Plate
Square

7966
Low Cordial

7966
Low Wine

147
8 oz. Marmalade & Cover
& Spoon

1532
3 pc. Mayonnaise Set

533
5½ in. Comport

GOLD DECORATED
D/Woodlily

P. 54
6½ in. Hld. Ftd.
Comport

P. 56
8 in. 2 Hld. Ftd.
Plate

P. 747
Cigarette Box & Cover

P. 306
6 in. Candy Box & Cover

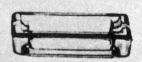

1711
2¼" x 3½" Ash Tray
Gold Edge Only

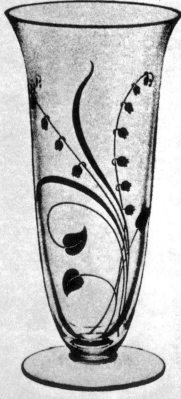

278
11 in. Ftd. Vase

1309
5 in. Globe Vase

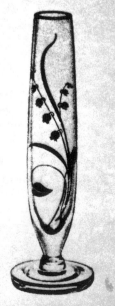

P. 604
8 in. Ftd. Bud Vase

Cambridge, Ohio - - - U. S. A.

"CAMBRIDGE ARMS"

SMART
TABLE APPOINTMENTS

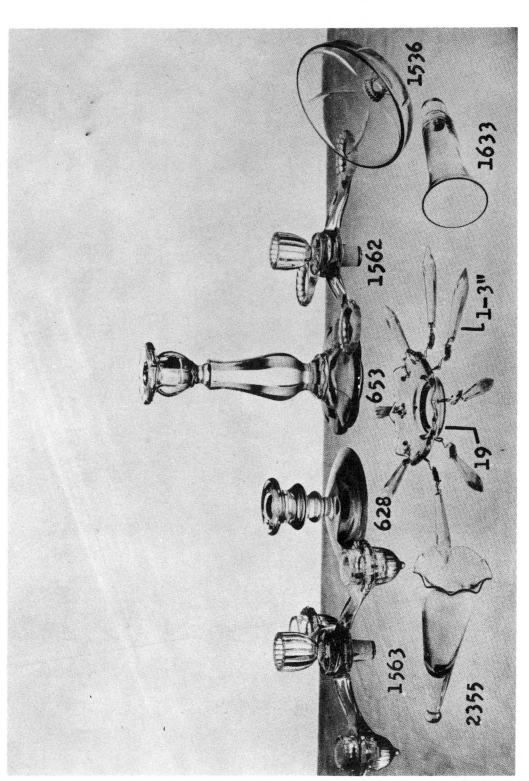

Designs For Dining

Patent No. D154701–D154796

"CAMBRIDGE ARMS"
Smart Table Appointments
DESIGNS for DINING

No. 1

No. 2

No. 3

No. 4

"CAMBRIDGE ARMS"
Smart Table Appointments
DESIGNS for DINING

No. 5

No. 6

No. 7

No. 8

"CAMBRIDGE ARMS"
Smart Table Appointments
DESIGNS for DINING

No. 9

No. 10

No. 11

No. 12

"CAMBRIDGE ARMS"
Smart Table Appointments
DESIGNS for DINING

No. 14

No. 15

No. 16

No. 17

"CAMBRIDGE ARMS"
Smart Table Appointments
DESIGNS for DINING

No. 18

No. 19

No. 20

No. 21

"CAMBRIDGE ARMS"
Smart Table Appointments
DESIGNS for DINING

No. 22

No. 23

No. 26

No. 25

"CAMBRIDGE ARMS"
Smart Table Appointments
DESIGNS for DINING

No. 27

No. 28

No. 30

No. 29

"CAMBRIDGE ARMS"
Smart Table Appointments
DESIGNS for DINING

No. 31

No. 32

No. 653

No. 5

"CAMBRIDGE ARMS"
Smart Table Appointments
DESIGNS for DINING

No. 16

No. 34

No. 12

No. 33

510/1537
Ball Candlestick
& Peg Nappy w/Candlewell

510/1537/1633
3 pc. Vase Set

510/1538/1606
3 pc. Hurricane Lamp

1636
4½ in. Bird Figure

437
13 in. 2 pc. Flower Center

510/1538/1636
3 pc. Set

HEIRLOOM

5000/1
9 oz. Goblet

5000/2
6 oz. Sherbet

5000/3
3 oz. Cocktail

5000/4
12 oz. Ftd. Tumbler

5000/5
5 oz. Ftd. Juice

5000/14
5 oz. Ftd. Tumbler

5000/13
6 oz. Sherbet

5000/12
10 oz. Ftd. Tumbler

5000/11
12 oz. Ftd. Tumbler

5000/15
Finger Bowl
5000/15
Finger Bowl Plate

5000/16
4½ in. Dessert or Fruit Dish

5000/17
Cup & Saucer

HEIRLOOM

5000/20
6 in. B. & B. Plate

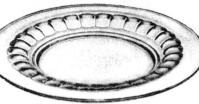

5000/22
8 in. Salad Plate

5000/24
9½ in. Dinner Plate

5000/40
Ind. Sugar & Cream

5000/38
3 pc. Sugar & Cream Set (40/37)

5000/37
Sugar & Cream Tray

5000/45
Sugar & Cream

5000/44
Ftd. Sugar & Cream

5000/41
Sugar & Cream

HEIRLOOM

5000/67
3½ in. Candlestick

5000/50
10 in. Ftd. Bowl

5000/62
12½ in. Bowl

5000/57
9½ in. Bowl, Salad

5000/70
9 in. Candlestick

5000/81
9½ in. Shallow Bowl

HEIRLOOM

5000/80
80 oz. Jug

5000/68
4½ in. Candlestick

5000/79
32 oz. Jug

5000/65
10 in. Oval Bowl

5000/138
Candy Box & Cover

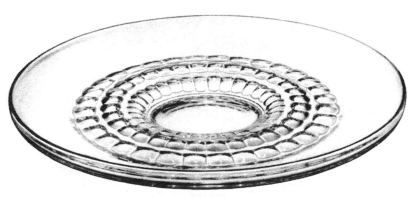

5000/33
14 in. Plate, r.e.

5000/72
9½ in. Candelabrum

5000/71
9½ in. Candelabrum Base

Cambridge, Ohio - - - U. S. A.

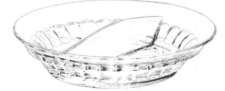

HEIRLOOM

5000/122
7 in. 2 Compt. Relish

5000/120
5¼ in. 2 Compt. Relish

5000/124
7 in. 3 Compt. Relish

5000/76
Salt & Pepper w/chrome top

5000/126
10 in. Oval 3 Compt. Cel. & Rel.

5000/100
Oil or Vinegar

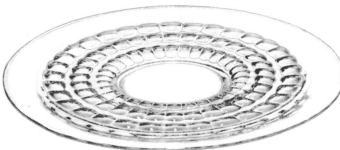

5000/26
12½ in. Plate

5000/32
13 in. Plate, r.e.

HEIRLOOM

5000/129
3 pc. Mayonnaise Set

5000/127/445
2 pc. Mayonnaise Set

5000/127
5½ in. Low Ftd. Comport

5000/136
Comport

5000/165
Candy Box & Cover

5000/78
11 in. Ftd. Vase

5000/77
8½ in. Fan Vase

MAGNOLIA

3790
Goblet

3790
Sherbet

3790
Cocktail

3790
Claret

3790
Cordial

3790
Wine

3790
12 oz. Ftd. Ice Tea

3790
5 oz. Ftd. Juice

3790
Oyster Cocktail

MAGNOLIA

P. 668
6 in. Bread & Butter Plate

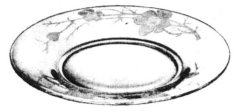

P. 556
8 in. Salad Plate

P. 933
Cup and Saucer

P. 360
Salt & Pepper w/chrome tops

P. 253
Individual Sugar & Cream

3900/37
Sugar & Cream Tray

P. 253/37
3 pc. Sugar & Cream Set

6 oz. Oil

P. 254—Sugar Cream

MAGNOLIA

P. 55
6 in. L.F. Basket

P. 54
6½ in. L.F. Comport

P. 56
8 in. L.F. Plate

3900/114
32 oz. Martini Jug

P. 1497
6 in. 3 Part Relish

P. 101
Cocktail Shaker
(Pat. D 133198)

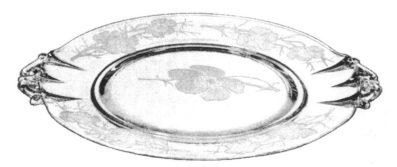

P. 1495
11½ in. 2 Hdl. Cake Plate

MAGNOLIA

3900/19
2 pc. Mayonnaise Set

P. 1532
3 pc. Mayonnaise Set

P. 1491
4 pc. Twin Salad Dressing Set

3400/1180
5¼ in. 2 Hdl. Bonbon

3400/1181
6 in. 2 Hdl. Bonbon Plate

P. 166
13½ in. Plate, r.e.

MAGNOLIA

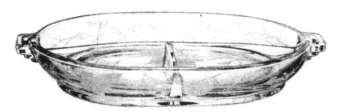

P. 214
10 in. 3 Part Relish

P. 306
Candy Box & Cover

P. 1498
8 in. 3 Part Relish

6004
8 in. Ftd. Vase

P. 247
11 in. Celery

278
11 in. Ftd. Vase

MAGNOLIA

P. 384
11 in. Oval Bowl

P. 628
3½ in. Candlestick

P. 430
12 in. Bowl, belled

3900/72
6 in. 2 lite Candlestick

3400/141
76 oz. Jug

AMBASSADOR ROCK CRYSTAL ENGRAVED

1953
Goblet

1953
Sherbet

1953
Cocktail

1953
Wine

1953
Cordial

1953
Ice Tea

1953
Juice

556
8 in. Salad Plate

JOAN OF ARC ROCK CRYSTAL ENGRAVED

1953
Goblet

1953
Sherbet

1953
Cocktail

1953
Wine

1953
Cordial

1953
Ice Tea

1953
Juice

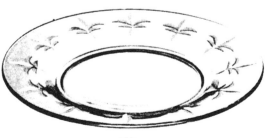

556
8 in. Salad Plate

SILVER WHEAT ROCK CRYSTAL ENGRAVED

1953
Goblet

1953
Sherbet

1953
Cocktail

1953
Wine

1953
Cordial

1953
Ice Tea

1953
Juice

556
8 in. Salad Plate

TROPICAL ROCK CRYSTAL ENGRAVED

3790
Goblet

3790
Sherbet

3790
Cocktail

3790
Claret

3790
Wine

3790
Cordial

3790
Oyster Cocktail

3790
Ice Tea

3790
Juice

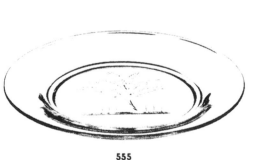

555
7½ in. Salad Plate

CATHEDRAL STEMWARE

1953
Goblet

1953
Sherbet

1953
Cocktail

1953
Cordial

1953
Wine

1953
Juice

1953
Ice Tea

DAWN

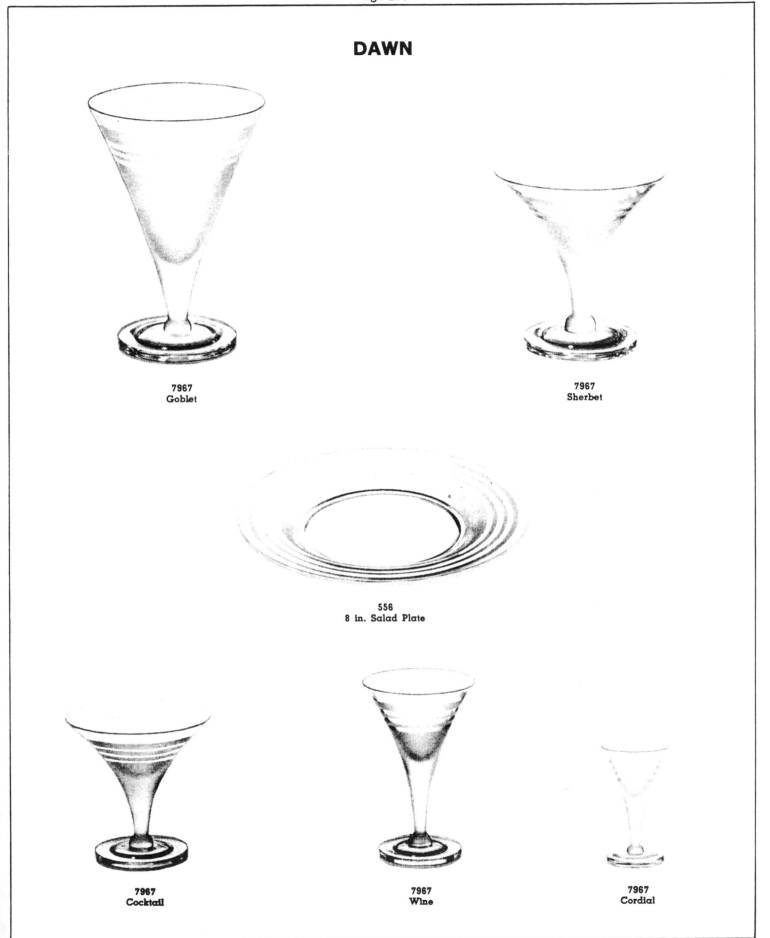

7967
Goblet

7967
Sherbet

556
8 in. Salad Plate

7967
Cocktail

7967
Wine

7967
Cordial

DECANTERS

1380
26 oz. Etched Scotch

1380
26 oz. Etched Bourbon

1380
26 oz. Plain

1380
26 oz. Etched Rye

1380
26 oz. Etched Gin

AMERICAN BEAUTY

P. 55
6½ in. Low Comport

P. 56
8 in. Ftd. Plate

P. 54
6 in. Ftd. Basket

P. 306
Candy Box & Cover

P. 628
3½ in. Candlestick

P. 532
6 in. Comport

P. 430
12 in. Bowl

6004
8 in. Ftd. Vase

P. 1495
11½ in. 2 Hdl. Cake Plate

278
11 in. Ftd. Vase

P. 166
13½ in. Plate, Rolled Edge

ROCK CRYSTAL ENGRAVED
Rondo
(1081)

7966
Low Goblet

7966
Low Sherbet

7966
Low Wine

7966
Low Cocktail

7966
Low Cordial

321—9 oz.
O.F. Cocktail

497
12 oz. Hiball

555
7½ in. Salad Plate

P. 360
Salt & Pepper w/chrome top

P. 254
Sugar & Cream

P. 290
6 oz. Oil g.s.

3700
5 in. Blown Comport

ROCK CRYSTAL ENGRAVED
Rondo
(1081)

3900/114
32 oz. Martini Jug

P. 101
32 oz. Cocktail Shaker
(Patent D-133198)

3900/115
76 oz. Jug

P. 427
10 in. Bowl

P. 426
8 in. Salad Bowl

ROCK CRYSTAL ENGRAVED
Rondo
(1081)

P. 533
5½ in. Comport

P. 671
Ice Tub

P. 1498
8 in. 3 Part Relish

P. 1532
3 Pc. Mayonnaise Set

P. 1491
4 Pc. Mayonnaise Set

P. 384
11 in. Oval Bowl

ROCK CRYSTAL ENGRAVED
Rondo
(1081)

P. 572
6 in. Vase

P. 247
11½ in. Celery

628
3½ in. Candlestick

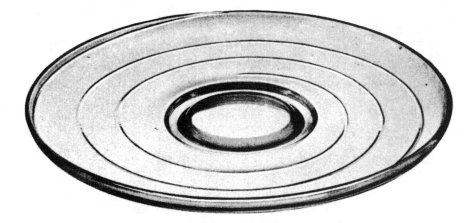

P. 166
13½ in. Plate (rolled edge)

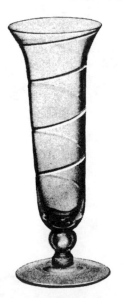

6004
8 in. Ftd. Vase

278
11 in. Ftd. Vase

CAMBRIDGE MILK GLASS

W 54
32 oz. Jug

W 55
10 oz. Table Tumbler to match Jug
(Not illustrated)

W 60
32 oz. Jug

W 62
Sugar

W 62
Cream

W 61
Ftd. Sugar

W 61
Ftd. Cream

W 63
Ind. Sugar

W 63
Ind. Cream

W 65
10 oz. Goblet

W 66
6½ oz. Sherbet

W 67
12 oz. Ftd. Tumbler

W 68
3 oz. Ftd. Tumbler

W 71
40 oz. Decanter

Cambridge, Ohio - - - U. S. A.

W-1

CAMBRIDGE MILK GLASS

W 69
1 oz. Ftd. Cordial

W 72
14 oz. Tumbler

W 73
10 oz. Tumbler

W 74
5 oz. Juice

W 70
11 oz. Decanter

W 75
3 in. Coaster

W 81
2 handled Open Salt

W 79
5 in. Ivy Ball

W 77
Covered Urn

W 76
4 in. Candlestick

W 83
Salt & Pepper

W 78
7½ in. Comport

W 80
6 in. Crimped Bowl

W 82
7 oz. Marmalade & Cover

W 84
Salt & Pepper

CAMBRIDGE MILK GLASS

W 85
4½ in. Puff Box & Cover

W 86
Honey Dish & Cover

W 87
12 in. Urn & Cover

W 88
5 in. Candlestick

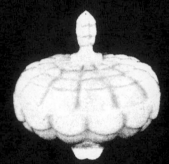

W 89
Candy Box & Cover

W 90
3 oz. Oil, g.s.

W 94
3 in. Swan

W 92
3½ in. Cornucopia

W 93
12 oz. Mug

W 95
4½ in. Swan

W 91
3 lite Candlestick

W 98
4½ in. Swan Candlestick

W 97
8½ in. Swan

W 96
6½ in. Swan

CAMBRIDGE MILK GLASS

W 99
16 in. Swan Punch Bowl
(5 Qts.)

W 101
Cigarette Box & Cover
(4½ x 3½ in.)

W 103
4 in. Ash Tray

W 102
2¼ in. Ind. Ash Tray
w/Placecard Holder

W 104
9 in. Comport

W 100
5 oz. Swan Punch Cup

W 105
9 in. 3 Ftd. Bowl

W 106
6 in. Comport

W 107
6 in. Ftd. Candy Box & Cover

W 108
8 in. Oval Dish

Cambridge, Ohio - - - U. S. A.

CAMBRIDGE MILK GLASS

W 109
8 in. Dolphin Candlestick

W 110
9 in. Dolphin Candelabrum
w/ ≠19 bobeche and
8—≠1 3 in. prisms

W 111
5 in. Bon Bon

W 112
Cream

W 112
Sugar

W 115
16 in. Tulip Plate

W 114
7 in. Salad Plate

W 113
5 oz. Seafood Cocktail
or Sherbet

W 116
12 in. Oval Bowl

W 117
Cake Salver or Table Centerpiece

CAMBRIDGE MILK GLASS

W 118
Deviled Egg Plate

W 119
Heron Figure Flower Holder

W 120
Girl Figure

W 122
Pigeon Book Ends

W 125
3½ in. Vase

W 123
3 in. Urn

W 124
4½ in. Vase

W 121
Scotty Book Ends

W 126
5 in. Vase

W 127
6 in. Vase

W 128
7½ in. Vase

W 129
12 in. Vase

Cambridge, Ohio - - - U. S. A.

W-8

CAMBRIDGE MILK GLASS

W 131
7½ in. Shell Vase

W 132
8½ in. Fan Vase

W 130
8 in. Horn of Plenty Vase

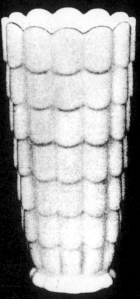

W 133
9½ in. Vase

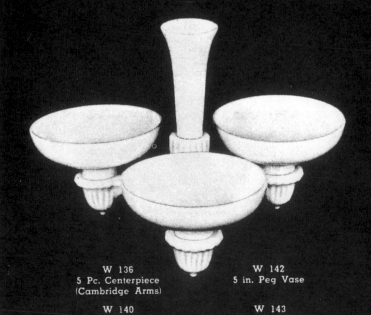

W 136
5 Pc. Centerpiece
(Cambridge Arms)

W 140
4 Candle Arm

W 142
5 in. Peg Vase

W 143
5 in. Peg Nappy

W 141
3½ in. Candlestick
(This is base for use in various
Cambridge Arm Units)

Ebon

by CAMBRIDGE

We are this year presenting Ebon.

Ebon is a black glass with a finish totally unlike any which has been on the market before. To describe this finish is difficult; to say it has a mat finish is incorrect, it really is a rough mat finish to which has been added a luster—a dull sheen which gives it a soft beauty. Borrowing, and changing a little, a phrase from a certain cigarette advertisement, Ebon is both a Treat and a Treatment.

Ebon is modern in that it harmonizes with the decorative trends of today; but its soft luster and flowing but distinct lines make it compatible with any period. It becomes a part of any color scheme and enhances any background against which it is shown.

The Cambridge Square Line has been noted for its correct lines and distinctive square base. The Ebon treatment brings out and emphasizes these predominate traits to such an extent that it could well be named "Silhouette".

THE CAMBRIDGE GLASS COMPANY
CAMBRIDGE, OHIO
. . . . fine American hand-made glassware . . . .

Ebon

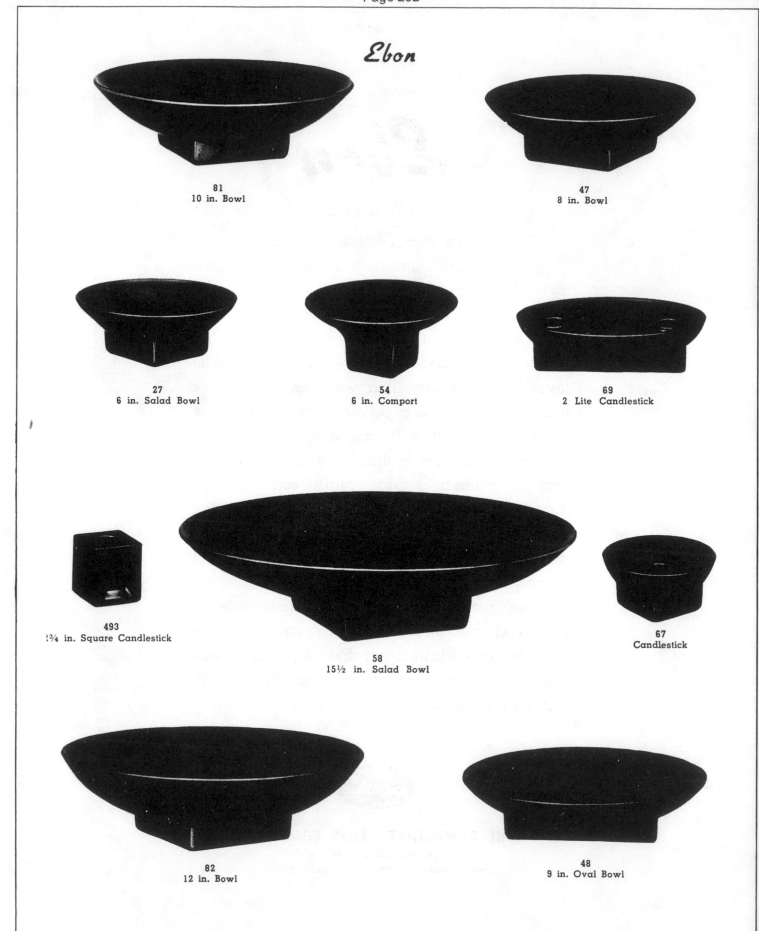

81
10 in. Bowl

47
8 in. Bowl

27
6 in. Salad Bowl

54
6 in. Comport

69
2 Lite Candlestick

493
1¾ in. Square Candlestick

58
15½ in. Salad Bowl

67
Candlestick

82
12 in. Bowl

48
9 in. Oval Bowl

E2

Ebon

747
Cigarette Box & Cover

151
3½ in. Ash Tray

40
Cigarette Urn

151
3½ in. Ash Tray

150
6½ in. Ash Tray

152
3 Pc. Smoker Set
(in white display box)

91
5½ in. Vase

628
3½ in. Candlestick
(Cambridge Arms)

165
Candy Box & Cover

1633
5 in. Peg Vase
(Cambridge Arms)

1536
5 in. Peg Nappy
(Cambridge Arms)

80
8 in. Bud Vase

78
9½ in. Vase

28
13½ in. Plate

PRICE GUIDE

Page 1 - Caprice		Cryst	M/Blu
CAP 13	3½" Coaster	6.00	18.00
CAP 17	Cup & Saucer	12.00	35.00
CAP 21	6½" B & B Plate	5.00	10.00
CAP 22	8½" Salad Plate	7.00	14.00
CAP 23	7½" Salad Plate	6.50	12.00
CAP 24	9½" Dinner Plate	25.00	85.00
CAP 38	Sugar & Cream	15.00	32.00
CAP 39	3 Pc. Sugar & Cream Set	22.00	48.00
	Also Alpine	25.00	50.00
CAP 40	Ind. Sugar & Cream	15.00	35.00
CAP 129	6½" 3 Pc. Mayonnaise	16.00	45.00
	Also Alpine	20.00	50.00
CAP 300	9 Oz. Goblet	12.00	34.00
CAP 300	5 Oz. Tall Sherbet	10.00	25.00
CAP 300	6 Oz. Low Sherbet	9.00	20.00
CAP 300	3 Oz. Cocktail	18.00	45.00
CAP 300	4½ Oz. Claret	25.00	65.00
CAP 300	1 Oz. Cordial	25.00	85.00
CAP 300	2½ Oz. Wine	20.00	55.00
CAP 300	4½ Oz. Oyster Cocktail	14.00	40.00
CAP 300	5 Oz. Ftd. Tumbler	9.00	22.00
CAP 300/2	12 Oz. Ftd. Tumbler	11.00	28.00
CAP 310	12 Oz. Ice Tea	12.00	34.00

Page 2 - Caprice		Cryst	M/Blu	E/Grn	M/Gld
CAP 30	16" Plate	45.00	85.00		
	Also Alpine	50.00	95.00		
CAP 32	11" Cabaret Plate, 4 Ftd.	25.00	45.00		
CAP 33	14" Cabaret Plate, 4 Ftd.	25.00	50.00		
	Also Alpine	30.00	55.00		
CAP 37	6" Oval Tray	10.00	16.00		
CAP 53	10½" Crimped Bowl, 4 Ftd.	22.00	50.00		
CAP 54	10½" Belled Bowl, 4 Ftd.	22.00	50.00		
CAP 61	12½" Crimped Bowl, 4 Ftd.	22.00	50.00		
	Also Alpine	26.00	55.00		
CAP 62	12½" Belled Bowl, 4 Ftd.	20.00	50.00		
	Also Alpine	26.00	55.00		
CAP 65	11" 2 Hdl. Oval Bowl, 4 Ftd.	22.00	45.00		
CAP 66	13" Bowl, Crimped, 4 Ftd.	25.00	50.00	50.00	50.00
	Also Alpine	28.00	55.00		
CAP 67	2½" Candlestick ......ea.	8.00	15.00		
CAP 70	7" Candlestick with Prism .....pr.	40.00	70.00		
	Also Alpine	40.00	75.00		
CAP 81	11½" 4 Ftd. Bowl, Shallow	20.00	40.00		
CAP 82	13½" 4 Ftd. Bowl, Shallow	22.00	45.00		
CAP 102	9" Pickle	12.00	35.00		
CAP 117	3 Oz. Oil, G.S.	25.00	70.00		
CAP 120	6¾" 2 Part Relish	10.00	25.00		
CAP 122	8" 3 Part Relish	12.00	33.00		
CAP 124	8½" 3 Part Celery & Relish	12.00	35.00		
	Also Alpine	18.00	38.00		

Page 2A - Caprice		Cryst	M/Blu
CAP 26	11½" Plate	20.00	45.00
CAP 28	14" Plate	25.00	50.00
CAP 31	2 Pc. Cake Salver	125.00	300.00
CAP 36	13" Cake Plate	100.00	245.00
CAP 183	80 Oz. Ball Jug	70.00	175.00
CAP 300	10 Oz. Ftd. Tumbler	10.00	25.00

Page 2B - Caprice		Cryst
CAP 301	Goblet	12.00
CAP 301	Sherbet	10.00
CAP 301	Cocktail	15.00
CAP 301	Claret	18.00
CAP 301	Cordial	35.00
CAP 301	Wine	18.00
CAP 301	Low Cocktail	10.00
CAP 301	Juice	10.00
CAP 301	Ice Tea	12.00

Page 3 - Caprice		Cryst	M/Blu	E/Grn	M/Gld	Mixed
CAP 96	Salt & Pepper Shaker	15.00	35.00			
CAP 130	7" Low Ftd. Comport	12.00	30.00			
CAP 131	8" Low Ftd. Plate	12.00	30.00			
	Also Alpine	14.00	33.00			
CAP 133	6" Low Ftd. Sq. Bonbon	12.00	30.00	30.00	30.00	
CAP 136	7" Tall Comport	20.00	55.00			
	Also Alpine	25.00	60.00			
CAP 151	5" 2 Handled Jelly	8.00	20.00	20.00	20.00	
CAP 152	6" 2 Hdl. Lemon Plate	7.00	18.00			
CAP 154	6" 2 Hdl. Square Bonbon	8.00	25.00			
CAP 165	6" 3 Ftd. Candy Box & Cover	30.00	65.00			
	Also Alpine	35.00	75.00			
CAP 207	Cigarette Box & Cover	15.00	30.00			
CAP 208	Cigarette Box & Cover	18.00	35.00			
	Also Alpine	20.00	40.00			
CAP 213	2¾" 3 Ftd. Ash Tray	4.75	10.00			
CAP 214	3" Ash Tray	4.00	10.00			
CAP 214/215/216						
	3 Pc. Ash Tray Set, Varitone Only					40.00

CAP 215	4" Ash Tray	4.50	12.00
CAP 216	5" Ash Tray	8.75	15.00
CAP 646	5" Candlestick	12.00	20.00
CAP 647	2 Lite Candlestick	15.00	25.00
CAP 1338	3 Lite Candlestick	20.00	40.00	40.00	40.00

Page 4 - Mount Vernon		Cryst
MT.V.1	10 Oz. Goblet	8.50
MT.V.2	6½ Oz. Tall Sherbet	7.00
MT.V.3	10 Oz. Footed Tumbler	7.25
MT.V.5	8½" Salad Plate	5.50
MT.V.7	Cup and Saucer	9.25
MT.V.9	Covered Urn	30.00
MT.V.19	6-⅜" B & B Plate	4.50
MT.V.19	Fingerbowl Plate	4.50
MT.V.20	12 Oz. Ftd. Tumbler	7.50
MT.V.21	5 Oz. Ftd. Tumbler	6.25
MT.V.22	3 Oz. Ftd. Tumbler	5.75
MT.V.23	Fingerbowl	5.75
MT.V.26	3½ Oz. Cocktail	7.50
MT.V.27	3 oz. Wine	8.00
MT.V.31	4½" Fruit Saucer	5.25
MT.V.87	1 Oz. Ftd. Cordial	12.00

Page 5 - Pristine		Cryst
P.101	32 Oz. Cocktail Shaker	25.00
P.102	48 Oz. Cocktail Shaker	30.00
P.123	8" Salad Plate	2.75
P.125	14" Plate	10.00
P.131	7" Blown Salad Plate	3.00
P.166	13½" Cabaret Plate, R.E.	11.50
P.169	16½" Cabaret Plate, R.E.	14.50
170	18" Plate	14.00
P.207	8" 3 Part Relish	9.00
P.212	10" 5 Part Celery & Relish	11.00
P.215	12" 3 Part Relish	12.50
P.7801	4 Oz. Cocktail	5.75

Page 6 - Pristine		Cryst	E/Grn	M/Gld	Ebony
P.245	6 Pc. Condiment Set	45.00			
P.246	11" Celery Tray	8.50			
P.285	5½" Twin Mayonnaise	8.25			
P.286	3 Pc. Twin Salad Dressing Set	14.50			
P.287	4 Pc. Twin Salad Dressing Set	15.50			
P.293	6 Oz. Oil	15.00			
P.306	6" Candy Box & Cover	20.00			
P.384	11" Oval Bowl	12.50	25.00	22.00	35.00
P.427	10" Salad Bowl	10.50			
P.430	12" Bowl, Belled	10.00			
P.431	13" Bowl	10.50			
P.440	10" Star Bowl	30.00			
P.671	Ice Tub	11.00			

Page 7 - Pristine		Cryst	Ebony
P.103	7" 3 Part Candy Box & Cover	17.50	
147	8 Oz. Marmalade & Cover	11.00	
P.151	3 Oz. Mustard & Cover	8.75	
P.300	6" 3 Ftd. Candy Box & Cover	40.00	55.00
P.454	8" Crescent Salad Plate	5.75	
P.477	9½" Corn Dish or Pickle	6.75	
P.531	7" Tall Comport	10.50	
P.532	6" Tall Comport	9.75	24.00
P.533	5½" Low Comport	6.25	
P.533	3 Pc. Mayonnaise Set	10.50	

Page 8 - Pristine		Cryst
P.138	Sugar & Cream	15.00
P.253	Individual Sugar & Cream	15.00
P.295	3 oz. Mustard & Cover	9.00
P.298	7 oz. Marmalade & Cover	9.75
P.555	7½" Salad Plate	4.50
P.556	8" Salad Plate	4.75
P.668	6" B & B Plate	3.00
P.810	9½" Dinner Plate	5.50
P.922	Cream Soup & Saucer	7.00
P.933	Cup & Saucer	5.75
P.1397	13½" Plate, Cabaret	13.50
P.1491	4 Pc. Twin Salad Dressing Set	13.50
P.1532	3 Pc. Mayonnaise Set	13.00
P.1534	5" Blown Nappy	3.00
P.1535	6½" Blown Nappy	3.50

Page 8A - Pristine		Cryst	E/Grn	M/Gld	Carmn	Ebony
P.41	2 Pc. Frappe Set	8.75				
P.126	13½" Gardenia Bowl	15.00				
P.426	8" Salad Bowl	9.75				
P.454	8" Crescent Salad Plate	5.75				
P.506	4" Candelabrum	20.00				
P.569	9" Crimped Vase	13.00	25.00	20.00	45.00	35.00
P.747	Cigarette Box & Cover	11.50				
P.1351	10½" Crimped Bowl	14.00				
P.1359	10½" Bowl	9.50				
P.1496	11½" Cheese & Cracker	15.50				

Page 8B -Pristine

		Cryst
P.214	10" 3 Part Relish	11.00
P.223	10" 3 Part Relish	12.50
P.248	11" Celery	7.25
P.254	Sugar & Cream	15.00
P.281	5½" 3 Pc. Mayonnaise	13.50
P.306	6" Candy Box & Cover	20.00
P.381	8½" Rim Soup	5.00
P.466	6½" Baked Apple	4.75
P.604	8" Ftd. Bud Vase	8.75
P.925	A D Cup & Saucer	15.00

Page 8C -Pristine

		Cryst
3700	5" Blown Comport	11.00
PRISTINE	11 Oz. Goblet	10.00
PRISTINE	6 Oz. Tall Sherbet	7.00
PRISTINE	6 Oz. Low Sherbet	6.00
PRISTINE	1 Oz. Cordial	25.00
PRISTINE	5 Oz. Oyster Cordial	8.00
PRISTINE	3½ Oz. Cocktail	9.00
PRISTINE	4½ Oz. Claret	9.00
PRISTINE	3 Oz. Wine	9.00
PRISTINE	12 Oz. Ftd. Ice Tea	8.00
PRISTINE	5 Oz. Ftd. Tumbler	7.00
PRISTINE	Finger Bowl & Plate	7.00

Page 8D -Pristine

		Cryst	E/Grn	M/Gild	Ebony
P.361	3 Pc. Salt & Pepper Set	18.00	25.00	25.00	30.00
P.424	13½" 2 Pc. Sandwich Set	30.00			
P.425	11½" 3 Pc. Relish	40.00			
P.436	13" 2 Pc. Sea Food Server	25.00			
P.437	13" 2 Pc. Flower Center	35.00			

Page 8E -Pristine

		Cryst
P.130	14" Blown Plate	15.00
P.421	2 Pc. Tidbit Tray	25.00
P.428	7" 2 Pc. Relish	28.00
P.432	9 Pc. Caster Set	70.00
P.510	2¾" Ball Candlestick	7.75
P.1410	6" Rose Bowl	12.00
PRISTINE	10 Oz. Ftd. Tumbler	8.00

Page 8F -Pristine

		Cryst
P.436/1902		
	8 Pc. Shrimp Server	40.00
P.442	3 Pc. Tidbit Set	40.00
P.443	3 Pc. Tidbit Set	36.00

Page 8G -Pristine

		Cryst
P.208	8" Oval Dish	7.50
P.247	11½" Celery	7.50
P.418	12" 5 Part Celery & Relish	16.00
P.419	12" 2 Pc. Relish	25.00
P.419	12" 6 Part Relish	18.00
P.435	7½" 2 Handle Bowl	7.50
P.461	10½" Shallow Cupped Bowl	9.75
P.1495	11½" 2 Handle Cake Plate	9.50
P.1497	6" 2 Part Relish	7.50
P.1498	8" 3 Part Relish	9.50

Page 8H -Cambridge Circle

		Cryst
3796	Goblet	8.00
3796	16 Oz. Ice Tea	8.00
3796	Sherbet	6.00
3796	Cocktail	6.00
3796	5 Oz. Ftd. Tumbler	7.00
3796	Cordial	20.00
3796	7" Salad Plate	6.00

Page 9 -3400 Line

		Cryst	E/Grn	M/Gild	Carmn	Ebony
3400/4	12" 4 Ftd. Bowl, Flared	16.00	25.00	25.00	50.00	40.00
	(See Page 31 for C/TUS)					
3400/35	11" 2 Hdl. Plate	10.00				
3400/45	11" 4 Ftd. Bowl, Fancy Edge	16.00				
3400/48	13" Bowl, 4 Ftd. Crimped	17.00	25.00	24.00	45.00	35.00
3400/52	5½" Butter & Cover	18.00				
3400/62	8½" Salad Plate	5.00				
3400/90	6" Hdl. 2 Part Relish	10.00	14.00	14.00	22.00	20.00
3400/160	12" 4 Ftd. Bowl, Oblong	16.00				
3400/176	7½" Salad Plate	5.00				

Page 10 -3500 Line

		Cryst	E/Grn	M/Gild
3500/5	8½" Salad Plate	5.75		
3500/54	6½" 2 Hdl. Ftd. Comport	10.00	14.00	12.00
3500/64	10" 3 Part 4 Ftd. Relish	14.50		
3500/69	6½" 3 Part Relish	7.75	14.00	12.00
3500/101	5-⅜" Comport, Blown	17.00		
3500/148	6" Comport	15.00		
3500/161	8" Footed Plate	7.25	12.00	10.00
3500/167	7½" Salad Plate	5.25		

Page 10A -Matched Barsemble Engraved Lattice

		Cryst
321	12 Oz. O.F. Cocktail	7.75

(Page 10A continued)

321	9 Oz. O.F. Cocktail	7.25
321	1½ Oz. Whiskey	8.00
497	14 Oz. Hiball	8.50
497	12 Oz. Hiball	8.50
3900/114	32 Oz. Martini Mixer	28.50
7801	4 Oz. Cocktail	8.00
7801	5 Oz. Whiskey Sour	8.50
7801	1 Oz. Pousse Cafe	14.00
P.92	26 Oz. Decanter	37.00
P.101	Cocktail Shaker	39.00
P.671	Ice Tub	16.50

Page 10B -Matched Barsemble Engraved Swirl

		Cryst
321	12 Oz. O.F. Cocktail	7.75
321	9 Oz. O.F. Cocktail	7.25
321	1½ Oz. Whiskey	8.00
497	14 Oz. Hiball	8.50
497	12 Oz. Hiball	8.50
3900/114	32 Oz. Martini Mixer	28.50
7801	4 Oz. Cocktail	8.00
7801	5 Oz. Whiskey Sour	8.50
7801	1 Oz. Pousse Cafe	14.00
P.92	26 Oz. Decanter	37.00
P.101	Cocktail Shaker	39.00
P.671	Ice Tub	16.50

Page 10C -Matched Barsemble Engraved Star

		Cryst
321	12 Oz. O.F. Cocktail	10.00
321	9 Oz. O.F. Cocktail	10.00
321	1½ Oz. Whiskey	10.00
497	14 Oz. Hiball	10.00
497	12 Oz. Hiball	10.00
3900/114	32 Oz. Martini Mixer	40.00
7801	4 Oz. Cocktail	10.00
7801	5 Oz. Whiskey Sour	10.00
7801	1 Oz. Pousse Cafe	20.00
P.92	26 Oz. Decanter	45.00
P.101	Cocktail Shaker	45.00
P.671	Ice Tub	25.00

Page 10D -Matched Barsemble Engraved FLEUR-DE-LIS

		Cryst
321	12 Oz. O.F. Cocktail	7.75
321	9 Oz. O.F. Cocktail	7.25
321	1½ Oz. Whiskey	8.00
497	14 Oz. Hiball	8.50
497	12 Oz. Hiball	8.50
3900/114	32 Oz. Martini Mixer	28.50
7801	4 Oz. Cocktail	8.00
7801	5 Oz. Whiskey Sour	8.50
7801	1 Oz. Pousse Cafe	18.00
P.92	26 Oz. Decanter	37.00
P.101	Cocktail Shaker	39.00
P.671	Ice Tub	16.50

Page 10E -Matched Barsemble Etched Vichy

		Cryst
321	12 Oz. O.F. Cocktail	8.25
321	9 Oz. O.F. Cocktail	7.75
321	1½ Oz. Whiskey	8.50
497	14 Oz. Hiball	9.00
497	12 Oz. Hiball	9.00
3900/114	32 Oz. Martini Mixer	35.00
7801	4 Oz. Cocktail	8.50
7801	5 Oz. Whiskey Sour	9.00
7801	1 Oz. Pousse Cafe	20.00
P.92	26 Oz. Decanter	39.00
P.101	Cocktail Shaker	41.00
P.671	Ice Tub	18.00

Page 11 -Candlesticks

		Cryst	M/Blu	Ebony	E/Grn	M/Gild
628	3½" Candlestick	10.00				
646	5" Candlestick	12.00	20.00	20.00	18.00	18.00
647	6" 2 Lite Candlestick	15.00	25.00	25.00	22.00	22.00
	(See Page 31 for C/TUS)					
1307	5" 3 Lite Candlestick	16.00				
1338	6" 3 Lite Candlestick	20.00	40.00		40.00	40.00
1357	6" 3 Lite Candlestick	30.00	100.00			
1457	6½" 3 Lite Candlestick	40.00				
M.494	4 " Candlestick	10.00				
M.495	5½" 2 Lite Candlestick	25.00				
CAP 67	2½" Candlestick ....ea	8.00	15.00			
P.492	1¾" Sq. Candlestick	6.00		10.00		
P.493	2¾" Sq. Candlestick	8.00		13.00		
P.495	3¾" Sq. Candlestick	10.00		15.00		
P.499	6½" Calla Lily	13.50		23.00	21.00	20.00
P.500	6½" Leaf Candlestick	15.00				
STAR 2	4" Star Candlestick	8.00	11.00			

Page 12 -Candelabra

		Cryst	M/Blu
648	6" Candelabra	25.00	
1268	6" 2 Lite Candelabra	50.00	
1356	7" 2 Lite Candelabra	70.00	

1440	9" Candelabra	35.00	
3121	7½" Candelabra	30.00	
M.496	6½" 2 Lite Candelabra	50.00	
CAP 70	7" Candelabra ......ea.	20.00	35.00

Page 13 - Candelabra

		Cryst
652	10" 3 Lite Candelabra	125.00
1358	7" 3 Lite Candelabra	70.00
1458	7½" 3 Lite Candelabra	110.00
1545	5½" 3 Lite Candelabra	35.00
1568	11" 5 Lite Candelabra	175.00
1569	8½" 5 Lite Candelabra	90.00

Page 14 - Epergnes

		Cryst
645	3 Lite Epergne	75.00
663	3 Lite Epergne	65.00
1357	3 Lite Epergne	85.00
1358	3 Lite Epergne	125.00

Page 15 - Hurricane Lamps

		Cryst
1603	10" Hurricane Lamp	50.00
1613	17" Hurricane Lamp	80.00
1617	9" Hurricane Lamp	40.00

Page 16 - Decanters

		Cryst	Carmn	Amyst	Amber
1070	36 Oz. Pinch Decanter, G.S.	30.00	50.00	35.00	35.00
1321	38 Oz. Ftd. Decanter, G.S.	30.00	60.00	40.00	40.00
1379	26 Oz. Colonial Decanter	30.00			
3400/92	32 Oz. Decanter, G.S.	18.50	45.00	29.00	28.00
3400/119	12 Oz. Decanter, G.S.	13.50	35.00	20.00	20.00
MT.V.47	11 Oz. Decanter, G.S.	24.00			
MT.V.52	40 Oz. Decanter, G.S.	32.00			

Page 17 - Flower Arrangers

		Cryst
518	8½" Figure Flower Holder.	50.00
1114	6" Figure Flower Holder	40.00
1136	9" Heron Flower Holder	60.00
1138	8½" Sea-gull Flower Holder	35.00
2899	2¼" Flower Block	4.25
2899	3" Flower Block	5.50
2899	3½" Flower Block	6.75

Page 18 - Punch Sets

		Cryst
111	Ladle	14.00
3600	15 pc. Punch Set	118.00
3600/129	18" Tray	21.00
3600/478	15" Bowl (13 qts.)	40.00
3600/488	5 Oz. Cups	4.25
P.169	16½" Tray	14.50
P.476	11½" Bowl (5 Qts.)	26.00
P.485	Ladle	14.00
P.486	5 Oz. Cups	3.25
PRISTINE	15 Pc. Punch Set	80.00

Page 19 - Punch Sets

		Cryst
111	Ladle	14.00
1221	15 Pc. Swan Punch Set	850.00
1221	16" Bowl and Base (5 Qts.)	550.00
1221	5 Oz. Cup	20.00
3200	15 Pc. Punch Set	225.00
3200	12½" Bowl & Foot (6 Qts.)	120.00
3200	5 Oz. Cup	10.00
P.485	Ladle	14.00

Page 20 - Salt & Pepper Shakers

		Cryst	M/Blu	E/Grn	M/Gld	Ebony
1177	Salt or Pepper	3.50				
1203	Individual Salt or Pepper	5.25				
1258	Salt or Pepper	6.25				
1262	Salt or Pepper	6.25				
1465	Cut Flower Salt or Pepper	6.50				
1476	Salt or Pepper	7.00				
1525	Open Salt	3.50				
CAP 96	Salt or Pepper ......ea	7.50	15.00			
MT.V.89	Salt or Pepper	6.25				
P.358	Individual Salt or Pepper	4.25				
P.360	Salt or Pepper	5.00		10.00	10.00	12.00

Page 21 - Smoker's Items

		Cryst	M/Gld	Ebony	M/Blu	Amber
390	6" Ash Tray.	5.25		14.00		9.00
391	8" Ash Tray	6.50		16.00	10.00	
1040	3" Swan Ash Tray	17.50	35.00		250.00	100.00
	See Additional Colors Below					
CAP 207	Cigarette Box & Cover	15.00			30.00	
CAP 208	Cigarette Box & Cover	18.00	30.00	45.00	35.00	
CAP 213	2¾" 3 Ftd. Ash Tray with Placecard Holder	5.00			10.00	
CAP 214	3" Ash Tray	4.00			12.00	
CAP 214/215/216	(See Below)					
CAP 215	4" Ash Tray	4.50			12.00	
CAP 216	5" Ash Tray	8.75			15.00	
P.721	2½" Sq. Ash Tray	3.50	5.00	6.00	5.00	5.00
P.725	3½" Sq. Ash Tray	3.50				
P.726	5" Star Ash Tray	8.50				
P.728	5 Pc. Ash Tray Set......ea.	20.00	35.00	40.00	40.00	35.00

P.731	6½" Star Ash Tray	8.25
P.732	3½" Sq. Ash Tray	3.75

Additional Colors		E/Grn	C/Tus	Carmn
1040	3" Swan Ash Tray	35.00	32.50	80.00
CAP 214/215/216	3 Pc. Ash Tray Set Varitone Only			40.00

Page 22 - Smoker's Items

		Cryst	M/Blu	Ebony	M/Gld	Amyst
CAP 207/213	5 Pc. Cigarette Set in White Display Box	35.00	70.00			
P.733	3" Ash Tray	3.50	8.00	8.00		
P.733/4/5	See Below					
P.734	4½" Ash Tray	4.25		10.00		
P.735	6" Ash Tray	5.50		12.00	10.00	
SS 33	4" 3 Ftd. Ash Tray	6.00	14.00		12.00	
SS 34	4" 3 Ftd. Ash Tray	5.25	7.25		7.25	
SS 34	8 Pc. Set, See Below					
STACK-AWAY	Ash Tray Set		23.50		23.00	22.00

Additional Colors		Mixed	E/Grn	C/Tus
P.733/4/5	3 Pc. Ash Tray Set (733-M/Blu 734-Ebony, 735-M/Gld)	25.00		
SS 33	4" 3 Ftd. Ash Tray		11.00	14.50
SS 34	8 Pc. Ash Tray Set in White Display Box-4 ea. M/Blu & M/Gld	55.00		

Page 23 - Swans

		Cryst	E/Grn	M/Gld	C/Tus	Carmn
1040	3" Swan	17.50	35.00	35.00	32.50	80.00
1041	4½" Swan	28.00				
1042	6½" Swan	33.50	100.00	100.00		225.00
1043	8½" Swan	47.00	150.00	135.00	150.00	275.00
1044	10" Swan	65.00				

Page 24 - Tumblers

		Cryst	M/Blu	M/Gld	Amyst	Amber
321	1½ Oz. Tumbler	2.25				
321	7 Oz. O.F. Cocktail	2.50				
497	14 Oz. Tumbler	2.75				
497	12 Oz. Tumbler	2.75				
497	10 Oz. Tumbler	2.50				
498	5 Oz. Tumbler	2.25				
498	10 Oz. Tumbler	2.50				
498	12 Oz. Tumbler	2.75				
498	14 Oz. Tumbler	2.75				
1206	12 Oz. Tumbler	3.50	6.50	6.25	6.25	6.25
3143/50	13 Oz. Gyro Optic Tumbler	4.00	7.25			6.25
3143/51	12 Oz. Gyro Optic Tumbler	4.00	6.75			6.50
CAP 310	12 Oz. Tumbler	15.00	40.00			

Page 25 - Tumblers

		Cryst	Amyst	Amber
319	9 Oz. Georgian Tumbler	15.00	15.00	15.00
	See Additional Colors Below			
400	14 Oz. Tumbler	3.50		
400	12 Oz. Tumbler	3.25		
400	9 Oz. Tumbler	3.00		
400	5 Oz. Tumbler	2.75		
400	3 Oz. Cocktail	3.00		
400	6 Oz. Fruit Salad	3.25		
400	1 Oz. Cordial	10.00		
1070	2 Oz. Pinch Tumbler	5.00	7.00	7.00
1341	1 Oz. Cordial	4.00	5.00	5.00
3400/92	2½ Oz. Tumbler	4.00	5.00	5.00
MT.V.51	10 Oz. Table Tumbler	6.25		
MT.V.55	2 Oz. Tumbler	5.25		
MT.V.56	5 Oz. Tumbler	5.25		
MT.V.57	7 Oz. O.F. Cocktail	5.50		
MT.V.58	10 Oz. Tumbler	7.00		
MT.V.59	14 Oz. Tumbler	7.50		

Additional Colors		E/Grn	M/Gld	Carmn	B/Blu
319	9 Oz. Georgian Tumbler	12.00	12.00	15.00	12.00

Page 26 - Vases

		Cryst	C/Tus	Amyst	Amber
274	10" Footed Vase	7.50	25.00	15.00	15.00
278	11" Footed Vase	12.50	35.00	21.00	21.00
279	13" Footed Vase	17.00		26.50	27.00
1066	7" Footed Ivy Ball	25.00		35.00	35.00
1237	9" Footed Vase	14.50	32.00	22.00	22.00
1238	12" Footed Vase	19.00	45.00	30.00	30.00
1239	14" Ftd. Vase	22.00		35.00	35.00
1299	11" Ftd. Vase	19.00	50.00	40.00	40.00
1309	5" Vase	11.00	35.00		

Additional Colors		E/Grn	M/Gld	Carmn	Ebony
1066	7" Ftd. Ivy Ball	30.00	30.00	45.00	38.00
1237	9" Ftd. Vase	21.50	22.00	40.00	35.00
1238	12" Ftd. Vase	30.00	30.00	45.00	40.00

Page 27 - Vases

		Cryst	E/Grn	M/Gold	C/Tus	Carmn
1236	7½" Ftd. Ivy Ball	30.00	35.00	35.00	45.00	50.00
6004	8" Footed Vase	10.00	14.50	14.00	26.00	27.00
6004	6" Footed Vase	7.25	15.50	15.00	22.00	22.50
P.563	6" Vase	12.50				

		Cryst				
P.565	Vase 5½" High 7½" Wide..........	12.00				
P.568	Vase, Height 6", Width 7"	11.00				
P.572	6" Vase..................................	8.25	15.50	15.00		
P.575	9" Cornucopia Vase.................	21.00			45.00	
P.580	8" Vase..................................	8.25				

Additional Colors

		Amyst	Amber
1236	7½" Ftd. Ivy Ball	35.00	35.00
6004	8" Ftd. Vase............................	16.00	15.50
6004	6" Ftd. Vase............................	13.00	13.00

Page 28 - Miscellaneous

		Cryst
1570	Cheese Preserver Jar & Cover (have been reproduced)...........	30.00
1571	Cheese Preserver Jar & Cover (have been reproduced)...........	30.00
M.156	Oyster Plate	20.00
M.156/69	Oyster Plate & Sauce Cup........	22.00
M.157	Deviled Egg Plate....................	18.00
V.134	10½" Cake Salver.....................	45.00

Page 29 - Miscellaneous

		Cryst	E/Grn	M/Gld	Amyst	Amber
1	4½" Muddler	6.00	18.00	18.00	20.00	18.00
604	5¼" Coaster	4.75				
968	2 Pc. Cocktail Icer	10.00				
1263	French Dressing Bottle	15.00				
3121	5⅜" Tall Blown Comport	18.00	30.00	30.00	30.00	30.00
M.122	8½" Salad Plate	4.75				
M.123	8½" Salad Plate	5.25				
M.250	Individual Sugar & Cream........	16.00	25.00	25.00		
3700	9 Oz. Goblet	7.75				
7966	2 Oz. Sherry............................	7.50			12.00	12.00
CAP 13	3½" Coaster	6.00				
MT.V.70	3" Coaster	4.25				
REGENCY	10 Oz. Goblet	15.00				

Page 30 - Crown Tuscan

		C/Tus
3011	9" Candlestick	100.00
SS 11	7" Ftd. Comport.......................	125.00
SS 15	6" Ftd. Comport.......................	35.00
SS 18	10" 3 Ftd. Bowl........................	60.00
SS 21	6" Ftd. Candy Box & Cover.......	50.00
SS 31	8" Oval Dish, 4 Ftd.	35.00
SS 40	10" Flower or Fruit Center	175.00

Page 31 - Crown Tuscan

		C/Tus
647	6" 2 Lite Candlestick	38.00
1040	3" Swan..................................	32.50
1043	8½" Swan................................	150.00
3400/4	12" Bowl, 4 Ftd.......................	44.00
3400/91	8" 3 Part Relish Tray	29.00
3500/57	8" 3 Part Candy Box & Cover	47.50
SS 10	5" Comport	100.00
SS 33	4" 3 Ftd. Ash Tray....................	14.50
SS 35	Cigarette Box & Cover	36.00

Page 32 - Crown Tuscan

		C/Tus
274	10" Footed Vase	25.00
278	11" Footed VAse......................	35.00
1236	7½" Ftd. Ivy Ball	45.00
1237	9" Footed Vase	32.00
1238	12" Footed Vase	45.00
1309	5" Vase..................................	35.00
6004	6" Footed Vase	22.00
6004	8" Footed Vase	26.00
P.575	9" Cornucopia Vase.................	45.00

Page 33 - Etchings

		Cryst
3111	Goblet, E Candlelight	23.00
3121	Goblet, E Portia.......................	20.00
3121	Goblet, E Elaine.......................	20.00
3121	Goblet, E Rose Point................	28.00
3121	Goblet, E Wildflower	22.00
3122	Goblet, E Diane	22.00
3130	Goblet, E Portia.......................	20.00
3500	Goblet, E Elaine.......................	20.00
3500	Goblet, E Rose Point................	28.00
3600	Goblet, E Chantilly	22.00
3625	Goblet, E Chantilly	22.00
3775	Goblet, E Chantilly	20.00

Page 34 - Rock Crystal

		Cryst
3121	Goblet, Eng Achilles.................	22.00
3130	Goblet, Eng Cordelia................	15.00
3130	Goblet, Eng Glendale................	15.00
3500	Goblet, Eng Adonis	22.00
3500	Goblet, Eng Croesus	20.00
3700	Goblet, Eng Ardsley	12.00
3725	Goblet, Eng Bijou	12.00
3725	Goblet, Eng Cadet	12.00
3750	Goblet, Eng Bexley	12.00
3750	Goblet, Eng Euclid	12.00
3750	Goblet, Eng Fuchsia	15.00
3778	Goblet, Eng Deerfield	15.00

Page 35 - Rock Crystal

		Cryst
3116	Goblet, Eng Lucia.....................	15.00
3139	Goblet, Eng Juliana..................	12.00
3139	Goblet, Eng King George...........	14.00
3139	Goblet, Eng Laurel Wreath........	14.00
3700	Goblet, Eng King Edward	15.00
3700	Goblet, Eng Laurel Wreath........	14.00
3700	Goblet, Eng Manor	12.00
3750	Goblet, Eng Hanover................	12.00
3776	Goblet, Eng Maryland	15.00
3776	Goblet, Eng Minuet	15.00
3778	Goblet, Eng Larchmont	16.00
7966	Goblet, Eng Lexington	14.00

Page 36 - Rock Crystal

		Cryst
1379	Decanter, Eng 1041..................	50.00
3130	Goblet, Eng Wedding Rose	14.00
3700	Goblet, Eng Montrose...............	15.00
3700	Goblet, Eng Tempo	14.00
3725	Goblet, Eng Plaza	12.00
3725	Goblet, Eng Star......................	14.00
3750	Goblet, Eng Minton Wreath.......	12.00
3775	Goblet, Eng Roxbury................	14.00
P.92	Decanter, Eng 1049..................	45.00
P.92	Decanter, Eng 1043..................	45.00
P.101	32 Oz. Cocktail Shaker.............	45.00
P.427	Bowl, Eng Celestial (600).........	22.50
P.430	Bowl, Eng Windsor (500)	22.50

Page 36A - Cambridge Square

		Cryst
3797	Goblet....................................	10.00
3797	Sherbet..................................	10.00
3797	Cocktail	14.00
3797	Cordial	22.00
3797	Wine	16.00
3797	14 Oz. Ice Tea	10.00
3797	5 Oz. Juice	10.00
3798	Goblet....................................	10.00
3798	Sherbet..................................	8.00
3798	Cocktail	10.00
3798	Cordial	22.00
3798	Wine	12.00
3798	12 Oz. Ice Tea	10.00
3798	5 Oz. Juice	9.00

Page 36B - Cambridge Square

		Cryst
3797/16	4" Dessert	10.00
3797/18	2 Pc. Cocktail Icer	20.00
3797/22	7" Salad Plate	10.00
3797/24	9½" Tidbit Plate.......................	15.00
3797/26	11½" Plate...............................	20.00
3797/27	6½" Ind. Salad Plate................	10.00
3797/28	13½" Plate...............................	25.00
3797/29	4 Pc. Buffet Set	40.00
3797/34	7½" Ice Tub	25.00
3797/35	7½" Rose Bowl........................	25.00
3797/36	9½" Rose Bowl........................	35.00

Page 36C - Cambridge Square

		Cryst
3797/37	8" Oval Tray	15.00
3797/40	Individual Sugar & Cream.........	16.00
3797/41	Sugar & Cream	18.00
3797/42	3 Pc. Ind. Sugar & Cream Set...	30.00
3797/47	8" Bon Bon	20.00
3797/48	10" Oval Dish	20.00
3797/49	9" Salad Bowl..........................	25.00
3797/57	11" Salad Bowl........................	30.00
3797/65	12" Oval Dish	25.00
3797/67	Cupped Candlestick	10.00
3797/76	Salt & Pepper w/Chrome Top (pr)	20.00

Page 36D - Cambridge Square

		Cryst
3797/77	7½" Footed Vase	18.00
3797/78	9½" Footed Vase	22.00
3797/79	11" Footed Vase	30.00
3797/80	8" Ftd. Bud Vase.....................	15.00
3797/81	10" Shallow Bowl	25.00
3797/82	12" Shallow Bowl	30.00
3797/85	32 Oz. Decanter	65.00
3797/90	6" Vase..................................	18.00
3797/91	5½" Belled Vase	20.00

Page 36E - Cambridge Square

		Cryst
3797/86	7 Pc. Wine Set	175.00
3797/87	7 Pc. Cordial Set	200.00

Page 36F - Cambridge Square

		Cryst
3797/100	4½ Oz. Oil	20.00
3797/104	4 Pc. Condiment Set	55.00
3797/105	5 Pc. Condiment Set	50.00
3797/120	6½" 2 Part Relish	14.00
3797/125	8" 3 Part Relish	18.00
3797/126	10" 3 Part Celery & Relish	20.00

		Cryst				
3797/127	Mayonnaise Bowl	12.00				
3797/127/445	Mayonnaise & Ladle	17.00				
3797/129	3 Pc. Mayonnaise Set	25.00				
3797/150	6½" Ash Tray	7.00				
3797/151	3½" Ash Tray	5.00				
3797/164	7" Bon Bon	10.00				
3797/165	Candy Box & Cover	25.00				

Page 36G - Cambridge Square

		Cryst
3797/35	7½" Rose Bowl	30.00
3797/35/493	3 Pc. Table Centerpiece	50.00
3797/36	9½" Rose Bowl	35.00
3797/36/495	5 Pc. Table Centerpiece	75.00
3797/47	8" Bowl	20.00
3797/47/492	3 Pc. Table Centerpiece	40.00
3797/492	1¾" Candlestick	10.00
3797/493	2¾" Candlestick	10.00
3797/495	3¾" Candlestick	10.00

Page 36H - Cambridge Square

		Cryst
3797/15	Teacup & Saucer	15.00
3797/15	Tea Cups, Stacked	10.00
3797/17	Coffee Cup & Saucer	15.00
3797/17	Coffee Cups, Stacked	10.00
3797/20	6" Bread & Butter Plate	8.00
3797/23	7" Dessert or Salad Plate	10.00
3797/25	9½" Dinner or Luncheon Plate	22.00
3797/54	6" Comport	18.00
3797/68	2 Pc. Hurricane Lamp	35.00
3797/92	5" Belled Vase	18.00
3797/103	11" Celery	20.00
3797/152	3 Pc. Smoker Set in Box	22.00

Page 37 - 3900 Line - Corinth

		Cryst
3900/17	Cup & Saucer	10.00
3900/19	2 Pc. Mayonnaise Set	11.00
3900/20	6½" Bread & Butter Plate	4.25
3900/22	8" Salad Plate	5.50
3900/24	10½" Dinner Plate	11.00
3900/26	12" 4 Footed Plate	15.00
3900/28	11½" Footed Bowl	14.50
3900/33	13" 4 Ftd. Torte Plate, R.E.	15.00
3900/34	11" 2 Handled Bowl	14.00

Page 38 - 3900 Line - Corinth

		Cryst
3900/35	13½" 2 Hdl. Cake Plate	14.50
3900/40	Ind. Sugar & Cream	15.00
3900/41	Sugar & Cream	15.00
3900/54	10" 4 Ftd. Bowl, Flared	13.00
3900/62	12" 4 Ftd. Bowl, Flared	15.00
3900/65	12" 4 Ftd. Oval Bowl	15.50
3900/67	5" Candlestick	10.50
3900/72	6" 2 Lite Candlestick	20.00
3900/74	6" 3 Lite Candlestick	20.00

Page 39 - 3900 Line - Corinth

		Cryst	M/Blu	E/Grn	M/Gld	Amber
3900/75	Epergne	65.00				
3900/99	4 Oz. Bitter Bottle w/Tube	13.00				
3900/100	6 Oz. Oil, G.S.	15.00				
3900/111	4 Pc. Mayonnaise Set	16.00				
3900/114	32 Oz. Martini Jug	22.00				
3900/115	76 Oz. Jug	20.00	38.00	34.00	34.00	34.00
3900/115	13 Oz. Tumbler	4.25	7.00	6.75	6.75	6.75
3900/120	12" 5 Part Celery & Relish	14.00				
3900/123	7" Relish or Pickle	7.25				
3900/124	7" 2 Part Relish	8.25				

Additional Color

		Amyst
3900/115	76 Oz. Jug	34.00
3900/115	13 Oz. Tumbler	6.75

Page 40 - 3900 Line - Corinth

		Cryst	E/Grn	M/Gld
3900/125	9" 3 Part Celery & Relish	9.75	14.50	14.50
3900/126	12" 3 Part Celery & Relish	13.00		
3900/129	3 Pc. Mayonnaise Set	14.00		
3900/130	7" 2 Hdl. Ftd. Bonbon	8.25		
3900/131	8" 2 Hdl. Ftd. Bonbon Plate	7.25		
3900/136	5½" Comport	14.00	22.00	20.00
3900/165	Candy Box & Cover	18.00		
3900/166	14" Plat. R.E.	16.00	21.00	21.00
3900/671	Ice Bucket w/Chrome Tongs	16.00		
3900/1177	Salt & Pepper Shaker ea.	4.50		

Page 40A - 3900 Line - Corinth

		Cryst
3900	9 Oz. Goblet	8.00
3900	6 Oz. Tall Sherbet	5.25
3900	6 Oz. Low Sherbet	5.00
3900	3 Oz. Cocktail	5.50
3900	2½ Oz. Wine	7.00
3900	4½ Oz. Claret	6.00
3900	4½ Oz. Oyster Cocktail	5.25
3900	1 Oz. Cordial	18.00
3900	5 Oz. Ftd. Tumbler	5.25
3900	5" Blown Comport	11.00
3900	10 Oz. Ftd. Tumbler	5.75
3900	12 Oz. Ftd. Ice Tea	5.75

Page 40B - 3900 Line - Corinth

		Cryst	E/Grn	M/Gld	Ebony
3900/18	2 Pc. Cocktail Icer	11.00			
3900/37	Sugar & Cream Tray	5.75	10.00	10.00	
3900/38	3 Pc. Ind. Sugar & Cream Set	20.00			
3900/39	3 Pc. Sugar & Cream Set	20.00			
3900/68	5" Candlestick	10.50			
3900/124	7" 2 Part Relish (Revised)	9.00			
3900/135	5" Comport	8.75	15.00	15.00	
3900/135	13½" Cheese & Cracker	19.50			
3900/244	7 Pc. Condiment Set	20.00			
3900/245	6 Pc. Condiment Set	20.00			
3900/575	10" Cornucopia Vase	21.00	35.00	35.00	40.00

Page 40C - 3900 Line - Corinth Jugs and Tumblers

		Cryst	M/Blu	E/Grn	M/Gld	Amber
3900/114	32 Oz. Martini Jug	22.00				
3900/117	20 Oz. Gyro Optic Jug	15.00	25.00	21.00	21.00	21.00
3900/117	5 Oz. Gyro Optic Tumbler	4.00	6.00	6.00	6.00	6.00
3900/117	20 Oz. Optic Jug	15.00	25.00	21.00	20.00	20.50
3900/117	5 Oz. Optic Tumbler	3.50	5.50	5.50	5.75	5.75
3900/118	32 Oz. Optic Jug	17.00	30.00	24.00	23.50	23.50
3900/118	5 Oz. Optic Tumbler	3.50	5.50	5.50	5.75	5.75
3900/118	32 Oz. Gyro Optic Jug	17.00	30.00	24.00	24.00	24.00
3900/118	5 Oz. Gyro Optic Tumbler	3.75	5.75	5.50	5.75	5.75

Additional Color

		Amyst
3900/117	20 Oz. Gyro Optic Jug	21.00
3900/117	5 Oz. Gyro Optic Tumbler	5.50
3900/117	20 Oz. Optic Jug	21.00
3900/117	5 Oz. Optic Tumbler	5.50
3900/118	32 Oz. Optic Jug	24.00
3900/118	5 Oz. Optic Tumbler	5.50
3900/118	32 Oz. Gyro Optic Jug	24.00
3900/118	5 Oz. Gyro Optic Tumbler	5.50

Page 40D - 3900 Line - Corinth Jugs and Tumblers

		Cryst	M/Blu	E/Grn	M/Gld	Amber
3900/115	76 Oz. Jug, Optic	20.00	36.00	34.00	34.00	34.00
3900/115	13 Oz. Tumbler, Optic	4.25	6.75	6.75	6.75	6.75
3900/115	76 Oz. Jug, Gyro Optic	21.00	36.00	34.00	34.00	34.00
3900/115	13 Oz. Tumbler, Gyro Optic	4.25	6.75	6.75	6.75	6.75
3900/116	80 Oz. Ball, Optic	25.00	40.00	35.00	35.00	35.00
3900/116	13 Oz. Tumbler, Optic	4.25	6.75	7.00	6.75	6.75
3900/116	80 Oz. Ball Jug, Gyro Optic	25.00	40.00	35.00	35.00	35.00
3900/116	13 Oz. Tumbler, Gyro Optic	4.25	6.75	6.75	6.75	6.75

Additional Color

		Amyst
3900/115	76 oz. Jug, Optic	34.00
3900/115	13 oz. Tumbler, Optic	6.75
3900/115	76 oz. Jug, Gyro Optic	34.00
3900/115	13 oz. Tumbler, Gyro Optic	6.75
3900/116	80 oz. Ball, Optic	35.00
3900/116	13 oz. Tumbler, Optic	6.75
3900/116	80 oz. Ball Jug, Gyro Optic	35.00
3900/116	13 oz. Tumbler, Gyro Optic	6.75

Page 41 - 4000 Line - Cascade

		Cryst	E/Grn	M/Gld
4000/1	Goblet	9.00		
4000/2	Sherbet	7.00		
4000/3	Cocktail	7.00		
4000/9	12 Oz. Ftd. Tumbler	9.00		
4000/11	5 Oz. Ftd. Tumbler	7.25		
4000/14	12 Oz. Tumbler	9.00		
4000/15	5 Oz. Tumbler	7.00		
4000/16	4½" Fruit Saucer	5.00		
4000/17	Cup & Saucer	9.00		
4000/21	6½" Bread & Butter Plate	5.00		
4000/22	8½" Salad Plate	6.75		
4000/26	11½" 4 Ftd. Plate	13.50		
4000/33	14" 4 Ftd. Torte Plate, R.E.	17.50		
4000/41	Sugar & Cream	12.50	25.00	25.00

Page 42 - 4000 Line - Cascade

		Cryst	E/Grn	M/Gld
4000/54	10" 4 Ftd. Bowl, Flared	13.50		
4000/62	12½" 4 Ftd. Flared Bowl	16.00		
4000/64	10" 3 Part Celery & Relish	10.50		
4000/65	12" 4 Ftd. Oval Bowl	16.00		
4000/67	5" Candlestick	8.25	20.00	20.00
4000/72	6" 2 Lite Candlestick	15.00		
4000/81	10½" 4 Ftd. Shallow Bowl	13.50		
4000/82	13" 4 Ftd. Bowl, Shallow	15.50		
4000/89	6½" Relish or Pickle	7.25		
4000/90	6½" 2 Part Relish	8.00		
4000/96	Salt & Pepper Shaker	12.00		

Page 43 - 4000 Line - Cascade

		Cryst	E/Grn	M/Gld
4000/129	3 Pc. Mayonnaise Set (Crystal Ladle)	14.00	25.00	25.00
4000/130	7" 2 Hdl. Ftd. Bonbon	8.75		

4000/131	8" 2 Hdl. Ftd. Bonbon Plate.......	8.00		
4000/136	5½" Comport........................	12.50		
4000/164	6" Bon Bon...........................	6.00		
4000/165	Candy Box & Cover..............	20.00	35.00	35.00
4000/214	4½" Ash Tray........................	4.00		
4000/214/215/216				
	3 Pc. Ash Tray Set...............	16.50		
4000/215	6" Ash Tray...........................	5.50		
4000/216	8" Ash Tray...........................	8.25		
4000/573	9½" Vase.............................	20.00	40.00	40.00
4000/574	9½" Vase, Oval.....................	17.50		
4000/616	Cigarette Box & Cover..........	16.00		
4000/671	Ice Tub Chrome Ice Tongs.......	16.00		

Page 44 - 4000 Line - Cascade — Cryst

4000/216	Base for Punch Bowl..............	8.25
4000/478	15" Punch Bowl (10 Qts.) & Chrome Punch Ladle..............	35.00
4000/478/479/488/216	16 Pc. Punch Set w/Chrome Ladle.........................	130.00
4000/478/488/216	15 Pc. Punch Set w/Chrome Ladle.........................	110.00
4000/479	21" Plate.............................	22.50
4000/479/216	21" 2 Pc. Sunday Evening or Buffet Supper Set..................	30.00
4000/488	5 Oz. Punch Cup....................	5.00

Page 45 - Rose Point — Cryst

3900/17	Cup & Saucer........................	35.00
3900/19	2 Pc. Mayonnaise..................	50.00
3900/20	6½" Bread & Butter Plate.........	14.00
3900/22	8" Salad Plate......................	16.00
3900/24	10½" Dinner Plate.................	110.00
3900/26	12" 4 Ftd. Plate....................	65.00
3900/28	11½" Ftd. Bowl.....................	75.00
3900/33	13" 4 Ftd. Torte Plate, R.E.......	65.00
3900/34	11" 2 Hdl. Bowl....................	65.00
3900/35	13" 2 Hdl. Cake Plate............	60.00
3900/40	Ind. Sugar & Cream..............	40.00
3900/41	Sugar & Cream.....................	35.00

Page 46 - Rose Point — Cryst

3900/54	10" 4 Ftd. Bowl, Flared..............	55.00
3900/62	12" Ftd. Bowl, Flared..............	65.00
3900/65	12" 4 Ftd. Oval Bowl..............	75.00
3900/67	5" Candlestick......................	45.00
3900/72	6" 2 Lite Candlestick.............	40.00
3900/74	6" 3 Lite Candlestick.............	45.00
3900/100	6 Oz. Oil, G.S.......................	85.00
3900/111	4 Pc. Mayonnaise Set..............	65.00
3900/115	13 Oz. Tumbler.....................	40.00
3900/120	12" 5 Part Celery & Relish........	60.00
3900/123	7" Relish or Pickle................	35.00
3900/124	7" 2 part Relish....................	40.00

Page 47 - Rose Point — Cryst

968	2 Pc. Cocktail Icer.................	65.00
3121	5⅜" Blown Comport...............	60.00
3900/125	9" 3 Part Celery & Relish.........	45.00
3900/126	12" 3 Part Celery & Relish........	55.00
3900/129	3 Pc. Mayonnaise Set..............	60.00
3900/130	7" 2 Hdl. Ftd. Bonbon............	33.00
3900/131	8" 2 Hdl. Ftd. Bonbon Plate.......	30.00
3900/136	5½" Comport........................	50.00
3900/165	Candy Box & Cover................	80.00
3900/166	14" Plate, R.E.......................	65.00
3900/671	Ice Bucket w/Chrome Handle....	110.00
3900/1177	Salt & Pepper Shaker, Pr..........	40.00

Page 48 - Rose Point — Cryst

274	10" Bud Flower Holder............	45.00
278	11" Ftd. Flower Holder............	100.00
279	13" Ftd. Flower Holder............	160.00
1237	9" Ftd. Flower Holder............	80.00
1238	12" Ftd. Flower Holder............	100.00
1299	11" Ftd. Flower Holder............	125.00
1309	5" Globe Flower Holder............	65.00
1603	Hurricane Lamp.....................	175.00
1617	Hurricane Lamp.....................	150.00
6004	6" Ftd. Flower Holder............	45.00
6004	8" Ftd. Flower Holder............	45.00

Page 49 - Rose Point — Cryst

3121	10 Oz. Goblet.......................	28.00
3121	6 Oz. Tall Sherbet..................	24.00
3121	3 Oz. Cocktail......................	30.00
3121	10 Oz. Ftd. Tumbler..............	25.00
3121	12 Oz. Ftd. Ice Tea................	28.00
3121	6 Oz. Low Sherbet................	18.00
3121	4½ Oz. Oyster Cocktail............	35.00
3121	4½ Oz. Claret.......................	65.00

3121	5 Oz. Ftd. Tumber.................	28.00
3121	3½ Oz. Wine........................	55.00
3121	1 Oz. Cordial.......................	65.00
3121	5 Oz. Cafe Parfait..................	65.00
3121	5⅜" Blown Comport...............	60.00

Page 50 - Rose Point — Cryst

3500	10 Oz. Goblet.......................	28.00
3500	7 Oz. Tall Sherbet..................	24.00
3500	3 Oz. Cocktail......................	35.00
3500	12 Oz. Ftd. Ice Tea................	28.00
3500	10 Oz. Ftd. Tumbler..............	25.00
3500	7 Oz. Low Sherbet................	18.00
3500	4½ Oz. Oyster Cocktail............	35.00
3500	4½ Oz. Claret.......................	65.00
3500	5 Oz. Ftd. Tumbler................	28.00
3500	2½ Oz. Wine........................	55.00
3500	1 Oz. Cordial.......................	60.00
3500	5 Oz. Cafe Parfait..................	65.00
3500/101	5⅜" Blown Comport...............	70.00

Page 50A - Rose Point — Cryst

3400/52	5" Butter & Cover..................	145.00
3400/71	3" 4 Ftd. Nut Cup..................	65.00
3400/91	8" 3 Part Relish....................	35.00
3900/38	3 Pc. Ind. Sugar & Cream Set.........	65.00
3900/39	3 Pc. Sugar & Cream Set..............	60.00
3900/75	Epergne.............................	125.00
3900/135	5" Comport..........................	40.00
3900/135	13½" Cheese & Cracker............	100.00
3900/575	10" Cornucopia Vase..............	125.00
3900/1177	Salt & Pepper Shaker.........ea.	21.00

Page 50B - Rose Point — Cryst

646	5" Candlestick......................	24.00
647	6" 2 Lite Candlestick.............	35.00
1338	6" 3 Lite Candlestick.............	50.00
3400/4	12" 4 Ftd. Bowl, Flared............	60.00
3400/48	11" Ftd. Bowl, Fancy Edge............	75.00
3400/160	12" 4 Ftd. Bowl, Oblong............	75.00
3900/68	5" Candlestick......................	45.00

Page 50C - Rose Point — Cryst

1321	28 Oz. Ftd. Decanter...............	250.00
1613	Hurricane Lamp.....................	275.00
3900/114	32 Oz. Martini Jug..................	300.00
3900/115	76 Oz. Jug...........................	175.00
3900/116	80 Oz. Ball Jug.....................	175.00
3900/117	20 Oz. Jug...........................	200.00
3900/117	5 Oz. Tumbler.......................	45.00
3900/118	32 Oz. Jug...........................	275.00
7801	4 Oz. Cocktail......................	40.00
7966	2 Oz. Sherry........................	75.00
P.101	32 Oz. Cocktail Shaker............	135.00

Page 50D - Rose Point — Cryst

103	2 Pc. Nite Set.......................	450.00
1066	5⅜" Candy Box & Cover............	125.00
1066	5⅜" Blown Comport...............	75.00
3400/141	80 Oz. Jug (Not Optic)............	225.00
3900/167	14" Plate.............................	65.00
P.721	2½" Ash Tray........................	30.00
P.728	5 Pc. Ash Tray Set.................	150.00
P.747	Cigarette Box & Cover............	145.00

Page 51 - Rose Point — Cryst

477	9½" Pickle...........................	50.00
3400/90	6" 2 Part Relish....................	27.00
3400/91	8" 3 Part Relish....................	35.00
3400/1180	5¼" 2 Hdl. Bonbon................	25.00
3400/1181	6" 2 Hdl. Plate.....................	22.00
3500/15	Ind. Sugar & Cream..............	45.00
3500/54	6" 2 Hdl. Ftd. Bonbon............	33.00
3500/55	6" 2 Hdl. Ftd. Basket.............	35.00
3500/57	8" 3 Part Candy Box & Cover......	65.00
3500/69	6½" 3 Part Relish..................	30.00
3500/161	8" 2 Hdl. Ftd. Plate...............	30.00
P.101	32 Oz. Cocktail Shaker............	135.00

Page 52 - Candlelight — Cryst

3111	10 Oz. Goblet.......................	23.00
3111	7 Oz. Tall Sherbet..................	20.00
3111	7 Oz. Low Sherbet................	17.00
3111	2½ Oz. Wine........................	32.00
3111	3 Oz. Cocktail......................	26.00
3111	4½ Oz. Oyster Cocktail............	26.00
3111	12 Oz. Ftd. Ice Teal...............	20.00
3111	5 Oz. Ftd. Tumbler................	18.00

Page 52A - Candlelight — Cryst

3121	5⅜" Blown Comport...............	50.00
3776	9 Oz. Goblet.........................	23.00
3776	7 Oz. Tall Sherbet..................	18.00
3776	7 Oz. Low Sherbet................	16.00
3776	2½ Oz. Wine........................	26.00

3776	3 Oz. Cocktail	22.00
3776	4½ Oz. Oyster Cocktail	20.00
3776	12 Oz. Ftd. Ice Tea	18.00
3776	5 Oz. Ftd. Tumbler	16.00
3776	4½ Oz. Claret	26.00
3776	1 Oz. Cordial	50.00

Page 53 - Candlelight — Cryst

3900/17	Cup & Saucer	28.00
3900/19	2 Pc. Mayonnaise Set	40.00
3900/20	6½" Bread & Butter Plate	12.00
3900/22	8" Salad Plate	14.00
3900/24	10½" Dinner Plate	60.00
3900/26	12" 4 Ftd. Plate	50.00
3900/28	11½" Ftd. Bowl	50.00
3900/33	13" Ftd. Torte Plate, R.E.	50.00
3900/34	11" 2 Hdl. Bowl	50.00
3900/35	13½" 2 Hdl. Cake Plate	48.00
3900/40	Ind. Sugar & Cream	35.00
3900/41	Sugar & Cream	32.00

Page 54 - Candlelight — Cryst

3900/54	10" 4 Ftd. Bowl, Flared	45.00
3900/62	12" Ftd. Bowl, Flared	50.00
3900/65	12" 4 Ftd. Oval Bowl	60.00
3900/67	5" Candlestick	30.00
3900/72	6" 2 Lite Candlestick	32.00
3900/74	6" 3 Lite Candlestick	36.00
3900/100	6 Oz. Oil, G.S.	75.00
3900/111	4 Pc. Mayonnaise Set	55.00
3900/115	13 Oz. Tumbler	30.00
3900/120	12" 5 Part Celery & Relish	45.00
3900/123	7" Relish or Pickle	28.00
3900/124	7" 2 Part Relish	32.00

Page 55 - Candlelight — Cryst

274	10" Bud Flower Hodler	35.00
968	2 Pc. Cocktail Icer	50.00
3121	5⅜" Blown Comport	45.00
3900/125	9" 3 Part Celery & Relish	36.00
3900/126	12" 3 Part Celery & Relish	45.00
3900/129	3 Pc. Mayonnaise Set	45.00
3900/130	7" 2 Hdl. Ftd. Bonbon	26.00
3900/131	8" 2 Hdl. Ftd. Bonbon Plate	24.00
3900/136	5½" Comport	40.00
3900/165	Candy Box & Cover	65.00
3900/166	14" Plate, R.E.	55.00
3900/671	Ice Bucket w/Chrome Handle	85.00
3900/1177	Salt & Pepper Shaker ....pr.	32.00

Page 56 - Candlelight — Cryst

278	11" Ftd. Flower Holder	60.00
279	13" Ftd. Flower Holder	75.00
1237	9" Ftd. Flower Holder	50.00
1238	12" Ftd. Flower Holder	70.00
1299	11" Ftd. Flower Holder	75.00
1309	5" Globe Flower Holder	45.00
1603	Hurricane Lamp	125.00
1613	Hurricane Lamp	200.00
1617	Hurricane Lamp	100.00
6004	6" Ftd. Flower Holder	30.00
6004	8" Ftd. Flower Holder	35.00

Page 56A - Chantilly — Cryst

3779	9 Oz. Goblet	23.00
3779	6 Oz. Tall Sherbet	20.00
3779	6 Oz. Low Sherbet	18.00
3779	3 Oz. Cocktail	22.00
3779	2½ Oz. Wine	25.00
3779	1 Oz. Cordial	50.00
3779	4½ Oz. Oyster Cocktail	20.00
3779	12 Oz. Ftd. Ice Tea	21.00
3779	5 Oz. Ftd. Tumbler	18.00
3779	4½ Oz. Claret	26.00

Page 57 - Chantilly — Cryst

3600	10 Oz. Goblet	22.00
3600	7 Oz. Tall Sherbet	20.00
3600	7 Oz. Low Sherbet	18.00
3600	2½ Oz. Cocktail	24.00
3600	2½ Oz. Wine	33.00
3600	4½ Oz. Claret	38.00
3600	4½ Oz. Oyster Cocktail	27.00
3600	1 Oz. Cordial	45.00
3600	12 Oz. Ftd. Ice Tea	22.00
3600	5 Oz. Ftd. Tumbler	18.00

Page 58 - Chantilly — Cryst

3625	10 Oz. Goblet	22.00
3625	7 Oz. Goblet	20.00
3625	7 Oz. Goblet	18.00
3625	3 Oz. Goblet	24.00
3625	2½ Oz. Wine	33.00
3625	4½ Oz. Claret	38.00
3625	4½ Oz. Oyster Cocktail	27.00

3625	1 Oz. Cordial	45.00
3625	12 Oz. Ftd. Ice Tea	22.00
3625	10 Oz. Ftd. Tumbler	20.00
3625	5 Oz. Ftd. Tumbler	18.00

Page 59 - Chantilly — Cryst

3775	10 Oz. Goblet	19.00
3775	6 Oz. Tall Sherbet	16.00
3775	6 Oz. Low Sherbet	15.00
3775	3 Oz. Cocktail	20.00
3775	2½ Oz. Wine	22.00
3775	4½ Oz. Claret	24.00
3775	4½ Oz. Oyster Cocktail	17.00
3775	1 Oz. Cordial	45.00
3775	12 Oz. Ftd. Ice Tea	18.00
3775	10 Oz. Ftd. Tumbler	17.00
3775	5 Oz. Ftd. Tumbler	16.00

Page 60 - Chantilly — Cryst

3900/17	Cup & Saucer	30.00
3900/19	2 Pc. Mayonnaise Set	42.00
3900/20	6½ " Bread & Butter Plate	12.00
3900/22	8" Salad Plate	15.00
3900/24	10½" Dinner Plate	65.00
3900/26	12" 4 Ftd. Plate	55.00
3900/28	11½" Ftd. Bowl	55.00
3900/33	13" 4 Ftd. Torte Plate, R.E.	55.00
3900/34	11" 2 Hdl. Bowl	55.00
3900/35	13½" Hdl. Cake Plate	52.00
3900/40	Ind. Sugar & Cream	38.00
3900/41	Sugar & Cream	35.00

Page 61 - Chantilly — Cryst

3900/54	10" 4 Ftd. Bowl, Flared	48.00
3900/62	12" Ftd. Bowl, Flared	52.00
3900/65	12" 4 Ftd. Oval Bowl	55.00
3900/67	5" Candlestick	32.00
3900/72	6" 2 Lite Candlestick	35.00
3900/74	6" 3 Lite Candlestick	36.00
3900/100	6 Oz. Oil, G.S.	80.00
3900/111	4 Pc. Mayonnaise Set	55.00
3900/115	13 Oz. Tumbler	30.00
3900/120	12" 5 Part Celery & Relish	46.00
3900/123	7" Relish or Pickle	30.00
3900/124	7" 2 Part Relish	33.00

Page 62 - Chantilly — Cryst

968	2 Pc. Cocktail Icer	55.00
3121	5⅜" Blown Comport	50.00
3900/125	9" 3 Part Celery & Relish	40.00
3900/126	12" 3 Part Celery & Relish	42.00
3900/129	3 Pc. Mayonnaise Set	48.00
3900/130	7" 2 Hdl. Ftd. Bonbon	30.00
3900/131	8" 2 Hdl. Ftd. Bonbon Plate	25.00
3900/136	5½" Comport	42.00
3900/165	Candy Box & Cover	65.00
3900/166	14" Plate, R.E.	55.00
3900/671	Ice Bucket w/Chrome Hdl.	85.00
3900/1177	Salt & Pepper Shakers ....pr.	34.00

Page 63 - Chantilly — Cryst

274	10" Bud Flower Holder	35.00
278	11" Ftd. Flower Holder	65.00
279	13" Ftd. Flower Holder	75.00
1237	9" Ftd. Flower Holder	55.00
1238	12" Ftd. Flower Holder	70.00
1299	11" Ftd. Flower Holder	75.00
1309	5" Globe Flower Holder	45.00
1603	Hurricane Lamp	125.00
1617	Hurricane Lamp	110.00
6004	8" Ftd. Flower Holder	35.00
6004	6" Ftd. Flower Holder	30.00

Page 64 - Diane — Cryst

3122	9 Oz. Goblet	22.00
3122	7 Oz. Tall Sherbet	20.00
3122	7 Oz. Low Sherbet	17.00
3122	3 Oz. Cocktail	27.00
3122	2½ Oz. Wine	33.00
3122	4½ Oz. Claret	38.00
3122	4½ Oz. Oyster Cocktail	27.00
3122	1 Oz. Cordial	45.00
3122	12 Oz. Ftd. Ice Tea	22.00
3122	9 Oz. Ftd. Tumbler	20.00
3122	5 Oz. Ftd. Tumbler	18.00

Page 65 - Diane — Cryst

3900/17	Cup & Saucer	27.00
3900/19	2 Pc. Mayonnaise Set	38.00
3900/20	6½" Bread & Butter Plate	10.00
3900/22	8" Salad Plate	12.00
3900/24	10½" Dinner Plate	55.00
3900/26	12" 4 Ftd. Plate	45.00
3900/28	11½" Ftd. Bowl	45.00
3900/33	13" 4 Ftd. Torte Plate, R.E.	48.00

Page 66 - Diane — Cryst

3900/34	11" 2 Hdl. Bowl	44.00
3900/35	13½" 2 Hdl. Cake Plate	45.00
3900/40	Ind. Sugar & Cream	34.00
3900/41	Sugar & Cream	28.00
3900/54	10" 4 Ftd. Bowl, Flared	45.00
3900/62	12" Ftd. Bowl, Flared	48.00
3900/65	12" 4 Ftd. Oval Bowl	52.00
3900/67	5" Candlestick	28.00
3900/72	6" 2 Lite Candlestick	32.00
3900/74	6" 3 Lite Candlestick	34.00
3900/100	6 Oz. Oil, G.S.	75.00
3900/111	4 Pc. Mayonnaise Set	50.00
3900/115	13 Oz. Tumbler	27.00
3900/120	12" 5 Part Celery & Relish	42.00
3900/123	7" Relish or Pickle	27.00
3900/124	7" 2 Part Relish	29.00

Page 67 - Diane — Cryst

968	2 Pc. Cocktail Icer	50.00
3121	5⅜" Blown Comport	48.00
3900/125	9" 3 Part Celery & Relish	37.00
3900/126	12" 3 Part Celery & Relish	40.00
3900/129	3 Pc. Mayonnaise Set	45.00
3900/130	7" 2 Hdl. Ftd. Bonbon	26.00
3900/131	8" 2 Hdl. Ftd. Bonbon Plate	23.00
3900/136	5½" Comport	36.00
3900/165	Candy Box & Cover	60.00
3900/166	14" Plate, R.E.	50.00
3900/671	Ice Bucket w/Chrome Hdl.	75.00
3900/1177	Salt & Pepper Shaker ....pr.	33.00

Page 68 - Diane — Cryst

278	10" Bud Flower Holder	32.00
278	11" Ftd. Flower Holder	50.00
279	13" Ftd. Flower Holder	60.00
1237	9" Ftd. Flower Holder	48.00
1238	12" Ftd. Flower Holder	60.00
1299	11" Ftd. Flower Holder	62.00
1309	5" Globe Flower Holder	40.00
1603	Hurricane Lamp	110.00
1617	Hurricane Lamp	95.00
6004	6" Ftd. Flower Holder	26.00
6004	8" Ftd. Flower Holder	32.00

Page 69 - Diane — Cryst

477	9½" Pickle	33.00
3400/90	6" 2 Part Relish	24.00
3400/1180	5¼" 2 Hdl. Bonbon	20.00
3400/1181	2 Hdl. Plate	18.00
3500/15	Ind. Sugar & Cream	34.00
3500/54	6" 2 Hdl. Ftd. Bonbon	24.00
3500/55	6" 2 Hdl. Ftd. Basket	26.00
3500/69	6½" 3 Part Relish	22.00
3500/161	8" 2 Hdl. Ftd. Plate	22.00

Page 70 - Elaine — Cryst

3121	10 Oz. Goblet	20.00
3121	6 Oz. Tall Sherbet	18.00
3121	6 Oz. Low Sherbet	16.00
3121	3 Oz. Cocktail	22.00
3121	3½ Oz. Wine	28.00
3121	4½ Oz. Claret	34.00
3121	4½ Oz. Oyster Cocktail	20.00
3121	1 Oz. Cordial	45.00
3121	5 Oz. Cafe Parfait	38.00
3121	12 Oz. Ftd. Ice Tea	20.00
3121	10 Oz. Ftd. Tumbler	18.00
3121	5 Oz. Ftd. Tumbler	18.00

Page 71 - Elaine — Cryst

3500	7 Oz. Tall Sherbet	18.00
3500	7 Oz. Low Sherbet	16.00
3500	3 Oz. Cocktail	22.00
3500	2½ Oz. Wine	28.00
3500	4½ Oz. Claret	34.00
3500	4½ Oz. Oyster Cocktail	20.00
3500	1 Oz. Cordial	45.00
3500	5 Oz. Parfait	38.00
3500	12 Oz. Ftd. Ice Tea	20.00
3500	10 Oz. Ftd. Tumbler	20.00
3500	5 Oz. Ftd. Tumbler	18.00
3500/1	10 Oz. Goblet	20.00
3500/101	5⅜" Tall Comport	48.00

Page 72 - Elaine — Cryst

3900/17	Cup & Saucer	27.00
3900/19	2 Pc. Mayonnaise Set	38.00
3900/20	6½" Bread & Butter Plate	10.00
3900/22	8 " Salad Plate	12.00
3900/24	10½" Dinner Plate	55.00
3900/26	12" 4 Ftd. Plate	45.00
3900/28	11½" Ftd. Bowl	45.00
3900/33	13" Ftd. Torte Plate, R.E.	48.00

3900/34	11" 2 Hdl. Bowl	44.00
3900/35	13½" 2 Hdl. Cake Plate	45.00
3900/40	Ind. Sugar & Cream	34.00
3900/41	Sugar & Cream	28.00

Page 73 - Elaine — Cryst

3900/54	10" Ftd. Bowl, Flared	45.00
3900/62	12" Ftd. Bowl, Flared	48.00
3900/65	12 " 4 Ftd. Oval Bowl	52.00
3900/67	5 " Candlestick	28.00
3900/72	6 " 2 Lite Candlestick	32.00
3900/74	6 " 3 Lite Candlestick	34.00
3900/100	6 Oz. Oil, G.S.	75.00
3900/111	4 Pc. Mayonnaise Set	50.00
3900/115	13 Oz. Tumbler	27.00
3900/120	12" 5 Part Celery & Relish	42.00
3900/123	7" Relish or Pickle	27.00
3900/124	7" 2 Part Relish	29.00

Page 74 - Elaine — Cryst

968	2 Pc. Cocktail Icer	50.00
3121	5⅜" Blown Comport	48.00
3900/125	9" 3 Part Celery or Relish	37.00
3900/126	12" 3 Part Celery & Relish	40.00
3900/129	3 Pc. Mayonnaise Set	45.00
3900/130	7" 2 Hdl. Ftd. Bonbon	26.00
3900/131	8" 3 Hdl. Bonbon Plate	23.00
3900/136	5" Comport	36.00
3900/165	Candy Box & Cover	60.00
3900/166	14" Plate, R.E.	50.00
3900/671	Ice Bucket w/Chrome Hdl.	75.00
3900/1177	Salt & Pepper Shaker ....pr.	33.00

Page 75 - Elaine — Cryst

274	10" Bud Flower Holder	32.00
278	11" Ftd. Flower Holder	50.00
279	13" Ftd. Flower Holder	60.00
1237	9" Ftd. Flower Holder	48.00
1238	12" Ftd. Flower Holder	60.00
1299	11" Ftd. Flower Holder	62.00
1309	5" Globe Flower Holder	40.00
1603	Hurricane Lamp	110.00
1617	Hurricane Lamp	95.00
6004	6" Ftd. Flower Holder	26.00
6004	8" Ftd. Flower Holder	32.00

Page 76 - Elaine — Cryst

477	9½" Pickle	33.00
3400/90	6" 2 Part Relish	24.00
3400/1180	5¼" 2 Hdl. Bonbon	20.00
3400/1181	6" 2 Hdl. Plate	18.00
3500/15	Ind. Sugar & Cream	34.00
3500/54	6" 2 Hdl. Ftd. Bonbon	24.00
3500/55	6" 2 Hdl. Ftd. Basket	26.00
3500/69	6" 3 Part Relish	22.00
3500/161	8" 2 Hdl. Ftd. Plate	22.00

Page 77 - Portia — Cryst

3121	10 Oz. Goblet	20.00
3121	6 Oz. Tall Sherbet	18.00
3121	6 Oz. Low Sherbet	16.00
3121	3 Oz. Cocktail	22.00
3121	3½ Oz. Wine	28.00
3121	4½ Oz. Oyster Cocktail	20.00
3121	1 Oz. Cordial	45.00
3121	5 Oz. Cafe Parfait	38.00
3121	12 Oz. Ftd. Ice Tea	20.00
3121	10 Oz. Ftd. Tumbler	18.00
3121	5 Oz. Ftd. Tumbler	18.00

Page 78 - Portia — Cryst

3130	9 Oz. Goblet	20.00
3130	7 Oz. Tall Sherbet	18.00
3130	7 Oz. Low Sherbet	16.00
3130	3 Oz. Cocktail	22.00
3130	2½ Oz. Wine	28.00
3130	4½ Oz. Claret	34.00
3130	4½ Oz. Oyster Cocktail	20.00
3130	1 Oz. Cordial	45.00
3130	12 Oz. Ftd. Ice Tea	20.00
3130	10 Oz. Ftd. Tumbler	18.00
3130	5 Oz. Ftd. Tumbler	18.00

Page 79 - Portia — Cryst

3900/17	Cup & Saucer	27.00
3900/19	2 Pc. Mayonnaise Set	38.00
3900/20	6½" Bread & Butter Plate	10.00
3900/22	8" Salad Plate	12.00
3900/24	10½" Dinner Plate	55.00
3900/26	12" 4 Ftd. Plate	45.00
3900/28	11½" 4 Ftd. Bowl	45.00
3900/33	13" 4 Ftd. Torte Plate, R.E.	48.00
3900/34	11" 2 Hdl. Bowl	44.00
3900/35	13½" 2 Hdl. Cake Plate	45.00
3900/40	Ind. Sugar & Cream	34.00

3900/41	Sugar & Cream	28.00

Page 80 - Portia — Cryst

3900/54	10" 4 Ftd. Bowl, Flared	45.00
3900/62	12" Ftd. Bowl, Flared	48.00
3900/65	12" 4 Ftd. Oval Bowl	52.00
3900/67	5" Candlestick	28.00
3900/72	6" 2 Lite Candlestick	32.00
3900/74	6" 3 Lite Candlestick	34.00
3900/100	6 Oz. Oil, G.S.	75.00
3900/111	4 Pc. Mayonnaise Set	50.00
3900/115	13 Oz. Tumbler	27.00
3900/120	12" 5 Part Celery & Relish	42.00
3900/123	7" Relish or Pickle	27.00
3900/124	7" 2 Part Relish	29.00

Page 81 - Portia — Cryst

968	2 Pc. Cocktail Icer	50.00
3121	5⅜" Blown Comport	48.00
3900/125	9" 3 Part Celery & Relish	37.00
3900/126	12" 3 Part Celery & Relish	40.00
3900/129	3 Pc. Mayonnaise Set	45.00
3900/130	7" 2 Hdl. Ftd. Bonbon	26.00
3900/131	8" 2 Hdl. Ftd. Bonbon Plate	23.00
3900/136	5½" Comport	36.00
3900/165	Candy Box & Cover	60.00
3900/166	14" Plate, R.E.	50.00
3900/671	Ice Bucket w/Chrome Hdl.	75.00
3900/1177	Salt & Pepper Shaker ....pr.	33.00

Page 82 - Portia — Cryst

274	10" Bud Flower Holder	32.00
278	11" Ftd. Flower Holder	50.00
279	13" Ftd. Flower Holder	60.00
1237	9" Ftd. Flower Holder	48.00
1238	12" Ftd. Flower Holder	60.00
1299	11" Ftd. Flower Holder	62.00
1309	5" Globe Flower Holder	40.00
1603	Hurricane Lamp	110.00
1617	Hurricane Lamp	95.00
6004	8" Ftd. Flower Holder	32.00
6004	6" Ftd. Flower Holder	26.00

Page 83 - Portia — Cryst

1321	28 Oz. Ftd. Decanter	150.00
1321/7966	7 Pc. Sherry Set	290.00
7801	4 Oz. Cocktail	18.00
7966	2 Oz. Sherry	23.00
P.101	32 Oz. Cocktail Shaker	95.00
P.101/-		
7801	7 Pc. Cocktail Set	200.00

Page 84 - Portia — Cryst

477	9½" Pickle	33.00
3400/90	6" 2 Part Relish	24.00
3400/1180	5¼" 2 Hdl. Bonbon	20.00
3400/1181	6" 2 Hdl. Plate	18.00
3500/15	Ind. Sugar & Cream	34.00
3500/54	6" 2 Hdl. Ftd. Bonbon	24.00
3500/55	6" 2 Hdl. Ftd. Basket	26.00
3500/69	6½" 3 Part Relish	22.00
3500/161	8" 2 Hdl. Ftd. Plate	22.00

Page 85 - Wildflower — Cryst

3121	10 Oz. Goblet	23.00
3121	6 Oz. Tall Sherbet	20.00
3121	6 Oz. Low Sherbet	18.00
3121	3 Oz. Cocktail	24.00
3121	3½ Oz. Wine	32.00
3121	4½ Oz. Claret	38.00
3121	4 Oz. Oyster Cocktail	20.00
3121	1 Oz. Cordial	48.00
3121	5 Oz. Cafe Parfait	38.00
3121	12 Oz. Ftd. Ice Tea	22.00
3121	10 Oz. Ftd. Tumbler	20.00
3121	5 Oz. Ftd. Tumbler	20.00

Page 86 - Wildflower — Cryst

3900/17	Cup & Saucer	28.00
3900/19	2 Pc. Mayonnaise Set	39.00
3900/20	6½" Bread & Butter Plate	10.00
3900/22	8" Salad Plate	12.00
3900/24	10" Dinner Plate	60.00
3900/26	12" 4 Ftd. Plate	45.00
3900/28	11" Ftd. Bowl	45.00
3900/33	13" 4 Ftd. Torte Plate, R.E.	48.00
3900/34	11" 2 Hdl. Bowl	48.00
3900/35	13½" 2 Hdl. Cake Plate	45.00
3900/40	Ind. Sugar & Cream	36.00
3900/41	Sugar & Cream	29.00

Page 87 - Wildflower — Cryst

3900/54	10" 4 Ftd. Bowl, Flared	45.00
3900/62	12" Ftd. Bowl, Flared	48.00
3900/65	12" 4 Ftd. Oval Bowl	55.00

3900/67	5" Candlestick	29.00
3900/72	6" 2 Lite Candlestick	34.00
3900/74	6" 3 Lite Candlestick	35.00
3900/100	6 Oz. Oil, G.S.	80.00
3900/111	4 Pc. Mayonnaise Set	50.00
3900/115	13 Oz. Tumbler	28.00
3900/120	12" 5 Part Celery & Relish	45.00
3900/123	7" Relish or Pickle	28.00
3900/124	7" 2 Part Relish	30.00

Page 88 - Wildflower — Cryst

968	2 Pc. Cocktail Icer	52.00
3121	5⅜" Blown Comport	48.00
3900/125	9" 3 Part Celery & Relish	38.00
3900/126	12" 3 Part Celery & Relish	42.00
3900/129	3 Pc. Mayonnaise Set	46.00
3900/130	7" 2 Hdl. Ftd. Bonbon	27.00
3900/131	8" 2 Hdl. Ftd. Bonbon Plate	25.00
3900/136	5½" Comport	37.00
3900/165	Candy Box & Cover	60.00
3900/166	14" Plate, R.E.	50.00
3900/671	Ice Bucket w/Chrome Hdl.	75.00
3900/1177	Salt & Pepper Shaker ....ea.	35.00

Page 89 - Wildflower — Cryst

274	10" Bud Flower Holder	33.00
278	11" Ftd. Flower Holder	50.00
279	13" Ftd. Flower Holder	60.00
1237	9" Ftd. Flower Holder	50.00
1238	12" Ftd. Flower Holder	60.00
1299	11" Ftd. Flower Holder	62.00
1309	5" Globe Flower Holder	40.00
1603	Hurricane Lamp	120.00
1617	Hurricane Lamp	100.00
6004	6" Ftd. Flower Holder	27.00
6004	8" Ftd. Flower Holder	33.00

Page 90 - Wildflower — Cryst

477	9½" Pickle	35.00
3400/90	6" 2 Part Relish	25.00
3400/91	8" 3 Part Relish	34.00
3400/1180	5¼" 2 Hdl. Bonbon	25.00
3400/1181	6" 2 Hdl. Plate	20.00
3500/15	Ind. Sugar & Cream	36.00
3500/54	6" 2 Hdl. Ftd. Bonbon	26.00
3500/55	6" 2 Hdl. Ftd. Basket	28.00
3500/57	8" 3 Part Candy Box & Cover	56.00
3500/69	6" 3 Part Relish	24.00
3500/161	8" 2 Hdl. Ftd. Plate	24.00

Page 90A - Roselyn — Cryst

1174	6" B & B Plate, Sq.	7.00
1176	8½" Sq. Salad Plate	9.00
3779	9 Oz. Tall Goblet	18.00
3779	6 Oz. Tall Sherbet	14.00
3779	9 Oz. Low Goblet	16.00
3779	6 Oz. Low Sherbet	12.00
3779	3 Oz. Cocktail	18.00
3779	2½ Oz. Wine	20.00
3779	4½ Oz. Oyster Cocktail	14.00
3779	4½ Oz. Claret	22.00
3779	1 Oz. Cordial	42.00
3779	12 Oz. Ftd. Ice Tea	16.00
3779	5 Oz. Ftd. Tumbler	12.00

Page 90B - Roselyn — Cryst

3400/35	11" 2 Hdl. Plate	28.00
3400/90	6" 2 Part Relish	17.00
3400/91	8" 3 Part Relish	22.00
3900/41	Sugar & Cream	30.00
3900/120	12" 5 Part Celery & Relish	28.00
3900/125	9" 3 Part Celery & Relish	24.00
3900/126	12" 3 Part Celery & Relish	32.00
3900/166	14" Plate, R.E.	38.00
P.248	11" Celery Tray	22.00

Page 90C - Roselyn — Cryst

646	5" Candlestick	16.00
647	6" 2 Lite Candlestick	22.00
1338	6" 3 Lite Candlestick	27.00
3400/4	12" 4 Ftd. Bowl, Flared	37.00
3400/48	11" 4 Ftd. Bowl, Fancy Edge	37.00
3400/160	12" 4 Ftd. Bowl, Oblong	44.00
P.533	3 Pc. Mayonnaise Set	33.00
P.1491	4 Pc. Twin Salad Dressing	38.00

Page 90D - Roselyn — Cryst

3121	5⅜" Blown Comport	42.00
3400/52	5" Butter & Cover	70.00
3400/1180	5½" 2 Hdl. Bonbon	13.00
3400/1181	6" 2 Hdl. Bonbon Plate	13.00
3500/54	6" 2 Hdl. Ftd. Bonbon	16.00
3500/55	6" 2 Hdl. Ftd. Basket	17.00
3500/57	3 Part Candy Box & Cover	44.00
3500/69	6½" 3 Part Relish	16.00

301

		Cryst
P.293	6 Oz. Oil	58.00
P.306	6" Candy Box & Cover	45.00
P.360	Salt & Pepper w/Chrome Top	28.00

Page 90E - Roselyn

		Cryst
274	10" Ftd. Bud Vase	20.00
278	11" Ftd. Vase	26.00
1237	9" Ftd. Vase	28.00
1238	12" Ftd. Vase	33.00
3900/115	76 Oz. Jug	70.00
3900/116	80 Oz. Ball Jug	82.00
3900/118	32 Oz. Jug	72.00
3900/671	Ice Pail w/Hdl. & Tong	50.00
P.101	32 Oz. Cocktail Shaker	65.00

Page 90F - Daffodil

		Cryst
1176	8½" Salad Plate	14.00
3779	9 Oz. Tall Goblet	22.00
3779	6 Oz. Tall Sherbet	20.00
3779	6 Oz. Low Sherbet	16.00
3779	9 Oz. Low Goblet	20.00
3779	3 Oz. Cocktail	22.00
3779	2½ Oz. Wine	28.00
3779	4½ Oz. Claret	33.00
3779	1 Oz. Cordial	48.00
3779	4½ Oz. Oyster Cocktail	20.00
3779	12 Oz. Ftd. Ice Tea	22.00
3779	5 Oz. Ftd. Tumbler	17.00

Page 90G - Daffodil

		Cryst
P.54	6½" 2 Hdl. Low Comport	22.00
P.55	6" 2 Hdl. Low Ftd. Basket	24.00
P.56	8" 2 Hdl. Low Ftd. Plate	22.00
P.166	13½" Cabaret Plate, R.E.	44.00
P.214	10" 3 Part Relish	38.00
P.248	11" Celery	33.00
P.253	Ind. Sugar & Cream	33.00
P.254	Sugar & Cream	30.00
P.293	6 Oz. Oil	80.00

Page 90H - Daffodil

		Cryst
628	3½" Candlestick	22.00
3400/141	76 Oz. Jug	135.00
3900/72	6" 2 Lite Candlestick	33.00
P.306	6" Candy Box & Cover	55.00
P.360	Salt & Pepper w/Chrome Tops	35.00
P.384	11" Oval Bowl	48.00
P.430	12" Bowl, Belled	44.00
P.1491	4 Pc. Twin Salad Dressing	44.00

Page 90I - Daffodil

		Cryst
278	11" Vase, Ftd.	50.00
532	6" Tall Comport	44.00
1495	11½" 2 Hdl. Cake Plate	38.00
3400/1180	5¼" Bonbon, 2 Hdl.	16.00
3400/1181	6" 2 Hdl. Bonbon Plate	15.00
6004	8" Ftd. Vase	28.00
P.533	3 Pc. Mayonnaise Set	44.00
P.533	5½" Comport	22.00
P.533/445	2 Pc. Mayonnaise Set	28.00

Page 91 - Rock Crystal Achilles (698)

		Cryst
3121	10 Oz. Goblet	24.00
3121	6 Oz. Tall Sherbet	22.00
3121	3 Oz. Cocktail	24.00
3121	12 Oz. Ftd. Ice Tea	22.00
3121	10 Oz. Ftd. Tumbler	20.00
3121	6 Oz. Low Sherbet	16.00
3121	4½ Oz. Oyster Cocktail	17.00
3121	4½ Oz. Claret	28.00
3121	5 Oz. Ftd. Tumbler	17.00
3121	3½ Oz. Wine	27.00
3121	1 Oz. Cordial	45.00
3121	5⅜" Blown Comport	50.00

Page 92 - Rock Crystal Achilles (698)

		Cryst
3900/22	8" Salad Plate	14.00
3900/35	13½" 2 Hdl. Cake Plate	42.00
3900/41	Sugar & Cream	34.00
3900/62	12" 4 Ftd. Bowl, Flared	44.00
3900/72	6" 2 Lite Candlestick	27.00
3900/111	4 Pc. Mayonnaise Set	44.00
3900/120	12" 5 Part Celery & Relish	42.00
3900/125	8" 3 Part Celery & Relish	38.00
3900/126	12" 3 Part Celery & Relish	42.00

Page 93 - Rock Crystal Achilles (698)

		Cryst
278	11" Ftd. Vase	55.00
968	2 Pc. Cocktail Icer	38.00
3900/129	3 Pc. Mayonnaise Set	38.00
3900/130	7" 2 Hdl. Ftd. Bonbon	24.00
3900/131	8" 2 Hdl. Ftd. Bonbon Plate	22.00
3900/136	5½" Comport	33.00
3900/165	Candy Box & Cover	48.00
3900/166	14" Plate, R.E.	48.00

Page 94 - Rock Crystal Adonis (720)

		Cryst
3500	10 Oz. Goblet	24.00
3500	7 Oz. Tall Sherbet	22.00
3500	7 Oz. Low Sherbet	16.00
3500	3 Oz.. Cocktail	24.00
3500	2½ Oz. Wine	27.00
3500	4½ Oz. Claret	28.00
3500	4½ Oz. Oyster Cocktail	17.00
3500	1 Oz. Cordial	45.00
3500	5 Oz. Cafe Parfait	27.00
3500	12 Oz. Ftd. Ice Tea	22.00
3500	10 Oz. Ftd. Tumbler	20.00
3500	5 Oz. Ftd. Tumbler	17.00

Page 95 - Rock Crystal Adonis (720)

		Cryst
968	2 Pc. Cocktail Icer	38.00
3500/101	5⅜" Blown Comport	44.00
3900/22	8" Salad Plate	12.00
3900/35	13½" 2 Hdl. Cake Plate	42.00
3900/41	Sugar & Cream	34.00
3900/62	12" 4 Ftd. Bowl, Flared	43.00
3900/72	6" 2 Lite Candlestick	27.00

Page 96 - Rock Crystal Adonis (720)

		Cryst
3900/111	4 Pc. Mayonnaise Set	44.00
3900/120	12" 5 Part Celery & Relish	42.00
3900/125	8" 3 Part Celery & Relish	38.00
3900/126	12" 3 Part Celery & Relish	42.00
3900/129	3 Pc. Mayonnaise Set	38.00
3900/130	7" 2 Hdl. Ftd. Bonbon	24.00
3900/131	8" 2 Hdl. Ftd. Bonbon Plate	22.00

Page 97 - Rock Crystal Adonis (720)

		Cryst
274	10" Ftd. Vase	27.00
278	11" Ftd. Vase	53.00
1321	28 Oz. Ftd. Decanter	140.00
3900/136	5½" Comport	33.00
3900/165	Candy Box & Cover	48.00
3900/166	14" Plate, R.E.	47.00
7966	2 Oz. Sherry	22.00

Page 98 - Rock Crystal Ardsley (1005)

		Cryst
555	7½" Salad Plate	8.00
3700	9 Oz. Goblet	13.00
3700	6 Oz. Tall Sherbet	10.00
3700	6 Oz. Low Sherbet	9.00
3700	3 Oz. Cocktail	12.00
3700	2½ Oz. Wine	15.00
3700	4½ Oz. Claret	15.00
3700	4½ Oz. Oyster Cocktail	10.00
3700	1 Oz. Cordial	28.00
3700	12 Oz. Ftd. Ice Tea	12.00
3700	10 Oz. Ftd. Tumbler	10.00
3700	5 Oz. Ftd. Tumbler	9.00

Page 98A - Rock Crystal Bexley (1072)

		Cryst
647	6" 2 Lite Candlestick	22.00
3121	Blown Comport	38.00
3900/41	Sugar & Cream	30.00
3900/115	76 Oz. Jug (Not Optic)	60.00
P.360	Salt & Pepper w/Chrome Top	22.00
P.384	11" Bowl	30.00
P.427	10" Salad Bowl	30.00

Page 98B - Rock Crystal Bexley (1072)

		Cryst
3900/120	12" 5 Part Celery & Relish	30.00
3900/126	12" 3 Part Celery & Relish	25.00
3900/129	3 Pc. Mayonnaise Set	25.00
3900/165	Candy Box & Cover	35.00
3900/166	14" Plate, R.E.	35.00

Page 99 - Rock Crystal Bexley (1014)

		Cryst
555	7½" Salad Plate	7.50
3750	10 Oz. Goblet	14.00
3750	6 Oz. Tall Sherbet	10.00
3750	6 Oz. Low Sherbet	9.00
3750	3½ Oz. Cocktail	13.00
3750	3 Oz. Wine	15.00
3750	4½ Oz. Claret	15.00
3750	5 Oz. Oyster Cocktail	10.00
3750	1 Oz. Cordial	32.00
3750	12 Oz. Ftd. Ice Tea	12.00
3750	5 Oz. Ftd. Tumbler	9.50

Page 99 - Rock Crystal Bijou (1011)

		Cryst
321	7 Oz. O.F. Cocktail	10.00
321	1½ Oz. Tumbler	10.00
497	14 Oz. Tumbler	10.00
497	12 Oz. Tumbler	10.00
555	7½" Salad Plate	7.25
3725	9 Oz. Goblet	12.00
3725	7 Oz. Tall Sherbet	10.00
3725	7 Oz. Low Sherbet	9.00
3725	2½ Oz. Cocktail	12.00
3725	2½ Oz. Wine	15.00
3725	4½ Oz. Claret	15.00
3725	4½ Oz. Oyster Cocktail	10.00
3725	1 Oz. Cordial	32.00
3725	12 Oz. Ftd. Ice Tea	12.00
3725	5 Oz. Ftd. Tumbler	9.50

Page 100A - Rock Crystal Cambridge Rose (1074)

		Cryst
555	7½" Salad Plate	8.00
3700	9 Oz. Goblet	15.00
3700	6 Oz. Tall Sherbet	12.00
3700	6 Oz. Low Sherbet	10.00
3700	3 Oz. Cocktail	15.00
3700	2½ Oz. Wine	18.00
3700	4½ Oz. Claret	18.00
3700	4½ Oz. Oyster Cocktail	12.00
3700	1 Oz. Cordial	30.00
3700	12 Oz. Ftd. Ice Tea	10.00
3700	5 Oz. Ftd. Tumbler	8.50

Page 100B - Rock Crystal Cambridge Rose (1074)

		Cryst
278	11" Ftd. Vase	44.00
556	8" Salad Plate	9.00
628	3½" Candlestick	15.00
1532	3 Pc. Mayonnaise Set	30.00
P.125	14" Plate	35.00
P.214	10" 3 Part Relish	25.00
P.254	Sugar & Cream	30.00
P.306	Candy Box & Cover (Cut Knob)	38.00
P.430	12" Bowl	32.00

Page 101 - Rock Crystal Cadet

		Cryst
555	7½" Salad Plate	7.00
556	8" Salad Plate	7.25
3725	9 Oz. Goblet	13.00
3725	7 Oz. Tall Sherbet	10.00
3725	7 Oz. Low Sherbet	9.00
3725	2½ Oz. Cocktail	12.00
3725	2½ Oz. Wine	15.00
3725	4½ Oz. Claret	15.00
3725	4½ Oz. Oyster Cocktail	10.00
3725	1 Oz. Cordial	30.00
3725	12 Oz. Ftd. Ice Tea	12.00
3725	5 Oz. Ftd. Tumbler	9.00

Page 102 - Rock Crystal Cordelia (812)

		Cryst
555	7½" Salad Plate	8.00
968	2 Pc. Cocktail Icer, Ftd.	27.00
3130	9 Oz. Goblet	17.00
3130	7 Oz. Tall Sherbet	12.00
3130	7 Oz. Low Sherbet	10.00
3130	3 Oz. Cocktail	15.00
3130	2½ Oz. Wine	18.00
3130	4½ Oz. Claret	18.00
3130	4½ Oz. Oyster Cocktail	12.00
3130	1 Oz. Cordial	35.00
3130	12 Oz. Ftd. Ice Tea	15.00
3130	10 Oz. Ftd. Tumbler	12.00
3130	5 Oz. Ftd. Tumbler	10.00
3400/62	8½" Salad Plate	9.00
3400/176	7½" Salad Plate	9.00

Page 102A - Rock Crystal Corsage (1075)

		Cryst
556	8" Salad Plate	9.00
3116	10 Oz. Goblet	16.00
3116	6 Oz. Tall Sherbet	12.00
3116	6 Oz. Low Sherbet	10.00
3116	3 Oz. Cocktail	15.00
3116	1 Oz. Cordial	38.00
3116	4½ Oz. Oyster Cocktail	12.00
3116	3 Oz. Wine	18.00
3116	4½ Oz. Claret	18.00
3116	12 Oz. Ftd. Ice Tea	15.00
3116	10 Oz. Ftd. Tumbler	12.00
3116	5 Oz. Ftd. Tumbler	10.00

Page 103 - Rock Crystal Croesus (722)

		Cryst
968	2 Pc. Cocktail Icer	38.00
3500	10 Oz. Goblet	24.00
3500	7 Oz. Tall Sherbet	20.00
3500	7 Oz. Low Sherbet	15.00
3500	3 Oz. Cocktail	22.00
3500	2½ Oz. Wine	25.00
3500	4½ Oz. Claret	25.00
3500	4½ Oz. Oyster Cocktail	16.00
3500	1 Oz. Cordial	45.00
3500	5 Oz. Cafe Parfait	25.00
3500	12 Oz. Ftd. Ice Tea	20.00
3500	10 Oz. Ftd. Tumbler	18.00
3500	5 Oz. Ftd. Tumbler	16.00
3500/5	8½" Salad Plate	10.00
3500/167	7½" Salad Plate	10.00

Page 104 - Rock Cry. Deerfield (1033)

		Cryst
555	7½" Salad Plate	8.00
968	2 Pc. Cocktail Icer	27.00
3778	10 Oz. Goblet	17.00
3778	7 Oz. Tall Sherbet	12.00
3778	7 Oz. Low Sherbet	10.00
3778	2½ Oz. Cocktail	15.00
3778	2½ Oz. Wine	18.00
3778	4½ Oz. Claret	18.00
3778	4½ Oz. Oyster Cocktail	12.00
3778	1 Oz. Cordial	38.00
3778	12 Oz. Ftd. Ice Tea	15.00
3778	5 Oz. Ftd. Tumbler	12.00

Page 105 - Rock Crystal Euclid (1017)

		Cryst
555	7½" Salad Plate	7.00
3750	10 Oz. Goblet	13.00
3750	6 Oz. Tall Sherbet	10.00
3750	6 Oz. Low Sherbet	9.00
3750	3½ Oz. Cocktail	12.00
3750	3 Oz. Wine	15.00
3750	4½ Oz. Claret	15.00
3750	5 Oz. Oyster Cocktail	10.00
3750	1 Oz. Cordial	28.00
3750	12 Oz. Ftd. Ice Tea	12.00
3750	5 Oz. Ftd. Tumbler	9.00

Page 106 - Rock Crystal Fuchsia (1019)

		Cryst
555	7½" Salad Plate	8.00
3750	10 Oz. Goblet	16.00
3750	6 Oz. Tall Sherbet	12.00
3750	6 Oz. Low Sherbet	10.00
3750	3½ Oz. Cocktail	15.00
3750	3 Oz. Wine	18.00
3750	4½ Oz. Claret	18.00
3750	5 Oz. Oyster Cocktail	12.00
3750	1 Oz. Cordial	37.00
3750	12 Oz. Ftd. Ice Tea	15.00
3750	5 Oz. Ftd. Ice Tea	10.00

Page 106 - Rock Crystal Festoon (1071)

		Cryst
555	7½" Salad Plate	7.00
3790	Goblet	12.00
3790	Low Sherbet	9.00
3790	Cocktail	12.00
3790	Wine	15.00
3790	Claret	15.00
3790	Oyster Cocktail	9.00
3790	Cordial	28.00
3790	12 Oz. Ftd. Ice Tea	12.00
3790	5 Oz. Ftd. Tumbler	9.00

Page 107 - Rock Crystal Glendale (1028)

		Cryst
555	7½" Salad Plate	8.00
968	2 Pc. Cocktail Icer, Ftd.	28.00
3130	9 Oz. Goblet	17.00
3130	7 Oz. Tall Sherbet	12.00
3130	7 Oz. Low Sherbet	10.00
3130	3 Oz. Cocktail	15.00
3130	2½ Oz. Wine	18.00
3130	4½ Oz. Claret	18.00
3130	4½ Oz. Oyster Cocktail	12.00
3130	1 Oz. Cordial	34.00
3130	12 Oz. Ftd. Tumbler	15.00
3130	5 Oz. Ftd. Tumbler	10.00

Page 108 - Rock Crystal Hanover (1015)

		Cryst
555	7½" Salad Plate	7.25
3750	10 Oz. Goblet	14.00
3750	6 Oz. Tall Sherbet	10.00
3750	6 Oz. Low Sherbet	9.00
3750	3½ Oz. Cocktail	12.00
3750	3 Oz. Wine	15.00
3750	4½ Oz. Claret	15.00
3750	5 Oz. Oyster Cocktail	10.00
3750	1 Oz. Cordial	30.00
3750	12 Oz. Ftd. Ice Tea	12.00
3750	5 Oz. Ftd. Tumbler	9.00

Page 108A - Rock Crystal Harvest (1053)

		Cryst
647	6" 2 Lite Candlestick	25.00
P.125	14" Plate	33.00
P.384	11" Oval Bowl	33.00
P.430	12" Bowl	33.00
P.499	6½" Calla Lily C/S	25.00

Page 108B - Rock Crystal Harvest (1053)

		Cryst
103	7" 3 Part Candy Box & Cover	38.00
278	11" Ftd. Vase	44.00
532	6" Tall Comport	38.00
1491	4 Pc. Twin Salad Dressing Set	38.00
P.212	10" 5 Part Celery & Relish	27.00
P.254	Sugar & Cream	30.00
P.306	6" Candy Box & Cover	38.00

| P.427 | 10" Salad Bowl | 33.00 |

Page 109 - Rock Crystal Harvest (1053)

		Cryst
532	6" Tall Comport	36.00
555	7½" Salad Plate	8.00
3750	10 Oz. Goblet	17.00
3750	6 Oz. Tall Sherbet	12.00
3750	6 Oz. Low Sherbet	10.00
3750	3½ Oz. Cocktail	15.00
3750	3 Oz. Wine	18.00
3750	4½ Oz. Claret	18.00
3750	5 Oz. Oyster Cocktail	12.00
3750	1 Oz. Cordial	35.00
3750	12 Oz. Ftd. Ice Tea	15.00
3750	5 Oz. Ftd. Tumbler	10.00
P.125	14" Plate	32.00

Page 110 - Rock Crystal Juliana (997)

		Cryst
555	7½" Salad Plate	7.25
968	2 Pc. Cocktail Icer	25.00
3139	10 Oz. Goblet	13.00
3139	7 Oz. Tall Sherbet	10.00
3139	4½ Oz. Oyster Cocktail	10.00
3139	2½ Oz. Cocktail	12.00
3139	2½ Oz. Sherry Wine	15.00
3139	4½ Oz. Claret	15.00
3139	1 Oz. Cordial	30.00
3139	12 Oz. Ftd. Ice Tea	12.00
3139	5 Oz. Ftd. Tumbler	9.00

Page 111 - Rock Crystal King Edward (821)

		Cryst
3700	9 Oz. Goblet	17.00
3700	6 Oz. Tall Sherbet	13.00
3700	6 Oz. Low Sherbet	10.00
3700	3 Oz. Cocktail	16.00
3700	2½ Oz. Wine	19.00
3700	4½ Oz. Claret	19.00
3700	4½ Oz. Oyster Cocktail	13.00
3700	1 Oz. Cordial	35.00
3700	12 Oz. Ftd. Ice Tea	16.00
3700	10 Oz. Ftd. Tumbler	14.00
3700	5 Oz. Ftd. Tumbler	12.00

Page 112 - Rock Crystal King Edward (821)

		Cryst
138	Sugar & Cream	32.00
321	7 Oz. O.F. Cocktail	11.00
321	1½ Oz. Whiskey	12.00
497	12 Oz. Tumbler	12.00
532	6" Tall Comport, Ftd.	35.00
533	6" Ftd. Comport	22.00
533	3 Pc. Mayonnaise Set	35.00
555	7½" Salad Plate	8.00
556	8" Salad Plate	8.00
628	3½" Candlestick	15.00
647	6" 2 Lite Candlestick	25.00
1491	4 Pc. Twin Salad Dressing	37.00
P.293	6 Oz. Oil	44.00

Page 113 - Rock Crystal King Edward (821)

		Cryst
103	7" 3 Part Candy Box & Cover	32.00
1321	28 Oz. Ftd. Decanter	85.00
1397	13½" Plate	40.00
P.101	32 Oz. Cocktail Shaker	65.00
P.212	10" 5 Part Celery & Relish	28.00
P.427	10" Bowl	35.00
P.430	12" Bowl, Flared	35.00

Page 114 - Rock Crystal King George (1027)

		Cryst
321	7 Oz. O.F. Cocktail	10.00
497	12 Oz. Tumbler	10.00
555	7½" Salad Plate	7.25
3139	10 Oz. Goblet	14.00
3139	7 Oz. Tall Sherbet	11.00
3139	4½ Oz. Claret	16.00
3139	2½ Oz. Cocktail	14.00
3139	2½ Oz. Sherry Wine	16.00
3139	4½ Oz. Oyster Cocktail	10.00
3139	1 Oz. Cordial	35.00
3139	12 Oz. Ftd. Tumbler	14.00
3139	5 Oz. Ftd. Tumbler	10.00

Page 114A - Rock Crystal Lily of the Valley (1069)

		Cryst
555	7½" Salad Plate	9.00
3790	Goblet	15.00
3790	Low Sherbet	10.00
3790	Cocktail	15.00
3790	Wine	18.00
3790	Claret	18.00
3790	Oyster Cocktail	10.00
3790	Cordial	37.00
3790	12 Oz. Ftd. Ice Tea	15.00
3790	5 Oz. Ftd. Tumbler	10.00

Page 114B - Rock Crystal Lynbrook (1070)

		Cryst
555	7½" Salad Plate	8.00
3790	Goblet	14.00
3790	Low Sherbet	10.00
3790	Cocktail	14.00
3790	Wine	16.00
3790	Claret	16.00
3790	Oyster Cocktail	10.00
3790	Cordial	32.00
3790	12 Oz. Ftd. Ice Tea	14.00
3790	5 Oz. Ftd. Tumbler	9.00

Page 114C - Rock Crystal Lynbrook (1070)

		Cryst
533	6" Comport	18.00
628	3½" Candlestick	12.00
1532	3 Pc. Mayonnaise Set	30.00
3600/495	6" 2 Lite Candlestick	25.00
P.214	10" 3 Part Relish	25.00
P.306	Candy Box & Cover	35.00
P.430	12" Bowl	30.00

Page 114D - Rock Crystal Lynbrook (1070)

		Cryst
3700	5" Blown Comport	27.50
3900/115	76 Oz. Jug	60.00
P.166	13½" Plate	30.00
P.254	Sugar & Cream	25.00
P.293	6 Oz. Oil	40.00
P.298	Marmalade & Cover & Spoon	25.00
P.360	Salt & Pepper	18.00

Page 115 - Rock Crystal Larchmont (1036)

		Cryst
555	7½" Salad Plate	8.00
968	2 Pc. Cocktail Icer	25.00
3778	10 Oz. Goblet	16.00
3778	7 Oz. Tall Sherbet	14.00
3778	7 Oz. Low Sherbet	12.00
3778	2½ Oz. Cocktail	16.00
3778	2½ Oz. Wine	20.00
3778	4½ Oz. Claret	20.00
3778	4½ Oz. Oyster Cocktail	12.00
3778	1 Oz. Cordial	40.00
3778	12 Oz. Ftd. Ice Tea	16.00
3778	5 Oz. Ftd. Tumbler	12.00

Page 116 - Rock Crystal Laurel Wreath

		Cryst
968	2 Pc. Cocktail Icer	30.00
3700	9 Oz. Goblet	14.00
3700	6 Oz. Tall Sherbet	12.00
3700	6 Oz. Low Sherbet	10.00
3700	3 Oz. Cocktail	14.00
3700	2½ Oz. Wine	16.00
3700	4½ Oz. Claret	16.00
3700	4½ Oz. Oyster Cocktail	12.00
3700	1 Oz. Cordial	32.00
3700	12 Oz. Ftd. Ice Tea	14.00
3700	10 Oz. Ftd. Tumbler	12.00
3700	5 Oz. Ftd. Tumbler	10.00

Page 116A - Rock Crystal Laurel Wreath

		Cryst
533	6" Comport	22.00
1532	3 Pc. Mayonnaise Set	30.00
3700	5" Blown Comport	27.50
3900/72	6" 2 Lite Candlestick	25.00
P.166	13½" Plate, R.E.	30.00
P.214	10" 3 Part Relish	25.00
P.254	Sugar & Cream	25.00
P.293	6 Oz. Oil (Polished Stopper)	40.00
P.298	Marmalade, Cover & Spoon	30.00
P.306	Candy Box & Cover (Cut Knob)	40.00
P.360	Salt & Pepper	25.00
P.430	12" Bowl, Flared	30.00

Page 117 - Rock Crystal Laurel Wreath

		Cryst
321	7 Oz. O.F. Cocktail	12.00
321	1½ Oz. Whiskey	12.00
497	14 Oz. Tumbler	12.00
497	12 Oz. Tumbler	12.00
555	7½" Salad Plate	8.00
556	8" Salad Plate	8.00
3139	10 Oz. Goblet	14.00
3139	7 Oz. Tall Sherbet	12.00
3139	2½ Oz. Cocktail	14.00
3139	2½ Oz. Sherry Wine	16.00
3139	4½ Oz. Claret	16.00
3139	4½ Oz. Oyster Cocktail	12.00
3139	1 Oz. Cordial	32.00
3139	5 Oz. Ftd. Tumbler	10.00
3139	12 Oz. Ftd. Ice Tea	14.00

Page 118 - Rock Crystal Lexington (758)

		Cryst
555	7½" Salad Plate	8.00
556	8" Salad Plate	8.00
968	2 Pc. Cocktail Icer	22.00
1321	28 Oz. Ftd. Decanter	75.00

No.	Item	Cryst
7966	9 Oz. Goblet	14.00
7966	6 Oz. Tall Sherbet	12.00
7966	3½ Oz. Cocktail	14.00
7966	3 Oz. Wine	16.00
7966	4 Oz. Claret	16.00
7966	2 Oz. Sherry	15.00
7966	1 Oz. Cordial	30.00
7966	12 Oz. Ftd. Ice Tea	14.00
P.101	32 Oz. Cocktail Shaker	62.00

Page 119 - Rock Crystal Lucia (824)

No.	Item	Cryst
3116	10 Oz. Goblet	17.00
3116	6 Oz. Tall Sherbet	19.00
3116	6 Oz. Low Sherbet	12.00
3116	3 Oz. Cocktail	17.00
3116	3 Oz. Wine	20.00
3116	4½ Oz. Oyster Cocktail	12.00
3116	12 Oz. Ftd. Ice Tea	17.00
3116	10 Oz. Ftd. Tumbler	15.00
3116	5 Oz. Ftd. Tumbler	12.00
3121	5⅜" Blown Comport	35.00

Page 120 - Rock Crystal Lucia (824)

No.	Item	Cryst
3900/22	8" Salad Plate	8.00
3900/41	Sugar & Cream	25.00
3900/62	12" 4 Ftd. Bowl, Flared	35.00
3900/72	6" 2 Lite Candlestick	25.00
3900/111	4 Pc. Mayonnaise Set	35.00
3900/120	12" 5 Part Celery & Relish	35.00
3900/125	8" 3 Part Celery & Relish	25.00
3900/126	12" 3 Part Celery & Relish	30.00
3900/131	8" 2 Hdl. Ftd. Bonbon Plate	16.00

Page 121 - Rock Crystal Lucia (824)

No.	Item	Cryst
278	11" Ftd. Vase	40.00
968	2 Pc. Cocktail Icer	27.00
3900/35	13½" 2 Hdl. Cake Plate	30.00
3900/129	3 Pc. Mayonnaise Set	32.00
3900/130	7" 2 Hdl. Ftd. Bonbon	20.00
3900/136	5½" Comport	25.00
3900/165	Candy Box & Cover	35.00
3900/166	14" Plate, R.E.	35.00

Page 122 - Rock Crystal Manor (1003)

No.	Item	Cryst
3121	5⅜" Blown Comport	35.00
3700	9 Oz. Goblet	12.00
3700	6 Oz. Tall Sherbet	10.00
3700	6 Oz. Low Sherbet	9.00
3700	3 Oz. Cocktail	12.00
3700	2½ Oz. Wine	14.00
3700	4½ Oz. Claret	14.00
3700	4½ Oz. Oyster Cocktail	10.00
3700	1 Oz. Cordial	32.00
3700	12 Oz. Ftd. Ice Tea	12.00
3700	10 Oz. Ftd. Tumbler	11.00
3700	5 Oz. Ftd. Tumbler	10.00

Page 123 - Rock Crystal Manor (1003)

No.	Item	Cryst
968	2 Pc. Cocktail Icer	25.00
3900/22	8" Salad Plate	7.50
3900/35	13½" 2 Hdl. Cake Plate	27.50
3900/41	Sugar & Cream	24.00
3900/62	12" 4 Ftd. Bowl, Flared	27.50
3900/72	6" 2 Lite Candlestick	22.50
3900/111	4 Pc. Mayonnaise Set	30.00
3900/129	3 Pc. Mayonnaise Set	25.00
3900/136	5½" Comport	25.00
3900/165	Candy Box & Cover	32.50

Page 124 - Rock Crystal Manor (1003)

No.	Item	Cryst
278	11" Ftd. Vase	37.00
1613	Hurricane Lamp	130.00
3900/120	12" 5 Part Celery & Relish	30.00
3900/125	8" 3 Part Celery & Relish	25.00
3900/126	12" 3 Part Celery & Relish	27.50
3900/130	7" 2 Hdl. Ftd. Bonbon	16.00
3900/131	8" 2 Hdl. Ftd. Bonbon Plate	14.00
3900/166	14" Plate, R.E.	30.00

Page 125 - Rock Crystal Maryland (985)

No.	Item	Cryst
968	2 Pc. Cocktail Icer	30.00
3121	5⅜" Blown Comport	35.00
3776	9 Oz. Goblet	17.00
3776	7 Oz. Tall Sherbet	15.00
3776	7 Oz. Low Sherbet	12.00
3776	3 Oz. Cocktail	17.00
3776	2½ Oz. Wine	20.00
3776	4½ Oz. Claret	20.00
3776	1 Oz. Cordial	40.00
3776	12 Oz. Ftd. Ice Tea	17.00
3776	5 Oz. Ftd. Tumbler	12.00

Page 126 - Rock Crystal Maryland (985)

No.	Item	Cryst
3900/22	8" Salad Plate	12.00
3900/35	13½" 2 Hdl. Cake Plate	37.00

No.	Item	Cryst
3900/41	Sugar & Cream	30.00
3900/62	12" 4 Ftd. Bowl, Flared	37.00
3900/72	6" 2 Lite Candlestick	27.00
3900/120	12" 5 Part Celery & Relish	37.00
3900/125	8" 3 Part Celery & Relish	27.00
3900/126	12" 3 Part Celery & Relish	32.00

Page 127 - Rock Crystal Maryland (985)

No.	Item	Cryst
274	10" Ftd. Bud Vase	35.00
278	11" Ftd. Vase	50.00
3900/111	4 Pc. Mayonnaise Set	40.00
3900/129	3 Pc. Mayonnaise Set	32.00
3900/130	7" 2 Hdl. Ftd. Bonbon	27.00
3900/131	8" 2 Hdl. Ftd. Bonbon Plate	20.00
3900/136	5½" Comport	35.00
3900/165	Candy Box & Cover	45.00
3900/166	14" Plate, R.E.	40.00

Page 128 - Rock Crystal Minton Wreath (1012)

No.	Item	Cryst
555	7½" Salad Plate	8.00
3750	10 Oz. Goblet	12.00
3750	6 Oz. Tall Sherbet	10.00
3750	6 Oz. Low Sherbet	9.00
3750	3½ Oz. Cocktail	12.00
3750	3 Oz. Wine	15.00
3750	4½ Oz. Claret	15.00
3750	5 Oz. Oyster Cocktail	10.00
3750	1 Oz. Cordial	32.00
3750	12 Oz. Ftd. Ice Tea	12.00

Page 129 - Rock Crystal Minuet (990)

No.	Item	Cryst
555	7½" Salad Plate	8.00
556	8" Salad Plate	8.00
3776	9 Oz. Goblet	15.00
3776	7 Oz. Tall Sherbet	12.00
3776	7 Oz. Low Sherbet	10.00
3776	3 Oz. Cocktail	15.00
3776	2½ Oz. Wine	18.00
3776	4½ Oz. Claret	18.00
3776	1 Oz. Cordial	35.00
3776	12 Oz. Ftd. Ice Tea	15.00
3776	5 Oz. Ftd. Tumbler	10.00

Page 130 - Rock Crystal Montrose (1004)

No.	Item	Cryst
555	7½" Salad Plate	8.00
3700	9 Oz. Goblet	15.00
3700	6 Oz. Tall Sherbet	12.00
3700	6 Oz. Low Sherbet	10.00
3700	3 Oz. Cocktail	15.00
3700	2½ Oz. Wine	18.00
3700	4½ Oz. Claret	18.00
3700	4½ Oz. Oyster Cocktail	10.00
3700	1 Oz. Cordial	35.00
3700	12 Oz. Ftd. Ice Tea	15.00
3700	10 Oz. Ftd. Tumbler	12.00
3700	5 Oz. Ftd. Tumbler	10.00

Page 131 - Rock Crystal Plaza (1018)

No.	Item	Cryst
555	7½" Salad Plate	7.25
3725	9 Oz. Goblet	12.00
3725	7 Oz. Tall Sherbet	10.00
3725	7 Oz. Low Sherbet	9.00
3725	2½ Oz. Cocktail	12.00
3725	2½ Oz. Wine	15.00
3725	4½ Oz. Claret	15.00
3725	4½ Oz. Oyster Cocktail	10.00
3725	1 Oz. Cordial	32.00
3725	12 Oz. Ftd. Ice Tea	12.00
3725	5 Oz. Ftd. Tumbler	9.00

Page 132 - Rock Crystal Roxbury (1030)

No.	Item	Cryst
555	7½" Salad Plate	8.00
968	2 Pc. Cocktail Icer	22.00
3775	10 Oz. Goblet	14.00
3775	6 Oz. Tall Sherbet	12.00
3775	6 Oz. Low Sherbet	10.00
3775	3 Oz. Cocktail	14.00
3775	2½ Oz. Wine	16.00
3775	4½ Oz. Claret	16.00
3775	4½ Oz. Oyster Cocktail	10.00
3775	1 Oz. Cordial	32.00
3775	12 Oz. Ftd. Ice Tea	14.00
3775	5 Oz. Ftd. Tumbler	10.00

Page 133 - Rock Crystal Star (1016)

No.	Item	Cryst
555	7½" Salad Plate	8.00
3725	9 Oz. Goblet	14.00
3725	7 Oz. Tall Sherbet	12.00
3725	7 Oz. Low Sherbet	10.00
3725	2½ Oz. Cocktail	14.00
3725	2½ Oz. Wine	16.00
3725	4½ Oz. Claret	16.00
3725	4½ Oz. Oyster Cocktail	10.00
3725	1 Oz. Cordial	32.00

Page 134 - Rock Crystal Tempo (1029)

No.	Item	Cryst
555	7½" Salad Plate	8.00
968	2 Pc. Cocktail Icer	22.00
3770	9 Oz. Goblet	14.00
3770	6 Oz. Tall Sherbet	12.00
3770	6 Oz. Low Sherbet	10.00
3770	3 Oz. Cocktail	14.00
3770	2½ Oz. Wine	16.00
3770	4½ Oz. Claret	16.00
3770	1 Oz. Cordial	32.00
3770	4½ Oz. Oyster Cocktail	10.00
3770	12 Oz. Ftd. Ice Tea	14.00
3770	5 Oz. Ftd. Tumbler	10.00

Page 135 - Rock Crystal Wedding Rose (998)

No.	Item	Cryst
555	7½" Salad Plate	8.00
3130	9 Oz. Goblet	14.00
3130	7 Oz. Tall Sherbet	12.00
3130	7 Oz. Low Sherbet	10.00
3130	3 Oz. Cocktail	14.00
3130	2½ Oz. Wine	16.00
3130	4½ Oz. Claret	16.00
3130	4½ Oz. Oyster Cocktail	10.00
3130	1 Oz. Cordial	35.00
3130	12 Oz. Ftd. Ice Tea	14.00
3130	10 Oz. Ftd. Tumbler	12.00
3130	5 Oz. Ftd. Tumbler	10.00

Page 136 - Rock Crystal Belfast (942)

No.	Item	Cryst
138	Sugar & Cream	30.00
278	11" Ftd. Vase	45.00
531	7" Tall Comport	37.50
P.166	13½" Plate, Cabaret	35.00
P.212	10" 5 Part Celery & Relish	30.00
P.246	11" Celery Tray	25.00

Page 137 - Rock Crystal Belfast (942)

No.	Item	Cryst
628	3" Candlestick	15.00
647	6" 2 Lite Candlestick	25.00
P.101	32 Oz. Cocktail Shaker	60.00
P.278	4 Pc. Twin Salad Dressing	35.00
P.427	10" Bowl	40.00
P.430	12" Bowl, Flared	42.00
P.671	6" Ice Tub	35.00

Page 138 - Rock Crystal Carnation (732)

No.	Item	Cryst
278	11" Ftd. Vase	40.00
3900/35	13½" 2 Hdl. Cake Plate	35.00
3900/41	Sugar & Cream	25.00
3900/62	12" 4 Ftd. Bowl, Flared	35.00
3900/72	6" 2 Lite Candlestick	25.00
3900/111	4 Pc. Mayonnaise set	35.00
3900/120	12" 5 Part Celery & Relish	35.00
3900/136	5½" Comport	30.00
3900/165	Candy Box & Cover	35.00
3900/166	14" Plate, R.E.	35.00

Page 139 - Rock Crystal Celestial (600)

No.	Item	Cryst
600/2	8" Flip Flower Holder	45.00
600/5	11" Ftd. Flower Holder	47.00
600/9	7" Tall Comport	40.00
600/17	10" 5 Part Relish Tray	25.00
600/25	7" 3 Ftd. Candy Box & Cover	50.00
600/628	3½" Candlestick	12.50

Page 140 - Rock Crystal Celestial (600)

No.	Item	Cryst
600/6	11" Ftd. Flower Holder	55.00
600/8	14" Plate	35.00
600/10	10" Bowl	35.00
600/11	12" Bowl	35.00
600/47	6" 2 Lite Candlestick	25.00

Page 141 - Rock Crystal Windsor (500)

No.	Item	Cryst
500/6	11" Ftd. Flower Holder	55.00
500/8	14" Plate	35.00
500/11	12" Bowl	35.00
500/628	3½" Candlestick	12.50
500/647	6" 2 Lite Candlestick	25.00
500/1491	4 Pc. Twin Mayonnaise Set	35.00

Page 142 - Rock Crystal Windsor (500)

No.	Item	Cryst
500/5	11" Ftd. Flower Holder	40.00
500/9	7" Tall Comport	40.00
500/10	10" Bowl	35.00
500/14	7" 3 Part Candy Box & Cover	40.00
500/17	10" 5 Part Relish Tray	25.00
500/25	7" 3 Ftd. Candy Box & Cover	50.00

Page 142A - Rock Crystal Ivy (1059)

No.	Item	Cryst
555	7½" Salad Plate	8.00
3750	10 Oz. Goblet	15.00
3750	6 Oz. Tall Sherbet	12.00

3750	6 Oz. Low Sherbet	10.00
3750	3½ Oz. Cocktail	15.00
3750	3 Oz. Wine	18.00
3750	4½ Oz. Claret	18.00
3750	5 Oz. Oyster Cocktail	10.00
3750	1 Oz. Cordial	35.00
3750	12 Oz. Ftd. Ice Tea	15.00
3750	5 Oz. Ftd. Tumbler	10.00

Page 143 - Rock Crystal Ivy (1059)   Cryst

103	7" 3 Part Candy Box & Cover	35.00
138	Sugar & Cream	25.00
278	11" Ftd. Vase	40.00
532	6" Tall Comport	40.00
647	6" 2 Lite Candlestick	25.00
1491	4 Pc. Twin Salad Dressing Set	35.00
P.125	14" Plate	35.00
P.212	10" 5 Part Celery & Relish	25.00
P.306	6" Candy Box & Cover	35.00
P.427	10" Deep Salad Bowl	35.00
P.430	12" Flower Bowl	30.00

Page 144 - Rock Crystal Maywood (1058)   Cryst

497	12 Oz. Tumbler (Star)	15.00
497	12 Oz. Tumbler (Classic)	15.00
497	12 Oz. Tumbler (Jewell)	15.00
497	12 Oz. Tumbler (Fern)	15.00
3400/90	6" 2 Part Relish	15.00
3400/1180	5¼" 2 Hdl. Bonbon	12.00
3400/1181	6" 2 Hdl. Plate	10.00
3500/15	Ind. Sugar & Cream	27.50
3500/54	6" Ftd. Bonbon	16.00
3500/55	6" Ftd. Basket	18.00
3500/69	6½" 3 Part Relish	17.00
3500/161	8" Ftd. Plate	12.00

Page 145 - Rock Crystal Miscellaneous
Kimberley (1043)   Cryst

321	1½ Oz. Whiskey	18.00
321	7 Oz. O.F. Cocktail	15.00
497	12 Oz. Hiball	15.00
P.92	26 Oz. Decanter	50.00
P.671	Ice Tub w/Chrome Ice Tongs	40.00

Lansdowne (1049)   Cryst

321	1½ Oz. Whiskey	18.00
321	7 Oz. O.F. Cocktail	15.00
497	12 Oz. Hiball	15.00
P.92	26 Oz. Decanter	50.00
P.671	Ice Tub w/Chrome Ice Tongs	40.00

Page 146 - Rock Crystal Miscellaneous   Cryst

1379	26 Oz. Decanter (Manhattan)	45.00
1379	26 Oz. Decanter (Norwood)	50.00
3700	3 Oz. Cocktail (952)	12.00
P.101	32 Oz. Cocktail Shaker (952)	50.00

Norwood (1041)   Cryst

321	1½ Oz. Whiskey	18.00
321	7 Oz. O.F. Cocktail	15.00
497	12 Oz. Hiball	15.00
P.92	26 Oz. Decanter	50.00
P.671	Ice Tub w/Chrome Ice Tongs	40.00

Page 146A - Rock Crystal (1064)   Cryst

3900/35	13½" 2 Hdl. Cake Plate	30.00
3900/41	Sugar & Cream	25.00
3900/62	12" 4 Ftd. Bowl, Flared	30.00
3900/72	6" 2 Lite Candlestick	22.50
3900/111	4 Pc. Mayonnaise Set	35.00
3900/120	12" 5 Part Celery & Relish	30.00
3900/125	8" 3 Part Celery & Relish	25.00
3900/126	12" 3 Part Celery & Relish	30.00
3900/129	3 Pc. Mayonnaise Set	25.00

Page 146B - Rock Crystal (1064)   Cryst

278	10" Ftd. Bud Vase	20.00
278	11" Ftd. Vase	35.00
3121	5⅜" Blown Comport	35.00
3900/130	7" 2 Hdl. Ftd. Bonbon	16.00
3900/131	8" 2 Hdl. Bonbon Plate	14.00
3900/136	5½" Comport	25.00
3900/165	Candy Box & Cover	35.00
3900/166	14" Plate, R.E.	35.00

Page 146C - Rock Crystal 1065   Cryst

3900/35	13½" 2 Hdl. Cake Plate	30.00
3900/41	Sugar & Cream	25.00
3900/62	12" 4 Ftd. Bowl, Flared	30.00
3900/72	6" 2 Lite Candlestick	22.50
3900/111	4 Pc. Mayonnaise Set	35.00
3900/120	12" 5 Part Celery & Relish	30.00
3900/125	8" 3 Part Celery & Relish	25.00
3900/126	12" 3 Part Celery & Relish	30.00
3900/129	3 Pc. Mayonnaise Set	25.00

Page 146D - Rock Crystal 1065   Cryst

274	10" Ftd. Bud Vase	20.00
278	11" Ftd. Vase	40.00
3121	5⅜" Blown Comport	35.00
3900/130	7" 2 Hdl. Ftd. Bonbon	16.00
3900/131	2 Hdl. Ftd. Bonbon Plate	14.00
3900/136	5½" Comport	25.00
3900/165	Candy Box & Cover	40.00
3900/166	14" Plate, R.E.	35.00

Page 146E - Rock Crystal Thistle (1066)   Cryst

278	11" Ftd. Vase	40.00
P.125	14" Plate	35.00
P.126	13" Gardenia Bowl	35.00
P.254	Sugar & Cream	25.00
P.306	6" Candy Box & Cover	40.00
P.532	6" Tall Comport	35.00
P.533	3 Pc. Mayonnaise Set	30.00
P.1491	4 Pc. Twin Salad Dressing	40.00

Page 146F - Rock Crystal Thistle (1066)   Cryst

3900/72	6" 2 Lite Candlestick	25.00
P.214	10" 3 Part Relish	25.00
P.384	11" Oval Bowl	35.00
P.426	8" Salad Bowl	30.00
P.427	10" Salad Bowl	32.50
P.430	12" Belled Bowl	32.50
P.499	Calla Lily Candlestick	25.00

Page 146G - Rock Crystal Silver Maple (1067)   Cryst

278	11" Ftd. Vase	40.00
P.125	14" Plate	35.00
P.126	13½" Gardenia Bowl	35.00
P.254	Sugar & Cream	25.00
P.306	6" Candy Box & Cover	40.00
P.532	6" Tall Comport	35.00
P.533	3 Pc. Mayonnaise Set	30.00
P.1491	4 Pc. Twin Salad Dressing	40.00

Page 146H - Rock Crystal Silver Maple (1067)   Cryst

3900/72	6" 2 Lite Candlestick	25.00
P.214	10" 3 Part Relish	25.00
P.384	11" Oval Bowl	35.00
P.426	8" Salad Bowl	30.50
P.427	10" Salad Bowl	32.50
P.430	12" Belled Bowl	32.50
P.499	Calla Lily Candlestick	25.00

Page 146I - Rock Crystal Miscellaneous   Cryst

3900/114	32 Oz. Martini Jug (King Ed)	70.00

3900/115	76 Oz. Jug (King Edward)	65.00
3900/117	20 Oz. Jug (King Edward)	75.00
NO. 29	Cambridge Arms Unit (1053)	125.00
P.437	13" 2 Pc. Flower Center (1053)	90.00

Page 146J - Rock Crystal Miscellaneous   Cryst

3900/115	76 Oz. Jug (1064)	60.00
3900/115	76 Oz. Jug (Laurel Wreath)	60.00
3900/115	76 Oz. Jug (1065)	60.00
3900/115	76 Oz. Jug (Bexley)	60.00

Page 146K - Rock Crystal Granada (1068)   Cryst

278	11" Ftd. Vase	35.00
647	2 Lite Candlestick	22.50
3121	5⅜" Comport	35.00
3900/35	13½" 2 Hdl. Cake Plate	30.00
3900/41	Sugar & Cream	25.00
3900/62	12" 4 Ftd. Bowl	30.00
3900/68	5" Candlestick	16.00
3900/166	14" Torte Plate	35.00

Page 146L - Rock Crystal Granada (1068)   Cryst

274	10" Ftd. Vase	20.00
3900/34	11" 2 Hdl. Bowl	30.00
3900/11	4 Pc. Mayonnaise Set	30.00
3900/120	12" 5 Part Celery & Relish	30.00
3900/125	9" 3 Part Celery & Relish	25.00
3900/126	12" 3 part Celery & Relish	27.50
3900/129	3 Pc. Mayonnaise Set	25.00
3900/130	7" 2 Hdl. Ftd. Bonbon	16.00
3900/131	8" 2 Hdl. Ftd. Bonbon Plate	14.00
3900/165	Candy Box & Cover	35.00

Page 146M - Rock Crystal Granada (1068)   Cryst

555	7½" Salad Plate	8.00
3139	10 Oz. Goblet	14.00
3139	7 Oz. Sherbet	12.00
3139	2½ Oz. Cocktail	14.00
3139	2½ Oz. Sherry Wine	10.00
3139	4½ Oz. Claret	16.00
3139	4½ Oz. Oyster Cocktail	10.00
3139	1 Oz. Cordial	30.00
3139	12 Oz. Ftd. Ice Tea	14.00
3139	5 Oz. Ftd. Tumbler	10.00

Page 146N - Rock Crystal Miscellaneous   Cryst

628	3½" Candlestick, Eng. Laurel Wreath	12.50
3900/120	12" 5 Part Celery & Relish Eng. Thistle	30.00
3900/120	12" 5 Part Celery & Relish Eng. Harvest	30.00
3900/137/445	2 Pc. Mayonnaise Set Eng. 1064	30.00
3900/138	Candy Box & Cover, Eng. 1064	45.00
P.419	12" 2 Pc. Relish, Eng. Laurel Wreath	40.00
P.419	12" 2 Pc. Relish, Eng. Harvest	45.00
P.419	12" 2 Pc. Relish, Eng. Thistle	45.00

Page 146O - Rock Crystal Engraved Rondo (1081) & Delhi (1078)   Cryst

555	7½" Salad Plate, Rondo	7.00
555	7½" Salad Plate, Delhi	8.00
7966	Low Goblet, Rondo	12.00
7966	Low Sherbet, Rondo	9.00
7966	Low Cocktail, Rondo	12.00
7966	Low Wine, Rondo	14.00
7966	Low Cordial, Rondo	22.00
7966	Low Cordial, Dehli	35.00
7966	Low Goblet, Delhi	15.00
7966	Low Sherbet, Delhi	13.00
7966	Low Cocktail, Delhi	15.00
7966	Low Wine, Delhi	16.00

Page 147 - Miscellaneous

		Cryst	Amyst	Amber	M/Blu	Carmn
657	7 Lite Candelabrum	175.00				
853	4 Lite Candelabrum	100.00				
1900	1 Oz. Cordial Tumbler	5.00	10.00	10.00		
1901	2 Oz. Wine Tumbler	5.00	7.00	7.00		6.50
#1	5 Pc. Tumbler Set	35.00				
#2	5 Pc. Tumbler Set	35.00				
#3	5 Pc. Tumbler Set	35.00				
3500/91	6" Sq. Tray	15.00				
3900/105	5 Pc. Condiment Set	65.00				
CAP 201	Ice Bucket w/Handle & Tongs	45.00				
P.105	6 Pc. Condiment Set	60.00				
STAR 1	2½" Star Candlestick	6.00			10.00	

Page 148 - Miscellaneous

		Cryst	E/Grn	M/Gld	Ebony
3400/90	6" 2 Part Relish	7.25	12.00	12.00	
3400/1180	5¼" 2 Hdl. Bonbon	6.25	10.00	10.00	
3400/1181	6" 2 Hdl. Plate	5.00	9.00	9.00	
3500/15	Ind. Sugar & Cream	15.00			
3500/54	6½" Ftd. Bonbon	7.00	14.00	14.00	
3500/55	6" Ftd. Basket	8.50	15.00	15.00	18.00
3500/69	6½" 3 Part Relish	7.75	12.00	12.00	
3500/139	5½" Sq. Honey Dish	6.50			
3500/161	8" Ftd. Plate	7.25	12.00	12.00	
3900/124	7" 2 Part Relish	8.25			
3900/151	5" Low Cupped Bonbon	5.25			
3900/152	6½" Shallow Crimp Bonbon	6.00			
3900/153	7¼" Shallow Cupped Bonbon	5.25			
3900/1177	Salt & Pepper Shaker..........pr.	10.00			
P.477	9½" Pickle	6.75			

Page 148A - Miscellaneous		Cryst	E/Grn	M/Gld	Amyst	Amber
1203	Shaker w/Chrome Top	10.00				
1258	Shaker w/Chrome Top	12.00				
1262	Shaker w/Chrome Top	12.00				
1465	Shaker w/Chrome Top	12.00				
1476	Shaker w/Chrome Top	12.00				
1596	6½" Candlestick	18.00				
3011	3 Oz. Cocktail (Plain)	80.00	80.00	80.00	80.00	80.00
	Stain Finish Stem & Foot		90.00	90.00	90.00	90.00
3400/71	3" 4 Ftd. Nut Cup	15.00	20.00	20.00		
3900/1177	Shaker w/Chrome Top ea.	4.50				
4000/39	3 Pc. Sugar & Cream Set	21.00	35.00	35.00		
4000/96	Shaker w/Chrome Top	6.25				
4000/235	5" Rose Bowl	25.00				
CAP 96	Shaker w/Chrome Top	10.00				
CAP 209	Cigarette Box & Cover	20.00				
M.W.43	7" 3 Part Candy Box & Cover	25.00				
MT.V.63	3½" Ash Tray	4.50				
MT.V.68	4" Ash Tray	5.50				
MT.V.89	Shaker w/Chrome Top	7.00				
MT.V.92	Ice Bucket w/Hdl. & Tongs	40.00				
P.358	Shaker w/Chrome Top	4.75				
P.360	Shaker w/Chrome Top	5.00	10.00	10.00		

Page 148A - Miscellaneous Additional Colors		Cryst Carmn	E/Grn Ebony			
3011	3 Oz. Cocktail	110.00	70.00			
CAP 96	Shaker w/Chrome Top	15.00				
P.360	Shaker w/Chrome Top		10.00			

Page 148B - Miscellaneous		Cryst	E/Grn	M/Gld	Amyst	Amber
496	12 Oz. Tall Joe	7.00	15.00	15.00	15.00	15.00
496	1 Oz. Little Joe	7.00	17.00	17.00	17.00	17.00
1401	8⅜" Salad Plate	5.75	7.50	7.25		
3011	1 Oz. Cordial	95.00	85.00	85.00	85.00	85.00
3011	3 Oz. Cocktail	80.00	80.00	80.00	80.00	80.00
	See Also Page 148A					
3400/142	3 Pc. Oil Set	35.00				

Page 148C - Colored Glassware Ebony		Ebony
390	6" Ash Tray	10.00
391	8" Ash Tray	12.00
1066	7" Ftd. Ivy Ball	85.00
1237	9" Ftd. Vase	40.00
1711	2¼" x 3½" Ash Tray	7.25
1713	4 Pc. Smoker Set	45.00
3011	3 Oz. Cocktail	70.00
3900/575	10" Cornucopia Vase	45.00
P.360	Salt & Pepper (Chrome Tops)	35.00
P.361	3 Pc. Salt & Pepper Set	35.00
P.733	3" Ash Tray	8.00
P.734	4½" Ash Tray	9.00
P.735	6" Ash Tray	12.00
P.747	Cigarette Box & Cover	25.00

Page 148D - Colored Glassware Ebony		Ebony
1174	6" Bread & Butter Plate	7.25
1176	8" Salad Plate	9.25
3400/4	12" Ftd. Bowl, Flared	35.00
3400/48	13" 4 Ftd. Bowl, Crimped	35.00
3500/55	6" 2 Hdl. Basket	20.00
P.300	6" 3 Ftd. Candy Box & Cover	45.00
P.384	11" Oval bowl	30.00
P.492	1¾" Candlestick	12.00
P.493	2¾" Candlestick	14.00
P.495	3¾" Candlestick	15.00
P.499	Calla Lily Candlestick	30.00
P.532	6" Tall Comport	30.00
P.569	9" Crimped Vase	32.50

Page 148E - Miscellaneous		Cryst
321	9 Oz. Old Fashioned Cocktail	4.00
321	12 Oz. O.F. Cocktail	4.00
3500/87	12" 7 Pc. Peg Relish Set	75.00
3600/157	Deviled Egg Plate	16.00
3900/137	6" Comport (No Ladle)	10.00
3900/137/445	2 Pc. Mayonnaise Set	13.50
3900/138	Candy Box & Cover	20.00
7801	5 Oz. Whiskey Sour	5.00
7801	1 Oz. Pousse Cafe	10.00
CAP 125	12" 3 Part Celery & Relish	45.00

Page 148E - Miscellaneous		Cryst	C/Tus
54	Hurricane Lamp	50.00	
55	Hurricane Lamp	50.00	
702	Miniature Cornucopia Coral		20.00
1040	3" Swan Coral		35.00
1539	6" Peg Nappy Blown	22.00	
1715	4 Pc. Stackaway Ash Tray Set	16.00	
1715	Ash Tray	4.00	
1715	Candleholder	5.50	
MT.V.102	Miniature Urn Coral		25.00
P.578	Miniature Cornucopia Coral		18.50

Page 149 - Emerald and Mandarin Gold		E/Grn	M/Gld
1401	Goblet	10.00	10.00
1401	Sherbet	9.00	9.00
1401	Cocktail	10.00	10.00
1401	12 Oz. Ftd. Tumbler	10.00	10.00
1401	5 Oz. Ftd. Tumbler	8.00	8.00
1401	8⅜" Salad Plate	7.50	7.25
4000/129	3 Pc. Mayonnaise Set (Crystal Ladle)	25.00	25.00
4000/165	Candy Box & Cover	35.00	35.00
4000/573	9½" Vase	60.00	60.00

Page 150 - Emerald and Mandarin Gold		E/Grn	M/Gld
3900/37	Sugar & Cream Tray	10.00	10.00
3900/125	9" 3 Part Celery & Relish	20.00	20.00
4000/39	3 Pc. Sugar & Cream Set	35.00	35.00
4000/41	Sugar & Cream	25.00	25.00
CAP 66	13" Bowl, Crimped, 4 Ftd.	65.00	65.00
CAP 133	6" Low Ftd. Bonbon, Sq.	30.00	30.00
CAP 151	5" 2 Hdl. Jelly	22.00	22.00
CAP 1338	3 Lite Candlestick	40.00	40.00

Page 151 - Emerald and Mandarin Gold		E/Grn	M/Gld	Cryst
1138	Sea Gull (Crystal)			35.00
3400/48	13" Bowl, 4 Ftd. Crimped	26.00	24.00	
3600/250	Ind. Sugar & Cream	20.00	20.00	
3900/37/M.250	3 Pc. Sugar & Cream Set	30.00	30.00	
3900/135	5" Comport	16.00	16.00	
3900/136	5½" Comport	20.00	20.00	
P.499	Calla Lily Candlestick	25.00	25.00	
SS 31	8" Oval Dish, 4 Ftd.	35.00	35.00	
SS 33	4" 3 Ftd. Ash Tray	12.00	12.00	
SS 35	Cigarette Box & Cover	30.00	30.00	

Page 152 - Emerald and Mandarin Gold		E/Grn	M/Gld
319	9 Oz. Georgian Tumbler	12.00	12.00
1040	3" Swan	35.00	35.00
1043	8½" Swan	125.00	125.00
1712	6 Pc. Stowaway Set	40.00	40.00
1713	4 Pc. Smoker Set	35.00	35.00
3400/71	3" 4 Ftd. Nut Cup	18.00	18.00
3900/575	10" Cornucopia	36.00	36.00
6004	6" Ftd. Vase	15.50	15.00
P.569	4 x 9" Crimped Vase	25.00	25.00

Page 152A - Emerald and Mandarin Gold		E/Grn	M/Gld
1066	7" Ftd. Ivy Ball	75.00	75.00
1237	9" Ftd. Vase	35.00	35.00
1238	12" Ftd. Vase	40.00	40.00
1711	2¼" x 3½" Ash Tray	5.50	5.25
3900/166	14" Plate, R.E.	30.00	30.00
6004	8" Ftd. Vase	20.00	20.00
P.360	Salt & Pepper pr.	20.00	20.00
P.361	3 Pc. Salt & Pepper Set	35.00	35.00
P.384	11" Oval Bowl	25.00	22.00
SS 11	7" Comport	400.00	400.00

Page 152B - Emerald and Mandarin Gold		E/Grn	M/Gld	Amyst	Amber
306	3" Vase	10.00	10.00	10.00	10.00
307	3" Vase Crimped	12.00	12.00	12.00	12.00
309	4½" Vase	10.00	10.00	10.00	10.00
310	3½" Vase	10.00	10.00	10.00	10.00
1042	6½" Swan	100.00	100.00		
1066	5⅜" Blown Comport	25.00	25.00		
1066	5⅜" Covered Candy Box	45.00	45.00		
1337	Cigarette Holder	35.00	35.00		
1714	3 Pc. Smoker Set	25.00	25.00		
3400/90	6" 2 Part Relish	12.00	12.00		
3400/1180	5¼" 2 Hdl. Bonbon	10.00	10.00		
3400/1181	6" 2 Hdl. Plate	9.00	9.00		
3500/54	6" 2 Hdl. Ftd. Bonbon	14.00	14.00		
3500/55	6" 2 Hdl. Ftd. Basket	15.00	15.00		
3500/69	6½" 3 part Relish	12.00	12.00		
3500/161	8" 2 Hdl. Ftd. Plate	12.00	12.00		
4000/67	5" Candlestick	20.00	20.00		
P.572	6" Vase	20.00	20.00		

Page 152C - Carmen		Carmn
555	7½" Salad Plate	10.00
3103	10 Oz. Goblet	20.00
3103	6 Oz. Low Sherbet	16.00
3103	3½ Oz. Cocktail	20.00
3103	3 Oz. Wine	22.00
3103	4½ Oz. Claret	22.00
3103	5 Oz. Oyster Cocktail	14.00
3103	1 Oz. Cordial	35.00
3103	12 Oz. Ftd. Ice Tea	18.00
3103	5 Oz. Ftd. Tumbler	14.00

Page 152D - Carmen		Carmn
319	9 Oz. Georgian Tumbler	20.00
1040	3" Swan	95.00
1042	6½" Swan	200.00

1043	8½" Swan	250.00				
1066	7" Ftd. Ivy Ball	45.00				
1066	5½" Blown Comport	40.00				
1066	Ftd. Candy Box & Cover	55.00				
1237	9" Ftd. Vase	45.00				
1901	2 Oz. Tumbler	10.00				
3011	Cocktail	125.00				
3400/48	13" 4 Ftd. Crimped Bowl	45.00				
3400/92	32 Oz. Ball Decanter	60.00				
6004	6" Ftd. Vase	35.00				
P.569	9" Crimped Vase or Bowl	40.00				

Page 153 - 1066 Line (Amyst, Amber & E/Grn made with Crystal Stem & Foot) Caprice

		Cryst	M/Blu	Amyst	Amber	E/Grn
556	8" Salad Plate	4.75	6.50	6.75	6.75	6.75
1066	11 Oz. Goblet	10.00	16.00	15.00	15.00	15.00
1066	7" Tall Sherbet	8.00	14.00	12.00	12.00	12.00
1066	3½ Oz. Cocktail	9.00	16.00	15.00	15.00	15.00
1066	3 Oz. Wine	10.00	16.00	15.00	15.00	15.00
1066	4½ Oz. Claret	10.00	16.00	15.00	15.00	15.00
1066	1 Oz. Cordial	20.00	40.00	35.00	35.00	35.00
1066	12 Oz. Ftd. Ice Tea	9.00	15.00	14.00	14.00	14.00
1066	5 Oz. Ftd. Tumbler	8.00	12.00	11.00	11.00	11.00

	Additional Color	M/Gld
556	8" Salad Plate	6.75
1066	11 Oz. Goblet	15.00
1066	7 Oz. Tall Sherbet	12.00
1066	3½ Oz. Cocktail	15.00
1066	3 oz. Wine	15.00
1066	4½ Oz. Claret	15.00
1066	1 Oz. Cordial	35.00
1066	12 Oz. Ftd. Ice Tea	14.00
1066	5 Oz. Ftd. Tumbler	11.00

Page 154 - Regency Stemware

		Cryst
REGENCY	10 Oz. Goblet	15.00
REGENCY	7 Oz. Tall Sherbet	12.00
REGENCY	7 Oz. Low Sherbet	10.00
REGENCY	3½ Oz. Cocktail	15.00
REGENCY	3 Oz. Wine	16.00
REGENCY	4½ Oz. Claret	18.00
REGENCY	4½ Oz. Oyster Cocktail	12.00
REGENCY	1 Oz. Cordial	25.00
REGENCY	12 Oz. Ftd. Ice Tea	15.00
REGENCY	10 Oz. Ftd. Tumbler	14.00
REGENCY	5 Oz. Ftd. Tumbler	12.00

Page 154A - 3790 Simplicity Stemware

		Cryst	Carmn
555	7½" Salad Plate	4.50	10.00
3790	Goblet	6.75	
3790	Low Sherbet	5.50	
3790	Cocktail	5.25	
3790	Wine	6.25	
3790	Claret	6.25	
3790	Oyster Cocktail	5.25	
3790	Cordial	15.00	
3790	12 Oz. Ftd. Ice Tea	6.25	
3790	5 Oz. Ftd. Tumbler	5.50	

Page 154B - 3795 Sweetheart Stemware

		Cryst
3795	Goblet	20.00
3795	Low Sherbet	18.00
3795	Cocktail	20.00
3795	Wine	25.00
3795	Claret	25.00
3795	Oyster Cocktail	15.00
3795	Cordial	40.00
3795	12 Oz. Ftd. Ice Tea	18.00
3795	5 Oz. Ftd. Tumbler	16.00

Page 154D - 7967 Melody Stemware

		Cryst
3796	7" Salad Plate	6.00
7967	Low Goblet	7.00
7967	Low Sherbet	6.00
7967	Low Cocktail	7.00
7967	Low Wine	7.00
7967	Low Cordial	20.00

Page 155 - 3109 Stemware

		Cryst	M/Blu	M/Gld	Amyst	Amber
556	8" Salad Plate	4.75	6.50	6.75	6.75	6.75
3109	9 Oz. Goblet	6.50				
3109	6 Oz. Tall Sherbet	5.25				
3109	6 Oz. Low Sherbet	5.00				
3109	4 Oz. Claret	5.75				
3109	3 Oz. Wine	5.75				
3109	3½ Oz. Cocktail	5.25				
3109	1 Oz. Cordial	10.00				
3109	4½ Oz. Oyster Cocktail	4.75				
3109	12 Oz. Ftd. Ice Tea	5.75				
3109	5 Oz. Ftd. Tumbler	5.00				

Page 156 - 7966 Stemware

		Cryst	Amyst	M/Blu	M/Gld	Amber
556	8" Salad Plate	4.75	6.75	6.50	6.75	6.75

3109	4 Oz. Oyster Cocktail	4.75		
7966	9 Oz. Goblet	7.75	12.00	
7966	6 Oz. Tall Sherbet	6.50	10.00	
7966	6 Oz. Low Sherbet	6.25	9.00	
7966	3½ Oz. Cocktail	7.00	12.00	
7966	2 Oz. Sherry	7.50	12.00	12.00
7966	1 Oz. Cordial	10.00	20.00	
7966	4 Oz. Claret	7.00	12.00	
7966	12 Oz. Ftd. Ice Tea	7.00	10.00	

Page 157 - Tuxedo

		Cryst
TUXEDO/1	10 Oz. Goblet	6.00
TUXEDO/10	14 Oz. Ftd. Ice Tea	6.25
TUXEDO/2	7 Oz. Sherbet	5.00
TUXEDO/3	2½ Oz. Cocktail	5.25
TUXEDO/4	2½ Oz. Wine	5.50
TUXEDO/5	4½ Oz. Claret	5.50
TUXEDO/6	1 Oz. Cordial	16.00
TUXEDO/7	12 Oz. Ftd. Tumbler	6.25
TUXEDO/8	8 Oz. Ftd. Tumbler	5.75
TUXEDO/9	5 Oz. Ftd. Tumbler	5.50

Page 157A - 1401 Line Stemware

		Cryst	E/Grn	M/Gld
1401	10 Oz. Tall Goblet	6.50	10.00	10.00
1401	6 Oz. Tall Sherbet	5.50	9.00	9.00
1401	10 Oz. Low Goblet	6.00	10.00	10.00
1401	6 Oz. Low Sherbet	5.25	8.00	8.00
1401	3 Oz. Cocktail or Wine	6.00	10.00	10.00
1401	1 Oz. Cordial	15.00		
1401	4½ Oz. Claret	6.25		
1401	12 Oz. Ftd. Ice Tea	6.00	10.00	10.00
1401	5 Oz. Ftd. Tumbler	5.25	8.00	8.00
1401	8⅜" Salad Plate	5.75	7.50	7.25

Page 157B - Cambridge 4 Pc. Game Set

		Mixed
	10 Oz. Ftd. Tumbler, Heart & Diamond Foot in Carmen, Spade & Club Foot in Ebony	160.00

Page 157C - Miscellaneous

		Cryst	E/Grn	M/Gld	C/Tus	Ebony
103	2 Pc. Nite Set	21.00				
1066	5⅜" Comport	16.00	25.00	25.00		
1066	5⅜" Candy Box & Cover	23.00	45.00	45.00		
1714	3 Pc. Smoker Set	15.00	25.00	25.00		30.00
3400/141	80 Oz. Jug	35.00				
3900/167	14" Plate	15.50				
7966	4½ Oz. Oyster Cocktail	6.00				
7966	10 Oz. Ftd. Tumbler	7.00				
MT.V.102	2 Hdl. Miniature Vase Coral				25.00	
SS 66	Candlestick Coral				40.00	

	Additional Colors	Carmn	Amyst	Amber
1066	5⅜" Comport	35.00	25.00	25.00
1066	5⅜" Candy Box & Cover	55.00	45.00	45.00

Page 157D - Gold Decoration D/1063 (Talisman Rose)

		Cryst
556	8" Salad Plate	14.00
7966	9 Oz. Goblet	20.00
7966	6 Oz. Tall Sherbet	18.00
7966	6 Oz. Low Sherbet	15.00
7966	4½ Oz. Oyster Cocktail	15.00
7966	4 Oz. Claret	20.00
7966	3½ Oz. Cocktail	18.00
7966	2 Oz. Sherry	18.00
7966	1 Oz. Cordial	40.00
7966	12 Oz. Ftd. Ice Tea	18.00
7966	10 Oz. Ftd. Tumbler	16.00

Page 157E - Gold Decoration D/1063 (Talisman Rose)

		Cryst
274	10" Ftd. Vase	30.00
278	11" Ftd. Vase	50.00
532	6" Tall Comport	40.00
628	3½" Candlestick	16.00
721	2½" Sq. Ash Tray (D/450)	8.25
747	Cigarette Box & Cover	35.00
P.125	14" Plate	45.00
P.306	6" Candy Box & Cover	45.00
P.430	12" Bowl, Belled	40.00

Page 157F - Gold Decorated D/Woodlily

		Cryst
147	8 Oz. Marmalade, Cover & Spoon	30.00
533	5½" Comport	22.00
1176	8½" Salad Plate, Sq.	12.00
1532	3 Pc. Mayonnaise Set	30.00
7966	Low Goblet	18.00
7966	Low Sherbet	15.00
7966	Low Cocktail	18.00
7966	Low Cordial	40.00
7966	Low Wine	16.00

Page 157G - Gold Decorated D/Woodlily

		Cryst
278	11" Ftd. Vase	40.00

1309	5" Globe Vase	30.00
1711	2¼" x 3½" Ash Tray, Gold Edge Only	7.00
P.54	6½" Hdl. Ftd. Comport	20.00
P.56	8" 2 Hdl. Ftd. Plate	17.00
P.306	6" Candy Box & Cover	35.00
P.604	8" Ftd. Bud Vase	25.00
P.747	Cigarette Box & Cover	30.00

Page 158 - Cambridge Arms — Cryst

628	3½" Candlestick	12.00
653	9" Candlestick	25.00
1536	Peg Nappy	10.00
1562	3 Vase Arm	17.50
1563	4 Candle Arm	17.50
1633	5" Peg Vase	12.00
19/1	Bobeche & 8 Prisms	22.00
2355	7" Epergne Vase	18.00

Page 159 - Cambridge Arms — Cryst

No. 1	Cambridge Arms Unit	35.00
No. 2	Cambridge Arms Unit	27.00
No. 3	Cambridge Arms Unit	42.00
No. 4	Cambridge Arms Unit	47.00

Page 160 - Cambridge Arms — Cryst

No. 5	Cambridge Arms Unit	100.00
No. 6	Cambridge Arms Unit	70.00
No. 7	Cambridge Arms Unit	70.00
No. 8	Cambridge Arms Unit	85.00

Page 161 - Cambridge Arms — Cryst

No. 9	Cambridge Arms Unit	90.00
No. 10	Cambridge Arms Unit	140.00
No. 11	Cambridge Arms Unit	188.00
No. 12	Cambridge Arms Unit	40.00

Page 162 - Cambridge Arms — Cryst

No. 14	Cambridge Arms Unit	70.00
No. 15	Cambridge Arms Unit	120.00
No. 16	Cambridge Arms Unit	155.00
No. 17	Cambridge Arms Unit	190.00

Page 163 - Cambridge Arms — Cryst

No. 18	Cambridge Arms Unit	65.00
No. 19	Cambridge Arms Unit	138.00
No. 20	Cambridge Arms Unit	180.00
No. 21	Cambridge Arms Unit	110.00

Page 164 - Cambridge Arms — Cryst

No. 22	Cambridge Arms Unit	57.50
No. 23	Cambridge Arms Unit	160.00
No. 25	Cambridge Arms Unit	135.00
No. 26	Cambridge Arms Unit	87.50

Page 165 - Cambridge Arms — Cryst

No. 27	Cambridge Arms Unit	165.00
No. 28	Cambridge Arms Unit	75.00
No. 29	Cambridge Arms Unit	72.00
No. 30	Cambridge Arms Unit	35.00

Page 166 - Cambridge Arms — Cryst

653	Cambridge Arms Unit	115.00
No. 5	Cambridge Arms Unit	100.00
No. 31	Cambridge Arms Unit	90.00
No. 32	Cambridge Arms Unit	87.50

Page 167 - Cambridge Arms — Cryst

No. 12	Cambridge Arms Unit	40.00
No. 16	Cambridge Arms Unit	150.00
No. 33	Cambridge Arms Unit	60.00
No. 34	Cambridge Arms Unit	82.50

Page 168 - Miscellaneous — Cryst

437	13" 2 Pc. Flower Center	45.00
1636	4½" Bird Figure	100.00
510/1537	Ball Candlestick & Peg Nappy	22.00
510/1537/1633	3 Pc. Vase Set	35.00
510/1538/1606	3 Pc. Hurricane Lamp	45.00
510/1538/1636	3 Pc. Set	140.00

Page 169 - Heirloom — Cryst

5000/1	9 Oz. Goblet	8.75
5000/2	6 Oz. Sherbet	6.75
5000/3	3 Oz. Cocktail	6.75
5000/4	12 Oz. Ftd. Tumbler	8.75
5000/5	5 Oz. Ftd. Juice	7.75
5000/11	12 Oz. Ftd. Tumbler	7.75
5000/12	10 Oz. Ftd. Tumbler	7.25
5000/13	6 Oz. Sherbet	5.75
5000/14	5 Oz. Ftd. Tumbler	6.50
5000/15	Finger Bowl	5.50
5000/15	Finger Bowl Plate	3.75
5000/16	4½" Dessert or Fruit Dish	5.50
5000/17	Cup & Saucer	9.00

Page 170 - Heirloom — Cryst

5000/20	6" Bread & Butter Plate	3.75
5000/22	8" Salad Plate	5.25
5000/24	9½" Dinner Plate	9.75
5000/37	Sugar & Cream Tray	5.75
5000/38	3 Pc. Sugar & Cream Set	23.00
5000/40	Ind. Sugar & Cream Set	18.00
5000/41	Sugar & Cream	19.00
5000/44	Ftd. Sugar & Cream	19.00
5000/45	Sugar & Cream	18.00

Page 171 - Heirloom — Cryst

5000/50	10" Ftd. Bowl	25.00
5000/57	9½" Salad Bowl	16.00
5000/62	12½" Bowl	18.00
5000/67	3½" Candlestick	15.00
5000/70	9" Candlestick	22.50
5000/81	9½" Shallow Bowl	14.00

Page 172 - Heirloom — Cryst

5000/33	14" Plate, R.E.	18.00
5000/65	10" Oval Bowl	15.00
5000/68	4½" Candlestick	8.25
5000/71	9½" Candelabrum Base	25.00
5000/72	9½" Candelabrum	40.00
5000/79	32 Oz. Jug	35.00
5000/80	80 Oz. Jug	45.00
5000/138	Candy Box & Cover	32.50

Page 173 - Heirloom — Cryst

5000/26	12½" Plate	15.00
5000/32	13" Plate, R.E.	16.00
5000/76	Salt & Pepper w/Chrome Tops	12.00
5000/100	Oil or Vinegar	19.00
5000/120	5¼" 2 Compt. Relish	8.00
5000/122	7" 2 Compartment Relish	10.00
5000/124	7" 3 Compt. Relish	10.00
5000/126	10" Oval 3 Compt. Celery & Relish	14.00

Page 174 - Heirloom — Cryst

5000/77	8½" Fan Vase	16.00
5000/78	11" Ftd. Vase	25.00
5000/127	5½" Low Ftd. Comport	10.00
5000/127/445	2 Pc. Mayonnaise Set	15.00
5000/129	3 Pc. Mayonnaise Set	18.00
5000/136	Comport	12.00
5000/165	Candy Box & Cover	25.00

Page 175 - Magnolia — Cryst

3790	Goblet	16.00
3790	Sherbet	14.00
3790	Cocktail	16.00
3790	Claret	16.00
3790	Cordial	40.00
3790	Wine	16.00
3790	12 Oz. Ftd. Ice Tea	14.00
3790	5 Oz. Ftd. Juice	11.00
3790	Oyster Cocktail	12.00

Page 176 - Magnolia — Cryst

3900/37	Sugar & Cream Tray	10.00
P.253	Ind. Sugar & Cream	22.00
P.253/37	3 Pc. Sugar & Cream	34.00
P.254	Sugar & Cream	25.00
P.293	6 Oz. Oil	35.00
P.360	Salt & Pepper w/Chrome Tops	18.00
P.556	8" Salad Plate	8.00
P.668	6" Bread & Butter Plate	7.00
P.933	Cup & Saucer	15.00

Page 177 - Magnolia — Cryst

3900/114	32 Oz. Martini Jug	47.00
P.54	6½ Oz. Low Ftd. Comport	16.00
P.55	6" Low Ftd. Basket	18.00
P.56	8" Low Ftd. Plate	14.00
P.101	Cocktail Shaker	60.00
P.1495	11½" 2 Hdl. Cake Plate	25.00
P.1497	6" 3 Part Relish	16.00

Page 178 - Magnolia — Cryst

3400/1180	5¼" 2 Hdl. Bonbon	15.00
3400/1181	6" 2 Hdl. Bonbon Plate	12.00
3900/19	2 Pc. Mayonnaise Set	22.00
P.166	13½" Plate, R.E.	25.00
P.1491	4 Pc. Twin Salad Dessing	32.00
P.1532	3 Pc. Mayonnaise Set	27.00

Page 179 - Magnolia — Cryst

278	11" Ftd. Vase	40.00

6004	8" Ftd. Vase	25.00
P.214	10" 3 Part Relish	27.00
P.247	11" Celery	25.00
P.306	Candy Box & Cover	37.00
P.1498	8" 3 Part Relish	22.00

Page 180 - Magnolia — Cryst

3400/141	76 Oz. Jug	75.00
3900/72	6" 2 Lite Candlestick	25.00
P.384	11" Oval Bowl	30.00
P.430	12" Bowl, Belled	25.00
P.628	3½" Candlestick	15.00

Page 181 - Ambassador Rock Crystal Engraved — Cryst

556	8" Salad Plate	7.25
1953	Goblet	14.00
1953	Sherbet	12.00
1953	Cocktail	14.00
1953	Wine	16.00
1953	Cordial	35.00
1953	Ice Tea	14.00
1953	Juice	12.00

Page 182 - Joan of Arc Rock Crystal Engraved — Cryst

556	8" Salad Plate	7.00
1953	Goblet	14.00
1953	Sherbet	12.00
1953	Cocktail	14.00
1953	Wine	16.00
1953	Cordial	35.00
1953	Ice Tea	14.00
1953	Juice	12.00

Page 183 - Silver Wheat Rock Crystal Engraved — Cryst

556	8" Salad Plate	7.75
1953	Goblet	15.00
1953	Sherbet	13.00
1953	Cocktail	15.00
1953	Wine	18.00
1953	Cordial	40.00
1953	Ice Tea	15.00
1953	Juice	12.00

Page 184 - Tropical Rock Crystal Engraved — Cryst

555	7½" Salad Plate	8.00
3790	Goblet	14.00
3790	Sherbet	12.00
3790	Cocktail	14.00
3790	Claret	16.00
3790	Wine	16.00
3790	Cordial	40.00
3790	Oyster Cocktail	10.00
3790	Ice Tea	14.00
3790	Juice	12.00

Page 185 - Cathedral Stemware — Cryst

1953	Goblet	9.00
1953	Sherbet	7.50
1953	Cocktail	8.25
1953	Cordial	25.00
1953	Wine	10.00
1953	Juice	7.75
1953	Ice Tea	8.50

Page 186 - Dawn — Cryst

556	8" Salad Plate	5.75
7967	Goblet	10.00
7967	Sherbet	8.00
7967	Cocktail	10.00
7967	Wine	10.00
7967	Cordial	30.00

Page 187 - Decanters — Cryst

1380	26 Oz. Decanter E Scotch	50.00
1380	26 Oz. Decanter E Bourbon	50.00
1380	26 Oz. Decanter	25.00
1380	26 Oz. Decanter E Rye	50.00
1380	26 Oz. Decanter E Gin	50.00

Page 188 - American Beauty — Cryst

278	11" Ftd. Vase	50.00
6004	8" Ftd. Vase	40.00
P.54	6" Ftd. Basket	20.00
P.55	6½" Low Comport	22.00
P.56	8" Ftd. Plate	18.00
P.166	13½" Plate, R.E.	35.00
P.306	Candy Box & Cover	50.00
P.430	12" Bowl	35.00
P.532	6" Comport	40.00
P.628	3½" Candlestick	16.00
P.1495	11½" 2 Hdl. Cake Plate	35.00

Page 189 - Rock Crystal Rondo (1081) — Cryst

321	9 Oz. O.F. Cocktail	10.00
497	12 Oz. Hiball	12.00
555	7½" Salad Plate	9.00
3700	5" Blown Comport	22.00
7966	Low Goblet	14.00
7966	Low Sherbet	12.00
7966	Low Wine	14.00
7966	Low Cocktail	14.00
7966	Low Cordial	27.00
P.254	Sugar & Cream	25.00
P.290	6 Oz. Oil, G.S.	30.00
P.360	Salt & Pepper w/Chrome Tops	20.00

Page 190 - Rock Crystal Rondo (1081) — Cryst

3900/114	32 Oz. Martini Jug	40.00
3900/115	76 Oz. Jug	45.00
P.101	32 Oz. Cocktail Shaker	50.00
P.426	8" Salad Bowl	25.00
P.427	10" Bowl	22.00

Page 191 - Rock Crystal Rondo (1081) — Cryst

P.384	11" Oval Bowl	25.00
P.533	5½" Comport	18.00
P.671	Ice Tub	25.00
P.1491	4 Pc. Mayonnaise Set	27.50
P.1498	8" 3 Part Relish	20.00
P.1532	3 Pc. Mayonnaise Set	22.00

Page 192 - Rock Crystal Rondo (1061) — Cryst

278	11" Ftd. Vase	27.50
628	3½" Candlestick	15.00
6004	8" Ftd. Vase	18.00
P.166	13½" Plate, R.E.	27.50
P.247	11½" Celery	20.00
P.572	6" Vase	22.00

Page W1 - Cambridge Milk Glass — Milk

W54	32 Oz. Jug	75.00
W55	10 Oz. Table Tumbler	20.00
W60	32 Oz. Jug	60.00
W61	Footed Sugar	19.00
W61	Footed Cream	19.00
W62	Sugar	15.00
W62	Cream	15.00
W63	Individual Sugar	15.00
W63	Individual Cream	15.00
W65	10 Oz. Goblet	18.00
W66	6½ Oz. Sherbet	15.00
W67	12 Oz. Ftd. Tumbler	15.00
W68	3 Oz. Ftd. Tumbler	12.00
W71	40 Oz. Decanter	90.00

Page W2 - Cambridge Milk Glass — Milk

W69	1 Oz. Ftd. Cordial	22.00
W70	11 Oz. Decanter	40.00

W72	14 Oz. Tumbler	14.00
W73	10 Oz. Tumbler	12.00
W74	5 Oz. Juice	12.00
W75	3" Coaster	8.00
W76	4" Candlestick	16.00
W77	Covered Urn	50.00
W78	7½" Comport	30.00
W79	5" Ivy Ball	45.00
W80	6" Crimped Bowl	35.00
W81	2 Hdl. Open Salt	25.00
W82	Marrmalade & Cover	30.00
W83	Salt & Pepper	19.00
W84	Salt & Pepper .... pr	20.00

Page W3 - Cambridge Milk Glass — Milk

W85	4½" Puff Box & Cover	34.00
W86	Honey Dish & Cover	50.00
W87	12" Urn & Cover	125.00
W88	5" Candlestick	30.00
W89	Candy Box & Cover	50.00
W90	3 Oz. Oil, G.S.	100.00
W91	3 Lite Candlestick	75.00
W92	3½" Cornucopia	16.00
W93	12 Oz. Mug	35.00
W94	3" Swan	65.00
W95	4½" Swan	75.00
W96	6½" Swan	145.00
W97	8½" Swan	200.00
W98	4½" Swan Candlestick	90.00

Page W4 - Cambridge Milk Glass — Milk

W100	5 Oz. Swan Punch Cup	35.00
W101	Cigarette Box & Cover	37.50
W102	2¼" Ind. Ash Tray w/Place Card Holder	15.00
W103	4" Ash Tray	17.00
W104	9" Comport	47.50
W105	9" 3 Ftd. Bowl	60.00
W106	6" Comport	40.00
W107	6" Ftd. Candy Box & Cover	60.00
W108	8" Oval Dish	43.00
W99	16" SwanPunch Bowl, 5 Qts.	1,000.00

Page W5 - Cambridge Milk Glass — Milk

W109	8" Dolphin Candlestick	125.00
W110	9" Dolphin Candelabrum w/#19 Bobeche & 8 #1 3" Prisms	150.00
W111	5" Bonbon	30.00
W112	Cream	25.00
W112	Sugar	25.00
W113	5 Oz. Seafood Cocktail or Sherbet	40.00
W114	7" Salad Plate	25.00
W115	16" Tulip Plate	100.00
W116	12" Oval Bowl	75.00
W117	Cake Salver or Table Center	100.00

Page W6 - Cambridge Milk Glass — Milk

W118	Deviled Egg Plate	40.00
W119	Heron Figure Flower Holder	700.00
W120	Girl Figure	150.00
W121	Scotty Book End	400.00
W122	Pigeon Book End	400.00
W123	3" Urn	16.00
W124	4½" Vase	65.00
W125	3½" Vase	65.00
W126	5" Vase	45.00
W127	6" Vase	70.00
W128	7½" Vase	85.00
W129	12" Vase	100.00

Page W7 - Cambridge Milk Glass — Milk

W130	8" Horn of Plenty Vase	100.00
W131	7½" Shell Vase	65.00
W132	8½" Fan Vase	40.00
W133	9½" Vase	65.00
W136	5 Pc. Centerpiece (Cambridge Arms)	275.00
W140	4 Candle Arm	75.00
W141	3½" Candlestick	40.00
W142	5" Peg Vase	50.00
W143	5" Peg Nappy	30.00

291 - "Ebon" Introduction

Page E2 - Ebon — Ebon

3797/27	6" Salad Bowl	14.00
3797/47	8" Bowl	30.00
3797/48	9" Oval Bowl	30.00
3797/54	6" Comport	30.00
3797/58	15½" Salad Bowl	45.00
3797/67	Candlestick	20.00
3797/69	2 Lite Candlestick	22.00
3797/81	10" Bowl	30.00
3797/82	12" Bowl	35.00
3797/493	1¾" Sq. Candlestick	17.00

Page E3 - Ebon — Ebon

628	3½" Candlestick	20.00
747	Cigarette Box & Cover	35.00
1536	5" Peg Nappy	45.00
1633	5" Peg Vase	50.00
3797/28	13½" Plate	35.00
3797/40	Cigarette Urn	16.00
3797/78	9½" Bud Vase	40.00
3797/80	8" Bud Vase	25.00
3797/91	5½" Vase	30.00
3797/150	6½" Ash Tray	22.00
3797/151	3½" Ash Tray	10.00
3797/152	3 Pc. Smoker Set	40.00
3797/165	Candy Box & Cover	40.00

National Cambridge Collectors, Inc.

P. O. Box 416,   CAMBRIDGE, OHIO   43725

A nonprofit organization dedicated to the preservation and study of Cambridge Glass

You Are Cordially Invited
To Become A Member Of The
NATIONAL CAMBRIDGE COLLECTORS, INC.

Benefits derived from membership include: receipt of our club publication, The Cambridge *Crystal Ball*; informative Quarterly Meetings; Antique Shows; Auctions; and other special events.

The Cambridge *Crystal Ball* is published the first of each month. This newsletter contains educational and interesting articles, questions and answers, information on reproductions and reissues, notices of all club functions, classified advertisements, dealers directory and many other features of interest to collectors of Cambridge glass.

Yearly dues are $15.00 for Individual Members and $3.00 for each Associate Member. All members have voting rights, but only one issue of the *Crystal Ball* will be mailed per household.

Name (please print) _____ $ 15.00

Mailing Address _____

City _____ State_____ Zip _____

Associate Members: (Must be at least 12 years of age and
                  living in the same household.)

1. Name _____

2. Name _____

3. Name _____

_____ Associate Members @ 3.00 each $ _____

Please make check payable to: National Cambridge Collectors, Inc.

TOTAL AMOUNT ENCLOSED: $ _____

Books on Antiques and Collectibles

Most of the following books are available from your local book seller or antique dealer, or on loan from your public library. If you are unable to locate certain titles in your area you may order by mail from COLLECTOR BOOKS, P.O. Box 3009, Paducah, KY 42002-3009. Add $2.00 for postage for the first book ordered and $.25 for each additional book. Include item number, title and price when ordering. Allow 14 to 21 days for delivery. All books are well illustrated and contain current values.

Books on Glass and Pottery

1810	American Art Glass, Shuman	$29.95
1517	American Belleek, Gaston	$19.95
2016	Bedroom & Bathroom Glassware of the Depression Years	$19.95
1312	Blue & White Stoneware, McNerney	$9.95
1959	Blue Willow, 2nd Ed., Gaston	$14.95
1627	Children's Glass Dishes, China & Furniture II, Lechler	$19.95
1892	Collecting Royal Haeger, Garmon	$19.95
2017	Collector's Ency. of Depression Glass, Florence, 9th Ed.	$19.95
1373	Collector's Ency of Amercian Dinnerware, Cunningham	$24.95
1812	Collector's Ency. of Fiesta, Huxford	$19.95
1439	Collector's Ency. of Flow Blue China, Gaston	$19.95
1961	Collector's Ency of Fry Glass, Fry Glass Society	$24.95
1813	Collector's Encyclopedia of Geisha Girl Porcelain, Litts	$19.95
1664	Collector's Ency. of Heisey Glass, Bredehoft	$24.95
1915	Collector's Ency. of Hall China, 2nd Ed., Whitmyer	$19.95
1358	Collector's Ency. of McCoy Pottery, Huxford	$19.95
1039	Collector's Ency. of Nippon Porcelain I, Van Patten	$19.95
1350	Collector's Ency. of Nippon Porcelain II, Van Patten	$19.95
1665	Collector's Ency. of Nippon Porcelain III, Van Patten	$24.95
1447	Collector's Ency. of Noritake, Van Patten	$19.95
1038	Collector's Ency. of Occupied Japan, 2nd Ed., Florence	$14.95
1719	Collector's Ency. of Occupied Japan III, Florence	$19.95
2019	Collector's Ency. of Occupied Japan IV, Florence	$14.95
1715	Collector's Ency. of R.S. Prussia II, Gaston	$24.95
1034	Collector's Ency. of Roseville Pottery, Huxford	$19.95
1035	Collector's Ency. of Roseville Pottery, 2nd Ed., Huxford	$19.95
1623	Coll. Guide to Country Stoneware & Pottery, Raycraft	$9.95
1523	Colors in Cambridge, National Cambridge Society	$19.95
1425	Cookie Jars, Westfall	$9.95
1843	Covered Animal Dishes, Grist	$14.95
1844	Elegant Glassware of the Depression Era, 3rd Ed., Florence	$19.95
2024	Kitchen Glassware of the Depression Years, 4th Florence	$19.95
1465	Haviland Collectibles & Art Objects, Gaston	$19.95
1917	Head Vases Id & Value Guide, Cole	$14.95
1392	Majolica Pottery, Katz-Marks	$9.95
1669	Majolica Pottery, 2nd Series, Katz-Marks	$9.95
1919	Pocket Guide to Depression Glass, 6th Ed., Florence	$9.95
1438	Oil Lamps II, Thuro	$19.95
1670	Red Wing Collectibles, DePasquale	$9.95
1440	Red Wing Stoneware, DePasquale	$9.95
1958	So. Potteries Blue Ridge Dinnerware, 3rd Ed., Newbound	$14.95
1889	Standard Carnival Glass, 2nd Ed., Edwards	$24.95
1941	Standard Carnival Glass Price Guide, Edwards	$7.95
1814	Wave Crest, Glass of C.F. Monroe, Cohen	$29.95
1848	Very Rare Glassware of the Depression Years, Florence	$24.95

Books on Dolls & Toys

1887	American Rag Dolls, Patino	$14.95
1749	Black Dolls, Gibbs	$14.95
1514	Character Toys & Collectibles 1st Series, Longest	$19.95
1750	Character Toys & Collectibles, 2nd Series, Longest	$19.95
2021	Collectible Male Action Figures, Manos	$14.95
1529	Collector's Ency. of Barbie Dolls, DeWein	$19.95
1066	Collector's Ency. of Half Dolls, Marion	$29.95
1891	French Dolls in Color, 3rd Series, Smith	$14.95
1631	German Dolls, Smith	$9.95
1635	Horsman Dolls, Gibbs	$19.95
1067	Madame Alexander Collector's Dolls, Smith	$19.95
2025	Madame Alexander Price Guide #15, Smith	$7.95
1995	Modern Collectors Dolls, Vol. I, Smith	$19.95

1516	Modern Collector's Dolls V, Smith	$19.95
1540	Modern Toys, 1930-1980, Baker	$19.95
2033	Patricia Smith Doll Values, Antique to Modern, 6th ed.,	$9.95
1886	Stern's Guide to Disney	$14.95
1513	Teddy Bears & Steiff Animals, Mandel	$9.95
1817	Teddy Bears & Steiff Animals, 2nd, Mandel	$19.95
2028	Toys, Antique & Collectible, Longest	$14.95
1630	Vogue, Ginny Dolls, Smith	$19.95
1648	World of Alexander-Kins, Smith	$19.95
1808	Wonder of Barbie, Manos	$9.95
1430	World of Barbie Dolls, Manos	$9.95

Other Collectibles

1457	American Oak Furniture, McNerney	$9.95
1846	Antique & Collectible Marbles, Grist, 2nd Ed.	$9.95
1712	Antique & Collectible Thimbles, Mathis	$19.95
1880	Antique Iron, McNerney	$9.95
1748	Antique Purses, Holiner	$19.95
1868	Antique Tools, Our American Heritage, McNerney	$9.95
2015	Archaic Indian Points & Knives, Edler	$14.95
1426	Arrowheads & Projectile Points, Hothem	$7.95
1278	Art Nouveau & Art Deco Jewelry, Baker	$9.95
1714	Black Collectibles, Gibbs	$19.95
1666	Book of Country, Raycraft	$19.95
1960	Book of Country Vol II, Raycraft	$19.95
1811	Book of Moxie, Potter	$29.95
1128	Bottle Pricing Guide, 3rd Ed., Cleveland	$7.95
1751	Christmas Collectibles, Whitmyer	$19.95
1752	Christmas Ornaments, Johnston	$19.95
1713	Collecting Barber Bottles, Holiner	$24.95
2018	Collector's Ency. of Graniteware, Greguire	$24.95
1634	Coll. Ency. of Salt & Pepper Shakers, Davern	$19.95
2020	Collector's Ency. of Salt & Pepper Shakers II, Davern	$19.95
1916	Collector's Guide to Art Deco, Gaston	$14.95
1753	Collector's Guide to Baseball Memorabilia, Raycraft	$14.95
1537	Collector's Guide to Country Baskets, Raycraft	$9.95
1437	Collector's Guide to Country Furniture, Raycraft	$9.95
1842	Collector's Guide to Country Furniture II, Raycraft	$14.95
1962	Collector's Guide to Decoys, Huxford	$14.95
1441	Collector's Guide to Post Cards, Wood	$9.95
1716	Fifty Years of Fashion Jewelry, Baker	$19.95
2022	Flea Market Trader, 6th Ed., Huxford	$9.95
1668	Flint Blades & Proj. Points of the No. Am. Indian, Tully	$24.95
1755	Furniture of the Depression Era, Swedberg	$19.95
1424	Hatpins & Hatpin Holders, Baker	$9.95
1964	Indian Axes & Related Stone Artifacts, Hothem	$14.95
2023	Keen Kutter Collectibles, 2nd Ed., Heuring	$14.95
1212	Marketplace Guide to Oak Furniture, Blundell	$17.95
1918	Modern Guns, Id. & Values, 7th Ed., Quertermous	$12.95
1181	100 Years of Collectible Jewelry, Baker	$9.95
1965	Pine Furniture, Our Am. Heritage, McNerney	$14.95
1124	Primitives, Our American Heritage, McNerney	$8.95
1759	Primitives, Our American Heritage, 2nd Series, McNerney	$14.95
2026	Railroad Collectibles, 4th Ed., Baker	$14.95
1632	Salt & Pepper Shakers, Guarnaccia	$9.95
1888	Salt & Pepper Shakers II, Guarnaccia	$14.95
1816	Silverplated Flatware, 3rd Ed., Hagan	$14.95
2027	Standard Baseball Card Pr. Gd., Florence	$9.95
1922	Standard Bottle Pr. Gd., Sellari	$14.95
1966	Standard Fine Art Value Guide, Huxford	$29.95
1890	The Old Book Value Guide	$19.95
1923	Wanted to Buy	$9.95
1885	Victorian Furniture, McNerney	$9.95

Schroeder's Antiques Price Guide

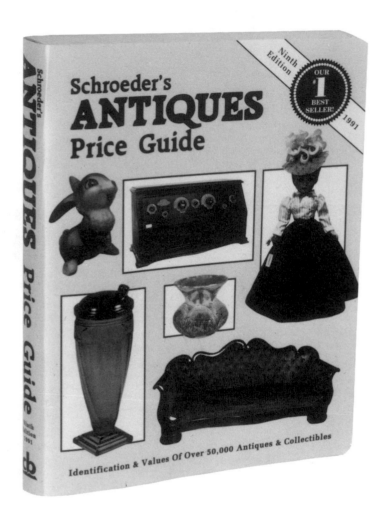

Schroeder's Antiques Price Guide has climbed its way to the top in a field already supplied with several well-established publications! The word is out, *Schroeder's Price Guide* is the best buy at any price. Over 500 categories are covered, with more than 50,000 listings. But it's not volume alone that makes Schroeder's the unique guide it is recognized to be. From ABC Plates to Zsolnay, if it merits the interest of today's collector, you'll find it in Schroeder's. Each subject is represented with histories and background information. In addition, hundreds of sharp original photos are used each year to illustrate not only the rare and the unusual, but the everyday "fun-type" collectibles as well -- not postage stamp pictures, but large close-up shots that show important details clearly.

Each edition is completely re-typeset from all new sources. We have not and will not simply change prices in each new edition. All new copy and all new illustrations make Schroeder's THE price guide on antiques and collectibles.

The writing and researching team behind this giant is proportionately large. It is backed by a staff of more than seventy of Collector Books' finest authors, as well as a board of advisors made up of well-known antique authorities and the country's top dealers, all specialists in their fields. Accuracy is their primary aim. Prices are gathered over the entire year previous to publication, from ads and personal contacts. Then each category is thoroughly checked to spot inconsistencies, listings that may not be entirely reflective of actual market dealings, and lines too vague to be of merit.

Only the best of the lot remains for publication. You'll find *Schroeder's Antiques Price Guide* the one to buy for factual information and quality.

No dealer, collector or investor can afford not to own this book. It is available from your favorite bookseller or antiques dealer at the low price of $12.95. If you are unable to find this price guide in your area, it's available from Collector Books, P. O. Box 3009, Paducah, KY 42001 at $12.95 plus $2.00 for postage and handling.

8½ x 11, 608 Pages $12.95

COLLECTOR BOOKS

A Division of Schroeder Publishing Co., Inc.

Sisi

This Large Print Book carries the
Seal of Approval of N.A.V.H.

SISI

EMPRESS ON HER OWN

ALLISON PATAKI

THORNDIKE PRESS
A part of Gale, Cengage Learning

 GALE
CENGAGE Learning·

Farmington Hills, Mich • San Francisco • New York • Waterville, Maine
Meriden, Conn • Mason, Ohio • Chicago

Copyright © 2016 by Allison Pataki.
Map copyright © Jeffrey L. Ward.
Thorndike Press, a part of Gale, Cengage Learning.

LIBRARY OF CONGRESS CATALOGING-IN-PUBLICATION DATA

Names: Pataki, Allison, author.
Title: Sisi : empress on her own: a novel / Allison Pataki.
Description: Large print edition. | Waterville, Maine : Thorndike Press Large Print, 2016. | © 2016 | Series: Thorndike Press large print core
Identifiers: LCCN 2016000761 | ISBN 9781410488596 (hardback) | ISBN 1410488594 (hardcover)
Subjects: LCSH: Elisabeth, Empress, consort of Franz Joseph I, Emperor of Austria, 1837-1898—Fiction. | Large type books. | BISAC: FICTION / Historical. | GSAFD: Historical fiction. | Biographical fiction.
Classification: LCC PS3616.A8664 S57 2016b | DDC 813/.6—dc23
LC record available at http://lccn.loc.gov/2016000761

Published in 2016 by arrangement with the Dial Press, an imprint of Random House, a division of Penguin Random House LLC

Printed in the United States of America
1 2 3 4 5 6 7 20 19 18 17 16

*To Dave: you are the reason
I can write about love.*

CONTENTS

9

10

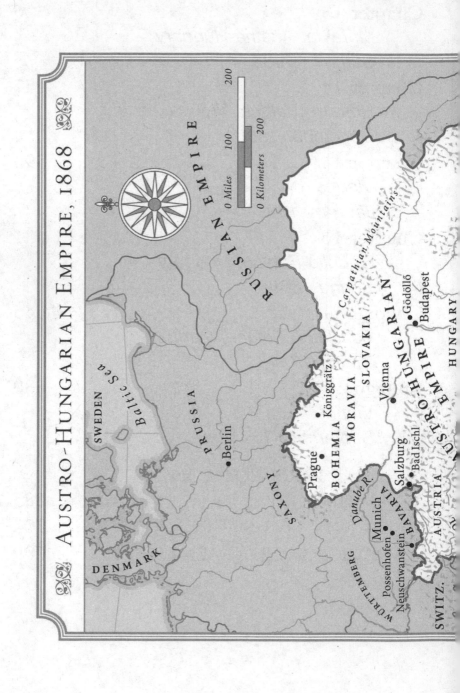

AUSTRO-HUNGARIAN EMPIRE, 1868

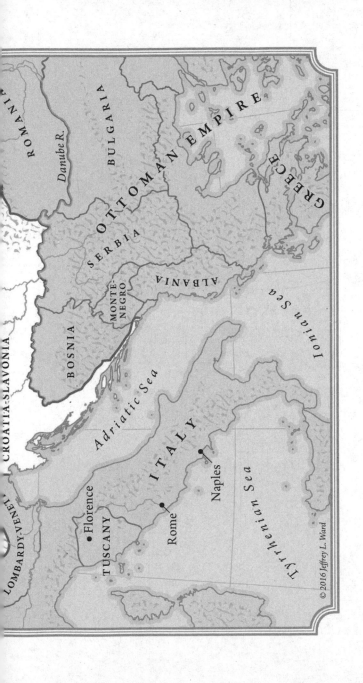

ROMANIA

Danube R.

BULGARIA

OTTOMAN EMPIRE

GREECE

SERBIA

BOSNIA

MONTE
NEGRO

ALBANIA

Ionian Sea

CROATIA-SLAVONIA

LOMBARDY-VENETO

Adriatic Sea

ITALY

Naples

• Florence

TUSCANY

Rome

Tyrrhenian Sea

© 2016 Jeffrey L. Ward

HISTORICAL OVERVIEW

Empress Elisabeth of Austria-Hungary, known to her people simply as Sisi, has just changed her empire forever.

All around her the great dynastic monarchies are crumbling as the world's most powerful kingdoms face rebellion from within and instability abroad. Not so in Austria-Hungary, however, and that's due to Sisi. The beloved empress has brokered the compromise by which Hungary, a dissatisfied but crucial constituent of the fractured Austrian Empire, opted to remain in the kingdom and allowed the Habsburgs to retain dominion over much of Europe — without firing a shot.

With this stroke, Sisi has asserted her right not only to her throne but also to her place beside her husband as a leader of the Habsburg Court. She has proven to rivals and critics that she is no longer the naïve and guileless girl of fifteen with whom Emperor Franz Joseph fell passionately in love. She is the mother of the crown prince, an activist beloved by her people and her emperor, and, at last, she will be the ruler of her own life.

But the perils and demands of life at the Habsburg Court only increase as Sisi works to expand her role within it. And how many enemies — known and unknown — has she made along the way? In mid-nineteenth-century Vienna, where the palace staterooms and bedrooms buzz not only with waltzes and champagne but also with temptation, rivals, and cutthroat intrigue, Sisi faces a whole host of new and unexpected perils and adversaries. Can the beautiful, charming, strong-willed "Fairy Queen" weather these challenges? Or is she doomed to fall as the latest sacrifice made at the altar of the world's most powerful empire?

PROLOGUE

Geneva, Switzerland
September 1898
She steps into view, and she is as they've all said she is: a beauty not of this world. When he spots the lady, his pale eyes narrow, focusing on her. The empress. Elisabeth. "Sisi."

She glides down the steps of the posh hotel, the Beau Rivage, clutching her parasol as bright early-autumn sunshine splashes the boulevard around her. Nearby, a small crowd has assembled, and they rouse to attention as they realize it's the empress.

"Here she comes!"

"Empress Elisabeth!"

"Sisi!"

Either she doesn't hear their cries or she chooses not to answer them, as she continues her stride, long legged and swift, away from the hotel. He shuffles a few steps from this crowd, refusing to be distracted by their chatter, their calls to her.

She makes her way along the quay toward

the boardwalk and the waiting steamer, her sole female companion hurrying to keep pace with her. Everything about her appearance distinguishes her from the common: luminescent skin the color of a pearl, her regal form tucked tight into a high-necked silk jacket and long black skirt, a black cap atop her pile of thick chestnut hair. That hair — so famous that even he has read about it — dark and wavy and laced with errant bits of silver. He looks down at his own ragged appearance, clucking with disapproval at the crescent moons of grime under his fingernails, the torn seam of his threadbare trousers.

From this close distance, he glimpses her face and notes how she blinks, wearing the skittish look of a hunted animal. Which she is, of course: hunted. Not only by him, by everyone. She, like him, is a runner. All her life she's been stalked and pursued, ripped apart and pieced back together, taking on whatever identity the people needed to foist onto her. The way she clutches her parasol to her side, he suspects it's more for her protection from people's eyes and words than to fend off the gentle sun. That parasol might pose a problem for him.

He falls in step behind her, his blood thrashing inside of him, his body surging with a heady brew of anticipation and exhilaration. Several hundred meters away her steamer waits, bobbing at the nearby dock as its stacks belch out black into the clear blue-sky day. He reaches into his pocket, and his fingers find the blade, stroking it, tenderly, as he might stroke a baby's cheek. It's only a small thing, no more than four inches long. And yet, he knows, with that tiniest of blades, he'll entwine his own fate with that of Empress Elisabeth, the most beautiful, most beloved woman alive. All those who love her will have to remember him, as well.

PART ONE

CHAPTER 1

Gödöllő Palace, Hungary
Summer 1868

Sisi could have offered any number of explanations as to why it was so different. Had someone asked her, it would have been simple enough for her to provide an answer. But what was the truth? she wondered. Why was it that twilight here in Gödöllő, her country estate just outside of Budapest, felt so different from twilight in Vienna?

She might have said that it was the view: the unruly, wild, perfectly inviting view. Here, in the soft light of the coming evening, the grounds rolled open before her, unfurling in waves of gentle green before meeting thousands of acres of virgin woodlands. Clusters of wildflowers dotted the meadows, so different from Vienna's imperial grounds and gardens, where sensible, stately tulips intersected lawns so symmetrical and tight clipped that it looked as though mankind had heeled nature into complete submission. Which of course, in Vienna, it had.

Or was it the sound of Gödöllő at dusk? Evenings out here echoed with the bark of her sheepdogs; the carefree laughter of the Hungarian stable boys as they scrubbed down her horses; the first stirrings of the crickets and frogs as they welcomed dusk from the overgrown fields, nature's unrivaled orchestra tuning up for its nightly symphony. It was a collection of sounds so entirely unlike those to be had in Vienna, where Sisi might hear the one-two of polished boots as the imperial guards paraded across the courtyards; the clatter of coaches rolling past the Hofburg gates; the cries of the Viennese mob gathered outside the palace at all hours, begging for her to give them a florin coin or a glimpse of her celebrated silhouette, her legendary hairstyles.

Perhaps it was the aroma in the air. Here, a medley of sweet scents traveled across the breeze: the faint trace of wild rose and acacia, the earthy musk of the stables, the heady perfume of overgrown grass and straw and mud. It was a lush bouquet of smells so natural and pleasing, entirely different from what she might breathe in back in Vienna, where she inhaled the cloying eau de parfum of obsequious courtiers; the stink of so many bodies and chamber pots jammed into the Hofburg Palace; the fear of the noble men and women who were always watching,

24

calculating as to how they might raise their own status or knock down a rival's. Yes, fear was something one could smell. Sisi knew that, after all of her years in Vienna.

But no, it was not the view, or the sound, or the scent that made twilight in Hungary so different from twilight in Austria. It was not anything outside of her or around her; it was a sensation entirely inside of her. It was how she *felt* each evening at dusk that made Gödöllő so different from the Hofburg.

In Vienna, by this hour of the day, Sisi would feel withered. Her head would ache from the unpleasantness of an argument with her husband or his iron-willed mother. Sisi's stomach would be coiled into a gnarled mess, her chest tight with anxiety from a day of sorting gossip and rumors from truth, of watching for and trying to address the judgment or disapproval that seemed to pass across every courtier's face. She would be looking drearily ahead to a night spent with the Imperial Court — a tedious evening ensconced in the damask and gold gilt of the staterooms, the sound of the violins overpowered by the chatter about trivial scandals. Hours spent watching women fawn before her husband, forcing a weary smile while men paid her the same trite compliments they used night after night. Days in Vienna were long, but the nights were interminable — and Sisi would limp back to her room each evening feeling spent, depleted. So fatigued that she already dreaded the next day before that day even came.

Here in Gödöllő she felt spent, too, but in the best way possible. Like a vessel poured out, light and free of burdens. Today, like all days at her Hungarian estate, she'd been free. She'd been outdoors since five in the morning, having risen at four. In keeping with her daily routine, she'd ridden hard and returned to the palace just briefly for a light broth at midday. The afternoon found her atop her horse once more and back in the fields and woodlands, where she practiced jumps, galloped to the point of breathlessness, and joined her charming neighbor, Prince Nikolaus Esterházy, in chasing foxes and racing across the untamed landscape.

That was why twilight in Gödöllő was always so different. By the time the sun began to sink over the western fields in the direction of Budapest, Sisi's body would ache with a pleasant, well-earned fatigue. Her cheeks, brightened by the clean country air and the physical exertion, would glow a deep rose. Her heart would feel light, her spirits buoyant, and her body strong.

And that was precisely how Sisi felt on this sultry late-summer evening, as she handed her horse off at the stables and thanked the Hungarian groom with an easy smile. She turned toward the palace, its red-domed roof cutting a fanciful outline against the fading sky. Even this structure, so whimsical and unpretentious, stood in contrast to the stately, solid form of Vienna's imperial residence, the Hofburg. As Sisi looked now over the strawberry-pink and cream façade, her eyes moved to the second floor, finding the window on the eastern wing of the house. She smiled, picking up her pace. She had almost expected to see the tiny cherubic face peeking back at her from within a glow of early-evening candlelight; and suddenly she couldn't wait to be back inside the palace, this place where she had made a home for herself, carving out a safe corner of domesticity and freedom away from the crushing hold of Vienna and the Imperial Court.

"Hello, Shadow." Sisi's favorite dog, an oversized mound of wagging white fur, trotted up, lapping a sloppy greeting on her as she reached the front door. "You miss me today?" She stroked the massive hound a moment before nodding at the nearby footman and walking into the front hall, her dog trailing behind her in accordance with his name.

"Empress Elisabeth." Ida Ferenczy, Sisi's attendant and longtime friend, curtsied as the empress entered. Beside her snored the empress's other dog, a heavy Saint Bernard named Brave. Her mother-in-law despised oversized dogs — the Archduchess Sophie only ever kept dogs small enough to sit in her lap. Perhaps that was why here, in Gödöllő, Sisi surrounded herself with the enormous, lovable beasts.

"Hello, Ida." Sisi tossed her riding gloves onto a nearby chair as she crossed the spacious, high-ceilinged front hall toward her attendant. "I will change quickly out of these riding clothes. I miss my little one. Is everything as it should be in the nursery?"

"The Archduchess Valerie is in perfectly good health this evening, thanks be to God."

"Has she cried today?"

"Only the normal fretting of any small baby. But the nurse reports that the little archduchess has had her milk without incident, and she should be in good spirits for Your Majesty's visit to the nursery."

"Good. I'll change and then go straight to her."

"Of course. And was Your Majesty's ride pleasing today?"

"Yes." Sisi nodded, making her way to the broad, curving staircase that led upstairs toward her suite of private rooms. "It was a wonderful day. The fox thought he had found a safe haven in the southern woodlands, but Nicky rooted him out, and we nearly —" Sisi paused on the steps, her mind pulled in several directions at once. "That reminds me, Ida, we shall be four for dinner tonight instead of three. Nicky — rather, Prince Esterházy — practically begged me for an

28

invitation, and I hadn't the heart to refuse him. He'll join the two of us and Countess Marie."

"In that case, Madame, I believe that we shall be five instead of four." Ida's lips curled upward in a sheepish smile, but she offered nothing more by way of explanation.

"Who?" Sisi asked, her hand bracing on the stairway's carved balustrade. "Who else is coming?" Had Franz decided to plan a last-minute visit? Sisi's stomach coiled — the emperor's presence, as rare as it was out here, had a way of disrupting the fragile, carefree peace she fought so hard to cultivate in this household.

As an answer, Ida held forth the small golden mail dish, piled with papers. "Your Imperial Majesty's personal correspondences."

"Thank you." Sisi took the dish, riffling through the pile. "You've forwarded all of the official petitions and letters on to my secretary in Vienna?"

Ida nodded.

Sisi's eyes landed on the one calling card, its lettering long and graceful — and familiar. No, this was not news of the emperor. This was a sight so longed for that Sisi felt her heart lurch in her breast, aching now with the first kindling of hope. *Andrássy!* But could it be? Was Andrássy back in Hungary? Sisi fixed a questioning gaze on her attendant,

29

aware of how her eager tone betrayed her as she asked: "Did he . . . did Count Andrássy come by today?"

Leaning forward, her voice low, Ida whispered: "Count Andrássy came calling while you were riding. He said he'd return for dinner."

Sisi clutched the banister, her heart feeling like it might trip down the carpeted stairs even as she stood frozen in place. "Well, that's a surprise. A most pleasant surprise. Come, I must dress at once."

★ ★ ★

As she dressed for the evening, Sisi made her way through the remaining pile of letters, her mind wandering every few moments back to Andrássy. Had he missed her these past months as she had missed him? How long would he stay? Would all be the same between them? She blinked, forcing herself to focus on the news from her family; she had only so much time to read these letters and visit the nursery before dinner. Before he arrived.

There were several letters from Bavaria, where Sisi's beloved older sister, Helene, had recently returned to the family home at Possenhofen to live with their parents. "Poor Néné." Sisi could almost see the tears that had fallen as her widowed sister penned this note. Helene, the eldest sister and the only

30

one of the five Wittelsbach girls to be happily married, had found her groom — a kindly prince of Thurn and Taxis — later in life. She hadn't married until her twenties, and yet she'd lost her husband just a few precious years after the wedding. Helene wrote of her own deteriorating health, of her daily sadness, but also of her deepening faith. She, who had once longed for a life in a nunnery, wrote Sisi now that daily prayer provided "the one balm against grief in the otherwise chaotic environment of our childhood household."

Sisi sighed, her heart heavy for Helene as she turned to her next letter from home. This one came from her darling younger sister Sophie-Charlotte.

My dearest Sisi,

I am to be married! You cannot possibly know how happy my heart is. Or perhaps you can, and do, understand my bliss; I was too young to witness it when you yourself fell in love with your husband and accepted his hand.

Sisi looked away for a moment, blinking as she absorbed the startling news. If Néné's letter had seeped sad resignation, a contemplative widow's acceptance that her life's dreams would never be realized, then Sophie-Charlotte's note burst with youthful cheer,

31

raw and naïve exuberance, an as yet unshaken optimism that felt as fragile and ill-fated as a bowl of blown glass in a child's hands. Sisi turned back to her sister's words.

Oh, my darling sister, you know our cousin Ludwig as well as I do. Perhaps even better, as he always tells me that you alone of the sisters (other than me, of course!) truly know him and love him. And how he returns that love to you! How he admires you! And how happy it makes me when he tells me that I, of all our sisters, most resemble you in beauty and sensitivity.

Oh, Sisi, mine is a blissful, giddy state of happiness. Ludwig, King of Bavaria, to be my husband!

He is a man without equal. Why, look at his palaces. He has taste and elegance enough to make me feel like quite the simpleton. And not to mention how beautiful he is to look on. I know that every girl in Bavaria is sick with envy, as they should be. I have won for myself the best husband in our country! Perhaps the world! (Your beloved Franz Joseph excluded, of course.)

You will come home to Bavaria for the wedding, won't you? I shall tell Ludwig that you will — the promise of seeing you

will induce him to name a wedding date!
I am now and shall remain your most
loving and devoted sister,
Sophie-Charlotte

Sisi put Sophie-Charlotte's letter down and folded it twice, an inexplicable sense of uneasiness settling over her. She was taken aback that the happy news filled her with such misgivings. Her sister was correct: Sisi *did* love Ludwig. He was her cousin and — other than Néné — her most cherished childhood playmate. She and Ludwig had spent so much of their youths together in Bavaria, the two of them running wild through the fields around Possenhofen and sharing their fantastic daydreams for both the present and the future. Perhaps Ludwig had even been a bit in love with the young Sisi. He had hinted at it enough.

But Ludwig — now to be Sophie-Charlotte's husband? The idea did not fill Sisi with the joy that such news ought to have aroused. Were they well suited? Certainly her mother, Duchess Ludovika, would be elated at such a match, thrilled by the fact that her youngest daughter would remain so close to her home in "Possi." And Sophie-Charlotte was euphoric, evidently. Sisi tucked her sister's note into her escritoire, determined to revisit the topic later. She did not wish to rob her darling baby sister of any of her bridal joy, but neither did she herself have the most optimistic view of matrimony these days. She'd need to think before crafting her reply.

Only two letters remained, and Sisi stared at them now. The top one bore the seal of ARCHDUCHESS GISELA, IMPERIAL PRINCESS OF AUSTRIA AND HUNGARY. Gisela, Sisi's twelve-year-old daughter, writing from the Imperial Court in Vienna. Gisela rarely wrote. She and Sisi were not close; they had never been given a chance at closeness. Gisela, from her earliest days as an infant, had preferred her grandmother, the Archduchess Sophie, the woman who could somehow be as soft and maternal with her grandchildren as she was cold and domineering with her daughter-in-law.

Sisi stared at the letter now, shifting in her seat as if troubled by a sudden bodily discomfort. The thought of her eldest girl pierced deep, to a hollow, hidden recess of her heart — to the place where time and distance failed to heal, failed to cover the wound with the scar tissue of acceptance and resolve. *No, not now,* Sisi thought. Not after the good day she'd had. Not when she was about to walk down the hall to the nursery to see her darling baby. Not when he — Andrássy — was only a few minutes away, expected for dinner. Sisi did not wish to weep now. She stiffened in her chair, tucking Gisela's letter into the inner folds of her dressing robe; she'd read it later. Later, when she might savor these rare words from her daughter. When the tears could come and the black night could enfold her in its inconspicuous privacy, where weeping went unwitnessed, where no one might see the extent of her longing or the depth of her despair over the loss of her two eldest children.

Sisi threw her shoulders back and flipped to the next and final letter. It bore a familiar handwriting, a recognizable crimson seal. And it stoked a familiar plunging feeling in her stomach, a brew of discomfort different from that stirred by Gisela's writing — this was a more muted discomfort, a dull throb where the pain at Gisela's letter had been a searing stab. But still, Sisi suppressed a groan as she ripped the seal. The letter came from Franz Joseph. Her husband, her emperor. This was the extent of their marital union these days: they wrote regularly between Hungary and Austria, though they hadn't seen each other in months.

Franz Joseph's letters were like he was: straightforward, reasonable, devoid of anything resembling the imaginative or sentimental. Dispassionate descriptions of his daily routine where he outlined the interminable hours he spent at his desk, surrounded by paper work and petitions and ministers, always summing up his accounting of the hours with the declarative statement: "But that is simply how it must be; one must work until one is thoroughly exhausted." He included brief accounts of Gisela and Rudolf; Sisi's heart always tripped when she saw their names in writing. *Gisela. Rudy.* The two children she had never been allowed to love. The two children who, upon their births, had been yanked from her arms and whisked away, installed in the imperial nursery where their every minute passed under the watchful and covetous eye of their paternal grandmamma, the Archduchess Sophie.

The children were both "in fine form," Franz assured her now. Of course. Everyone in the imperial family was always expected to be "in fine form." Sophie saw to it that no chink ever appeared in the gilded luster of the perfectly ordered and respectable imperial household. Not in the House of Habsburg, where custom and order and tradition dictated the unbending routine of every day, keeping the machine of imperial authority humming smoothly, ensuring that everyone knew precisely what was expected of him or her. Sophie had seen to that years ago, for though Franz Joseph wore the emperor's crown, it was his mother who ran the imperial household.

Sisi rarely spoke to her mother-in-law directly, but Sophie was present in every letter sent by Franz. She loomed large over her son's written words, just as she loomed large over the daily comings and goings at his court. Any mention of life in Vienna inevitably included Sophie, the emperor's closest advisor and the dominant figure in his — and Sisi's precious little ones' — days. Sisi groaned, balling Franz's letter in her fist and throwing the paper across the room.

But Sisi reined in her thoughts before they galloped headlong down that dark and disconsolate corridor — that familiar clutch of agony against which she fought so regularly. *Valerie.* She said the name aloud, as if to banish the demons circling her, as if to soothe herself with its sacred sound. Her darling, her youngest child. The baby safely cocooned in the nursery here at Gödöllő. The baby whose conception had finally compelled Sisi to leave Vienna and her mother-in-law and the whole Imperial Court behind. To come here, to Hungary, where she might at last be free of Sophie's authority and be allowed to raise at least one child as her own, to pour out all of the denied maternal longings with which her soul had throbbed.

"Are we finished? I long to hold my Valerie." Sisi fidgeted in her chair, eyeing the imperial hairdresser, Franziska Feifalik, in the mirror as the woman arranged the finishing touches on Sisi's braided hairstyle. Yet another thing that was more pleasant about her life here away from court: Sisi could wear her famous ankle-length hair in loose braids with crowns of wildflowers instead of the formal hairdos and heavy, jewel-encrusted diadems she wore at court and events of state. Hairdos that inevitably caused a headache by the end of the evening.

"Just one more moment, Empress." Franziska wove one last thread of wildflowers through Sisi's chestnut curls, her fingers skillful and quick. "*Et voilà,* done! Another masterpiece, if I say so myself."

Sisi rose from her seat and crossed to the wardrobe, where she selected a tight-fitting gown of cream-colored satin trimmed with gold-stitched flowers. She covered her neck and ears and wrists with pearls to match the dress and the fragrant white petals in her hair. As her ladies buzzed around her, fastening buttons and adjusting the folds of lush fabric, Sisi nodded at her reflection in the mirror, satisfied. "Good," she said, "I believe we are done here." She could all but hear the collective sigh of relief from her three attendants in the room: Franziska, the Polish hairdresser; Ida, her Hungarian attendant; and Marie Festetics, the Hungarian countess and longtime member of Sisi's personal retinue. Not one person in the Austrian empress's inner circle was Austrian. Just the way Sisi wanted it.

"A bit overdressed for the nursery, but perhaps darling Valerie will enjoy these splendid pearls." Sisi smiled as she turned from side to side, scrutinizing her appearance one final time before the full-length mirror. She was always exacting when it came to her dress and hair. She hadn't garnered her reputation as "the most beautiful woman alive" — even more beautiful than that French enchantress, Empress Eugénie — by being careless. But tonight it was even more important than usual, for tonight Andrássy would be joining her at dinner.

★ ★ ★

And now it was Sisi's favorite hour of the day. "Is everything as it should be?" Sisi swept into the bright nursery, its walls painted a cheerful blue, a shade that she herself had selected, free of her mother-in-law's unsolicited opinions. Sisi crossed straight to the bassinet and lifted the baby into her arms, breathing in Valerie's powdery, milky fragrance. She covered Valerie's cheeks with kisses. The baby answered with a soft, rolling coo, and Sisi pulled her even closer, overwhelmed by a fresh wave of bottomless, intoxicating love for the little girl.

"Indeed, Empress, the archduchess is pink and merry today." The governess was a soft-spoken British girl by the name of Mary Throckmorton. Even-tempered and unexcitable, Miss Throckmorton was the opposite of Sisi, who was tempted to respond to every gurgle and whinny from the baby with the

39

utmost alarm and solicitousness.

"Her crying has ceased? And she's eaten enough?" Sisi asked, shifting the baby in her arms so that her eyes might take in every inch of Valerie's plump, rosy flesh. Just perfect, her little girl was. Her own little angel.

"I believe her crying was due to this," Miss Throckmorton said, leaning forward. With skilled hands, she pulled Valerie's tiny lips apart and revealed a lone white tooth.

"Her first tooth," Sisi gasped, placing a fresh round of kisses on the baby's cheeks. "Oh, my darling girl! My most precious angel! Growing up so quickly. Already cutting her teeth! Oh, the poor little lamb. Miss Throckmorton, you are to provide the archduchess with any comfort she requires during this time that she is cutting her teeth. Do you understand?"

"Of course, Empress," the governess replied, her tone remaining even.

"My girl!" Sisi said, her own voice humming with maternal pride.

In response, Valerie let out another coo, her chubby hand reaching for her mother's face. Sisi sat with the baby on the nursery floor. There they played, the two of them so absorbed in each other that it was difficult to say which was more enamored. Valerie was dazzled by the spectacle of her mother's glossy waves, the shine of her pearls, her wide and constant smiles. And Sisi was besotted, delighted by every single detail of her darling daughter. Her "only child," as Sisi often described Valerie when speaking to Ida and Marie Festetics. The sole recipient of the outpouring of the natural mother-love that, for years, had been stifled within her, drying up like the milk that she had never been allowed to feed to her first little loves.

Of course Sisi still felt love for Gisela and Rudy as well. And of course she had loved her darling firstborn, the Princess Sophie, who had died of a fever while still a toddler. A part of Sisi had never recovered from that blow. But it was simply that, with the other two children installed back in the imperial nursery in Vienna, Sisi had never been allowed to form any meaningful sort of bond with them. They had never been allowed to suckle at her breast or take comfort in her arms, to know her as a mother, and she had never been allowed to cherish them as she had longed to. Her visits to the imperial nursery, when sanctioned by her mother-in-law, had always been quick and dictated by protocol. Accompanied by Archduchess Sophie's ministers and attendants and over-seen by Sophie herself. Visits filled with critiques and censures and thinly veiled reminders of Sisi's inadequacy. Sisi knew what Sophie had said at their births; she'd heard the whispers, the reports of her mother-in-law's scorn. *Of course Sisi should not raise*

the children — why, she is only a child herself!
And with their natural preference tending,
after a time, to their grandmother, Sisi's
children had filled her heart as much with
aching anguish as with warm and maternal
affection. Until Valerie. Her fourth and final
babe. A surprise, an unexpected gift of grace,
and Sisi's chance, at last, to be *Mamma*.

After putting Valerie to bed, ensuring that
she would be neither too warm nor too chilly
in her sleep, Sisi left the nursery and made
her way with Countess Marie and Ida to dinner.

It was as she descended the stairway, her
heart still aglow from the visit with Valerie,
that Sisi spotted the tall silhouette in the front
hall, a figure darkened just slightly by shadow
where the candlelight did not quite reach.
Sisi paused, midstep, taking a moment to
gather her composure. It was either that or
fly down the stairs and into his arms — a
response that would hardly be appropriate.

Andrássy must have heard Sisi's descent,
because he turned in that moment, his dark-
eyed gaze landing squarely on her. "My
queen." He strode across the hall toward the
bottom step. He always used her Hungarian
title of "queen" rather than the Austrian one
of "empress." She belonged to *his* land, to
his people. She loved that.

"Andrássy."

42

"Sisi."

She forced her pace to remain steady as she descended the final steps and glided toward him, yet she was unable to suppress the smile that burst across her face.

"The sight of you dazzles me anew each time." He extended his hand, taking hers in his grip and lifting it to his lips. *So many breaches of protocol,* Sisi thought. No one, with the exception of the ladies-in-waiting who dressed her, was permitted to touch her. And certainly no man other than Franz should dare to place a kiss on her hand. But even worse, she wasn't wearing gloves, so that Andrássy's lips now touched her bare flesh, that most sacred of imperial surfaces. Oh, how she loved being in Hungary!

"How are you?" He spoke in a low voice, as if they alone occupied the massive hall. Which they might as well have, since Marie and Ida — experts in discretion — had excused themselves into a side conversation.

"I've been very well. And now I'm even better." She beamed at him. "How was your journey from Vienna?"

"Long. But I had something to look forward to." His eyes held hers a moment too long before traveling down to her gown, her waist, taking in her whole appearance. He smiled approvingly, and she felt a warm flush travel from the base of her spine up to her cheeks.

And then, because he knew her heart so

well, his next question followed quickly: "And how is Valerie?"

Sisi couldn't help but grin even more broadly now. "I've just come from the nursery. She has cut her first tooth."

"Her first tooth already! My, have I been away that long?"

"You've been away far too long," Sisi said, her eyes remaining fixed to his. The very fact of him — his indisputable physical presence after so long away — seeped into her and through her, soothing her, like the cooling balms with which her ladies plied her sore muscles after too much riding, or the fragrant almond oil with which the hairdresser massaged her scalp and tamed her layers of unruly hair. He was here, once more, before her. His mind and his words and the longed-for sight of his tall, striking figure. She breathed out slowly before saying, "I was tempted to use my imperial power to summon you back to me; I didn't know how much longer I could bear it."

Andrássy smiled, an open, relaxed look. "Well, now I'm here. And glad of it." Never mind that the gossipers in Vienna and across Austria whispered that Valerie was his, Andrássy's child. That people claimed he had given her this home at Gödöllő as a gift from the Hungarian parliament purely so that the two of them might have a haven for their private meetings. Never mind that some

44

called the youngest princess "the Hungarian child" and theorized that of course the mother had chosen to raise the girl in Hungary, as that was the land of her parentage. Both Sisi and Andrássy knew that it was untrue. As did the emperor. Even Valerie's pale blue eyes and faultless ivory skin attested clearly to Franz's paternity — they had nothing of the swarthy darkness of Andrássy. *But never mind all that,* Sisi thought. As long as Franz Joseph wasn't troubled by the rumors, Sisi did nothing more than laugh at their viciousness and give thanks for the distance between herself and her critics.

"The night is a splendid one, and you would look splendid in it. Shall we?" Andrássy scooped Sisi's arm into his and escorted her through the French doors into the back gardens, where they stepped into the indigo light of Gödöllő's thickening evening. Behind them, Marie and Ida trailed at a discreet distance.

"Will you stay here?" Sisi asked. Their footsteps landed in unison on the terrace as, from the nearby stables, a horse let out a long, languid whinny.

"I confess I would like nothing more than to stay. But I thought that, to avoid any whisper of scandal, perhaps I should stay in Budapest."

"No," Sisi said, her tone decisive. "You'll tell them you are staying in Budapest. But in

45

fact, you'll stay here. Oh, at least for a few days?"

Andrássy paused their walk and, his arm still linked with hers, stared sideways at Sisi, deliberating. He cut a tall, fine figure in his full dinner coat and tails.

Sisi sighed. "Let them whisper. Let them gossip. I want you here."

Andrássy still looked at her appraisingly.

Sisi forced herself to keep her breath steady, noting how his dark eyes caused her insides to thrash about. "Besides," she said, "it's not the people in Budapest who start the rumors; it's the Viennese."

Andrássy resumed their walk. "That is true. The Hungarians would never utter a word against you, their queen. Their Sisi."

"Or you. Their beloved prime minister."

Andrássy cocked his head, considering this. "So you'll stay."

Andrássy's lips spread into a reluctant smile as he acquiesced. "If that is what my queen commands, then who am I to disobey?"

"Good," Sisi said, turning her smile back toward the garden path before them. She loved that Andrássy let her win on matters close to her heart. Loved that he accounted for and nurtured her feelings with such tenderness. It was something Franz had always been less inclined to do.

"I will confess that I am chastising myself," Sisi continued. "Thanks to my support back

46

in Vienna, you were made prime minister here in Hungary. And now, due to that very same title, you are forced to go so often to Vienna or to stay walled up in Budapest's parliamentary chambers while I myself have decamped here."

"We are quite the star-crossed pair, aren't we?" Andrássy was deliberately shortening his long stride, allowing her to set a slow, meandering pace.

"I love you for the statesman you are . . . and yet, I hate it as well." Sisi sighed. "I suppose I should ask you how Vienna was?"

Andrássy thought a moment before answering. "Your husband's council has pretty much entirely turned over in recent months. As I'm sure you are aware."

"You'd be surprised how little I know from Vienna."

"But you and Franz — er, the emperor — write regularly, don't you?"

"Oh, he keeps me updated on the children. And all of the inconsequential facts of his daily life — what he ate at the previous day's supper, what show is being put on at the Court Theater." Sisi paused, looking out over the darkening grounds, where unseen crickets filled the night with their soft strands of pastoral music. "But Franz has never liked me to speak about anything that goes deeper than courteous small talk, so that most certainly precludes politics. I've only ever found him willing to listen to me on one political question: Hungary."

Andrássy leaned close now, and she caught a whiff of his fragrance, shaving soap and cigar smoke. His lips nearly grazing her ear, he whispered: "Hungary. The cause closest to your heart."

"Indeed." She felt his arm grip hers tighter — a gesture so minor that she might have missed it, and yet, there was no missing the jolt that his touch sent rippling through her entire body.

But Andrássy's voice turned suddenly serious. "And that is precisely why the emperor's advisory council has seen such a turnover."

"Because of his willingness to grant Hungary autonomy? Because he signed off on the creation of the Austro-Hungarian Dual Monarchy from the Austrian Empire?"

Andrássy nodded, and Sisi thought about this, eventually shrugging. "A change of blood in Vienna was long overdue. Franz knows that the Austro-Hungarian Compromise was the right thing to do, even if his ministers now protest it. It was the only way to keep Hungary from open rebellion, to preserve the borders of his empire. He didn't want a civil war across his lands — a war that might well have engulfed all of Europe. Especially so soon after he suffered such a decisive defeat against Prussia and Italy. No, Europe can't have any more war."

"He does see that, and he said as much," Andrássy agreed, his tone still heavy with thought.

"My husband's ministers are like weeds," Sisi said. "Mow one down, two more shall pop up in the same place."

Andrássy paused, angling his body so it tilted toward hers. "Come now, you think so little of me?"

She turned to him, a mischievous smile pulling her lips apart. "You were mine before you were his. You're different."

"I should hope so."

As they resumed walking, Sisi was tempted to ask Andrássy which highborn courtier or vulgar actress her husband's ministers had found to warm the emperor's bed these days, but she swallowed that bitter thought. Her time with Andrássy was sacred — she wouldn't allow the old scars of her broken marriage to seep into this moment. Plus, the days when she had truly cared about all of that had passed. She was no longer the naïve girl Franz Joseph had married; the guileless sixteen-year-old provincial who had confused infatuation for love and promises for deeds. The girl who hadn't understood *how things are done* at the Imperial Court and who had been broken when the time had come for her to learn.

Franz couldn't hurt Sisi now, not like he once could. Her heart, battered by the crushing blows issued first by her mother-in-law, then by her husband, and then by the death of one child and the emotional loss of the other two, had, miraculously, revived in recent years. Somehow, slowly and stubbornly, the heart that Sisi had presumed wasted and ruined had continued to beat. Had developed a layer of scar tissue and had refused to give way. And so she had decided anew to live. On her own terms. And with that decision had come acceptance and a new potency — and freedom. Franz was far away from her now, made so not only by the physical distance she had put between them but also by the shield she had raised for herself; there was nothing that Franz could do to hurt her now.

Besides, their marriage hadn't had that physical element to it in years — almost a decade, now that she thought about it. Save for that brief reconciliation when she had returned to the imperial marital bed while working with Franz Joseph to forge the Austro-Hungarian Compromise. A fleeting encounter that, miraculously, had given her Valerie, as well as the kingdom of Hungary.

And now Andrássy stood before her, his dark-eyed gaze as soft as black velvet, and glorious evening had fallen over Gödöllő. So Sisi pushed Franz and the years they had spent hurting each other out of her mind. She had wrestled with and found some sort of peace with the fact that Franz had allowed her first three children to be taken from her, making her feel like a broodmare and an outcast in her own court. That her life with Franz had never been theirs, but had always been overcrowded and overstructured, overshadowed by the demands of his role as emperor. That he had neglected her, keeping his emotions closed off from her understanding and never striving to know hers, either. That he had instead sought the company of his generals and his ministers and his mother and other women. That he had wandered from their marriage — but what did any of that matter? For now she herself was the wanderer, wasn't she?

Andrássy broke into her silent reverie, raising his finger to stroke her forehead. "You look as if you are doing battle."

"I am."

"Who is winning?"

She offered half a smile. "I am."

"Good." He leaned down and kissed her brow; it was too bold of a move for a place as public as the gardens, but the last light of the day had slipped away, and the seam of darkness had closed in around them.

A sound traveled into the yard through an open window — the laughter of a servant in the kitchens. Andrássy pulled his lips from her brow. "I suppose we should get you in to dinner."

51

"I suppose you are right." Sisi sighed, agreeing. They both turned back toward the palace. "I must warn you, we will be joined by Nicky — Prince Esterházy — at dinner."

Andrássy groaned, pausing in their walk.

"Well, I didn't know you would be here," Sisi said, somewhat amused by his apparent jealousy. "Had you written, I might have made sure that he —"

"I like to surprise you, you know that. The look of delight on your face makes the pain of the separation worth it."

"Ah, but you came by while I was riding with Nicky, so the surprise was thwarted."

Andrássy leaned close to whisper now, his words tickling her ear: "Then perhaps I might have to find another way to summon the look of delight to your beautiful face."

★   ★   ★

Prince Esterházy awaited them in the dining room. He stood expectant and formal, much like his impeccable posture in the saddle. Esterházy, like Andrássy, wore a full coat and tails, and he looked fresh and rosy after a day spent chasing foxes.

"Oh, Queen Elisabeth, you are not alone." Esterházy's face sagged, betraying the same frustration that Andrássy had just voiced. "Andrássy," he said, forcing an upbeat tone even as he clenched his jaw. "Good to see you."

"And you, Esterházy." The two men shook hands.

"Have you recently returned from Vienna?"

"Just today," Andrássy answered.

Esterházy cocked a dark eyebrow. "And you've already left Budapest for the queen's dinner table? Don't you have business to see to back in the city?"

"What business could be more important than paying my respects to our sovereign and seeking her counsel on my recent trip?"

Esterházy frowned, fiddling with the sleeves of his dinner jacket.

"But I must commend you, Esterházy," Andrássy continued, his tone one of forced amiability. "It seems that you have taken great care of our queen — I hear you've been a most devoted companion while I've been away. She's had no shortage of Hungarian hospitality from you."

Sisi couldn't help but chuckle to herself as she took her seat at the center of the table, directing the men to either side of her. She continued to revel in their rivalry throughout dinner as they traded verbal barbs. Nicky's jealousy came as no surprise: he was a charming, wealthy, attractive nobleman. He had ladies all over Hungary in pursuit of his smiles and his family fortune. The fact that he owned the largest stable of thoroughbreds in the country, and that his estate bordered Gödöllő Palace, had made Prince Nikolaus Esterházy a most pleasant companion for Sisi the past few months. Not to mention that he was perhaps the only rider in the country who could keep up with her, a legendarily skilled horseback rider herself.

Andrássy seemed taken aback by Nicky's presumptuousness, by the familiar manner in which he spoke to Ida and Marie, by the amount of time his rival had clearly spent at this dinner table and in the presence of Sisi during his most recent absence. It was cruel of Sisi to do so, and she knew it, but she watched Andrássy frown and fidget throughout dinner with a sense of something akin to relief, if not outright pleasure. Andrássy's jealousy was the surest sign that his feelings for her had not altered during their separation. That he still longed for her — needed her — with the same yearning that she felt for him. And so, as dinner progressed and the footmen marched out the endless parade of plates and dishes, Sisi sipped her wine and allowed herself to grow tipsy on the meal and the company.

"I presume then, Count Andrássy, that you will be returning to Budapest this evening after supper? To Countess Andrássy?" Esterházy smoked throughout dessert, addressing the footmen by name and calling them over for frequent refills of his wineglass.

"I have asked the prime minister to stay in Gödöllő," Sisi interjected, sensing that the tension at the table might mount to an undesirable level at this latest remark. Andrássy looked down at his dessert plate, his exhale audible. He hated any mention of his wife, so long estranged from him but still, legally, his spouse. He knew, as did Sisi, that they were both married. That the love that existed between them was wrong — even if it didn't feel so. He hated for Sisi to be reminded of Countess Andrássy's existence. Like all burdens, this was yet another one from which he tried to protect Sisi.

"I've asked Count Andrássy to stay," Sisi continued, her voice remaining clear and calm. She scooped herself a taste of her favorite dessert, a violet ice cream made and transported especially for her by one of Budapest's confectioners. "Only for a few days. I haven't been back to Vienna in months, and I want a full report."

Esterházy turned to Sisi now, his lips scowling under his full, dark mustache. *All these Hungarian men,* Sisi thought, *was it a requirement of their upbringing to have these dark mustaches?* It made them appear so dashing when they smiled — but so brooding and fearsome when they frowned.

"Now, then." Sisi sat up tall, shifting the conversation. "Shall it be cards or charades tonight? Or perhaps we should have some music or poetry?"

Following dinner, the group moved to the drawing room for drinks and entertainment, and nighttime in Gödöllő settled into its easy, familiar rhythm. Here, the late hours were passed before a cozy fire, with Ida reading aloud from the Hungarian poet Mihály Vörösmarty or Marie plunking her way through a Franz Liszt sonata on the piano. Everyone was free to come and go, to propose whatever enjoyment they wanted. Shadow and Brave would avail themselves of the patch of carpet at Sisi's feet. Ida would sit to Sisi's left with a smile, accommodating and pliant, always willing to do whatever the group — or rather, whatever Sisi — wanted. Meanwhile Marie Festetics, ever solicitous, would buzz around the room, fretting that Sisi sat too close to the open window where she might catch the cold breeze, or wondering aloud if perhaps her seat close to the fire made Her Majesty overly warm. Sisi would smile and assure her lady, "I am perfectly content."

In Vienna, even the most intimate family gatherings were dictated by centuries of rigid Habsburg tradition and imperial protocol. The most natural of interactions became somehow stilted and uncomfortable — made so by the unceasing need to pay homage to that royal deity, etiquette. Even in the private family sitting room, even when it was just

Sisi and the children with Franz and his mother, no one was permitted to speak unless first addressed by the emperor. No one was to sit down to the table without dining gloves on. No one was to rise from a chair until His Majesty rose. No one was to eat once His Majesty had finished eating. The rules were limitless and unyielding, so that all that seemed to pass between the family members were short, meaningless scraps of small talk or polite comments on the day's happenings.

Here, as hostess, Sisi encouraged the exact opposite ambience. As she nestled into her plush chair now, her glass of sweet *tokaji* in her ungloved hands, she gave thanks for the tenth time that day that she was far away from the imperial capital. That she was here, where Valerie slept safely in the nursery and the nights were relaxed and merry, full of wine and laughter and candid discussion.

Or at least, where the nights here were *usually* relaxed and merry. Tonight, things were noticeably tenser. Sensing the possibility of a quarrel should the topic veer toward the personal, Sisi steered the conversation toward politics, relatively safe ground by comparison. It seemed that, however much enmity existed between Esterházy and Andrássy, they could agree on one thing: their dislike of their neighbor to the north. Prussia under Chancellor Bismarck was growing alarmingly strong and increasingly militant. Having already defeated Austria in a war several years earlier, Bismarck now sought to make Franz Joseph his ally. And then, once assured of Vienna's friendship — or submission — it seemed that the iron fist of Bismarck was poised to strike France, where Emperor Napoleon III was accused of being more preoccupied with his lavish palaces and Empress Eugénie's sultry figure than the affairs of state. Both Andrássy and Esterházy agreed: if Prussia were to fight and defeat France, it would upset the entire balance of power in Europe.

"But I think the queen and her ladies grow weary of our political talk, Andrássy." Esterházy, appearing more relaxed than he had at dinner, leaned forward in his chair, fixing his eyes on Sisi. "Come, let's talk of Your Grace's favorite topic: riding. Why, we almost had that fox today, didn't we?"

Sisi couldn't help but perk up at the memory. "We did! My goodness, Nicky, when you took that final hedgerow at a full gallop, I was sure you were about to be unseated."

Esterházy erupted into a full-belly laugh, the type of laughter that's not necessarily the expression of some authentic inner delight but rather seems somehow like gloating. As if the individual laughing wishes for others to see that he has cause to laugh. "Have you so little faith in my skills in the saddle, even after all this time we've spent riding together, Queen Elisabeth?"

Sisi handed her glass to Ida for a refill, avoiding Andrássy's glower. But then, before she could answer, a footman appeared and bowed before the entrance to the room, his gloved hands carrying a silver mail tray.

"Yes?" Sisi sat up in her armchair, lowering her drink to the nearby table. "Come in. What is it?"

The footman bowed once more before approaching Sisi, his eyes angling downward as he proffered the tray carrying a single telegram. Sisi made swift work of opening the message. It was from Gisela — how strange to have had two correspondences from her daughter in the same day. Sisi read the words quickly:

MY ESTEEMED MADAME, YOUR IMPERIAL HIGHNESS STOP HAS YOUR MAJESTY RECEIVED LETTER? STOP REPLY REQUESTED AT ONCE STOP MOST URGENT MATTER STOP HUMBLY AND RESPECTFULLY YOURS, GISELA FULL STOP.

Sisi felt her spine go rigid. The letter — Gisela's letter. She'd put it away, tucked it into a fold of her dressing gown to be read at a later hour. She had been so eager to get to Valerie, to see Andrássy, she had put it off.

"Your Majesty?" Marie leaned forward.

"What is it? Is everything all right?" Andrássy strode toward where Sisi sat, his dark brows knitting together.

"I'm so sorry, but I must —" Sisi looked back at the telegram in her hands, dazed. When she finally spoke again, it was with a faint voice: "But I must excuse myself. I . . . I . . . wish you all a good night." And with that, Sisi rose from her chair and left the room, her ladies and her two hounds trailing after her.

Upstairs, an unseen servant had tidied while Sisi had been at dinner, arranging the queen's bed for sleep and replacing her dressing gown into the armoire. Sisi strode briskly across the large room, marching straight for the gown as Marie and Ida ordered more candles lit. Sisi riffled through the folds of fabric until her hands touched on Gisela's letter, deep in the pocket where she had left it.

Sisi sat at her desk and tore the letter opener along the seam, her eyes landing on her daughter's elegant, well-trained hand.

To my most esteemed and admirable mother,
Her Blessed and Imperial Majesty the Empress Elisabeth of Austria, Apostolic Queen of Hungary:

Sisi could not help but sigh at the salutation; Gisela had always been like her father — dutiful in her formality, toeing Sophie's line and heeding court protocol so that even a greeting to her own mother became unwieldy and unnatural. Unlike Rudy, Gisela had none of her mother's sensitivity or imagination. Sisi read on.

Dear Madame,
   I pray that this note finds you and my sister, the Archduchess Valerie, in good health. I must also begin with an apology: I wish that the circumstances of my writing were happier, but in fact, this letter carries distressing news.

Sisi's frame stiffened. What distressing news could Gisela be reporting? She turned back to the paper.

   As you may know, my brother, Rudolf, the crown prince of Austria-Hungary, has been for some time under the supervision and tutelage of the military officer Count Leopold Gondrecourt. The count is a stern and exacting man, but those qualities need not be considered negative traits in and of themselves. Be that as it may, not all is as it should be in the relationship between the count and my brother the crown prince.

61

I have watched for months now with a tortured heart, made ever heavier by what I see happening, but lacking any means with which to address the less-than-favorable situation to which I am witness. I did not know to whom I might confess my burden. Papa dismisses my concerns, and Grandmamma scolds me whenever I raise the topic. But, dear Madame, here it is: Count Gondrecourt subjects my darling younger brother to a whole host of agonies, all in the name of "education."

I might label what Count Gondrecourt and Papa and Grandmamma call "education" as more akin to torture. And the toll is evident when I look at Rudy, who, the poor dear little soul, is diminishing before my very eyes. (Not that I get to see him often — so seldom is he free of his "lessons." However, when I do see him, I am so saddened by his ongoing deterioration that I weep for hours.)

I know it is sinful to argue with a parent, and I mean no disrespect to my father, the All-Highest, the most esteemed Imperial and Royal Majesty. Nor to my beloved grandmamma, the admirable lady Archduchess Sophie, who is a paragon of excellence for us all. Be that as it may, I must confess my worries to you. What I see as the sensitivities and charms of Rudolf's compassionate and gentle nature, my father and grandmamma and Count Gondrecourt view as stumbling blocks in the little boy's ability to someday assume the role of emperor. The count believes that my brother, a boy of barely ten years, must therefore be subjected to the harshest of drills in order to rid him of what Grandmamma and Papa call his "delicate constitution."

I've known the count to rip my little brother from bed in the middle of a winter's night and force him to march, barefoot, around the frozen palace grounds. The count takes Rudy to our family's private zoo, a place intended to delight, but then locks him in the same space as the lions, yelling that the boy must kill the beasts or be killed. He pulls him from bed each day before sunrise and submerges him in tubs of ice-filled water, sometimes convincing the boy that he will be drowned. He shoots pistols right before the crown prince, aiming near to the little boy's trembling figure. If Rudy cries out in fear or retreats in panic, the count repeats the activity, aiming his weapon even closer.

Dear esteemed Madame, I always try to obey my blessed grandmamma and His Imperial Majesty the Emperor my father, but I am in agony as I watch this go on. I know that you avoid Vienna. I do not understand the reasons, and Papa frowns whenever I ask why you stay away, but I write now to beseech you: please, for the sake of your son, who grows paler and more shrunken every day, please return to Vienna and see for yourself. If you, like Grandmamma and Papa, reach the same conclusion that all of this "education" is an essential part of the process by which my brother — a darling, sensitive little soul — becomes a man fit to serve as emperor, then I will have no choice but to cease my protestations. I will understand that this is simply how things must be done, and I shall willingly submit to the superior wisdom of my elders.

But if you, like me, see these practices and determine that they are cruel and unnecessary, then perhaps you, at last, may be able to put an end to the little boy's senseless suffering.

I am and shall remain Your Majesty's
most devoted and ever humble,
Gisela

Sisi lowered the letter to the desk, her frame trembling with a noxious mixture of fury and anguish. Each word had struck her anew, a fresh pain worse than the crack of a whip, and yet she forced herself to reread the note a second time and then a third and again until she had absorbed the ghastly words more than a dozen times. The message filled her with new horror with each pass. She dismissed her ladies abruptly, offering no answer to their concerned looks and questions, and she remained before her desk with the hated letter, weeping. She kept trying to find some logic to it, some explanation for these incomprehensible words — but there was none to be had. Imagine torturing a little boy with water cures and terror and physical deprivations!

Sisi pushed herself away from the desk. Still dressed in her formal dinner gown, she left the bedchamber and slipped down her private staircase, the passage that led directly from her suite out into the backyard by the stables.

Sisi knew that she would find him out there. They never met at night, alone, inside the house. He'd never dream of approaching her bedchamber. It was too risky in this house full of servants who might notice or whisper. Esterházy's estate was just beyond the distant tree line, and another estate nestled beyond that one, and beyond that another, all the way to Budapest. Surely the servants of these country households knew one another, their news and gossip joining together like the links of a necklace until the chain reached the Hungarian capital. From there, it was an easy leap to Vienna.

But out here, under the expansive stretch of black sky, with no streetlamps or lights of any kind other than the brilliant scramble of stars overhead, Sisi knew of a secret space, removed from the household's witnessing or judgment. It might look ordinary enough: an alley of red chestnut trees leading to a grove of dogwood saplings, their leafy boughs heavy and shimmering in the moonlight. They were tucked in behind the stables, close to where Sisi's twenty-six hunting horses slept, and at a safe distance from the palace. Both she and he knew of this place as a refuge.

And now, on this night, she fled there, like some haunting apparition seeking the soul that might deliver her, might console her after the torture of the words she'd just read from Vienna.

She heard his voice before she detected the shadowed outline of his tall figure. "Sisi."

Her whole body went slack as she exhaled. "Andrássy." The sound of her own voice surprised her, how breathless and raspy it was — full of despair and desperation. His body was before hers, and he found her in the dark. She surrendered into his arms as he leaned forward to kiss her.

"Oh, my darling." Taking her chin in his hands, he angled her gaze upward so that the faint glow of moon and starlight illuminated their faces. "What caused you to run away so quickly? What's the matter?"

She didn't answer, but rather slipped the letter into his hands. He pulled a match, usu-

66

ally used for his cigars, from the pocket of his trousers and read the note by its flickering glow. Sisi stood silently. A spear of moonlight slid back and forth across Andrássy's face as the leaves overhead quivered in the soft breeze. Sisi watched his expression darken as the meaning of Gisela's words took hold.

When he had finished reading, Andrássy lowered the paper and stood before her, wordless. Other than a stifled groan at the back of his throat, he made no noise, but simply began pacing, his long stride quickly crossing the small space lined by dogwood and red chestnut trees. His silence, Sisi suspected, indicated an ire more potent than had he railed and cursed. At last he paused and turned to her and spoke, his tone low and resolute. "You must go back."

Sisi felt her throat and neck tighten, and she swallowed rather than reply. It was what she had expected him to say.

"You must return to Vienna." He turned and punched his fist into the nearest sapling, and Sisi saw his frame go rigid with fury. "This can't go on. Such treatment of the crown prince? A small boy? No."

Sisi took the letter from his hand, her eyes falling on the ghastly words, and fresh tears hurled themselves from her eyes. She had barely stopped weeping since first reading her daughter's account. She lowered the let-ter, shutting her eyes to its horrifying mes-

67

sage. To the fact that she, as a mother, had utterly failed her son. She shifted from one foot to the other, her body overly warm and covered in a slick of perspiration even though the late-summer evening had turned cool. "But what can I do, once I'm back there?" She looked to Andrássy. "I tried and failed for years to stand up to Franz and his mother. I've never once succeeded. I have no influence at court."

"That's not true, Sisi." Andrássy paced the small clearing again, his footsteps landing heavily on the soft earth.

The yard smelled fragrant with the aromas Sisi loved: the nearby horses, the damp earth, the grass and wildflowers, but tonight she found such ripeness overpowering and repulsive. She blinked, trying to make some order of her thoughts. "Gisela writes that she has tried to reason with them," Sisi said. "How can I possibly hope to prevail where she has failed?"

"You are stronger than you think," Andrássy said. "Why, look at you here. You are here because you stood up to them. You won the Hungarian nation for them and then claimed Valerie as your own."

That final point made her head feel fuzzy, and Sisi steadied herself on a nearby sapling. *Valerie!* "What if I go back and she takes Valerie from me?" The words of her question quivered as they came out. "No, I can't risk that. The only way to keep my child is to keep her away from Sophie."

Andrássy shook his head. "You won't let that happen. You are stronger now."

"But how can I know that? How can I protect myself? I never could before —"

"Because you are stronger than you've ever been. Don't you see that?"

"How can you say that, Andrássy?" She was only strong because she was far enough away to be invulnerable.

"You are stronger now because you have the one thing that the emperor wants more than anything else." Andrássy paused his steps and ran his hands through his dark waves, setting them into further disarray. "You have the means to grant him or deny him his most sacred wish."

Sisi looked at Andrássy, frowning in confusion.

"The one thing he wants most," Andrássy said.

"What . . . what is that?"

Andrássy crossed his arms, sighing audibly before he answered. *"You."* With that he collapsed into the tree opposite where Sisi stood, its trunk supporting the weight of his tall frame. "Franz Joseph wants *you.* The emperor wants his wife back. It's a constant source of embarrassment for him that you've left him. But more than embarrassment, it causes him pain. He misses you, Sisi."

Sisi considered these words, offering no reply.

"It is so plain for all to see," Andrássy continued, his tone like that of a tortured confessor. "Your portrait hangs in every single room of his. It's the first thing he sees over his bed each morning, the last thing he stares upon before shutting his eyes at night. And that one portrait you sat for, the one Herr Winterhalter painted of you a few years ago . . ." Andrássy's words withered midsentence, as if it was too difficult for him to finish his thought.

Sisi's cheeks flushed warm; she knew of which portrait Andrássy spoke. It was the most intimate, most alluring, most brazen portrait she had ever commissioned. She'd posed for it as a gift for her husband only a few years earlier, when she and Franz had become close again, briefly, while working together for the cause of Hungarian autonomy. In it she stood sideways, dark hair loose and tumbling over her shoulders in the free-flowing style in which only her husband had the right to behold it. Her body was covered in nothing but a delicate white dressing gown, the draped material just seconds away from slipping off her bare and glistening ivory shoulders. It was such a private view of her that the emperor had sat speechless when she'd first presented it to him. He'd then hung it in his private study, right over

70

his desk, where only he might see it. Well, perhaps he saw it, *and* his most trusted advisors saw it as well, since Andrássy seemed to have glimpsed the portrait.

Andrássy continued now, pulling Sisi from the clutch of her agitated thoughts. "The way he stares at your image, it's as if he wishes that, by his imperial will, he might replace the likeness with the real thing. You are the only subject he has ever had who has openly defied his royal wishes — and yet, he remains powerless before you. Franz Joseph would do anything you asked of him, Sisi, in order to get you back. Goodness, what man wouldn't?" Andrássy's words had a choked, tortured quality, but he pressed on. "He wants his wife; he wants to know his youngest daughter."

Sisi considered this for a moment. Franz, still in love with her . . . Could Andrássy be correct? What he said now surely brought him no pleasure to admit. She leaned across the clearing, her hands reaching for his. He let her take them up, but he avoided her gaze. "Andrássy . . . you know that my heart is hopelessly and irreversibly yours."

In the glint of moonlight, she saw how Andrássy's features pulled tight across his dark, brooding face. He drew in a long breath, keeping her waiting several minutes before he responded. Finally, his eyes found hers, and he spoke: "When I think about all the reasons why you should not love me. About all of the reasons why I should not love you, Sisi . . . all of the reasons why it is so foolish — and *dangerous* — for me to love you. Why, about how jealous Esterházy is, clearly. And the rumors that are growing. . . ." He pulled his hands from hers as if, even here, they weren't safe.

She leaned forward to reach for him, but he denied her embrace. "Andrássy, what's the point of torturing yourself like this?" she asked, pressing herself to him. "You know I love you. I've tried not to. We both have, but some things are simply greater than either of us."

At last, he wavered, his resolve faltering as he grasped her, pulling her into his arms, and she willingly yielded to his kiss. Andrássy ran his fingers through her hair, pressing his weight into hers as they fell backward into the support of a nearby sapling. She heard her own breath, heavy, as it matched Andrássy's. Their bodies, like their exhales, folded into each other, meeting in the dark in that most natural and necessary of unspoken languages. As Andrássy held her, Sisi looked up at the stars, a fire kindling within her to match theirs. But it was over almost as soon as it began.

"No," he said, shaking his head as he stepped back. "What if we were ever discovered? How could we ever explain ourselves?

To think that I might be the source of your ruination. Why . . . I'd never forgive . . ."

"But we are safe here," she said, trying, and failing, to sound self-assured as she reached for him once more. "We are free here."

"*Free* here? How can you say such a thing?" Andrássy dragged his hands through his hair. "Can we really delude ourselves so? Can we really allow ourselves to get lulled further into the supposition — the very false supposition — that we can get away with . . ." He waved his hands back and forth between them.

Sisi felt her heart hammer angrily inside her rib cage as she sensed the conviction hardening behind his words. When she spoke, her voice had a hollow sound to it: "Andrássy, you can't possibly mean . . ."

"Sisi, all I have ever wanted to do is lift your burdens. To be your solace. To bring you joy, as you've done for me. And yet, don't we both know that we are not free . . . not free to love each other?"

"Andrássy, my darling." She stared up into his face, his features so twisted with anguish. She kissed him, her spirits crushed by the way he turned away, rebuffing her affection. "How can we help it, if we love each other?"

"Sisi, it's as you just said: some things are simply greater than either of us. We both know that your place is in Vienna. With your family. With the crown prince, who needs you."

She felt her body go limp, and she knew her words would feel the same, should she offer them in protest, because Andrássy was correct. She knew that. How could she remain here, knowing how her child suffered? How could she choose her own heart's need for Andrássy over the all-powering need of her child? Hadn't the whole plan been to come here to find peace? She'd never have peace here, not now, not when she knew what was happening back in Vienna. Even if she could put one thousand more miles between herself and the Imperial Court, the fragile wall of tranquility and freedom that she had labored so long to erect around her had now crumbled. She could have no peace; she could have no separation. The pull of her family and her capital and her duty was too strong. Stronger, even, than her desire to love and live freely.

Andrássy looked sideways at her now, endeavoring to sound more upbeat as he said, "I go to Vienna often. Why, you yourself say I go *too* often. Well, I'll just have to go even more."

She shook her head, struggling to wrangle the threads of her tormented thoughts into something she could understand and accept. Struggling to find a way that she could return to save Rudy while also keeping her freedom,

74

keeping Andrássy. "You know it's not the same. You and I . . . we couldn't possibly live there as we can here. I'm not free there."

His hand went to her cheek now, cupping her face in his palm. She nuzzled into it, craving his touch and feeling certain that she could never live without it. His expression had softened, the pinched strain of his features now replaced with sadness. Resignation. "My Sisi, was either of us ever free, really?" He sighed, his dark eyes holding hers, catching the glow of moonlight. "I don't want to give you up — why, I'd sooner give up my own heart, if I could. Believe me. But these are things larger than ourselves. We can't allow our love to make us selfish."

But that was all that Sisi wanted. As empress, wasn't she supposed to get what she wanted?

II

Reason and love keep little company
together nowadays.
— WILLIAM SHAKESPEARE,
A Midsummer Night's Dream,
SISI'S FAVORITE PLAY

CHAPTER 2

Vienna, Austria
Summer 1868

Sisi's response, as the imperial carriage pulled her along Vienna's wide boulevards toward the Hofburg Palace, was visceral and involuntary. The scene outside the windows caused her to tremble as surely as it had on the day she'd first arrived, a bride of sixteen, new to the capital and terrified of the court — of the life — that awaited her.

Sisi noted now how much had changed in the city since she'd left it. As Franz had explained in his letters, Vienna's medieval wall had been completely demolished, replaced by the Ringstrasse, a grand loop of boulevard encircling the center of the city and opening it up for outward growth and expansion. The streets felt more spacious, more fluid and modern. The opera house on the Ringstrasse, after years of work, appeared near completion, its magnificent white façade as fanciful as a confectioner's cake, as grand

and imposing as the empire it would now entertain.

And the women throughout the city, Sisi noticed, appeared different as well. They no longer wore their hair à la Sisi as they once had, wreathing their heads with loose braids to emulate the style of their beloved young empress. No, having been abandoned by their empress, the Viennese women had apparently eschewed her hairstyle, instead fashioning their coifs in sensible buns with two clusters of tight curls that framed each side of the face, hanging like ripe bunches of grapes. The style, Sisi noted, that her mother-in-law had made popular at court.

And yet, much felt the same within the pulsing, throbbing *Kaiserstadt,* the imperial capital city, its streets still full of noise and people, of stately stone buildings and slapdash traffic. Looking out over the city — over *her* city — Sisi marveled that the time she had spent here hadn't familiarized the capital for her. Instead, she still felt foreign there. Unsure of her place. She still noted the tremor in her hands and the coiling of the nerves in her belly as she beheld the grandiosity of her husband's imperial seat.

Curious vendors and pedestrians lined the boulevards, staring up from amid the noise and chaos and traffic as the imperial coach wove its way toward the Hofburg. As she gazed back at them, Sisi understood why the

Viennese imagined themselves to be living at the center of Europe's greatest empire. Their backdrop, every single day, was an immaculate city of grand new government buildings and glistening white theaters and museums. Their emperor ruled by divine right, the latest in a family that had held tight to the reins of power for centuries. What better fate was there in this world of revolutionary countries and combustible liberalism than to be a subject, safe and sound, in Franz Joseph's steady and stable Habsburg Empire?

And yet, Sisi thought, wasn't their status constantly imperiled? Did they know, as she knew, about the forces that would gladly have knocked Austria down from its imperial pedestal? Did they not know the danger of having a leader whose motto was *Ich weiss nicht ändern*? "I don't change." How many times had she heard Franz and his mother, Sophie, repeat that motto? And how many times had she thought that it spelled certain disaster for a future where change was necessary — even inevitable?

The crowds thickened as the streets narrowed, winding farther into the center city, toward the imperial palace. Some of the people called out cheers of delight, shouts of welcome to the long-absent empress. Others offered jeers and hisses. Many in the city were not quick to forget that their empress had left them a year earlier to forge the dual monarchy and receive a crown from Hungary, that she had made her preference for Budapest so evident, the sister city they considered less grand and less worthy.

★ ★ ★

Inside the Hofburg, the jeers and hisses were more muted and subtle; whispers behind gloved hands, morsels of gossip shared behind closed doors. "It's a terrible pattern, really," Sisi said, as she settled back into her old apartments in the Hofburg Palace's Amalia wing. These rooms she had first moved into with so much ceremony and hope as a young bride. These rooms where she had conceived and delivered her babies and then schemed as to how to fight to keep them. These rooms where she and Franz had driven each other mad, first with the tenderness and passion of their love and then with the fury of their quarrels — more of the latter in the later years. Now she was back in these same rooms, looking at the same lavish surroundings of red damask, porcelain vases, and shimmering gold-gilt chandeliers, and reliving the same heart-wrenching memories of the years she had spent in them.

"It's a terrible pattern," Sisi repeated, as she thought back to the expressions of the courtiers she'd passed in the hallway moments earlier. The stunned, inquiring looks

80

that had gripped their faces. The way they had barely waited until she had passed to erupt into gasps and whispers. The genteel and well-dressed courtiers may have been more restrained than the commoners who shouted out their reactions in the streets, but only barely.

"They mock and revile me, so I stay away," Sisi said, watching Marie and Ida riffle through one of her dozens of clothing-filled trunks. "But the longer I stay away, the more they revile and mock me. There's no winning. Which is precisely why I decided to just give up entirely."

Ida and Marie exchanged uneasy looks. Sisi, sitting on the silk settee with a sleeping Valerie in her arms, didn't acknowledge their troubled expressions but turned back to the peaceful face of her sleeping baby. "But now . . . I don't know how long we shall be back, my baby," Sisi said, her voice low and expressionless. She tightened her grip on the little girl.

Marie, always trying to conjure an environment of cheeriness around Sisi, ventured a tenuous reply. "I bet there are many more courtiers here who are happy to see Your Majesty return than those who are not."

"Oh, what does it matter anyway?" Sisi sighed. "I didn't come back for them." And with that, she rose and carried Valerie to the small bassinet that she'd had placed right beside her bed. Seeing her sleeping child tucked safely under a blanket, Sisi crossed the room to her desk and picked up the small portrait of her son, the one she'd had made of him as a toddler. She wiped the dust off its frame to study the soft, fine-featured face. He really was her child in so many ways. The bright hazel eyes, the chestnut curls. But especially in the sensitive disposition so evident in the way he looked at his portrait-ist. An earnest expression that betrayed what Franz had always labeled *a weak constitution.*

The first thing Sisi did, after settling herself and Valerie into her own apartments, was visit her son's suite of rooms. Before leaving her chamber, Sisi issued the sternest of orders to Marie and Ida that they were not to let Valerie out of their sight. Under no circumstances was the baby to be taken from the empress's bedroom. Nor was Archduchess Sophie to be admitted into it.

Sisi arrived at the crown prince's suite shortly before the dinner hour expecting to find the little prince returned and resting after a long day. She was shocked to learn instead from the uniformed guard that Rudolf was still out with his tutor. "When is he expected to return?" Sisi asked the man, whose face she had never before seen.

"I do not know, Your Majesty."

Sisi crossed her arms in front of her waist,

frustrated by this guard's stingy withholding of information. "Well, when does he *ordinarily* return?"

"The Crown Prince Rudolf ordinarily returns to his chambers at approximately eight in the evening, Your Majesty."

"Eight in the evening?" Sisi frowned. "When does he leave in the morning?"

The man hesitated now as if uncertain whether he might share such information. Apparently Sisi's stern face convinced him he'd be in more trouble if he *didn't* answer, because he said, "The Crown Prince Rudolf and Count Gondrecourt quit this suite at approximately five in the morning, Your Majesty."

"*Fifteen* hours of study?" Sisi knit her hands together and began to pace across the small receiving area in front of the guard. Fifteen hours of study for a boy of just barely ten years old? It was madness.

"It's not just study, Madame. It's drilling, and marching, and —" But the guard remembered himself, checking his words as he stiffened his posture, his face going blank once more.

"I know quite well," Sisi said, nodding. "I'll wait in his room until they return." Sisi made for the door that would lead her into Rudy's bedchamber, but the guard remained motionless before it. He blocked her way, looking at Sisi as if she had suggested trespassing.

83

"Yes? What is it?" She heard the bristling in her own tone.

"It's just that . . ." The man shifted his weight from one polished boot to the other, his eyes drifting downward to the parquet floor. "No one is admitted to the Crown Prince Rudolf's rooms without a previously scheduled appointment, Your Majesty. The Count Gondrecourt's orders."

"I don't give a damn about Gondrecourt's orders."

★　★　★

Though suppertime came and went, Sisi had no appetite. Evening crept through the windows of the crown prince's bedroom, and she glanced around as the space succumbed to shadow. It looked nothing like a child's room ought to; there were no toy drums or train tracks or picture books, no cozy fire or warm dinner tray awaiting the prince after his long day. Not even any toy soldiers. There was a plain bed, a desk and chair, some simple dressers. It was a comfortless, joyless place.

Finally, the door opened and two figures appeared, one broad shouldered and heavy footed, one slight and sickly, the body of a tiny invalid. The first glimpse of her son nearly caused Sisi to cry out in anguish. She knew enough from Gisela's letter to expect

84

her son's poor health, but the reality now presented before her was far worse than she had imagined. Rudy was dressed in an officer's uniform, the same stiff and starched attire his father wore, only with proportions tailored for his small body. He was ten years old, yet he appeared no sturdier than a boy of seven. Rudy's hair, once resembling his mother's russet waves, now hung limp and dull around a pallid face. But it was the expression on that face that caused Sisi to wring her hands in the darkened bedroom. Rudy's eyes were sunken and heavy lidded, his brow creased into a crumpled mass that spoke of his exhaustion and anxiety. His body was that of a tiny boy — his face wore the cares of a full-grown man.

On spotting the unfamiliar, beautiful female figure in his room, the boy leapt back in fear — an instinctive response that had clearly been conditioned into him by daily startlings and shock tactics. *My God, the little boy must tremble every time he enters a room,* she thought. He could never know what terrible torment or spectacle his tutor had arranged to await him on the other side of any door.

"Rudy." Not wanting to startle him further, Sisi spoke his name as softly as she could. She walked to him and bent to her knees. "Rudy." She took his hand in her own, feeling the cold of his fingers, noting how he trembled. She kissed his palm. Still, he looked

85

distrustfully at her. His eyes, so familiar in their shape and color, could have been her own eyes staring back at her except for the frantic, haunted look in them.

"Rudy, it's me, your mamma. Oh, Rudy, my darling." Tears slid down Sisi's cheeks as she reached forward and pulled him into her arms. He had always been small; he had his mother's lean, narrow build. And yet, now she felt as if even her gentlest hug might crush him, so spindly and insubstantial was his frame. "My darling boy. It's all right now. Everything will be all right. I am here."

"Empress Elisabeth." Count Gondrecourt stood over them, his hand landing proprietarily on Rudy's narrow, uniformed shoulder.

"Count Gondrecourt." Sisi pried her arms from Rudy and stood, staring into the tutor's broad, stern face. It looked as if his lips had never formed a smile in his entire life. She turned once more to her son, repressing her shudder and instead managing a soft tone for him. "My darling boy, I am going to speak with your tutor in the next room. And then I will return, and we will have dinner together."

The little boy shook his head, casting a nervous glance toward his tutor as if to beg him: Please don't punish me for this woman's infractions.

Sisi resisted the urge to wail. She wouldn't cry; she would not give that added discomfort to Rudy — or that added pleasure to the sadistic man who stood over him. She turned back to the tutor. "Gondrecourt, a word with you outside."

But the man stood motionless, as still as an oak. "I will see to it that the crown prince has his supper and performs his evening cleansing and prayers. Once my daily duties are complete, I can speak with you, if that is the emperor's will." And then, as an afterthought, he added: "Empress Elisabeth."

Sisi felt her entire frame go rigid. "No, Gondrecourt, you will come out into the hall with me, and we will speak now." The unflinching firmness of her tone startled even her, and the tutor acquiesced, frowning at the little boy as he followed his mother out of the room.

In the antechamber, Sisi tried to keep her voice quiet. She didn't want to upset Rudy by raising it. Also, she suspected that her antipathy for the tutor might be even clearer in her calm, measured voice than it would be if she railed and stomped. "Count Gondrecourt, you are dismissed. We no longer require your services."

The military man's face remained unresponsive, his expression an inscrutable mask. Sisi continued: "You are to leave the palace at once. If you need assistance making alternative arrangements for lodging, a palace aide will help you secure temporary housing outside of the Hofburg walls. I don't want to hear that you've come near the crown prince's suite ever again. You are to have no further contact with him. Do you understand?"

Gondrecourt crossed his arms now, still no hint of emotion on his face. When he spoke, it was with the fraying patience of one who must address a dim-witted child. "Empress Elisabeth, I serve at the pleasure of His Imperial Highness, the Emperor Franz Joseph."

"Not any longer," Sisi answered, shaking her head, attempting to remain calm. "You are dismissed."

Now the man smiled. Not the sort of smile she'd hoped to find on the face of the man who worked with her child but instead a bored smirk, a condescending way of telling Sisi that he didn't place much store in what she said.

She balled her hands into two tight fists but then unclenched them, forcing her voice to stay quiet. "Do you have any questions? Or shall I summon a guard to see you out?"

The man's eyes slid back toward the bedroom door, as if he were ready to return to his sadistic duties on the other side. He spoke after a moment, his voice like a challenge as he asked: "If I leave, who's going to oversee the crown prince's studies and discipline?"

Sisi hadn't thought about that question, but the answer came to her quickly: "I will."

Back in Rudy's room, the little boy was missing. "Rudy, my darling?" Sisi lit several candles and called in a maid to build a fire in the white porcelain stove. She ordered two bowls of broth, a pot of hot chocolate, and a warm bath — emphasizing the warmth — for her son.

She found Rudy cowering behind a massive armoire in the corner of the bedroom. The sight of his body curled up, the way his face became panicked when he saw that he had been discovered — like an abused animal's — was enough to break Sisi's heart all over again, but she summoned all the strength she could. There would be time to weep later. Not now, not in front of her son, who needed her strength more than her tears. And besides, couldn't she understand his urge to hide? How many times had she felt the same urge? The desire to flee the rooms of this palace? "Come here, my darling." She offered a hand, but the boy didn't take it. "Come. You're safe, I promise. That awful — er . . . that man is gone."

At this, Rudy stood slowly and followed her, step by tenuous step, from the corner of the room, still not taking her outstretched hand. His eyes darted around the candlelit space as if to verify the truth of what she had just said.

"It's well past suppertime. Are you hungry?"

The boy didn't answer, but his hunger became apparent as he watched the footmen who now entered with the dinner dishes Sisi had ordered. "Will you have dinner with me, my darling Rudy?" They sat down at a small wooden table, and Sisi lifted her spoon to taste her broth.

"Wait," Rudolf said, lifting a small gloved hand.

"Yes?" Sisi asked, pausing with her spoon raised to her lips.

"Count Gondrecourt says I must always begin my meal with a prayer."

"Oh, yes, of course," Sisi said. She prayed quickly, wondering how that man could fathom speaking to God when he treated the child before him the way he did. "Now, Rudy, my dear, eat."

The boy sipped his bowl of broth with polite and measured gestures, but even his obedience to table etiquette could not hide his obvious hunger. "When was the last time you ate?" Sisi asked, watching him from her seat across the small table.

Rudy looked at her, then looked around the room, as if certain that Gondrecourt still lurked somewhere, waiting to berate him for speaking to this strange woman who had appeared, like a beautiful apparition, to disrupt the all-important imperial routine.

"My darling," Sisi said, pushing her own half-eaten bowl of broth toward him. "You've finished yours. Eat this."

He looked at her, his eyebrows sliding upward in mute disbelief.

"Go on," she urged him. "I'm not hungry." It was the truth.

Once he had slurped down the second bowl of broth and the entire pot of hot chocolate, Sisi tried again. "Rudy, my darling, that bad man is gone."

Rudy looked at her appraisingly, his opinion of her credibility clearly still undecided. How many tricks had Gondrecourt played on him, each with some hidden moralistic lesson? Surely he thought this was just another such test. Oh, but to have Gondrecourt come back now would be the cruelest one!

"Rudy, you can trust me. I am your mamma." Sisi swallowed, reaching into the fold of her skirt. "See here? This is you. As a little boy. I carry it with me always." She showed the miniature portrait to the boy, who looked at it but would not take it into his own hands, as she suggested. She replaced the portrait into her pocket. "And see?" She lifted another miniature likeness. "I carry this one, as well."

"Gisela," Rudy said, the faintest hint of a smile touching his lips as he said the name of his elder sister.

"Rudy, I was away for a bit. But I'm back

91

now. And I promise that you will never see that man again. Do you know what a promise is?"

The little boy didn't answer.

"A promise," she explained, "is when somebody says that they will do something, and you know that they will do it. You can trust them." Andrássy's face burst into her mind, but Sisi forced herself not to think of him, not to think of the yearning she felt for that man. How he had once told her this very same thing when she had been wounded. *I want to show you that you can trust again, Sisi.*

She folded her hands in front of her on the table and looked squarely at her son. "I promise you, Rudy, you are done with that man."

After supper, she convinced him to take off his military uniform, averting her eyes at his clear bashfulness. "My darling, the bathwater is warm. I promise you." Rudy walked distrustfully toward the tub, clearly not believing her. He put his hand in and, noting that it was in fact warm, looked at her in mild surprise.

He sat in the tub for a few moments, motionless. She recalled, her heart thrashing inside of her, how bath days had been such a wild and unruly time in her childhood home at Possenhofen — how she and Néné had played and sung and made such a mess of the weekly event. Such a carefree contrast to

92

the little boy who sat before her now like a block of ice that needed thawing.

Once he was dressed in his nightclothes, Sisi tucked Rudy into bed and curled up beside him, wrapping her arms around him, breathing in the scent of his freshly washed chestnut waves. "Do you see your papa or grandmamma at night?" she asked.

"Not on nights when I have lessons," he said. The sound of his voice slipped so softly from his lips that Sisi was taken aback for a brief moment. But he had spoken to her, at least!

"When do you see them?"

"In the mornings, Your Majesty."

"Please, my darling, please call me Mamma."

Rudy gave her a quizzical look, as though he believed that he hadn't heard correctly. She nodded to encourage him, but the boy remained unconvinced.

"You see them in the mornings then, you were saying?"

"Yes, Your Maj—" Rudy paused, catching himself. He was nothing if not conditioned to obey the orders of adults. "For an hour. When I'm good."

Sisi nodded, chewing on her lip as she considered this. It shouldn't have come as a surprise. Eventually, she spoke again, trying another strategy for entering into the boy's confidence. "Would you like to hear about

93

Mamma's farm in Hungary?"

Rudy didn't answer.

"I have horses," she continued. "And chickens. And dogs. Big dogs."

"Grandmamma has dogs, but hers are little."

The little rats that she has trained to growl at me, Sisi thought.

"She says she despises big dogs," Rudy added.

"Precisely," Sisi said, omitting the remainder of her thought: *Precisely why I have them.* "And you know what else, Rudy?" Sisi kept her tone bright. "You have a sister named Valerie."

"I have a sister named Gisela."

Sisi winced, momentarily silenced. "That's right, you have an elder sister named Gisela. And you also have a baby sister named Valerie. You might not remember her very well — she is much younger, and she was born in Hungary, but you'll get to know her now. She has big, bright blue eyes. And she has her first tooth now, too. Would you like to go with Valerie someday, to Mamma's farm?"

He considered the question a moment before asking: "Are the dogs nice?"

Sisi frowned, her heart breaking at the fear lurking behind what otherwise might have been a child's innocent question.

"Because Count Gondrecourt told me he

94

was going to take me to see dogs that looked like wolves. Dogs that hunt little boys in the woods, and then, if the little boy is not strong and brave, they —"

"No, Rudy, these dogs are nothing like wolves. If they scare you for even an instant, we will lock them up. But I promise you . . . they are very friendly. All they will want to do is kiss you and lick you."

She touched the tip of his nose with her finger, and he smiled, just a faint hint of a smile. A flimsy look that she might have missed had she blinked, but Sisi thought in that moment that it was the most beautiful look she had ever seen. Except, perhaps, for Valerie's baby smiles.

"Good," she said, trying not to react too vociferously for fear of startling the skittish boy. "Good, then I shall take you with me to Hungary someday. But first, I shall speak to your father."

★ ★ ★

The emperor was out for the evening, having already made plans to attend the night's showing at the Court Theater with a delegation of visiting ministers from France. And Franz Joseph would never have considered canceling.

Sisi appeared outside his apartments early the next day, bathed and dressed and looking

95

as lovely as she could manage, given the circumstances. She hadn't slept a minute of the previous night, hadn't even looked at her breakfast tray, and she knew she wouldn't be able to eat until she had Franz's assurances that Rudy might be saved.

Sisi knew Franz Joseph's daily schedule — and she knew that he of all people would not have modified it in her absence. His personal motto, after all, was "I don't change." First he would wash and say his prayers; then the mornings were his time alone at his desk with his ministerial reports and letters and endless paper work. She also knew that the emperor did not allow visitors during these hours and that no one, save for perhaps his mother, ever dared to approach his study without an invitation or previously scheduled appointment.

"I must speak to the emperor," Sisi said now, standing before the impassive guard, his face as rigid and unmoving as the starched military uniform he wore. "I know that he is in there. Tell him that his wife wishes to speak to him."

The guard hesitated a moment, as if not quite sure whether to heed the order, but he turned and left to dispatch the message. A few minutes later, the heavy door groaned open, and Sisi was led into her husband's study by a small army of footmen wearing the black-and-gold Habsburg livery. Her

96

presence was announced, and Emperor Franz Joseph rose from his desk, nodding as his wife bowed before him.

"Your Majesty," Franz said, his tone guarded, his voice betraying no hint of his deeper emotions at seeing her after so long.

"Your Majesty," Sisi said in return, her eyes lowered to the hemline of her dress.

"Welcome back to Vienna," he said. "It is my pleasure to see you. Please, please . . . rise." Sisi stood back to her full height. With a nod of his chin, Franz dismissed all attendants from the room so that only the two of them remained. Man and wife, alone. He raised a gloved hand and asked: "Some refreshment? Shall I order coffee? Cakes? You look thin."

"No, thank you." Sisi looked toward his desk piled high with papers, then toward the settee and chairs upholstered in red damask, their rich color matching the drapes and carpet. "Habsburg red," it was called, because of her husband's — or, perhaps more precisely, her *mother-in-law's* — clear preference for the scarlet color in decorating. Sisi gestured toward the settee. "May we sit?"

She wouldn't sit across from him at his desk like some minister or bureaucratic supplicant. She was his wife. Rudy's other parent. And she was here to discuss something no less important than the very survival of their child.

"Oh, yes, yes, of course," Franz answered, raising his hand to direct her.

They kept several inches between their bodies, perching stiffly on the sofa with their legs angled toward each other. Sisi took in the long-unseen face of her husband; the time they had spent apart showed itself in his appearance. His hair now grew in thinner on top, giving the impression that his forehead had stretched. His beard was thick, meeting his sideburns in a tangle of strawberry blond and silvery gray — more of the latter than when Sisi had last seen him. His blue eyes were as she remembered them, light and clear and ever alert, but surrounded by a soft webbing of lines. He seemed to be fending off fatigue, though he would never have dared admit to such a human weakness.

"You look very well, Elisabeth."

"Thank you, Franz." Had he just read her own thoughts about his aging? "You do, too."

"No need to lie," he said, cracking half a smile. He put his hands on his knees, looking straight ahead now. "It's good to see you. Very good to see you."

"You, too."

"What did I say about lying?"

Sisi laughed in spite of herself. Looking up, she noted how her portrait, the Winterhalter masterpiece she had given him, still hung over his desk. A second Winterhalter painting of her hung just beside it — this one similarly intimate, but with Sisi flashing a beguiling smile rather than looking off into the distance. Smaller framed images of her also decorated his desk, accompanied by miniatures of each of their children. So Andrássy had been correct: her husband *did* stare at her likeness every day. She shifted now, folding and unfolding her hands in her lap.

"How was everything in Hungary?" Franz asked.

"Good."

"Gödöllő continues to please you? Does the house lack anything?"

"No."

"You'll let me know if there is anything that I can do to make it more comfortable for you?"

"Franz, I know that a separation as long as ours necessitates some sort of polite small talk. Some exchange of niceties." She angled her body toward his, waving her hand. "But I have something very important to discuss with you."

Franz looked toward her, nodding once. He hadn't changed, but now he saw that neither had she. His voice was even as he said, "I heard that you tried to dismiss Gondrecourt."

"Not *tried*," she said, a cold lump of panic forming in her gut. Was that terrible man back in the palace, tormenting Rudy even at this very moment? Making a cruel deceiver

99

of her after she had promised her son that Gondrecourt was gone? "That man must go."

The emperor shifted in his seat, sighing as he patted down a nonexistent wrinkle in his immaculately starched pants. So he still dressed daily in his military uniform: cream-colored tunic and scarlet trousers, the attire from his days as a young officer in the Austrian cavalry. The daily apparel that had earned him the friendly nickname of "Old Red Pants" from some in the empire.

"Elisabeth, you have been gone a long time."

"I know. And I am back now, because I was made aware of what that horrid man was doing to our son."

"It's hardly appropriate for you to come in here and disrupt the course —"

"It is even worse than I had imagined. After seeing Rudy, I am convinced it's essential for his mental, physical, and emotional well-being, his very existence, that we put a stop to this madness."

"Who told you? Who went to you with these drummed-up and exaggerated reports?"

"It doesn't matter who told me." And it didn't. Besides, she would never betray Gisela's confidence. It would be her own private secret with her daughter, her first secret with her daughter. "What matters is that the situation got so desperate that the news reached me all the way in Budapest."

"Elisabeth, you have been gone. But you must try to understand, there are certain ways that things are done, and you can't just come here and —"

"*How things are done.* Subjecting a small child to water cures and perpetual fear? Shock tactics taken directly from the battlefield? It's incomprehensible."

"It's military training. It's what I went through. Mother had me in the uniform by age four."

"She was wrong to do so. It doesn't mean we must subject Rudy to the same abuse. Why, he's only a small child. He's petrified! He's made ill by it." As the heat in her voice rose, Franz kept his tone steady, controlled, as if she herself were an unruly child in need of reasoning.

"The boy has a weak constitution." Franz Joseph scratched at his sideburns, looking away from Sisi and across the room. "Someday he will be expected to assume his rightful role as leader of the Austro-Hungarian Empire. He will require strength, both inner and outer, to carry on our dynasty. To lead our army into battle. The only way to strengthen Rudolf is to —"

"Strengthen him? Why, have you *seen* him? The boy is an invalid! He is malnourished. He trembles like an epileptic. He wakes in the dark from night terrors."

Franz sighed. "Then we shall simply have

101

to redouble our efforts to fortify his constitution. Gondrecourt knows what he is doing. Gondrecourt will see to it that the crown prince —"

"Gondrecourt is a sadist and a fool, and I will no longer allow him near my son."

"Elisabeth." Franz paused now, weary of her interruptions, her impassioned entreaties so different from his own measured statements. "The boy is too sensitive. He is not of the right mold to become emperor. We must turn him through practice and discipline into what he is not, by nature, inclined to be. Rudolf is not enough like . . . He's too much like . . ."

"Too much like his mother?" Sisi said, the words bitter on her tongue. "Not enough like his stoic father? Oh, and how often your mother likes to say it, right?"

Franz didn't answer, but his silence resounded louder than a hearty agreement.

Sisi exhaled, exasperated. "Franz, I've seen our son. I've spoken to him."

"I visit the crown prince regularly. If the situation were as dire as you claim it to be, I would know. Rudolf would have expressed some of his discomfort to me. Or to his grandmother. He's very close to the archduchess."

Sisi ground her teeth hard but forced herself to remain focused. "The boy is petrified. He's practically mute. Trust me — your efforts to toughen him through this regimen of brutality are having the opposite effect. Instead, he —" But Sisi was interrupted by the figure that appeared in the doorway at that moment. She swallowed the rest of her words, her body stiffening on the couch with the instinctive need to assume a coating of protective armor. Both Sisi and Franz turned their gazes to the entryway.

Archduchess Sophie paused on the threshold as the two women made eye contact. Neither one moved, and Sisi thought in that moment: *It's remarkable, really, how much can be said between two women without a word being spoken.*

"Elisabeth."

"Sophie."

"Franzi," the archduchess said, turning her steely, pale-eyed gaze on her son.

Sisi could feel her husband's body tense as he rose from the sofa. "Mother, hello." Franz hated nothing more than to be caught between these two women. It had happened hundreds of times, and yet he'd never quite figured out how to manage. He, the man who ruled a fractious empire, had never been able to bring peace to his own household. *Except,* Sisi thought, *when I'm hundreds of miles away.*

"It's good to see you, Elisabeth. You make your old Aunt Sophie happy." Sophie swept forward into the room now, and Sisi let her head fall to the side, eyeing her mother-in-law with a look that said the archduchess fooled no one. Sophie ignored Sisi's gaze and continued: "I'm comforted to see that you've finally realized that your place as wife and mother — as empress — is here. Not off on that Hungarian horse farm."

Sisi looked away, not responding. Franz, still standing, shifted his weight.

"How is the child? Valerie?" Sophie asked, her lips exaggerating the name — the only grandchild's name that she herself hadn't picked. Sisi felt her heartbeat quicken involuntarily, the instinct to run or fight pulsing through her insides; she didn't like her mother-in-law speaking the baby's name.

"She thrives," Sisi answered, forcing herself to meet the archduchess's gaze directly.

"God is good," Sophie said, knitting her fingers together before her bell-shaped skirt. "I pray for her . . . and you . . . and all of my loved ones. Daily."

"Indeed," Sisi said, keeping her tone level. "I am back here for my other child, though. Rudy's health is quite another story. I am here to rescue my son from that barbarian you have installed in his household."

Sophie addressed her son directly. "I presume that you have tried to explain to her what is best for Rudolf?"

Franz Joseph nodded, looking from his mother to his wife with a grim expression.

"I remain unconvinced of the merits of your

way of doing things," Sisi said.

Sophie made to answer, but a coughing fit interrupted her. Franz called for water, which Sophie refused to drink, shaking her head. "I'm fine, I'm fine." Clearing her throat, tears pooling in her eyes, the archduchess inhaled a slow and unsteady breath, her splotchy breast rising visibly with the intake of air. She put a hand on her son's desk but then quickly removed it, as if trying to hide the need for such support.

"Mother." Franz crossed the room to Sophie, putting a hand on her arm. "Please, at least sit."

"Don't worry about me, Franzi. You have enough to worry about, my darling boy." Sophie made a visible effort to appear recovered, but her breathing was labored, Sisi noted. It hit Sisi in that moment just how aged the archduchess appeared. This woman, once so robust and round from her butter creams and thick stews and prime cuts of beef, a figure who had clipped down the halls of the Hofburg issuing orders and outpacing the imperial guards, was now, somehow, finding it difficult to stand. This woman who stood before her, coughing and wheezing, was entirely altered.

Sisi allowed herself to forget the woman's former strength and stared at her now through fresh eyes, and she saw that Sophie's body indeed appeared shrunken and weak, her face pale. Her mother-in-law, her aunt, had become an old woman. The change caught Sisi completely unaware; it was as if Father Time, having granted the formidable woman a reprieve for so many years, had now come to collect his payment, and greedily so.

Sisi looked up once more at the portrait of herself where it hung over her husband's desk, and she grasped in that moment something she had never before believed possible: she was stronger than Sophie. True, it was only because of the deficit of youth and energy and bodily strength that existed between herself and the older woman, but regardless of the reason, she, Sisi, had the advantage. She would outlast this woman. She knew it, and Sophie knew it. Her husband had to know it, too.

Franz made to break the silence, but Sisi raised her hand, beating him to it. "Franz dear, I am back. I am here for my son. And I will stay. I will be his mother, and I will be your wife." Sisi said it with a firm authority, and she noted the sudden attentiveness in her husband's face as he turned from his mother to listen to his wife. Before Sophie could interject, Sisi pressed her advantage: "But I can't stay if that man is allowed to continue on. I cannot stand by and watch that. You have a choice: Gondrecourt goes, or I go."

And surely, all in the room knew that what

Sisi might as well have said was: *It's your mother's way or mine.*

★ ★ ★

Vienna's leaves burst from green into a riot of color — flame red, mustard yellow, warm gold, and honeyed ochre — before falling from the branches and carpeting the imperial boulevards with their used remnants. That autumn and winter, as the days grew short and chilly, Sisi settled in to a regular, if not contented, routine in Vienna. As always, she found that her days passed more quickly when she kept busy, and so she filled her hours with the concerns and cares of her household and her children.

Her first task was to follow through on the dismissal of Count Gondrecourt. Though bits of the insulted military man's gossip reached her ears (*All I ever did was faithfully enact the orders of the emperor and his mother. But then, the empress never did know her place.*), Sisi ignored the controversy that Gondrecourt tried to foment, never even acknowledging his slander.

In Gondrecourt's place Sisi installed Colonel Joseph Latour, a soft-spoken man with a kind smile and liberal ideals for educating children. Latour, like Gondrecourt, was a military man by training, but Sisi gave him the strictest orders not to behave like one with her son. "Latour, you are to find the best teachers possible, regardless of pedigree or social standing at court," Sisi said to the man when he visited her in her study to discuss the crown prince's new schedule.

"But, Empress . . ." Latour hesitated. "I beg to humbly remind Your Majesty that the Habsburg hiring rules, in place for centuries, mandate that only military officers, members of the aristocracy, and clergymen might be permitted to interact with and teach a crown prince."

"You are to ignore those ancient rules," Sisi answered, offering a decisive flick of her wrist. In response to the tutor's visible disbelief — or was it discomfort? — she added: "These are your *new* orders. I will deal with any opposition you might encounter. I care only about the character and the scholarly training of the crown prince's teachers. In fact," Sisi whispered, "members of the bourgeoisie and common classes would be perfectly acceptable, even preferred, as I hope to gain for my son a liberal education. That's how I was educated, and that's the program I have advocated since his birth."

Under the watchful eye of his mother, his kindly tutor, and the new court physician, a mild-mannered gentleman named Dr. Widerhofer, Rudy was slowly and cautiously introduced to a new way of life. He began to eat and gain some weight. He shed his habit of trembling upon entering a new room, as if anticipating some horrific shock. It became not uncommon to hear the little boy laugh. Nobody was to ever speak the name Gondrecourt in his presence, and soon enough the only symptoms from his former torment that persisted were occasional night terrors and difficulty sleeping. From time to time, Sisi might catch him staring quietly off into nothingness, his face pinched in some unspoken agony, as if recalling a past torment or fearing some future event. When this happened, Sisi's heart would break anew, and she would recall why she had left the peace and freedom of Gödöllő to be here with her child.

When she was not following Rudy's progress and approving lesson proposals from Colonel Latour, Sisi spent the rest of her time doting on Valerie, ensuring that the baby made a smooth transition from Gödöllő to the Hofburg. Sisi guarded her daughter like the fiercest of she-wolves, not allowing Valerie out of her apartments unless accompanied by the empress herself. Though Sophie issued invitations for both Sisi and Valerie to join her for tea in her suite or a stroll through the imperial gardens, Sisi never accepted, nor did she ever return the invitation to her mother-in-law.

Valerie was a healthy girl who experienced the usual ailments of any baby: pain from her new teeth, the occasional upset stomach, small fevers or tumbles as she experimented with her unsteady legs. Each small incident, however minor Governess Throckmorton labeled it, sent Sisi into a terror, so solicitous was she for her child's well-being.

The only child who didn't seem to need — or want — Sisi's presence was Gisela. She had, after all, grown to adolescence without her mother playing a significant role in her life; she seemed perfectly content to continue without her now, carrying on her busy days within the relative autonomy of her own little household, overseen by her solicitous grand-mamma. From the limited interactions Sisi had with Gisela during their occasional family dinners or official gatherings, Sisi saw that Gisela seemed perfectly comfortable in her own place at court. She was nothing like her mother physically, already round in her figure before having reached ripe maturity. Nor was she like Sisi in temperament, having inherited — or adopted — her father's reserved formality, where Sisi had been free-spirited and sensitive in her youth. And Gisela was on the cusp of young womanhood, only a couple of years younger than Sisi herself had been upon meeting Franz Joseph. Gisela would marry soon and leave the court entirely, Sisi realized. Sensing her daughter's emotional distance, and yet seeing the closeness that existed between Gisela and her grandmother,

Sisi couldn't fight back a feeling of bitterness, so she willingly ceded the girl's affections, pouring out what might have gone to Gisela onto little Valerie instead.

As the year drew to a close, Sisi marked her thirty-first birthday with a small family dinner in her apartments and looked glumly ahead to the remainder of the Viennese winter. While the rest of the court eagerly anticipated *Fasching,* the merrymaking period before Lent that saw a flurry of carnivalesque masquerades and nightlong parties, Sisi longed for Budapest and its freedom. She longed for Andrássy, who visited her now only in his letters, sent to Ida to avoid censors or snoops. She began to think that perhaps Rudy was strong enough that she might slip away for a quick trip to Budapest with Valerie and her ladies. But then, some troubling news would come to her from the crown prince's tutor — news of some relapse: an attack of anxiety, a night terror waking the prince, or a refusal to eat — and she would be reminded that she was needed in Vienna.

And so the best Sisi could do was carve out her own small sanctuary in what she viewed as an otherwise hostile environment. She kept to her own private rooms, avoiding her mother-in-law and all but the most official obligations. She would plead a headache or cold as a reason to skip most state dinners, balls, and ceremonies. She saw her husband

111

for regularly scheduled visits in his staterooms and at dinner once a week in her private rooms, but otherwise she allowed into her confidence only Ida Ferenczy and Marie Festetics. To help her with the administrative work that inevitably piled up in Vienna, Sisi invited a Hungarian nobleman, a discreet, bespectacled man by the name of Baron Ferenc Nopcsa, to manage her household. Hungarian, not German, was spoken in her apartments at all times. And so, with Valerie in her lap and Shadow and Brave at her feet, Sisi cultivated as safe and cozy a cocoon as she could.

Franz Joseph, accustomed as he was to his wife's prolonged absences from court, seemed content to have even the scraps of odd hours with her a few times a week. When she did join him for an official appearance, he seemed positively delighted. He knew that she would never return to his bed, nor would she invite him back into hers — that had been established years earlier. What he most longed for was an end to the rumors and an occasional visit. Sisi's return had satisfied both desires and thus appeared to satisfy him.

But not everyone shared the emperor's happiness at the empress's return. Surely the emperor knew that his new adjutant general, a conservative Austrian officer by the name of Count Bellegarde, disliked Her Majesty the Empress. Everyone in the palace knew what Bellegarde whispered about her, excoriating "the Bavarian" for her liberal policies, her meddling in Rudolf's education, and her flagrant preference for Hungarians over Austrians. He railed against her "offensive submission to Andrássy's compromise." He noted every state function from which the empress was absent, lamenting the "heavy cross our emperor is forced to bear."

Though Sophie's age was advancing and her robust health waning, it appeared that Bellegarde was all too happy to take up the archduchess's banner. The general slandered Sisi so loudly that even she, almost entirely removed from the court gossip circles, couldn't help but hear his criticisms. She saw in the papers how she was referred to as "the resident guest at the Hofburg," that there were bets being placed on when she would next abandon her family and flee from her role. She heard how the courtiers scoffed at her, mocking her "rustic Hungarian hunting lodge." Even the diplomatic Baron Nopcsa, whose quiet and inoffensive manner often lulled people into disclosing perhaps too much in his presence, had to acknowledge to Sisi that she seemed to have a number of detractors at court.

★　★　★

Egypt was so rarely at the center of news.

113

The civilized world followed the updates out of Vienna, where Master Strauss, the court composer and unrivaled "Waltz King," was hard at work on a new masterpiece for his imperial patrons. Or out of Paris, where new hoopskirt designs and tight corsets had inspired a flurry of female excitement and fainting across Europe. Or London, where Queen Victoria had workers tunneling beneath the city streets to create a vast network of trains that ran *under* the ground. But Egypt? The glory of that Nile kingdom belonged to antiquity and Rudy's schoolbooks.

And yet, the opening of the Suez Canal promised to be a party worthy of the world's elite, a massive project that made even the construction of Vienna's Ringstrasse or Queen Victoria's underground trains seem like unambitious odd jobs in comparison. The project, undertaken with France's leadership, had carved a water passage through Egypt, linking the Mediterranean to the Red Sea, promising a new and lucrative era of easy trade between East and West. The project had taken ten years, cost one hundred million dollars, and had claimed the lives of thousands of workers. A project such as that, naturally, necessitated a party as lavish and splendid as the canal's building had been costly and destructive. And no one would want to miss a party given by Napoleon III

114

and his Empress Eugénie.

Franz Joseph and Sisi were expected to join the crush of crowned heads who prepared to travel to the northern shores of Africa in the autumn of 1869 to mark the long-awaited opening. In the weeks leading up to the journey, Marie and Ida had begun to buzz with questions: "When shall we begin packing, Empress?" "What shall Your Majesty need for Egypt?" "Will it please Your Grace to have us begin your trunks?"

"I cannot go." Sisi broke the news to Franz Joseph several weeks before their planned departure. The emperor looked up from his letters, pen poised midsentence, his shock immediately apparent on his face. "I shall explain why," Sisi said, sitting down opposite her husband at his desk. It was one of their scheduled weekly meetings in his study, often the only hour in a week they shared alone as man and wife.

Franz seemed to think he hadn't heard Sisi correctly. "Cannot go? But you must — surely you don't wish to miss the opening of the Suez Canal."

Sisi was careful to keep her tone soft, plaintive, as she ventured, "Valerie has been fighting a cold for over a week now. And Rudy? Why, he makes gains, to be sure, but just yesterday his tutor informed me that the boy awoke in the middle of the night gripped by a terror and cold sweat. I am reluctant to

115

leave the children behind. I feel that it is my . . ." And then, emphasizing the one word to which she knew her husband would surely yield, Sisi said, "It is my *duty*." She nodded, letting the word ring in his ears in the otherwise quiet study.

Franz lowered his pen onto the paper in front of him, folding his hands before himself on the desk as he mulled this over. As was his habit, his eyes drifted toward the massive portrait of his wife where it hung over his desk, as if he found its presence to be a soothing balm when he became overburdened by cares. It reminded Sisi of how her baby, Valerie, seemed to cling to one particular blanket of hers when she was upset.

Sisi had offered only a portion of her reasoning for not wanting to go to Egypt, leaving out the other and perhaps more significant piece. But Franz — unimaginative, unquestioning, practical Franz — would never have guessed at his wife's deeper thoughts, would never have surmised that a more complicated emotion lurked behind her straightforward words.

"Are you certain, Elisabeth?" Franz looked back to his wife now. "Eugénie will be there. She's going to accompany the French emperor."

Yes, Sisi knew that the French emperor and his wife would be there. She knew that she shouldn't allow her rival — the only woman

116

who was ever held up as a contender to Sisi's fashion sense or skill atop a horse — to go alone and seize the international headlines and glory.

But Empress Eugénie wasn't the person whose planned presence in Egypt unnerved Sisi. Just a day prior, Franz had shared with his wife the news that he had invited Andrássy to join the Austrian delegation on the trip. It would be a show of unity, Franz declared, proof of the stability and harmony that reigned in his empire since the establishment of the dual monarchy.

Sisi had received the news with quiet agony. She longed to see Andrássy more than anything, to be near him and with him. But that longing was precisely why she didn't trust herself to go. She knew that Bellegarde, also selected to be a part of the imperial delegation, would be watching each step she took, would notice every look that passed over her face.

The adjutant general had been so vicious in his attacks on the empress of late, so critical of Sisi anytime she declined to attend a formal state occasion with the emperor, and Sisi knew that he would be poised to catch any error she might make on the trip, happily reporting back to Archduchess Sophie's camp, as well as the Viennese press, ensuring that news of Sisi's failings and shame could be served up like scrumptious pastry to the entire empire.

Andrássy, the model of self-discipline, would behave flawlessly throughout the trip. He knew of Bellegarde's vitriol, and he would never dream of putting Sisi at risk. But being so near to Andrássy and yet being forced to act like an aloof acquaintance, to conceal the way she truly felt about him, would be more agonizing for Sisi than being apart. She had never acquired that essential palace skill of repressing her true feelings or masking her troubled thoughts. Andrássy always teased her about this, told her that she wore her thoughts and emotions so plainly on her face that she barely needed a mouth to speak them.

No, she couldn't go on this trip. For she knew that, while she stood holding her husband's arm, her eyes would travel to the Hungarian count beside her, and it would be plainly obvious to all that the man she loved and the man to whom she was married were not one and the same.

But here, in Franz's study, Sisi didn't divulge any of this, and she knew that as long as she stuck to the lines she had prepared she would most likely be granted a reprieve. "Besides," Sisi said, smiling at her husband where he sat at his desk, hemmed in by his papers, "I know how fond you are of *la belle Eugénie*. Without me there, you'll be free to flirt and declare your admiration for France's beauty without fear of your wife growing jealous."

Franz looked down, the skin under his thick beard flushing the same scarlet hue as his trousers. It *was* indeed common knowledge that Franz Joseph admired Eugénie greatly, having extolled to his ministers the exotic and full-figured charms of Napoleon III's empress. But oh, how ironic that this line of logic would now work to Sisi's advantage!

"I understand," Franz said eventually, unknotting his hands and pressing them down onto his desk, like a judge passing a verdict. "You feel that your place is here with your children. While I regret that I won't have you beside me, I commend you for your maternal devotion. And your willingness to put your sacred duty and the concerns of our children ahead of your own joy. You may stay."

And so, while the palace buzzed around her and the two most important men in her life prepared to leave for the lush and alluring land on the Nile, Sisi looked ahead to yet more time in Vienna.

As soon as the Viennese newspapers learned of Sisi's plans to forgo the trip, the criticisms began to swirl anew. The most widely accepted theory was that Sisi, jealous of the preeminent role that Eugénie and the French would play in hosting the opening ceremonies, had declined out of vanity and bruised pride. Other papers printed that Sisi was fearful of a "beauty contest" with her shapely, coquettish rival. Others wrote that she, "the houseguest," would never miss an opportunity to be unsupportive of her husband, the long-suffering Emperor Franz Joseph, whose wife only stayed in the capital when His Majesty had to be out of it. Sisi would read the reports and editorials each morning over breakfast, feeling her appetite flee. Surely stories such as these sold papers — otherwise they wouldn't be printed with such frequency. And surely if they sold, it was because this was what the people wanted to read and discuss. She'd toss the papers aside, but it was always too late; the words had already crawled into her mind and body and gripped her with an overwhelming feeling of self-rebuke, a bitter loathing for the vicious, unrelenting gossips in this city.

Sisi and the children bid farewell to the imperial delegation, waving as the carriages swept the emperor and his retinue through the palace gates and out into the streets, where the crowds hoisted the Austrian flag and called out prayers for a safe journey.

Both Franz Joseph and Andrássy wrote to Sisi throughout the journey, and their letters were as different as they themselves were. Franz Joseph gave Sisi detailed accounts of every day of the trip. Like a dutiful bureaucrat taking notes, he outlined for her the details of the lavish reception given by Turkey's sultan on the banks of the Bosporus Strait. He explained how the Turks had built their own palaces over the crumbling walls of the ancient Christian city of Constantinople. He wrote of the way the sultan collected women in his harem and horses in his stables. And he boasted proudly of the massive green emerald he had procured for his wife from the sultan's personal treasury of jewels.

Once safely in Egypt, Franz wrote with boyish pride about how he had climbed the greatest pyramid in Giza in just seventeen minutes. He recorded in detail the thirty courses he had eaten beside Empress Eugénie at the grand opening of the Suez Canal. He proclaimed that thousands of people had turned out in the port city of Suez for the occasion, yet he bemoaned the fact that "the ceremony days were very hot and not at all well organized. We monarchs in attendance were expected to elbow and push our way through the crowded city with the rest of the uncivilized mob." After that, he listed the many ways that, had the event occurred in Vienna, he might have done things differently, more efficiently.

Andrássy's letters, by contrast, were pure poetry, his words painting a picture for Sisi of the far and foreign lands that the Austrian delegation visited:

One night during our stay in Jordan's ancient city of Petra, after all the others in our party had retired, I quit our lodgings and set out alone on foot. I found myself exploring a deserted garden under a low-hanging moon. The night was heavy with that sweet, almost painfully seductive scent of jasmine, and I had nothing but the sound of the gurgling water to accompany my thoughts. Naturally, they turned to you. I sent a prayer up into the night, a wish that, wherever you were and whatever you were doing in that moment, you would know that you were also with me in that fragrant garden, looking up at Petra's star-strewn sky. I stayed there with you, in that pleasant, trancelike reverie, until the morning prayers were called out from the tower of the nearby mosque, and I knew that my companions would begin to stir and notice my absence. Before leaving the garden, I plucked a small cluster of jasmine and breathed in its fragrance, noting how its beauty, though exquisite, fell far short of yours.

And Andrássy told Sisi about the meandering streets of Jerusalem:

Paths so narrow that I could touch walls on both sides simply by spreading my arms. What dark secrets do you suppose have been whispered on such winding, ancient pathways? What hearts have been broken or delighted down those discreet and darkened lanes? I wondered, and I wished — for perhaps the hundredth time that day — that you had been there to wonder it with me.

He recounted his visit to Constantinople's ancient Byzantine cathedral, now a mosque called the Hagia Sophia, writing:

The dome soared so high that birds flew overhead beneath the colorfully painted ceiling. This sight, like all the other sights of exquisite beauty, made me long for you — for I knew that its beauty might only have been improved, indeed, perfected, by your presence beside me. I couldn't help but smile to think of you and what joy you would have derived at each moment of discovery and delight. You would have been particularly amused by the sultan's menagerie of wild beasts. I say, that colorful collection would have pleased you far more than his treasury of crown jewels.

Sisi delighted in Andrássy's descriptions, envisioning him on the journey and herself beside him. She found it easy to close her eyes and imagine the sights as she savored his words. In the Holy Land, only Andrássy swam in the Jordan River, the others in the

123

group protesting that the water was too cold in the late autumn. Andrássy did it because the waters there, once the bathing place of the Christ himself, were purported to give the bather miraculous powers. "Miracles, they say. Something both I and my nation could use."

* * *

"Rudy?" Sisi sought out her son one afternoon, having completed the latest letters from both Franz and Andrássy. "Rudy, just wait until you hear what Papa has written today! Would you like to hear about the giant statue they call the Sphinx?" She had gone into her dressing room to read the letters in private, leaving Rudy with his toys in the drawing room and Valerie sleeping in the bedroom. She was like a mamma bird — she would devour the news from the two men and then digest it before delivering the morsels that would be appropriate for the eleven-year-old boy's ears.

"Rudy?" Sisi looked for her son as she reentered the large room. But the boy wasn't there, and her voice rang unanswered throughout the empty space. "Rudy?" she called out again, thinking that perhaps her son was hiding and wanted to be found.

And then she heard a yelp coming from the bedchamber, a jarring, disturbing sound that

124

pierced the closed door and the silence in which Sisi stood. Valerie's cry, but its tone more urgent — more distressed — than the ordinary whimpers of a baby waking from her nap. Sisi's heart leapt against her rib cage, and she flew into the bedroom. "Valerie?" Sisi found Rudy standing over the cradle. "Valerie!" Sisi gasped, running toward the baby, her little cries still spilling out high-pitched and shrill. "Rudy, what's happened to your sister?" In her haste to reach the baby, Sisi pushed the little boy away from the cradle, accidentally sending him tumbling to the floor.

"Ouch, Mamma!" Rudy protested, but Sisi was so preoccupied with reaching into the cradle, pulling her daughter and a fistful of blankets into her arms, that she didn't acknowledge her son's fall. She held Valerie close, rocking the baby up and down and wondering where Marie and Ida were. "Hush, my angel. There, there, Mamma is here. What is the matter, my dearest one?"

Still Valerie wailed, and with a shrillness that Sisi had heard only once before, when the baby had fallen over her own unsteady feet and crashed against the jagged edge of a side table.

"My darling, my darling, what ever is the matter?" Sisi examined the baby, peeling away the layers of blankets and her sleeping dress. There, on the bare skin of one of

Valerie's short, chubby legs, Sisi saw the source of the child's distress. *"No!"* Sisi gasped, lifting a hand off the child. She examined her own palm, the small drop of blood from the child's white skin now coloring her own, too. "Good heavens, are you bleeding?" Sisi turned to look at Rudy for the first time, his little frame still in a heap on the floor. He gazed up at his mother and sister through narrowed, sulky eyes.

"Rudy, why is your sister hurt? What happened?" Sisi looked suspiciously into the cradle for some sharp object, sweeping the border of the bed and finding nothing. She turned back to her son. "Rudy? You were in here. Answer me. Did you see how your sister got this cut?"

Rudy shook his head once as he averted his gaze. A feeling of discomfort seeped through Sisi as she sensed, inexplicably, that her son was lying to her. She looked from the boy back to the baby in her arms. Valerie had calmed down, her hushed cries now mere whimpers as she nuzzled into her mother's embrace.

Sisi examined her baby's leg more closely. The cut was not deep or severe. Though it bled, it was nothing more than a small scrape, as though she had been pinched by a set of tweezers or a small pair of fingernails. Sisi's gaze fell once more on her son, her voice trembling. "Rudolf?" She swallowed hard as

126

she clutched her baby girl with a tighter grip. "You are telling Mother the truth? You did not pinch your sister?"

The little boy shook his head again, angling his entire frame away from his mother, like a guilty thief hiding a stolen handful of silver. But it was impossible, Sisi reasoned. This sweet, sensitive boy, himself the victim of torment — he wouldn't turn around and inflict pain on an innocent toddler. The boy might have been mistreated, but he wasn't a sadist. Her son couldn't be capable of malice toward her most precious, most beloved baby. Could he?

★ ★ ★

The mild autumn weather turned raw, and winter rolled in. Franz Joseph returned to the capital, and the court resumed its customary, unchanging routine. Often throughout that long, cold season, Sisi felt as though she spent more time and effort corresponding with people who were outside of Vienna than she did communicating with people within her own palace. She wrote daily to Andrássy — through Ida — begging him to visit. She wrote home to Bavaria, telling her mother how deeply she longed to leave court for Budapest "where everything was so much more pleasant."

Sisi heard from home as well. There it

seemed that Sophie-Charlotte's initial euphoria at her engagement to their cousin King Ludwig had been replaced with first a low-grade anxiety and now an outright panic. Months had passed, and still Ludwig would not answer his future father-in-law, Duke Max, when pushed to select a wedding date. Sophie-Charlotte complained to Sisi in her letters:

People are beginning to gossip — I know they are. I believe it is envy that causes them to whisper about my relationship with King Ludwig. Oh, the vile things they say! They point out how the king proposed marriage to me but then refused to set a date for the wedding when Papa pressed him. They whisper about the fact that our closeness arose, initially, out of our shared passion for and admiration of the music of the composer Richard Wagner. They say that Ludwig has spent his entire fortune on his fantastic castles and on financing the musical endeavors of Herr Wagner. They say that Ludwig will have me spend my days playing Wagner's music on the pianoforte while Ludwig busies himself professing his love to Wagner in the next room. Can you imagine anyone saying anything so vile and malicious? So what if my fiancé has a close friendship with Herr Wagner? I am not jealous of it, so why should they be?

Ludwig possesses a brilliant mind and deeply sensitive soul; of course he would surround himself with other individuals of brilliance and depth. Doesn't Herr Wagner top that list? And yet, there's little old me, somehow deemed worthy to stand beside Ludwig — my marvelous Ludwig — even though I am so much less brilliant than he is, and so much less sophisticated!

And so, I try to be patient with him. I write, and I beg Ludwig to end my embarrassment and sadness by simply setting a date for our marriage. And yet my letters to my fiancé often go unanswered. Worse still, my latest offers to visit him at his palace in Munich or his estate near Possenhofen have been declined. The one time I did see him, at a recent ball in Munich, Ludwig fled suddenly in the middle of a waltz, leaving me standing alone on the dance floor for all to witness my shame and utter bewilderment. Sisi, what am I to do?

Ludwig wrote to Vienna instead of to Possenhofen, and Sisi took it as an even more troubling sign that not once did he mention the name of her sister, his fiancée. Instead he wrote at length about his dear friend Richard Wagner. About the composer's genius, about how the two men had teamed up once more, and that Wagner was working on yet another opera. Ludwig offered no details, just outlandish hints: "This project, if we succeed, shall change the course of music forever. In fact, it shall alter the entire course of history."

That was Ludwig: always impassioned, always full of big dreams and giddy, extravagant language with which to express his hopes. Flattering and fulsome with his loved ones and his plans for the future. Except, it seemed, when it came to his future domestic life with his bride.

The other source of Ludwig's joy, Sisi learned from his letters, was his new castle. He'd undertaken his latest profligate building project atop the cliffs of Bavaria. He planned to call the castle Neuschwanstein, or "New Swan Stone." Ludwig wrote to Sisi: "The spot is one of the most beautiful places that one could ever find. It is sacred and out of reach, touched only by celestial breezes and the steep heights. It shall be a worthy temple to him. I hope he will come to me here to work and never leave." Sisi did not need to ask for the name of the male figure to whom Ludwig referred.

It was not just Sophie-Charlotte who struggled in Possi. Néné continued to wrestle with melancholy and physical weakness. The sister who had early in life sought the nunnery now lived like a novitiate in the secluded setting of her parents' countryside castle. And Sisi's other sister, Marie, was in even worse trouble. This sister, who had once seemed so happy in her own marital match, was now besieged in Rome with her half-witted husband, the deposed king of Naples. Sisi had learned from Marie's letters that the royal pair had been formally exiled from their kingdom in the south by revolutionaries who were calling for a free and unified Italy. Even the pope himself seemed under siege by Victor Emmanuel and Giuseppe Garibaldi and the lawless rabble that had spread across the Italian peninsula.

Sisi would look up from her letters and around her room, sighing as her eyes feasted on the gilt-framed oil paintings of long-dead Habsburg relatives, the polished mahogany that glistened under the candles of her crystal chandelier, and the porcelain clock that kept the time of her tedious days; she'd pace her imperial rooms, a suite that she dared not leave — fearful of what she would confront in the halls — and she would think that perhaps being royal was not the privilege that others might believe it to be.

III

Geneva, Switzerland
September 1898
He arrives in Geneva, his cheeks chapped by
the early-autumn sun, his feet rubbed raw and
aching from the dusty road. As he has no
money with which to pay for a lodging, he plans
to spend the night on the lakeside quay. Not so
bad, he tells himself, his view overlooking Lake
Geneva and the spikes of the Alps that enfold
it. It's still warm at night this time of year, but he
pulls his threadbare jacket close as he watches
the cruise boats gliding off across the lake, their
wealthy passengers tucked neatly belowdeck,
enjoying candlelight and violin music and
spreads of dinner and champagne laid out for
them on linen-covered tables. Not even realizing how hungry the man is who sits, watching, from the darkened shore. Not even knowing he exists.

He settles in on a wooden bench, listening to
the waves that lap the landing berths just feet
away. A sudden noise, a plop, interrupts their

regular rhythm. A fish jumping. There are fish in this water — loads of perch. If only he could get at one now, he'd take it in his dirty hands and eat it raw, in two bites. That is how much his stomach burns with hunger.

He looks up at the starry Swiss sky wanting to cry out in frustration and anger. In hunger. In desperation and ravaged surrender. But then his fingers touch the edge of his coat pocket and find the blade — the small, hidden blade. The tool that will deliver him from this solitary, starved obscurity. The tool that will help him make sense of it all.

It won't be long now, he reminds himself, feeling the small flicker of purpose ignite once more in his empty belly. Once he has done the Great Deed, he won't be thinking about money or food or sleeping out under a sky of Swiss stars. Once he has done the Great Deed, he will be immortal. And she, a mortal, will be no more.

CHAPTER 3

Schönbrunn Summer Palace, Vienna
Summer 1871

"But *why* can't I go with you?" Rudy's lip quivered, and though Sisi regretted to see her son so upset, it was promising, at least, that the boy felt comfortable enough to express normal childish emotions once more.

"My darling boy, come here." Sisi pulled her son into her arms, her heavy travel cloak making it hard to bend down to him. Behind her, Marie Festetics struggled to keep Valerie from fussing while, outside, Ida oversaw the loading of their luggage into the imperial coaches. "I won't be gone long. Mamma must make a quick trip to Bavaria to see her family about a most urgent matter. Grand-mamma Ludovika has some toys for you — shall I bring you back a toy from Possen-hofen?"

"But why does *she* get to go with you, and not me?" Rudy looked accusingly at the tod-dler in Marie's arms, and the heartbreak apparent on his face pierced Sisi; she felt her resolve momentarily weaken.

Sisi sighed, straightening back up. "Because, my darling boy, Valerie is a little girl. You are the crown prince; you must stay here and continue your lessons with Colonel Latour. You like Colonel Latour, don't you?"

"But I want to be with *you*, Mamma."

Sisi couldn't explain the rest of the truth to her son: That Valerie was the only child over whom she had direct authority. That she would have given her own life rather than risk leaving Vienna without Valerie, thereby allowing Sophie to gain control of her baby. That Rudy, the heir to the Habsburg dynasty, would always have to accept certain obligations to which his baby sister would not be bound. That life was always going to be more difficult for him, requiring more sacrifice and awarding less freedom. Instead, she sighed and prepared to take her leave. "Farewell, my darling boy." Sisi put her hand once more to his soft cheek. "I shall write to you from Bavaria."

"Farewell, Mamma," Rudy answered, his hazel eyes drifting to the floor. And then, as Sisi turned to leave him, she was halted in her steps by his parting words, by the sudden woodenness that came over his tone as he said, "I shall try my best to be brave. And to keep Papa company while you are gone." Now the boy stood tall, his chin jutting out

135

in a posture of forced stoicism entirely unlike the vulnerability of a moment earlier.

Sisi stared at him, marveling. *My word,* she thought. A little boy clearly her own son in the depth of his emotions, but already so well trained at how to suppress those feelings. How to speak like a Habsburg. A small, sensitive boy who felt a perfectly natural attachment to his mother, but already seemed to understand, to accept, *how things were done.*

Sisi frowned as she stepped through the doorway and left him behind. Whether she agreed with it or not, the Habsburg heir could not be permitted to take off with his mamma when she was called home to Bavaria on a family crisis.

And it certainly was a crisis that awaited her at home. All of Bavaria was in an uproar over the standoff between Duke Max and King Ludwig. The young king, once so popular and full of promise, had now postponed his wedding to Sisi's youngest sister twice, each time with increased embarrassment and insult to the bride and her family, and with mounting exasperation from his subjects, who longed for a royal wedding and the feasts and heirs that would follow.

But it had gotten worse than just the postponements and rescheduling. Now Ludwig was flatly refusing to name a new date, offering the construction of his castle and the debts he had undertaken to finance Wagner's latest work — an operatic trilogy of some sort, something about magical rings and an epic German saga — as his reasons.

Duke Max had fired back with an uncharacteristically stern ultimatum: the king could not keep humiliating his daughter like this. Either Ludwig must set a wedding date or Duke Max would withdraw his approval for the union entirely. Since that ultimatum, the two sides had reached an impasse, with neither party making a move.

Ludovika and Sophie-Charlotte, in a panic, had begged Sisi to return to Bavaria to serve as a mediator — a third party who might, because of her close relationship with her cousin, prevail upon the king to see reason. Franz Joseph, disapproving of the gossip and growing scandal that this cousins' feud was generating, had heartily agreed that Sisi should go to Bavaria and try to help her family resolve this conflict.

As Sisi crossed the courtyard and stepped into the waiting imperial coach, Valerie in her arms and Marie and Ida on either side, she noticed the mixture of emotions she took with her from Vienna. She had left her secretary, Baron Nopcsa, in charge of her household and administrative duties in her absence. She had bid farewell to Franz and Gisela and Rudy. Ordinarily she would have felt a thrill, a sense of freedom, upon quitting the court for someplace else. But now, however, she did not feel that elation. She was not going toward Hungary, and Andrássy, and freedom, after all. Instead, as she rode toward Bavaria, a thickening sense of uneasiness settled within her, a disquiet over the task that awaited her.

★　★　★

The sights of her homeland, the oft-trodden views of her happy, carefree childhood, lifted Sisi's spirits considerably. She arrived back at Possi at her favorite hour of the day, shortly before dusk. The diagonal light of the setting sun fell over the glassy surface of Lake Starnberg like dazzling strings of diamonds, and a gentle breeze blew the lake's mist over the newly sown fields, cloaking the area in a delicate haze. The peasants and villagers waved as Sisi's coach drove past, shouting out greetings of "Welcome home!" and "Long live Sisi!"

The castle itself was exactly as Sisi remembered it — squat and thick, with bits of its white paint chipped away, revealing the scarred and ancient stones beneath it. *Shabby,* was how Aunt Sophie always referred to Possenhofen Castle. *A beggar's household in total disrepair.*

Sisi stepped out of the coach, looking out over the unruly fields and the tree-lined lake that stretched before her, their beauty unchanged since her last visit. Let Sophie disparage this place as much as she liked, but neither the Hofburg nor Schönbrunn was anything compared to the raw and untamed loveliness of Possi, Sisi thought. In that moment, amid her joy at seeing her childhood home once more, Sisi felt a sharp pang of longing, as she couldn't help but think of Andrássy. How she would love to show him this place, to share it with him so that he could learn about this past piece of her. So that he could see where she had lived before it all, back when she had simply been Sisi.

Her mother stood before the house, her tall frame sentry-like and erect. As Sisi walked toward her, Ludovika's well-trained stoicism seemed to waver ever so slightly, and she greeted her returning daughter with a weary hug and an anxious smile. "Sisi, you've made it." Duchess Ludovika took her daughter's shoulders in her hands so that she might gain a full view of Sisi's appearance. "My, you look as healthy as I've ever seen you. Oh, thank God you are here."

Ludovika ushered Sisi, Valerie, and their attendants directly into the drawing room. There sat Helene, whose own appearance presented the opposite of that impression of health and vigor. Her eyes, always serious and dark, were ringed in shadow. Her lean frame, cloaked entirely in widow's black, had shrunk even further, and she appeared decades older than her age.

"Hi, Néné." Sisi pulled her favorite sister into a long hug, wishing she could transfer some of her own strength through the embrace.

"Sisi, you're here." Néné didn't wipe the tears that had pooled in her eyes. "Oh, how I have missed you."

"And I've missed you, my darling big sister. No, please, do not get up." Sisi knelt beside Helene, thrilled to be near her once more, even if she did look frail and careworn.

"Is she here yet? I saw the coach out front!" Sophie-Charlotte burst into the room, looking young and beautiful and positively vibrant in comparison. She was no longer a girl, and her figure had bloomed like the fertile fields outside the castle. Of all Sisi's sisters, Sophie-Charlotte, the youngest, bore the greatest resemblance to Sisi; her hair was just a shade lighter, and she was not quite as tall, but she was a pretty girl and full of youthful vigor. It would be a hard-hearted person who found the young lady's charms unappealing. And yet, it seemed that was the case with King Ludwig.

Once little Valerie had been passed from woman to woman, her cheeks sufficiently kissed and her flawlessness sufficiently proclaimed, Sisi dismissed Marie and Ida to take the little girl to the nursery for the evening. A fire was lit in the drawing room, and Sisi settled into an overstuffed chair beside her mother and her two sisters. Her brother Karl, she knew, was serving his military duty and living away from home.

"Where is Papa?" Sisi asked, looking around the room, noting the dust that clung to the wall hangings, the fraying seams that crept across the upholstery. Precisely as it had been during her childhood. *A beggar's household.* And yet, the polished and gilded halls of the Hofburg could never feel so welcoming, so cozy.

"Your father . . ." The duchess exchanged a meaningful look with Helene before continuing. "Only God knows. He left on one of his . . ." Ludovika paused to order tea for the four of them. "Shortly following his harsh declaration to Ludwig, he took off, and we haven't seen or heard from him since."

Sisi nodded, disappointed but not surprised. She knew enough from her mother's letters to understand that her father continued with his excessive drinking. She had already heard that the gossipers in town had named yet another illegitimate peasant child as her father's offspring. Sisi sighed now at her father's ongoing and habitual philandering, at all that her mother had to bear in the name of ducal and familial duty.

"All those who say that Ludwig is too eccentric for Sophie-Charlotte . . ." Ludovika waved a hand. "It does not get more eccentric than your father. And your father does not have the excuse of being king."

Sisi looked from her mother to her younger sister. "So tell me — what is happening?"

Their mother answered first: "I make no allowances for Ludwig's behavior to Sophie-Charlotte. And I do not excuse it. But . . . but I do not think these differences are irreparable. I would very much like to salvage the engagement, if at all possible. And I think it *is* possible."

"Have you seen Ludwig?" Sisi asked, knowing that her cousin's new castle, Neuschwanstein, was just southwest of Possi, an easy trip for a king who had the finest carriages and horses in all of Bavaria at his disposal. All three women shook their heads. Ludwig had not come.

"But have you heard from him at least? Has Ludwig offered any reply to Papa's message?"

Again the women answered in the negative. Sisi sighed.

"It would not do to break it off, though," Ludovika continued, her tone slightly defensive. "They have such a dear friendship. And Ludwig is a kind boy. Let the gossipers say what they want about him, but no one can deny his sweet and gentle nature. And it would be so nice to have Sophie-Charlotte always nearby."

A servant brought in tea for the four of them, and Sisi took a warm cup in her hands.

She felt a tug on her heart toward the nursery, a yearning to go and make sure her little girl was all right, but she forced herself to focus on the matter before her. "Well, now, Sophie-Charlotte." Sisi turned to her younger sister. "What do *you* think? That's what matters, after all."

Sophie-Charlotte didn't reach for the tea before her, but weighed her sister's question. After a pause, she said, "I confess that I am quite confused by Ludwig's behavior."

Sisi nodded, letting her continue.

"Initially, he was so effusive and so generous with his praise and affection. I never would have thought him the type to abandon me, to simply vanish at a ball that he himself was hosting, and without telling me where he went."

Sisi blew on her tea, listening to her sister.

"And why he keeps postponing our wedding, I could not tell you. I trust that he does not mean to hurt me. I know him to be kind. And good. And of course, he is so very handsome. . . ."

"But do you think he could make you happy, as a husband?" Sisi asked.

"Could he make me happy?" Sophie-Charlotte cocked her head to the side, thinking the matter over for a few moments before replying. "Yes, I do believe he could make me happy. Or at the very least . . . content. Ludwig has a sharp mind and a gentle spirit.

I believe he would make a perfectly sweet husband."

Sophie-Charlotte knit her hands together in her lap, looking down as she continued. "And if my feelings no longer soar toward the rapture I initially felt . . ." She paused, and Sisi nodded, remembering that first giddy letter in which her sister had announced her engagement.

Sophie-Charlotte wore a chastened smile now, as if acknowledging her previous silliness. "Well, that is quite all right, isn't it? All raptures must give way eventually, do they not? And then what does one hope for? What must remain is a friendship and respect. I believe that I would feel those things for Ludwig, if he were my husband."

So very reasonable, Sisi thought. So the opposite of how she had approached her own marriage. In her case, the rapture had not worn off until after the wedding day, leaving her hopelessly lost and bitterly disappointed.

Perhaps it *was* better this way, Sisi reasoned. Perhaps it was better to know the flaws of one's spouse, to take a more measured look at what marriage actually meant before cleaving one's life to an imperfect individual. "Well" — Sisi leaned forward, taking her sister's hands in her own — "you are far less naïve than I was as a bride, that's for certain."

"We just need someone to speak to Ludwig," Ludovika declared, leaning toward Sisi.

144

"To make him see reason! He's shut up in that castle with nobody daring to challenge him or speak the truth to him. His parents are both deceased" — the duchess paused to make a sign of the cross before her face — "and he keeps no ministers with him. But surely someone need only make the case to him that, as king, he *must* marry. He must have heirs. And who could make him happier than our sweet girl?"

Sisi looked from her mother to her younger sister, their faces so heavy with concern. Staring at Sophie-Charlotte, she asked: "Is it what *you* want? Will it make you happy to be Ludwig's bride?"

The younger sister nodded, biting her lower lip.

Sisi sighed. "If that is so, I am happy to make your case to Ludwig and to try to see what our fool of a cousin is thinking."

Sophie-Charlotte's face burst into a relieved smile. "You will do it?"

Sisi nodded, returning her sister's smile but not feeling certain that they ought to be celebrating just yet. "My, but he would be mad to pass up the chance to marry you, Sophie-Charlotte."

"You'll tell him that?" The hope now lit Sophie-Charlotte's delicate, young features. She really was quite pretty. Was that how sweet and fresh she herself had once looked? Sisi wondered. "Oh, thank you, Sisi!" Sophie-

Charlotte leaned forward and squeezed her sister's hands.

"I will dash off a note to him tonight telling him I am home in Bavaria and I wish to visit him tomorrow. Besides, don't you think he'd like to meet little Valerie?"

Her younger sister smiled once more in girlish delight, and Ludovika's sigh of relief was audible.

Later that night, after the servants had withdrawn and the household retired for bed, Sisi found her way to her childhood room, where she and Néné had shared a bed for all of their girlhood years. There was no discussion, no questioning; Néné simply smiled when she saw Sisi enter, bearing her flickering candle toward the bedside table.

"You'll sleep in here tonight?" Ludovika appeared on the landing outside the chamber, peering in at Sisi and Néné as they settled into the oversized canopy bed.

"Yes," Sisi said, pulling back the goosedown blanket and climbing into bed. Valerie was tucked happily into the Possi nursery with Ida sleeping nearby, and Sisi longed for nothing more than to be here, beside Néné. Here in this room where she'd slept the sleep of the innocent, where she'd dreamed without knowing that dreams didn't actually come true.

"It's like old days," Ludovika said, her graying hair woven tight around her bedtime curling papers. "How nice to have my two girls together once more. I don't doubt that you'll stay up half the night whispering and giggling, as you always did."

"Good night, Mamma," Sisi said, suppressing a yawn.

"And don't forget . . ." Ludovika said from the door.

"We know," the sisters replied in unison. "We shall not forget to say our prayers."

"Good girls." With that, Ludovika shut the door, closing them into silence and the dim lighting of their two candles.

Sisi burrowed deeper into the bed. "Néné! Your feet are still cold." She felt the icy shapes of her sister's feet as Néné pushed them under Sisi's legs, just as she'd always done as a girl.

Néné giggled. "Well, you'll warm them up."

"Just like old days, indeed," Sisi said, not at all irritated.

"And let's hope that *you* don't still snore," Néné answered.

"Snore?" Sisi gasped. "I never snored! I *don't* snore."

Néné cocked a dark eyebrow, a teasing smirk on her shadowed face.

"What? I don't!" Sisi insisted. And then, after a pause, she asked: "Do I?"

"Franz never told you that you snore?" Helene burrowed into the pillow, her face op-

147

posite Sisi's. Close enough to see Sisi's features tighten at the question. *No, Franz wouldn't know that I snore,* Sisi thought. Not when they hadn't shared a bed in years.

Sisi looked around at the room, its furniture lumpy and sagging, its comforts so basic after the decadence of Vienna. Here, the bedside comb and mirror did not match, were not part of a flawlessly engraved ivory set. The mirror hung cracked and in need of dusting, where in Vienna, her mirrors were trimmed in gold leaf, her mantels carved from glossy marble. "Do you know," Sisi said aloud, "that in the palace back in Vienna, even our chamber pots are engraved with the Habsburg imperial seal? The double-headed eagle of the House of Habsburg."

"Ah," Néné said, "lest you forget your divine-right status while nature calls."

Both girls giggled, but Sisi wondered: Did Helene ever think of Franz? Of Sisi and the palace? Did she ever think about how her own life might have been so different had *she* been the one to marry Franz, as Archduchess Sophie had intended? Doubtful, Sisi reasoned. Néné had never wanted that life, the life beside the emperor. She'd never wanted the role that Sisi had so willingly — so naïvely — stepped into. And now here they both were, back home at Possi, with their lives as far apart as two lives could be.

Sisi's eyes fell on the windows that opened

148

over the darkened fields and black Bavarian night. In the distance, a lone owl droned its melancholy cry into the surrounding pines. How many evenings she had lain awake in this exact spot unable to find sleep, her restless mind wandering. Her imagination craving adventure, to travel someplace far. To find love and leave home and seek out whatever it was that she had thought she was missing. Why hadn't she just enjoyed being *here*? Being home? Being safe and free.

She was about to confess these very thoughts to her sister, but Helene's voice interrupted her reverie. "Sisi, I need to talk to you about something."

Sisi turned back toward her sister, alarmed to see an intense flicker in Néné's eyes where her black irises were illuminated by the dim candlelight.

"There's something you should know," Néné whispered, her tone suddenly low and serious.

"What is it?"

Helene exhaled. "It's just that . . . I don't think . . . well, I don't think you should bring Valerie with you tomorrow when you visit Ludwig."

Sisi shifted under the bedcovers, slightly relieved. That had hardly been what she had expected to hear from her sister. "To see Ludwig? Whyever not? I bring Valerie everywhere I go."

"No." Helene shook her head, an assertive movement, a very uncharacteristic gesture for the timid Néné. "Not tomorrow, not up to that mountaintop. It would be far too frightening for a child."

"Frightening?" Sisi pushed back the blanket. "Néné, you are confusing me."

Helene chewed on her lower lip, her black eyes catching the quiver of her candle's flame, giving her an almost otherworldly look. Like some sort of conjurer beside a sorcerer's fire. "You will find Ludwig quite changed," Helene said, her expression grim.

From somewhere outside the castle walls, a wolf howled, sending its eerie dirge out into the dark Bavarian wilderness. It was a familiar sound from the nights of her childhood, and yet, at hearing it, Sisi felt her frame begin to shiver.

"Ludwig is not as you remember him," Helene continued. "He's not the golden boy of our youth. He's become quite . . ."

"Ludwig was always eccentric." Sisi shook her head, confident in her memories of the romantic young prince. Forcing herself to feel that confidence now. "He was always a dreamer. Passionate enough to make me look stodgy and reasonable in comparison." Sisi kept her tone light, but there was no way to ignore the heavy, wide-eyed look Helene offered in response.

"No, Sisi, there is eccentric, and then there

150

is something else. . . ." Helene held Sisi's gaze for a moment without saying anything, as if she were picking her words carefully. And then, at last, she leaned close and whispered the words: "They call him Mad King Ludwig."

★ ★ ★

Sisi narrowed her eyes, trying to peer through the thick black forest of pine and fir that bordered the steep lane, as if through increased effort her vision might pierce the impenetrable forest wall. But no, she could not see farther than an arm's length to either side of the road, so densely packed were the trees.

"It can't be much farther up this hill now," Sisi said, turning back toward Marie and Ida. The two women let their pinched expressions serve as reply even though they dared not voice their concerns aloud.

The three of them were riding in one of Ludwig's covered carriages. Her cousin, on receiving word that Sisi wished to pay a visit to his new cliff-top castle, had insisted on sending his own carriage. "You'll never find the palace otherwise," he had written. "I must insist — my sense of chivalry will not allow you to get lost atop the Bavarian peaks."

Yet his sense of chivalry would allow him to repeatedly jilt her sister? But Sisi had accepted the offer and had climbed in when his coach had arrived at Possi that morning.

True to Ludwig's sensibilities, it was an outrageously lavish conveyance, burnished in gilt. Carved angels sat on its top, their flawless naked bodies raising a massive crown skyward. The four white horses that pulled it, themselves elegantly adorned in golden tassels, now panted as they led Sisi and her attendants up a meandering mountain lane that seemed to have no end.

Overhead, the canopy of pine and fir needles grew thick and close, creating a damp tunnel all around them. The air hung cold and dark, redolent with the scent of bark and sap and sweet pine. Higher and higher they climbed, the ladies across from Sisi seeming to share her confusion — and mounting unease — as the coach spiraled farther upward in the black forest.

"Perhaps Néné was right, after all," Sisi said, attempting a tone of levity. "Valerie might have been afraid of the wolves in these woods." She tried again to see through the dense wall of trees, as if by spotting the menaces that lurked nearby she might be made less frightened by them. She gave a silent prayer of thanks that the coach was covered and enclosed.

"It's not the wolves, Empress," Marie Festetics said, her voice hushed. "I'm more frightened of what awaits us at the top of this

152

mountain."

Sisi frowned at the countess, surprised by this uncharacteristic expression of dissatisfaction, however veiled it was. "Oh, don't tell me you pay any heed to the silly gossip," Sisi snapped, folding her hands in her lap. "Ludwig is a darling. I, for one, am very eager to see him."

"Of course, Your Majesty," Marie said, chastened. Beside her, Ida, ever obedient, avoided Sisi's eyes and stared out the window.

But Néné was the opposite of silly and the furthest thing from a gossip; Sisi had never known her sensible, circumspect elder sister to utter a negative remark about anyone. Even the Archduchess Sophie. The fact that even Néné had expressed concerns over Ludwig's recent behavior told Sisi that perhaps all was not as it should be at the top of the mountain they now climbed.

And what was best for her younger sister? Sophie-Charlotte would be removed from the entire world if she moved up here as Ludwig's bride. Sisi couldn't help but feel troubled; she couldn't deny that her dread thickened as the forest around her did, and as the road continued to wind skyward.

Finally, after what felt to Sisi like an eternity, the forest wall seemed to thin out, with patches of blue sky becoming visible ahead. Sisi sat up, relieved as she looked out the window at the scene that opened before her.

She saw for the first time just how high they were. Far below, a stretch of green pastures came into view. And then, just ahead, at the top of the craggy cliff before them, Sisi caught her first glimpse of Neuschwanstein Castle.

The first thought to strike Sisi was that such a building defied explanation. It was a colossal structure of white stone perched atop the summit; in keeping with its name, "New Swan Stone," it appeared like a massive white body poised in momentary rest atop the weather-beaten peak, waiting to spread its wings and take flight into the sky that encircled it.

"Oh!" Sisi pulled a hand to her mouth as she gasped. She noted that, across from her, the two attendants were struck just as speechless by the sudden appearance of the castle.

"It's remarkable!" Marie said after a moment, her jaw falling open.

And it was. Neuschwanstein was the most extraordinary structure Sisi had ever beheld. Even in her tours of the ancient ruins at Corfu and Egypt and Rome, she had never seen this castle's equal. That such a palace existed — its ornamentation as delicate as the ethereal mists that enshrouded it, and yet, its frame sturdy enough to blend so flawlessly with the stone peak out of which it sprung — eluded logic. Sisi couldn't help but gape.

The coach sped past a red gatehouse, and

Sisi noticed the uniformed attendants peeking up at her as she passed, eager to catch a glimpse of the famously beautiful empress. The horses trotted up the remainder of the steep drive, and they rolled to a halt before the largest front door Sisi had ever seen.

Birdsong filled the air around her now as Sisi was helped out of the coach. She was amazed that the birds had managed to ascend to this remote height; she looked down on the entire world from up here, with even the neighboring peaks appearing like distant lowlands far beneath them. And yet, as high as she was, the castle vaulted upward even higher before her.

Everything about the building and its setting gave a sense of the vertical, of the soaring climb toward the heavens. The castle was a spectacle of pointed turrets, arches, and vaulted towers. Ludwig, the dreamer, the romantic — even he, with his penchant for bold proclamations and fantastical language, had not overstated the majesty of his mountaintop masterpiece. Oh, perhaps Sophie-Charlotte wasn't as unlucky as Sisi had feared her to be!

Before the front door hung a large plaque, and the words carved into it were so typically Ludwig that Sisi could practically hear her cousin bellowing the greeting: WELCOME WANDERERS! GENTLE LADIES! PUT YOUR CARES ASIDE! LET YOUR SOUL GIVE ITSELF

"Ludwig is not mad; he's just misunderstood," Sisi said, thinking aloud as she was ushered through the door, her mood soaring as high as the towers of this castle. If building such a home as this made a person mad, then she would gladly accept a similar diagnosis. Didn't one *have* to be a bit mad to conceive of such a spectacular place as this? And then, what's more, to turn it into reality? It reminded her anew of why she had always loved Ludwig so much, why she had admired his indomitable spirit, his limitless dreams. It was all so romantic; she even wished Franz might be touched by a bit of this same madness.

As Sisi stepped through the opened doorway, she heard Ludwig's voice before she located him. "Sisi!" Her host stood in the front hallway of his castle, clearly expecting her, and his appearance so distracted Sisi that she fixed her eyes on him before taking in any more of her surroundings.

"Oh, she's here! She's here!" Ludwig skipped toward her, his tall frame a riot of colored silk and giddy energy. "The empress is here! Let the joyous news be proclaimed from my mountaintop!" Ludwig was well built, the tallest man she knew other than Andrássy. At well over six feet, he crossed the room in several strides.

"Hello, my dear cousin," Sisi said, smiling

at him. Ludwig's clothing made her — a famously elaborate dresser — feel bland in comparison. He wore cropped breeches of soft blue velvet and rose-colored stockings underneath them. A flouncy cape draped over his broad shoulders, and his hair looked as if it had been coiffed and curled with the same attention that she herself paid to her toilette.

Sophie-Charlotte called Ludwig handsome. Yes, Sisi thought, she supposed he was handsome. He had Sisi's coloring, and in fact, the villagers and farmers had always thought them brother and sister when they were together as children in Possenhofen. They had the same bright hazel eyes, long lashed and almond shaped. They had the same hair, golden in their youth, thick and chestnut colored now. Though he was not necessarily virile or swarthy in the imposing way Andrássy was, no one could deny the beauty of Ludwig's features, the flawlessness of the way he groomed himself.

"Sisi, oh, I am dizzy with delight at seeing you!" Ludwig took her in his arms, spinning her around as his uninhibited giggles echoed off the muraled walls. As she spun in his embrace, Sisi's eyes took in the whirling view of frescoed figures, glistening chandeliers, and high-vaulted ceilings.

"It's marvelous to see you, too." Ludwig lowered her to her feet, and Sisi waved Marie and Ida forward so she could introduce them.

As Ludwig greeted the ladies, Sisi looked once more over her cousin, studying this buoyant man who seemed perfectly content to live alone at the top of the world.

"You look splendid, Sisi, as always. I told the servants, I said, 'Now, be prepared to fall in love today, for my cousin is known as the most beautiful woman alive.' "

With that, Ludwig giggled again, and Sisi lowered her eyes to the floor. "You look very fine, too, my dear cousin." Her eyes couldn't help but study his wide-legged pants and his colorful pink hose.

"Do you like this?" Ludwig spread his arms wide. "I'm dressed as a troubadour today."

Sisi nodded. Perhaps Ludwig simply needed human company. Perhaps this mountaintop was so lonely and isolated that he was bored — growing eccentric for lack of outlets for stimulation or diversion. She commented, "On the way up, Lud, we felt as if we would climb —"

"Forever and ever," Ludwig interjected, rocking in his heeled shoes. "Up, up, up! So" — Ludwig waved his hands around, his heavily ringed fingers fluttering, adding to the cacophony of color that Sisi's eyes now tried to take in — "what do you think of my humble abode?"

"What do I think? I think I'm a bit stunned. My word . . . Ludwig, it's magnificent."

Ludwig clapped, delighted to have her approval. "And you haven't even seen anything. How about *le grand tour*?" At that, Ludwig took Sisi's hand in his own and set off at a skip, pulling her toward a hallway so long that she could barely make out its end. Marie and Ida jogged behind, attempting to keep pace with Ludwig's long-legged strides.

They swept past room after room, each one grand and imposing, each one large and lavish enough to serve as a ballroom, even by the standards of the snobbiest court — Vienna's. Only, Sisi suspected that Ludwig did not intend to host many balls here at Neuschwanstein. One did not build one's castle so far removed from society if one craved a steady stream of guests and visitors in one's halls.

Ludwig had pleaded incompletion of his castle as his reason for not being ready to marry, but the structure Sisi now saw appeared nearly finished. She supposed she could see the incompletion if she looked closely: figures only half painted on the colorful murals, chandeliers not yet stocked with candles, floorboards still being laid and polished and buffed. But certainly Sophie-Charlotte would not be in any way uncomfortable if she were to move here.

They walked on. Behind her, Sisi could hear poor Marie Festetics panting. Ludwig, on the other hand, seemed to be growing more effervescent as he guided them on, and

159

his voice bounced off the interminable corridor as he chattered. "I wanted hallways long enough that I could race my horses down them. I've succeeded, haven't I?"

Sisi gave her cousin a sideways glance, certain that he was teasing. But though he smiled, there was nothing about his expression to indicate that he had made a joke.

"And, at night, sometimes I suit up in my armor, and I pick a lucky servant to do the same, and we mount our steeds and joust in these hallways. We pretend we are medieval knights on the quest for the Holy Grail. Isn't that marvelous? Ah, here we are, the stairs! Prepare to climb." Ludwig took the first two steps at a leap. The ladies followed behind, Sisi growing tired and short of breath even though she imagined herself in better condition than most people of her age, thanks to her strenuous horseback riding. Poor Marie was now wheezing behind the empress.

"Ludwig, wait," Sisi said, pausing on the endless stairway. "Perhaps Ida and Marie should wait for us downstairs? We've had a tiring trip. They might prefer to rest."

"Fine." Ludwig didn't seem to care, and didn't wish to be delayed. Sisi nodded and let the attendants go down as she reluctantly continued her climb, picking up her pace to try to keep up with her cousin. At the top of the stairway, Ludwig raised a hand like a conductor, his breath barely labored. *"Après vous,* after you, *ma belle cousine."*

At the top he directed her into a room, this one the biggest space Sisi had seen yet. "The Singers' Hall," Ludwig proclaimed, looking around with proprietary pride. Sisi, still panting from the dash up the stairs, couldn't help but gasp anew. They were at the top of one of the castle's soaring towers, and the entire wall was made of windows so that they had a panoramic view of the world below.

Sisi may have thought that they were high up before, but this was an even more remarkable vista. Looking north, she peered out over jagged peaks dotted with fir trees and a wispy mist that hugged the seam where the mountains met the sky. Beyond the mountains curved a shimmering ribbon of blue, the gentle river carving its way through rural countryside and green pastures.

The room itself was almost as staggeringly beautiful as the view it afforded. The roof soared overhead, covered with crimson and gold panels. On the panels were painted angels and saints and demons and dragons, supernatural figures locked in an epic battle for the earth below. Sisi couldn't decide which side looked more beautiful — the armies fighting for God or the armies fighting for Satan.

The wall space that wasn't pierced with pristine floor-to-ceiling windows bore a series of frescoes. Sisi studied them now, intrigued, but unsure of their meaning. "The quest," Ludwig said, standing over her shoulder to survey the scenes alongside her, "for the Holy Grail. It's just as Richard —"

Sisi turned and saw how Ludwig's golden eyes flickered, flashing with a quick burst of lightning as he spoke the name of the world-famous composer Richard Wagner.

"Richard wrote about the quest in his opera *Lohengrin.*" With that, Ludwig raised a hand, gently touching the image, stroking the cheek of the delicately painted knight.

For the first time since she'd arrived, Sisi noticed, her cousin wasn't bouncing or fidgeting or darting giddily about — Ludwig stood completely still. Transfixed. Staring longingly at the mural inspired by his friend and composer. When he spoke again, Ludwig's previously feverish voice was soft, even tender: "I wanted this room to be a place where he could come to be inspired."

Sisi swallowed, turning away from the vivid mural and glancing back toward the windows, staring out over the expansive wilderness below. A bird soared beneath the castle's clifftop peak, and it looked as if it was a world away, so far below them it flew.

Ludwig's achievement was remarkable, Sisi had to concede it. Here his most outlandish fantasies had been made solid; through sweat and masonry and his millions, Ludwig had turned his wild thoughts and illogical dreams into stone and marble and fresco. The result was nothing short of breathtaking. One had to be a bit mad to conceptualize such a place, Sisi reasoned. And even more so to have the audacity to build it once it had been imagined.

"Sisi?"

She turned now, back toward her cousin. "Yes?"

"Can we go down?"

"Yes, of course. Is everything all right?"

Ludwig shrugged. "I don't like to be in this room without Richard; it makes me . . . well, I don't know. I suppose it makes me sad."

Once down from the tower, they traipsed along the interminable hallway in the other direction. "Remember how I told you that I wanted the hallways to be long enough to ride horses in them?"

"Yes." Sisi nodded, wondering how she would ever find her attendants among these endless corridors.

"Well, it was making it very difficult for the servants to serve me a warm meal. The food always grew cold on the long journey from the kitchens to my table. So you'll see the solution I conceived!" Ludwig, his high spirits apparently recovered, now ushered Sisi into a monstrously oversized dining hall where the longest table she had ever seen was set for two — one chair at each end of the sprawling table. She would need to shout in order for him to hear her.

They took their places at opposite ends, and Ludwig stood, holding his hands aloft like a conductor. Sisi noticed there was no food on the table. Then, with a flourish of his wrists, he shouted, "*Tischleindeckdich!* Table, lay yourself!"

At that command, the table disappeared, sinking into the very floor on which it had stood an instant earlier. Sisi watched in open-mouthed silence, dumbfounded, as the table reappeared through the floor a moment later, its previously bare surface now heaped with steaming platters.

"Isn't it splendid?" Ludwig clapped, his high-pitched voice sounding distant at the far end of the table. "It was my very own idea!"

"But . . . how?" Sisi stared at the now fully set table before her.

"They said it couldn't be done, but I told them to find a way! The kitchens are right below us, so we simply lower the table down, they load it up, and *voilà*!"

Now servants appeared, as if themselves emerging through the walls, and they transferred food from the porcelain platters onto a plate, which they placed before Sisi. "Thank you," she said, looking up at the footmen before her. Even her cousin's servants were beautiful — each one more attractive than the most well-groomed courtiers in Vienna.

"Won't you be eating with me?" Sisi asked, noting how no one placed a plate before Ludwig.

"No." He shook his head. "I take my lunch at midnight."

Sisi cocked her head to the side, wondering, once more, whether he was joking.

Ludwig waved a hand. "I keep all sorts of strange hours these days. I'm only awake right now because I didn't want to miss a minute of your visit!"

A footman appeared beside Sisi and poured her wine. He might have had the most beautiful face she had ever seen. She waited until the servant stepped out of the room and then glanced at her cousin. "My, Ludwig, these attendants of yours. Each one is more attractive than the next."

"Of course! You wouldn't imagine me to have *ugly* servants, would you?" Ludwig blinked in exaggerated horror — or was he being perfectly earnest? Sisi could not tell.

"It was the first command I gave as king," he continued, staring idly at his tidy fingernails, adjusting his colorful rings. "I sacked all of Daddy's and Mummy's ugly servants and replaced them all with the finest young grooms that Bavaria had to offer."

Sisi sipped her wine.

"Oh, and see this?" Ludwig flicked his wrist, calling out the word "Flowers!" Just then an enormous vase of blooms emerged, as if on a set of ropes and pulleys, from under the table.

"Now I can't see you," Sisi said, shifting in her chair, trying to see around the sprawling floral arrangement.

"Precisely the point. I arranged this so that if I *have* to dine with ugly guests, I don't have to look at their faces. I wish only to be surrounded by beauty."

Sisi frowned, relieved that her cousin couldn't see her puzzled reaction to such an outlandish statement.

"But of course, such measures are hardly necessary with you as my companion!" Ludwig clapped, and the vase was removed by one of his handsome manservants. "Why, your face, Sisi — I could look on it all day. One of the reasons why I love you so much."

"Thank you," Sisi said, adjusting her napkin in her lap. She gazed at the food before her but felt very little appetite. And where had Ida and Marie gone off to? She hoped that one of Ludwig's beautiful servants would make sure they were served luncheon.

"But enough about me." Ludwig's voice practically echoed, he sat so far away. Sisi realized that this distance, like everything else in the palace, was by design. He must have had it in mind when he commissioned the largest dining room table she had ever seen. "How are you, Sisi? Your farm in Hungary sounds delightful, as you describe it. I should like to come visit you there."

"I fear you'd find Gödöllő terribly plain in comparison to this."

"Plain? Nothing about you could ever be plain to me, Sisi."

"You are kind."

"And how's . . . the *Austrian*?" Ludwig always used that nickname for Franz. Ever since catching wind of the early marital discord between Sisi and Franz Joseph, he'd become fiercely mistrusting of the emperor.

"Franz is doing well. Thank you for asking. He's the same as ever. Duty bound, over-worked."

"That man needs to learn to take more amusement."

Sisi sighed. She might have said a similar thing, but it didn't seem like the same point coming from Ludwig. "My little daughter, Valerie, is a great joy to me. In fact, I wanted to bring her with me so that you could meet her. Perhaps I'll bring her next time."

"Oh, I wish you wouldn't!" Ludwig gasped, as if disturbed by the thought. Then seeing the wounded look on Sisi's face, he clarified: "Not that I wouldn't love her. I'm sure I'd love her, because she is a part of you. But . . . it's just that . . . well, children make me so terribly uncomfortable. How they frighten me!"

Curious, Sisi thought, considering the concern Helene had expressed, the fear that

167

Ludwig would have frightened the child. And considering his bright pink stockings and fancifully curled hair and sudden outbursts of hysterical laughter, she suspected that Helene had been correct.

But even as Ludwig uttered these bizarre remarks, there seemed to be nothing deliberately malicious or hurtful in their delivery. He meant no offense and seemed oblivious of the fact that he might cause any. He had the unselfconsciousness of a child, a trait usually shed sometime around adolescence but preserved, somehow, in him. It was the self-assured frankness of someone who was never opposed, someone with whom no one ever dared to disagree or argue.

Something like Franz, Sisi realized — though that was as far as any similarity between the two men extended. Perhaps, she reasoned, it was a trait unique to sovereigns. Babies who, from the time they were in the royal nursery, heard only *Yes, Your Highness* and *If it pleases Your Highness.* Sisi saw, suddenly, the risk that she might become that way, as she recalled how she often glared at Marie when the countess ventured to express even the slightest disagreement. And Ida never even dared. Sisi decided then to always surround herself with people who would disagree with her. Andrássy, she thought. Andrássy would dare to challenge her. All the more reason she needed him in her life.

Ludwig prattled on at the distant end of the table, unaware of her daydreaming. Sisi pulled her focus back to her cousin, listening as he said, "I remember how Daddy had me flogged once, when I was little. It was because I was rude. We had this *hideous* manservant — I was positively petrified of his pockmarked face. Whenever he'd appear in the room, I'd turn away in horror and shut my eyes. Daddy told me to stop and to apologize, but I wouldn't. So he had me whipped."

Sisi nodded without offering a reply, taking another sip of wine instead.

"Richard is not beautiful . . . in the traditional sense," Ludwig said, his voice suddenly softening.

"Oh?" Sisi picked up her fork and forced herself to dig into the slaw before her.

"No, at least, his body isn't. Not in the way that you and I are beautiful," Ludwig continued, his tone guilelessly frank. "And yet, I've never known a soul to be more embodied in beauty. With Richard . . . ah, with Richard, I don't look and see a body. With Richard, I look, and I see the divine."

"Excuse me, Your Majesty?" A footman knocked at the door.

"I told you not to interrupt me when I am with my cousin." Ludwig sighed, throwing an irked look at the servant.

"Yes, I apologize, Your Majesty. . . ." The footman cast his gaze downward. "But, begging Your Grace's pardon, Your Majesty also said that we were to bring this to you — the moment it arrived. A parcel from Herr Richard Wagner."

"It came?" Ludwig's voice climbed an octave, taking on a shaky, quivery quality. "Oh, it's here! Glorious, glorious news!" Ludwig sprung from his chair and flew across the length of the room, running to the servant and taking the package from the man's outstretched hands.

"Oh, Sisi, forgive me. I must go," Ludwig said, his rouged cheeks flushing an even deeper red. "I must leave you at once. I have been waiting for Richard's pages. Oh, I have been waiting an *eternity*. Eat, drink! Enjoy your feast! I shall find you later. But now . . . now I must . . ." And without another word, Ludwig fled from the room, leaving Sisi alone with her barely touched lunch plate, her mind filled with the story her sister had told her — about how Ludwig had left her at the ball in the middle of a waltz, without so much as an explanation.

Hours passed, and the afternoon wore on as Sisi looked out over the world beneath Ludwig's remote peak. Given how dark and unwelcoming the trail had been during the bright daylight, descending those desolate, winding roads at night struck Sisi as something to be avoided at any cost. But the thought of spending the night here, alone with her cousin on this remote summit — Sisi felt a chill even considering it.

So as the afternoon slipped away and the sun dropped closer to the horizon far beneath them, Sisi redoubled her efforts to find her cousin and have her intended chat with him before taking her leave and returning to the cozy, welcoming world of Possenhofen.

Sisi knew that her cousin had received some pages from the composer Wagner and that he had fled to read them, presumably to some private place. Knowing his affinity for all things beautiful, she had supposed such a place would be outside where he might commune with the nature she knew he loved. But as she traipsed the environs of the palace on foot, Sisi did not find Ludwig anywhere among the grounds or gardens. Thwarted, she returned inside.

She scoured the long hallways but didn't find Ludwig in any of the oversized rooms. She climbed several winding stairways but found him in none of his towers. Finally, back in the front hall, having been unable to locate even a footman who might direct her to Ludwig, Sisi found a narrow passage almost like a secret corridor. She followed it.

As she walked on, Sisi had the sense that she was walking deeper and deeper into the chilly stone structure, as if tunneling toward the center of the castle. And then, the candlelit corridor gave way, and she was in a massive hall, a space at once cavernous and celestial.

Sisi gasped on entering the hall, and she chided herself for being so consistently astounded by Ludwig's rooms. By now, shouldn't she expect nothing but glorious fantasy and impractical lavishness? But this room surpassed all the others. The ceiling flew high overhead, a dramatic dome of shimmering blue with the sun and stars twinkling across it. Beneath her, the floor was painted in a swirling scene of grass and greenery and flowers, with every animal present in the Garden of Eden romping and playing. Sisi felt wrong treading on such flawless art. The walls around her, too, were covered in glorious frescoes: lions, the symbolic beasts of Bavaria, growled and roared, as massive images of Jesus Christ and the Virgin Mary gazed out over the sprawling hall.

At the heart of the room was a flight of marble steps. Sisi's eyes traveled upward with them to a broad platform carved out of an alcove. It was almost like an altar, or a stage, Sisi thought; there, in a prostrate heap, reclined her cousin. "Ludwig?" Her voice echoed off of the cold walls and domed ceiling. He didn't look up as Sisi approached, her heels clicking on the floor. He didn't even acknowledge her as she climbed the marble steps and approached him.

172

"Ludwig?" She didn't know if he was sleeping, weeping, or simply ignoring her approach. Goosebumps pricked her flesh, and that was not due to the cold and damp of the room.

Ludwig moved for the first time when Sisi reached the top of the platform, and she saw the tears in his eyes, the anguish clouding his face. She looked at the papers sprawled all around him, a jumbled flurry of poetry and musical notes. Had this package been the source of his present devastation? "Ludwig, what's the matter? Why do you weep?" She knelt beside him.

"This!" Ludwig held up a piece of paper and threw it skyward as his head dropped once more, too heavy for his neck. He cupped his face in his hands.

Sisi put a hand on his broad shoulder, comforting him as she might do for Rudy, but he shrugged her off. And then, he looked up at her, his amber eyes blazing as if touched by otherworldly flames. "He did it again! Do you believe it? He did it again!"

Sisi wasn't certain to what her cousin was referring, but she resisted the urge to back away, to flee this room and run back down the mountain to Possi and her mother and her darling baby, Valerie.

Ludwig took her hand, pulling her toward him. The force of his grip frightened Sisi; she was certain that, should she need to, she would not be able to rend herself free from Ludwig's hold. But when he spoke now, his voice was a gentle whisper: "This changes everything." Fresh tears gathered in his beautiful, flickering eyes.

"I'm sorry, Ludwig, I don't . . . I don't understand." She tugged, but her hand did not move within his clutch.

"This!" Ludwig released her and picked up another piece of paper from the pile scattered around him, hurling the sheet into the air. Then he did it with another, and then another, so that sheets of white paper covered in musical notes rained down about them. "Sisi, he said he could do it, and I believed him. Of course I believed! I, alone in this world, believed him. And now he's done it."

Sisi looked, confused, at the papers falling to the floor around her. She picked up the nearest sheet and read the words at the top: "Der Ring des Nibelungen." She said the name aloud: "The Ring of the Nibelung."

Hearing the words spoken aloud caused Ludwig to shudder in a fit of excited energy, like a supplicant in the midst of some trance-like communion with his deity. He sprung to his feet, wringing his hands before her. "Don't you see? Richard and I . . . we are about to change the entire course of musical history."

Ludwig's eyes blazed as he looked at her, his irises shining brighter than the glistening sun and stars painted overhead. "No, forget musical history . . . *history* itself. We are about to change all of history!"

"Of course." Sisi stood slowly, being sure to keep her tone calm and measured. "Ludwig, would you come with me?" She pointed down the marble stairs. "Let's take a walk. There's something about which I must speak to you."

Ludwig had told her there was one more room that she had to see, so Sisi suggested that they walk there now. He seemed to calm down, somewhat, as they strolled, and Sisi followed him in silence. Eventually he led her into a space that had the appearance of a museum. "Hello, my friends!" Ludwig called out, and Sisi half expected to see a crowd of people waiting for them. Instead, what she saw was a forest of marble busts — human heads on pedestals, staring at her with colorless eyes and impassive facial expressions.

"My collection of heads!" Ludwig said, cheerful once more after his weeping fit of a few moments earlier. My, how his emotions seesawed. He made her moodiness seem trivial in comparison.

Sisi looked over the collection, reading the plaques beneath the busts. She saw the face of Louis XIV, the French monarch who had called himself *le Roi-Soleil,* "the Sun King," the man who had given the world Versailles

175

Palace. No surprise that Ludwig admired him. And then there was a bust of Marie Antoinette, the infamous French queen who had lived in Versailles before losing her head at the guillotine. She was a Habsburg princess before all of that. *A great-aunt of Franz Joseph's,* Sisi thought. *Oh God, what would Franz think if he saw his cousin here?* She shuddered at the thought of what her reasonable husband would make of any of this.

"Here he is," Ludwig called out from across the room, waving Sisi toward a male bust. "I told you he was not beautiful." Ludwig stood before the likeness, his hands cupping the marble cheeks of this face as he might caress a lover.

"No, Richard, you aren't so beautiful, are you?" Ludwig spoke directly to the bust, his voice soaring an octave higher than was natural. "So serious all the time. This frown. Oh, but I think you are the most beautiful thing I have ever seen!" And with that, Ludwig placed a kiss on Wagner's brow and trotted on to the next bust.

"But where is it? Oh, you have to see, Sisi." Ludwig pounced and swerved around the pedestals, seeming to search for one face in particular. "Ah! Yes, here it is!" Ludwig paused now. Sisi followed him and saw the bust before which he stood, her breath momentarily catching in her lungs when she realized she was staring at her own face.

"Here *you* are." Ludwig leaned toward her marble likeness, giggling and making faces as one might before a baby one hoped to make smile. "She's pretty, my Sisi! This is for when I miss you. When you are so far away, with the *Austrian.*"

Sisi, on realizing that he meant to pay her the highest of compliments, recovered her composure. "My, Ludwig, thank you. But . . . however did you manage it?"

"I went on and on and on about your beauty. I showed the sculptor your portrait. I think he did you justice. Do you approve?"

"Do I? Well, I believe that you did me more than justice. I think you have improved upon the real thing."

"Nonsense!" Ludwig tossed his curly-haired head back and tittered.

Sisi looked once more at the bust, then at the one immediately to its right. Was it yet another likeness of her? But no, that was a bust of Sophie-Charlotte. Ludwig's fiancée. And suddenly Sisi recalled her purpose. "Ludwig, you have my sister as well! Sophie-Charlotte. My, she is quite pretty, isn't she?"

"Hmm?" Ludwig turned reluctantly from the bust of Sisi to the marble likeness of Sophie-Charlotte beside it. "Oh, yes. A lovely girl." And then he sighed, walking from the row of statues to the window, where he looked out over the world, his mood suddenly deflated.

Sisi followed him, her voice quiet and calm as she spoke. "Surely you know that I must ask, Ludwig, what is happening? Why do you avoid her?"

He turned to Sisi after several moments, his eyes no longer glowing. "She's a nice girl. A lovely girl."

"And yet?"

Ludwig sighed again. "Do you know how I first came to know about Richard's work?"

"Please, enough about Richard Wagner. Won't you please answer my question?"

"I *am*," he protested.

Sisi frowned, confused.

"I first learned about Richard's work at your home," Ludwig said.

"At Possi?"

He nodded. "Your father had left some of Richard's sheet music on the pianoforte at Possenhofen. I saw it when I was a young boy . . . shortly after you had moved to Vienna. Married the *Austrian*. I was so sad. I missed you terribly; I hated to be at Possenhofen without you. But then . . . that day . . . everything changed."

"But what does this have to do with Sophie-Charlotte?"

"Your sister is a lovely girl."

"Yes, you keep saying that."

"Well, it's only natural, given the fact that your father, my dear uncle, first introduced

178

me to Richard's genius, that I would want one of his daughters to be my wife."

Sisi turned away, swallowing hard as she clutched the windowsill at which they stood. She saw a distant bird flying beneath them, and her mind circled and swerved in a similar loop.

"Your sister was always so charming and welcoming when I would visit your home. We would have nice enough conversations. But then . . . one day . . . she played the piano for me. I asked her if she could play Wagner, and her face lit up. She loved his music as much as I did! Or . . . *almost* as much as I did."

Sisi listened in silence, the situation becoming clearer with each of Ludwig's impassioned words.

"We would sit for hours at the piano, side by side, while she played and sang for me. She's truly talented, your sister. And his music? His music puts me into such a state of divine intoxication. I think that was it. Sophie was playing it for me, and I became utterly intoxicated. . . . I mistook the love aroused by *him* as love intended for *her.*"

Sisi nodded, crossing her arms before her breast. Eventually, she asked: "But why did you propose marriage, Ludwig?"

He turned away from her, leaning forward and pressing his brow into the glass of the window as he looked down at the cliff drop below. "Your mother saw the way I gravitated toward your sister. The way I visited and sought her out. And she saw how Sophie returned my affection. She pulled me aside one day and told me how Sophie felt. She guessed at my feelings, too, mistaking them for romantic love. She told me that it had gone on long enough. That Sophie could have any number of suitors and that it wasn't fair for me to toy with her. That either we must get engaged, or I must cut all ties and allow her to find love elsewhere."

Sisi's head was spinning as she imagined her mother — her protective, practical, well-meaning mother — doing precisely what Ludwig now described.

"I realized then how far down that road I had allowed myself to travel, so enraptured was I by Sophie's and my common passion. I felt genuine sympathy for Sophie, who I knew loved me. And I feared losing her. So . . ." Ludwig shrugged once, an irresolute gesture. "But . . . as with any intoxication . . . a feeling of disgust follows in the morning. Regret. And I do regret what I've done, what I must do, to poor Sophie-Charlotte."

Sisi considered this, her mind racing to understand all the twists of this fruitless love story. She should have felt sadness, knowing the disappointment her sister would experience. As well as embarrassment for her family members, who would no doubt face a public scandal when King Ludwig jilted his

180

bride. And yet, all that Sisi felt in that moment was an overwhelming sense of relief — both for Sophie-Charlotte and for Ludwig. Relief at knowing that they could avoid a loveless marriage that would have imprisoned them both, made them both so very unhappy.

Exhaling heavily, she said, "But it's what's best." And it was; Sisi was sure of it. "My sister is a strong girl. She will recover from this."

"You think so?" Ludwig asked, turning to Sisi with a pained look.

"Yes. This is what's best for both of you."

Ludwig nodded, his face slackening with relief. He sighed, lifting his hands and placing them over his heart. "And surely she must know, in her heart — well, I never pretended to care about her more than I care about him. She knows of the . . . friendship . . . I feel for him."

"Does Wagner . . . Richard . . . share your feelings of . . . friendship?" Sisi asked.

"I think so," Ludwig said, his voice suddenly faint. "At least, I certainly hope so. Sometimes it maddens me the way he avoids me. I build this place just for him; I take note of every detail, large and small, all with only one question in mind: will it please Richard? I have designed it to his exact desires, using his own words as my blueprint, hoping to draw him to me."

Ludwig gestured jerkily now, waving his

181

hands all around the room. When he spoke next, he sounded confused. "And yet, he always has some reason why he can't come to me. He always reminds me of his wife . . . as if I don't remember who she is!" Ludwig's voice was sour with resentment now. He paused a moment, sighing as he turned back to the bust of the composer. He walked toward it, and Sisi followed.

Standing before Wagner's likeness, Ludwig said, his voice quiet, "Sometimes I feel as if I only hear from him when he needs more money."

This confession struck Sisi, and she put her hands on her cousin's shoulder. "Then say no. If he ignores you, if he is ungrateful to you, don't continue to spend your fortune on his writing and his productions."

Ludwig shook his head, a sad smile of resignation spreading across his features.

"I mean it, Ludwig. Don't hurry to fund a new opera or build him a new theater every time he asks you for one. It's not fair of him to —"

But Ludwig held up a hand, pleading for her to be quiet. "It's useless, Sisi. Don't talk to me of that. I am powerless to say no to Richard." He sighed again, crossing his arms, his tall frame drooping as he stared at the marble face. "I would give my palaces, my entire fortune, my very life, if it allowed him to keep creating such beauty. He tells me I

182

am his guardian angel. I tell him that he is more than my guardian angel — he is my god."

Sisi had no words with which to respond. After a long pause, Ludwig shifted on his feet and walked down the aisle between the marble heads. When he arrived before the statue of Marie Antoinette, he paused, lifting a finger to trace the outline of her elaborate hairline. "I'm building a replica of Versailles. Did you know that? At Linderhof."

Sisi shook her head. She had heard that her cousin was millions in debt due to his lavish building projects and his patronage of Richard Wagner, but she had not heard that he was attempting to build a second Versailles. "Is it wise, Ludwig? Is it the right timing to undertake such a costly . . ."

"It will be a perfect imitation — only better," Ludwig said, stroking Marie Antoinette's stone cheek. "Isn't she beautiful? Sometimes I think, if I could have had her, then perhaps I would have been happy to marry. Her . . . or you. But no one else will do. No other female could have enticed me to marry."

★ ★ ★

Back at Possi, Sisi added her voice to the growing chorus of those who were urging Sophie-Charlotte to break off the engagement. Even the duchess came around to the

183

inevitability of a severing of ties once she heard Sisi's brief recounting of her visit to Neuschwanstein. Sisi didn't elaborate too much, didn't tell Sophie-Charlotte many of the specifics of her day spent with Ludwig. Perhaps she didn't want to entirely admit to the others, or even to herself, how disturbing she'd found her time with her beloved cousin. Perhaps she felt some need to protect Ludwig, to allow him peace on his mountaintop, where he would not be a menace to anyone but himself. But she did remain resolute in her belief that Sophie-Charlotte should end the engagement.

"I can't help but feel, Sophie-Charlotte, that it is for the best," Sisi said that evening, safely ensconced back in her childhood home.

"But . . . surely you don't mean —" the younger sister began, leaning forward to protest.

But Sisi continued: "I do mean it, my dear. Having visited Ludwig, and the place that you would call home, I now believe that you would find much more happiness elsewhere. Even that you have been saved, somehow, from a most undesirable fate." Sisi repeated that phrase, and others like it, many times in the days following her visit to Neuschwanstein and her return to Possi.

And yet, her sister still clung to the hope that her fiancé would amend his ways. Sisi, Néné, and their mother took turns sitting

184

beside the distraught girl, who had taken to her bed to weep for her absentee groom. Or perhaps it was the embarrassment more than the grief that drove Sophie-Charlotte to cling to the idea of Ludwig. But either way, the young bride seemed reluctant to give up on her dreams of happiness as Queen of Bavaria.

In the end, Sisi didn't need to convince Sophie-Charlotte to end it, as Ludwig wrote a letter doing just that. The news arrived several days after Sisi's visit to his castle. The letter was as overwrought and impassioned as Sisi would have expected, coming from him, but he had done the right thing.

Sisi remained at Possi for a few more days to comfort her sister; meanwhile, her heart flew to Budapest. She longed for the familiar and beloved countryside of Gödöllő. She longed for her horses and her freedom. But, even more, after the rigid months in Vienna and the draining days in Possenhofen and, especially, that bizarre and disheartening day she'd spent on Ludwig's cliff top, Sisi longed for Andrássy. She longed for his strong presence and his steady words and the calm certainty and equilibrium that he always restored for her.

She told her mother that, rather than return straight to Vienna, she and Valerie would instead go on for a brief visit to Gödöllő. She hadn't been there in far too long, and she wished to check on the stables and the household. Of course she longed for several weeks of strenuous riding, as well.

But Sisi's plans were disrupted the next afternoon when she received word from Franz Joseph — an urgent request from the emperor that his wife return to court. The Archduchess Sophie was in poor health and getting worse. Rudolf and Gisela were beside themselves to see their matriarch suffering and so often confined to her bed. Franz couldn't leave Vienna with his mother in this condition, but he missed his wife, and he begged the empress to return to her rightful place beside him and the children. Sisi's heart seethed with a tangle of conflicting desires and emotions as she read Franz's words. However, the postscript, as meaningless an afterthought as it must have been to Franz, flew off the page when Sisi read it.

Postscript: "I've appointed Count Andrássy as foreign minister of the crown and have asked him to relocate, for a time, to Vienna. He will be on hand at the palace to welcome you and provide your official greeting if I am indisposed at Mother's bedside."

Suddenly, Vienna didn't seem like such a terrible place to be after all.

IV

Where I am not, there lies happiness.
— HEINRICH HEINE,
SISI'S FAVORITE POET

Chapter 4

Schönbrunn Summer Palace, Vienna
Autumn 1871

But it was not Andrássy, as expected, who stood in the courtyard to greet Sisi. It was Franz Joseph and the two older children.

The court remained at the summer palace just outside of the city for the last few pleasant days. Though Sisi preferred this palace, with its cheery, lemon-yellow walls and its sprawling, flower-strewn gardens, the mood she felt from her family members was far from warm. "Hello, Elisabeth," Franz said, nodding to her before offering a perfunctory kiss on the cheek.

"Hello, Franz. How is your mother?"

"She is a strong woman," was all he offered by way of reply, and Sisi sensed that he was choking back further emotion — perhaps even tears.

"Rudy, darling." Sisi turned from her husband and leaned toward her son, taking in his serious face, his soft features crinkled in too-heavy worry for such a young boy.

"Mother." Rudy glanced sideways at his sister as if for reassurance. Then, turning back to Sisi, he added: "Welcome back. I trust that your travels were smooth?"

Sisi leaned back, so caught off guard was she by the stiffness, the formality of Rudy's reception. As if all the progress between them had gone cold during her time away. Perhaps he had not forgiven her for her sudden departure, her decision to take only Valerie with her. She straightened, turning now to Gisela. "Hello, my dear."

"Mother." Gisela's response was even chillier. The girl fixed her eyes — the same pale blue eyes as her father's, rimmed in red from tears over Sophie — on some distant point across the yard but offered no other greeting. Not entirely surprising, such brusqueness, but still, it saddened Sisi.

"Well, I am sorry that I've been away. I am eager to pay my respects to your mother," Sisi said, turning back to Franz where he stood, stiff and upright in his military uniform.

"She sleeps now. I think today has seen enough stimulation for her, what with all of the physicians and nurses surrounding her. Perhaps tomorrow will be better."

"As you wish," Sisi agreed.

"Right, then," Franz said, nodding. "I shall take the children back to her room now. We

189

will tell her that you will visit her bedside tomorrow." Franz made a small bow toward Sisi. "I've ordered a family dinner this evening in your honor. Mother won't be able to join, of course, but she knows that you are expected home, and she will be glad to see us off to a family meal. I will see you then."

And with that, the emperor turned, his children following devotedly behind him as he marched back toward the palace. Back toward the ailing woman whose loss they would all feel so much more deeply than her own. Sisi stood still in the courtyard, watching them recede, wondering why he had called her home.

★   ★   ★

Though word of the Archduchess Sophie's miraculous improvement spread throughout court, lifting the nobles' spirits and prompting prayers of thanksgiving, these celebrations were soon cut short. More troubling news followed shortly after, this time from beyond the palace walls, where the dark storm clouds of war had gathered to the west.

It was a damp, chilly evening in late autumn, several weeks after the court's relocation to the Hofburg for the winter. Sisi sat at dinner, having been summoned to a gathering that there'd been no opportunity to decline. While the court musicians stood in the far corner of the room, filling the space with their lilting waltz melodies, and while the table setting was as lavish and splendid as ever, with piles of sweetmeats and glistening platters of gilded bronze, the mood of the assembly was noticeably dour.

She looked across the table, waiting, like everyone else, for the emperor to speak. Between every few bites of food, Franz would pause to wipe at his mouth, or take a quick, tight-lipped sip of wine, before cutting back into his dinner. Without his initiation, no one else might utter the anxious words or voice the uneasy questions that rippled through their minds.

At last, Franz glanced out over the small group, his eyes noncommittal as he scanned two columns of concerned faces. "But for the grace of God . . ." Though he did not finish his sentence, Sisi and everyone else at the table knew precisely what he meant.

But for the grace of God, it would have been them suffering, in Vienna, as opposed to the Parisians. It could have been the Habsburgs besieged and dethroned by Otto von Bismarck's Prussians as opposed to Napoleon III and Eugénie. It could have been the fall of the Austro-Hungarian Empire as opposed to the fall of the French Empire.

It *had* been them only five years earlier, embarrassed and defeated by Prussian military might and Bismarck's cunning. And yet it was staggering now to read the headlines and hear the reports. To see how, in only a handful of years, Bismarck's forces had grown even stronger, making easy work of the legendary French army — believed just months earlier to be the strongest fighters in Europe and the world. And yet, now all the world could read how Prussian men and field guns had mowed down entire French divisions, capturing Emperor Napoleon in battle and swiping huge swaths of French land for themselves.

But it was the news that traveled to Vienna from Paris — more so than the news from the battlefields — that made Sisi shudder: tales of daytime murder and looting of the shops, accounts of Empress Eugénie being chased through the streets of the capital by the blood-lusting Prussians. How the French citizenry, surrounded and defenseless, had suffered during the long siege, forced to fend off the freezing weather by burning their furniture and combat starvation by eating rats and dogs in their city that prided itself on its unrivaled culinary tradition.

"This spells a very dark future," Franz said aloud to no one in particular, before wiping at his gnarled beard with his napkin.

A very dark future, perhaps, and a grim present. Sisi looked around the table now at the muted and stunned faces gathered for their decadent Austrian dinner. No one in any of Europe's ruling classes, the Habsburgs very much included, quite understood what had just happened. How Bismarck had so quickly and decisively handed the French defeat and, in doing so, established the new and formidable German Empire. How he had so swiftly wiped out the French Empire, knocked Austria from its place as the leading German entity, and upset the entire balance of power — not only in Europe, but in the world.

Franz Joseph stabbed absentmindedly at his dinner plate, his hands finding their way every few minutes to his graying whiskers. Unless he spoke, no one else could, so a tense silence hovered around them.

Rudolf shifted in the chair next to his father, uncomfortable with his new status at the adults' table, his eyes darting between his father, his grandmother, and his elder sister for cues as to how to cut his fish or wipe his still-unwhiskered mouth. Gisela sat quietly and dutifully, eyes angling downward, though Sisi suspected the girl's thoughts were elsewhere, with her suitor. Prince Leopold, a distant relative in Bavaria, had recently made his intentions for marriage clear to the very distracted Franz Joseph.

Farther down the table, Andrássy sat grim faced and silent, his dark eyes ragged with fatigue. He most likely longed for Hungary, Sisi guessed. How could he not regret his decision to come to this capital? How could he not miss the freedom of Budapest compared to the solemn, worry-stricken Viennese Court? International politics and the demands of Franz's role for him had consumed Andrássy since his move here. And yet, Sisi was relieved beyond explanation to have him at the Hofburg, even if they had barely had a moment together or a meaningful word spoken between them.

But Sophie, the archduchess, was the one who took news of the new German Empire the hardest. Sophie, who had rallied to come to this dinner with her son and the family, looked as if she now yearned for her bed. For Sophie, the triumph of the hated Prussians — first over her own son five years earlier and now over France — was perhaps the harshest blow in a string of devastating losses. All around her, her enemies and rivals seemed to be ascending. Sophie had been stunned when her son had been so quickly defeated by Bismarck, in a war that she herself had advocated. Then she had publicly decried the Austro-Hungarian Compromise and establishment of the dual monarchy, a move she considered far too liberal and weak, and that was engineered, no less, by her daughter-in-law and the former revolutionary Count Julius Andrássy. Then she had watched, overridden, as Franz had granted Sisi the reins of Rudy's education.

And now Sophie faced the joint blows of Prussian supremacy in Europe and the appointment of her Hungarian nemesis, Andrássy, who sat at her family's dinner table, the newly minted foreign minister and the most powerful man in the empire after her son. It was too much for the old and ailing matriarch to bear. Sophie cleared her throat loud enough for her son to hear.

Franz looked up. "Yes, Mother? Is there something you'd like to say?"

The old woman nodded.

"Yes?"

"To think," Sophie leaned forward, her voice shaky, her entire demeanor somehow depleted as she slouched in her chair. "To think that I, as a young bride, came to Vienna under such different circumstances. Why, when Prince Metternich sat in the foreign minister's seat" — she threw a distrustful look at Andrássy — "the whole world slept soundly at night. With Austria at the helm of Europe, it was the age of the great monarchs. Dynasties were assured; all was in its proper order. People knew who their leaders were. There was none of this bickering over constitutions and revolutions and laissez-faire governments. There was peace. There was *order*!" Sophie uttered the last word with the sacred reverence it was due, looking down at her dinner plate, seemingly exhausted by her outrage. "I fear . . . oh, my Franzi, I fear for the age of the great monarchs. . . ."

"There, now, Mother . . ." Franz Joseph said, his words tapering out as he perhaps found no reply with which to comfort his stricken mother. Perhaps she was right.

Andrássy leaned forward, and Franz turned to him. It was remarkable, Sisi thought; these two men, once sworn enemies, now sitting together at a small dinner table in Vienna. Franz turning his attention from his mother to hear the counsel of a onetime Hungarian rebel and exile. And she, Sisi, the one who had brought them together, silently looking on.

"Yes, Count Andrássy, would you like to speak?" Franz asked.

"If I may, Your Majesty."

Franz nodded, and Andrássy sat up a bit taller, pushing his plate away, apparently done with his stewed beef. "Prussia seeks our friendship once more," Andrássy said, clearing his throat. "Bismarck knows that — given a choice among France, England, and Austria-Hungary — it is our friendship he most needs."

"The Prussians — our friends?" Sophie's tone was biting.

"It's a new world, Archduchess Sophie," Andrássy said, turning slowly to Sophie before looking back to Franz. "Prussia's . . . or, shall I say, *Germany's* . . . victory over France has made it so. We must adapt, or per-ish. Your Majesty."

"We are the Habsburgs. We don't change," said Sophie, repeating the family motto, but her son did not nod his usual agreement.

"I tell you," Franz replied to Andrássy, not to his mother, "I worry less about the Prussians — No, I am being serious. Hear me on this: it's not going to be the Prussians who bring about our undoing, and it's not going to be the Hungarians." Franz bowed his head to Andrássy as if to credit him. Sisi bristled at this. Hadn't *she,* too, been critical in brokering peace between the Austrians and Hungarians?

Franz continued, looking neither at his wife nor at his mother but only at his foreign minister. "After all of this, it won't be the Prussians or the Hungarians or the Italians who ruin us. I swear it: if this empire crumbles" — he raised a hand, waving his finger at the table — "it will be the threat coming from the Balkans. The Serbs could be the end of the Habsburgs."

Andrássy, Sisi, and Sophie considered this silently. The Serbs who lived within Habsburg lands were volatile and constantly clamoring for independence, yes, but they were a disorganized band of anarchists, fascists, and communists; lone gunmen, each man out for his own glory. No Serbian could pose a serious threat to unified and resolute Austro-Hungarian might.

197

Franz Joseph lifted his napkin to his lips, wiping his whiskers before placing it down on the table before him. "I've finished," he said, rising, and with that, custom dictated that all the other diners, too, had finished eating, whether in fact they had or not.

Sisi had barely touched her food. She had come to dinner hoping to voice some of her own concerns to her husband and Andrássy. Her own sister Marie had been driven from her husband's palace in Rome and had fled like a refugee to Possenhofen, where she was now living in exile, a disgraced queen without a crown or kingdom. Wasn't there anything Austria could do to help Sisi's sister drive that revolutionary criminal Victor Emmanuel from Rome so that Marie and her husband might win back their Italian thrones?

But Sisi saw that she would not have the occasion to plead for her sister the former Queen of Naples, as Franz cleared his throat, standing tall at the head of the table. "I shall go through to the other room for a smoke. Andrássy, would you join me?"

"Of course, Your Majesty."

The two men left the room, and Sisi remained behind. Her mother-in-law coughed beside her. Gisela and Rudolf whispered a small joke between them, instantly more relaxed now that the emperor and foreign minister had gone. Sisi looked down at her lap, adjusting the folds of scarlet silk and

198

beadwork of her gown. *How curious,* she thought. She had once been Andrássy's closest ally, his only champion in the Habsburg Court. He had needed her to get even a word to Franz's ears. But lately those two men spent nearly every evening together, locked in Franz's study, drinking and smoking cigars and discussing the endless list of international crises that battered and beleaguered them, like an unceasing assault of ocean tempests. Andrássy seemed to have forgotten entirely about Sisi, replacing her with her husband and his bottomless workload. Franz's personal work philosophy, "One must work until one is thoroughly exhausted," seemed to be Andrássy's new motto, as well. The two men had become inseparable, bound together by the shared cares of the imperial ship they steered.

She looked down once more at her elaborate gown, feeling foolish. She had dressed magnificently for dinner — wearing a high-necked gown of beaded scarlet. She had had her hair woven into a coronet of braids. She had covered her skin in rose water and diamonds and rubies. She had come to dinner looking her best. And yet, Andrássy had barely noticed her.

Fool! she thought. It was a lesson she had learned long ago, as a young bride — she could never compete with the cares of running the empire.

"I ought to be so terribly mad at you, Andrássy, the way you have neglected me."

It was the first moment Sisi had had alone with Andrássy since his return to court. She had been inviting him to luncheon in her formal staterooms for weeks, and he had only just accepted the invitation.

Outside the palace the air was crisp and snow flecked, sweetened with the scent of the roasted chestnuts and fried dough peddled by the vendors beyond the gates in Michaelerplatz — St. Michael's Square. The opera house had opened its doors, dazzling Vienna's upper classes with its gold-gilt chandeliers and walls covered in violet silk, a setting as resplendent and glittering on the interior as the stone exterior was imposing and grand. The tinkling sound of bells pierced the air as sleighs glided along the icy Ringstrasse, while all along the boulevards, bundled pedestrians dashed about to purchase sweets and gingerbread cakes and holiday gifts. Master Strauss was hard at work on a waltz dedicated specifically to the city of Vienna, and the emperor had just announced a glorious new alliance with the powerful German Empire. It promised to be a peaceful Christmas. The Austrians, their emperor declared, had much to toast as the year's end approached.

And yet, there was an underlying current of

tension that pulsed within the palace. The alliance with Germany had been forged out of necessity, out of the need to appease Austria's more powerful neighbor, more than any true affection between the two states. The emperor was overburdened and harassed by simmering discontent from the Balkans in the south up to Bohemia in the north. And the Archduchess Sophie's health continued to deteriorate. Count Bellegarde, meanwhile, hated Andrássy almost as much as he hated the empress, and he viewed the Hungarian patriot's presence at court, at Franz's side, as an affirmation of the empress's toxic influence on the emperor. The general had redoubled his efforts to discredit and defame Sisi at court to anyone who would listen — and there were many receptive ears.

Sisi, for all of these reasons, dreaded the thought of a long winter in Vienna. The busiest season came after New Year's Day and before Lent, during which time she would be expected to make merry alongside the rest of the courtiers, waltzing and gossiping and dining late into the evenings. She longed for the peace and freedom of Gödöllő, and even more, she longed to understand and somehow fix the distance that seemed to keep spreading between herself and Andrássy.

"I think you've forgotten all about me," she said now, sitting down to lunch in her formal state dining room. It was just the two of them, as she had dismissed her secretary, Baron Nopcsa, as well as her ladies. She attempted to keep her tone light, but her words spoke of a much deeper hurt.

"Please don't be cross with me, Empress."

"Empress? You're so formal these days." *Like a seasoned Viennese bureaucrat,* she thought.

Andrássy fiddled with his napkin, taking a long time to unfold it. "You know that I have so many masters to serve."

Sisi looked at him, noticing the way his dark eyes, once so radiant and mischievous, stared seriously ahead. She couldn't remember the last time she had seen him smile — an authentic, reckless smile, not the polite and measured expressions he offered to her and her husband in their formal exchanges and conversations.

Sisi wasn't certain how this gulf had grown so wide between them. It was as if the distance necessitated by the more formal setting of the Viennese Court had now become their accepted way of interacting, as if their aloof and protocol-dictated public style had taken root, becoming a very real coolness and habitual disinterest. Now when they spoke to each other with such stiffness, it was no longer them simply acting their parts; they truly had become little more than formal acquaintances.

"How is your family?" Andrássy asked,

tucking into his *Rindssuppe,* a warm broth with dumplings and onions.

"Rudy is . . . well, he excels in his studies. He's intelligent. But he remains . . ."

Andrássy looked up, spoon poised in hand.

"He's still so incredibly nervous."

Andrássy nodded.

"I don't know if he'll ever be fully . . ." Sisi sighed and took a sip of her wine. "Gisela, on the other hand, couldn't be less sensitive. That girl has the emotional depth of her father in addition to bearing his likeness. The two of them can be . . . oh, as dull as a pair of bricks."

"Sisi!" Andrássy looked up at her, and for a moment, his censure of her was so familiar, so casual and authentic, that she could have smiled in relief to see him scolding her. But he quickly recovered himself, clearing his throat. Sisi saw how, as Andrássy looked back down at his soup, the candor on his face from just a moment ago had been reined back in.

When he spoke next, he reassumed his formal tone: "The Archduchess Gisela is a very poised and pious girl. She's displayed an admirable forbearance in the face of the Archduchess Sophie's failing health . . . in preparing to bid farewell to her. . . ." Andrássy's words sputtered out, and Sisi couldn't help but bristle. *What about me?* she thought, her stomach tightening. *Who commended me on my* admirable forbearance *when I lost my own children? Surrendered them and their love to another?*

But before she could voice these tormented thoughts, Andrássy continued: "You have much to be proud of. You've raised an impressive girl."

The words pierced Sisi like an arrow, and she snapped her quick reply, her tone biting: "I had little to do with it."

"You *are* her mother, Sisi."

"In name only."

"The Archduchess Gisela admires you greatly. I am sure of that," Andrássy replied, his elbows propped on the table.

Sisi didn't know whether to groan at this reply or to reach across the table to take Andrássy's hand and plead with him to stop being so stilted and unnatural around her. He knew how difficult it had been for Sisi, how little intimacy and love she felt between herself and Gisela — he knew that the girl didn't take after her mother in disposition or physicality. Not any more than she seemed to want her mother around. Gisela hardly ever spoke more than three words together to Sisi, and only when they were together in formal group settings.

"And what news from Bavaria? How is your family at Possenhofen?" Andrássy said, sipping his way efficiently through his soup. He was probably eager to finish lunch and get back to his papers . . . to Franz, Sisi thought bitterly. "I saw that your sister Sophie-Charlotte married the Duke of Alençon."

"Yes," Sisi said, her fingers tracing a flower stitched into the tablecloth.

"That's good," Andrássy said, nodding at his soup. "I'm glad she did not spend long pining over Ludwig. That was a road to a very unhappy ending."

Sisi didn't know why, but she grimaced at the remark. Perhaps it was Andrássy's veiled jab at Ludwig that irked her. Or perhaps it was the familiar and presumptuous manner in which Andrássy passed judgment over the members of her family — as if he had that right, when he himself had been so removed and aloof to Sisi lately.

"And how about the rest of your family?" Andrássy seemed eager to fill the silence, to direct the conversation to a safe ground that focused on others, not on the two of them. "Your parents? Your other sisters?"

Sisi sat up in her chair, clearing her throat. "Actually, my sister Marie —"

"Yes, how is she?"

"Not good," Sisi said.

"Is she still in Bavaria with your parents?"

Sisi nodded. Her sister was still living in exile, while Victor Emmanuel had declared himself the king of Italy. To make matters worse, Marie had lost her only child to illness during the midst of her political crises.

Between Marie's anguish, her father's immoderation, reports of Ludwig's increasing eccentricity, and Helene's ill health, Sisi didn't know how her mother managed to keep that household at Possenhofen running. She looked now at Andrássy. "Can't we do something to support Marie's claim to the Italian throne? It would mean so much to my family."

Andrássy sighed, propping his elbows on the table as he broke apart a piece of bread. "You know that your husband lost his own Italian lands just a few years ago, and since then he's —"

"Yes, but he is still the Emperor of Austria-Hungary. Surely his support counts for something?"

"He supports your sister, of course. She is family. But what can he do? Words alone won't make Victor Emmanuel give up his hard-earned throne."

"Then, can't we do something else?" Sisi pushed herself back from the table, rose, and began pacing the room, her appetite nonexistent.

Andrássy watched her walk, thinking for a few moments. "What — declare war? You understand that that is not an option, not with things as they currently are. Not while we are trying to solidify this alliance with Prussia — I mean, the German Empire."

"Ah, yes, Bismarck, Bismarck, Bismarck. Our onetime enemy, now the belle of the ball, suddenly," Sisi said, sick of the man's name. Strange how these leaders swapped foes and bedfellows so often. Was nothing real, nothing authentic in this court?

"Come back to the table, Empress. You've barely touched your luncheon. I will explain to you the absolute necessity of our friendship with Bismarck."

"I have no appetite — either for that rich food or your talk of politics." She lifted a handkerchief and coughed, her entire chest heaving as she did so. It took her several moments to recover.

"That is quite a cough, Empress."

"Would you stop calling me that?" Sisi grumbled, lifting her handkerchief and coughing once more.

"You really ought to take care of yourself," Andrássy said, eyeing her from his seat.

"Yes, I know," she said. *Andrássy,* she thought, *rise and take my hand, won't you? Where have you gone? Talk to me of something other than politics.*

"This whole empire needs a strong and healthy empress." As he said it, he folded his napkin and placed it on the table, and for a moment she thought that in fact he did plan to rise, to come to her. But instead he stood tall, straightening the folds of his jacket as if preparing to go. "I shall leave you in peace, since you are not feeling well. Thank you for the luncheon, Empress."

Her heart plummeted to her stomach. So he was going to leave, just like that? When this was the only chance they'd had to speak alone in months? "You . . . you've only just finished your soup. You won't stay for the rest of the meal?" Her entreaty sounded feeble given that she herself had barely touched her soup. But she didn't want him to leave, not yet.

"I do not wish to impose on you further. You are unwell. Please, Empress, rest. Take care of that cough. You must recover your strength." He bowed toward her, and then, before taking his leave, he added: "We all depend upon it."

It was the way he said it — more so than his choice of words — that shattered her. Her health was a matter of state importance. *We all depend upon it.* As if she had become, to him, nothing more than a vessel of imperial significance. He, Andrássy, didn't care about her well-being so much as he, the foreign minister, recognized the need for a strong empress. It made the blood inside of her simmer.

"I plan to recover," she said, jutting her chin out and standing a bit straighter. This was the first time she had thought of the idea that she now voiced: "Valerie has the same persistent cough. I was thinking I might take her south, somewhere warm for the winter, to take a water cure."

Andrássy didn't miss a beat, bowing forward to take his leave as he answered: "If that is what you wish, Empress."

She stood stunned, deeply hurt by the quickness of the reply, of his acquiescence that she might just go away, far away from him. So, too, was she hurt by the calm, emotionless mask Andrássy wore on his face, revealing no sadness at the thought of her departure.

"Yes, then, in that case . . ." She knit her hands together in front of her waist. "It's already been decided; I plan to leave with Valerie immediately. Besides, I can't stand to be in this court a minute longer — the only person I care about is Valerie anyway."

She thought she saw him wince. That there was, at last, a flicker of emotion in his dark, silky eyes. A fleeting glimmer of his true feelings. But he recovered his composure before she could be sure he had even lost it, and he nodded, the perfect bureaucrat once more, and a complete stranger.

★ ★ ★

"Over the hedge! Run! You have the fox in your sights!" Sisi called out to her daughter Valerie, who was darting across an expanse of green grass before a cluster of cypress trees. Valerie, having declared her wish that she might be just like her mamma, was

209

pretending to race atop a horse. Her mother looked on from the patch of shaded grass where she sat lazily thumbing her way through her book of Heinrich Heine poetry.

"I got the fox, Mamma! I caught him!" The little girl came running up to her mother, her cheeks rosy, her breath uneven from giggles.

"Did you, my darling? Bravo!" Sisi leaned forward and covered her daughter in kisses. "Soon we'll have you doing more than make-believe, my love. Soon we'll have you atop a true Hungarian thoroughbred."

That clear spring day found Sisi in the southern spa town of Merano. She and Valerie had both recovered from their coughs months earlier, yet Sisi had resisted the gentle hints and frequent requests from her husband that she return to court. Here her days were her own to enjoy with Valerie and Marie and Ida, to read her poetry and ride her horses and take in the clean mountain air. No, the thought of returning to court filled her with such anxiety that her ladies warned her she threatened to make herself sick all over again. She would stay away as long as she possibly could, ignoring her mother's entreaties and the vicious newspaper reports that tallied her days away. Even Franz seemed to have accepted it.

Or so Sisi had supposed. Until she received his telegram bearing a message to his wife that was not so much a request as a summons:

HER MAJESTY THE ARCHDUCHESS SOPHIE IN INCREASINGLY POOR HEALTH STOP PHYSICIANS AGREED: NOT MUCH TIME LEFT STOP ENTIRE IMPERIAL FAMILY CALLED TO HER BEDSIDE TO BID FAREWELL AND RECEIVE FINAL BLESSING STOP PLEASE RETURN AT ONCE FULL STOP.

★ ★ ★

Spring had bloomed across Vienna, with curtains fluttering in open windows and boxes of bright flowers enlivening the stately white façades of the Ringstrasse, but inside the Hofburg, a somber mood hovered like a dark, wintry fog. The courtiers haunted the long halls, covered in black, whispering in hushed voices as Sisi swept by, clutching Valerie's hand in her own as the little girl struggled to keep apace with her mother.

The antechamber adjoining Sophie's private rooms was packed with long-faced ambassadors, courtiers, ministers, and relatives, all dressed in black and clutching prayer books and rosary beads. Dozens of eyes fell upon Sisi as she entered, setting off a wave of bows and curtsies.

"Empress Elisabeth."

"Your Majesty."

"God bless and keep Your Grace."

Sisi swept the room with her eyes. She nodded toward Count Bellegarde, then Colonel Latour. Half a dozen priests and cardinals stood together in the corner.

"Empress." Andrássy strode forward, extending his hand but then remembering himself and withdrawing it, offering nothing more than a formal bow.

"Andrássy," Sisi answered, leaning close to him, turning her back on the narrowed eyes of Bellegarde.

"Thank goodness you have arrived in time. The emperor is anxious to have you beside him." Andrássy guided Sisi toward the door to the old woman's bedchamber. "You are to enter, right this way."

A liveried footman pulled the bedroom door open, and Sisi reeled as she walked through it, her mind awhirl at the fact that Andrássy, her mother-in-law's sworn rival, was keeping vigil outside the archduchess's door. At the fact that she was now ushered into this room so swiftly — this room that had been barred to her all of those years when her little babies were kept in the nursery off of their grandmother's suite. How she'd haunted this doorway, aching to be let in but so often finding a guard or minister to turn her away, telling her that the archduchess and the children were napping or that she had not made an appointment and had missed her opportunity to visit the babies.

"Keep Valerie," Sisi said, ignoring the little girl's protests as Miss Throckmorton took the child's hand. "You three," Sisi said, looking at Ida, Marie, and Miss Throckmorton, "stay out here. I don't want Valerie to be scared or put at any risk of illness." The little girl began to cry as her mother left her behind, but Sisi, for perhaps the first time in her life, did not grant the little girl her wish.

Inside the large, elegant bedroom, a small, sad assembly sat in shadow. The scarlet curtains were drawn so that the whole room appeared to be steeped in gloom, filled only with the sounds of faint whispers. Several priests and nurses darted about, dispatching various orders pertaining to the sick woman's body and soul, pausing only to offer a cursory bow at the empress's entrance. The family members knelt and huddled around the oversized bed where Sophie's frame lay, inanimate and unresponsive.

Sisi saw her son first, noticing that he had barely grown during her months-long absence. "Rudy, my dear." He looked only slightly thicker than a young boy even though he was an adolescent. Perhaps it was his face that made him appear so young, Sisi thought — his eyes were red-rimmed and puffy, his cheeks raw from wiping away tears.

"Mother," he said, bowing toward Sisi but

otherwise keeping to his post beside his grandmother's bed. Perhaps he was hurt that she had left him once more, Sisi considered. Or perhaps he felt that the woman who lay dying on the bed had been more of a mother to him than this latecomer ever would be.

"Gisela." Sisi greeted her daughter next. If Rudy still looked like a boy, Gisela had become a woman, plumper and rounder than she, Sisi, had been when she herself had married. And then Sisi remembered: her daughter was engaged. Sisi had found out about it from a letter, but had yet to see her daughter since it had happened. Oh, she should utter some words of congratulation to her daughter, and how she wished they were meeting under different circumstances!

"Mother, welcome home." Gisela shuffled closer to Rudy, putting her arms around her brother rather than greeting her mother with any particular show of affection, or even familiarity.

"Hello, Elisabeth." Franz Joseph stood from his place at his mother's bedside, and Sisi crossed the room toward him.

"Franz," Sisi said, placing her hands on his arms. "Oh, Franz, I'm so sorry. How does she do?" Sisi looked down now. She could barely conceal her alarm as she stared into Sophie's pale, waxy face. The woman looked like a wraith, a withered, vestigial shell of her former self. Her hair, once so dark and thick, flew away from her face like errant wisps of a spiderweb. Her eyes, closed in sleep, were ringed by a webbing of fine purple veins, and her lips were spread apart, so she appeared as though she were trying, and failing, to speak.

"She hasn't awoken in several hours." Franz's voice was low and hoarse, and he seemed to swallow his words in an effort to choke down the threat of tears that accompanied them. "We hope this sleep is a restful one. And that she will wake at least one more time so that we may all . . ." Now he brought a gloved hand to his face, hiding the emotion — the anguish — that would not heel to his imperial will.

Sisi put a hand to his shoulder and stared back down at the motionless figure of her aunt. Her mother-in-law. Her most ruthless rival at court. And in that moment, Sisi wondered how it was possible to hold such powerful feelings of both love and hate in her one heart.

This was, after all, the woman who had haunted Sisi since her earliest days as a bride, exercising complete dominion over her choices, her husband, her household, her children. This was the woman whom Sisi had fled, traveling to other countries and continents but never entirely escaping her meddling or influence.

And yet, this was the woman who had

welcomed Sisi to Vienna as a young girl, who had been the constant in her life, more present as a daily companion, perhaps, than even her distracted and overburdened husband. The woman who had given her Franz. The woman who had loved Sisi's children and nursed her through her pregnancies and held her hands through her painful deliveries.

As Sisi looked now at the aged woman, silent at last, she wondered: how had this woman had the power to terrify her as she had? Sophie looked so feeble as she lay there, her features expressionless, her skin as white as parchment. Incapable of hurting anyone, especially a strong and robust young woman like Sisi. Had she been unfair to the older woman? Sisi wondered. Had she let the early tension between them color every action and word from the woman since? Hadn't Sophie simply done the best she could for the son she adored — the son who had been forced to shoulder so many burdens, to fill a role where more-than-humanness was expected of him? Wouldn't she, Sisi, do the same for Valerie, now that she understood what it was to be enamored with, to be utterly devoted to one's child?

And Sisi was struck by the Heine quote she had circled that morning, on her trip back to Vienna: *Before death I shall, moved in my heart, forgive them all the wrong they did me in their lifetime. One must, it is true, forgive one's enemies — but not before they have been hanged.*

Sisi turned away from the bed, pacing the large, shadowed chamber. Her eyes fell on the opposite wall, where the large oil painting of Maria Theresa looked down over the room, the face plump and proud. Maria Theresa — the most beloved Habsburg ruler to ever occupy this palace. The strong, prolific, infallible empress. Devoted wife. Model mother. Pious Christian. Formidable and just ruler of her people. Maria Theresa was the Habsburg ruler against whom every Habsburg had measured him- or herself since. She was the woman upon whose face Sophie had chosen to look every single day. The woman on whom Sophie had tried to model her every behavior, both personal and public. Had she succeeded? Sisi crossed her arms, holding herself. Yes, she conceded, Sophie had succeeded. She had earned for herself a spot in the brightest constellation of Habsburg stars. "The Only Man at Court," that had been Sophie's nickname. She had been the strongest figure at a court where strength was the highest virtue and most necessary trait.

Sisi turned away from Maria Theresa's stern, all-knowing gaze and crossed to the other side of the room. Sophie's desk was scattered with papers and a hastily discarded pen, as if the old woman had been busy at work when death had finally come to claim

217

her. Sisi brushed her finger against the surface of the woman's rosewood desk; not a speck of dust. She startled, ever so slightly, when she realized that on top of the desk rested two small framed portraits. Sisi reached forward and picked them up. She stared into a pair of youthful, smiling faces. Herself and Franz Joseph. The portraits they had sat for just before their wedding. How bright and carefree and hopeful those two individuals looked — the faces of children, really. They were the only portraits that occupied the space of Sophie's desk, the place where the woman had sat and worked every single day. Fingers trembling, Sisi replaced the pictures where they had been these past twenty years.

Just below the portraits sat a leather book, its pages left open. So Sophie *had* been in the middle of work when she had taken ill. But this was her diary, Sisi realized, recognizing the old woman's familiar, elegant handwriting. Her throat dry, Sisi read just the last few words the woman had scrawled: "Liberalism will triumph, I fear. God help us all. If only my son could —" That was Sophie, indeed. The woman had worried about her son and her empire with her very last bit of strength.

Sisi glanced over her shoulder and saw where the rest of her family remained huddled and focused on the inanimate figure in bed. She turned back and leaned over the diary. Her heart racing now, she picked it up and began riffling through the pages. They fell naturally to a section far earlier in the thick book. Clearly a section that the woman herself had visited often, for the writing was faded, and the pages were worn. Sisi narrowed her eyes and read the words, the book shaking in her hands: "Some are now predicting that my son might choose the younger one, Sisi, rather than the elder one. What an idea! As if he would look twice at that little imp!"

Farther down the page: "When I tried to praise Helene, to extol her virtue, her intellect, her slim figure, he would not listen. Instead he said to me: 'No, but see how sweet Sisi is! She is as fresh as a budding almond, and what a splendid crown of hair frames her face, she is a vision. How can anyone help loving her, with her tender eyes and her lips as sweet as strawberries?' But what my bewitched son doesn't see — Sisi is just a child!"

Sisi stifled the gasp that tried now to burst from her throat. She threw a glance toward Franz, who didn't look toward her, and then flipped farther through the pages. She came next to a passage in which her mother-in-law described the morning after their wedding night: "I found the young pair at breakfast, my son radiant, a picture of happiness (God be thanked). Sisi was as timid and frightened as a little bird. I wanted to leave them alone but my son stopped me from going with a heartwarming summons to join them."

A page later, Sophie — always watching, always observing, always judging — described Sisi's behavior at a church service: "The young couple looked perfect, inspiring, uplifting. The empress's demeanor was enchanting; devout, quite wrapt in humble meditation." And then, Sisi realized, came a passage from during her first pregnancy: "I feel that Sisi should not spend too much time with her parrots. If a woman is always looking at animals in the first months, the children are inclined to resemble animals. Far better that she should look at herself in the mirror, or at my son. *That* would have my entire approval."

Sisi's heart constricted with each word she read, and yet, she could not stop. Several pages later came a description of Franz's journey to the wars in Italy. Sisi's earliest devastation as a young bride. She still recalled how she had begged Franz to take her with him to the Italian campaign rather than leave her alone at the frightening, hostile court. He had refused, and his mother had had this to say on the matter: "Poor Sisi's scenes and tears only serve to make life even harder for my unfortunate son." But then, just after that, came more praise from the woman: "Sisi at a Christmas party for her twenty-second birth-

220

day, looking as delicious as a sugar bonbon, in a strawberry-pink dress of watered silk."

It kept going — page after page of the woman's most intimate and honest thoughts. So much ink spent on her constant concerns for the court, her care for her soul, and above all her love and devotion to her son. Second only to the attention spent on her son were the writings on her son's wife, and the older woman's seesawing opinions on whether Sisi was performing her role appropriately beside him. "Poor Sisi, gone, and for how long? We know not. Leaving her poor husband behind, as well as her children. I was shattered to see her go." Sisi's stomach seized. She looked at the date: October 1860. Right after her departure from court. Her first time fleeing Vienna, shortly after she had become ill. Just after she had heard the rumors of Franz's infidelity. The first real rupture in her marriage — and one that had proven insurmountable. She remembered how sick she had felt, how frantic she had been to escape, not only from Franz, but from his mother, as well. "I was shattered to see her go." Sophie's own take on the departure. It was too much, reliving these moments through Sophie's eyes and her own memories, and Sisi pressed the book shut, replacing it on her mother-in-law's desk.

She turned back, her mind spinning, her eyes filling with tears. She looked on the inanimate frame of Sophie once more, surrounded by the family members who loved her. In that moment, Sisi realized that she had not said a nice thing to or about this woman in over a decade. She had avoided her and rebuffed her and presumed every word and gesture from this woman to be malicious and hostile. Perhaps Sophie, in all her attempts to be with Sisi these past few years, had longed to apologize. To begin again in a new relationship. Or, at least, to allow both of them the opportunity to right the wrongs of the past before it was too late . . . for surely Sophie, ever the pragmatist, had known that her end approached. Perhaps *she,* Sisi, had been the more antagonistic of the two, had prevented either of them from seeking any absolution for the troubles they had created for each other. And now, perhaps, it was too late. The immense weight of all of this suddenly overwhelmed Sisi, and she flew to the bedside where she fell to her knees, clutching her hands together. Leaning up against her mother-in-law's bed, she gasped, "Oh, Aunt Sophie, forgive me!" And with that, unsure of whether the tears rose up out of a pool of grief, or guilt, or both, Sisi wept.

She had carried her anger toward this woman like a heavy stone for so long; she had spent so much time and energy avoiding the very sight of her, so many words expressing the injustice she'd suffered at Sophie's hands. And now, in spite of that — or perhaps because of that — Sophie was the only person who could relieve Sisi of the burden of her hatred.

Later that night, after Gisela and Rudy had been urged by their father to take several hours of rest, Sisi and Franz remained in the bedroom, keeping their silent, watchful vigil beside Sophie. The archduchess's waking came as a quiet and unexpected occurrence, one that they might easily have missed but for their inability to sleep and their orders that the candles around the bed remain lit. Franz noticed first. "Mother, are you awake?" Sophie stirred at the sound of her son's whisper.

"Aunt Sophie!" Both Sisi and Franz rose, their bodies hovering on either side of the bed like sentries.

Sophie took in her surroundings. "Sisi?" Seeing her niece's face through the shadows, the old woman gasped. "Sisi, is it you?"

"Yes, Aunt Sophie."

"You came." The woman's voice, as weak as it was, carried the tinge of surprise.

"Of course I came."

"Oh, my little niece. Thank you for being here for Franzi." The woman reached for Sisi's hand, and Sisi returned the grip, noticing how fragile the bones felt beneath the old woman's cold, papery flesh. "Sisi, my girl."

"Yes, Aunt Sophie?"

Now Sophie turned from her niece to her son, before looking back to Sisi. "Sisi, you will be the sole comfort to my poor Franzi now. Please, be good to him. Be good to the children. Your place is . . ." But Sophie stopped, struggling to breathe. When she had recovered several moments later, Sophie seemed to have lost the thread of her thoughts, for now she turned to her son. "Franzi?"

"Yes, Mother."

"You are here, Franzi?"

He held her hand tighter, leaned in a little closer. Sisi had never seen any likeness of her son in Franz, but in that moment, she caught a glimpse of the boy's soft, emotive face. "I am here, Mother," Franz said.

"Franzi, you are ready. You've been ready for a long time. I've prepared you for this."

Neither Sisi nor Franz said anything. Did the old woman not realize that it was her forty-one-year-old son to whom she spoke and not the eighteen-year-old boy, newly ascended to the throne? The throne she had won for him.

"It falls on you now, my son. Remember, it's your sacred duty to be strong. Always be strong." Sophie took a pause, her breath wheezy and labored. "If you show weakness, even if it's with the best of intentions to help the people, you shall simply end up hurting them. For any sign of weakness will only

224

encourage revolution and lawlessness."

That was Sophie, Sisi thought. Exerting her will up until her last breath, always thinking about duty even as she barely clung to life. Sisi listened to what she supposed would be the last lecture by the old woman with a strange and indecipherable swirl of emotions.

"You know . . . both of you know, right?" Now Sophie looked back and forth between her son and his wife, the old woman's eyes watery but watchful, as if she feared that she might never teach them all that they needed to know.

"Know what, Mother?" Franz leaned forward, his voice tender in a way Sisi had never heard it.

"You know that . . ." Sophie coughed, and the effort seemed to consume her last bit of strength. "You know that . . . all I ever wanted . . . was for you two . . ."

One final spasm shook Sophie's chest, and it looked as if she spent the final reserves of her breath to whisper: "Please, a priest."

"I am here, Your Imperial Highness Archduchess Sophie." A robed priest glided forward.

"It is time. My rites. My last rites. For soon . . ." Sophie struggled to breathe. "I shall be with my Lord and Savior."

Clutching a cross and a string of rosary beads — the same cross and rosary beads that had once belonged to Empress Maria

Theresa — Sophie was granted her last rites. She listened with a somber expression, eyes open and mouth shut, displaying the same stoic dignity with which she'd presided over the court during her many formidable years. When the priest was done, Sophie's face seemed to slacken into a more peaceful look as if, at last, she might rest.

From that point, Sophie slipped in and out of wakefulness, uttering the occasional sigh or small, inaudible prayer. Rudy and Gisela came and went, keeping vigil with their parents during the daylight hours, retreating to their bedchambers at night on their father's orders. Only Sisi and Franz Joseph stayed around the clock.

Sisi lost track of time, slipping into an almost trancelike, meditative rhythm. She noticed, absently, how Marie Festetics entered on occasion to urge her to leave for a bit to rest and eat. "No." Sisi would shake her head, still clinging to Sophie's hand while, across the bed from her, Franz did the same. Her husband didn't seem to register anyone's presence, didn't even see the room around him. And yet, Sisi felt as if she needed to be there with him. And with Sophie. "No, Marie, I shall stay here until she has breathed her last."

Neither Sisi nor Franz rose from the bedside. Food was brought in and left, growing cold on the trays because of their fear that if they turned away, they might miss the final moment. But Sophie's last breath didn't come. The woman's strength and will to fight had never been in question, and they were proved all the more clearly in her final days. The archduchess, the member of the royal family most diligent about protocol and punctuality, now kept everybody waiting for days. So strong was her spirit that even death itself would not defeat her without a hard-fought battle.

Sisi thought it a small miracle that when the time finally came, when Sophie let out her final breath, her chest heaving high before collapsing in on itself and pushing out a raspy puff of air, both Rudy and Gisela were in the room. It was how they had wanted it.

Franz stirred, clutching his mother's hand. The doctor stepped forward and felt the woman's chest and neck before nodding to the waiting priest.

"The archduchess is with her Maker," the priest said aloud to the dark room, making a sign of the cross over the bed. At that pronouncement, both Franz Joseph and Rudy began to weep, burying their faces in their hands. Gisela sat in the corner silently praying, as the holy water was splashed over Sophie's resting figure.

Sisi, aware that the hand to which she clung now belonged to a corpse, slid her fingers free and rose. Her head swam as she stood, dizzy with exhaustion and hunger and — yes, she supposed — grief. She made to walk around the bed toward Franz, but suddenly the room spun so violently that she could not remain upright.

She reached for the nearby bedpost, hearing her son and her husband weeping as the priest recited the Latin prayers. She realized, in that moment, that it was the first time she had seen her husband cry since the death of their child. She thought of her daughter Sophie in heaven, and then of her mother-in-law joining the little girl there. So they would be together again, the loving grandmother and the darling princess. Inseparable, just as they had been in life. Sisi wasn't sure if she felt glad that they were together, or jealous, or something else, but before she could decide, everything went dark.

★　★　★

Sisi awoke in her own bed, daylight slipping through the curtains and testifying to a warm spring day outside. Disoriented, aware of her parched throat, she looked around before pressing the buzzer that rang Ida in the adjacent room.

"Your Majesty!" Ida swept into the bedchamber several moments later, her face ragged with fatigue even as she wore an immaculately pressed gown and offered a quick smile. "How does Your Grace feel?"

"I'm . . . I'm fine, but what time is it? Why am I in bed?" Sisi shifted under the bedsheets, feeling weak as she attempted to sit up.

"Your Majesty didn't eat or sleep for days. You took yourself to the verge of exhaustion and starvation remaining beside the archduchess's bed."

That was when Sisi remembered everything — the scenes coming to her like patches of a horrific, shadowy dream. "Sophie!" Sisi kicked aside the covers. "I must get up. I must go to Franz. And the children."

"Please, Empress Elisabeth, wouldn't it please Your Majesty to eat something first?"

"No, I must go to Franz." Sisi shook her head. "Fetch me a black gown."

Ida frowned, making clear her disapproval even as she obeyed without protest. Sisi dressed quickly, covering her unruly waves with a veiled cap of black silk. "Tell Valerie that I will come to her later. The poor girl must be confused; she must be so terribly upset that I've left her alone." With that, Sisi swept from her suite and strode briskly toward Franz's apartments, aware that Ida and Marie fell in step behind her.

Franz's antechamber was as crowded as Sophie's had been, the dark-paneled space filled with black-clad ministers, ambassadors, courtiers, and clergymen, all eager to express their condolences and prayers to the bereft emperor. They all turned now as Sisi entered, and she paused, as if paralyzed by the intensity of their collective stares. She should have known they'd all gather here, and yet, she wasn't prepared to see them, didn't wish to share this moment with so many others. She stood still, pulling her veil tighter around her face. Immediately the whispers began.

Sisi stepped forward into the room, fighting the desire to flee from this bowing crowd, to be gone from their probing stares and expectant expressions. "Please, as you were," she said, her voice quiet and without authority. My, she was thirsty; why hadn't she at least taken a sip of water before leaving her rooms?

The crowd splintered off into small clusters as Sisi glided through, whispering, "Excuse me, please," as she made her way toward her husband's door. She just wanted to be near him, to provide whatever small comfort she could. *Poor Franz,* she thought. He was so devoted to his mother. The way he had stayed beside the old woman's bed, the way he, always so strong, had broken down at her passing. Her heart was soft for her husband in a way it hadn't been for years — perhaps in over a decade. It had been Sophie's last wish that she, Sisi, would be there for Franz. Now, for the first time in years, Sisi felt her own wishes aligned with those of her mother-in-law.

And then she heard one courtier's voice louder than all the others. He spoke to a companion, but he had to know that everyone else in the room could hear. "It's exactly what I said. You can see it here, the newspaper's words, not mine. 'With the Archduchess Sophie's passing, Austria loses its real empress.'"

Sisi looked around the room, trying to locate the figure who had spoken these words.

The low voice continued, its owner obscured by the crowds: "And here, you see they go on to say, 'This was a respectable, devout, and significant woman, the most significant woman in Austria since Maria Theresa. She leaves no worthy female successor at court, only a void greater than we can fathom.' And it's not just a void in the government. Without his mother, the poor emperor will feel the void more intensely than anyone. Now he is stuck only with his selfish wife, and there will be no domestic comfort for him from now on. You heard how she collapsed the minute after Sophie died? That's her — always demanding that the attention be on her. Even when she runs away, it's always a ploy to pull his attention back to her."

Sisi's eyes, falling on a familiar face, finally found the origin of the hateful voice. Count Bellegarde stood at the center of a small circle of ministers, his hands clutching a thick pile

231

of newspapers from which he read aloud.

Sisi swallowed hard, freezing midstride. Bellegarde looked toward her now, staring her straight in the eyes, a muscle twitching in his jaw. And then, without a touch of reverence or apology, he bowed his head just an inch as he said, "Empress Elisabeth, my condolences. We all know how *fond* you were of that remarkable woman. This must be a bitter ordeal for you, indeed."

Inside the emperor's room, Franz sat motionless in a chair, staring out the window at his well-groomed, sunlit grounds. He didn't look up when Sisi entered, nor did he respond with anything more than a shrug of his shoulders when she asked if there was anything she might do.

Rudy and Gisela clung to each other, weeping on the nearby couch as maids darted in and out, offering tea and biscuits and asking whether or not Their Majesties wished the windows to be opened or the curtains drawn. No one answered with anything more than a blank expression.

Sisi found Andrássy in the corner of the room, her stomach in knots as she continued to digest the vitriol of Bellegarde's words. But it wasn't Bellegarde alone who felt that way. Why, he had simply been reading from the front page of one of the national newspapers. So then all of Austria felt that way!

And now the whole world would see it!

Sisi had always suspected — no, known — that she had vocal critics at the Viennese Court. They resented her long absences from the capital; they had sided with Sophie in past family quarrels; they had heard of her and Franz's periods of marital estrangement and had begrudged her affinity for Hungary. But that their enmity toward her was so ripe and well known that the newspapers railed against her, at a time such as this — this was too much for her to bear.

"I must leave, Andrássy," Sisi whispered, her voice low and hollow. Her heart pounded against her rib cage, and she thought that perhaps she might even run from this room and take off through the palace gates on foot. When she said she must leave, she meant right at that moment. She knew it was selfish — she knew it would mean abandoning her husband and children in their grief. But if everyone agreed she was selfish to begin with, what did she have to lose in confirming that impression of herself? "I can't stay here, not where they all hate me. I need to leave."

Andrássy looked at her, and his own expression registered alarm. She was certain that her appearance warranted such concern: she had barely slept in days, she hadn't eaten a bite of food, she was pale and haggard, and tension surely pulled tight across her features.

Andrássy confirmed this by saying, "Perhaps you are right, Empress. Perhaps you should go somewhere else to grieve and recover from this blow in private." He paused a moment, as if weighing his next words, before he added, "The last thing the emperor should do right now is worry about your health, too. He needs you strong."

Sisi had to sit down. She steadied herself on the nearby table, knocking over the miniature portrait of herself that rested there, as she said, "Yes, you're right. Then that's what I'll do. I'll take Valerie and . . ." Sisi nodded, casting a nervous glance toward her other two children, preparing herself for the unpleasantness of taking her leave from them. But then again, the way they clung to each other in grief, ignoring her to mourn their grandmother . . . they made it perfectly clear that she was no mother to them, not as Sophie had been.

"I myself must return to Hungary," Andrássy said. "The parliament is to meet next month, and I will be laying out the emperor's agenda to them."

"Hungary," Sisi repeated. "Hungary? Yes. I will go to Hungary."

"It's a good idea." A faint voice, choked with grief and the threat of tears, spoke from the corner of the room. Sisi looked over, startled, at Franz. She hadn't known he could hear her and Andrássy. "Hungary," Franz repeated, still with his back to the room as he stared out the window. "We shall all go to Hungary. I think that even I am entitled to a bit of a break."

V

Geneva, Switzerland
September 1898
He walks into the Café du Pont, a bistro just off the Mont Blanc Bridge. The hour is between breakfast and lunch, and the place is empty. A mustached man glances up from behind the bar, where he stands wiping cups with his apron. He has the well-groomed and tidy appearance of all of the Swiss, and he eyes Luigi for just a moment too long. There it is, Luigi thinks, that familiar look, a visible mixture of mistrust and disdain. The man doubts whether Luigi can pay, and he's weighing whether to kick him out now or to wait until after he's admitted that he can't afford a meal. "No charity in here," the bartender says, apparently deciding on the former.

Luigi smirks. He begins to whistle as he pulls a Swiss franc from his pocket, rubbing it between his thumb and pointer finger. Charity indeed, Luigi thinks, but this man doesn't need to know it. Doesn't need to know that a well-dressed lady tossed the coin toward Luigi when she found him this morning, sleeping on the quay. The coin catches the sunlight, and the barkeeper's entire demeanor changes. He places the cup on the bar and says, "My apologies, Monsieur. Long journey? How about a round on the house."

Luigi props his elbows on the cleanly polished bar counter and nods, looking squarely into the Swiss man's eyes. He accepts the drink and then orders another one with a bowl of soup. When it comes, he forces himself to eat slowly, even though his stomach begs for him to lift the bowl and pour the entirety of its contents down his throat in one swallow. In order to slow the pace of his eating, he makes conversation. "Duke of Orléans is expected here, in Geneva."

The bartender, back to polishing his cups, looks over at Luigi. His lips pressed tight under his neat mustache, he doesn't offer a reply.

"How long until the big man arrives?" Luigi puts his spoon down and wipes his mouth. Even just talking about the duke sets his heart to racing. The Duke of Orléans. The man who imagines himself next in line for the French throne, one of the richest, most powerful men in the world! Luigi thinks once more of the blade in his pocket, of his plans for the Great Deed. "He's expected today or tomorrow, right?" He manages nonchalance, even a shrug, as he asks the all-important question.

The bartender lowers his cup, wipes his

hands on his pristine apron. "You don't know? Haven't heard?" The Swiss man's tone drips with condescension.

Luigi bristles. He doesn't like being made to feel stupid, not by this bartender. His hand goes to his pocket, and he fingers the blade, considers plucking it out right now and giving the bartender with his thin mustache a bit of a shave.

But he keeps his cool, reminds himself not to waste the Great Deed on someone as lowly and inconsequential as this barkeep. He removes his hand from his pocket and picks up the soup spoon once more. With a cool shrug, he says, "No, heard what?"

"The Duke of Orléans is not coming to Geneva," the bartender says, and Luigi feels his stomach plummet.

The Duke of Orléans — not coming? But Luigi has spent all summer trying to catch up to the man. Not coming to Geneva? Well, then where is he going? And how will Luigi carry out the Great Deed? The royal Luigi has been hunting so methodically, now sprung free from his trap. So, what then is Luigi to do in Geneva?

CHAPTER 5

Gödöllő Palace, Hungary
Autumn 1872

"Surely you are too young to be a grandmother, Queen Elisabeth." Nikolaus Esterházy glanced sideways at Sisi, his dark hair escaping his riding cap in unruly tufts that fell around his strong, angular face, and Sisi couldn't help but think how attractive he was. "But then, if you are to be one, allow me to say that you shall be the most beautiful grandmother who ever lived."

"You are too kind, Nicky." Sisi adjusted her seat in the saddle, flashing her most beguiling smile at the Hungarian nobleman beside her. It felt so good to flirt once more, to parry a man's flattery with wit and laughter.

"Kind, perhaps. But I'm only stating the truth," Prince Esterházy said.

"I, too, am telling you the truth, Nicky. Gisela is to be married to that Leopold of hers. And I must make my peace with the fact that I'm getting old."

"Hardly. You look as youthful as a bride yourself."

"And yet . . . when I insisted that they have a long engagement," Sisi continued, "do you know what the court response was?"

"No, what was it?"

"That I was postponing my daughter's happiness to appease my own vanity. That I am terrified of becoming a grandmamma and thus won't allow Gisela to marry."

"And is that the truth?"

Sisi cocked her head. "I confess I don't wish to be a grandmother! But no, that was hardly my reasoning. I'm not *that* selfish. I arranged for Gisela to have a long engagement so that she would not be married while still a girl, as I was."

Esterházy fidgeted in his saddle, uncertain how to reply.

"But let's leave all of that in Vienna, shall we?" Sisi sighed. "For here I am, far away from all the gossips."

They rode slowly toward her stables in Gödöllő, the sun sinking low over the fields to the west. Sisi felt spent and more relaxed than she had in weeks, her skin salty with the remains of hard-earned perspiration. The day had been a clear one, and the evening air felt crisp, tinged with the scent of log-burning fires and dry leaves. She and Prince Esterházy had been riding since dawn, while Franz and Rudolf had taken half a day off of their work to hike in the surrounding woodlands. Gisela had been preoccupied with planning her bridal trousseau and writing love letters to her soon-to-be husband.

Sisi pulled the reins in tighter to slow the horse as they approached the stables. The grooms rushed out to meet their arrival, with Shadow joining them as the happiest member of their welcome party. Sisi leaned her head to the side as she pulled her horse to a standstill and looked up at the house, where Gisela's bedroom windows were aglow. "I cannot understand how people can look forward to marriage so much and expect so much good to come from it."

Esterházy hopped down and extended his hand to help Sisi out of her own saddle. She continued, speaking perhaps more to herself than to her riding companion: "When I think of myself, sold as a child of fifteen and taking an oath which I did not understand . . ."

Esterházy kept his tone light, not sensing the depth of Sisi's thoughts. He shrugged and answered: "Probably why I prefer to remain a bachelor." Esterházy offered his arm, and Sisi looped her own through his to be escorted back to the house. The massive maidenhair gingko tree in the yard had shed its bright leaves, carpeting the ground in yellow, and Shadow now rolled in the colorful pile as they passed. "Besides," Esterházy continued, "I have not yet found anyone who could pull

241

my fidelity from you, Queen Elisabeth."

She laughed off the comment, knowing that this dashing rogue would eventually make himself into a husband, as soon as his appetite for hunting and flirting had been sated. And he'd have no shortage of willing partners when the time came. But he was a wealthy man, and thus, the freedom of choice was his prerogative. Sisi sighed and recited one of her favorite verses: "Music played at weddings always reminds me of the music played for soldiers before they go into battle."

"Pardon?" Esterházy glanced sideways at her.

"It's a Heine quote," Sisi answered.

"Who?"

"My favorite poet." *Andrássy would have known that,* she thought, a stab of anguish piercing her. With that, she slid her arm out of Esterházy's and picked up her pace, marching toward the house. "I must hurry if I wish to visit my Valerie. Thank you for the ride, Nicky. I'll see you at dinner."

★   ★   ★

Sisi hadn't known — neither Franz nor Andrássy had told her — that Andrássy would be joining them that evening in Gödöllő. She barely concealed her pleasure at beholding him when she entered the dining room with Marie and Ida.

"Good evening, Empress." Andrássy was pristine in a dinner coat and tails even after his journey.

"Count Andrássy, hello."

"You look well."

"Thank you," she answered, her heart leaping in her breast. When she looked into his eyes, she felt her cheeks flushing warm. *Your face always betrays your emotions . . .* That was what Andrássy had once told her, and she recalled it now. *Oh, well,* she thought; no one here would gossip and send word to Bellegarde that the empress had smiled too broadly throughout dinner.

Several hours later, Sisi perched on the armrest of her husband's chair. The evening meal was over, and the group had moved through to the drawing room. Nicky sat across from them sipping on sweet *tokaji* wine. Marie and Ida were enveloped in a game of cards with Gisela and Rudolf. At the far end of the room, Andrássy stood alone, smoking in the corner as he looked out the window at the dark, chilly night that had fallen over Gödöllő.

"Franz, there's something we must speak about," said Sisi.

"Yes?" Franz turned toward his wife. "Will you have a drink, Elisabeth?"

"No, thank you," she said, shaking her head. "But you must speak to Nicky — Prince Esterházy . . . about his stable full of

243

thoroughbreds. My birthday is approaching, as is Christmas, and I'd quite like a new horse. I think I've completely worn my poor old creatures out."

"Is that so?" Franz looked at his wife as a footman filled his wineglass. There always seemed to be so many more footmen present in every room whenever Franz was around, Sisi thought. "Nikolaus, have you already exhausted my wife's fine Hungarian thoroughbreds?"

"Please don't be angry with me, Your Majesty. Besides, with a petitioner such as she is, my guess is that you obey the empress as willingly as the rest of us do." Esterházy glowed from wine and food and the imperial companionship.

"Not only willingly, but quickly, too." Franz looked to the Hungarian prince as if to indicate that he had learned his lesson, had learned of the consequences of choosing *not* to obey. "Tell me about your horses, Prince. Elisabeth has praised your stables to no end."

Sisi seized her moment, seeing that Franz would now be drawn into a long, wine-filled conversation with Esterházy — the nobleman couldn't resist any opportunity to boast about his superbly stocked horse stalls. She rose from the chair and glided quietly to the far side of the room. She nodded at Ida as she passed.

"Ida, some music?"

Her attendant obeyed, rising from the game of cards to take a seat at the piano. Now, between the piano, the laughter erupting from around the card table, and Esterházy's booming monologue on horses, there was plenty of noise to fill the room. "Hello, Andrássy." Sisi stopped at his side.

He glanced sideways at her, as if emerging from deep thought and only now noticing that he was not alone in the room. "Good evening, Empress Elisabeth." He stood tall, throwing a look toward Franz and Esterházy on the far side of the salon. They were nearly concealed behind the piano and a nearby bookshelf, but nevertheless, his body language was perfectly formal, suitably reserved.

"How are you?" she asked, angling her body so that it appeared as if she was looking out the window, though in fact she was looking at him.

"I'm fine," he said. His face sagged with fatigue, and his tone carried no hint of cheer. "And you?"

"I'm very well, thank you." She paused, drawing in a long breath, and then she added: "I'm happy to see you." And she was; it was the truth.

"You look as if you have been restored to your former splendor." He turned and admired her appearance — her brocade gown the color of silvery charcoal, with bows on the sleeves and glass beading on the skirt and collar. It was almost time for them to be out of mourning attire, and this charcoal dress had just the appropriate amount of modest decoration. Andrássy turned back toward the dark gardens once more.

"Thank you," she said, then paused. "I suppose it is because I am back where I belong."

He nodded, not looking at her.

"And *you* are back where you belong," she added quietly as she studied his profile. "Here. In Hungary."

"It is a relief to find both you and the emperor looking and feeling so well, Empress."

She wished he would stop calling her that, but she knew he never would. Not in front of Franz Joseph or anyone else. "Have things been very busy for you with the parliament in Budapest? We have barely seen you."

He nodded.

She attempted a light tone as she continued. "I suppose you've heard our joyous news? You know that I am to be the mother of the bride?"

"Indeed," he said. They both looked toward Gisela, whose plump face shone a rosy pink as she laughed with her brother at the card table. "My best wishes for the Archduchess Gisela."

"And I am feeling very old," Sisi said, sighing.

He looked at her, his features indicating —

what was it? Terrible fatigue, or else sadness?

"But we shall send one girl off and pull another one in," Sisi said. "I've invited a relative of mine, a young Bavarian girl by the name of Marie Larisch, to attend to me in my household. I told Ida and Marie that we're getting too old and that the only way to keep us young is to get some fresh blood into my rooms."

"Marie Larisch . . ." Andrássy repeated. "I don't know the young lady."

"No, you wouldn't. She's the child of an actress."

"She's your relative?"

"Oh, well, her mother's an actress; her father is one of my relatives in the Bavarian ducal line. So, she's half noble. Not enough to count by Viennese standards. All the better: she shall never be embraced by the court. And so I shall never have to fear her turning on me."

A massive eruption of laughter signaled the end of the nearby card game, with Marie Festetics throwing her hands up in triumph. Across the room Franz and Esterházy were still speaking while Ida plunked away on the piano. Gisela began prattling on to Marie at the card table about her plans for the upcoming wedding, explaining that she had decided on a pattern for her new porcelain, and marveling that the pieces of her bridal trousseau had already begun to arrive from as far away as London and Paris.

Rudolf sank into a brooding silence as the two women chatted about Gisela's wedding. He wore the military uniform now, and though that forced him to sit up erect and stiff, his facial expression undid his otherwise arresting appearance. He looked glum, even on the verge of tears. Sisi guessed at the source of Rudolf's melancholy: the boy dreaded his sister's upcoming departure. The crown prince and his father were not close, their dispositions being so entirely opposite. With his grandmother deceased and his mother so often out of reach, Gisela was Rudolf's closest family member and only confidante.

"Come now, how can you keep the empress all to yourself over there, Andrássy?" Nicky called from his seat near the emperor. "That's not very gallant!"

Both Sisi and Andrássy turned, an instinctive response, and walked back toward the others, their private interlude over.

"We are over here plotting your birthday present, Empress," Esterházy said.

Franz looked sleepy in the chair opposite him. "Rudy." The emperor turned now to his son. "What are you doing over there, listening to talk of wedding gowns with a pair of women?"

Sisi nearly winced at the insensitivity of the remark. "I was playing cards with them,"

248

Rudy answered, his voice quiet.

"Even worse, losing at cards to a pair of women. Come now, son, you should be over here. Drinking with the men."

"I'm tired," Rudy said, rising from his chair. "If you don't mind, I shall excuse myself and retire for the evening." With that, Sisi watched her son exit the room, his uniformed frame moving in tight, brittle motions.

An uneasy silence hung suspended in the air for several minutes before Esterházy filled it. "It's a shame you won't ever come out riding with us, Andrássy." Esterházy lit a cigar and exhaled a cloud of smoke around his face. "You deny yourself all fun."

"You have no idea," Andrássy replied, his voice so low that even Sisi, who was standing beside him, barely heard. But then, speaking more loudly so that the others might hear, Andrássy said, "I can't divert my energy and time with child's play and sport when I have the important work of running the kingdom on my desk each morning."

Sisi should have been insulted — the remark was, after all, just as pertinent to her manner of spending time as it was to Esterházy's. But she wasn't mad. No, in fact, she was delighted because, as he said it, Sisi saw the jealousy plainly across Andrássy's face.

Andrássy was not jealous of Franz; she understood that much. Andrássy knew that Sisi and Franz's bed had gone cold years earlier and that Sisi felt no desire to return to her husband in that capacity. But Nicky Esterházy was bold and virile and could potentially grab her eye. He *did* grab her eye, in fact, and Andrássy saw it. The way he himself had first grabbed her eye all those years ago as the dangerous and dashing young Hungarian patriot who had asked her to dance. Seeing that drove Andrássy mad with jealousy, and this kindled in Sisi some small, stubborn flame of hope.

Later that night while the entire household slept, Sisi walked to the spot under the leafless dogwood trees, her cloak wrapped tight around her shivering frame. They hadn't planned it, hadn't discussed it at all. And yet, there they both stood, their shapes illuminated by the soft glow of the half-moon overhead. "Andrássy."

"Sisi." His voice sounded hoarse, tortured. "You came."

She flew the final steps to him.

"I've fought so hard," he said. "And I've succeeded — or, at least, I thought I had. I've been loyal to my king, and I've served him. Oh, but Sisi, it destroys me every day to be away from you."

He pulled her into his arms, and she gladly folded into him, receiving his embrace as she would an absolution. She could have wept with joy. Their bodies found each other in the dark, after so long apart, weaving will-ingly together in ravenous treason.

★ ★ ★

Sisi was actually relieved the next morning when Miss Throckmorton told her at break-fast that Valerie had awoken with a fever. Sisi called the physician into the nursery, ordered her daughter to be put under constant surveil-lance, and canceled her ride, telling Nicky that she planned to remain in the palace while her child needed her.

But there was something else, too, which she did not share with Nicky. Sisi was relieved to have an excuse to skip the day's hunting excursion because she had awoken that morning to other news: Andrássy was gone. It was so abrupt that she wondered if the previous night had been nothing more than a glorious dream. But no, Marie announced while Sisi dressed that he had left early that morning. He had returned, Sisi guessed, to parliament in Budapest. With that abrupt departure, the happiness of the previous night was replaced by a bitter sadness, and Sisi was certain that Nicky, solicitous and jealous Nicky, would have seen that something was wrong.

So Sisi spent the morning in her room, dismissing her attendants and brooding in bed. By midday, bored and still unhappy, Sisi decided to take a walk by herself. The afternoon was a chilly one, gray with the promise of rain, so she returned to the palace after only a short outing. Feeling as though she'd go mad with restlessness, she poured herself into the activity of catching up on her letters. She read and responded to the notes from her mother, and Helene, and Sophie-Charlotte. She saved her letter from Ludwig for last. If news from Possi had lifted her spirits some, the news from Ludwig caused her mood to plummet once more.

My dearest Sisi,
I greet you with a crushed and demoralized soul, for just today, I have feuded with Richard, and I fear that the rupture may be beyond repair.

Perhaps you ask yourself how two souls who are knit so closely together as Richard and I are — two people who share such deep understanding, and intimacy, and common dreams and purpose — could find vile discord to exist between them. To such a question, I offer this defense: it is not my fault! It is the fault of that despicable consortium of apes in Munich, that so-called government of mine!

My ministers have recently complained to me of the dire financial state of my kingdom, and they have most brusquely insisted that I curb new spending projects until my situation becomes more solvent. They tell me that I have driven Bavaria deep into debt and that the government in Munich, henceforth, shall need to approve of all new expenditures that would exceed ten thousand marks. Imagine them telling me, their KING, what I may or may not do?

When I tried to explain this to my dear Richard, he did not understand. He is a genius — he does not (and should not) concern himself with matters as filthy and mundane as money! What does money even matter when we are speaking of creating pure and divinely inspired art? Richard urged me to disregard the tyrannical orders being issued from Munich, from my own ministers. Oh, how I wanted to bend to his will!

And yet, fool that I am, I begged him to give me some time to consider it. To see if there might be a way to beseech the apes to come around, to make them understand and acknowledge the supreme significance of our projects. Richard did not like this, and he roared the most unbearable things at me, storming out of the castle and telling me that he would never see me again.

He is, as you know, the god of my life, and I question whether there's any reason to go on living without him in it.

    With a most heavy and burdened heart, I
pray that you remember your devoted

                cousin,
                Ludwig

Sisi kept the letter in her hands as she paced across her bedroom, fuming. Soon the space grew too confining, and she burst from the bedroom, crossing the hallway with angry footsteps and descending the stairs. She marched out the back door and into the garden, her mind racing.

Her poor cousin! Her foolish, eccentric, naïve cousin! Ludwig was clearly unhinged, driven mad by his passion and his dreams and their incongruity with the harsh reality of the world. There was no longer any denying his troubles. Though he was not quite mad enough to belong in an asylum, he had no business being king.

The tales of his patronage of Richard Wagner made Sisi's blood roil. Wagner's profligacy was legendary across Europe. The man might have been a genius when it came to composing music — but his exploits with women, liquor, gambling, and brawling were just as epic. How could anyone even say that Ludwig's money went toward the art that he thought he was financing?

Sisi traipsed across the yard, ignoring Shadow as he found her and ambled along beside her. She did not even acknowledge her surroundings until, with a stab of longing, she noticed that she stood before the dogwood copse. Andrássy! She could have wept with her yearning for him. But it was then that she noticed the thin, hunched figure hiding behind the nearby bushes.

"Rudolf?" She knew it was her son; she had caught a glimpse of his military uniform. Her heart lurched — had the boy found out about her and Andrássy? Was that why he had come to this particular spot?

"Oh, hello, Mother." The boy emerged from the bushes, acting as if he were surprised to see her there, though, clearly, he had noticed her approach and had taken cover.

"What are you doing here?" Her voice sounded stern, surprising even her.

"Nothing." His cheeks flushed a scarlet red, giving him an almost feverish look. She could tell he was lying — about something. He threw a furtive glance back toward the cluster of bushes, and Sisi followed his stare with her steps. There, in the shrubs, she found it. A vile, putrid, rotting mound of small carcasses. Dead and bloodied birds. The worst part of her discovery, however, was that not all of the birds were dead. Some of them were still writhing and whimpering, clearly clinging to life while in the throes of agony.

Sisi shrieked, stepping back. "What? Rudolf, what is the meaning of this? Why are there so many dead and injured birds?"

And then she noticed the small rifle beside the pile. Her mouth fell open. "Rudolf? Did . . . did you . . . shoot all of those poor animals?"

"No," Rudolf said, stepping away from the bushes. "No," he said again, shifting from one foot to another. "I found them," he added, not at all convincingly. And then the boy spotted the dog beside Sisi, its furry tail wagging with dumb and innocent joy. "Shadow must have killed them," Rudolf said. "I . . . I brought them here to bury them."

Sisi could have wept in relief. How would she have recovered from the shock of discovering that she had a sadist and an animal torturer for a son? But then a troubling thought struck her. "Then . . . then why is your rifle right there?"

Rudolf paused, swallowing, casting his eyes downward. "I . . . I brought them here to bury them. I thought it would be a nice spot."

"But why the gun?" Sisi asked, her voice low and toneless.

"I had my gun on me. I always have my gun on me when I'm out in the wild. Father told me there are wolves all about. I had it, but I put it down to bury the birds."

Sisi thought about this for a moment, her heart thrashing in her breast. Nothing about the story could be proven wrong, however odd it seemed to her. She'd never known her dog to hunt birds, but she didn't know Rudolf to be a killer, either. She nodded once, choosing to believe her son's story. The other alternative was too horrifying for her to consider.

Back inside the house, Sisi admitted to herself that she wished her family would leave and return to Vienna. She and Franz had had a good autumn together, it was true. He had recovered from his grief over his mother's death with his usual stoicism and had even made for pleasant company lately. They had ridden together on occasion. They had enjoyed regular family dinners in the more casual setting that Hungary allowed them. As always, he, like her, grew more relaxed the longer he was away from court. Though they weren't lovers, they were friends, and she didn't dread his company the way she once had.

And yet, now that autumn was nearly over, Sisi couldn't deny that she wanted her house to herself again. She wanted the flood of Franz's footmen and servants and ministers gone. She wanted the return of her quiet evenings with just her and Valerie and Ida and Marie before the cozy fire. She wanted to be there, without everyone else, if Andrássy were to return. And though she regretted to admit it, she was tired of Gisela's constant

257

and naïve chatter about her upcoming wedding.

But, even more important than all of this, Sisi had grown increasingly uncomfortable around Rudolf. She was unsettled by his rapidly shifting moods — sweet and sensitive one moment, withdrawn and melancholy the next. She was made anxious by the tension that so clearly existed between father and son; Franz Joseph would attempt to draw Rudolf into some conversation about the military or the government, and the young man would reply with a bit of poetry or a fact he had read in one of his botany books. The two men had nothing in common except for the fact that Rudolf was destined for the same throne that Franz now occupied, and they regularly depended on Gisela or Sisi to serve as interpreter. But even more than all of this, Sisi was unnerved by the fact that, lately, she could not quite tell whether Rudolf was telling the truth when he spoke to her.

So when Franz announced that evening at dinner that he had given orders for the household to be packed up, Sisi had to struggle to hide her relief. "Yes," she said, nodding at the announcement. "I imagine you do need to get back to Vienna."

Franz nodded, cutting into his breaded schnitzel with his quick, controlled motions. "We'll leave next week."

"I shall stay for a while," Sisi said, her tone

258

tenuous at first. But then she drew in a long inhale. "Valerie and I will stay."

Rudolf and Gisela exchanged a meaningful glance across the table, one that Sisi ignored. She was more concerned that Franz had stopped cutting his meat, placing his fork and knife down and propping his elbows on the table. He stared at his wife. "Elisabeth, you know that I appreciate your independence. And I honor your wishes, whenever possible, even to the detriment of my own desires and the well-being of our two older children. . . ." He looked toward Rudolf and Gisela, and they nodded, as if this was something about which the rest of the family regularly conferred. "But on this occasion, I cannot grant your request."

"But . . . it wasn't a request." Sisi bristled, both offended and frustrated. "I will come back, eventually. It's just that, for now —"

Franz raised a gloved hand, silencing her. "We *must* go back. All of us."

"Why?" she asked, her tone defiant. He had granted her her freedom years ago. Her freedom to live where she wished, to travel where she wanted. They had reached this understanding after so many years of unhappiness together; why did he now renege on that?

"Because, my dear wife, the entire world is about to descend on Vienna. I've already sent Andrássy back ahead of us — that's why he left so early this morning. You and I are to host the world's fair."

The world's fair? The international event that had driven London to erect the Crystal Palace and had brought millions of visitors and francs to Paris? Was she so removed from Vienna and the news of her capital that she hadn't even known that her family was next in line to host the spectacle?

"This event . . ." Franz was stroking his graying whiskers, nodding at his wife as if to tell her that she had no choice. "It promises to boast all sorts of marvels and thrilling sites — but a glimpse of the surpassingly beautiful Empress Elisabeth is what the people most want to see."

VI

This is not life, but a fantasy! The world's fair . . . devours everything. All other interests seem to have disappeared, and the craze for making merry as wildly as possible prevails over everything else, as if in truth all seriousness had disappeared. It is almost frightening.

— *COUNTESS MARIE FESTETICS,*
SISI'S LADY-IN-WAITING

CHAPTER 6

Vienna
Spring 1873
Even the stoic and sensible Viennese, a
population who prided themselves on not
often being impressed, couldn't help but look
twice, some of them even pausing to gawk, at
the colossal rotunda that seemed to rise
higher each day, climbing upward from the
capital's Prater park. Sprawling outward into
a vast maze of alleyways and arcades, exhibition booths and imposing pavilions, the
fairgrounds of Vienna's World Exposition
promised to play host to the greatest show
the world had ever seen. Millions of spectators were expected to descend on the city
from around the world, each person ravenous
to behold the inventions and wonders
peddled by the tens of thousands of exhibi-
tors who had been fortunate enough to
secure booth space on the fairgrounds, with
vendors and visitors coming from as far afield
as America, Japan, and northern Africa.

If the sights, sounds, and scenery of the world's fair provided the lure to pull these millions to the city, the party's hosts, Franz Joseph and his famously beautiful Empress Elisabeth, were expected to dazzle them all once they arrived, for the Viennese press loved to write about nothing more — save for the empress's setbacks at court — than the empress's elaborate wardrobe tastes and her otherworldly beauty, the natural riches that made her and the emperor the envy of all other world rulers.

It was a bright morning in early May, the first week the exhibition was officially open to the public. Sisi stood in her bedroom sipping her tea and considering different dress options with Marie and Ida. Valerie played with a doll on the carpet while the hairdresser, Franziska, stood nearby, diligently preparing her ivory combs and crystal hair ornaments like a soldier readying swords and daggers before battle.

"How about this one?" Sisi pointed toward a magnificent gown of shimmering indigo silk, its skirt broad beneath a tight waist and glittering sapphire ornamentation. "Will it impress those stern Germans?"

"Marvelous choice, Your Majesty." Marie nodded her approval, relieved to have Sisi's deliberations over, as Ida crossed to the wardrobe to select the matching shoes and appropriate corset. "We don't have much time, Empress, as we are expected to meet the emperor downstairs in just a few hours," Marie prodded gently. "Would it please Your Majesty to finish breakfast so that you may begin to dress?"

"And I still need a couple of hours for the hair," Franziska interjected. Marie threw the woman an irritated glance, and Sisi suppressed the urge to smirk at their daily rivalry. Marie resented how long it took the woman to comb and braid and style the empress's thick, floor-length locks. Hours every day. Yet Marie did not protest this morning, for she knew that the ornate hairdos that this stylist fashioned — having originally trained backstage on the elaborate coiffures of the opera house — were a large part of Sisi's striking overall appearance.

Outside the spring weather was mild and clear, a welcome reprieve after a damp spell of chilly rain. Days like this never failed to make Sisi think of the fields outside of Vienna and the woods as far as Gödöllő, and she wished herself outside of the city and atop her new horse. But that would not be happening any time soon, not while the world's fair was going on.

Sisi sighed. "Don't you think our grand new fairground rotunda looks like a giant wedding cake topped with *Schlag* cream?" She settled into a chair as Franziska began to ply her thick chestnut waves. While the hair-dresser worked, Sisi flipped through the morning's newspapers. "Our world-famous Viennese pastry chefs have outdone themselves once more." She continued to riffle through the pages. "Ah, and there I am, looking like a potted plant at one of our endless opening ceremonies. Goodness, does my brow really crinkle like that when I'm trying to look serious?"

Hours later, once her hair had been sufficiently pinned and braided, each wave adorned with strands of sapphire, crystal, and diamond ornaments, Sisi rose. "Now, time to get into the harness," she sighed, looking at the corset held forth by Ida.

"We're going to have to sew you into this gown, Your Majesty," Ida said. "It's so snug, there's no other way."

Sisi nodded, clutching the frame of the bed as she held her breath. "They've all claimed that they wish to see my figure — and see it they shall." As her midsection was cinched ever tighter to its famously narrow eighteen inches, Sisi thought aloud: "If only they would all come together, at the same time, for one nightmare of a week. Instead, it shall consume the entire spring and summer."

It had already been a frenzied spring, what with Gisela's wedding the previous month and the feasts and parties that such an event had included. Then Johann Strauss had debuted his new waltz, "Wiener Blut," dedicating it as a wedding gift to the young bride. Next the Court Theater had put on *A Midsummer Night's Dream* especially for the empress, as it was known to be her favorite play, and Sisi didn't dare decline the performance. Already she was exhausted by the court calendar and the chaos of the crowded city, and yet she was staring ahead to the busiest few months of her life with the hosting of the fair.

Andrássy had filled her and Franz Joseph's schedules with a ceaseless stream of foreign dignitaries and crowned heads who would be traveling to Vienna. They would all be coming on social visits, yes, looking to be entertained, but Sisi was under no illusion that these would be enjoyable visits for her or Franz. Andrássy expected her to work — to strengthen and solidify the bonds with new allies such as Germany and Russia, to show gratitude and appreciation to loyal friends such as Saxony and Belgium, to reassure the skeptical satellites such as the Balkan states and Bohemia, and to charm or neutralize the potential foes such as England and Spain. And then, inexplicably, there would be the visit at the end of the summer from the shah of Persia, that outlandish man who apparently dyed the manes of his horses pink and traveled in the company of his astrologers, his "ladies of pleasure," and his own equipage of goats and rams.

Just days earlier on May Day, the first of the month, Sisi and Franz Joseph had attended the fair's opening ceremony and feasts, declaring Vienna's World Exposition officially open to the public. It had been an exhausting ordeal from the moment that her imperial coach was swarmed by the crowds on her entrance into the Prater park grounds. The mob, a mixture of Viennese and foreign visitors, had waited outside for hours in the freezing rain. Upon seeing Sisi's coach, a rare sight given her recent travels, they had charged her, sending her horses into a paralyzed panic as the crowd climbed up onto the wheels of the coach, fighting to peek through the windows and catch a glimpse of her stunned face.

Inside the rotunda was an almost blinding explosion of color and fabric and ostentatious wealth — the opposite of the gray, rain-soaked day outside. The Viennese who had been fortunate enough to win a place at the opening ceremonies had spared no small detail, and Sisi had looked out over a sea of feathered hats, pearl-trimmed gowns in every color, corsages bursting with fresh flowers, and mustached men in top hats.

Sisi sat beside Rudolf on the dais while Franz welcomed the giddy crowd and pronounced the world's most anticipated — and expensive — fair officially open. Next they attended a concert during which Master Strauss led the orchestra through several of his waltzes and a Handel march. Rudolf sat sulky and withdrawn throughout the ensuing feast, his deep melancholy all the more noticeable because of the otherwise festive feel all around them. Sisi hadn't seen him smile since saying farewell to Gisela.

And today, Sisi and Emperor Franz Joseph were poised to welcome their first and most important official visitor — Crown Prince Frederick of Germany. Germany's favored nation status had been made clear by Frederick's prime billing in the roster of royal visitors. "The crown prince shall be joined by his wife and mother?" Sisi asked, confirming with Marie what she had spent the previous night reviewing.

Her attendant now consulted the detailed program, a pamphlet the palace aides had distributed with the coming week's schedule. "That is correct, Madame." Marie nodded. "His wife, the Crown Princess Victoria, as well as His Majesty's mother, Germany's Empress Augusta."

"Poor Franz," Sisi said as she turned toward the mirror to admire the different views of her elaborately braided hairdo. She marveled at the way Franziska had placed the sapphires and diamonds in her waves to catch glints of spring sunshine. As she slipped on a pair of white gloves, she added: "I think that *my* outfit is a burden. How must he feel?"

As was dictated by custom, Franz Joseph would not appear in his usual Austrian cavalry uniform but instead would honor his foreign guest by wearing the military uniform of the visiting nation. Putting on the white and gold of the Prussian grenadier would be a bitter experience for Franz indeed, as that was the uniform that had defeated his own forces just a few years earlier during the Austro-Prussian War.

"I feel as if I am doing battle against my own self when I put it on," Franz had confessed to Sisi the night before.

Nevertheless, as Sisi swept into the courtyard, trailed by Rudolf, Marie, Ida, and Baron Nopcsa, she found her husband dutifully stuffed into the white-and-gold jacket and trousers. A ridiculously shiny helmet rested atop his head, its feathers quivering as her husband paced, turning his head from side to side to inspect the members of his entourage. He stopped in his place when his wife's entrance was announced.

While everyone else bowed, Franz strode toward Sisi and reached out his hand, taking in her appearance with an appreciative smile. "There is my secret weapon," he said. Sisi let him gawk — let all the members of the retinue gawk. She knew she looked fresh and lovely in her indigo gown of delicate silk and gossamer, her diamond and sapphire jewels accenting her thick tresses while the snug fit of the gown highlighted her trim figure and narrow waist.

"Did you sleep at all last night?" she asked, stepping toward him.

"Not a wink."

"That makes two of us," Sisi said.

Andrássy stood behind Franz and avoided eye contact with Sisi. Franz scanned the courtyard, asking, "All here? Then we are ready to go. Let's be off — we don't want to keep our precious *brother*, Prince Frederick, waiting."

Frederick and his wife, a young English princess named Victoria, after her mother, England's Queen Victoria, were lodging with their retinue at the nearby Habsburg property of Hetzendorf Castle during their visit. Because this was imperial Vienna, everything had been scheduled down to the minute. Sisi and Franz were to depart shortly before their German counterparts so that they could be on hand at the fairgrounds to provide a formal and official welcome as their most esteemed guests arrived.

As the footmen opened the doors of the imperial coach, one of Franz Joseph's generals, Count Grünne, stepped forward. "If you please, Your Majesty?"

"Yes, what is it, Grünne?"

The general appeared nervous now, hesitating a moment before answering. "We've received word that the crown prince and princess were ready . . . and rather than wait, it was Their Majesties' wish to depart for the fairgrounds."

Franz stood silent and still, eyeing his general. "And, have they? Departed for the fair?"

Grünne nodded once, a tight jerk of his chin, his gaze falling to the ground.

Sisi felt Franz stiffen beside her, and she turned to see that his cheeks had flushed scarlet beneath his thick beard. His words, though quiet, contained a frightening fury. "Then they shall arrive before us? And we won't be there to greet them?"

Again, Grünne nodded.

"This is entirely unacceptable!" Franz spat. Protocol hadn't been kept. His carefully orchestrated plans had not been heeded — this, Sisi knew, was a cardinal sin in Franz Joseph's view. All eyes in the courtyard now rested nervously on the emperor, whose mustache had begun to quiver. "It makes us look disorganized and terribly *rude* for not being on hand to welcome our guests!"

The courtyard pulsed with an agitated quiet. Rudolf slid away from his father, as if to seek refuge behind his mother's broad skirt. Andrássy and Grünne shuffled on their feet, exchanging a quick glance. Franz remained motionless, frozen in silent anger, his

271

face appearing dark against the pristine white of his Prussian tunic. And then he barked his question to no one in particular: "Who allowed this to happen?"

Everyone in the courtyard began to fidget, the emperor's fury all the more discomfiting because Franz Joseph so rarely displayed any chink in his well-rehearsed composure. So rarely betrayed a temper. But his anger continued to mount when no one answered, and he yelled, "And against my orders? A gross breach in protocol! This is an embarrassment! Someone will be punished for this error!"

Now even the imperial guards, usually so impassive as to resemble statues, seemed to shiver as Franz's words filled the courtyard. Seeing that nobody else would dare to do so, and sensing that this outburst stemmed from nerves and exhaustion rather than any authentic rage, Sisi stepped forward, her tone low and conciliatory. "Franz, my dear." She put her hand on her husband's arm and he turned to look at her, his cheeks puce under the thick tangle of his sideburns.

Sisi offered an entreating smile, speaking so softly that it seemed she was whispering only to him. "Please, my dear, let's not waste any more time. If Frederick and Victoria are ahead of us, then let's go at once. We may be able to catch them." And then, searching out the words that she knew would resonate with her husband, Sisi added: "Let's you and I stay calm, for the others."

Franz considered her appeal, drawing in a long, slow breath. As he exhaled, he nodded, his lips pressed in a tight line. The wild stallion of his temper reined in, heeled once more. Finally, he said, "Yes. I apologize for forgetting myself." He offered his hand to help her into the coach, and Sisi took it.

"Let's be off," Franz called now to the crowd in the courtyard, and everyone, it seemed, let out a collective sigh of relief.

A small party was sent out to intercept and divert Frederick's coach with a tour along the Danube so that it worked out that Franz and Sisi arrived just moments before the German cavalcade and were ready to officially welcome their guests as they arrived.

Crown Prince Frederick stepped down from his coach into the balmy May morning, a stern and unsmiling man. Sisi studied his appearance with interest. He cut an imposing figure; though he wasn't tall, he stood broad shouldered and sturdy in the same Prussian military attire worn by Franz.

As Franz and Rudolf conducted the formalities of greeting the heir to the German Empire, Sisi stepped forward to meet his wife, a young woman with pale eyes and dark hair against fair skin. "Princess Victoria, it is such a pleasure to meet you. Welcome to Vienna."

"Empress Elisabeth, the pleasure is mine. You are famous from my homeland of England all the way to my new home in Berlin!" Victoria was not exactly a beauty — she had too much of her mother's boxy build — but she was warm and agreeable, and she spoke German with the hint of a charming English accent.

"I hope that your journey from Berlin was not too tiring, Princess?"

"Not at all, thank you, Empress Elisabeth. And it was worth it. Look around us! Vienna is as splendid as I've always heard it to be. But, if you please, Empress Elisabeth, meet my mother-in-law, Her Imperial Majesty the Empress Augusta of Germany."

The Crown Princess Victoria slid gracefully aside as a giantess stepped forward. Empress Augusta was even more imposing than her surly son, standing at over six feet tall and with shoulders so expansive that Sisi understood, instantly, why Prussian men made for such formidable warriors, since even their women were built like Goliath. "Welcome to Vienna, Empress Augusta," Sisi said, smiling up at the woman.

"Empress Elisabeth!" When Augusta spoke to Sisi, it was with a voice so deep and booming — a sound that seemed to originate from

274

somewhere deep inside her cavernous chest — that Sisi had to suppress the instinct to erupt in a gale of startled laughter.

"Goodness," Sisi whispered to Franz as the party fell into a procession, making its way toward the massive rotunda. "I shall have to call her Madame Foghorn."

"Sisi!" Franz shot his wife a scolding look, but she noticed the hint of his smile.

Franz and Sisi were to play host and hostess, showing off the millions of marvels and exhibits assembled within the massive grounds making up the largest world's fair ever planned. But first, as this was a Habsburg party, there had to be a proper nod to protocol and tradition. The imperial party stood solemnly while the two national anthems were played — first Austria's, then Germany's.

That formality out of the way, Franz led the group on a course that he and his ministers had already mapped out, the crowds gently and efficiently pushed aside like a parting sea by a column of imperial guards.

"The motto we settled upon is *Kultur und Erzsiehung,* 'Culture and Education,' " Franz explained, gesturing from left to right. "Every exhibitor accepted to display here — and there were *hundreds of thousands* of applicants — had to show how he was advancing one cause or the other. In Austria-Hungary, it is always about achieving greatness in those fields."

Frederick stood beside Franz, listening, and Rudolf stood on his father's other side. Sisi trailed just behind with Victoria and Augusta, looking at the men. Their three silhouettes could not have been more different, she thought. In the center walked Franz, the cordial and conscientious host, advanced in his years and dignified because of his well-trained posture, his silvering hair, and his position as accomplished patriarch of his people. On his one side stood the thick and stern German officer, a man who had come of age fighting battles and forging a new empire from blood and iron and willful determination. To the other side was Rudolf — youngest of the three, slight of frame, timid and soft-spoken, his eyes roving restlessly across the space as if seeking out a path by which he might escape.

These two younger men would be rulers at the same time; allies, even, if the course set by Franz Joseph and Andrássy continued. Would Rudolf ever grow into his role? Sisi wondered. Would he ever carry himself with the same authority and self-assurance that Frederick so clearly displayed, even now when he was a guest in a foreign country?

As they entered the rotunda, all eyes from the crowd landed on them, so that Sisi felt as if she were on exhibit, even more so than the goods bursting from each of the booths. As the guards kept the crowds at bay, Franz ignored the gawking and gaping and plowed his way forward, treading determinedly down the long and colorful aisles. Andrássy, the highest-ranking minister present, kept a respectful distance behind with the nonroyal members of the entourage, accompanied by Marie and Ida.

Four massive halls sprouting off of the rotunda comprised the central core of the exhibition: the halls of agriculture, art, machinery, and industry. Franz did not skip a single aisle, paying his respects with a formal nod to each bowing exhibitor as he passed. Sisi's favorite sight was the Ethnographic Village, a sprawling plot filled with European farmhouses that were actually inhabited by peasants and farmers of many different nationalities. She sought out the Hungarian enclave and greeted the peasants there in their native tongue.

Farther on, Victoria marveled at the mock-up of a Croatian seaside port, telling her husband that she should very much like to visit Croatia. Augusta found the collection of Japanese furniture and clothing — more than six thousand pieces — to be especially entertaining, and she expressed her appreciation in her deep baritone that seemed to startle the Japanese craftsmen and craftswomen.

When the royal party came to the model of

the city of Jerusalem, Sisi exchanged a glance with Andrássy, recalling the letters he had written to her from that city, notes in which he had detailed its ancient streets and hidden gardens. How he had bathed in the Jordan River, hoping it would bring his nation good fortune. She pulled her eyes away from him now. "Come, Victoria, let's go find that new communication device they have invented, the *telephone,* isn't that what they call it? I hear that someday I shall be able to speak to my family as far away as Bavaria."

Though Frederick remained mute and inexpressive as the group perused the stalls, Sisi noted how his eyes took in the rows of restaurants and cafés, the manicured gardens where flowers burst forth as if in their natural environment, the full-sized ships that looked as if they had been marooned on Viennese soil after Noah's floodwaters receded.

Equally as dazzling as the exhibits and inventions were the Viennese visitors who gawked at the displays, filling the halls with their appreciative *oohs* and *aahs.* The women had all come with the obvious hope of spotting their imperial hosts, and they were covered in diamonds and pearls and feathers and silks. The young maidens giggled and smiled at Rudolf as he passed, turning only in time to catch a glimpse of Sisi. When they spotted the empress, they took in her appearance like devoted pupils, studying her hairstyle and her jewelry so that they might return to their parents' new mansions along the Ringstrasse and find the best way to imitate her.

"Your Viennese women dress with more flair than we do in Berlin," Victoria noted, staring at one woman in an elaborate gown of shimmering fawn satin, her hair festooned with more feathers than a plump wild pheasant.

"Ah, yes." Sisi nodded. "In Vienna, one must always concern oneself with the appearance of things."

The booths delighted the fairgoers, and the cafés pleased them, luring people in with the promising aromas of strong Turkish coffee and sweetly fried dough. Most impressive of all, however, were the soaring proportions of the central rotunda. Even Frederick — impossible-to-impress Frederick — asked whether they might return to look at the domed hall from the inside once more. Franz agreed with an obliging smile.

"Cost us enough! Twice the original amount my engineers projected." Franz shrugged with indulgent, fatherly exasperation. Sisi guessed that, had he to do it over again, Franz would spend just as much, if only for the satisfaction of this present moment, having clearly dazzled his unimpressionable German rival-turned-ally. "It's larger than St. Peter's in the Vatican," Franz said, looking up at the soaring ceiling appreciatively, perhaps hoping his guests would do the same. "And more than twice the size of your Crystal Palace in London, Princess Victoria. What would the mighty Queen Victoria think of that? After all of that British boasting, eh?"

Franz made the comment not with the intention of deriding England, but merely to prop up Austria — Sisi knew that. But the literal Germans seemed to have taken offense at this, because they turned toward Franz now with their mouths falling slightly open. Even Madame Foghorn went quiet.

Veiled boasting was one thing; an outright statement that one's own kingdom might have done something better than another — why, wars had been started over less. Victoria's light skin went a shade paler as she offered no reply.

Franz, realizing too late the coarseness of his remark, looked to his wife, his own mouth now falling open, too, but lacking the words with which to absolve himself. The world's most seasoned, most self-disciplined host had forgotten himself, had committed a mortifying blunder.

"Victoria?" Sisi intervened, looping her arm through the princess's, as if they were long-time confidantes whispering in a school yard. She set off at a slow walk, guiding Victoria toward a nearby booth of hand-painted Greek vases. "You must tell me about horseback riding in the English countryside. I've heard such fantastic things."

"Oh?" Victoria turned, somewhat surprised but flattered by Sisi's sudden gesture of intimacy.

Sisi leaned close now, beaming at the younger woman. "I believe your family is acquainted with Prince Nikolaus Esterházy?"

Now the princess smiled, a sheepish, eyes-tilting-downward expression — Nicky seemed to have that effect on most women.

"I ride with him in Hungary," Sisi continued, "and he is always telling me that I *must* go to England if I wish to experience a true hunting season."

"If Your Majesty enjoys riding to hounds in a fox chase, then truly, there is no better place than England," Victoria agreed, the offense by Franz clearly forgotten. And, with that, what began as an attempt by Sisi to distract the young princess turned into a conversation of genuine and shared interest. Princess Victoria was intelligent and chatty, and she happily regaled Sisi with stories from her childhood at her mother's countryside estate, Osborne House, where members of her royal family would ride out for fox hunts.

"And you will meet my brother Edward soon, won't you?" Victoria asked.

"Yes," Sisi said, "I believe the English delegation is due to arrive just after you leave. I look forward to meeting the crown prince."

"Oh, I wish my stay could have overlapped with Edward's . . . even just for one day."

Sisi couldn't help but notice the longing in the princess's voice. "Do you miss home, England, ever?" Sisi picked up one of the Greek vases before them and admired it. She knew to tread cautiously in moving from talk of hunting to a topic that touched on the personal.

Victoria cast a fleeting glance toward the thick, unyielding frame of her husband, her smile faltering momentarily, like a candle flickering in a chilly breeze. But then she remembered herself, and her entire posture became more stiff. She was, after all, Queen Victoria's daughter. She understood — had been made to understand from a young age — her role in this world. "Berlin is my home," Victoria answered matter-of-factly, turning back to Sisi, her face inscrutable. She picked up a nearby clay amphora and appeared suddenly very taken with the bronze artwork along its rim. And then, as if fearful that she hadn't sufficiently convinced Sisi — or perhaps herself — Victoria added: "I was honored to leave England for Germany. I'm blessed in my role as Prince Frederick's wife."

Spoken like a true royal, Sisi thought. But she lowered her voice and whispered: "I miss my home in Bavaria all the time."

Victoria flashed a surprised look at her hostess, her pale eyes suddenly wide and inquiring, as if she was wondering whether she had understood Sisi correctly. Had she actually just heard the empress of Austria-Hungary, the hostess of all of this surrounding splendor, confess that sometimes she found her imperial role to be anything other than wonderful?

But Victoria was clearly more disciplined than Sisi, or else simply more content, because she did not agree with Sisi. At least, not out loud. Placing the vase back where she had found it, pulling her shoulders back so that her posture was once more impeccable, Victoria said, "But if you love hunting, Empress Elisabeth, then you simply must visit my family in England during the hunting season."

"I would like that," Sisi said, sighing as she turned to look at the line of nearby booths.

"Mother would be delighted to have you as a guest. Lord Spencer — he's the nobleman you'll want to know; he organizes the best riding parties in the whole country. Near his estate in Althorp."

Sisi nodded. "You have me convinced, Victoria."

"My, just look at all of this," Victoria said, glancing down a long row lined with stalls featuring spices from Morocco, leather saddles from Spain, hand-crafted jewelry from Tyrol, and heavily plumed hats and veils and bonnets from Paris. "Anything one could ever want . . . it's all right here. We are young, our new German Empire. But here, you Austrians, why, your people must enjoy such satisfaction, such fulfillment, such pride knowing that they come from such a productive and advanced society."

Sisi surveyed the scene before her, her gaze falling on her husband, his stiff frame dressed in the hated Prussian uniform to please Frederick. Next she looked at Andrássy, who caught her eyes every few minutes before dutifully turning away. At Rudolf, who watched nervously as his father spoke to Frederick about the innovative architectural advances his engineers had pioneered in propping up the domed ceiling overhead. And then Sisi looked at the people all around her: At the ladies dressed in their brightest silks, staring at Rudolf and Sisi and Franz Joseph. At the massive hall that had cost her family millions to erect, built in such a rushed and slipshod manner that it would likely begin to decay as soon as the fair closed. Why, the people didn't know this, but Franz had confessed to Sisi that even the ground beneath them was soggy and unstable, threatening to cause the buildings to sink and collapse. But none of these fissures or weaknesses mattered, did they, as long as nobody knew of their existence?

And now, turning back to Victoria, Sisi leaned close as she said, "It is as our court composer said to me once. You are familiar with Master Strauss?"

"But of course, all of Europe has waltzed to the music of Johann Strauss the Second. He's yet another reason why Vienna's court is the envy — I mean, admiration — of the world."

Sisi nodded, continuing: "Well, I once asked Master Strauss why he thinks his waltzes are so popular."

"And what did he say?"

"He laughed and told me, 'Illusion makes us happy.' "

★ ★ ★

Later that night, following a long dinner and an interminable ball given in honor of Crown Prince Frederick and his wife, Sisi sat opposite Franz in the coach returning them to the Hofburg. "Would it pain him to smile, even just once?" Sisi asked, remembering the crown prince's implacable scowl throughout the entire ball. "Victoria is so lovely and warm. And his mother — the foghorn — even she is pleasant, though she speaks about Berlin too much. But Frederick . . ."

"He's a Prussian. What do you expect?" Franz yawned, quickly lifting his gloved hand to conceal such an undignified display of weakness.

"It's quite all right, you know," Sisi said,

smiling at her husband.

"Pardon?"

"You may yawn in front of me. You're tired." Sisi shrugged. "Is that such a crime?"

Franz let the remark go unanswered, looking out the window, his face catching the regular intervals of light from the streetlamps as the carriage rolled past them in quick succession. Sisi shut her eyes and leaned her head back against the coach. After a moment, his voice so quiet as to be barely audible, Franz said, "Thank you, Sisi."

Sisi opened her eyes and looked across the shadowed coach. "For what?"

Franz's face was drawn with fatigue, his lips curling downward as if defeated by the effort of having worn a smile all day. "For all of it," he said. "For being here. For this morning. And this evening. You are the reason today was a success." Franz turned back toward the coach window, sighing as if he could fall asleep before even reaching the palace gates.

Because it was dark and because the din of the horse hooves and carriage wheels clamored so loudly outside the window, Sisi wasn't sure she heard the next part correctly. From where she sat, across from Franz Joseph, she thought — but wasn't certain — that she heard him say, "You will never know how badly I need you."

* * *

No sooner had the German royals left than Queen Victoria's heir and representative, her eldest son, the Prince of Wales, arrived from England. If Frederick had been dispassionate and stern, his entire countenance like that of a soldier who had declared war on all cheer and merriment, Prince Edward proved to be his opposite in nearly every way. A handsome young man, Prince Edward did not dress in military uniform but instead wore a cool summer suit and a hat that dipped rakishly to one side. He carried himself more like a dapper bachelor looking to enjoy himself than a royal dignitary visiting on official state business.

On his first day in Vienna, Edward arrived late to the exposition grounds, having kept Franz, Sisi, and Rudolf waiting for nearly an hour. Sauntering up, a relaxed grin on his face, his long gait as easy as if he'd already enjoyed an entire bottle of wine — which Sisi suspected he might have — the crown prince offered no apology for his tardiness.

"Well, then, shall we make our way into the rotunda?" Franz asked, a tone of forced joviality in his voice as he examined this offender of protocol. It was a muggy day in early summer, and the Austrians in their full dress had already grown quite warm — and irritable — while waiting for their English guest.

"Yes, my dear, let's go in," Sisi said, sweeping her husband along with her.

Edward was closer in age to Rudolf than Frederick had been, and he seemed to want to make an ally — or a drinking companion — of his fellow crown prince. As the small group made its way into the hall, Sisi overheard the young prince, while slapping Rudolf on the shoulder as if they were old buddies from university, whisper: "Right, then, let's get this over with so we can cut right to the ball, shall we? How are these Viennese women, huh, Rudy? As warm and creamy as your famous strudel? The few I've seen so far have definitely stoked my appetite."

Edward had his sister's pleasant affability as well as her pale coloring and dark hair, but he seemed to lack any of Princess Victoria's restraint or sense of the decorum expected of his station. At the ball given in his honor, Edward flirted openly with Sisi and several of the pretty young Viennese debutantes, asking multiple girls to dance and resting his hand brazenly on their waists long after the songs were over.

Later in the evening, the crown prince slid up to Sisi's side, his hands full with a pair of champagne glasses. "Join me in a toast, Empress?"

"Of course, Prince Edward." Sisi took the crystal flute he now extended toward her, offering him a measured grin.

His features, by contrast, were relaxed and merry, his dark waves falling haphazardly around his flushed face, his collared shirt unbuttoned. "To you, Madame." Edward lifted his glass, spilling a splash of champagne down his front as his unsteady hands wobbled. He ignored — or didn't notice — the wet spot as he continued: "This city is filled with many beauties. Why, look around this hall! But let me simply say that you . . . Empress Sisi . . . stand out alone. And I'd love nothing more than to go inside . . . your rotunda."

"Cheers to Your Majesty's health," Sisi said, sipping from her glass before turning toward her husband. Franz was clearly horrified, muttering to his wife that he had never seen such a mortifying display, but Sisi simply giggled with bewildered amusement. As the night progressed, there was no denying that Edward danced well and possessed a certain uncouth charm. He might have been a cad, but he was young and harmless and far more agreeable than Germany's Frederick had been, and he'd certainly piqued the interest of many of Vienna's young ladies. Sisi was grateful that, at last, Rudolf seemed to be enjoying himself. Her son had shed some of his customary surliness beside the gregarious and cocksure English prince, and Sisi even saw him dance throughout the course of the evening.

Apparently not of his mother's school of thought on sobriety or personal piety, Edward continued to partake liberally of the wine and champagne as the gala stretched on. At one point, complaining that the pavilion in which they were dancing was too hot, he tried to open a window. Failing to do that, Edward simply picked up a chair and hurled it through the window, causing a spray of shattered glass and female shrieks to spill across the hall. The horrified gasps of Franz and the rest of the courtiers in the room were overshadowed only by the sound of Edward's uproarious guffawing laughter.

★　★　★

"I think more than one young Viennese lady feels her heart leaving on this train back to London," Sisi said as she stood beside Franz Joseph, waving farewell to the departing Prince of Wales. A silent Rudolf stood with them, sulking as if he wished he could leave with his new English friend.

"He takes some of the ladies' hearts," Franz said, offering one final wave to the vanishing train, "and I daresay, perhaps their virtue, too."

"He certainly came to conquer." Sisi suppressed a chuckle. It was nice, for once, to have someone take her place as most gossiped about in the newspapers and court circles, even if it wouldn't last.

"And now it's time to prepare for a Russian winter," Franz sighed in reply.

The climate in Vienna did in fact go from wild and frivolous to frosty and serious as Edward left and they looked ahead to the arrival of the Russian tsar and his entourage. Andrássy, the diplomat and conductor, playing his role as foreign minister with aplomb, warned both Sisi and Franz to prepare for a taxing few days.

"It's not fair, really," Sisi complained to Franz the night before the Russian tsar and tsarina were to arrive. "They come one at a time and have all the energy needed for a few frenzied days. But you and I? We are expected to keep this show going at a breakneck pace, day in and day out, for months on end. And each guest thinks that *he* is the most important visitor."

"If we wish to avoid making enemies," Franz sighed, "then, indeed, each visitor must continue to think that he *is* our most important visitor."

But Sisi felt less like a diplomat than a marionette, dancing on display and entertaining with rehearsed lines and acts. Her stomach was in coils from constantly wearing a corset and tight-fitting dresses; her head throbbed from the elaborate hairdos and diadems that pulled on her scalp. She had had her fill of feasting and champagne and the overheated, crowded halls, of exchanging cheery, tiring pleasantries with demanding guests. And she had barely seen Valerie in weeks. "I wish I could just take off to Gödöllő and actually enjoy this summer," she muttered in the coach on the way back to the palace after yet another Viennese ball.

Franz sighed, perhaps agreeing with her, but he never would have said so. For him, his own personal happiness or comfort mattered little when compared to the demands of the empire and his role in it.

Andrássy spent days fastidiously preparing for the arrival of the Russian imperial party. He warned Franz and Sisi that the Russians were now second only to the Germans as the most important friends and allies of Austria-Hungary. With his vast realm bordering the Habsburgs to the east, Tsar Alexander ruled over an empire of millions, as well as crucial wheat crops and rich mineral stores. And the tsar's waterways would only grow more critical for Austro-Hungarian trade and military security in the coming decades. Tsar Alexander was a most desirable ally — and would prove an even more undesirable foe.

"And to them, as hereditary rulers for centuries, ritual and tradition are sacred," Andrássy said. He and Bellegarde were standing with Sisi and Franz on Vienna's train platform, awaiting the Russian cortege.

"We know a thing or two about ritual and tradition." Sisi sighed.

"No." Andrássy shook his head. He leaned in close now, speaking in a low voice so that only Sisi might hear over the roar of the approaching train. "The Habsburgs believe they rule by the blessing of God. Well, the Romanovs have convinced their pious and down-trodden people that they themselves *are* gods."

Sisi considered this, her eyebrows gliding upward as the train slowed to a halt before them.

"The Romanovs make the Habsburgs look pliant and easygoing in comparison," Andrássy added.

"Goodness."

As Tsar Alexander stepped onto the platform, his mustached lips tight and unsmiling, Sisi bowed her head, careful not to look directly into his eyes. Next she turned to kiss the Tsarina Maria's hand before accepting kisses on her own hand from the remaining female members of the imperial Russian party. Perfectly rehearsed — perfectly executed. So far, she seemed to have avoided a misstep, and Andrássy looked on approvingly.

"Welcome, Your Imperial Highness," Franz greeted the tsar, stepping forward in his own crisp and starched version of the Russian military uniform. Sisi had dressed for them, as well — she wore a tight-fitting gown of lilac silk under a jacket of white Siberian fox fur.

"Of course there is no creature more beautiful than your Siberian fox," she said to the tsar, her eyes lowered, hoping he didn't notice the beads of sweat that dappled her brow. *Or with a warmer coat,* she thought, panicking. She was already overheated in the summer weather, and they hadn't even begun their day at the packed, swarming fairgrounds and the parade that they were scheduled to watch with delighted smiles. Would the Blessed Tsar be irreparably offended if she had to shed the Siberian fox coat?

The tsar smiled only once throughout his whole stay in Vienna, and it was at dinner on his final evening, when Sisi told him of her desire to ride her horse along Russia's Neva River. "You have somehow bewitched that stern old Romanov," Andrássy said, pulling her aside the next day in the halls of the Hofburg. "Well done, Sisi."

Next came the magnates from the Balkans. While their kingdoms were not as vast or influential as Russia or Germany, these diverse regions had long and interwoven histories with the Austrian Empire. Franz Joseph hoped that in ingratiating himself with the regions' leaders, he might gain additional support from them in suppressing their restless and often hostile populaces in his southern lands. First came Prince Milan of Serbia, who was unshaven and tardy to nearly every scheduled appointment, often appearing as if he had just tousled his dark hair in a fight with a gambling rival or an angry lover. Or perhaps both. There was Prince Nicholas of Montenegro, a swarthy, staggeringly handsome man with ruddy features and a full Montenegrin uniform covered with a collection of blades and weaponry draped across his chest and waist.

Next came King Leopold of Belgium, a solicitous and fawning man whose only shortcoming was that he brought his presumptuous daughter Princess Stéphanie with him. Sisi took an almost immediate dislike to Princess Stéphanie; she found the girl unbecoming with her frumpish wardrobe and boxy build, and she didn't like the way Stéphanie flirted openly with Rudolf in front of the others, making her ambitions plain. Nor did Sisi like the girl's combustive and artificial laughter. She noted how Stéphanie erupted in fits of giggling any time Rudolf spoke, more, it seemed, to flatter him than to express any genuine mirth. Fortunately Rudolf still thought like an underdeveloped boy, and he seemed as unimpressed by the Belgian princess's inauthentic flattery and artless attempts at coquetry as his mother was.

Leopold and Stéphanie left and were replaced by Queen Isabella of Spain, a tall and imposing woman with black hair and dull, yellowing skin. Isabella dressed well enough and held herself with a certain regal dignity, but she was not at all pleasant to be around, giving Sisi the impression that she would much rather have been back in Madrid. *Just as well,* Sisi thought, *for I'd rather be elsewhere myself.* Isabella's reticence spared Sisi some of the forced and cheerful chatter she was finding so increasingly wearying as the days dragged on.

The fair — with both its architectural feats and its endless rows of booths — was universally acclaimed as a success. But though the exhibitions and the halls both dazzled and impressed, news of the troubles occurring elsewhere in Vienna couldn't help but seep into the grounds. The crowds were not coming in the numbers Franz's ministers had projected. Nor was the fair earning money at the rate it needed to in order to be profitable, or simply break even. Adding to these concerns, a cholera epidemic had broken out across the city, causing many to flee to the countryside in search of cleaner air during the hottest months of the year.

More bad news came when the city's cab drivers decided to go on strike, preventing many who might have gone to the fair from getting there. As news of the fair's lackluster performance spread, the stock market crashed, the impact rippling from the lowest to highest tiers of society and setting off a sudden spike in suicides; during the summer when it had hoped to be named the world's capital of culture and art, Vienna was instead dubbed the suicide capital of the world.

Franz weathered these repeated and recurrent blows with his usual stoicism and resilience, withdrawing inward whenever he was not attending to a public appearance, but by the time of the King and Queen of Saxony's visit, Sisi felt exhausted and ravaged. She did not have the energy for one more parade, dinner, ball, or exhibition tour. She was petrified of the cholera epidemic, both for her own sake and for Valerie's. Plus she had come down, inexplicably, with a summertime cough and was now suffering from daily headaches.

"Please, can we leave the capital, only for a week? What does the visit from the King of Saxony mean anyway? Have one of your ministers show them around. They don't need the Emperor of Austria-Hungary. Bellegarde can manage it. Besides, he's more on their level."

"Sisi, we cannot insult the Saxons like that," Franz said, his voice carrying a twinge of disapproval — or was it simply fatigue?

"Saxony was our most faithful ally against the Prussians. They have always been there for us." How could Franz do it, honoring his duty day after day? Sisi wondered. Subjugating all personal desires and needs to serve, work, and fulfill? She marveled at his fortitude, chastising herself for her own human frailties and petty selfishness, and yet, she could not imagine living like that.

"And besides, after the Saxons, we have our greatest visitor of all. . . ." Franz said, perking up slightly. "And I'm certain you will not want to miss him."

"Who is that?"

"The shah of Persia."

★ ★ ★

"Tell me one more time. I can hardly believe it." Sisi sat in her bedchamber, preparing for the dinner during which she and Franz would welcome the shah of Persia to Vienna. Outside, it was a roasting summer evening, and inside, the palace buzzed with a current of anticipatory giddiness, so outlandish had this foreign ruler proven to be before even setting foot in the palace.

"Nor can I believe it, Empress!" Marie Festetics could barely keep from giggling as she laid out Sisi's evening gown. "They say that he has traveled here with his own horses, their manes colored pink, as well as forty rams, a herd of gazelles, and a pack of dogs, all because he heard that Your Majesty adores animals. He plans to give the gazelles to you as a gift, Madame."

"And what of the people with whom he travels?" Sisi asked.

"He has brought his entire family, numbering in the dozens, as well as several 'ladies of pleasure.' "

Sisi's eyes widened.

"I apologize, Empress. I've offended you."

"No, Marie." Sisi clutched her stomach, trying not to laugh for fear of the corset's punitive pinch. "Go on, go on."

"Also in his entourage are dozens of ministers, his soothsayers, his doctors, his grand vizier — who he insists must be with him at all times — and his astrologers."

"Ah, yes, the blessed astrologers!" Sisi said, rising from her chair. "The shah canceled his appointment earlier in the day, refusing to meet me and Franz at the exposition grounds because his astrologers had declared 'the stars were not propitious for the meeting.' "

Sisi strode to the bedside to inspect the silver gown she had selected for the evening. "And what's more," she continued, "you know that he complained at being housed at Laxenburg Castle, as he wished to be closer to Franz . . . the emperor? And yet, do you know what he has insisted on doing at Laxenburg?"

"Dare I ask?" Marie allowed the hint of a smile to plump her cheeks.

"He has insisted that they construct an open hearth in his bedroom so that his rams may be slaughtered daily and roasted right before him on the open flame. And he's using the neighboring bedroom as his slaughtering room!"

Marie put a hand to her mouth, hiding her giggles. Serious Ida stood in the back preparing Sisi's jewelry for the evening — she never indulged in such gossip.

"I think my days of visiting Laxenburg are over," Sisi said, her mind awhirl. "And people called me demanding? And Ludwig eccentric?"

"He is telling everyone, Empress, that he is more excited to see you than the fairgrounds," Marie said.

"Well, then, let's finish getting ready. If the stars are propitious for the meeting tonight, I shall finally meet the man who so humbly calls himself the Blessed Center of the Universe."

Sisi and Franz welcomed the shah and his massive entourage that evening at the feast. Having heard of the visitor's colorful and extravagant tastes, Sisi had dressed even more opulently than usual. She wore a wispy gown of silver and cream, her waist wrapped tight in a violet sash, strands of amethysts and diamonds trimming her loose chestnut waves. Upon his introduction to his hostess, Shah Naser al-Din lifted his golden pince-nez to the bridge of his nose and allowed his eyes to rove freely and unabashedly over her entire figure. Then, turning to his grand vizier, a tall man with black eyes lined in heavy kohl, he muttered in French, as if Sisi couldn't hear or understand: "My Lord, but she is as lovely as they say she is."

Sisi turned to Franz, barely suppressing the urge to giggle. She didn't know what she found more amusing, the shah's unselfconsciousness or Franz's clear discomfort.

Throughout dinner, the shah sat beside Sisi like a shy schoolboy, looking at her but barely speaking to anyone but his vizier, who sat to his other side. "Are you looking forward to visiting the fairgrounds tomorrow, Your Majesty?" Sisi asked in French, valiantly attempting to draw the shah into conversation as the dessert was served. Farther down the table, Franz was chatting dutifully with one of the shah's many brothers. When the shah did not answer her, Sisi posed a second question. "Perhaps there is some exhibit in particular you look forward to?"

"No," the shah answered, his tone as direct as his staring.

"Oh?" Sisi sat back, momentarily at a loss.

He continued: "But I would like to invite you out to my lodgings at Laxenburg. I hear that Your Majesty is a great admirer of horses, and I would be honored if you would allow me to show you mine."

"You are too kind, sir." Sisi lowered her head, nodding. She was saved just then by the announcement of dancing. The evening progressed with waltzes and quadrilles, during which the shah observed but did not participate. Afterward, there were fireworks in the gardens in his honor.

The successful night was followed by a trying day, one in which Sisi saw even Franz's well-practiced hospitality worn down until he was teetering uncharacteristically close to overt frustration with his guest. The shah arrived at the grounds two hours late for his official tour with the emperor and empress, leaving them both to stand in the harsh midday sun without explanation. As they milled through the exhibits, seeing sights that Sisi had now beheld dozens of times, Shah Naser al-Din was decidedly less interested in the goods on display than he was with the pretty and well-dressed Viennese women he passed. Several times he looked squarely in the face of a young girl and pressed his tongue to his lips in a provocative manner.

His ministers assured Sisi that the Blessed Center of the Universe meant no offense with this gesture, however lewd it may have appeared to those who didn't understand; it was simply His Majesty's habitual way of tell-

302

ing a woman that her looks pleased him. At one point the shah went so far in his zeal to express his pleasure that he reached out to a passing woman and grabbed her arm, pinching it before allowing his fingers to glide toward her breasts.

The young woman began to shriek, attracting an embarrassing amount of attention to the scuffle, and Sisi and Franz Joseph hurried ahead as the imperial guards intervened to usher the girl to safety while Andrássy swept forward to divert the shah.

The most awkward part of the day occurred when a particularly buxom young woman fell before the shah's appreciative eyes and the Persian monarch whispered an order to his vizier. The vizier then approached his host and hostess, eager to dispatch his leader's will. "Emperor Franz Joseph?"

"Yes?" Franz turned from Sisi to the minister.

"You have an opportunity to make your holy guest, the Blessed Shah, most happy."

"Anything," Franz said, somewhat coolly, but nevertheless expressing his eagerness to be an accommodating host.

"If you would — that beautiful woman over there . . ." The minister pointed, and both Franz and Sisi followed his finger with their eyes to a pretty young girl, dressed in perhaps fewer layers of clothing than propriety would have dictated. But then, it was a wretchedly hot day.

The grand vizier continued: "She has greatly pleased Shah Naser al-Din, and His Excellency would like to know how much he might pay in order to enjoy her company . . . in private."

* * *

After the shah departed, Sisi stood firm and told Franz that she needed to leave the capital for a brief stay in the country. Her cough, rather than improving in the summer heat, was worsening, and now she broke out with rose-colored spots on her chest. An incapacitating pain had taken hold of her abdomen. On top of that, she had come down with a fever and was still experiencing persistent headaches. The court doctor had diagnosed her as suffering from typhoid fever coupled with exhaustion and had urged the empress to leave the city. Sisi almost celebrated the diagnosis; at last, she could get away, and not even Franz, with his steadfast adherence to duty, could protest.

The day before her planned departure to Gödöllő, Andrássy found Sisi walking in the gardens of Schönbrunn accompanied by Valerie, Miss Throckmorton, Ida, and Marie. "If you wouldn't mind, Empress, might I join you on the stroll?"

"Of course," Sisi said. They stood before the Neptune Fountain, a fantastical pool filled with the naked bodies of ancient Roman gods, their muscular forms of white stone writhing and wrestling, as their open mouths spit gurgling water. Swans skimmed the glassy surface beneath them, unfazed by the epic battle of the gods overhead.

"We were just about to climb the hill up to the Gloriette." Sisi gestured up the slope toward the magnificent stone structure that rested atop Schönbrunn Hill. The miniature palace adorned the summit like a delicate puff of cream and pastry and looked down over the private grounds of Schönbrunn. "Valerie said she wishes to see the giant wedding cake."

Andrássy laughed. "In that case, I will gladly accompany you." He fell in step beside Sisi. As they made their way up the meandering path that scaled the hilly grounds, Sisi couldn't help but remember a night, years earlier, when she had snuck out of the palace to climb this same hill. It had been dark and rainy, but sleep had eluded her, as it still so often did. She had been surprised and delighted to find that Andrássy, too, had followed his midnight restlessness to the same picturesque spot. They had sat on the summit, sheltered from the rain by the creamy stone archways of the Gloriette, speaking about their love for Hungary and their dreams for peace between their two lands. Sisi wondered if he remembered that night. Whatever it was he now thought about, he seemed restless.

For her part, Sisi was enjoying a finer mood than she had in weeks; she was looking forward to the break from court, a brief reprieve from the trying pace she'd kept all summer. As soon as her fever was cured and her cough was fully gone, she planned to enjoy the remaining warm months in the saddle, riding through the wilderness around her Hungarian estate. But Andrássy fidgeted beside her as they walked, as if he needed to confess something. "What is it? Why do you appear so nervous?"

Andrássy didn't respond to her question. He didn't even turn to look at her as they continued up the pebbly lane.

"What is it?" She studied his profile, unnerved by his silence.

"Empress, I wish . . ." He turned to face her for the first time. "I would most humbly request . . . that you would consider postponing your departure from the capital."

Sisi paused her steps, unsure of how to respond. It was Andrássy the bureaucrat who stood before her now; she could see that clearly, and she found it endlessly frustrating. She drew in a long breath, looking out over the magnificent grounds of Schönbrunn that spread before them. "Andrássy, I'm ill. The

306

doctor has diagnosed my fever. Even Franz understands that I must get away for a bit."

"But . . . the timing is not good, Empress. It will not reflect well if you —"

"*Will not reflect well?* I've stood dutifully by Franz's side the entire summer. What could possibly be more important now than my health?" Sisi asked, the edge in her tone sharpening. "The doctors are in agreement that I must go and recover my strength."

"But we have someone coming who might be offended."

"Haven't we already played host to every single crowned head of Europe . . . of the world? Who remains?"

"The King of Italy . . ."

"Victor Emmanuel?" Sisi spat out the name as she would the name of a criminal. Which was what he was. "The man who besieged my sister Marie and then drove her out of her kingdom entirely? The man who now wears her crown and sits on her throne as she lives as an exile in Possenhofen?" Sisi didn't wait for Andrássy to say more. Instead, taking two fistfuls of her skirt in her hands, she set off at a brisk walk, her heart thrashing angrily in her chest as she continued to climb the hill.

She did not pause until she arrived, panting, at the summit, which afforded a bird's-eye view over the grounds and gardens of the palace. Far below, the royal maze unfolded within a series of tight-clipped hedgerows and bushes. Sisi saw the faint outlines of courtiers strolling through the maze, perhaps discussing some secret business or whispering of a hidden love affair. Her mind darted and weaved as if she herself were stuck in some maze far more labyrinthine; what was Andrássy asking of her? He was asking her not only to stay, at the risk of her own well-being, but also to play gracious hostess to the man who had ousted her sister? How could he ask such a thing of her? Had he so completely turned into the bureaucrat that he now entirely disregarded her feelings?

"Sisi, please, wait." Andrássy trotted to catch her. "Please don't run away from me. Listen to me."

"No, Andrássy, you have some gall asking that of me. Forget that I am sick — regardless of that, how can you possibly expect me to remain here to receive that impostor? My sister's tormentor. Does Franz . . . the emperor . . . know about this? No, he can't possibly. He has already told me that he does not expect me to receive that . . . *man.* Not when he has abused my sister so. Franz would never ask me to —"

"The emperor recognizes that this is a matter of state importance and not a game of petty grudge holding."

"*Petty . . . grudge . . . holding?*" Sisi repeated his words back to him, her tone going low.

Andrássy simply looked at her, stone-faced, his demeanor unwavering. "You are allowing your personal feelings to interfere with important matters of state."

Sisi tossed her shoulders back, straightening to her full height. "So, what then? I betray my sister . . . hop quickly onto the side of some lawless revolutionary simply because he has grabbed the reins of power?"

"It's what is best for the empire. Your husband sees that. Your sister should understand that it's your duty. And so should . . ." He didn't finish his thought. But he didn't need to. *And so should you,* he wanted to say. His unspoken words hung in the air, his meaning encircling them like a ring of smoke.

Sisi shifted on her feet, grinding her teeth to prevent herself from lashing him with her words. And then, turning to her ladies, who had nearly reached the summit with the little princess, Sisi said, "Ida? Marie? Prepare my bags. Miss Throckmorton, prepare Valerie. I don't want to wait until tomorrow. We'll leave for Gödöllő this afternoon."

★　★　★

The world's fair came to an end just as its hastily built halls and rotundas began to chip and crumble. As workers set to the task of dismantling the fairgrounds, the busy summer turned inevitably toward autumn. The court relocated to the Hofburg, settling in for the colder months and shorter days, and Sisi returned, reluctantly, to the capital. Andrássy found Sisi back at the Hofburg shortly after she had returned for the upcoming holidays and her husband's silver jubilee celebration. He wrote requesting a visit, and Sisi granted it.

"Emperor for twenty-five years already," Andrássy said, lowering himself onto the settee in her formal receiving room. Ida and Marie had just left the room, heeding the empress's orders to go check on Valerie in her new nursery.

"Twenty-five years," Sisi repeated, looking out the window. Outside, the frozen grounds were dusted with a thin layer of the winter's first snowfall. Beyond the Hofburg gates, all of Vienna was in a state of anticipatory excitement, preparing for the parades and festivals that the emperor's silver jubilee celebration promised.

"And nearly twenty years that you have been married. Does it feel like it has been that long already?"

Sisi turned to look at Andrássy, considering his question. Her anger toward him had lessened slightly over the past few months — the acute sting fading to a more dull but persistent ache. Had he really come here today to talk about her marriage to Franz? She crossed the room and sat on the settee opposite him. "Married nearly twenty years, yes. And yet I'm only in my thirties and have this preposterous idea that I still have a lot of life to live."

Andrássy nodded, looking down at his hands. "As well you should, Empress."

"You know I hate it when you call me that."

Andrássy shifted in his seat, looking around the room now for the tenth time to ensure that they were alone. Sisi wondered how they had ever sat so companionably together — and where that ease between them had gone.

"Should you order some tea?" Andrássy suggested, perhaps only to fill the silence.

"Would you like tea?"

"Not especially. But I don't know" — he shrugged — "I feel as though an afternoon visit should be accompanied by tea?"

Sisi sighed. "Andrássy, your timing could not be worse; if you've come here hoping to find me charming and agreeable, I fear your suit will be an unsuccessful one."

"Why is that? Are you still so very cross with me over Victor Emmanuel? I had hoped to find you returned from Hungary and Bavaria with your spirits restored."

"Yes, well." Sisi riffled through the pile of papers before her — the dozens of letters, petitions, and prayers that had awaited her upon her return to the capital. "Ah, here it is. What a lovely homecoming." She handed Andrássy the article she'd clipped from that morning's newspaper. It was an open letter penned by the editor in honor of Franz Joseph's jubilee. After praising the emperor for providing his people with the gifts of peace, stability, and progress, the editor went on to contrast Franz Joseph's successes with the failings, both personal and public, of his wife.

"The Strange Woman." Sisi read the title of the article aloud now, masking the hurt she felt behind a tone of bitterness. Bitterness was easier to admit to than deep sadness, both to oneself and to others. "There are so many good bits in here," she said, trying to keep a calm voice as her eyes scanned the article. "Let's see. Here they critique me for my long absences from court. The 'imagined health conditions' that I use to justify my negligence as a wife and mother. Then there's a nice passage on my 'illogical love of and dangerous preference for the Hungarian minority.' And then there's the review of my vanity. And then they've printed these lovely interviews with anonymous courtiers who swear to have heard Franz and me 'in the throes of violent quarrels.' How mortifying, whether those are authentic interviews or not. But here's my favorite bit: 'As the emperor this year commemorates the triumphs of his twenty-five years, he has every right to look back over these decades with tremendous satisfaction in his record and his service. We can't help but feel, however, that the only grave error he made in this otherwise exemplary tenure was the one he made in 1854.' " Sisi looked up at Andrássy now. "Marrying me — you understand their point, yes?"

"Why would you even read such filth?" Andrássy reached for the paper, snatching it from her hands and rending it apart in one quick, decisive gesture. His face was expressionless, but she saw that he had gone pale.

"Because it's on the front page of the newspaper. I can't very well miss it, can I?"

"You should never have been allowed to see that paper."

"Oh, Andrássy, I'm not like Franz. I don't have my papers read ahead of time, cut up with just the positive bits put on my desk. I *like* to know the truth. It's just . . ." Sisi looked at the shreds of paper in his hands now. "Well, I pick up the journals, looking to see what I've missed while I was away, and it's right there. For all to see."

"Has Franz . . . has the emperor seen it yet?"

"Oh, yes, I told him he must read it."

"And?"

"He's livid. He's penning an open reply and demanding that they print it on the front page of every paper, as well as read it aloud in parliament."

"Good," Andrássy said, nodding. "It's one bitter man's opinion. He's staunchly pro-Austrian and he resents your support for

313

Hungary; he rails that you've been away from court, but you're back now. I wouldn't give it another thought, Sisi."

She inclined her head to the side, looking at him for a moment in silence. "You don't really suppose that he alone feels that way, do you? I know that members of this court say the same. Why, he has included their interviews."

"Enough of that," Andrássy said, shifting in his chair. "They do not warrant your attention. How was Possenhofen? And Hungary?"

Sisi thought about this, weighing her answer. In truth, rather than reviving and restoring her, as they had in the past, her trips that autumn had left her feeling weary and disheartened. While in Bavaria she'd had several visits from Ludwig and had been discouraged to see his health in such steep decline. Regardless of what people thought of his eccentricity, Ludwig had always been an unequivocally handsome, well-groomed man. He prized beauty perhaps above any other virtue. But this past autumn, he had arrived at Possenhofen looking like a stranger. The first thing Sisi had noticed was that her previously fastidious and vain cousin had grown bloated and thick with self-neglect. His smiles, which had a fleeting, frenzied quality to them, revealed receding gums and rotten teeth.

Their time together had been filled less with

meaningful conversations and long pleasant walks than with Ludwig's illogical monologues, his speech veering, at times, toward the disturbing. He had spoken to Sisi of his recent reconciliation with Wagner, and of the composer's upcoming operas, and of the work he was doing on his newest castle, modeled to look just like France's Versailles. When she'd asked him how he had managed to raise the funds to finance these undertakings, Ludwig had erupted in shrill laughter. "I won't allow my divine calling to be thwarted by something as base and vile as the want of money, Sisi." When the time had come to bid Ludwig farewell, Sisi had sent her cousin home to Neuschwanstein with a feeling of relief — and deep foreboding.

Elsewhere in the Wittelsbach household, the mood had been bleak. Valerie had come down with the same cough that Sisi herself had been fighting. Her mother and father were as unhappy as ever — the Duchess Ludovika overburdened with the cares of her duchy and her family, and Duke Max claiming that he wanted to take off on another one of his rambling hunting expeditions. Helene remained cloistered in silence and solitude. She barely spoke to anyone but a local priest whom she invited to the home for her daily confession. But Marie — the time with Marie had been perhaps the most trying portion of Sisi's stay. Marie walked around the home in a state of utter denial. With the haughtiest of smiles, she would declare that she was so happy to have this "brief respite" from her cares in Italy, predicting that it would be only a matter of time before "the crown would be restored to its rightful owner." And somehow, inexplicably, both Marie and the Duchess Ludovika seemed to think that it was Sisi who would get that Italian crown back for her sister.

Sisi turned back to Andrássy now, groaning at the recollection of this chore that had been placed on her by her family. "You can't think that I will let you and Franz forget that we owe my sister a response. Victor Emmanuel continues to —"

"Please." Andrássy raised a hand. "Enough. We've discussed Italy ad infinitum. Franz has recognized Emmanuel's kingship. The sooner your sister accepts that, the better. It is done."

"Done? But it can't be done! Why, he is not a legitimate king. My sister and her husband are the legitimate regents."

"Victor Emmanuel . . . and the people of Italy . . . would say otherwise."

"But this can't be borne!" And even though Sisi had looked at her sister and seen only denial and self-delusion, now she railed at Andrássy on Marie's behalf. She was so angry with him for so many reasons — reasons even she herself could not understand — and now, at last, she had an outlet. "You have no loyalty," she declared. "Why, my sister waits in Possenhofen like a refugee — her rightful home seized from her, her crown snatched from her head. And that criminal pretends to have a claim! How can Franz, a legitimate monarch, recognize a usurper? And don't you feel any sense of loyalty to me? If I tell you this is important to me, does that mean nothing?"

Andrássy let her rail against him, sitting motionless opposite her, studying her with a quizzical look. Eventually, when she fell silent, he spoke. "I always thought you the populist among the Habsburgs."

Sisi smarted at this, at his cruel calm. At the veiled mockery that lurked behind his words. At the way he had avoided her last, and most urgent, of questions — *if I tell you this is important to me, does that mean nothing?*

Narrowing her eyes, Sisi answered: "You know that I put loyalty to my family above anything else."

Andrássy landed his elbows on his knees and let out a long, slow exhale. "Do you not realize that your own husband — how did you say it? — *snatched* the throne for himself? Taking it from a weak uncle? And we will mark his silver jubilee this year, celebrating the fact that he did so."

Sisi shook her head. "That's different."

"How is it different?" Andrássy's voice was

317

quiet, patient. "Aren't all crowns stolen — in some way or another? If not from a predecessor, then from the people, who make up the only legitimate ruling power."

Sisi waffled, her mind reeling. "But you work for the empire," she replied, her tone defiant, even argumentative.

Andrássy nodded, tenting his fingers before his thoughtful face. "I'm a realist who works toward ideals. This is an empire in which we live, so I work for the people through this imperial structure. I simply seek to bring power and prosperity to my people. I thought you felt the same. And, it seems the people of Italy have chosen their authority figure decisively. If they wish to reject an ineffective king's power, replacing him with a populist ruler who better represents their interests, and they are strong enough to do so . . . well, it isn't the first time that a throne has been toppled. And it won't be the last."

Sisi crossed her arms. It was true; she had always advocated liberalism, had always labeled herself a supporter of the constitution and the parliament and ever-greater rights for the people. And yet, to hear Andrássy so openly dismiss her sister's claim, to hear him diminish her husband's authority — and, by proxy, hers — made her question whether in fact she truly believed what she had been saying all of these years.

Andrássy seemed to sense her inner turmoil, because he leaned forward, inclining his head toward her. "Perhaps that's difficult for you to hear, being a Habsburg?"

★   ★   ★

The next day, Sisi took a ride through the Vienna Woods. The day was bitter cold beneath a steel-gray sky, too cold even for snow, and Sisi had faced the disapproving frowns of Ida and Marie as they'd helped her into her white fox fur cap and cloak.

Though she rode alone, she spent the afternoon arguing with Andrássy, berating him in her mind and cutting him with her imagined words. She'd gone for this frigid ride out of desperation — being in the saddle and free of all company was the only way she could fathom sifting through her warring emotions. Here, where the wind whipped so relentlessly that her tears froze and vanished before slipping down her cheeks, she could rail at him in the way she knew she never otherwise would.

After several hours, her lungs aching like the stab of a cold knife, Sisi slowed her horse and guided the tired animal toward a small hunting lodge. She knew this spot — Franz had brought her here in the earlier days of their marriage. The place was called Mayerling Lodge, and it was an imperial camp tucked deep in the Vienna Woods, reserved

319

exclusively for the royal family's use as a retreat during hunting or riding excursions.

The grounds at Mayerling, a former church, now comprised little more than a dingy, haphazard hunting cabin neighbored by the ruins of a small, ancient chapel. The grounds' best feature were their large horse stables. The household was run by a sparse staff of servants, kept at the woodland retreat on the rare chance that a member of the imperial family made a visit as impromptu as this one. As Sisi approached now, a thin ribbon of black smoke curled upward from the cabin's main chimney. At least it would be warm inside.

In the yard, Sisi spotted a hunched figure carrying two armfuls of kindling toward the cabin's main door. The man turned in response to the unexpected sound of horse hooves. "Good afternoon." Sisi slowed her horse in front of the cabin and smiled at the caretaker, a small, thickly built man with weather-beaten skin and a heavily patched winter cloak. "I hope I'm not disturbing you. I thought I'd stop in for a quick rest."

The man's face showed first confusion, then mute shock. "Your . . . Imperial Majesty . . . Empress Elisabeth?" He dropped his armfuls of wood onto the hard ground, bowing as he did so. "Welcome to Mayerling Lodge, Your Grace. But I am all apologies; I've got no meat. I was not prepared for —"

"I only want a fire, please." Sisi hopped down from her saddle and handed the man her reins. "I'll see myself in if you will see to this poor, cold horse."

Inside, the cabin was dim and chilly, the small fire in the corner seeming to contribute more soot than flame as it sputtered on the hearth, barely warming the open space. "Took you long enough!" A wiry woman in heavy wool skirts, her hair pulled back in a thin gray bun, crouched before the fire, stabbing at it with a rusted poker, as if trying to coax the reluctant embers into providing more warmth. "Chimney's still blocked up. But bring me that wood anyway; we'll try to thaw ourselves just the same. It'll be stew again for supper — more roots than meat unless you've finally caught something."

Turning, she saw that it was not her fellow servant to whom she had spoken so gruffly, but rather her imperial mistress. "Empress Elisabeth!" The woman's face registered the same shock that the man's had a moment earlier. "Can it be?" Rising, she dropped the poker to the stone floor and wiped her hands on her apron, bowing her head.

"Good afternoon," Sisi said, sweeping into the front room.

"My, you are a vision in white, coming into our dark space." The woman studied Sisi's entire appearance with stunned, rounded eyes. "But I must apologize. I . . . we . . . had no warning of your visit."

"I gave none." Sisi shook her head, removing her fur cap and allowing her hair to fall loose. "Please, do not worry. All I want is this fire, and perhaps some hot tea. I'll only be here a short time, an hour at most, just to warm myself."

"As you wish, Your Majesty." The woman nodded and shuffled off toward the kitchens, mumbling to herself as she did: "Tea, tea, tea at once. But they might have sent us word Her Majesty was coming. . . ."

Sisi took off her gloves, tossing them along with her cap onto a nearby chair, its upholstery worn and dust covered. As she stood before the fire thawing her raw fingers, she heard another horse outside. She stiffened. Had someone found out where she was and come looking for her? she wondered. Some imperial guard sent by Franz? A moment later, the door to the lodge opened, and a tall figure blocked out the slice of gray daylight that seeped in.

"Andrássy?" Sisi stood still before the feeble heat of the fire, staring at him. After a moment, she pulled her gaze away and turned back to the hearth. "Close the door; you're letting all the warmth out."

"I'm happy to see you, too, Sisi," Andrássy said, stepping into the room. She did not answer him.

Andrássy looked around the lodge, lifting

his fur-lined hat from his head and placing it beside her white cap on the chair. Sisi stole a sideways glance and saw that his cheeks were tinged pink from the cold, his tall frame covered in a long, fur-lined coat. He crossed the room and approached her, raising his own hands over the fire. "I know you are wondering how I found you."

Sisi did not say anything, keeping her gaze fixed on the flames.

"Marie Festetics told me you were riding in this area."

Sisi fumed, silently forming a censure for her attendant. But Marie couldn't have known the extent of her rupture with Andrássy — or the fact that Sisi had come here today specifically to be away from him. Meanwhile, she now stood next to him, in a secluded lodge in the pine- and snow-covered Vienna Woods, and he was staring at her, his face just inches from hers. She thought of all the times she had longed to be alone with him — and now here he was, the one person whose presence she most dreaded.

"It's remarkable, really."

She turned to him, curiosity gaining the upper hand as she asked: "What is?"

He paused a moment before answering. "How much you tell me with your face."

She frowned at this and then, realizing that she was only making herself more readable, composed her features, assuming the mask so necessary at court.

"Ah, there it is." Andrássy nodded, making her uncomfortable under the intensity with which he studied her. "Much better. Hide it all."

"You are insufferable to be around." She turned away, slipping off her fur coat and tossing it on the couch. Already she felt overheated, and she wasn't sure whether it was from the fire, or her fury with him, or both. "I am not the one who has become a Habsburg lackey."

"I wish you'd tell me how you truly felt."

"In that case, I shall gladly oblige." She turned, her tone biting. "I've found you to be insufferable of late. In fact, I feel as if I hardly know you, what with how much you've changed. I did not wish to see you today. That was why I left the palace, in fact. I came here to be alone."

And now Andrássy's face slackened entirely, and she saw his hurt so plainly across his features; she knew what she saw, because it was what she herself hid under her own bitterness and anger. What she beheld in Andrássy's face was a pain that she knew so well — a pain that had no easy cure.

"Sisi." He turned from the fire, taking off his coat and approaching her. She could smell him — he smelled like the cold, and the pines, and the smoke of this hearth. She shut her eyes, angling her body away, forcing

324

herself to stay mad. If the anger gave way to the gnawing sadness beneath it, she'd have no hope of composure.

Andrássy reached forward and put a hand on her shoulder, and she stepped away to pull her body out of his reach. Just then the woman reentered with the tea. "Oh?" She nearly dropped the tray when she saw that yet another well-dressed visitor had arrived, also unannounced, at Mayerling Lodge. "Another one? My, we don't have a visitor from court for five years straight, and on this afternoon we get two. Do I . . . shall I go and fetch another cup?"

"It's fine; he's not staying. Leave it," Sisi said, her tone flat as she nodded at the tray with the single cup of tea. The woman did as she was told, depositing the tray and scurrying from the room.

Left alone with Andrássy once more, Sisi stood silently, then walked toward the window and looked out over the stark, frozen vista of the Vienna Woods. She didn't touch the tea, nor did she look at Andrássy. On the hearth, a log popped before decomposing, sending a spray of ash onto the stone floor. When Sisi hadn't spoken for a long stretch of minutes, Andrássy filled the silence: "I wish I knew . . . how we got here."

"On horseback, it would appear," Sisi said, throwing a glance toward the stables outside the window.

"You know what I mean, Sisi. How we — you and I . . ."

"Don't," she said, lifting a hand as she turned to face him. She shook her head once. "Don't."

She couldn't say more; she knew her voice would break if she tried. Besides, they both knew how they had gotten here. They loved each other, but they both served a master — the Habsburg Empire — that cared not for love or the hopes or the heartache of any individual. After a pause, she managed a reply. "No words can change anything now, Andrássy. Perhaps it's better if we just . . . don't say anything."

Andrássy seemed to be reading her thoughts, because he nodded once. Sisi saw the tears filling his dark eyes, giving them that velvety glimmer that had always struck her as so disarming, so impossibly inviting. "Yes," he said, his voice low. He swallowed. "It's better this way."

She nodded, because she herself had decided the same thing. She knew what had to be done; she had come out here, riding and weeping across the frozen woods, to mourn it, in fact.

His voice sounded strangled when he continued: "Before we can break it, or be broken by it."

She laughed to herself — a tormented, choking sound. She was pretty certain that she was already broken by it. But at least this way, they might escape with their dignity intact. With the memory of what they had felt — what they had shared — intact. Their love would be just the latest sacrifice brought to the altar of the empire, but at least it would be brought pure and beautiful.

This time, as he reached forward, Sisi allowed Andrássy to take her hands in his, knowing that it would be the last time she ever did. She looked down, saw the way their fingers intertwined. "How it began," she said, keeping her voice low, but still hearing its tremor.

"Hmm?"

"How it began," Sisi said, squeezing her own hands and his. "When I took your hand. So many years ago."

He smiled, suddenly remembering, too. The night he had found her alone, heartbroken, in the halls of the Hofburg. It had been a troubling evening with Franz. She had bumped into Andrássy on her way back to her apartments, her spirits shattered, her confidence broken. She had taken Andrássy's hand out of desperation. She had needed someone — a friend — to listen. To prove to her that she wasn't alone. He had later confessed that it was on that night that he had fallen in love with her.

"How it began." He nodded, stroking the top of her hand with his finger. *And how it shall end, too,* she thought, meeting his eyes. As he looked at her now, she saw a fleeting glimpse of every other time he had ever looked at her this way: their first meeting in the Viennese opera house; the balmy summer evening when he had asked her to dance in Budapest; the night he had found her weeping in the halls of the Hofburg; their rainy evening stroll across the grounds of Schönbrunn on the eve of peace with Hungary; the night she had found him, alone, on Castle Hill overlooking Budapest and the River Danube. Oh, those times and so many other times!

Andrássy inclined his head toward hers, his voice thick with grief as he spoke to her: "It's better, Sisi, if I never tell you how deeply and achingly and permanently I shall love you. If I never tell you that you saved not only my country, but my very life. And how, knowing that, I would gladly lay my own life down for you, if I thought it could help you or bring you any more happiness." He paused, fighting against himself. Eventually, his voice shaky but calm, he continued: "It would not do for me to tell you that I've agonized over this, and that I've come to realize that I cannot change you, or change whom you're married to, or alter the purpose that God has for you in your life and your role. That I've realized that to keep loving you is selfish of me. That I think you, alone of all women, are perfect. And yet, by knowing you and loving you, I've come to see that in fact the best thing I can do — for you, for me, for this entire empire — is to release you." He stopped now, his eyes shutting as his words expired, choked as they were on the sobs he fought against.

The way they held hands, their bodies facing each other, it was almost as if they were making sacred vows. Affirming that, because they loved each other, they would spend their lives together. But, instead, they were doing the opposite. When Andrássy spoke next, his words confirmed that. "Sisi, in ending it now, you, to me, shall remain perfect."

She lowered her eyes, feeling the tears that slid down her cheeks, salting her lips. Lips that had no words with which to reply.

"I will always love you," he said, whispering the words. Was it a good thing for her to know all of this, or would it have been better had he never said it? She blinked, ever more tears slipping from her eyes and cutting warm lines down her wind-chapped cheeks. His words, shattering as they were, did not come as a surprise. In fact, he echoed precisely what she herself had come to know — what she had spent the past months in Gödöllő preparing herself for. Her return to Vienna and their immediate quarrel had only made it all the more apparent. They could not go on like this, she had finally admitted that to herself.

There could be no more of her seeking her fulfillment or freedom or happiness in this man — this good, wonderful man who, in spite of his goodness, could not help but fall short, as the two of them were battered by so many needs larger than the yearnings of their own two human hearts. This man, whose love had been just the latest idol she had grown disappointed in and disillusioned by. It wasn't fair for him. And it wasn't good for her.

Sisi drew in a long, fortifying breath, slipping her hands from Andrássy's, noticing that they were no longer cold. She turned back to the window. There, her breath fogging up the panes of glass, she looked out over the frozen yard. Beyond that grew the dense, snow-covered pines, and farther still, the naked hills shivered beneath a threatening winter sky. Studying this vast, desolate view, so lonely and forbidding that it made her want to weep anew, Sisi thought: *life has to return at some point.* Spring would come eventually, even to this bleak and barren landscape. It had to; it was ordained by a divine plan more steadfast and inevitable than anything she herself could understand. "I'm going to leave," she said after a while, turning to look back at Andrássy. "For the winter. Valerie has been sick for months. The doctor has told me to seek out a different climate. I shall heed his advice."

Andrássy nodded, not surprised. He knew

her well enough to know that she followed every grief or disappointment with a flight. She weathered heartache by fleeing the court, where she was not allowed to mourn. "Where will you go?" he asked.

Sisi sighed, her breath coming out as a visible mist even inside the lodge.

"To Possenhofen?"

She shook her head. "Not to Bavaria . . . it's too difficult to be there. What with Father drinking himself to death. And my sisters Marie and Helene both so upset all the time. And Ludwig . . . oh, poor Ludwig. He is more besieged by the day."

"Then to Gödöllő?"

"No." She stared at him. How could she tell him that she couldn't stand to be there now, in that place where she had once been her happiest? That he, Andrássy, was all over Gödöllő, and yet he would never be there again. Not as he had been. "No, not to Gödöllő, either. I must go somewhere far, far away. Someplace where they don't know me, and I don't know them. Someplace where everything shall be new. New and untouched by memory."

"Does such a place exist?" he asked.

"I don't know," she answered, her eyes meeting his one last time. "But if it does, I shall find it."

PART TWO

VII

"The bright star of Europe" her kingdom
    has left,
And Austria mourns of its Empress bereft.
Firm seat in the saddle: light hands on the
    reins,
As e'er guided steed over Hungary's
    plains:
She has come — with her beauty, grace,
    courage, and skill —
To ride, with our hounds, from old
    Shuckburgh Hill.

        — ENGLISH POEM WRITTEN
           ABOUT EMPRESS SISI

CHAPTER 7

Easton Neston House, Northamptonshire,
  England
Spring 1876
"If he insists on saying such spiteful things
against me, then I shall have to insist on prov-
ing him wrong."

It was a clear morning in early spring,
bright and mild, and the scene outside Sisi's
bedroom was a lush English tapestry of newly
budded leaves and thick hedgerows. The
estate she had rented for the hunting season,
a grand old home in Northamptonshire,
seemed to grow a more vibrant hue of green
as the morning sun climbed higher from the
horizon, drying up the slick sheen of dew that
glistened across the landscape like a scatter-
ing of emeralds and diamonds.

"But I can't stay cross, even upon hearing
this unpleasant gossip." Sisi sighed, gazing
out the window at the gardens, bordered by
unruly myrtle and populated by lively birds
that darted from bush to hedge to branch,

filling the yard with their songs. Beyond the gardens stood the estate's vast stables, where her horses were being put through their morning steps, and farther away was the private woodland park. It was nothing like the view from her imperial rooms in Vienna, and Sisi had the entire day to explore this pastoral playground atop her horse.

"These English are fortunate in their land-scapes, are they not?" Sisi posed the question aloud to her busy bedchamber, the large space bustling with the members of the empress's household who had traveled with her from Austria. She had with her Baron Nopcsa, dispatching his duties as master of the imperial household, and Countess Marie Festetics and Ida Ferenczy to attend to her daily needs, and Franziska Feifalik, of course, to style her hair. Valerie traveled with the imperial retinue as well, and she and her governess were completing the morning lessons in their nearby room.

The newcomer to Sisi's household, a pretty young countess named Marie Larisch, who had been hired recently, was the woman who had supplied Sisi with the gossip that she now considered. Countess Larisch had been Sisi's pick when the empress had declared the need for a fresh addition to her suite. At the time, Ida and Marie had hardly welcomed the news of another attendant joining the empress's household — Sisi had deduced that from their scowls — but they had submitted to her wishes with their pliable and self-restrained acquiescence. "Come now, ladies," Sisi had added, a note of finality to her tone, "we need at least one among us who will keep our blood young."

Sisi's selection had come from her homeland of Bavaria. Countess Marie Larisch was indeed young, the same age as Rudolf in fact, and in the full bloom of her eighteen years. As the reluctant bride of a stern, pockmarked German, a lieutenant by the name of Count Georg Larisch, the pretty little countess had been all too happy — even giddy with gratitude — to accept the invitation to join Empress Sisi's household and attend the empress on her travels abroad. Anything to get her away from her dull husband and his dilapidated, lonely castle — a need for escape that Sisi could understand and even sympathize with. Countess Larisch seemed to view each trip as an audition for a role she was determined to win, and she'd immediately set about charming Sisi with her quick wit, her fresh and vivacious laughter, and her morsels of salacious gossip.

The hiring of Marie Larisch had caused a minor scandal in Vienna. The court had quickly gleaned that Countess Larisch was related by her father to the empress but that Marie's mother was lowborn — an *actress*, of all things. Sisi laughed to think what her mother-in-law would have made of it — the hiring of such an entirely unsuitable woman as an attendant in the empress's household.

Sisi *liked* that Countess Larisch wasn't of pure blue blood and a pristinely noble pedigree; it would ensure that the lively young brunette remained loyal and close to the empress. Marie knew from where her patronage and protection came. Plus, perhaps it was Countess Larisch's questionable parentage that made her so fun and enjoyable to have around. She could sing, dance, and offer retorts as quick and entertaining as a Shakespearean comedienne. In her time in her post, Countess Larisch had filled Sisi's rooms with laughter, music, and plenty of delicious chatter.

"Now, Countess Larisch, come sit by me." Sisi patted the empty seat beside her. She was having her hair styled, the last step of her toilette before she was to be sewn into the day's riding habit. "And tell me everything you heard about this Captain Middleton. How does he already know so much about me when I've only just arrived to England?"

In fact, it was Sisi's third full day in Northamptonshire, the imperial party having arrived on Sunday to the pealing of church bells and a cheering village square. Though she was traveling incognita — or trying to — word seemed to have spread throughout the region that Austria-Hungary's famed Empress Elisabeth had come to try her equestrian skills in the legendary English hunting season. As she waved bashfully to the curious, smiling onlookers who lined the entirety of the country lane to the estate, Sisi had realized that she would be as pursued and stalked here as she was everywhere else.

On Monday, her first full day, Sisi had ridden around the private acres of her rented estate. Heeding the warnings of Nicky Esterházy and all who had ridden the English countryside before, Sisi worked to familiarize herself with the brambly, thawing terrain, its features entirely foreign and, as she had been warned, much more challenging than the flat plains of Hungary. "I don't see what can be so difficult," she had declared when she had returned home at the end of that first day. "Spring thaws the plains of Hungary just as it does the meadows and fields of England." Ida and Marie had pressed their lips together and lowered their eyes, allowing their rumpled brows to speak their concerns plainly enough.

On Tuesday Sisi accepted an invitation to lunch at Althorp palace, the nearby estate of Lord and Lady John Spencer. Lord Spencer, an earl from one of England's elite families, was the resident Northamptonshire aristocrat and Sisi's official host for the hunting season. His Lordship had been the one to recommend and secure the lodgings at Easton

Neston for the imperial party. An energetic man with an obliging smile and abundant fiery-red facial hair, just barely tinged by the gray of middle age, Earl Spencer had clearly decided to take his duties as the empress's host quite seriously.

Luncheon at Althorp was a lavish spread paired with claret wine and a detailed discussion of the English countryside — the unique obstacles presented by the shire landscapes and the special skills required of the horses that would carry the empress across them. Once more, Sisi was warned what a formidable challenge it would be to traverse the spring terrain of Northamptonshire in pursuit of the fox and stag.

It was also during this lunch at Althorp that Sisi met Captain Bay Middleton. Sisi had first noticed Captain Middleton when she arrived at the earl's palace. He stood somewhat removed from the rest of the guests, a thick-shouldered, unsmiling man in the English officer's uniform. Captain Middleton looked to be about ten years younger than she. Lord Spencer formally introduced them before the luncheon began. "We know, Empress, of your skill atop a hunter, and so I've selected Captain Bay Middleton to pilot you on tomorrow's hunt. He served in my cavalry unit back in Ireland, and I tell you, there's no better rider in Her Majesty's kingdom than Middleton here."

Captain Middleton barely acknowledged either these flattering words from his merry host or the imperial guest to whom he was being introduced. He simply looked about the room as if this luncheon and Sisi's presence were an imposition on what might otherwise have been a pleasant day.

Sisi cast quick, furtive glances toward this rude officer throughout the meal. A man of middle height — he was nowhere near Andrássy's stature — Captain Middleton nevertheless presented an imposing figure. He was sturdily built with a thick, broad chest and a haughty, square-jawed face. His hair, a coppery brown, was neatly clipped and matched by a tidy mustache under which his lips remained closed and unsmiling. Sisi groaned inwardly as she completed her survey of Middleton, discouraged that such a bad-mannered, arrogant man would be her companion on what was supposed to have been such a pleasant, enjoyable occasion. She disliked Captain Middleton immediately, and that was before she had even heard the vicious things he had said about her.

And now it was Wednesday, her third full day. Sisi had the morning to get ready before she was expected to take her place in Lord Spencer's hunting party, riding behind his hounds across the fields and forests of Northamptonshire with Captain Bay Middleton scowling beside her.

"Tell me once more, Countess Larisch." Sisi was sitting before the mirror as Franziska Feifalik wove her hair into a series of loose plaits that would be tamed and tucked under her riding cap.

"Are you certain you wish to hear such gossip, Empress?" Marie Festetics interjected from her spot by the bed where she was brushing down Sisi's riding habit, a skirt and jacket of royal blue etched with golden trim.

"Hush, Marie." Sisi raised her hand. "My experience with being gossiped about is that it's better to know what's being said than to be caught unaware." With that, Sisi nodded at her young confidante, once again patting the chair beside her.

Countess Larisch took the empty seat offered to her and threw a self-satisfied smirk at Marie Festetics before leaning toward Sisi. "Well, Empress, he's a cavalry captain by the name of George, but his friends know him simply as 'Bay.' "

"And how old is this *Bay*?"

"Thirty years old, Madame."

"And a bachelor?" Sisi asked, feeling the weight at the back of her neck grow heavier as Franziska wove more and more of her thick chestnut locks into an upswept hairstyle.

"A bachelor, but apparently a well-known favorite of the ladies." Countess Larisch giggled as Marie and Ida sighed audibly from the other side of the bedroom.

Sisi ignored her disgruntled attendants. "Is that so?"

"Yes." Countess Larisch nodded. "Apparently he's just concluded quite the scandalous affair with a noblewoman. A *married* noblewoman."

Sisi put a hand to her lips, concealing the undignified smile that tugged on them. She knew it was vile to gossip so, but Countess Larisch made it so delicious!

The young woman continued in a low voice, leaning in so that only Sisi might hear: "But now he's got to be on his best behavior because he's recently engaged."

"To whom?" Sisi asked, wondering who would willingly attach herself to such an infamous seducer, and an unpleasant one from the look and sound of it.

"A young lady by the name of Miss Charlotte Baird. A great beauty and an heiress to a vast coal and iron fortune up north. It's *her* father who has bought the last of the Middleton lands. It seems that this Bay, though skilled in riding all sorts of . . . *thoroughbreds*" — Larisch paused for effect, allowing Sisi to gasp out a scandalized laugh — "has very little cash to his name. A situation he will rectify when he marries the twenty-two-year-old heiress, Miss Charlotte Baird."

"Oh, the poor little Charlotte Baird. This is too scandalous!" Sisi tossed her head back, stifling a giggle.

"Empress, please! Be still!"

"Sorry, Franziska." Sisi sat back up, her mind still abuzz with Larisch's report. Suddenly Bay Middleton's arrogance struck her as confounding but far less unnerving. He was without land and penniless — what right did he have to show such conceit toward *her*, Empress Elisabeth of Austria-Hungary? And how had that surly man from the previous day's luncheon succeeded in seducing so many different women? But perhaps most perplexing of all — how had the news of Middleton's reputation and adventures already reached her young attendant's ears? Sisi narrowed her eyes, focusing back on the countess. "Larisch, how do you know all of this?"

Now Countess Larisch cocked her head to the side, flashing a dazzling, big-eyed smile at once both charmingly innocent and dangerously coy, and Sisi was certain that any man on the receiving end of that smile would have no choice but to fall in love with the young lady. "I have my ways, Empress."

"Never mind, I'm not certain I even wish to know. But now to the most important point, Larisch." Sisi reached over and took the young lady's hand in her own. She could practically feel Marie's and Ida's watchful, simmering disapproval from the other side of the room, but she ignored them. "Tell me once more, what vile words has this Bay Middleton said about *me*?"

Marie Larisch paused, angling her long-lashed eyes to the floor as if it pained her to repeat this next part. "He said" — she cleared her throat — "when told by Lord Spencer that he would be Your Majesty's pilot for the riding season: 'What is an empress to me? She'll only hold me back.'"

Though Sisi had already heard Captain Middleton's insults once, the night before from Larisch, hearing these words anew only quickened her indignation and caused her heart to speed up, defiant, in her breast. She knew that Bay Middleton wasn't alone in his skepticism of the empress's oft-lauded skills in the saddle. Many others had warned her of the difficulties of riding the English shires. Both Franz and Andrássy had begged her to be careful when she had departed the court in Vienna. Rudolf had looked as if he might cry when he had heard of his mother's decision to join an English hunt for the season. Even Franziska, unflappable Franziska, had suggested a hairdo that might provide cushioning to the back of Sisi's head, just in case the empress was launched from her mount and hurled to the earth.

Everyone seemed to agree that English riders were unrivaled in their skills at following hounds in the hunt and that the English countryside presented the most uniquely challenging of all hunting terrains. These were not the plowed, flat fields of Hungary. The shires presented mile after mile of untamed pasture, wild grazing land for fat livestock portioned off by hedgerows and formidable stone and wooden fences. In addition to that, the land was littered with what the locals reverentially referred to as "Pytchley bottoms," unmarked ditches and gulleys carved out of the earth for irrigation. At these points the earth yawned wide and deep, swallowing not only water, but also galloping horses and the riders unlucky enough to sit atop them as they tumbled in. These hidden ravines could be ten feet deep and more than six feet wide, and were usually bordered by fences that obscured their presence and presented further jumping obstacles.

The hounds leading English hunters had been bred to outpace the wind. They knew this terrain instinctively and did not break for prudence or addled nerves as they raced across it. The horses, trained for centuries to keep up with the hounds, showed the same disregard for caution. Falls from these hunters happened at breakneck speed and often proved fatal. If the falling rider happened to be a lady, she faced the additional disadvantage of wearing an elaborate skirt whose folds of fabric often became entangled in the saddle or stirrups and caused her to suffer any number of grisly disfigurements and harrowing ends on her way to the ground.

For all of these reasons, Sisi knew that Captain Middleton's skepticism was not entirely unfounded, even if he was incredibly rude to voice it so unabashedly. He was probably not alone in wondering whether this empress was up to an English fox hunt. Ida and Marie had not stopped frowning since their arrival to England.

And yet, since her earliest days, Sisi had always been at her most comfortable and confident atop the saddle of a horse. Rather than deter her, the fears and doubts of others now stirred her inner fire and quickened her drive to succeed. That morning, facing the concerns of her attendants and the disparaging words of Bay Middleton, she resolved that this hunting season would be a success. She would prove herself not only worthy of her reputation as the best horsewoman in Europe, but the equal of Bay Middleton himself.

Sisi fidgeted throughout the remainder of her morning toilette, moving on to dress once her hairstyle was in place. In order to be light and unencumbered, she decided to discard her petticoat, prompting quite scandalized looks on her ladies' faces. She was sewn directly into her habit, a matching blue cap set atop her thick chestnut hair. As she surveyed herself, adjusting the row of golden buttons down the front of her jacket, their luster matching the golden trim on her cuffs and neck, she nodded approvingly.

"Well, Empress," Ida Ferenczy said, as all in the room stared at her tight, statuesque figure. "You certainly look the part."

"Not yet," Sisi said, glancing sideways at the flawless line of her silhouette. "I'll look the part when I am seated happily in my saddle."

★ ★ ★

The hunting party assembled shortly after noon at Lord Spencer's Althorp estate. On spotting her, the host hurried to Sisi's side. "Empress Elisabeth, allow me to be the first to welcome you to the Pytchley fields." The nobleman bowed deeply, his long, fiery beard catching glints of the spring sunshine.

"Thank you, Lord Spencer," Sisi said, surveying the scene around them. A huge crowd had gathered, both fellow riders and onlookers on foot. Townspeople had turned out in droves to gain a glimpse of the famous empress, and many of them now cheered as she walked out to join the horses.

Sisi spotted Bay Middleton, who turned upon hearing her name called out, his face still unsmiling. He excused himself from the conversation in which he was already in-volved, turning to walk toward the empress. Sisi steeled herself, standing tall as she studied his approaching figure. For someone who was purported to be without an inheritance, Bay Middleton certainly dressed well, looking like the consummate country gentleman. He wore a scarlet coat and tails, his tight-fitting breeches hugging thick, strong legs, his leather boots climbing up his calves. His hair was combed back neatly, his top hat in his gloved hands.

"Empress Elisabeth." He offered half a bow as he paused before her, barely enough to be polite.

"Good day, Captain Middleton."

From across the field, several bugles began to sound, their upbeat notes ringing across the bright, sunlit scene. Cries of "To saddles! Take your mounts!" now joined the bugle notes.

Without speaking, Bay extended his arms to help Sisi into her saddle. Sisi submitted to his assistance, aware that so many eyes watched and not wanting to fuel the rumors that were surely circulating about her and his doubts of her. He lifted her easily, his strong arms making her feel featherlight as he hoisted her onto her mount.

The crowds began to roar all around her, cheering and waving and clapping. Sisi was accustomed to this; her appearances in public always caused an uproar. But, as she listened, she noticed, to her astonishment, that it was not her name that they yelled.

"Bay!" "Brave Bay!" "Bay Middleton!"

Sisi stole a furtive glance toward Bay where he stood beside her, his hands guiding her leather heels into the stirrups. Was he some sort of local hero? A celebrity, even? Bay Middleton looked up at her now, his eyes seeming to voice once more his lack of faith in her, even his mockery. She shifted in her saddle, tossing her chin forward as she straightened up to her full height. "You know, Captain Middleton, I've told —"

"Call me Bay."

Sisi stopped short, stunned to speechlessness at having been interrupted. And by *him,* a nonnoble, penniless cavalry officer! She twisted the reins in her gloved hands, pausing a moment before continuing. "Fine, *Bay. . . .* I've told Lord Spencer that under no circumstances are you to go easy on me."

Bay stared directly up at her now, his light blue eyes flickering as they caught a flash of afternoon sunlight. After a pause, he cracked the first smile she had ever seen on his face. "If you say so, Empress Elisabeth."

Sisi settled into her seat atop the chestnut hunter as Bay mounted his own horse and joined her. They were in a hunting party of about three hundred people, from the look of it. Sisi studied her company, aware from the previous day's conversation that these assemblies, numbering in the hundreds at the outset, usually ended with only four to six riders making it through the entire hunt. Everyone around her would fall, be thrown, be thwarted by an obstacle, or give up from fatigue or fear before the day's ride was over. She clutched tight to the reins, adjusting her leather gloves and offering a silent prayer that she might be one of the few to last the day.

As Sisi shifted in her saddle, the horse beneath her began to respond to her nerves with its own twitchy pacing, and so she reminded herself to remain calm. She had grown up in a saddle; this was where she was most comfortable. She shut her eyes and took in a deep breath, allowing herself to tune in to her horse's mood and movements. Her senses slipped into a familiar state of hyper-alertness, her body cleaving to and communing with the saddle and the horse beneath it, preparing the animal to move with her as one. As an extension of her own frame, an executor of her determined will.

Lord Spencer took his mount now, and the crowds cheered ever louder as the horses shifted and paced to the front of the field, a large throng of anxious and anticipatory energy pulsing from human and horse alike. The bugles played out the call once more, and the hounds were brought out, braying and barking and pulling on their leashes. The dogs' agitation seemed to make the horses — and the riders — even more feverish, and Sisi fought her horse's attempts to fidget beneath her.

The hounds were unleashed, and several of them caught a first whiff of fox, and before Sisi was aware of what was happening, they were off, barking and howling as if they would outrun the riders of the Apocalypse. Without a word to her, Bay took off, urging his horse to follow right behind the hounds, and Sisi propelled her hunter forward, determined to keep close to him.

They flew across the first field at the front of the pack, the wind whipping her face as she heard the thunder of hooves and the blood-lusting howls of the hounds all around her. The first fence was upon them before she knew it, and she felt her entire body tighten in anticipation, every muscle within her alert and engaged. It was a stake-and-binder fence, not too high. She had cleared these before, she reminded herself, holding tight to her reins as she matched her body to the rhythm of the horse. Bay took the fence a few paces before her. She watched him out of the corner of her eye and then prepared for her own jump, throwing her weight forward to join the horse in the thrust. She cleared it effortlessly and couldn't help but laugh out in delight as she and the horse felt solid ground beneath them once more.

She noticed how Bay peered over his shoulder, making sure that she had landed, and she met his gaze with a defiant smile, her eyebrows gliding upward as if to ask: *Did you expect anything less?*

What was the expression on Bay's face in that moment? Sisi wondered. Approval? Surprise? Whatever it was, Sisi pressed her legs into her horse and urged it to speed up, no longer content to be a few paces behind Bay.

Already the crowd around them had thinned as some of the riders had sought a way around the first fence while others had fallen back to take the field and its fences at a slower pace. Sisi felt the full intoxicating effects of adrenaline coursing through her veins now, and she breathed happily and quickly, turning to glance at Bay beside her.

They crossed another field side by side, taking a small brook at a gallop and easily overcoming several rows of thick hedges. By the end of the first half hour, they were out front alone, the only riders still clipping at the same pace as the hounds. Sisi took the next fence, a stone barrier, right beside Bay.

"Good," he shouted, his voice loud enough to surmount the roar of their horses' hooves and his and Sisi's panting. A wide, unobstructed field stretched out before them now, and Sisi's heart soared at the pleasure of it all: the green countryside; the crisp, clean air; the welcome ache of exertion in her muscles. Even Bay's skepticism was visibly diminishing as he kept glancing at her, his rigid facial expression thawing into what almost resembled a smile. Regardless of whether she finished the day's hunt apace with the hounds, Sisi would consider it a success. She had at least ridden well enough not to have embarrassed herself or compromised her good reputation.

"You have it already, Empress." Bay panted beside her, and Sisi noticed, with delight, that his breathing seemed even more labored than her own. "Your Majesty thinks, and the beast intuits. You have your horse in communion with your desires and commands."

Sisi tilted her head to the side, stunned at Bay's words of approval. "Would that it were so easy with the other men in my life," she said. Her heart leapt with delight when she saw how Bay smiled at this.

At the end of the field, Sisi's spirits still soared, but though she was tireless, she felt the troubling signs of fatigue in her horse. She'd had him at a run for most of the past hour, and his steps were landing with increased heaviness. His breath seemed to come louder and more labored with each pace.

Sisi and Bay entered a dense, damp woodland. "There will be ruts up ahead," Bay cried over his shoulder, his body assuming a position of readiness as the world around them fell under the shadow of thick, leafy branches.

Sisi clutched her reins tighter and narrowed her eyes, trying to scan the soggy earth for the signs of upcoming trouble. The first obstacle was a small hedge. The horse cleared it, but not with the same agility as earlier in the day. Sisi began to worry, wishing she could transfer some of her seemingly inexhaustible energy to her horse.

She was falling behind Bay now, her horse struggling to keep up. She was lucky for this, because he reached the next gulley several paces before her, giving her time to prepare for it. "Ditch!" Bay yelled, glancing back to warn her once he was safely on the other side. "Take it full on!"

Sisi leaned forward, readying herself as she urged her horse onward. She kicked to speed him up, but his legs were spent, and he failed to summon enough spring before leaping across the deep rut. Before Sisi knew what was happening, she felt her horse falter on his landing, his body pitching forward at a downward angle. Sisi flew forward now, too, her body's inertia launching her over the head of the tumbling horse. It all happened quickly, and her body reacted with instinct more than reason or purpose. She didn't have time to think much of anything — in fact, the only thought that even vaguely crossed her mind in that instant was a fleeting image of Valerie. She couldn't die — she couldn't leave Valerie.

Sisi tightened every muscle in her frame, drawing herself into a ball and rolling as her body met the ground. She shut her eyes, begging God to keep the horse from landing on her. *What an awful way to die, horse hooves shattering one's skull,* she thought. She noticed with a detached sense of relief, her mind whipping about, how soft the earth felt beneath her as she tumbled across grass and mud. Perhaps this made it less likely that she would snap her neck.

The horse had stumbled a few feet away, miraculously not landing on her, and he was quickly righted to his feet. Sisi stopped rolling and lay motionless on the ground, blinking up at the patches of sky that filtered in through the leafy branches, her mind and body in a state of dazed and foggy inertness. She was alive, she realized; but was she paralyzed? she wondered. And then her mind leapt to the next logical question: would it be preferable to be paralyzed or dead?

Bay was off his horse and standing over her, his face twisted tight in concern. "Empress!" He crouched down beside her, his eyes just inches from hers. She noticed, absently, that she had not lost consciousness. And her lungs, temporarily stunned from the impact of the fall, now gasped for air. She inhaled, tasting dirt and grass on her lips. She could breathe; a promising sign, she thought.

"Empress, it was not your fault!" Bay

hunched over her supine figure, speaking to her with an uncharacteristic softness. "Are you hurt?" Kneeling beside her, he removed his gloves and then wrung his hands, apparently unsure of the protocol for touching his imperial companion to check for signs of injury. "May . . . may I?"

"Yes."

As Bay's hands reached tentatively toward her, pressing gently into her legs, Sisi performed her own scan of her body. "Can . . . can you feel that?" Bay asked, tapping gently on her knees.

"Yes," Sisi answered.

"Does it hurt terribly?"

"In fact . . . no." She realized, to her utter relief, that nothing ached.

"And what of your arms?"

As Sisi moved her fingers and then her arms and wrists, she marveled that she might actually have escaped the fall completely uninjured. She hadn't broken her neck; she hadn't even broken a finger.

"Not your fault at all, Empress!" Bay was less assured of her well-being, still in a state of visible distress beside her. "No rider could have stayed in the saddle through such a fall. The horse was spent. I'm sure no one could have taken it better than you thus far."

Sisi absorbed the meaning of Bay's complimentary words as, simultaneously, she realized that she was entirely unhurt. She was so happy at these two realizations — and so ecstatic that Bay was clearly disabused of his skepticism of her — that she broke out into laughter, reaching for Bay's arm and pulling herself up to a seated position. "Thank you, Bay!" she exclaimed, still giddy with relief and the great fortune of having survived, both her body and her ego intact. "Oh, thank you, thank you!"

"But . . . Empress . . . are you . . . are you hurt?"

"Entirely unhurt!" With Bay's help she rose to a standing position. She looked over her body once more. Her hat had fallen off, her hair had been shaken loose and now fell in disheveled waves about her face, but other than that, everything was as it should be. Even more astounding, she and Bay stood entirely alone in the copse, their lead ahead of the pack having been so substantial that they remained a few minutes' ride, still, in front of the others.

Bay leaned over, retrieving her hat from the ground a few paces away. He held it out to her. "Again, I say, not your fault at all."

"I know," Sisi said, putting her hand to his arm, losing herself for a moment in her joy. Bay's eyes flew to her hand where it rested on him, and she withdrew it quickly, remembering herself. She took the hat he held out to her. "Thank you." She replaced the cap on her hair and stood up straight, patting down her skirt. Just then she heard a bark in the not-too-distant field beyond the small wood. "Bay, I think we can still do it; we can still catch the hounds."

He looked at her now, his features making plain that he was impressed, perhaps even a bit incredulous. He had a slick of perspiration across his brow, and his chest still heaved in uneven, labored breath. "Really, Empress? You're ready for it — getting back on your mount?"

Sisi nodded, striding toward her hunter and taking the reins in her hands. "I am."

"If . . . if you think so . . . But I don't wish to overtax —"

"What did I tell you, Bay? You are not to go easy on me."

He smiled now, his features spreading in an expression of open approval. Staring at him, Sisi noted how his cheeks shone rosy from the exertion, how his tousled, rust-colored hair fell around his strong-featured face, and she caught a glimpse of just why Bay Middleton had the reputation he had. Why the townspeople cheered when they spotted him, why women found it impossible to resist his unique brand of virile and haughty charm.

Bay, meanwhile, extended his hands, taking Sisi's waist in his still-ungloved grip as he lifted her effortlessly once more into the saddle. After she was up, easily seated, his hands lingered just a moment longer around her waist, his body pressed close to her legs as he looked up into her eyes. And then, flashing his relaxed smile, he said, "I'm beginning to think, Empress, that perhaps I had better ask *you* to go easy on *me.*"

VIII

Geneva, Switzerland
September 1898

"No, he's not coming." The bartender stares at Luigi and shakes his head once. "The Duke of Orléans has changed his plans. Wanted to go hunting . . . and I don't think it was for wildlife. The man loves his women, from the sound of it." The barkeep smirks, holding up a cup to make sure it has reached an appropriate luster.

Luigi could cry out in agonized frustration; the French pretender has evaded him. After everything he has planned. After his plotting of the Great Deed. Now what is he supposed to do? His entire errand appears foolish — his life's purpose is suddenly rendered null. How unjust it all is! These nobles can simply change their plans from one day to the next on a whim. They know that their gilded coaches will carry them from town to town, country to country, as if miles mean nothing. But how is Luigi to track the duke down when he has only his blistered feet to carry him?

But then, as soon as he is pierced, he is saved. He looks down on the bar counter and sees, beside his soup, the newspaper. The front page bears the photo of a beautiful, dark-haired woman, her fine-featured face flashing a coy, timid smile. Below the image sits the headline:

EMPRESS ELISABETH OF
AUSTRIA-HUNGARY IN GENEVA!
HER IMPERIAL MAJESTY HONORS
THE HÔTEL BEAU RIVAGE WITH A VISIT

The Hôtel Beau Rivage. Why, that's just up the avenue. The nicest, most decadent hotel in town. The one with the snobbiest porters and most dismissive patrons filing in and out of its doors. Empress Elisabeth. The most beautiful woman in the world. Wife to Emperor Franz Joseph, the most powerful man in Europe.

"Even better." Luigi whispers the words. Who is the Duke of Orléans, when Luigi can have Empress Elisabeth of Austria-Hungary instead? He can't believe his own great luck. His heart begins to race, his blood churning so wildly that he has to force himself to remain calm. It's just his secret. At least, for now, though soon enough, the whole world will know.

Chapter 8

Easton Neston House, Northamptonshire, England

Spring 1876

That evening Sisi insisted, over the disapproval of her entire household, on keeping her plans to host a small dinner party.

"But is it wise after your fall, Your Majesty?" Ida asked.

"Perhaps Your Grace ought to retire early tonight to let your body recover from the shock?" Marie Festetics added.

"I shouldn't even have told you it happened," Sisi answered, sighing, as her ladies suggested yet again that she postpone the dinner party. "I should have known you'd be as disapproving as Franz. Lord, I definitely will not be telling *him.*"

In truth, the spill had left Sisi without so much as a scrape. If anything, it had added to the heady sense of pleasure with which she'd left the day's ride. She and Bay alone had lasted the entire hunt. The difficult

English terrain had thrown its worst at her; her horse had struggled while she had prevailed, even excelled. Now, as twilight settled over the gardens and evening crept in through her opened bedroom windows, as the servants downstairs clamored and hustled about in their preparations for the evening meal, Sisi felt spent but exultant.

Sisi greeted her guests that evening wearing a simple, tight-fitting gown of black and white, rose and camellia petals laced through her hair, pearls trimming her collar and wrists. She suspected that her most radiant adornment, however, was her smile. She was happy, and she knew that it showed. "Lord Spencer, welcome to Easton Neston. How can I thank you enough for the splendid day we had today?"

"It is Your Majesty who must be thanked. I don't think Northamptonshire has been the center of so much chatter and excitement ever before." The nobleman's fair skin was kissed a soft pink by the day's sunshine, almost matching his beard and sideburns.

"And Lady Spencer, good evening." Sisi turned, smiling warmly to the noblewoman before her. "Welcome to Easton Neston."

"Thank you, Empress Elisabeth." Lady Spencer curtsied, her manners gracious, though more reserved than those of her affable husband.

At the last minute, Sisi had decided to

invite Bay to dinner, mentioning it to him only after the hunt had ended. When he arrived now, dressed once again in his tidy officer's uniform, his face more relaxed than it had been when he'd greeted her at luncheon the day prior, Sisi felt her cheeks flush warm, and she couldn't help but smile at him, remembering the afternoon they had passed together in the countryside. "Captain Middleton," she said, nodding at him as he bowed before her, "thank you for joining us."

"What did I ask, Empress? That you call me Bay."

"Very well, Bay, welcome," Sisi said. "Please allow me to introduce you to Countess Marie Larisch, and this is Countess Marie Festetics, and my attendant Ida Ferenczy."

Bay nodded at each of them in turn before turning back to Sisi. And then, with an easy grin, he said, "So many beautiful ladies, I think I might have to visit Easton Neston with some regularity, Empress."

Dinner was a casual, festive affair, with the distance from Vienna and the court allowing Sisi to eschew the formal procedure and etiquette that encumbered such gatherings in Austria's capital. Rather than holding to the imperial rule that allowed a diner to speak only to those seated immediately to his or her left and right, Sisi allowed the talk to flow freely, along with the food and the wine. Before long, the conversation turned into quick-paced banter between Spencer and Bay. Sisi called for more wine as the meat was cleared, and by the time dessert was served, Spencer was chiding Bay good-naturedly on some of his recent practical jokes. Bay cast repeated glances in Sisi's direction, attempting to exculpate himself in front of his hostess, but Spencer proved relentless.

"I'll tell you the most challenging thing about sharing your lodgings with Bay Middleton," Lord Spencer said, wiping his bright beard with his napkin before taking a large gulp of wine. "It's that you never know what you'll find under your sheets."

Sisi and the other ladies lowered their eyes in appropriate modesty at the remark. Sisi helped herself to another drink, laughing into her cup.

"Come now, Spencer, you make me sound like a villain!" Bay said, glancing apologetically toward Sisi. He spoke informally to Spencer, even though the older man was his senior in military service and a member of the peerage, while he himself was not of noble birth. And without even an inheritance, if the rumors were true.

Nevertheless, it was clear that Bay was a special favorite of Spencer's and that the casual rebuttal from his subordinate not only didn't offend the earl but in fact cheered him on. "Well, you *are* a villain, Middleton, so I can't very well make you *sound* like something that you already are. But no, ladies, ladies, I don't mean to be vulgar." Spencer lifted his hands, turning first to Sisi and then to his wife with a look of exaggerated contrition. "It's nothing so uncouth as it sounds. Simply that Captain Middleton here is a great joker."

"Oh, we know that well at Althorp, John," Lady Spencer said, allowing a modest chuckle to escape her thin, aristocratic lips.

Her husband continued, less restrained now. "Bay loves to alarm his friends by planting little surprises for them so that, after a long night of port and billiards, when they lay their heads down to rest, they don't know what awaits them. What was it you did to poor George Lambton? Was it a dead frog you put in his bed when we were in Leicestershire?"

"A toad," Bay said, his cheeks flushing scarlet as his eyes darted to Sisi. "But I can promise you this: the toad I put in that bed was a lot better looking than any other creature that George has had between his sheets."

A peal of scandalized but hearty laughter rose up from around the table, and Sisi laughed the loudest. Such talk would never be appropriate in Vienna — or even in Hungary, for that matter. These English had such a jovial way of ribbing and jesting with one another; there was an ease about their gatherings that she hadn't enjoyed since her childhood in Possenhofen.

"Now, then, Bay, has Doggie Smith ever forgiven you for the prank you pulled in Combermere?" Spencer asked. "The time you swapped out his riding jacket for the lady's coat?"

Bay propped his elbows on the table and rested his chin on his hands, chuckling to himself. "Must you undo me like this, Spencer? I was hoping not to entirely offend the empress."

"Has he? Has he forgiven you?" Spencer rapped the table with his knuckles, guffawing. "Come now, Bay, you must tell the empress what you did to the poor chap. I insist; otherwise I'll ship you back off to Ireland as punishment for disregarding my orders."

Bay protested, but when Sisi also insisted, he relented. "I'll tell you, Empress, but only if you promise to believe me when I say that he deserved it."

Sisi cocked her head to the side, smiling at Bay. "I'll decide that once I've heard."

Bay nodded. "Doggie is a friend of ours who —"

"*Was* a friend of yours! Perhaps no longer," Spencer said.

Bay smirked. "*Was* a friend of mine who . . . How shall I say this, Spencer?"

"He takes great pride in his appearance," Spencer said, providing the words, looking at Sisi and then his wife as he tipped the wine decanter toward his glass.

"Indeed," Bay said, nodding his agreement. "By the way, Spencer, save some wine for us, won't you? Anyway, Doggie is a man who is always well turned out. And likes to point out the superiority of his own appearance to anyone else's."

Lady Spencer chuckled knowingly. Sisi listened, growing merrier with each passing minute in Bay and Spencer's company.

"So on our final afternoon at Combermere, we were to hunt, and there was a certain lady scheduled to join, a lady in whom Doggie . . . Captain Smith . . . had expressed an interest."

"Ah, yes. Wasn't it Marjorie Thurston?" Spencer asked.

"It was," Bay replied.

"Marjorie can ride well enough," Spencer mused aloud, "but it's not as though she's —"

Bay interjected, "She's nothing compared to you, Empress."

Sisi blushed at this, then asked herself why Bay's approval had brought out this response.

Bay continued. "Anyhow, given Marjorie's presence that day, I knew that Doggie would wear his scarlet jacket and take great pains to look his best. And so I bribed Doggie's valet to let me swap out Doggie's very well-tailored and well-fitted riding jacket with . . ."

"With the exact same jacket, only made for a woman!" Spencer howled, leaning forward to erupt in good-natured laughter.

"Don't forget the bows, Spencer."

"The bows!" Now Spencer was practically clutching his sides, his face turning crimson as he devolved into hysterics.

"John, really." Lady Spencer raised a hand to her brow, scandalized, but she smirked at Sisi as if to say that this hilarity was a regular occurrence between her husband and Bay Middleton.

"It was quite a nice jacket," Bay said, shrugging as he drained his glass of wine. "The bows down the front really gave Doggie a bit of flair."

Spencer was choking, he was laughing so hard. "He had no choice, you see? No gentleman would dare go out riding without his jacket. He'd already sent everything else with his valet to be cleaned, having saved his best coat for the final day with Marjorie. And no one had another one to lend to him — Bay had seen to that."

"But how did he fit into it?" Larisch asked, flashing her merriest smile as she leaned toward Bay. Sisi bristled slightly at the young girl's advance, suddenly aware that she felt a proprietary possessiveness over Bay and that she didn't want her pretty, young attendant diverting his attention. She sat up straighter.

Bay answered: "It was a bit . . . snug." He winked at Larisch. "I fear it had ripped down the back before the afternoon was over."

"And what did the lady think?" Sisi asked, angling her body to face Bay, noting with satisfaction that, as she did so, his attention was pulled from Larisch to her.

"Oh, she liked it well enough. Asked where he had had it made. Said she fancied one exactly the same for herself."

After dinner the group retired into the drawing room, and Spencer entertained the party with a recap of the day's hunt. "Truly, Empress, you have impressed even those of us who began the day's event feeling confident of your skills. And those of us who were skeptical" — Sisi did not miss how Spencer threw a teasing look toward Bay — "well, those individuals, you have completely won over."

Sisi forced herself not to smile too broadly. "You are too kind, Lord Spencer. I can't remember a day in which I enjoyed myself as much, perhaps ever."

"I marvel," Spencer said, holding out his port glass for a refill. He looked from Sisi to Bay. "Only the two of you left at the end, out of hundreds. Bay, I think you might have finally met your match."

Bay, meeting Sisi's eyes, flashed half a grin as he answered, "Indeed I have."

The next day dawned clear and mild, and Bay greeted Sisi in the field with a warm smile rather than a cold scowl. "I am to be your pilot once more, Empress, if you'll have me."

"Gladly." Sisi felt her stomach tumble as Bay lifted her into the saddle, his strong hands holding tight to her waist before taking her feet and guiding them into the stirrups.

Once more, they found themselves far out in front of the pack after the first half hour of the chase. They loped happily across a field, granting their horses a brief respite as the hounds struggled to regain the lost fox scent. Bay moved his horse close to Sisi's so that they rode side by side. "How did you learn to ride so, Empress?" Bay asked.

Up ahead of them, the hounds had their snouts pressed determinedly to the ground, sniffing through the underbrush for the lost trail. Above them, large clouds slid slowly across a bright sky, like lazy white sailboats manned by phantom crews. Sisi inhaled, marveling at the beauty of the English countryside all around them. At the early buds that colored the branches with shoots of green. At the fields that rolled across the horizon in slopes of soft, fertile earth. She turned to Bay. "How about when we're alone out here, you call me Sisi?"

Bay cocked a single eyebrow, a restrained smile lighting his red-cheeked face. "If you insist?"

"I do."

"Right, then. How did you learn to ride so well, Sisi?"

Sisi smiled, liking the way her name sounded on his English tongue. "It was when I was a child," she answered. "My father always joked that, had we not been born a duke and duchess, he and I could have been circus riders."

Bay considered this in silence. A few paces away, the hounds were still scouring the ground, desperately trying to locate a hint of the fox. "I will confess," Bay said a moment later, "I so look forward to my time in the hunting fields. I long for these months all year. I was desperately afraid I'd have to hang back for you when Spencer told me I'd be your pilot. Or, even more dreadfully, I feared that I'd have to keep to the road with you, leaving the fields and brooks and fences to the others."

Sisi gasped in mock indignation. "Keep to the road?"

"I see now that my fears were unfounded," Bay said, quick to undo any offense.

"I knew I'd win you over eventually," Sisi said. "Even when I heard the things you were saying about me."

Bay allowed his mouth to fall open, a look

374

of raw mortification. "But . . . Your Majesty . . . you heard?"

Sisi nodded.

"But . . . if you don't mind my asking so . . . how did you hear? You had only just arrived to England."

Sisi shrugged, her face expressionless. "My spies."

Bay gasped. "Then you *do* have spies? Spencer and I were wondering, but I thought surely —"

Sisi couldn't help but laugh now, and she covered her lips with her gloved hand. "I'm only joking. Goodness, I don't have *spies* with me. Who do you think I am?"

"The Empress of Austria-Hungary."

"No spies in my retinue. Sorry to disappoint you." Though Larisch might have been a spy, considering how effective she'd proven at tracking gossip.

"Then how did you hear?" Bay asked.

Sisi threw him a sideways glance, allowing herself half a smile. "I guess you were speaking so loudly of your unhappiness that news of it reached my household."

"Well, now I'm dreadfully embarrassed."

Sisi chuckled at his blush. "At least you didn't replace my riding coat with something that didn't fit. Or put a toad in my bed. I suppose I should feel fortunate in comparison."

■ ■ ■ ■

The hounds never reclaimed the fox's scent, but Sisi and Bay stayed out for hours, racing across the countryside on their own and leaping the hedges and fences as if they were giving frantic chase. When they returned, hours later, Sisi's legs burned, and her lungs felt scrubbed clean by the fresh country air. She could have ridden for hours more, had the sun only been willing to remain high in the sky.

Back at the stables, Bay helped her down from her mount, and she paused a moment, taken aback by his expression as she landed on the ground opposite him. "Bay? What is it?"

"Nothing, Empress . . . Sisi." But he looked at her so intensely that she shifted, all the while keeping her hands in his own.

"Tell me, what is it? Why do you look at me as if I've grown a second head?"

"It's just that . . ." Bay swallowed, apparently struggling for the words as his eyes continued to scour hers.

"What?"

"Your eyes."

"Yes, what about them?" She blinked.

"They are hazel, aren't they?"

Sisi nodded.

"Well, right now they appear as if they are full of fire."

Nighttimes most often found Sisi back at Easton Neston, pleasantly fatigued and ready for sleep. Late at night, after supper — a meal Sisi usually ate in private with Valerie, unless the Spencers invited her to a more formal dinner — and after she'd had her limbs massaged and her clothes sorted for the next day, she'd dismiss Ida and Marie and Franziska and Larisch, and she'd curl up with a journal. She wrote nightly that spring, noting, as she flipped back through the pages, how often Bay's name appeared — in every entry, usually more than once.

> Today Bay showed me a woodland where I am convinced fairies must live.
> Bay showed me how to leap a double stone fence with very little impact on the landing.
> Bay and I lost the others even sooner than usual today.
> Great success for Bay and me today.

Her letters home to Franz and Rudy also mentioned Bay, though she made certain to mute her enthusiasm and curtail the frequency with which she included his name in her anecdotes, even though there wasn't a single minute of her riding that didn't include him beside her.

They rode all day, every day except Sunday. Even that small break, required by church law, began to feel like an interminable agony for Sisi. On their rides, once they had found themselves alone with no one but their horses and the hounds, Bay would ask Sisi about life in Vienna and Budapest. She told him about Gisela and Rudolf, but spoke mostly of Valerie. He told her about his time serving in Ireland under Spencer. She rarely mentioned Franz, never mentioned Andrássy. Not once did Bay speak the name of Charlotte Baird, and Sisi never asked about her.

"But why don't you ride like this in Austria?" Bay asked one afternoon, several weeks into her stay. It was a moody spring day, and a thick cover of bruised clouds threatened to drop rain on them at any moment.

Sisi considered the question, ignoring the weather as her horse carried her farther from the stables. "In Vienna, everything is dictated by protocol," she said. "Even the question of to whom one speaks at dinner or how much wine one may drink must be answered by pre-written rule. The emperor decides who gets to taste which dishes and in what order. How long we may all sit at the table. Nothing is natural; nothing is free. This . . . this is living."

Franz wrote daily, but the news he reported

was so horrid that Sisi dreaded his letters. In Bulgaria, the Ottoman authorities were killing people to put down a rebellion. Turkey was threatening a war with Russia after the tsar's imperial navy had made a threat to seize the Dardanelles strait. Andrássy and the Hungarians were pushing Franz to side with Turkey, so persistent was their hatred of Russia since the tsar had helped crush their own revolution of 1848, but Franz was unwilling to make an enemy of the most powerful kingdom in the east. Nor did he wish to do anything to upset Germany.

Rudolf, now seventeen, was also a cause of daily stress for his father. Franz Joseph, usually so dispassionate and patient, railed to Sisi about their son's mounting gambling debts, about the reports of disgruntled husbands and outraged brothers and sons and fathers who vowed to take vengeance on the crown prince for seducing their wives and sisters and mothers and daughters. Franz wrote:

It seems that our son, who put off entering manhood longer than other boys his age, is now fully embracing the more base pleasures of said manhood. And apparently he possesses an appetite and a prowess to match a man of twice his age and experience. From the sound of it, he seeks companions for himself no longer just among the more pliable and discreet ladies of the court, but with women throughout the capital city, perhaps even the empire. It is most troubling for me to hear these reports of his indiscretions. It is most anathema to the character and comportment that I would hope to see in my son. Most contradictory to the example I have always tried to model.

And then there were the almost daily articles excoriating her, Sisi, for her prolonged absence from court and the exorbitant cost of her trip to England. Franz included glimpses of the articles: "My dear, the paper today said you 'live only for your horses.' The sooner you consent to return home, the better for us all."

But for Sisi, these letters only confirmed that she had made the right decision in leaving. What could she do to help Franz, even if she were beside him at court? He wouldn't listen to her advice on politics any more than Rudolf would take orders from his mamma on his romantic indiscretions.

And besides, her love for the English countryside was growing more impassioned each day. The people loved her, and the terrain was challenging her in a way in which she had never before been challenged. Bay, too, was challenging her in a way in which she had never before been challenged. And she was meeting the challenge! How could her days out here not delight her when her handsome, strong riding companion made her laugh so, and took such pleasure in showing her all of the beauty and excitement of his native land? How could she return home right now, right as she was finally finding happiness and fulfillment? And what would even be the point?

When guilt nagged at her, drawing her focus back toward Vienna and her obligations there, Sisi would remind herself that Rudy was a man now. He was impenetrable, foreign to her — as lost to her as Gisela had become. Franz had his ministers and his bureaucrats — the only people whose advice he ever sought anyway. No, only Valerie needed her at this point, and Valerie was here. There was no reason to cut short such a pleasant sojourn. And so, she continued to relish her freedom and her days in the English fields.

"I have only one concern," she said to Bay one mild afternoon in mid-April. The night before had dropped a heavy rain over the countryside, and the earth beneath them was sodden, the air still heavy with a thick, warm dampness. "It is that my horse is not up to the task."

She had tumbled a few times in the past few weeks, when her horse had failed to clear a brook or a gulley. Each time she had escaped unhurt, but she wondered if her luck might eventually run out.

Bay considered her statement, eventually nodding. "You are right."

"Really?" She turned to him, the surprise evident in her voice. "But you never agree with me."

Bay smiled at this teasing. "In this case, you are right."

After that, Bay insisted that Sisi borrow one of his own English hunters. "I have more than I need, Sisi. You would do me great honor to ride one of my hunters. Besides, this way you shall stop slowing me down with your frequent tumbles."

The horse Bay loaned to Sisi was named Merry Andrew, and he proved to be as tireless as Sisi and Bay. His gait was smooth and steady, and Sisi's rides atop him were entirely different. What had previously been enjoyable for Sisi now became almost a source of rapture. When Bay took to repeating the quip "Merry Andrew, you're the luckiest male in Victoria's realm," Sisi couldn't help but laugh, opening her fan to hide her scarlet blush.

What was it about Bay? Sisi would ask herself each night as she relived the highlights of the day. She'd sit before the mirror and note how her cheeks glowed from sun and fresh air and a feeling of intense delight. She'd look into her own eyes, half alarmed as she saw what Bay had seen — that the amber of her irises seemed to hold some bewitching, latent flame. She'd recall some bit of laughter they had shared and find herself in fresh spasms of giddiness, eager for the night to pass quickly so that the next day could dawn and bring Bay to her once more. She'd think of the pressure of his hands on her waist as he'd hoisted her so smoothly into her saddle. Of the way they'd lingered in the stables at the end of the day, both of them eager to prolong the time in each other's company rather than take their leave.

Bay was unlike any man she had ever known. Andrássy was all soul and tortured idealism and poetry. That was probably why she and he could not work together; a pair of dreamers couldn't get by in the hard reality of their world. They needed a realist's grounding influence. That was Franz, she supposed. Opposite Andrássy's idealism and yearning, Franz was reasonable and unyielding. A large dose of solid, dependable, unwavering practicality. No, there was nothing whimsical about Franz Joseph.

But Bay. Bay "The Bravest of the Brave" Middleton. Bay was something else entirely. He was built like a strong, sturdy man, yet he laughed and behaved like a mischievous boy. So entirely unlike Franz, who had never behaved like a boy, even as a child. Bay evaded her understanding. She didn't know why she craved his approval so greedily, but she did. Out in the fields, his moods were blustery and capricious. He could be solicitous and cheerful one moment, and the next minute he'd retreat behind a haughty scowl, critiquing her form or telling her that she could do better. He would howl at her any number of times over the course of an afternoon, his deep voice roaring over the clamor of horse hooves with commands that would sound forceful, even impolite, to others:

"Take the fence directly, Sisi!" "Move left, left, now!" "Get up; you're not hurt."

But Sisi took it in stride because it was an unspoken part of their contract. Out there, she wanted to be free of the trappings of the empire. She wanted to be Bay's equal in skill. And if she was going to be his equal, Bay had to be allowed to speak to her as a riding partner, not as an attendant addressing an empress. She, in turn, could not expect the same obsequious adoration and censored civility that she received from every other person in her life, her husband included. Horses and hounds didn't care about protocol and formality, so if they were to master horses and hounds together, neither could Sisi and Bay.

Bay was direct with her in a way that no man had ever dared to be. He was free and raw and candid in her company, so she found herself behaving in the same way. In carving out this dynamic with him, Sisi allowed Bay to play a role in her life that no other man

had ever played, at least, not since her childhood and her ascension to empress. After
decades on her isolated, exalted pedestal,
never knowing a man or woman who would
dare to so brazenly buck her, she found this
manner of Bay's to be refreshing and energiz-
ing and maddening, in the best ways possible.
Each time Bay raised his voice to express his
honest frustration with her, each time he
scowled to disagree with something she said
or did, she found herself pulled even closer
to him, her desire for him warming and coloring her cheeks with a flush more potent than
anything the fresh spring breezes and hours
of exertion could summon. She craved nothing so much as she craved Bay's strong and
earnest smiles, his hard-earned words of approval, and the prospect that, out here, when
she excelled and thrived, she might earn his
admiration.

★ ★ ★

"I've puzzled it out," Bay said at the end of
one of their afternoons together. It was a
sultry Saturday evening, unseasonably warm,
the sun slanting down from a clear sky as, all
around them, birds warbled out their last
notes before dusk. Sisi and Bay were making
their way back to the Althorp stables after a
long afternoon. The horses ambled slowly,
their coats slicked in a gloss of sweat, and

neither Sisi nor Bay urged them to speed up. Tomorrow being Sunday, Sisi knew she would have to take the day off and wait an entire day before seeing Bay again.

"What have you puzzled out?" Sisi asked, glancing sideways at Bay. She didn't know how, but his appearance seemed entirely changed from their first meeting. She had been unimpressed when they'd been introduced; she'd found him to be an average-looking man of middling height and a squat build. Now, when she looked at Bay sitting atop his horse, she saw the most agonizingly desirable man she had ever seen.

"The riddle I've been sorting through in my head," Bay answered.

Sisi smiled. Bay often filled their afternoons with riddles and jokes. "And the riddle is?"

"What makes *you* so much more beautiful than all the other ladies?" Bay posed the question matter-of-factly, his light eyes facing straight ahead. Sisi stiffened in her saddle. Bay had never before commented on her beauty, not once. True, she came to him each day looking her best, putting even more than usual attention into her toilette here in Northamptonshire than she had in Vienna. She thought she looked good enough. She knew that other men fancied her — they made their admiration plain in the way their eyes found and rested upon her. They studied her hair, her waist, her long, lean figure. But

Bay never seemed to notice. And he certainly never commented on it. He would compliment her on a good jump or a particularly good run, but that was the extent of his flattery.

Which was why as he continued now, speaking as if he were remarking on something as mundane as the weather, Sisi was caught completely unaware. "I've figured it out," he said. "You have a beautiful face, certainly. But that matters little."

Sisi glanced askance at him, finding the remark odd. Up ahead, the stables of Althorp came into view. Her stomach sank; she didn't want the day to be over. Didn't want to say goodbye to Bay. Not yet.

Bay continued to speak as they rode toward the estate. "I could find any number of faces as pretty as yours . . . prettier, even . . . on any given London street."

Sisi forced out a startled laugh. "And here I was thinking that perhaps you were about to pay me an uncustomary compliment."

"It's not the collection of features on your face that sets you apart," Bay continued, not being diverted by her interruption. He turned to her now and met her eyes for the first time. Without a smile, he said, "It's the expressiveness."

Sisi arched an eyebrow, unclear of his meaning.

"You wear your emotions so brazenly across

your face, Sisi."

"I . . . I do?" It was precisely what Andrássy had always told her.

Bay continued, pulling Sisi's thoughts from Andrássy back toward himself. "You offer glimpses of what is deeper. Remember what I told you on our second day together?"

She shook her head. All she remembered from their second day together was that she hadn't fallen and that Bay had told her that she rode better than any woman he had ever known. "No."

"I told you that your eyes were full of fire."

Sisi swallowed, saying, "Oh, yes. Now I remember."

Bay continued. "Well, now that I know you a bit better — now that I've seen you angry, and determined, and scared, and so happy that I thought the joy would tear you apart — now I know that those eyes of yours that had me so entranced, why, they merely hint at a fire that hides deeper within. A far more powerful blaze, I would imagine. You give me a hint of it every now and again, and that has the effect of being entirely disarming. And impossibly inviting."

Sisi broke from his gaze, aware that her heart was beating furiously against her chest, even though she and her horse were doing nothing more than a slow walk.

Stable boys began to cluster around them, eager to help, but Bay dismissed them with a flourish of his wrist, and they scattered, leaving the two of them in private conversation once more. "There."

She turned back to Bay. "What?"

"There, you're doing it again. You're showing me exactly what you feel."

She sat up a bit taller in the saddle. "Which is?"

"You're happy that I've finally admitted that you're beautiful. And you're wondering why it took me so long to admit it, to admit the obvious."

"Oh, please, Bay, you really think me so vain?" she scoffed, squirming in her seat.

"And now you're uncomfortable. And your cheeks are scarlet."

"Would you please stop looking at me?" She turned away, feeling as modest as a girl.

"No, I won't."

She swallowed hard, slowing her horse because they had reached the wide doors to the stables. Why did it have to be Saturday evening?

Bay hopped down from his mount, ignoring his horse as he strode to Sisi's side and placed his hands on her waist to help her down. She slid forward, and he caught her, landing her effortlessly on the ground in front of him. They did this every day, twice a day. Why, now, did it feel as if what they were doing was forbidden?

Bay's hands remained around her waist,

and she stood motionless, facing him. As if they were about to begin dancing. Could he feel her heartbeat, how it raced within her? she wondered.

Their faces were immodestly close now, but neither one stepped away. When Bay spoke, his voice was quiet. "I imagine very few people have met you without falling under your spell." He paused, staring at her, his own blue eyes aglow. She was terrified he might try to kiss her. What would she do if he did? But instead, he leaned forward and said, even more softly, "I certainly have." And with that, he bowed and took his leave.

★   ★   ★

When they reconvened on Monday, it was as if the conversation had never happened. Bay's smile was bright and carefree that morning, and he whistled as he helped Sisi into her saddle.

"How was your Sunday?" he asked, once they were out in front and apart from the others. Sisi turned to him, knowing that he was teasing her. Bay knew how her Sunday had been; all of England knew how her Sunday had been, thanks to the malicious newspaper articles that had been printed that morning. The Viennese might even know by now of her disaster — if they didn't yet, they soon would.

Having been in England for weeks now, Sisi had been unable to delay any further a visit to Queen Victoria. The strong-willed old matriarch had made it plain to her advisors — who had made it plain to Franz Joseph's advisors back in Vienna — that it was very offensive that the Austrian empress was staying in Her Majesty the Queen's realm and had not yet gone to pay her respects.

"But I'm not here in any official capacity," Sisi had written back to her husband. "An incognita ruler does not travel in state."

"It matters not, Sisi," he had responded. "You are a head of state, whether you will acknowledge it or not, and Victoria knows you are there and that you have paid house visits to members of her peerage — and not to Her Royal Majesty."

So, not wanting to inflict any further offense, but also not wanting to skip even a day in the hunting fields — a day with Bay — Sisi had selected Sunday for her long-overdue visit to the English queen. Sisi, who found formal state visits tedious, thought that her plan was a good one. Wouldn't Victoria also have other things she needed to do on the other days, and wouldn't she be happy to have this formality out of the way, just as Sisi was?

But when Sisi had arrived at Windsor Castle at midday on Sunday, having sent word ahead that she had selected that day to

391

pay her respects, she was quickly made to understand that her hostess was displeased with having to receive a visitor on a Sunday, a day usually reserved for church services and private family time.

As Sisi was announced into Victoria's formal receiving room, a dark-paneled chamber that seemed to creak and groan with age, she bowed and flashed her widest smile, hoping to offset any offense she had unintentionally inflicted. The clock in the room ticked unusually loudly as it kept time. Victoria looked up from where she sat, her ample, black-clad frame filling the entirety of her upholstered armchair. She spoke with the tone of a disapproving grandmother addressing her unruly offspring. "Elisabeth, it is good of you to come, at last."

Sisi took the chair offered to her and nodded to accept a service of tea. She raved about England, mentioning numerous times that she was there on a trip of leisure and not in any official capacity, sprinkling in copious compliments to the beauty of Victoria's countryside and the hospitality of her people.

The unsmiling English matriarch replied by mentioning multiple times that she had had to have her parish minister cut short his sermon so that she could be back at Windsor Castle in time to receive Sisi on her ill-considered Sunday visit. Hearing this, Sisi determined to make the visit quick so as not to disrupt any more of her hostess's day — a decision that was made easier by Victoria's frosty demeanor.

When the clouds outside turned ominous, dropping a slick rain on the thick-paned windows that threatened to turn into a late-spring ice, Sisi determined it best to travel back to Easton Neston before the route became more difficult. She declined Victoria's very tepid invitation to stay on for luncheon. "I won't keep you any longer, Your Majesty, as I'm certain that you would like to enjoy the rest of your Sunday in peace."

All of these were miscalculations, Sisi learned when she spotted the newspaper reports the next morning. Sisi had offended Victoria in everything from her selection of the day of the visit, to the time of the visit, to the short duration of the visit, to the topics of conversation she had discussed while paying said visit. Franz was no doubt at his desk in Vienna this very minute penning an exasperated note to his wife, begging her once more to return to his court before she could do any more damage at home and abroad.

Bay, having clearly seen the reports himself, now made a joke of them as they rode out ahead of the others. "I see that things got quite chilly at Windsor Castle yesterday, and I don't refer to the freezing rain."

Sisi couldn't help but frown at this, her eyes looking straight ahead but, for once, not enjoying the lush English scenery before her. The last thing she wanted was for the burdens of her official duties to tarnish this free time out in the fields; this was supposed to be the one place where she was not bothered by all of that.

But Bay continued: "The reports say you've declined not one but two of old Vicky's dinner invitations? And so then you called on Her Majesty yesterday, rather unexpectedly, and angered her even further by declining luncheon?"

Sisi didn't respond, and Bay at last seemed to pick up on the annoyance he had caused. "I'm only teasing, Sisi." He glanced at her, but she avoided his gaze. "But one thing confuses me: rather than make such a scandal, why didn't you just stay for luncheon? Or accept on one of the nights when she invited you to a formal state dinner?"

She turned to Bay now, wondering how she could explain. How could anyone possibly understand how sacred her time away was, how hard she had fought to carve out these stolen moments in which she was free of the crushing burdens of the empire? How she had loved, these past weeks, sitting down to simple meals with friends and not having protocol dictate the order in which they could cut into their meat, which topics she might discuss; not fearing, always, that she had somehow offended someone by veering off a script that so often eluded and confounded her? And how, now that she'd finally found a glimmer of happiness and freedom for just these few months, she wanted to cling to her liberty, her privacy, however selfish or impolite that made her appear?

She couldn't make Bay, or Franz, or anyone understand; she didn't even want to waste any more of her time that day trying to explain. She didn't wish to defend or justify her actions, not here, and she didn't want to be asked to do so. So instead, all she said was: "That sort of thing bores me. If I wanted state dinners, I'd return to Vienna."

Bay, as expected, didn't understand the depth of her exasperation. "Why do you loathe Vienna so?"

She sighed. "Bay, please, let's not talk about it."

"Fine," he said, his tone turning light-hearted. "Well, you're the empress. You tell me what we shall talk about."

So she did. She filled the hours telling Bay about Possenhofen and Bavaria and her father. She confessed that, since arriving in England and riding hard every day as she had as a girl, she had been dreaming of her father with startling regularity. Recalling their time together in the riding ring and out in the countryside. She found herself missing him in a way she never had before. She confessed to Bay how strained her relationship with her father had become. Once so close to him because of their shared passion for horses, Sisi had given up on her father after his years of dissolution, philandering, and excessive drinking.

Bay didn't try to calm Sisi or urge her to assume mastery over her emotions, as Franz would have. Nor did he try to offer some sensitive advice, to fix it for her, as Andrássy would have. He did neither; he said nothing. He simply listened, nodding occasionally. And then, when her confessions were over, he shrugged and changed the subject. It was odd, an unusual way to react, and yet, something about it soothed Sisi. It was all so simple. He didn't dismiss her troubles, but he didn't dwell on them, either. And she knew, somehow, that everything she told him was safe in his confidence. And she found it unusual and refreshing that his face showed no reaction — no judgment. It made her want to keep confiding in him.

So she spoke about Hungary, too. She described the hunting season there, outlining how different it was in the wilds outside of Budapest from the shires of Northamptonshire. She explained how the woods and forests around Gödöllő allowed the fox to escape, often making it difficult for the hounds to track the scent. She explained that the jumping there was more often over ditches than pasture fences and lush hedges.

"You'll have to come and see a Hungarian hunting season for yourself, Bay," she said one afternoon in late spring. "Would you like that?"

"If you were there, Sisi, then yes, I'd like it very much."

She nodded at this, twisting the reins in her hands as she tried not to smile.

"But am I invited?" Bay asked, turning sideways to glance at her.

"I think I just invited you."

"Then I think I just accepted the invitation."

★ ★ ★

As spring ripened into full, glorious English summer, Sisi knew that her time abroad was drawing to a close, and she faced the grim reality of returning to Vienna with a sense of deepening melancholy. She dreaded resuming her official role beside Franz at formal state dinners, making small talk with stiff ministers and gossipy courtiers. She dreaded the thought of confronting Rudolf's debauched behavior, and facing the vicious Viennese press, so angry with her for the prolonged absence. She grew so anxious about it all that soon even her time in the saddle surrounded by the green and glorious shires failed to lift her spirits.

Bay, sensing her unhappiness, proposed a

grand celebration before her departure, something to which she might look forward. "You should host a steeplechase." When Sisi didn't respond, Bay continued: "Easton Neston has plenty of land for a course."

"A steeplechase?" Sisi was pulled from her unhappy daydreams as she turned to Bay to repeat his suggestion.

"Yes. With riders, and a prize, and a fun lawn party. Invite everyone you've met in England. You can present a cup to the winner."

"But I wouldn't know the first thing about setting up a steeplechase course."

"I'll help you," Bay said. "It'll be quite fun."

And so, with Bay's enthusiastic support and Lord Spencer's dependable assistance, Sisi declared her intention to host a race that she named the Grafton Hunt Steeplechase. As the day of her departure drew closer, the course was set up over the park grounds of Easton Neston, and Sisi invited the entire population of Northamptonshire.

After a week of fog and drizzle, the morning of the steeplechase dawned clear and warm, a perfect day for racing and lawn-party revelry. Sisi had ordered a tent put up in the garden, and there in the shade, she served champagne to the hundreds of guests who came. She had made the invitation open, and many who had participated in one of the hunts with her or worked in the surrounding grand homes turned out for the day. As Sisi greeted her guests, her hair pulled back in a loose coronet, her gown sheathing her frame in lightweight lilac silk, she realized just how many local faces she now recognized. All of her visitors expressed their fondness for her, and they thanked her profusely for honoring their shire with such a prolonged stay.

"It is I who must thank all of you for making me feel so at home," Sisi said, repeating herself throughout the day.

Marie Larisch giggled with Lord and Lady Spencer, having thoroughly charmed them both with her questions about English fashion and customs. Valerie smiled at the guests, clapping happily as she watched the horses assembling for the races. More champagne bottles were ordered and popped, and as Sisi looked around, she knew that the party was an undeniable success. But the high point of the event came when the crowd assembled around the course for the steeplechase. Bay, riding his thoroughbred Musketeer, took the lead just at the last jump and won handily. Sisi couldn't help but beam when he joined her at the front dais, erected especially for the day, to receive the trophy from her hands. The crowd clapped and hollered, yelling out her name and Bay's. So loud was the applause that Sisi was certain only Bay heard her when she leaned toward him and said, "I didn't want anyone to win but you, Bay."

Bay didn't pause a moment before offering his reply: "Empress, I've got the invitation to come see you in Hungary this autumn. I've already won."

IX

Our dreams are always fairer when
they are not realized.
— *EMPRESS SISI OF AUSTRIA-HUNGARY*

CHAPTER 9

Gödöllő Palace, Hungary
Autumn 1876

Franz posed the question to Sisi over breakfast on the morning of Bay's scheduled arrival to Hungary. "He's only a commoner, this Captain Middleton. And an unmarried one at that. He'll be happy in one of the outbuilding cottages, won't he?" Outside the air was sunny and brisk, with the earliest scent of fall tingeing the gentle breeze. *A perfect day for traveling,* Sisi thought, her own spirits as bright and clear as the weather.

Inside Gödöllő Palace, the imperial household hummed and hustled as efficiently as on any other day, the tasks of making up spare bedrooms and airing out guest cottages easily managed by the emperor's large staff of servants. Only Sisi seemed to feel, with the imminent arrival of Bay and Lord Spencer and the rest of her guests, that it was a day far different from any other. How would Bay like Gödöllő? How would it be, riding with him here, where it was so unlike Northamptonshire?

"Well? What do you think?" Franz interrupted his wife's reverie, gazing at her across a table heaped with breakfast sausages, steamed fruit, and wispy pastries. "Shall one of the cottages suit your much-lauded cavalry rider? I don't think it's appropriate to have him sleep in the castle, given that he's of the common class, if that's all right with you."

Sisi nodded her absentminded consent. "Certainly, yes. Bay — Captain Middleton — will be perfectly happy in one of the guest cottages." She looked back at the table, sipping her glass of milk but abstaining from the platters of food, her nerves leaving no room for an appetite.

Franz thought of Bay as he would a stable groom or riding instructor, that much was evident. Keenly aware as he was of how caste and the social order governed habits and people, Franz couldn't understand how a man of nonnoble birth had found himself in such proximity to the likes of Lord Spencer — or, even more surprisingly, Empress Elisabeth of Austria-Hungary — unless he interacted with them as a servant would.

It was a good thing that Franz saw it that way, Sisi had reminded herself when he had expressed his confusion as to how Bay had secured an invitation to her hunting party. It was what had prevented Franz from experiencing even a scrap of jealousy when Sisi had raved about Bay's skill in the saddle and insisted that the English sportsman join them at Gödöllő. Confused as he might have been, Franz would never have felt anything even close to suspicion on hearing that his wife, an *empress*, spent so much time with someone who functioned like any other nonnoble attendant. At best, perhaps he thought of Bay as some sort of elevated riding instructor.

But if Bay *hadn't* been an attendant or an instructor, what had he been? Sisi wasn't sure that she could have answered that question, even to herself. Empresses did not have friends, let alone male friends with whom they rode unchaperoned and unattended. So, if he hadn't been a friend, and he wasn't a nobleman in her retinue, and he wasn't an attendant, what was Bay Middleton?

In her world, where everyone knew their place and everyone understood the rules that dictated each interaction, Bay somehow existed outside of such a framework. It had been fine — pleasant, really — when *Sisi* had been allowed to exist outside of the framework, as well. It hadn't mattered in the relaxed, free-form environment of the shires, where she had been the mistress of her own home, without Franz or the court or protocol to answer to. But how Bay's relationship with her would translate here, into the imperial household, Sisi didn't know. All she knew was how eager she was to see Bay once more — and how fluttery her stomach had been all morning in anticipation of his arrival.

"Ah, you'll wish to see this," Franz said, fanning out the morning's journal and pulling Sisi's focus back to the breakfast table. "Ludwig's latest success."

"Hmm?" Sisi leaned forward to look at the paper.

Franz read aloud now. "Richard Wagner's new operatic masterpiece, the *Ring Cycle,* opened to popular and critical acclaim in Bayreuth, Bavaria, in a brand-new theater made possible by the generosity and patronage of Bavaria's King Ludwig. The king was so involved, in fact, that even His Majesty's horse was featured in the production, appearing onstage to the delight of all present."

Sisi grumbled, "Of course, now that Wagner's show is a smashing success, everyone is in a flurry to offer the highest praise to Ludwig, when just months ago they were lambasting him as a spendthrift and an eccentric."

Franz took a sip of coffee, still studying the paper. "Well, the man knows his operas and castles, that much I will concede. Even if I can't agree with the millions he has thrown away on them." Franz placed his coffee cup back in its saucer and picked up a roll. "But then again, they criticize me similarly for how much I spend on your horses and your trips

405

abroad."

Sisi bristled at this, throwing a sharp look toward her husband. Though she had defended Ludwig in the previous breath, she didn't appreciate the comparison Franz now made between her and her cousin. Certainly, the Austrian papers had excoriated her for the length of her trips abroad and the sums she had required for them. But she spent a mere fraction of what Ludwig dispensed on his ventures. She inhaled, preparing to defend herself, but instead, she sighed audibly, brushing her irritation aside. Bay and Spencer would arrive in just a matter of hours, and she had the prospect of a Hungarian hunting season before her, in their company, and she wouldn't let anything spoil her mood this morning. Especially not a quarrel with Franz.

★　★　★

Sisi stood between Franz and the ladies of her household as she greeted her guests, listening to the giggles of Larisch even as she kept her own expression poised and appropriately regal. A series of carriages rolled up to Gödöllő to drop off the invitees, all arriving in time to dine that evening before officially beginning the weeks-long hunting party the next morning. Nicky Esterházy arrived first, bringing with him a cheerful friend named Rudi Liechtenstein who professed to love horses as much as Esterházy and the empress.

"Well, then you've come to the right place," Sisi said, greeting the newcomer warmly.

"Good to see you again." Nicky flashed a self-assured wink as he stepped in front of his friend and bowed before Sisi.

"You, too, Nicky."

Next came Rudolf, looking haggard and pale after what had most likely been a raucous few days in nearby Budapest. Sisi heard Franz sigh beside her when he saw his son approach, when he noted Rudolf's disheveled hair and tired, bloodshot eyes.

"Father, hello."

"Son," Franz said, nodding at the young man who looked nothing like him, resembling only his mother in his build and coloring.

Rudolf turned next with a slack expression toward Sisi. "Mother, good to see you."

"Hello, dear. Now let me see my boy." Sisi looked her son up and down, noticing two things as she did so. The first was that Rudolf wore his military tunic over the navy pants of the infantry officer, a direct challenge to his father, who always wore the red from his own days in the cavalry and who had been rebuffed in his request that his son follow in his footsteps into the cavalry. The second thing that Sisi noticed was that Franz, seeing the taunt, scowled, looking barely happy to

407

welcome his son and heir.

"It's good to see you, Rudolf." Sisi forced a smile, already aware of the tension that would now fill the house, seeping outward from both father and son. She just hoped she could remain as removed from it as possible, and spare Bay from it entirely.

"So who is this Middleton fellow?" Rudolf asked. "I'm all for welcoming an Englishman, but shouldn't it be the Prince of Wales, and not some common *officer*?"

Sisi ignored the remark, allowing her son to move farther down the line, noticing out of the corner of her eye how Rudolf lingered before Marie Larisch for several moments too long.

Finally the carriage carrying Lord Spencer and Bay arrived at the palace. As the horses halted before them, Sisi forgot protocol and glided forward to greet her final guests. "Bay!" She called out, aware that she practically cooed the name, so happy was she to utter it again.

If the emperor picked up on Sisi's too-familiar tone, he made no acknowledgment of it, but offered a formal smile and courteous nod as he met the two Englishmen, inquiring after their journey and welcoming them to Gödöllő.

Rudolf, on the other hand, greeted her mother's guests with tight-pressed, unsmiling lips. "Lord Spencer, it is a pleasure to have *you* here. Welcome. And Captain Middleton."

Bay surely sensed the hostility in her son's icy tone, Sisi thought, shifting uncomfortably as the two men stared at each other.

"Crown Prince Rudolf, an honor to meet you." Bay offered a slight, measured bow.

Rudolf continued: "We've certainly heard enough about you, the commoner who can outride England's nobles. I only wonder, what does that say about England's nobles?"

Bay ignored the remark, turning back to Sisi with his bright, strong-featured smile. "Heavens, it's good to see you."

Sisi smiled, looking only at Bay even as, beside her, she felt her son's frame stiffen with fury.

★　★　★

The next day officially began the hunting party, with the group taking their mounts after lunch and riding off into the fields and woodlands around the palace. Though nothing like the size of the groups in Northamptonshire, they were a large enough assembly, with Sisi and Larisch, Franz and Rudolf, Nicky and Rudi Liechtenstein, and of course Spencer and Bay.

It was a mild September day, and Bay professed to be enjoying himself throughout the afternoon, but Sisi couldn't help but admit that, for her, the day was missing something; it was uneventful and unexciting compared to the breakneck pace and exhilarating obstacles of riding across the shires. With Franz present, it wasn't Bay who helped Sisi in and out of her saddle, and she missed the jolt of delight she'd received in those moments, however fleeting they had been. Because of the density of the woods, the hounds proved entirely unable to pick up any scent long enough for the horses to work up to a good gallop. As a result, the entire pack of riders remained close together all day, not splitting up as the stronger, more skilled riders disappeared out front. The smaller size of the party, in allowing them all to stay so close together, in fact led to a more cramped feeling.

As a result, Sisi had almost no time with Bay. Rudolf, who had consumed too much wine during luncheon and at the previous night's dinner, was uncomfortable in the saddle and blamed his horse, uttering curse words with liquor-steeped breath and kicking the animal repeatedly with his spurred boots. Nicky remained at Sisi's side throughout the hunt like a jealous shadow, refusing to be shaken and speaking only in Hungarian, a language that he knew Bay and Spencer could not understand.

Nor did the night afford the same carefree camaraderie that Sisi had enjoyed in Northamptonshire. Given the presence of the emperor, the evening began with the necessary ritual, the *Feuersitzung,* or "fireside session." During this ceremony, all present were to sit around Franz Joseph, waiting until he addressed each guest personally with some form of chatter or greeting. No one could speak until addressed directly by the emperor. Sisi caught Bay's eye at one point during the sitting, hoping he sensed her apology for the stilted and tedious nature of this house party.

Dinner didn't improve things. Sisi longed for the laughter that came from Spencer and Bay exchanging good-natured jabs and quips, and she attempted to draw them into remembering their time together in Northamptonshire, but the two Englishmen seemed cowed by the formality of the setting and all of the rules that struck them as impenetrable and entirely foreign. Rudolf was sulky, glowering at Bay throughout the meal, and Nicky dominated the conversation with talking — or, more precisely, boasting — about his past Hungarian hunting seasons with Sisi. He, more than anyone but Rudolf, seemed to sense that Bay stood high in the empress's esteem, and Sisi understood that, as long as Nicky was around, she would get absolutely no time to enjoy Bay's company.

"Larisch, I need you to do me a favor." Sisi was dressing for dinner the following evening, and desperately hoping that the group's third night together would prove less unpleasant than the previous two had been. She had dispatched Marie and Ida on quick errands to Valerie's nursery, sending them out from her bedchamber so that she might steal a moment alone with Larisch — she knew that the other two ladies would never approve of the topic she now raised.

"A favor? What's that, Empress?" Larisch stood in front of the full-length mirror, inspecting her own appearance as Sisi finished her toilette.

"I wish for you to charm Nicky Esterházy tonight."

Larisch cocked a playful eyebrow, taking a strand of Sisi's pearls off the dressing table and twirling it in her hands. "Why is that?"

"Oh, I don't know. I'm just finding him tiresome. I need a break from him."

"I think I know why," Larisch said, flashing a round-eyed smile, her singsong voice dripping with meaning.

"Oh?" Sisi sat up tall in her chair, indulging in the girl's playfulness. "And what do you think you know?"

"I think you want more time with *Brave Bay Middleton.*" Larisch erupted in giggles as Sisi threw a look at the door, making sure that neither Ida nor Marie had reentered to hear this. She turned back to the young girl, savoring her easy, lighthearted brand of frivolity for the moment.

"Empress, I see it every time he walks into a room." Larisch leaned close to Sisi, breaking protocol by placing her own hand atop the empress's.

"What do you see?" Sisi asked, allowing her attendant's presumptuousness to go unchecked. It was nice for once to speak so candidly.

"Why, Empress, you bloom whenever Bay is present."

Sisi absorbed Larisch's words, noting how they kindled a small but strong heat somewhere deep within her belly. "Perhaps I do want a bit of time with Bay," she admitted, her voice quiet.

Larisch smiled, her large eyes lively with the thrill of the conspiracy. "Then I shall get it for you."

"You don't mind?" Sisi asked. "Diverting Nicky for just a bit?"

Larisch shook her head, still clutching Sisi's pearls in her hands. "Not in the slightest. Nicky is very handsome. I may be married . . ." Larisch scowled, but it was only a moment before the buoyancy returned to her expression. "But that doesn't mean I'm not allowed to fall in love, as long as it's just for a little while."

Sisi nodded at this. "Well, then," she said, "thank you."

"Anything for you, Your Majesty." Larisch squeezed Sisi's hand before holding the pearls up against the empress's neck for consideration. Sisi was reminded in that moment of a complaint Marie Festetics had recently made, when Sisi had pressed her and Ida on several occasions to confess why they both disliked Larisch so fiercely. Ida had refused to comment, but eventually Marie had capitulated: "I have the feeling that she is insincere. As if she has a talent for acting."

But wasn't that precisely what Sisi needed her to do now?

The evening was, as a result of Larisch's charms and collusion, a more upbeat affair. Following dinner Franz became involved in a conversation with Spencer and Rudi Liechtenstein comparing English and Austro-Hungarian politics, noting how each kingdom had faced a dissatisfied but strong minority in the Irish and the Hungarians, respectively. Ida and Marie Festetics tried valiantly to lift Rudolf from his surliness, offering to join him in a game of cards. Larisch, acting upon Sisi's request, had attached herself to Nicky Esterházy, begging the handsome nobleman to play piano duets with her and peppering him with nonstop questions and compliments.

Slowly, over the course of the evening, Sisi and Bay slid toward two chairs by the window until finally they sat, partly removed from the rest of the assembly, as Larisch's piano playing and singing provided a pleasant barrier of noise for them. Sisi breathed out slowly. It felt like such a relief to be near Bay once more. In some ways, the past few days had been even harder for Sisi than the months since her departure from England. Having Bay so close and yet being denied the carefree, candid rapport that she had previously enjoyed with him had been excruciating.

She had to be mindful, now that she had a few moments with him, not to appear too eager. Even when they weren't speaking, there was an unmistakable magnetism between them, and Sisi knew it. Larisch had pointed it out. Ida and Marie Festetics had noticed, too. "Be careful, please, I beg Your Majesty," Marie had whispered earlier that day, when she'd noticed Sisi staring in unabashed delight upon Bay's arrival to luncheon.

"Whatever did you mean by your warning at lunch, Marie?" Sisi had asked later, still smarting somewhat.

"I mean no offense. I simply . . . I only wish the best for Your Majesty." It wasn't as barefaced as how Larisch had put it, but it was the same message. *You bloom whenever Bay is present.*

Rudolf's mood indicated that he had noticed, as well. Nicky's insistence on always being at Sisi's side meant that surely he had noticed, too. It seemed the only one who hadn't sensed the attraction was Franz.

"What do you think of all of this?" Sisi asked, keeping her face calm and her voice low. She wanted, at last, a conversation just for her and Bay.

Bay weighed his words a moment before answering. "It's certainly different . . . than Easton Neston. I understand, now, what you meant."

Sisi breathed out a stifled laugh. "Yes, it is."

"The fact that they must fold every dinner napkin in such an elaborate way, as if it's a matter of state importance. And that the fold must be done according to strict guidelines that only two living people know!" Bay repeated this piece of mealtime trivia he had gleaned from that evening's dinner, about the top secret "Imperial Fold" of the Habsburg linen. "I feel terribly disruptive simply for sitting down to the table and unfolding my napkin."

"And if you think this is something, you should see what it's like in Vienna. This is relaxed by comparison."

"I shudder to think that *this* is relaxed."

"The *Feuersitzungen* are, to me, the worst part of it all."

"What?"

"The silly ritual at the beginning of the night," Sisi clarified. "When Franz holds court, and we all sit around him, and he makes idle chatter with each of us, one by

416

one. It's just so . . . *unnatural.*"

"I actually don't mind that part of the night," Bay said, leaning toward Sisi with a quizzical smile.

"Really?" Sisi shifted in her chair. Something about the way Bay looked at her prompted her to glance around the room to make sure that no one else was watching. Satisfied of that fact, she turned back to Bay. "And why is that?"

"Because I take that opportunity to watch you. Even though you look bored and unhappy, you are as bewitching as ever." Bay paused, eyeing her intently. She wished they were alone in the room now — wished Bay could lean all the way forward and pull her into a kiss. When he spoke next, his voice was low and intended only for her: "I could watch you forever."

The next morning Lord Spencer remained in bed, complaining of the beginning of a cold, and Franz and Rudolf decided not to ride, pleading paper work and a headache, respectively. As the pared-down party readied their mounts for the day's ride, Sisi asked Bay to help her into her saddle, ignoring Nicky's protestations as she did so.

They set off into a gray, blustery afternoon. Larisch, still committed to her imperial assignment, positioned her horse beside Nicky's early on. One of the hounds picked up a scent and took off, the hunters giving chase behind.

Though neither Sisi nor Bay spoke about doing so, they found themselves, somehow, alone in the woods.

They rode side by side, an uncharacteristic silence between them. Sisi wanted to enjoy this stolen time with him; she wanted to laugh and tease and feel the familiar glow that Bay's company stoked within her. But, even though the others weren't with them, the realization that they would soon be found served to dampen her spirits and prevented her from feeling as if she truly had Bay to herself. She retreated into a gloomy, restless reverie.

Bay spoke first. "You're . . . you're different here."

She heard his words and thought about them. Eventually, she nodded.

"Less at ease," Bay said, glancing at her sideways. Her stomach seized; he really was impossibly good-looking, his scarlet coat a dash of bright color against the browning woods of the Hungarian autumn.

Just then their horses both halted, as if startled by something up ahead, and Sisi clutched her reins. Had they come upon one of the packs of wild dogs that the servants and local peasants always spoke of with such terror? But no, it wasn't a pack of dogs. There, ahead of them in the shadowy distance, two figures stood pressed up against a tree, intertwined in an embrace. Sisi narrowed her eyes, the blood draining from her face as she tried to determine what, exactly, she looked upon. The scrim of branches and brush obscured the view, but Sisi heard a familiar sound — the bouncy giggle of a young lady. Within a minute, the laughter turned to a low, amorous sigh. Sisi stiffened in her saddle, certain, even at this great distance, that she recognized the taller of the two silhouettes. Nicky had discarded his riding coat. Another noise followed, this one the low, throaty groan of a man. Then the lady's dark hair became entirely obscured by the brush.

"Let's go this way," Bay whispered, redirecting both his horse and Sisi's off to the side, his quick movement making plain that he, too, had seen what was occurring up ahead. Before they could be noticed, and before Sisi knew what was happening, Bay trotted them both behind a small copse and in the opposite direction. The two woodland lovers continued their liaison, unaware and uninterrupted.

That night, without offering an explanation, Esterházy announced that he was cutting short his time in the hunting party, declaring his need to leave the very next day. Sisi noticed how Larisch blanched at the announcement, but she kept her eyes downward, her full lips pressed in uncharacteristic silence for the remainder of the evening.

Sisi offered no protestation and did not ask Nicky to reconsider his early departure. She wanted him gone. She didn't know what precisely had transpired between her lady-in-waiting and the nobleman in the woods, but whatever it was, she, Sisi, felt partly to blame. She had meant only for Larisch to flirt with the man — to distract him and charm him. But she knew that Larisch was an unabashed coquette and that Nicky, a bachelor, was nearly mad with his unrequited attempts to win Sisi's attention; she felt sick with the realization that she had practically pushed the girl into his arms.

Sisi remained in bed the entire next day, feeling heavy with guilt and leaving her chambers only for a brief visit to Valerie's nursery. She avoided Larisch for fear that she'd have to ask the girl what had happened. Or worse, apologize for her role in making Larisch think that it was all right that it had happened. She avoided Bay, for he had seemed so mortified when they had discovered the illicit meeting together. However, Larisch seemed to recover her cheerful, carefree demeanor within a matter of days, and Sisi decided that the damage must not have been too terrible.

The mood lightened noticeably with Esterházy gone, and over the next few days, Sisi and Bay managed to take a few solo rides together. For the first time since his arrival at Gödöllő, Sisi found herself truly savoring

Bay's company. They spent hours together galloping across the fields and leaping the ditches at their old breakneck speed. When they grew tired, they allowed the horses to walk, and Sisi enjoyed the feeling of fatigue, looking around at the auburn and gold of the autumn, savoring the free, unchecked manner in which Bay chattered to her about her form and the challenges of a Hungarian countryside versus an English one. Out there, with fields and woods between them and the palace, Sisi found the old Bay, and he found the old Sisi.

Her only source of sadness was how quickly these days passed. She dreaded the moment when the sun would begin to sink toward the western horizon each afternoon. Sisi noticed how both she and Bay took far longer than they needed to in returning to the palace, allowing their tired horses to tread impossibly slowly back to the stables at the end of each outing. When Bay helped her down from her saddle, they would linger, pausing opposite each other, his hands around her waist for longer than was necessary. Sisi wondered, each night, if he would kiss her. She also wondered what she would do if he did. Here, in her home, where her husband and son awaited her at the dinner table. Would she have the power to resist Bay, if he finally did what she longed for him to do?

But Bay never forced Sisi to make that decision, because he never kissed her. He never spoke to her of wishing to, either. Instead, all he did was look at her with an intensity and a longing that caused her to blush deeper than any kiss ever would. She didn't need him to voice his desire — his light eyes spoke so plainly of it. And they only seemed to grow more desirous with each passing day. Sisi didn't know how long they could go on like this before being found out. But — found out in what? They weren't doing anything wrong, were they?

After several weeks had passed like this, Bay announced at dinner one night that he couldn't possibly come all this way and not see Budapest. He would go to the capital the next day, he declared. Sisi smarted at this, disappointed to hear that Bay had decided on these plans without first telling her. He had only a few more days in Hungary; why would he want to miss even an hour in her company? But Bay was adamant — so much so that she wondered if perhaps there was something he wasn't telling her. All he said, when she probed him further, was that he had heard marvelous things about the Hungarian capital and he simply had to see it.

Franz agreed wholeheartedly with Bay's plan — perhaps he had grown weary of his many houseguests. Sisi merely succeeded in convincing Bay to take her secretary, Baron Nopcsa, with him. The baron would serve as guide and interpreter in the foreign city. But Sisi had a second motive, too, in insisting that the old man accompany Bay; she couldn't deny that she'd want a full report from the baron when they returned so that she'd know what Bay had done and whom he'd seen.

When Sisi wished Bay farewell for his visit to Budapest, it was with a gloominess that frightened her. If she dreaded saying good-bye to him for just one night while he went to the nearby city, how would she deal with his upcoming departure when he would be leaving to return to England?

Not wanting to ride without Bay, Sisi passed the entirety of the next morning with Valerie, taking whatever solace she could in her daughter's company. When the appointed time came for the men's return that after-noon, Sisi stood before the front door ready to greet them, having prepared herself as lav-ishly as if she were going to host a ball. But she saw with dismay that only Baron Nopcsa stepped out of the coach.

"But where is Bay — Captain Middleton?" Sisi asked the aide. The usually fastidious gentleman looked a bit ragged, his clothes wrinkled and his hair uncombed.

"Your Majesty." The baron shrugged, his frown weary and apologetic. "I wish I knew. I lost Captain Middleton almost as soon as we arrived in the city. It was as if he was trying to shake off my presence."

On further questioning, Baron Nopcsa confessed that Bay had been adamant that he needed a few hours alone and that he would meet the old man later that same evening in the casino. But when the baron went to the casino at the appointed hour, there had been no sign of Bay Middleton. The baron remained there all night, staying until the casino closed, but Bay never appeared.

Returning to the hotel where they had taken a suite of rooms, the baron found no sign of Bay. Upon learning from the hotel staff that Middleton had never come back to the hotel, the baron had allowed himself a few hours of sleep and then, on waking, had resumed his search for the still-missing Englishman.

The baron had spent the morning scouring the city's cafés and other hotels, even returning to the casino, but still had found no trace of Bay. Not wanting to further disrupt the plans he had made with the emperor and empress, he had decided to return to Gödöllő to report on these unusual events and to see what else might be done in the search.

"Seems you've done everything you can, Baron," Franz declared, shrugging as if to indicate that he didn't understand the ways of horse grooms. "We shall simply have to wait for the prodigal son to return."

Evening came, and Bay still didn't arrive,

424

nor did he send word to Gödöllő of his whereabouts. Larisch filled the hours with lighthearted chatter, giggling to Rudolf about the places where Bay might have vanished. "Perhaps he drowned in the Széchenyi bathhouses," she said. "Or perhaps he took a tumble up on Castle Hill and plummeted into the Danube? No, no, I'm only joking."

Rudolf picked up the thread, pinching Larisch's bare arm as he leaned forward and whispered, just loud enough for Sisi to overhear: "I'm sure there's nothing to worry about. I'm sure Brave Bay is simply passing his hours, happy as can be, riding one of Budapest's legendary . . . thoroughbreds."

"Enough!" Sisi scowled at the young pair, finally silencing them with the fury of her stare. She retreated to her bedroom, irate. The next day, after Sisi awoke, she found the baron, who informed her that there was still no word from Budapest. It was then that her anger changed to fear — what if something truly awful had happened to Bay?

The following day Andrássy arrived for pre-scheduled meetings with Franz. Sisi saw him briefly, and they exchanged a few cordial words. He asked her how the hunting season was going so far. She inquired about his time in Vienna. His face appeared more heavily seamed than she had remembered it, his dark hair traced with wisps of silver. Still, he offered her his kind, striking, black-eyed smile, and Sisi wondered if age had perhaps made Julius Andrássy even more handsome. It had certainly made him more distinguished.

As she stared at him, Sisi was aware of something that stirred from within the deepest recesses of her being, flames glowing from the faintest, most persistent of embers, reminding her that their fire had not been extinguished. It would likely never go out. Was she doomed to carry this deep, unremitting love for Julius Andrássy, like an ache that she could ignore but never entirely cure, until the day she died? And yet, she was not as distracted by Andrássy's presence as she might have otherwise been, so preoccupied was she with Bay's ongoing, unexplained absence. Perhaps it was even a little bit of a blessing, the dilemma with Bay. It gave her something to focus on, even as Andrássy moved around in the same house as her, dispatching his duties for the empire and sitting in the private office with her husband, the man he so steadfastly served.

And then, finally, a telegram arrived shortly before lunch from Budapest's police headquarters. The message said that a certain Captain Middleton was in police custody in the Hungarian capital. The police chief apologized for the disturbance to Their Imperial Majesties, informing them that Middleton had been insistent that he was in fact Their Majesties' houseguest and that he was expected back at Gödöllő. After much deliberation, the officer had decided it was best to relay a message about Middleton's whereabouts in case the dapper Englishman *was* indeed expected by any members of the imperial household. Franz replied immediately, telling the chief that Middleton spoke the truth and that he was in fact their guest. The lawman replied that Middleton was safe but bankrupt, having been robbed by a certain lady after seeking her services in a house of questionable repute.

Franz burst into scandalized laughter at reading the telegram over lunch. Andrássy, perhaps noting the paleness of Sisi's face, lowered his eyes and retreated into unobtrusive silence. As Franz continued to laugh, Sisi's fury at Bay threatened to erupt in a loud, bloodcurdling outburst. That fury was compounded now by a swell of other violent emotions — outrage, shock, embarrassment. And what else was it? Jealousy? Yes, maddening jealousy. But she forced herself to focus, instead, on her fury and outrage.

"How could he?" she gasped, her blood thrashing around in her veins as she pushed her lunch plate away, disgusted. She needed to excuse herself from this table.

"Come now, Elisabeth," Franz said, wiping his laughing eyes as he looked once more over the vile telegram. "You hadn't guessed that the young bachelor wanted a bit of fun on his trip to Hungary?"

"But he . . ." And then, noticing how the two men — her husband and Andrássy — awaited her next words, Sisi stammered: "He . . . he makes us look bad!"

"He's a cavalry officer and a stable groom." Franz shrugged. "What did you expect?"

Sisi chewed over the question in silence, rising from the meal and offering her apologies. "A sudden headache," she mumbled, leaving the room without looking in Andrássy's direction. She exited the house and took off into the fields on foot, walking at a brisk pace, alone. Franz was right, she supposed: what *had* she expected?

X

Hôtel Beau Rivage, Geneva, Switzerland ·
September 1898
It doesn't surprise him, how grand the building
is. The Hôtel Beau Rivage. Of course she's
selected the most luxurious place in town. He
stares up at it now, studying the structure, its
flags billowing lazily in the intermittent lakeside
breeze. A front staircase covered in plush red
carpet, a limestone façade testifying to money
— old money. The careless, unwarranted
money of the patrons who file in and out of the
front doors, coming from shopping trips or boat
rides, going to the theater or eight-course dinners.

Daylight softens and thins until eventually
dusk descends across the city. As the last wisps
of sunlight slip behind the Jura Mountain peaks
to the west, he remains still, posted on the quay
across from her hotel, like a sentry keeping
watch. Only, he's not a sentry; he's not here to
protect.

Velvety black settles over the scene, and the

lights of ships pop up across the glassy surface of the lake. The windows of the hotel and neighboring buildings begin to glow, their warm brightness seeping like puddles out onto the street where he stands. He crosses his arms in front of his chest, the autumn air turning chilly around him. He's hungry once more, the day's soup now completely digested, the heavy knot of emptiness returned to his gut.

He's thinking about this hunger when the corner room on the third floor becomes bright, its inner space glowing a warm amber that spills out into the night.

Luigi's heart lurches as his eyes fix on that lit, warm space. Is she in there? Getting ready for bed? Getting ready for tomorrow? Perhaps even saying her evening prayers, without the smallest clue as to what awaits her. Without knowing that God has already abandoned her. That he, Luigi, a black angel of death, is the only spirit she need concern herself with now.

His hands fly instinctively into his pockets where he feels for it, just to be sure. Yes, the blade is still there. Ready. One more black night to endure, and then, tomorrow will come.

CHAPTER 10

Summerhill House, Meath, Ireland
Winter 1879

There was no evading Viennese news, Sisi realized, even in a place as far-flung and remote as Ireland.

Word of Andrássy's resignation caught up to Sisi upon her arrival to the British Isles, where she and Valerie and the rest of her household were to pass the late winter and early spring in the region of Meath, Ireland. The letters awaited Sisi at her rented estate, stiff and sealed and carrying news of faraway places, distant conflicts; like uninvited guests who now demanded her immediate attention, unwelcome but impervious to the unpleasantness that their presence imposed. Sisi's head spun as she tried to absorb all that she read: Russia had defeated Turkey to the east and now sought to make its power even greater across Europe. Given his extreme dislike of Russia and his inability to chart a course forward for Austria-Hungary that wouldn't be affected by his enmity for the Slavs, Andrássy decided to retire after a lifetime of public service.

Though Meath was itself an area that threatened revolution and roiled with discontent from its local Irish populace, Sisi had hoped to find there a temporary reprieve from politics. What she had wished to concern herself with during her stay was her stable full of thoroughbreds, stocked with Bay's expert advice and buying prowess, along with the thousands of acres of fields and hills that surrounded her estate. She'd planned to leave the tensions of British politics to Victoria and the stresses of Austrian politics to Franz back in Vienna.

That was, until she read this news of Andrássy. The announcement filled Sisi with an odd and dazed feeling of disorientation. It felt like a disruption in the proper order of things. Andrássy, whose personality had loomed large over the court since her earliest days as a young bride, would be gone when Sisi returned to Vienna. Having served his entire life as a tireless statesman for the causes of first Hungary and then Austria-Hungary, he would, at long last, retire. He'd return to his estate in Hungary and enjoy — or at least try to enjoy — the peace that he had never before allowed for himself. She'd no longer see him. She'd no longer bump into him in the halls, or find him in Franz's study, or see his dark-eyed smile of greeting.

Sisi consoled herself with the bald facts of her current situation: she was so far away, at the lovely Irish mansion of Summerhill, and she never saw much of Andrássy these days anyway. The distance from Vienna and Budapest was well-timed, as it offered her a bit of a shield, softened the blow of his sudden and permanent absence. She'd already bid Andrássy farewell, hadn't she? He was already out of reach; what difference did it make whether he was out of reach in a remote Hungarian castle or in a separate wing of the Hofburg?

And so Sisi put the letters aside and forced herself not to grow melancholy. She turned to look out the window, over a rolling expanse of emerald green, willing herself to recall the rapture that such views usually roused. The pleasures that such landscapes held. How could she remain melancholy when Bay was expected to come and fetch her for their afternoon ride at any minute?

★ ★ ★

"The Queen of the Chase!
The Queen! Yes, the Empress!
Look, look, how she flies,
With a hand that never fails,
And a pluck that never dies.
The best man in England can't lead her —

433

he's down!
Bay Middleton's back is done beautifully
    brown —"

"I must stop you right there." Sisi raised a
hand, fighting back laughter. "Bay, you hear
how they speak of you?"

"I take great offense!" Bay leaned forward,
his cheeks rosy, his voice roaring merrily
across the long table. "I'm glad you do the
empress justice, but must you have such a go
at me? My 'back is done beautifully brown'?"

They were in the grand dining room at
Summerhill: Sisi, Bay, the Spencers, her
ladies, as well as a wealthy family who had
been staying in the area, the Rothschilds.
Supper had been cleared, but they remained
at the table. The room was warm with the
postprandial glow of good food and convivial-
ity, and Spencer was reading aloud from a
poem that the locals had composed in honor
of Sisi's arrival in Meath, Ireland.

"I must say, Empress, it is good to have you
back in Britain," Lord Spencer said now, tip-
ping his glass toward the wine for a refill.

"And I'm glad to be back. Especially here,
where the things written about me in the
newspapers are so uncharacteristically favor-
able."

"You are quite popular in the British Isles,"
Spencer said, nodding. At that, Sisi's eyes
couldn't help but land on Bay, who stared at

her with a look of such intensity that she felt her cheeks ignite with warmth.

Later, well past midnight, Lady Spencer succeeded in coaxing her garrulous husband and the rest of the guests out of the hall and into their waiting carriages. "We must allow the empress her rest, John."

Sisi hid her urge to yawn as she wished them farewell. She was tired, yes, but she regretted to see them go. She, who retired first from any evening assembly in Vienna, would have gladly stayed awake all night to enjoy their company and their easy, good-natured laughter. She couldn't remember the last time she had felt this happy. And she had the entirety of the hunting season still stretched out before her!

The next afternoon while out riding, she and Bay found themselves caught in a sudden downpour, a common occurrence, he explained, in the moody, soggy climate of Ireland. Too far from the stables to return without becoming thoroughly soaked, they guided their horses into a thick copse, taking refuge under the cover of its leafy branches. "Are you terribly drenched?" Bay asked, both of them laughing as they watched the furious rain pound the slushy earth around them.

Sisi looked down at her riding skirt, its crimson silk ringed with brown at the hem. "Only a bit of mud," she said, "no worse than on the days when I tumble out of the saddle."

"You're not covered enough. Here, step closer." Bay reached forward, pressing his hand ever so gently to her lower back as he guided her farther out of the rain, closer to him. Sisi turned, her breath catching at the back of her throat as she felt the soft press of his palm on her body. Bay returned her stare, neither of them speaking. Eventually, he leaned even closer, saying in a low voice: "Just a passing shower; nothing that comes on this sudden and furious can last. It'll move off in no time."

"Yes," she agreed, lowering her eyes. In truth, she didn't mind the delay in the slightest, even found herself hoping that the storm might linger for hours, holding them close in this spot.

"Sisi?"

"Yes?" Her eyes lifted to meet his.

"I have something for you."

"Oh?"

"Nothing fancy, I'm afraid." He reached into the pocket of his scarlet riding coat and pulled out a small pinch of bright green. "For you. A welcome gift, I suppose."

Sisi looked at his fingers. "A clover?" Already she knew that Ireland was practically carpeted with the plant — clovers with leaves so green and bright she thought they put the Habsburg emerald collection to shame.

"It's not just any clover," Bay said, holding

it forward. "Don't you notice something? This one . . . is different. Special."

Sisi gasped. "It has four leaves."

"That's right," Bay said, nodding. "It's incredibly rare to find one. They say it brings good luck to its carrier."

Sisi looked more carefully, opening her palm for Bay to place the clover in it. He did, his fingers touching her palm before he took her hand in his own, threading his fingers through hers. He leaned forward now. The closeness of his lips, the way his breath landed on the soft, sensitive skin of her neck — she felt a shiver pulse through her entire body. She shut her eyes, hyperaware of his body beside hers, of how his nearness set her skin to tingling. "But . . . wouldn't you like to keep it for yourself?"

"No," Bay whispered, allowing his lips to graze her ear. "My good luck came to Ireland in the shape of a beautiful lady, the lady who rides with me by day and haunts my dreams by night." And then, before she understood what was happening, his lips slid to her neck. They lingered just a moment; so fleeting was their touch that Sisi thought she might even have imagined it. Before she could open her eyes, Bay had removed his lips from her bare, shivering flesh, pulling his face away and dropping her hand from his.

Sisi opened her eyes and looked to him, aware that the moment had passed. A feeling of dizziness hummed through her. She longed to ask: *Did that even happen?* She couldn't be sure, but she thought, she hoped, that she had felt Bay Middleton kiss her.

But the next day brought another interruption, this one threatening to disrupt her fragile and precious happiness even more than the news of Andrássy's departure. This note came from Rudolf. The sight or mention of her son's name always, these days, filled Sisi with a wave of unpleasant anxiety, mixed with guilt and discomfort. He and Franz were always at odds, and he seemed to thrive on shocking his parents with his indiscreet behavior and intemperate statements. But as Sisi read Rudolf's words now, that feeling of dread thickened, settling into her gut like a hot brick.

Dearest and most esteemed Madame,
  News of your *special closeness* with Captain Bay Middleton has reached as far as my own ears. I express my deepest disappointment in your choice of constant companion, as well as my most ardent wish that you might, going forward, conduct yourself in a manner that will, if not extinguish, then at the very least not further inflame these vicious reports — stories that are damaging both to your

own name and the name of our entire family.

Sisi crushed the paper in her hands, flew to the hearth, tossed the vile words over the logs, and watched them crinkle and turn to ash before anyone else might see her shame and her son's censorious words. "Marie?" Sisi said, hands clenched at her sides as she watched a flame lick the charred remnants of the paper, devouring Rudolf's message in the small blaze.

"Yes, Empress?" Marie Festetics said.

"Cancel my ride. Send Bay away. I'm not well." These words, spoken like a series of frantic pleas, set off a flurry of excitement as Ida helped Sisi into bed.

Hours later, with just Marie Festetics and Ida beside her, Sisi thought it over. She was regretting burning the note — she would have liked to read it one more time to see if, on a second reading, she might be able to make more sense of Rudolf's words.

Rudolf was wrong; that was all there was to it. Sisi and Bay had never overstepped propriety's line. They had behaved like the closest of friends. Certainly she didn't think of Bay as she thought of other friends, but they had never done anything improper. She was simply enjoying a few months of freedom away from her suffocating role at court. Was that not her right?

And yet, these rumors existed, and they were pervasive enough to have reached her son. Dangerous rumors. And if someone had dared utter them to the crown prince, it was only a matter of time before someone might whisper them in the presence of the emperor. And then, whether what she was doing was wrong or not, her days of riding with Bay would be over.

"But who would have said such vile things to Rudolf?" Sisi asked aloud to the room, her voice raspy from the hours she'd spent weeping. She was embarrassed that she was so clearly being gossiped about. She was frightened that Rudolf had heard these rumors — had Franz, too? She was smoldering with shame that her own son had thought it necessary to rebuke her. She was indignant, too, that he had dared to do so, when he himself led such a debauched life. She was outraged that she was being chastised when she and Bay had never even acted on what they both so clearly longed to — But she cut that thought short, stamping it out like a dangerous flame. She asked once more: "Who would dare?"

Ida and Marie exchanged a meaningful glance before turning to Sisi. Marie sighed. "Empress, there is one in your household who speaks with the crown prince regularly, even more often than Your Grace does."

"There is?"

"Yes," Marie said, as Ida nodded somberly. "Who is that?"

The dislike hung heavy on Marie's lips as she spoke the name: "Countess Larisch."

Sisi fidgeted in bed, rumpling the covers in her hands. It shouldn't have come as a surprise. They were the same age, Rudy and Larisch. Rudolf, though he wore a perpetual frown in the presence of his parents, was apparently quite the charmer with ladies. And he was handsome, with his mother's slender build and honey-colored eyes. And Larisch, well, she was an energetic and lively young woman in a loveless marriage; there was no containing her coquetry, no missing the way men admired her soft, youthful body and her easy, frequent smiles. Why, Nicky had certainly been taken with her, Sisi reasoned, and she all too happy to be taken by him.

Of course Larisch and Rudolf would have found each other's company enjoyable, especially given how much time they had spent together in Vienna and Budapest. Perhaps they'd even begun some sort of flirtation. But would Larisch be stupid — or wicked — enough to gossip about Sisi to Rudolf?

Just then, as though she'd heard her name spoken, Larisch swept into the room carrying an armful of lace riding kerchiefs, freshly pressed for Sisi. The young lady's entrance brought with it the scent of her pleasing floral

441

perfume, and she smiled innocently at the three women gathered in and around the empress's bed. "Empress." The girl curtsied before crossing the room to sort the kerchiefs.

Larisch had been the only one to whom Sisi hadn't explained the contents of Rudolf's letter earlier. For some reason she hadn't quite understood in the moment, Sisi hadn't wanted to confide in Larisch. And she was certain that neither Marie Festetics nor Ida would have filled Larisch in, so strong was their dislike of her. So, the girl didn't know anything, for once.

"Larisch." Sisi forced calmness into her tone as she said the girl's name aloud. "Leave those kerchiefs. Come sit with us."

Larisch obeyed, placing the pile down and skipping happily to the bed. "Is everything all right, Empress?"

"Fine, just fatigued," Sisi lied. "I'm trying not to fall ill. But answer me one question, my darling girl."

"Anything, Empress." Larisch perched on the edge of the bed, ignoring Ida's unwelcoming scowl.

"You speak regularly to the crown prince, don't you?"

"I do, Madame." Larisch, silly girl that she was, didn't even attempt to mask the way her cheeks flushed now.

"Tell me, then, what is the latest news from him?"

"Well, you know that he is close by, Madame," Larisch said. "That the crown prince is on an international tour of his own."

"Yes, he's in London," Sisi answered. It had struck her as odd — and vaguely sad — that though they were both in the British Isles, neither one of them had put much effort into seeing the other.

"He's a smashing success in London," Larisch continued, with a blushing, almost proprietary pride. "They say that the English ladies love him even more than they love the Prince of Wales."

"He is . . . ? They do . . . ?" Sisi asked, incredulity momentarily throwing her off her purpose.

"Why, yes, Your Majesty!" Larisch said, her chest puffed out like a boastful bird's. "Even old Queen Victoria has spoken openly about how charming she finds Rudy . . . I mean, the crown prince."

This struck Sisi as curious and incomprehensible. Queen Victoria — that unsmiling, irascible, surly old widow? Charmed by Rudolf? But how had her son managed such a feat? And how could he present such a different image in public compared to the moody, argumentative persona he showed to his family? Did he save all his virtues for the outside world and show only his vices when in the presence of his family? But Sisi pushed these questions aside. She'd worry about

Rudolf's idiosyncrasies later. For now, she turned her focus back to Larisch, who remained perched beside her. "It makes me so happy that you speak with my son so often. I'm going to depend on *you* to keep me filled in on his life."

"Happily, Empress! We write almost every day."

This was all the confirmation that Marie Festetics and Ida needed, as Sisi could tell from the expressions that now passed between the two ladies. She felt her own body go rigid beneath the covers, but she forced herself to flash a placid smile as she leaned forward and patted the girl's heavily ringed hand. "Good girl."

Sisi decided, in that moment, not to confide anything else in the pretty little countess. In fact, a part of her was tempted to dismiss Larisch right then and there, to send her back to Georg Larisch's isolated, gloomy castle, where she'd be out of sight and out of trouble. But there was no guarantee that this girl, having tasted the excitement of the Empress Elisabeth's household, would return to her husband's castle. What if she chose to make a life for herself instead in Budapest or Vienna? She was pretty enough and smart enough, and she certainly knew how to get what she wanted for herself — some rich gentleman would fall prey to her beguiling ways and would happily support her; Sisi was sure of it. And then what sort of trouble would the careless girl get herself into? Liberated and at large, with a smitten patron to fund her lifestyle and the credentials of her time at court to propel her into society; how would she reflect on Sisi? And what of Sisi's private information would this girl share? As she felt such little trust in Larisch, Sisi decided that, for now, the best course was to keep the girl close. Only not quite as close as Sisi had once allowed.

And besides, Sisi reasoned, the young lady was so valuable in providing other gossip *to* Sisi that she kept the empress far more informed than modest Marie Festetics or pious, tight-lipped Ida ever would. So, Sisi kept Larisch in her household, only taking care to no longer confide any secrets to the girl. Instead, she'd use her to find out what she, Sisi, needed to know.

This, of course, concerned Bay Middleton. At Sisi's request, Larisch soon brought home the news that, yes, in spite of his reticence on the topic, Bay Middleton was still most certainly engaged to Charlotte Baird.

"But why does he continue in the engagement to Miss Charlotte Baird when he so clearly does not love her? Why, he never even sees her. . . ." Sisi mused aloud one evening, hoping that Larisch would hear the question and take the bait. Sure enough, like a bloodhound bred to catch the whiff of fox, Larisch returned several days later having sniffed out her own prize, which came in the form of juicy gossip.

"It's a matter of finances, really," Larisch declared. "Bay Middleton is only engaged to Charlotte Baird because her family has bought up all his family's land, and he has absolutely no means for himself, other than his measly stipend as an officer." Larisch sat opposite Sisi as the empress got ready for bed. Outside, the distant neighing of one of Sisi's horses filled the dark evening. Larisch continued: "Hardly enough money to live off of as a professional man of hunting and sport. Charlotte will bring him an income of twenty thousand pounds a year."

So Bay didn't love Charlotte Baird, Sisi assured herself, not bothering to ask why she herself cared so much, or what she would do now that she possessed such information.

★   ★   ★

The news from Rudolf worsened when he wrote from London to tell his mother that he had accidentally shot himself in the hand. "Misfire of the sporting rifle," he explained. He was in incredible pain and seemed embarrassed that the British papers had caught wind of his mishap, but he assured his mother that he was being given the best possible medical attention by Victoria's physicians.

446

Sisi glowered at the letter. No doubt Rudolf's wits had been dulled at the time of the accident by too much alcohol.

Franz Joseph's next letter railed against their son, calling him "reckless and irresponsible." The only solution, Franz declared, was that it was time for Rudolf to marry and assume his role as the head of his own family. He was twenty years old now, after all, and finished with his formal education. If he wouldn't grow up on his own, it was time that some responsibility be placed on him.

Sisi didn't know that this was the right solution — nor did she share Franz's belief that matrimony caused one to suddenly become mature. All she had to do was think back to what a disaster her own early years of marriage had been to see the fallacy of that theory. But she didn't want to be bothered with all that, at least not at that particular moment. She had only a few weeks left to enjoy her freedom in Ireland, and she wouldn't allow anything — not sadness over Andrássy's departure, nor the disastrous news of Rudolf's injury, nor even Franz's calamitous rants from Vienna — to ruin her time.

She and Bay loved Ireland. They marveled at the soft earth rippling with clover, at the stone walls that presented endless challenges, even to them. She loved the briny ocean air that filled her lungs and made her feel as if she were being scrubbed clean from the inside out. She delighted in the droll, clipped cadence with which the locals spoke. She mingled whenever she could with the peasantry, ignoring protocol and opting instead to enjoy impromptu meals in public restaurants during her rides and smiling at the fair, freckled children and auburn-haired farmers she passed on the country lanes.

"I am in love with the Irish," she declared one evening as she undressed for bed, a hearty fire warming her bedroom against the damp, blustery air outside. "They remind me of the Hungarians. Brave and spirited, humorous, even a bit irreverent. Nothing like our serious and stern Austrians. And what's even better? There's no 'Royal Highness' on this island who expects my visit." Sisi chuckled, recalling her frigid encounters with Queen Victoria.

But it seemed the more Sisi enjoyed herself, the more Franz urged her to depart Ireland and return to Vienna at once. His protests began as mild statements, not so much complaints as hints and thinly veiled insinuations. He started out by telling Sisi that, given his renewed efforts to forge a friendship between Austria and England, it didn't help his cause that his wife was so publicly enjoying her time in Ireland, a region that caused constant trouble for Queen Victoria.

Sisi ignored these statements, pretending she didn't see the implications lurking behind

Franz's words. She instead filled page after page to him with the details of her daily rides and her lighthearted meetings with the locals around Meath. But then Franz's words grew bolder. Before long, his daily letters contained regular and increasingly forceful urgings for Sisi to return until, finally, they reached such a level of sternness that Sisi could practically feel his anger seeping out of his cramped and formal penmanship.

I've received with misgivings the news that you attended Catholic mass at the seminary at Maynooth College and that you made a formal visit to the priests there. I applaud your piety, and yet, surely you must know that the Catholic priests in that region of Ireland are some of the most vocal and combative agitators for Irish rebellion within all of Queen Victoria's empire. Your public praise and acknowledgment of them, coupled with the fact that you have yet to pay a formal visit to Her Majesty during this trip, has caused great offense to the queen and great embarrassment to me. Your travels, far from simply causing me personal sadness and private loneliness, have now become a source of public stress to the entire kingdom, threatening to undo the work I have undertaken with the hope of forging amity between our two thrones. I was willing to endure it when I was the sole victim of your prolonged absences and frequent removal from our family life, but I grow increasingly uncomfortable when I see that others now suffer as well.

"Oh, for heaven's sake," Sisi grumbled, lowering the paper, not needing to read more. "I smile at a few people in public, I attend a mass at the nearby church, and it becomes the cause of an international scandal?" Sisi tossed the letter onto the hearth to be gobbled up by the flames.

This was just the latest entreaty from her unhappy husband, his well-practiced patience clearly fraying. There would be another letter tomorrow, perhaps even more strongly worded. Franz's correspondence was getting so tiresome that Sisi began to think that perhaps she should in fact draw her trip to an early close. When she floated the idea to her ladies, both Ida and Marie Festetics agreed wholeheartedly with the emperor, causing Sisi further irritation. Only Larisch seemed to understand how badly Sisi needed this time away.

But she should have known that it wouldn't last. Anything that was stolen would have to be returned eventually, and that applied not just to jewels and goods, but to time, as well. Only a few days later, Franz Joseph sent yet another stern letter. This one, rather than boldly entreating, instead insisted that Sisi leave Ireland at once. The entire trip had been ill-advised from the start, just as he had warned her, and he could not allow it to continue.

Sisi looked up from the note in panic, wondering if, somehow, this new sense of urgency meant that Franz had learned of her feelings for Bay. Had he learned of the afternoon under the leafy copse, when Bay had pressed the four-leaf clover into her palm? But no, as she read on, she saw that Franz's motives were, as always, of an entirely political nature. With tensions mounting to the point of violence between Ireland and England, Victoria's ministers had conveyed to Vienna that they were unequivocally furious at the fact of Sisi remaining in Ireland.

We cannot allow our fragile — and highly necessary — friendship with England to be compromised, Sisi. Especially given Andrássy's recent departure and the uncertainty we face with the changes in our ministry and advisory council. We have no choice but to honor Victoria's position, deferring to her preeminence as ruler of that realm, and so I must insist that you return at once to your own lands.

The offense was so bad, in fact, that Sisi learned from a subsequent telegram that she was to travel through London on her journey home. Franz insisted that she make the trip — more like a pilgrimage, Sisi thought — to pay homage to the insulted queen.

It would be a tense visit to Queen Victoria; Sisi knew that. She hoped it would be over quickly, lasting just long enough to be acceptable to protocol, but not so long that she might inadvertently do something to add further offense. Just long enough so that Victoria could have its happening reported in the London newspapers. Just enough that Victoria could boast that Austria's queen was *her* friend, and not the friend of the rebels who loved Sisi — and hated Victoria — throughout Ireland.

★ ★ ★

"I appreciate your *delicacy* in handling these most difficult, most unfortunate of circumstances." Queen Victoria did not rise as Sisi joined her in the receiving room at her ancient seat, Windsor Castle. The queen appeared older than she had during their last visit, her expansive body covered, as always, entirely in black crepe, a tribute to the long-ago passing of her beloved Albert.

"I meant no offense, Your Majesty," Sisi said, feeling like a chastened child. But Victoria turned away at this, casting her gaze toward the windows. They sat in silence for a moment as the elderly woman fanned herself,

452

her hands skittering in a restless motion. Sisi studied the woman's profile, noticing the loose, flaccid flesh that dangled beneath her chin, like molten wax oozing down a candle. The pale, rubbery skin trembled as the older woman continued to fan herself. *Lord, don't let me grow rotund as I age,* Sisi thought.

Sisi pushed this fear aside, refocusing her thoughts. The sooner this meeting was over, the sooner she could take her leave. Even Vienna seemed a haven compared to this damp, somber English palace. "I was traveling in no official capacity to Ireland, Your Majesty."

Victoria turned to face her now, the soft flesh of her chin and neck following at a slight delay as she moved.

Sisi continued: "I did not intend to express any formal support for the rebellious armies of Ireland. I simply longed for a few weeks of leisure."

"Traveling in no official capacity?" Victoria repeated Sisi's claim, tapping her fan against a small table three times, like a headmistress weighing punitive measures for an unruly pupil. Eventually, the old woman drew her pale, fleshy features into a measured smile, the look of an indulgent and long-suffering elder who pardons the errors of someone too young and wayward to understand. Leaning forward, Victoria said, "But my dear, now you understand, a queen is *never* in any capacity

453

other than her official capacity."

No wonder she and Franz got along so well, Sisi thought, swallowing her urge to reply along with a large gulp of lukewarm tea.

* * *

The morning sun rose over London, but daylight barely seeped in through a thick cover of soot-gray clouds and chilly drizzle. Even a heavy travel cloak, hooded with velvet and trimmed in fur, did not entirely shield Sisi from the raw, damp air. The train station pulsed with frenzied activity, the locomotives belching out their columns of smoke as conductors clad in top hats whistled and called out commands across the tracks. Sisi and Marie Festetics took refuge in the warmth of a room removed from the public platform as the rest of her imperial staff buzzed about nearby, readying the private train car that would bear the empress from London.

Baron Nopcsa entered the waiting room, allowing in a slice of cold outdoor air with him. "Your Majesty, this comes from Crown Prince Rudolf." The secretary bowed and then held forth a telegram. "It looks as if we shall have to alter our route back to Vienna, making an unplanned stop in Brussels to see the crown prince."

"Brussels? Why Brussels?" Sisi took the

telegram in her hands and glanced down at the message.

She read the words quickly, as the baron answered: "To meet the crown prince and his soon-to-be in-laws, Their Majesties the King and Queen of Belgium, who wish for Your Grace to join in their celebrations."

The baron's spoken words mingled with the type on the page as Sisi understood. Rudolf was engaged to be married. The bride was to be Princess Stéphanie, the daughter of Belgium's King Leopold. "Princess Stéphanie?" Sisi remembered back to the world's fair and her first meeting with Stéphanie. She recalled a plain, uninteresting, pretentious girl. An artless coquette who laughed too often, but never from what seemed like genuine mirth. A girl who had surely not caught her son's eye with her great beauty, or her wit, or even her sweetness. Rudolf — a voracious pursuer of female charms and allures — was to marry *that* girl?

No, surely this was not a love marriage. Were they really doing it again, these Habsburgs? Sisi wondered. Repeating the mistakes of the past hundreds of years — condemning yet another generation to these marriages, arrangements of state. Alliances forged at the altar and in the marital bed, but at what cost to the individuals? At what cost to the family? To the empire? The news felt quite wrong, settling like a cold stone in the pit of Sisi's belly.

Marie Festetics stepped forward. "Empress, what is the matter? You've gone white."

Sisi put her hand on the back of a nearby chair, glancing once more at the telegram in her hand. "Rudolf is engaged."

Marie's hand rose to her breast as she let out a loud exhale. "Oh, thank heavens. From the look on your face, I thought it was news of some disaster."

Sisi blinked, looking down once more at the words as she thought about her complicated, tormented son. Now he was to be someone's husband. Did he even understand what marriage meant? He was to join his life to that of Stéphanie, a girl who'd filled Sisi with such an inexplicable yet innate dislike. Sisi's reaction to the girl had been quick and instinctive — but perhaps she had been unfair, she reasoned. She sighed, folding the telegram and tucking it into a pocket in her skirt. "Heaven hope that it not be one."

★　★　★

Spring bloomed across Vienna, and the city came to life as the palace prepared for the upcoming Imperial Silver Wedding Anniversary Festival. During this time, Sisi and Franz would join their empire in marking their twenty-five years of marriage. Outside the

Hofburg gates, the capital buzzed with anticipatory excitement as the crowds swelled, with new celebrants arriving each day from the far reaches of the realm.

It was to be a grand party, a party celebrating Habsburg stability and continuity; there were no feats that the Habsburgs celebrated with greater pomp and revelry than stability and continuity. Restaurant owners opened their terraces and stocked their wine cellars with reserve liquor while tradesmen and street vendors elbowed and fought to claim prime locations for their booths along the parade and party routes.

Twenty-five years of marriage, Sisi mused, sitting still as Franziska fashioned her hair into loose waves that fell down her back. It was the morning of the parade, during which she and Franz would process along the avenues and boulevards of Vienna, waving to the throngs, just as they had done as bride and groom a quarter of a century earlier. They'd seen four children born, and their daughter Gisela was now a mother herself. They'd seen the birth of a crown prince, the inception of the Austro-Hungarian Empire. They'd weathered wars and famines and the construction of the Ringstrasse and the madness of hosting the world's fair. But did she and Franz understand each other any better on this day than on the day when they had married, a pair of young and naïve strangers, twenty-five years earlier? She didn't know. Nor did she know what twenty-five more years would bring. But what she did know was that she did not wish to appear twenty-five years older than she had on her wedding day.

"See the headline here?" She pointed at the journal in her lap, holding it up for Franziska to see as she read aloud. " 'Twenty-Five Years That Should Have Been Spent in Homemaking Have Instead Been Spent in Horseback Riding.' Oh, well, let them judge me." She continued to riffle through the pages, seeing how the headlines alternated between criticizing her as a foreigner and a spendthrift and venerating her as an unparalleled beauty and a saintly counterpoint to the stolid Habsburgs. "Only, they can't seem to make up their minds," Sisi sighed.

"Sit still, Empress. Almost done," the hairdresser said, her tone well seasoned with patience.

"Ah, here they've called me 'The World's Most Beautiful Grandmother.' "

"You don't look like a grandmother, Empress," Franziska said, her tone appropriately dubious.

"I certainly hope not. Please, Franny, you must do everything you can today to make me look like a bride."

Knowing how desperate the need was for her to dazzle, to win back some of the goodwill she had spent during her frequent and prolonged absences from court recently, Sisi dressed for the Viennese festivities with great care. She selected a gown of pale green satin that hugged her narrow waist and shimmered in the spring sunlight. She wore her hair loose down her back, trimmed with diamonds and emeralds and flower petals. Matching jewels glistened from her wrists and ears and around her neck.

The parade through Vienna took Sisi and Franz along the new loop of the Ringstrasse and through the public parks and gardens, with thick walls of people lining the entire route. The crowds — ten thousand strong, Franz said — waved flags and sang the national anthems of Austria, Hungary, and Bavaria. Most of them shouted Franz Joseph's name, the emperor being the more popular of the two monarchs, but there were enough cries for Sisi that she didn't feel like a total impostor.

While the imperial household returned to the palace to feast and waltz with members of the court, the rest of the city roiled with parties and fireworks and dancing in the streets, courtesy of the Habsburgs. People had traveled great distances to be here, and they now seemed determined to extract enough amusement to make their arduous journeys worthwhile. Sisi's image had been plastered alongside her husband's outside every café, beer garden, dance club, and hotel. Unlike inside the palace walls, where Sisi noticed the stares of the women and the gloved hands covering whispering mouths, the people outside of the court seemed to forget all of their grievances with their wayward empress as the festivities got under way. Perhaps that was because she and her husband had gifted them with days of free entertainment and endless wine and beer.

It was during the reception that Sisi realized just how well her son, Rudolf, knew the courtiers, and just how many faces she no longer recognized, those of the women especially. Sisi had missed the formal introductions of this year's crop of fresh Viennese debutantes, the blue-blooded young maidens presented at court and declared eligible for suitors. My, how young they looked! And she had been even younger when she had been made empress! No wonder some of the older women at court had disapproved of her from the start.

One woman in particular made a pronounced impression on Sisi, but not because of her youthful, fresh-faced beauty. This woman, with dark, wide-set eyes and thick brunette hair, appeared to be of middle age. And yet she stared around the room like the most starry-eyed of debutantes, her dress so expertly stitched, her neck and limbs covered in so many strands of pearls that only Sisi, and perhaps pretty little Larisch, outshone her. The lady was introduced to Sisi as the Baroness Helene Vetsera; when she paused before Sisi in the receiving line, she had the nerve to look the empress in the eyes and flash her a bewitching, dark-eyed smile.

★　★　★

"Larisch, who was that woman?" Sisi had retired to her rooms shortly after midnight. She sat now before the mirror, Franziska and Larisch picking the diamonds from her hair as Marie Festetics sorted her gown and jewels and Ida readied her bed.

"Which woman, Madame?"

"The striking middle-aged woman I met at the end of the evening. The one covered in pearls."

Larisch nodded knowingly. "Oh, that was Baroness Vetsera, Your Grace."

Sisi took a finger's pinch of beeswax ointment from the spread of creams and balms laid out on her vanity table, massaging it into her hands before dabbing it around her eyelids. "And who is Baroness Vetsera?"

"She's an up-and-comer in Viennese society. Not noble by birth, but she married well. Now, conveniently for her, she's a rich widow, having inherited both her husband's title and his fortune."

It was odd for Larisch to relate the baroness's story so judgmentally, Sisi mused; had the girl forgotten that she herself was the bastard of an actress? And ennobled only by her own unhappy marriage? But Sisi let the point go unnoticed, for she had further questions for the pretty young gossip. "Rudolf seemed to know Baroness Vetsera well," Sisi remarked. "He spoke to her in the corner for what must have been half an hour."

Larisch lowered her eyes but didn't respond. This silence served to offer a reply much louder than any words she might have spoken.

"How does Rudolf know the Baroness Vetsera?" Sisi asked, keeping her tone indifferent, hoping to coax more information from Larisch.

"She holds a salon at her home on Salesianergasse," the young girl said after a moment, not meeting Sisi's stare in the mirror.

"Ah, a salon." Sisi spread the ointment over her forearms now, massaging the skin at her elbows. "Yes, of course, so many of the fashionable Viennese ladies host salons these days. And does Rudolf attend her salons?"

"I believe he does."

"And what sort of reputation do Baroness Vetsera's salons have? Do her conversations attract those concerned with politics? The arts? Music?"

"I believe that many . . . gentlemen . . . from this court frequent Baroness Vetsera's salons. Men of varying interests," Larisch said, her voice sounding uncharacteristically timid. "The baroness — well, it is said that she does much to entice them to her home."

Sisi cocked her head to the side. "Oh?"

Larisch nodded. "They say that when rich men come knocking, the baroness opens more than just her door."

Sisi dropped the jar of ointment, creating a sudden noise and a puddle of spilled lotion on the floor. Her other ladies looked over, startled, as Sisi eyed her own mess. After a moment, her voice low and breathless, she said, "I do apologize. Oh, it's just . . . this is a wicked city." She kept her gaze on the floor before her, where the shattered glass and the spilled balm had splattered her skirt and the carpet. "I've made a terrible mess now." She didn't utter what she was truly thinking. *Oh, Rudolf,* she agonized, *how I have made a mess of things. How I have failed you.*

XI

If only you had never seen a saddle.
— *FRANZ JOSEPH TO SISI*

CHAPTER 11

Combermere Abbey, England
Winter 1881

With a return to Ireland flatly forbidden, Spencer and Bay found Sisi a wonderfully picturesque alternative in England's wind-swept western region of Cheshire. The house was Combermere Abbey, an ancient estate passed down through the Cotton family since the reign of Henry VIII, its rooms older than William of Orange. Marie Festetics was quite unhappy to be staying in the abbey's "Orange Bedroom," where it was reported that William of Orange himself had once slept. Bay's frequent teasing that he swore he had glimpsed William's ghost lurking in the corridors outside the chamber brought Marie great anxiety, and prompted great fits of laughter in Sisi.

"Shame on you, Bay," Sisi would scold him each time he terrorized her lady-in-waiting, smiling to let him know that in fact he had not angered her in the slightest. "You are wicked."

Bay. He was by her side as devotedly as ever that season, riding out with her each day. And Sisi found herself craving his companionship even more than she craved the sunshine and the fields. She drank in his constant presence, feeling a more delicious state of intoxication than that which any wine could induce. She longed for the moments when he'd take her hand to help her over a patch of mud or wrap his hands around her waist to hoist her into the saddle. He confessed to her one afternoon that he loved the way his name sounded on her lips, touched with the traces of her bewitching German accent. *Bay.* She found herself saying his name aloud to herself when she was alone in her bed at night. She'd think back to that moment when he had given her the four-leaf clover, how he had leaned close and pressed his lips to her neck, ever so softly and fleetingly. That was the closest they had ever been; that was the only time his self-control had ever appeared to fissure. How she wished it would rupture open!

But what about *her* self-control? She'd think about him in his own bedchamber just down the hall, and she'd fight back the maddening desire to slip down the dark passage and knock on his door. *Bay.* She'd imagine what she would say when he answered the door, his hair tousled, his body covered in

466

nothing more than a nightshirt. But something always kept her in her own bed. Something kept her from crossing propriety's line, from acting on these musings, at least in the flesh, if not in her mind and her dreams.

If Bay tried, well, she'd have to see what happened. She wasn't entirely sure that she'd possess the discipline to put him off. But she couldn't be the one to begin it. Not her, the empress. A mother four times over. Not when he was engaged to a young lady. What if he rejected her? Her pride couldn't sustain that, wouldn't venture the risk.

And besides, hadn't she told herself, years earlier, that this flame of erotic passion led down a false road? A maze littered with signs of promise that turned quickly to nothing more than disillusionment? Hadn't she learned not to make an idol of another person? Hadn't that been what had ruined Andrássy for her? She wouldn't allow it to ruin Bay, too. *Bay.* Part of her suspected that the version of Bay she held in her mind was more perfect than anything the flesh-and-bone man could ever be. The Bay in her mind was a delicious diversion that tantalized and inflamed and inspired. If allowed, she'd carry on like this forever, not quenching the desire, for fear that the quenching would only make the flame shine less bright.

And yet, Sisi couldn't shake the troubling feeling, as the weeks went on, that there was something slightly different about him this season. At times she felt as if he was bridling himself, as he would a restless thoroughbred. Forcing himself not to smile too broadly. Cutting himself short before indulging in his usually hearty laughter. She noticed how he would divert his eyes from her, looking away and replacing the longing of his stares of seasons past with a self-disciplined and intentional determination to gaze straight ahead.

And then, most different and troubling of all was that, this season, Bay found frequent occasions to sprinkle Charlotte Baird's name into their conversations.

"Charlotte tells me that the weather is this damp up north as well."

"Charlotte and I enjoy this . . ."

"Charlotte and I believe that . . ."

Sisi would hear these remarks and nod, biting back the unpleasant jealousy that the name Charlotte Baird invoked within her. Perhaps she wouldn't have minded it so fiercely if she had felt that Charlotte was a legitimate rival, a beguiling lady who had truly won Bay's affection. If she had sensed that Bay's heart really belonged to the other woman. She could have understood that and yielded to the signs of his irrefutable preference for another. But when Bay spoke of his intended bride, it struck Sisi almost as though he was trying to remind everyone, but especially himself, that Charlotte existed.

Larisch, as dutiful as ever in her role as household sleuth, had relayed the news to Sisi that Charlotte Baird was mad with jealousy — everyone in London was whispering about it. The reports were that Charlotte had flatly forbidden her fiancé from speaking the Empress Elisabeth's name in her presence. And it wasn't just the bride who found Bay's imperial acquaintance a source of displeasure. The Baird brothers, growing increasingly impatient with the prolonged engagement between their eligible sister and her wayward sportsman, had apparently asked Bay to spend this hunting season anywhere but at Empress Elisabeth's side.

Bay had bucked the Bairds' request, thank heavens, as was evident by his daily presence on Sisi's rides. He'd probably pleaded loyalty to Earl Spencer, reminded the Baird brothers that the earl needed someone to pilot the visiting empress. It was his duty, a matter of state diplomacy.

But would he be able to continue to defy the Baird family? Did he *want* to continue to do so? Surely he'd have to marry the girl at some point, Sisi admitted to herself. And if Charlotte was already so jealous of the relationship — so unhappy to be left behind while her groom spent yet another season in the presence of a famously beautiful foreign queen — how would Charlotte feel once she was the wife? Mrs. Charlotte Middleton. How would Mrs. Charlotte Middleton stake her claim and protect what was duly hers once she'd secured Bay as her husband?

As the weeks passed, Sisi spent increasingly more evening hours agonizing over these questions, sensing somehow that Charlotte Baird, with her massive coal fortune and her expiring patience, haunted the halls of Combermere Abbey that season much more determinedly than the expired soul of William of Orange.

These thoughts, coupled with the dread Sisi felt about Rudolf's upcoming wedding, made the late winter and early spring pass with a palpable hum of tension so unlike the feeling of the British hunting seasons of years past. Gone was the pure, carefree escape she had come to savor in her time away. While letters in Charlotte Baird's elegant handwriting arrived daily for Bay, letters arrived for Sisi from Vienna with a tone of ever-increasing urgency. What awaited her back at court promised to be the largest state event since the world's fair. And what came *after* that event worried Sisi even more. She didn't know what the marriage would mean for Rudolf or Stéphanie or the rest of the family, and yet, for some nagging reason, the dread of it thickened in her gut like heavy spring mud.

While Franz Joseph and his ministers oversaw the arrangements for the state wedding back in Vienna, Larisch dutifully dispatched Sisi's orders to discover anything she could about Rudolf's Belgian bride. The news with which Larisch returned only added to Sisi's dismay. "One of the papers in Vienna said the crown prince would have been better off picking any old Belgian hausfrau, because at least a housewife would be less homely, and she'd know how to cook."

"Goodness! I'm almost tempted to feel sorry for Stéphanie, even if I don't think she's the right girl for my son," Sisi said. It was a cold morning in March, and Sisi stood in her bedroom bundling into a cashmere riding coat for the day's hunt. "The Viennese are as harsh on the Belgian princess as they are on me."

"Perhaps even harsher, Empress," Larisch said, holding forth Sisi's kid leather gloves. "Another report said that Stéphanie's eyes may be small, but at least her dowry is large."

How would Stéphanie hold up against this crush of scrutiny and judgment that awaited her? Sisi wondered. Stéphanie was sixteen, the same age Sisi had been when she'd married her imperial groom. The Belgian princess had only just experienced her first monthly courses; Sisi felt sorry for the poor girl that she and everyone else in the Habsburg family knew such a private thing, that the girl's menses were a matter to be discussed so openly by ambassadors and ministers and gossipy courtiers. Monthly courses or not, the girl was far too young to understand what marriage meant. Far too young, in spite of her clear desire for the role, to understand what it would mean to be married to Crown Prince Rudolf of the Austro-Hungarian Empire.

Even swayed by a mother's love, Sisi had to admit that Rudolf would likely not be the most sensitive, most attentive of grooms. At least Sisi had had an ally and supporter in her young groom. At least she and Franz had married in the belief that they were wildly in love. At least she'd had the shelter of trusting in his affection and fidelity in those earliest, most difficult of years. Sure, she'd come to understand the errors and snares of those suppositions all too brutally. But that was later. At least, at sixteen, she had entered the marriage with the most noble and hopeful of naïveties, with the two of them joining their lives together in the happiest of fogs.

Rudolf was not in love with Stéphanie, and Sisi knew it. He had not curtailed his liaisons with other ladies, nor did he have any intention of doing so after he made his marital vows. He said that loudly and often enough that everyone knew it. Even — most troublingly, in Sisi's opinion — Stéphanie knew it. And yet, the girl didn't seem to care.

Reports from Franz's ministers indicated that Stéphanie seemed more excited about Rudolf's title than Rudolf himself. Did the girl have no genuine feelings? Sisi wondered.

Rudolf had chosen his bride after only the briefest, most formal of state visits. A conversation with the girl's father and an examination of a checklist had, ultimately, made the crown prince's decision. Stéphanie was the least unacceptable young lady in a lineup of unpalatable alternatives.

The landscape of eligible young royal virgins had been especially sparse for Rudolf — entirely different than it had been decades earlier for the fortunate young Franz Joseph. Victoria's many daughters had been raised in the Church of England and were therefore not suitable for the throne room of the world's most powerful Catholic kingdom. *Thank heavens,* Sisi thought. Imagine having that frigid old cow as an in-law. Rudolf had rejected the hefty Mathilde, niece of Saxony's King Albert, announcing publicly that he'd never be able to submit to the job of making an heir on top of her. He'd rejected Spain's princess, the sickly, yellow-skinned infanta, on similar grounds. Belgium's princess was not pretty, and she had a very homely, charmless demeanor, and yet, Stéphanie wasn't in ill health or offensively unattractive. Her father offered a generous dowry, and she was of the right religion. Next to the other options, Stéphanie was really the *only* option. Poor Rudolf, Sisi kept thinking, as spring crawled closer and the wedding date approached. And poor, poor Stéphanie.

* * *

As if God himself shared Sisi's misgivings about the marriage, it snowed on the May morning of Rudolf's wedding to Stéphanie. So unseasonably harsh and bitter was the weather that the shivering newlyweds barely lingered outside the Augustinerkirche, Vienna's Church of the Augustinians, to greet the crowds that had assembled in the square to bless and applaud them.

Back at the Hofburg, Sisi stood beside Franz as they welcomed an endless stream of ministers, courtiers, and heads of state. She was the gracious hostess, the smiling mother of the groom. And yet, Sisi couldn't help but notice that Rudolf drank far too much wine at the wedding feast. She couldn't help but worry at the look in his eyes — the look of a hunted animal — as a stream of ministers and courtiers congratulated him on his initiation into married life. Her eyes stayed fixed to the newlyweds as she thought of the Habsburg family motto: "Let others wage war; you, happy Austria, marry."

Happy Austria? How had these Habsburgs not come to understand that, as long as their heirs were forced to marry purely for the interests of the state, no one in the imperial household would be *happy*?

Stéphanie, for her part, wore a permanent smile on her doughy features, greeting each minister with the correct title and the perfect scrap of small talk. The girl had clearly studied ahead of time, and based on the distracted look of her groom beside her, one would have supposed that Stéphanie was the more seasoned royal, the one who had been raised and schooled in this court. *How different,* Sisi thought, remembering her own wedding day decades earlier. Recalling how she had trembled with each step along the church's massive aisle. Remembering with a fresh blush how she had fumbled and forgotten the names of the important dignitaries and ambassadors, even eliciting Aunt Sophie's visible ire at multiple points throughout the day. How all she had wanted was to bid farewell to the crowds and to escape, unobserved and unjudged, with the man she loved.

At the end of the evening, Sisi and Franz blessed the newlyweds and saw them out of the palace. A waiting coach would carry them to Laxenburg, where they would honeymoon as man and wife. Laxenburg — the site of Sisi's own unhappy honeymoon. Sisi sighed, remembering how Franz had left her each day, alone with her new mother-in-law.

Whatever misgivings Sisi now held in her breast, however much she disliked Stéphanie for her son, she was resolved that she would not behave as her own mother-in-law had. She would be perfectly polite and even respectful of Stéphanie; she would keep herself out of their domestic affairs. While Sophie had insinuated herself directly into the earliest days of Sisi's marriage, an invasive and ever-present force, Sisi would do the opposite. Her son and his bride would have to find harmony in their own union, and she would give them all of the space that they needed in which to do that.

"Perhaps the cold weather is a blessing," Sisi said, turning to Franz Joseph as they reentered the palace. They had just bid their farewells to the young couple.

"Snow in May? How is that a propitious sign?" Franz asked.

Sisi sighed. "It might make them more eager to remain in bed together."

"Doubtful," Franz replied, showing a rare emotion — what was it, anxiety? — on what was usually his implacable mask of a face.

In accordance with her intention to let the newlyweds adjust to their new domestic life and to allow Stéphanie to settle into her own role at court, free of the shadow of a meddling mother-in-law, Sisi spent most of her summer with Valerie in Hungary and at the

476

imperial villa in Bad Ischl, receiving the occasional visit from Franz when he could get away from his desk.

Valerie, now thirteen, was Sisi's daily companion. It amazed Sisi to see the girl transforming before her very eyes, as if this was the summer in which Valerie would bid girlhood farewell and ripen into a young woman. And yet, that realization filled Sisi with a rush of panic. Stéphanie, her son's wife, was only three years older than Valerie. And Valerie, given the largesse of her dowry and the power of her father's empire, would surely be one of the most desirable and sought-after brides in all of Europe as soon as she reached a marriageable age. That day would be sooner than Sisi had allowed herself to consider. Where had the years gone? How long before the foreign envoys would arrive, stealing glances toward the princess and making inquiries as to her father's hopes for a suitable match? How long before she would lose Valerie, too, the only child who had ever really been hers to care for?

And so Sisi resolved that she would not push Valerie toward marriage for many years. If ever. If Valerie declared her hope never to marry at all, that would be perfectly acceptable as well. And if and when the time *did* come for marriage, Valerie would under no circumstances be forced to walk down the aisle toward a groom selected *for* her. She would not be offered as a prize to advance the considerations of the Habsburg state or its governors. *Let others wage war; you, happy Austria, marry.* No, not so for her darling little baby. Years of this mercenary Habsburg outlook on marriage would cease right then and there. Valerie would be allowed to choose her own groom; in that, she would have her mother's fierce support and protection.

Sisi held Valerie especially close that summer, sensing that maturity lurked just out of sight, perhaps in the early, shorter days of coming autumn. Her daughter, Sisi found, was like a beautiful melody that kept her guessing at its next verses. At times, Valerie even proved confounding to her doting mamma. Valerie had her mother's beautiful hair but almost nothing else of hers. She had Franz's lips and eyes, and — most shockingly, since she spent far more time with her mother than her father — she seemed to have her father's even disposition. She had a frank, matter-of-fact way of seeing the world. Sisi noticed how Valerie wore Franz's stern expression when she deliberated, concentration weighing heavily on the fair facial features inherited from her papa. Valerie struck Sisi as mature beyond her thirteen years, highly practical, and not at all given to flights of whimsy. Valerie didn't like to compose poetry with her mother, nor did she show a particular interest when Sisi would read

478

aloud to her from the poetry of Shakespeare or her favorite writer, Heinrich Heine.

Nevertheless, however little she saw of herself in Valerie, nothing, absolutely nothing, could diminish the fierce mother love Sisi felt for her youngest girl. The girl whom Rudolf jokingly called, a tense pinch tightening his brow, "the Little Favorite." The girl whom Franz had once referred to as "the only Habsburg she loves."

Sisi didn't correct her son or her husband when they remarked on her preference. Valerie *was* her favorite. Valerie was the only vessel into which Sisi had been able to pour from her deep well of maternal love and affection. Her life's primary purpose was to protect Valerie, to ensure that the girl felt loved. As long as Valerie was happy, then Sisi was proving all of those wrong who, early on, had said that she wasn't fit to mother her own children. Valerie was the repudiation of all of that.

★ ★ ★

Winter found mother and daughter back in England, where Sisi felt almost giddy with happiness to return to Combermere Abbey. She loved the large windows of her bedchamber, loved the wild view she enjoyed as she looked out at the nearby lake and, beyond that, the woodlands. She found even the dark, candlelight-flecked rooms and drafty passageways to be cozy and welcoming in the memories they evoked of her past season there, and the company she'd enjoyed within the abbey's walls. Most of all, she looked forward to the upcoming reunion, when she would be greeted once more by the broad, smiling face of Bay Middleton.

And yet, when Sisi rode out the next morning for her first day of hunting, Bay was not to be found among the assembly of cheery, chattering riders.

It was a frosty, gray day in early February, with low-hanging clouds and a brisk wind that would make it difficult for the hounds to track the scents. No bother; Sisi cared very little about actually catching a fox. All she needed in order for a hunt to be successful was the chance to ride at the speed of the hounds and a stretch of uninterrupted hours to enjoy Bay's company by herself.

Lord Spencer was already at the hunting grounds, discussing the weather and hunting conditions with a small crowd. On spotting the empress, he excused himself from the others and glided toward her. "Empress Elisabeth! How good it is to see you back where you belong."

"And you, Lord Spencer." Sisi beamed at her friend, his fiery beard matching the wind-chapped flush of his cheeks. Surely Bay had come with him? Sisi glanced once more toward the nearby crowd, seeking out the scarlet riding coat, the one face she longed to see.

"How we have missed you, Empress. The hunt is never quite the same without Your Majesty." Spencer seemed slightly ill at ease, for he fidgeted now, looking at her horse, around the field, up at the pewter-gray sky. "It'll be a cold day," he added, clearing his throat.

"Indeed," Sisi answered.

"Hard on the hounds with this wind."

"Lord Spencer, where is Bay?" Sisi asked, hearing the tinge of panic that she had tried — and failed — to conceal.

"Bay, ah, yes, Bay!" Spencer tugged on his leather gloves. "You've heard about Bay's upcoming wedding? That he and Miss Charlotte Baird are to be married this year?"

Sisi's heart plummeted to her stomach, but she forced herself to smile as she answered: "I . . . No, I hadn't heard that they had settled upon a date. . . . How wonderful for them both."

"Indeed!" Spencer said, appearing slightly relieved that the news had been shared and that the empress seemed to have taken it so evenly.

"I'll have to congratulate him." Sisi twisted the reins in her hands. "When is he expected here?"

"Ah!" Spencer crossed his arms. "I'm afraid

the planning of the blessed occasion didn't allow our friend Captain Middleton to sneak away this season."

Sisi's mind reeled, as if whipped about by the harsh wind that now skittered across the fields all around them. "He's . . . he's not coming?"

Spencer forced out a gust of sputtering laughter. "One must keep one's bride happy, as I'm sure your husband, the emperor, knows."

Sisi absorbed the blow in silence: Bay wouldn't be with her this season, at all. Charlotte Baird had exerted her authority as the fiancée. Bay, being the gentleman he was — or perhaps, having exhausted all other options — had yielded to her. And now Sisi was alone, and facing the prospect of the English hunting season without the one person who had made the times out in these fields the happiest in her recent life.

"Fear not, however, Empress Elisabeth!" Lord Spencer was still standing beside her, and he spoke now with a tone of forced cheer. "We would never place you anywhere but in the best hands! Which is why I've asked Major Rivers-Bulkeley over here to pilot you through this season."

Just then a man to whom Sisi had not given a moment's notice approached on foot. He paused before her, keeping his eyes down on the brown, frozen earth. Sisi felt the February wind ripple through her very insides, turning the glow of her excitement into an icy freeze. Bay was to be married. This man was to be Bay's replacement. Bay would not be joining her this season. Or ever again.

Meanwhile, the man who stood before her — what had Spencer said his name was? — appeared unimpressive in every way. He lacked Bay's thick, sturdy build. Rather than possessing Bay's roguish, cocksure swagger, this man seemed entirely unenthusiastic to the point of dullness. As he stood now, waiting to be addressed by the empress, the mustache above his lips seemed to tremble.

Spencer shifted on his feet. "Empress Elisabeth, allow me to introduce you to Major Rivers-Bulkeley here."

"Major," Sisi said, nodding once, wishing she could turn her horse around and gallop back to the abbey.

"Empress Elisabeth." The man bowed before her, his voice so quiet that Sisi barely heard it.

Out in the field, Rivers-Bulkeley proved to be a fine enough horseman. Spencer wouldn't have paired her with him otherwise. But that was where the similarities between Rivers-Bulkeley and Bay ceased. He was as dull as Sisi had feared he would be. Either nervous in her presence or simply nervous by nature, he proved unwilling to call out to her. Whereas Bay was constantly whooping and shouting, guiding Sisi over the obstacles with his booming voice and irreverent humor, Rivers-Bulkeley seemed too timid to address her directly.

So, as they approached fences and ditches, places where Bay would have cried out, his voice roaring with exhilarated gusto — *Take it full on, Sisi! Lean into it! Don't embarrass me!* — Rivers-Bulkeley muttered tentative, barely audible statements: "I shall take it full on, Empress."

After several such declarations, Sisi deduced that Rivers-Bulkeley meant these statements as his piloting calls and that *she* should do what he said he would do, as well. These pinch-lipped statements were as close as he could come to issuing her advice or orders. A few times she didn't even hear his words and barked out in frustration that he needed to speak up. Rivers-Bulkeley seemed as uncomfortable with the arrangement as Sisi was. The afternoon passed as a tense and unenjoyable few hours, as depressing as the weather overhead. For the first time since coming to Britain, Sisi longed for the day's hunt to be over.

The next day, rather than face another outing like the previous day's, Sisi remained in bed, declaring that she was ill and not up for riding. "Tell Spencer that they may go on without me."

"Empress, we must keep you warm." Ida hovered by Sisi's bed, spreading out another covering. "Never in all of your years coming to England have you skipped a day of riding."

"I'm not well."

"Shall I fetch the doctor?"

"No."

"What ails you, Madame?"

How could Sisi explain — how could she answer that question? She couldn't, so she didn't try. She simply rolled over and, eyes wide open, wondered what Bay was doing in that moment. Did he long to be here with her? She shut her eyes and begged sleep to steal her away for a few hours.

As if to compound her melancholy, the bitter February weather hovered in and around Combermere, keeping the earth locked in a deep freeze as the wind howled down the abbey's ancient stone hallways. The home, once so cozy and welcoming to Sisi, began to feel like the haunted house that the locals claimed it to be. Yet even a dark, haunted house was preferable to the hunting fields without Bay beside her. So Sisi skipped many days, blaming the weather, though a bit of wind and cold had never been considerations for her in the past.

Spencer, seeming to pick up on Sisi's melancholy, invited her often to his lodgings to dine with him and the Rothschilds, whose company Sisi had so enjoyed in previous seasons. Sisi declined as often as was acceptable without being rude. Even Spencer's merry dinner table somehow felt dull to her without Bay sitting at it.

She kept thinking, hoping, that Bay would come. Each morning that she arrived at the hunt, dressed in her finest silk and fur riding habits — just in case this was the day that he finally appeared — she'd face a fresh tide of despair as she'd spy Rivers-Bulkeley waiting for her, his timid face tilting downward. The poor man — it wasn't his fault that he wasn't Bay. She didn't blame him, even if she did hate to see him each time. And she was grateful to him for one thing; she was grateful that Rivers-Bulkeley always looked away rather than staring directly at the empress, as Bay had done. This way, the man didn't see the tears that warmed Sisi's cheeks before freezing in the biting wind, stiffening into hard, stiff patches on her pale, unsmiling face.

As the days passed, Sisi became ever more resolved that she couldn't leave England without at least seeing Bay once. He would be married soon — and then, surely, she'd *never* see him. This might be her last chance. But how could she get him here when he was not permitted to ride with her? She decided she'd host a grand dinner party, a gathering to mark her last night in England. She'd send an invitation to Bay, and should he decide to bring his fiancée with him, fine. All that mattered was that she had to see him.

Sisi threw herself into the plans for the dinner party with the same zeal with which she'd approached her riding in the past seasons. She had no use for her saddle now, but the thought of seeing Bay filled her with a small flicker of hope. Would he come? Panicked that he might decline, Sisi asked Spencer to implore him on her behalf. Spencer reported back that Bay had been honored by the invitation and that he would indeed be there. "Like a moth to the flame, he shall come, Empress," Spencer predicted, smiling kindly.

Knowing that Bay would be there, Sisi spent the afternoon preparing herself for the reunion. She hesitated before her wardrobe for nearly an hour before selecting the most dazzling gown she had brought with her, a violet dress of wispy crepe de chine. She had Franziska wash her hair and perfume it with rose water before pulling it back in a loose chignon trimmed with diamonds and crystal. Sapphires dripped from her ears and around her neck, and she colored her pale cheeks with rouge.

When she spotted Bay that evening, she felt herself trembling with relief. He had come alone, without Charlotte. "Bay." She smiled at him, keeping her voice low.

"Sisi." He was here. Charlotte, wherever

she was, was most likely furious, but he was here.

"How I've missed you. You have been so unkind to stay away."

Bay's eyes held hers, his gaze as direct and intense as she remembered it. "And I have missed you." He looked her over approvingly, and she felt her entire face flush with heat.

"I might have to be incredibly cross with you, Bay." She remembered then what he had once said, how he loved the way his name sounded on her lips.

"Please don't be cross with me."

He leaned forward, and she absorbed the fact of his closeness, feeling as if her entire body had surged back to life in his presence. *You bloom whenever Bay is present.*

"I've suffered enough, Sisi, simply by being kept away from you. If you punish me, I might not survive."

She lowered her eyes at his statement, dizzy with relief to hear that she was not the only one who had suffered these past weeks.

Like a moth to the flame, he shall come. That was how Spencer had called it, and he had been correct. The time apart had seemed only to intensify the magnetic pull between them. Bay remained close to Sisi's side the entire night, at times allowing his hands to accidentally brush the bare skin of her arms, to quickly graze her waist or back as he hovered in such close proximity. Each time she felt the warmth of him so close to her, she went almost light-headed with the loveliest fog of desire. She seated him beside her at dinner and focused her conversation entirely on him, not caring in the slightest what her ladies or the Spencers or the Rothschilds thought of her negligence as a hostess.

After dinner, as the others retired to the drawing room for Marie Festetics to play music, Sisi and Bay, made restless by the reality that the dinner party would soon be over, strolled the hallways of Combermere Abbey. "Shall we go and find William of Orange?" Bay asked, his gaze sliding sideways toward Sisi. She nodded her agreement.

It was a dark, chilly night, and the abbey seemed to groan around them, its ancient bones creaking against the relentless English wind. Sisi did not mind the cold. Her footsteps clicked and echoed off of the ancient walls as the two of them meandered down the candlelit passageways, laughing as they recalled Marie Festetics's past horror over Bay's ghost talk. "Besides, if old William *did* bother to raise up his old carcass to come a-haunting, I doubt it'd be *Marie* he'd wish to visit. No doubt he'd want a glimpse of you, Sisi."

Whenever they shared a laugh, whenever their eyes met in loaded, meaningful stares, Sisi longed for him to take her hand in his.

She wanted him to take her in his arms and pull her into any one of these shadowy, private rooms and lay her down and . . . She blinked, pausing her steps to steady herself on the wall. Bay paused beside her. "Are you all right?"

"Fine . . ." she said, smiling weakly at him. "Just a bit dizzy. Perhaps I had too much wine at dinner."

He nodded, half a grin pulling his lips apart. "Yes, perhaps it was the wine."

As they resumed walking, Bay resumed his scattered and restless chatter, telling Sisi about a new horse he had acquired, a thoroughbred named Domino. Sisi didn't care about his horses, not now. "How is Charlotte?" she asked eventually, her jealousy gaining mastery of her. She wanted to see his reaction. Wanted to exorcise the ghost of Charlotte that stood between them, knowing it would remain a menace until she confronted it.

Bay's response to his fiancée's name being spoken aloud was curious. He paused and shut his eyes a moment and then, opening them, turned to Sisi. His voice without emotion, he said, "She's cross with me at the moment."

Sisi resumed walking, and Bay fell into step beside her. "I hope the disagreement is not a serious one?" Sisi stared straight ahead down the shadowed hallway, holding her breath as she awaited his reply.

Bay shook his head. "She will forgive me. She is a very patient and forbearing girl." And then he turned to Sisi, waving his hand back and forth between the two of them. "Clearly."

Sisi found the comment odd, and it gave her heart a jolt. Did Bay mean that he knew there was something — something wonderful and undeniable — between the two of them and that poor, patient Charlotte Baird knew it, too? Or did he mean that what they were doing was wrong, filling him with guilt over how he misused the forgiving girl? Sisi didn't know what he thought or how he felt — about her, about Charlotte, about himself. They'd been so close all of these years, and yet he had never revealed that to her.

She swallowed hard now, forcing her voice to remain calm as she asked: "So tomorrow you shall return to your bride and beg her forgiveness?"

Bay nodded once, stuffing his hands into his trouser pockets.

Sisi stopped midstep and leaned her back against the wall. The stone felt cold on the bare flesh of her arms and shoulders and neck. Overhead, a candle's flame quivered, setting the world atremble, and Sisi shut her eyes. Her throat constricting, she pulled her hands to cover her face as a shudder of tears overtook her self-control.

Bay, apparently at a loss, said nothing as

she began to weep.

After a moment, Sisi continued. "And tomorrow," she said, fighting to contain the tears, "tomorrow, I shall return to captivity."

Bay angled his body so that he faced her squarely now, standing opposite her where she leaned into the cold wall. He didn't speak, and he didn't touch her, but his body was so close that, even with her eyes shut behind her hands, she sensed him there, felt how near he stood. After several moments, she lowered her hands, wiping aside her tears and opening her eyes. Bay stood before her with his arms raised, his hands pressing against the wall behind her so that he fenced her in, his intense expression holding hers from just inches away. She stared back at him through the gloss of her tears.

Bay spoke first. "If it were in my power . . . If I could, I would . . ." He sighed, changing courses. "Are you really so upset?"

"I'm always sad to leave." She paused, wiping at the moisture on her cheeks. "But at least in the past I have left with wonderful memories, enough of a reserve to get me through the gloom that awaits me back in Vienna." She inhaled, willing herself not to resume crying. "But this year, without you, I didn't even have that."

"Sisi, what do you expect from me?" He groaned, running a hand through his rust-colored hair. He still stood just inches from her, but his eyes drifted down, from her face to her body. "It's been *years.*" His tone was heavy, loaded with — what was that? Longing? Frustration? He looked back into her eyes now. "We know what we can be for each other . . . and what we can't be. How much longer do you expect me to keep this up?"

He was right, and she knew it. She was married to the emperor, and he was engaged to Charlotte Baird. Their . . . friendship . . . had become untenable. Of course she must release him to live his life. How could she explain the depths of her selfishness? To explain that, even though she couldn't have him and wouldn't give herself to him, she didn't want anyone else to take him from her? It wasn't fair, and she knew it. And yet, how could she let him go? "Bay, these months are . . ." How could she say that she lived her entire year for these few stolen months with him? "These months are what get me through my year."

Bay thought about this, puffing his cheeks full of air before breathing out an audible sigh. "Sisi, I can't live my life for a few stolen months each year."

The words hit Sisi like a blow, just as a gust of drafty wind skittered down the hallway, extinguishing the candle that flickered overhead. She shut her eyes and absorbed his meaning, the shadows now encasing them in the quiet, darkened hallway. What they had

— this dangerous dance with which they had been deluding themselves — was no longer enough for him, and so he was determined to find more. He'd take Charlotte Baird as his wife, and she, Sisi, would recede from his life like an ocean wave that had crested and now had no more power remaining. He'd choose the path that could give him contentment and satisfaction and an agreeable life. But she, she had no hope of doing the same. Her decisions had been made decades ago; her life was set, and on a course that she had never truly understood.

Sisi was jealous now, not only of Charlotte Baird, but of Bay as well. Bay would move on from her. He could and he would, while she had no such freedom. She looked over his shoulder, down the darkened hallway of the abbey that spread out in both directions. A vast maze of corridors, ancient and mysterious, trod by the feet of both the living and the dead. Sisi began to shiver as she realized that perhaps it wasn't only in this house that, from now on, she would feel haunted.

XII

Geneva, Switzerland
September 1898

As he stands vigil outside her hotel, the Swiss night turning ever darker, he thinks back to a time years ago. He's seen her, he realizes. Once before. It was on a dusty road across eastern France. He didn't know who she was at the time, only that she was a noble lady, well dressed and surrounded by a cadre of self-important attendants. They met on a road where he'd been working as part of a labor crew digging a ditch. She'd been strolling — for pleasure. Because everything that the poor do out of necessity, the rich do for pleasure. Probably on one of her lavish trips, journeys where she rented castles and rode horses through the countryside.

He stepped forward to approach her as she passed him by on the lane. Extended his hand and begged: "Madame, a coin so that I may get something to eat? My work here is done, and I have no more wages."

495

She stopped, frozen, looking at him with soft, slanted eyes. Eyes the color of honey. Warm, even. But before she had the chance to answer, a haughty guard stepped forward, arm lifted for a blow. "Back, scum!"

A lady shuffled in front of her, uttering something about continuing onward. "These local beggars show no respect." And she nodded, absentmindedly, to the lady. Sped on, continuing briskly up the road without glancing back at him.

He wished in that moment that she'd starve. Someday, that she'd know hunger as he did. That all of them — the haughty attendant, the brutish guard, even the pretty lady with the kind, honey-colored eyes — that the lot of them would know pain and deprivation. What right did they have to the riches that filled their lives? What hard work had they ever done? What food had they earned? No, no, no. Only those who work should eat.

CHAPTER 12

Schönbrunn Summer Palace, Vienna
Spring 1884

"I can't eat," Sisi sighed, waving her hand at the table. "You might as well take the breakfast away."

Sisi sat in her "Riding Chapel," a good-sized receiving room off of her bedchamber that she had converted into a sort of private shrine or museum. In this space Sisi had collected the various mementos from her happy, bygone days in England and Ireland. The walls were lined with portraits of her English hunters and thoroughbreds, as well as landscapes of the lush fields across which she had raced. There were also the journals she'd kept, as well as small keepsakes — her riding gloves, the pressed four-leaf clover Bay had given her.

Bay. No portrait of his hung on any of the walls, and yet, his presence loomed large over this sacred space. Perhaps it was just as much an altar to consecrate him as it was a shrine to commemorate those blissful days riding to the British hounds. It was to remind Sisi that, yes, Bay Middleton had existed. Bay, whose loss meant that now England, too, was lost to her. She couldn't go back, not without him. Not when Bay had made Charlotte Baird into Charlotte Middleton.

"Come now, Empress Elisabeth, I can't abide seeing you in such low spirits." Marie Festetics shuffled about the room, busying herself with the small chores of tidying the books, dusting the gilded frames. "It's a lovely day out there. How about we take a walk through the *Tiergarten*? You love that park in the spring, when everything is in bloom." As if to invite in the mood-lifting influence of spring, Marie crossed the Riding Chapel and opened one of the full-length windows, allowing in the gentlest of breezes.

Sisi turned to her lady-in-waiting, smiling appreciatively but offering a feeble shake of her head. "I just can't bear the thought of it . . . the crush of people. All of them pointing and staring and crying out vulgar things."

"We could take the covered coach and go to —" But Marie's suggestion was cut short as, just then, they heard a loud noise, like the pop of gunfire, come in through the opened window. It was followed by what sounded like the horrifying shriek of a child or a cat, and then several more rounds of gunfire mingled with a man's raspy yell. Sisi rose from her chair and flew to the window to see the cause of the disturbance below. It was one thing to hear the ever-present imperial guards in their marching or in their changing of shifts, but she was not accustomed to such a barrage of erratic and bloodcurdling noises.

"Heavens! Have the guards broken out in fighting?" Sisi looked out over the courtyard. There, to her shock and horror, she didn't spot a guard but Rudolf, standing before the bloodied carcass of what appeared to be a giant wildcat. "God help me, is that . . . ?"

"The crown prince." Marie stood beside Sisi at the window.

"And one of the wildcats from our imperial zoo?" Sisi asked, narrowing her eyes.

"Empress, I fear you are correct."

Both ladies looked on as Rudolf held his gun over the cat. One final round of fire issued from the gun's barrel, the sound ripping across the yard as the dead cat offered no further protest. Blood now seeped from the animal's limp carcass, pooling on the cobblestones before its empty cage. Rudolf was shouting, laughing like a demon dancing over a bonfire as he swung his rifle over his head. Several guards looked on from their posts in the courtyard, their faces customarily stoic, but pale.

"I got him! I killed him!" Rudolf let out a whoop, his words muddled by what sounded like the effects of alcohol.

Sisi stared in horror as understanding took root: Rudolf had ordered one of the imperial zoo's wildcats delivered to the palace just so that he could kill it in cold blood. But why? How was that an entertainment that Rudolf sought? She rode after foxes, and her husband liked to stalk game in the wild, yes, but this just seemed unnaturally cruel.

"Come away from there, Empress." Marie put her arms around Sisi. "Why don't you sit down?"

Sisi allowed herself to be guided to the plushly upholstered sofa, her mind spinning. Try as she did, she could make no sense of having witnessed her son's irrational brutality. What had driven him to such an act? After several moments, her voice feeble, all she managed to say was: "He's just . . . he's just so unhappy. And marrying Stéphanie only sealed his fate." Was she offering this as explanation to Marie — or to herself?

And could Rudolf's odd — and, at times, seemingly sadistic — behavior be blamed on anyone, really, but himself? Clearly the marriage was an unhappy one, as unhappy as Sisi had feared it would be. The ink of their marriage proclamation had barely dried when Rudolf had fled the newlywed suite, moving back to his bachelor apartments in the Hofburg. Even the birth of their first child, a daughter named Elisabeth, had brought little happiness to the union. In fact, Rudolf had recently been sent away from court by the physicians to be treated for conditions labeled "bladder infection" and "rheumatism," ailments that Sisi and everyone else knew had come from one of his many lovers and could more accurately be described as gonorrhea. There were so many lovers: actresses, duchesses, courtesans vulgar enough to petition the imperial secretaries for payment when Rudolf did not adequately compensate them for their hired services. Rudolf's behavior had become so infamous that even Sisi, as removed as she was from court gossip, couldn't help but catch whispers of what was being said about her son. Franz could barely look at his heir, and the two men had almost no daily interaction.

"Empress, perhaps you can speak to him?" Marie Festetics said now, her hesitant voice pulling Sisi from her troubled musing back to the room. Back to this place where, below her window, she heard Rudolf's maniacal laughter as he stood over his kill.

Sisi looked at the other woman, dazed. "What did you say, Marie?"

"Rudy. The crown prince. Perhaps Your Majesty might speak to him?"

Sisi stared at her attendant, noticing for the first time how Marie's face had lost all the glow of youth — how her skin had lost its elasticity, how her cheeks bulged and her eyes stared out from a border of careworn lines.

Was there no limit to the cruelties imposed by time? Sisi sighed, even as Marie continued to speak.

"If the crown prince is so unhappy, perhaps you might provide some comfort to him, Empress. Serve as an ear into which he might confess. Offer advice that might help him find some peace. As his mother, you might be able to . . ."

"No," Sisi said, shaking her head. "No, I won't interfere in their lives, in their marriage. I made that vow the same day they made their marriage vows. I won't do to Rudolf and Stéphanie what Sophie did to me."

"Then don't speak to Stéphanie," Marie said, displaying uncharacteristic boldness in continuing with the matter. "Just speak to your son. I think he is a kind boy — *man* — a kind man. Perhaps he's simply misunderstood. Perhaps he needs someone to guide him back to . . . well . . ." Marie's eyes slid back to the opened window where, below, Rudolf was still laughing, gloating over the dead carcass of the cat. Sisi wondered if Marie was thinking the same thing she herself was — that, while he was still a young boy, Rudolf's sadistic tutor had locked him in cages with those same wildcats, terrifying the boy. No wonder he longed to kill them now.

Sisi sighed. "The damage was done so long ago, Marie. He was so young, and I had no say. I blame Franz, and I blame his mother. I hope God will know that the fault does not rest on my shoulders."

"But it's not too late, Empress. Rudolf — think of him. Don't you remember the sweet boy? Why, I remember, when you could draw a smile from him, it was like letting the sunshine into the room. He's like you, Empress. He's so very sensitive. He can be so very tender."

"Oh, Marie, he *is* like me. Don't you see? That's the point. Rudolf is like me. He is meant to be free. Since that will never be an option, he will never be happy. There is nothing I can do. I learned that long ago." Sisi knew Marie well enough after all of these years to know what she was thinking. The woman said it plainly enough with her sad frown, if not with any further words. The woman thought that she, Sisi, was being selfish. Selfish and removed. That she was using her own mother-in-law, using her old resentments and scars from so many years past to justify the fact that, in the present, she would not take up this struggle. That she lacked the energy for another battle against the Habsburgs and the court and their suffocating rules, against *the way things are done.* She was too mired in and crippled by her own unhappiness to intervene, to be a good mother to a son who was clearly as unhappy as she herself had ever been.

But who could blame her? Why, Rudolf wasn't the only one who was miserable in this court. Rudolf wasn't the only one who had vicious things whispered about him. Why, just recently she'd heard the latest bit of gossip the courtiers were bandying about *her* — that Nicky Esterházy was her lover. That he came to the capital and slipped into the palace for illicit visits with the empress, dressing himself like a priest to gain entry into her rooms for trysts and unholy communion.

"Even worse, Marie, they say you are complicit! They say that the love affair happens in your bedchamber, away from the rest of my servants, while you keep watch at the door."

"It's too vile for comprehension, Empress," Marie had said when Sisi had reported the rumor to her. "Do not let it weigh on you."

But of course it weighed on Sisi. That latest rumor, coupled with a new flood of health problems — soreness in her joints and back pain so severe she sometimes could not sleep at night — had convinced Sisi that she needed to get away from court. "Everything about this court makes me unwell. I must get away."

But where could she go to find peace?

★ ★ ★

"Let's get away to Hungary for a couple of months, my darling," Sisi proposed to Valerie a week later. The days were long and hot, and Sisi was feeling the itch stronger than ever to be out of the capital city. "I long for Gödöllő. I long for its privacy, for its quiet, and its wild views."

They sat at breakfast, just the two of them, but Valerie's focus seemed to be on the bowl of coffee before her. "I do not wish to go to Hungary," Valerie said eventually, her voice uncharacteristically firm.

Sisi sat up a bit straighter, staring at her daughter. "You don't? But why not?"

"I hate Hungary."

This caught Sisi entirely unaware. "You . . . do?"

Valerie nodded once, her features stern as she sipped her coffee, offering no further reply.

"Why? How could you hate Hungary? Gödöllő is the only place that has ever been our home."

Valerie turned her eyes on her mother for the first time that morning. "Gödöllő is not my home. I am *not* Hungarian. Even though I know what they all say about me. What they say about *him* being my father."

Sisi felt as if the blood in her veins had frozen. She knew perfectly well what Valerie was saying. Andrássy. The rumors that had existed since the time of Valerie's birth, the nickname given to her: "the Hungarian child." The statements throughout court that

505

of course Sisi has decided to raise her child in Hungary, as the child is Hungarian by birth and paternity. They weren't true. She and Andrássy and Franz all knew it. Why, look at Valerie! She had more of her Austrian father in her mannerisms and appearance than the other children combined. And yet, for Valerie to have heard such malicious reports — it roiled Sisi. She wished to cry out, to take her fists to whoever had been vile enough to pass this rumor along to the poor, innocent child. But who would have repeated such poisonous filth to a young girl?

Just then Marie Larisch swept into the room, humming a merry racing tune. "Hello, Empress! Hello, Valerie. Good morning."

Sisi felt nauseous. Was it Larisch? Who else had close enough access to Valerie? Who else would have the chance to whisper such a lie? Who would have the audacity? The complete lack of shame? She'd grown ever more wary of Larisch as time had passed; she'd come to believe that Ida and Marie Festetics had been correct from the beginning about the girl, that she was duplicitous and self-serving. But still, Sisi feared letting her go. Larisch knew too much at this point. She had traveled with Sisi for years, including all of those trips with Bay. She knew Rudolf better than even his own parents. Perhaps she even knew things about Valerie, as she was so adept at coaxing secrets and observing private behaviors. Sisi couldn't have this woman at large. No, the better option — the only option — was to keep her close while carefully edging her out. But it had to be done in such a way that Larisch didn't take offense, didn't see that it was happening and turn hostile toward her patroness. And most important of all, Sisi would make absolutely certain that Larisch had no further direct contact with Valerie, ever again.

"Hello, Larisch, darling," Sisi said now, turning to her attendant, her tone sugary. "My daughter and I are just discussing a private matter. Do you mind giving us a moment?"

"Oh . . . well . . ." Larisch wavered momentarily, searching for words. "Yes, yes, of course." Larisch curtsied and left the room. Sisi turned back to her daughter. Valerie, her coffee bowl poised between her fingers, showed her surprise. "But you never dismiss Larisch, Mamma."

Sisi spoke low now so that only Valerie could hear, just in case Larisch was crouched outside the door. "I wish for time alone with you, my dear. We were in the middle of an important decision. Very well, we will not go to Hungary, then. I can't ride anyway, with my back pain as severe as it is. The court physicians tell me it's a condition called sciatica. With that and my rheumatism, I should go to a place where I can be treated. There's this doctor they tell me about in the north, a Dutchman near Amsterdam called Dr. Metzger who treats patients with ailments like mine. Shall we go there?"

Valerie put her coffee down, pressing her palms together on the table before her. *My, how she resembles her father when her brow knits in concentration,* Sisi thought.

Eventually, Valerie looked up, clearly still weighing her mother's proposition. "Leave here for Amsterdam? And abandon poor Papa once again?"

The words hit Sisi with a stab of guilt, but she forced that aside. Sighing, she answered: "Oh, darling, it's the summer. Papa knows we like to get away in the summer."

★ ★ ★

Sisi rented a villa outside of Amsterdam on the North Sea, near the village of Zandvoort. During the first few weeks there, she found her mood lifting, her nights becoming less interminable and sleepless. The wild seascape, weather-beaten and untamed, matched and spoke to her own restlessness. She saw Dr. Metzger for regular visits. Under his care, the pain in her back and inflamed joints began to lessen. She and Valerie took long walks along the rocky beach, listening to the shrill caws of the circling sea gulls and watching as large steamers glided toward the immeasurable horizon.

The sky was almost always moody, with a thick cover of bruised gray clouds that hovered, perpetually threatening rain, and there was always a chilly wind from the north. At night, Sisi sat by a blazing fire, curled up under a woolen blanket as she read aloud from the poetry of Heine, oftentimes taking up her own pen to play with a pair of verses of her own.

When Valerie declined to join her on walks, Sisi used the time for daydreaming and thinking, her feet marching determinedly down the strand of pebbly beach until she grew short of breath. She thought of Andrássy and what life must have been like for him now that he had retired from public life. She thought of Bay, wondering how he found married life with Charlotte. And she thought often of Franz. Tireless, dutiful Franz, back in Vienna, sitting at his heavy desk, hemmed in by papers, while she and Valerie had fled as far from court as was possible. Sisi found herself feeling increasingly guilty at the space she had put in between them. At the ease with which she so often left him to his never-ending duties. She'd never felt such pangs of guilt before. Not since they'd worked out, years earlier, that she was free to pursue her own happiness as repayment for the years in which she'd suffered. But now this guilt settled in and stayed with her, weighing her down like a bundle she'd be forced to carry, even on her most far-flung travels. It was in part, she was sure, because of Valerie's repeated mentioning of him. *I wonder what Papa is doing today. I hope Papa isn't too terribly sad in our absence. Poor, dear Papa, he must be so lonely.*

Valerie, as a young woman, was a conundrum to Sisi. Her whole life, the girl had been beside her mother — loved by her, protected by her, coddled by her. Yet she seemed to nurse some indelible affection for and loyalty to the father from whom she'd so often been absent. Perhaps that was the easiest way to love Franz, Sisi thought. Perhaps, from afar, he could not disappoint. Perhaps, in keeping her daughter from Franz, she had inadvertently instilled in Valerie a deep and idealistic love for the man who, in person, could be bureaucratic and cold. Whatever it was, the attachment between the girl and her father persisted. She spoke of him daily, mentioned her longing to return to him often. By the end of the summer, Valerie had convinced Sisi that they ought to go back to Vienna. The bargain was worked out, with Sisi's urging and Valerie's agreement, that they would return as long as they could travel home through Bavaria.

"I believe we owe Cousin Ludwig a visit," Sisi said. Something about the desolate, wild environment of Zandvoort and the North Sea had prompted her to think often of Ludwig, too, throughout those summer months. Poor Ludwig. Wagner's opera had debuted to unmitigated acclaim and popular enthusiasm, but it had finally bankrupted Bavaria's coffers. How was Ludwig holding up against that reality? Sisi wondered. Had the recognition and accolades of the world, at last, been enough to sate his manic drive to build and spend and create?

Sisi and Valerie and the rest of her small traveling household arrived at Neuschwanstein in late summer, when just the hint of the coming snows tinged the pine-scented mountain air. A handsome groom waved their coach through the front gates, and Sisi fixed her eyes eagerly ahead. Though she had been to this place before, the first glimpse of the castle stole her breath anew, its beauty as majestic and imposing as she remembered it. Beside her, Valerie cried out in girlish delight. "Mamma, look!"

"I know." Sisi nodded. "Breathtaking, is it not?"

Though the castle dazzled, the first look at Ludwig had the opposite effect, stirring within Sisi a deep and immediate discomfort. Ludwig greeted her and Valerie at the wide front door. She remembered her past visits when he had barely been able to contain his excitement at receiving her as a guest, how he had been positively giddy to show off his home. He greeted her now, however, with a drawn expression, his eyes listless and unsmiling. "Hello, Sisi. Come in."

Overhead the sign still hung at the entrance of the castle — WELCOME WANDERERS! GENTLE LADIES! PUT YOUR CARES ASIDE! LET YOUR SOUL GIVE ITSELF OVER TO POETRY'S GAY MOOD! — but the lettering was chipped and faded, the plaque showing the signs of age and of the harsh winters atop this remote mountain.

"Ludwig, darling, it's wonderful to see you." Sisi forced a smile as she hugged her tall cousin, but she pulled away from the embrace as quickly as she could. An unpleasant trace of fear had clutched her. Was she afraid *of* Ludwig? Or afraid *for* Ludwig? She didn't know. But, as she studied her cousin's appearance — seeing how his teeth had begun to brown and decay from lack of proper care, noting how the once-fastidious dresser now appeared shabby in too-tight, threadbare clothing — she felt that everything about Ludwig was in a state of disorder and disrepair. She shivered, recalling how this man had nearly been her sister's husband. Thank goodness Sophie-Charlotte had been spared! Imagine if Sophie-Charlotte had to live with this man every day atop this isolated peak? Sisi suddenly regretted bringing Valerie with her, even for this briefest of visits. She held Marie Festetics and Ida and Baron

Nopcsa with her eyes, flashing an urgent look that she hoped they would understand: *You are to stay at my side at all times.*

"Come in." Ludwig looked at her, unblinking. "I'll have them tend to your horses, and I'll see that your groom gets something in the kitchens."

"Thank you, Ludwig." Sisi followed as he led them into the castle. "They need not concern themselves with the coach, however — we can't stay the night, unfortunately."

Ludwig paused, turning his pale hazel eyes on her. "But you told me you would."

Sisi fidgeted, looking around at the high ceilings. She saw how Valerie, beside her, was enchanted by the castle. She leaned toward her cousin now with an apologetic crease of her brow. "I'm sorry. I wish I could. But my time in Bavaria is limited. Franz wants me back to Vienna. And I promised Mother that I would spend the evening with her at Possi."

Ludwig nodded, running a hand through his unkempt, graying hair, once a chestnut hue as vibrant as her own. Could he tell that she was lying? "As you wish, Sisi."

They stood in the front hall, and it was there that Sisi was struck anew by the sheer size of the place — and just how much bigger it must have felt for Ludwig, alone in it each night. Ludwig offered Sisi and Valerie refreshments, and then Sisi suggested a walk. As they trod the gardens that encircled the castle, Ludwig answered Sisi's questions about the premiere of the *Ring Cycle.* He explained how Richard had been a smashing success in Bayreuth. How Ludwig had insisted that Richard hold special, private performances just for him so that he might watch and enjoy the operas in peace, shielded from the prying eyes of the crowds that otherwise gawked at him and made him feel as if *he* were the "spectacle, rather than spectator."

Sisi told Ludwig about Rudolf's bouts of ill health; about the new baby, Elisabeth; about her stay in Zandvoort. "I think you'd love it there, Ludwig. I really do. It's so rugged and untamed."

Ludwig looked ahead of them, then back toward the walls of his castle, then toward Sisi, his eyes listless. As if he were waiting for company to appear from any direction at any moment. The longer they walked, the more restless he seemed to grow beside Sisi.

"Do you think you'd ever want to take a visit there? To Zandvoort? Or perhaps to come and visit me in Hungary?" Sisi asked, trying to settle his spirits.

Ludwig shook his head. "I have no desire to leave my palace."

"I can't entirely blame you for that," Sisi conceded. "It is indescribably lovely here, after all."

"It's even more that I fear the rest of the

world. The nasty, brutish, terrifying world out there."

Sisi let the comment go unanswered.

After several moments, Ludwig asked: "What did you do there? In Zandvoort."

Sisi looked out over Ludwig's view, glancing down the surrounding cliffs to a vista of fields and the lake and distant white-tipped summits. "Well, it's a landscape entirely unlike this one. We were on the North Sea. I'd walk along the beach every single day. I'd see the doctor. I'd get seawater massages. I'd read; I'd write. In fact" — she riffled through her pocket, retrieving a paper now — "I wrote this for you."

Ludwig took it, and sliding a pair of spectacles onto his nose, he read aloud:

"To the eagle of the mountains, dwelling
    amidst eternal snows,
Sends the sea gull fervent greetings from
    the watery waste below."

Ludwig read it twice before letting out a peal of giddy laughter, his mood somehow shifting to entirely buoyant in a matter of seconds. "I love it!" He laughed once more, a tight, high-pitched cackle sputtering out, echoing off the mountains that hemmed them in. "The eagle — that's me! From the sea gull! You!"

Sisi continued to walk beside him, edging

515

her body just the slightest bit away. She didn't know what unnerved her more — the glimpses of his deep gloominess or his sudden, unexpected bouts of hysterical laughter. She continued in a measured tone: "I'd watch the sea gulls for hours. I'd never seen so many birds. I found myself, at times, envying them. Such freedom, that each gull might take wing and pursue her next adventure across the sea with nothing — no one — to hold her back."

She hoped he'd understand, from her telling him this, that he wasn't the only one who suffered from loneliness. The only one to wrestle against waves of despair, what Heine called *Weltschmerz,* "world-weariness." That she, too, understood melancholy. But Ludwig didn't seem to gather her meaning, because when he looked at her now, his eyes were restless and giddy, and he clapped his hands. "Speaking of the sea . . ." Ludwig paused his steps, looking out over the cliff at the lake below them, its basin carved by the ancient glaciers into the edge of his mountain. "How about a boat ride before you go?"

Sisi glanced over her shoulder to where Valerie trailed just a few steps behind with Marie Festetics and Ida and Baron Nopcsa. She turned back to her cousin. "If you think we can all fit?"

They descended the hill in Ludwig's coach and stepped into his private boat. It was a calm, windless late-summer day, and the waters were eerily placid, like a sheet of glass nestled in between the stark, pine-dotted Alpine cliffs. The boat cut across the still surface of the lake as Ludwig rowed them toward the distant side.

As he rowed, Ludwig hummed to himself. A doleful, romantic melody — something from Wagner, Sisi presumed. Valerie chattered with Marie Festetics and Ida as the ladies pointed out the different marvels in the breathtaking scenery. Staring at her cousin, Sisi felt her discomfort thickening in her belly; she simply longed for this boating excursion to be over so that she might bid farewell to Ludwig and be gone from this place.

Ludwig looked at her now, holding Sisi in his amber-eyed gaze, his features seeming to pulse with intensity as he continued to hum the song. Sisi shifted on the wooden seat. "What is that you hum, Ludwig?"

"It's Richard's."

Sisi nodded.

"Richard . . ." Ludwig continued, still staring squarely at Sisi, "he's not well."

Neither are you, Ludwig.

"We don't have much time," Ludwig said.

Sisi swallowed, crossing and then uncrossing her hands in her lap. When she spoke, she forced herself to keep her tone measured. "Time for what?"

Still rowing, Ludwig smiled at Sisi. A fever-

517

ish, trembling smile. "Why, for our divine work, of course."

"Your music?"

Ludwig nodded.

"There's more?"

Again, Ludwig nodded. "It's Richard. Of course there is more; there is always more. It never ends. And the world needs it."

"But, Ludwig . . . I thought that . . . I heard that your coffers had run dry. You've been a most generous patron, but perhaps you ought to take a brief respite from funding these works so that your ministers —"

Ludwig raised a large, long-fingered hand, cutting her short. "No, Sisi." He shook his head, a fitful, jumpy gesture that set his graying locks aflutter. "Come now, don't tell me that you've joined their side?"

"I'm on no one's side who would be against you, Ludwig. You know that. I only wish for you to be . . ."

"Don't join them, don't join them. You *must* understand. You know the divine, Sisi; you know what I must accomplish. I have important work to do, and I can't be forever waiting on them."

Them meant his ministers, the men who ran the government in Munich, Sisi deduced. The men who collected taxes and paid for the kingdom, the men who had cut their King Ludwig off from the Bavarian treasury, putting an end to his boundless spending until

518

his government could become solvent once more.

When Ludwig spoke next, his voice had an eerie calm to it, a wiry softness that had the effect of rendering Sisi even more uncomfortable than his loud, effervescent manner of a moment earlier. "Richard and I are running out of time."

Sisi heard these words, offering no reply. She looked from her cousin up toward Neuschwanstein, where the castle soared atop the cliff like a stone swan poised to take flight. It really was breathtaking. Ludwig had achieved perfection. The *Ring Cycle* was being heralded as the most perfect operatic masterpiece ever written. His castles were the most impressive dwellings any ruler had ever built. Ludwig's works would inspire imaginations and stir hearts for centuries to come, Sisi was sure of it. And yet, he wanted to continue to build and spend and create, even though he was bankrupt, even though his ambitions were driving him to the brink of madness. But was there any way to speak reason to a mind and heart such as his? A mind that imagined and a heart that dreamed the way his did? Sisi turned back to her cousin, laboring to keep her tone even. "What more do you feel you must accomplish, Ludwig?"

"What more?" He repeated the question as he would an accusation, his eyes ablaze.

"Why, everything."

"But you have paid for the finest castles and operas of your time. And now you are out of money, my dear cousin."

"I only need ten million more."

"Ten *million*?" Sisi gasped, finally unable to hide her shock. She knew, from Baron Nopcsa's briefings and Franz's audible disapproval, that her cousin was already at least ten million marks in debt. And yet he wanted ten million *more*?

Ludwig continued, undaunted: "But they tell me I can't have it. How am I to sit idle and listen to them? If I had listened to them, I'd never have built this." He gestured toward the castle on the hill. "I'd never have given Richard the freedom to . . ." He choked on these last words, dropping the oars into the water, disrupting the placid calm of the surface. Sisi turned to Valerie, trying to assure her with a comforting look. Marie Festetics reached over the side of the rowboat and retrieved the oars as Sisi let Ludwig weep. Eventually, when he looked back up, his eyes glazed with moisture, he said, "I won't let anyone get in our way. I can't. Not now. I'll just have to dismiss them."

Sisi followed his logic, incredulous. "Dismiss your ministers? Your entire government?"

Ludwig waved a hand, shrugging, as if to say it could be easily done. "I have men here who can serve better than they can. Why, my stable boys and hairdressers would be better equipped. They understand my sacred mission."

Sisi leaned forward and pressed her hands onto his. "Oh, Ludwig, my dear one." She loved his romance; she admired his dreaming, his longing to create beauty. And yet, those same passions that drove him to conceive of such splendor would now be his undoing, rendering him entirely unable to function in this world. She feared for him.

But her disquiet ran even deeper than that, and she could not delude herself about that fact. In her cousin, Sisi caught a terrifying glimpse of what she herself could potentially become, if time dealt with her as cruelly as it had so many other members of her family. Hadn't she always been the one most able to understand Ludwig? Hadn't her own papa, Duke Max, similar to his favorite daughter in so many ways, fought against this same shiftless mania in his life? Sisi knew that the seeds of this madness lurked latent in her own core, too, threatening to sprout like a petrifying, strangling weed.

And with that thought, she offered up a silent prayer to God that she'd never find herself as lost as her cousin. She looked to her daughter — at reasonable, steady Valerie — and couldn't help but smile. Thank God her daughter was so much like the father she resembled, Sisi thought, for the first time in her life. And now she, like her daughter, suddenly longed to return home to Franz Joseph.

PART THREE

XIII

At first I was almost for giving in;
I thought I never could bear it. Yet, in spite
   of all, I've borne it —
Only ask me not how.

          — HEINRICH HEINE QUOTATION,
              KEPT ON SISI'S DESK

CHAPTER 13

Moravia, Austria-Hungary
Summer 1885

"Let's see now. You've charmed the emperor of Austria-Hungary, clearly. We know he's the most doting husband in Europe. And you're well on the way to warming my cold Russian blood. But how shall Germany's impenetrable Chancellor Bismarck hold up against your famous charms, Empress Elisabeth?" With that, Tsar Alexander erupted in deep-bellied laughter at his own joke, his gaze swinging from Sisi to Franz before he helped himself to another long, hearty glug of wine.

Sisi and Franz sat opposite Russia's tsar and tsarina in the garden at Kremiser's summer palace, in their northern region of Moravia. It was a sultry evening in late summer, and the fountains gurgled as all around them birds filled the garden with song, hopping between the trees and flower beds. The small royal dinner party sat in the soft indigo twilight; once dark descended, a pair of actresses would arrive from Vienna for an outdoor performance. *It might not have been an entirely unpleasant evening,* Sisi thought, *if not for the awkward and tiresome company.*

Joining the Russian and Austro-Hungarian rulers was the third prong of the new alliance, Chancellor Otto von Bismarck, representing Germany's interests in the place of his ailing kaiser. Sisi had to marvel at this group, as unlikely as it was uncomfortable. An alliance that, years earlier, she would never have imagined possible. But with Andrássy and his liberal administration gone from Vienna, Franz's new ministers had pressed on him the necessity of Austria-Hungary realigning itself with its onetime friend Russia, while also maintaining its close ties with Germany. With a powerful ally on both its eastern and western borders, Austria-Hungary could be assured of its safety — no one would dream of starting a war with a member of such a trio. Franz had agreed. And so, now, the three leaders sat together, toasting the so-called *Kaiserbund,* the League of the Three Emperors, gathered on this summer evening to solidify the bonds between them and set their foreign policy agendas together.

As the men chatted about England and France and the far-flung nation of America, Sisi studied her companions, eager for night to fall so that the show might begin and the tsar might cease his bawdy winking in her direction. Russia's ruler had grown impossibly jowly, his face swollen under a thinning patch of strawberry-colored hair. A full beard of the same shade colored his bulbous cheeks, its whiskers moist where it had dipped into his wine cup, already refilled too many times this evening. Beside him sat the Tsarina Maria, who appeared her husband's opposite in nearly every way. Maria had a long face, a shock of black hair pulled tight atop her head, and matching black eyes. She, like Bismarck, didn't smile, nor did she speak.

Having inherited his throne following his father's assassination, Alexander was known for his paranoia, and he had traveled to Moravia with an abundance of imperial Russian guards. Those stern-faced men now filled the garden, interspersed throughout the lush space, standing alert beside the plump marble figures of the grounds' baroque statues. Their watchful eyes seemed to indicate that Russia's imperial guards feared a new attempt at an assassination at any moment. That, too, was why the *Kaiserbund* had chosen such a remote and unvisited corner of the Austro-Hungarian Empire for this meeting; Vienna, Berlin, or St. Petersburg would pose far too many security risks.

Like his guards, Alexander wore the Russian military uniform, a heavy jacket of dark blue and gold, his massive barrel of a chest bedecked with ribbons and medals. Hereditary awards, Sisi presumed, earned at birth in St. Petersburg's imperial nursery, rather than in battle.

Beside the tsar sat Chancellor Bismarck. This formidable minister, once Franz Joseph's sworn enemy, now sat quietly. His stern eyes darted back and forth between Franz and Alexander, as if to size them up even though they were now, allegedly, his friends. Though the hair had receded from around his forehead and temples, a plentiful mustache overhung Bismarck's unsmiling lips. He wore the Prussian military uniform — the gray blue of his jacket drawing out the pale color of his hard, observant gaze. But where he seemed stingy with his words, his Russian friend proved the opposite. "You know what the German kaiser once confided in me, Empress Elisabeth?" Tsar Alexander continued, his voice growing louder and merrier with each cup of wine.

"If it was said in confidence, Your Majesty, perhaps it would be better off not repeated," Sisi answered, trying to conceal her ennui.

Alexander waved a hand, its fleshy bulk more like that of a bear's paw. "He told me that he couldn't look at you for too long, Empress Elisabeth. He said . . . *it inflames his soul too much.*" With that, Alexander roared out a fresh volley of laughter. Bismarck

529

lowered his eyes, his lips tightening beneath his mustache.

Sisi could sense Franz's disapproval, could practically feel his frame going more rigid beside her with each passing moment. He was all for being a gracious host, but the tsar's flirtatiousness was taxing even Franz's limitless patience. Sisi leaned forward, her voice quiet as she answered Alexander: "What need have I, Your Imperial Majesty, for Russian or German admiration, when I have the one heart that sets my own to waltzing?" With that, she threw a tender glance toward Franz, who nodded his reply. She hoped that this might finally be enough to put Alexander off.

It was all a charade, but only Franz and Sisi knew it. In truth, they had grown tired of each other's company this summer, almost as tired as Sisi now felt of this dreadful summit with these foreign leaders. Franz, as much as he professed to long for his wife during her absences, quickly grew irritated and confounded by Sisi after any prolonged amount of time in her presence. He didn't understand her restlessness, her need to take off into nature for hours-long walks. Her desire to spend her evenings alone, reading Heine's depressing poetry or speaking with Marie Festetics and Ida rather than attending state dinners with him.

While he found her overly emotional and perplexing, she found life with him dull and painfully hard-edged. He accused her of daydreaming and evading reality; she didn't understand how he lived with so little curiosity or imagination. How he could stand it when all he ever did was pore over his papers, discuss government business with his ministers, and attend formal, tedious state dinners in which he never actually spoke to anyone on any topics of interest or substance.

They'd spent the recent weeks of late summer unhappily together in Bad Ischl. Sisi had longed to take off for Hungary or on some other enriching pilgrimage, but Valerie, inexplicably, had taken her father's side. She really had grown quite stubborn, Sisi noted, as the girl had refused to travel with Sisi, suggesting instead that the family should pass a summer as one for the first time in years.

Much good that had done. Now, at the end of the summer, Sisi sat at this meeting, bored to tears and sensing Franz's relief that the season was nearly over. That he would soon be allowed to return to Vienna. Back at the Hofburg, they both knew, he could throw himself even more fully into his papers and meetings and his imperial duties, and the two of them might easily go days without seeing each other and arguing.

Sisi supposed that part of Franz's frustration arose from the fact that he would have loved an invitation back into her bed. He'd return to her this very night if she gave the signal that it was an option. But that would not happen. Not when he, years ago, had invited so many others into their marriage. No, it had been more than a decade since she had even been able to think of him in that way. That flame in her heart, that spark warming her body with desire for him, had long ago foundered and extinguished. Especially as she knew so well that he continued to seek his pleasure elsewhere.

The best she could give him now was companionship — but even that was proving excruciatingly tedious and tiresome. What she wanted was to take another trip. To have another adventure. But how could she convince Valerie to come with her, and Franz to let her go, without a terrible quarrel?

The sky overhead pinkened and then darkened as the birds fell quiet and the fireflies emerged, reflecting the flickering of the freshly lit candles. But though the night was balmy and the breeze glided pleasantly through the lush greenery all around them, the conversation at the table sputtered to a halt. Alexander, finding no willing partner in his wine-soaked jesting, retreated into his cup, and an uneasy silence settled over the group. At last, the actresses were announced, to the visible relief of the small gathering.

"*Now* we'll have some fun, shall we?" Tsar Alexander watched appreciatively as two young women were ushered in by palace attendants. It had been Franz's idea: the actresses had come from Vienna's Court Theater to perform a series of scenes for the imperial assembly. Sisi, who hadn't been to the theater in the past season, didn't know the ladies, but they were introduced as Josephine Wessely and Katharina Schratt.

"Ah, yes, Miss Schratt." Franz nodded approvingly from his seat beside Sisi. "She's quite good. She made a splendid Kate in *The Taming of the Shrew.* I try never to miss a show at the Burgtheater when she's the lead."

Franz tipped his glass for a refill of champagne. His whole countenance brightened as he kept his eyes on the pretty young actress, whose dark hair framed a plump face before falling loosely down her back. Sisi noticed this, slightly amused at Franz's sudden mood shift, at how quickly her surly husband had turned chipper, even as giddy as a young student.

Sisi found her own attention continually drawn to Katharina Schratt as the two ladies performed — she agreed with her husband that, yes, the actress did have a certain charisma in her bearing. Katharina Schratt was not a great beauty, but her round figure and ivory skin enhanced a very feminine, very alluring performing style. It was Miss Schratt's eyes that struck Sisi most — they were big and bright and guileless, and when she smiled, they seemed to overflow with her youthful energy.

The champagne was refilled as the garden darkened, and the ladies performed several scenes from the show *Town and State*. Bismarck, though decidedly less chatty than the tsar, nevertheless proved able to keep apace with his drinking. But unlike his Russian drinking companion, whose tongue loosened with each glass, Bismarck seemed to retreat further into ever more determined silence as the evening progressed.

The fountains babbled in the darkness, echoing the laughter of the imperial assembly as they enjoyed the performance. By the end of the show, the tsar seemed thoroughly drunk, and Franz, it seemed, was completely intoxicated by the charming performance of Miss Schratt. Franz then did something shocking, and entirely unprecedented: he invited Miss Wessely and Miss Schratt — both commoners, both *actresses* — to sit at dinner with three of Europe's most powerful rulers. The young ladies, stunned to speechlessness, humbly accepted, and two additional places were set.

It was a mild, star-filled evening, and the pleasant hum of the fountains mixed with the pop of champagne corks and Franz's lively conversation. Sisi noticed that he seemed, suddenly, as relaxed and happy as the tsar. "I remember you well, Miss Schratt. You played the lead in *The Taming of the Shrew*," Franz said, his light eyes smiling on a speechless, blushing Katharina.

Sisi watched this with a mixture of wonder and bemusement. She had never seen her husband so at ease, so irreverent to protocol in addressing a commoner — and inviting her to his dinner table, no less!

Over the course of the dinner, Alexander and Franz drew out Miss Schratt's story, leaving poor Miss Wessely nearly ignored. Miss Schratt had been an actress for more than ten years. She had tried her luck on the stage in America but had recently returned to Vienna. "And is there . . . is there a Herr Schratt?" Franz asked, his stare suddenly fixed on the folds of his napkin. The woman lowered her eyes and answered that she was estranged from her husband, her cheeks coloring scarlet at the admission.

As the night wore on, while Franz asked respectful questions of Frau Schratt about her acting and her life in Vienna, Tsar Alexander became visibly more forward, his entire frame stooping toward Frau Schratt. The actress, flushed from the wine and the warmth of the evening, seemed overwhelmed by the heaps of imperial attention she was receiving.

Late that night, once they had eaten and drunk to fullness, there was a fireworks display. Through the flickering candlelight and the pops of color overhead, Sisi saw how the Russian ruler inched his massive body closer to Frau Schratt's. As an explosion of orange light burst above them, Sisi noticed that the man's giant hand had wandered to the actress's lower backside. She saw the horrified, pale face of Katharina Schratt a moment later, and might have heard the actress's squeal of shocked protest if not for the next firework explosion that ripped across the night.

And then Sisi turned and saw for the first time the expression of her husband beside her — he was looking at Katharina Schratt and the hovering tsar, and his features were tight in silent, jealous fury.

* * *

The next morning Franz was in a sulky mood when he sat down opposite his wife at breakfast.

"Good morning, Franz."

"Good morning. How did you sleep?"

"Fine, thank you, and you?"

Franz ignored the question as he pressed his hands together, tenting his fingers in front of his plate. "You know what I heard? You know what my guards told me this morning? Most troubling."

Sisi arched an eyebrow as she nibbled on a small square of toast. She noted the uncharacteristic tightness in Franz's usually calm features. "What did you hear?"

"That Alexander . . ." Franz said the name as he would the name of a vile sickness. "He tried to get himself into Frau Katharina Schratt's rooms last night. Can you imagine? It's unpardonable."

Sisi put her toast down, stunned by her husband's revelation.

Franz continued: "Good thing I had the sense to dispatch a small unit of guards to the ladies' quarters last night; otherwise, I shudder to think . . ." Franz cut into a link of sausage before saying, "I invite that poor woman here to perform, and then she is treated so rudely by my other guest. I'm mortified — it's really indefensible."

Sisi nodded, clearing her throat as Franz went on. "And then, when he couldn't gain entry into Frau Schratt's bedroom, you know what he did? He stood outside and declared that he was in love with her. And then, shameless man that he is, he had his valet deliver one hundred roses and an emerald necklace to her. And this is all while his wife sleeps in a bed nearby!"

Was it outrage on Frau Schratt's behalf that so angered Franz? Sisi wondered. Or something else entirely? She saw plainly how jealous Franz was. She imagined how jealous Tsarina Maria would be, too. And then she noticed, to her considerable surprise, that she, upon seeing her own husband's clear infatuation with another woman, felt nothing akin to jealousy.

*　*　*

Back in Vienna, as autumn turned the sycamore and chestnut trees into a medley of rich burgundy and orange and gold, the Imperial Court decamped to the Hofburg for the coming cold season. The New Year passed with a hum of familial tension, as Rudolf had recently taken a harrowing spill from a horse while riding. Though his life had never been in danger, the crown prince was now being treated by the court physicians with morphine and other potent drugs, a prescription that Franz considered excessive.

As Vienna fell headlong into winter's icy clutches, Sisi noticed that her husband went regularly to the Burgtheater, almost once a week. It seemed to be the one bright spot for him after his otherwise tedious and dark days. Sisi noticed his mood worsening as the months passed — her usually stoic husband grew more and more surly in response to Rudolf's addled behavior, Germany's rude treatment of its allies, and instability in the Balkan states.

Seeing this, Sisi made a decision. She wrote to Katharina Schratt, telling the woman how much she had enjoyed meeting her in Moravia and how much she and the emperor admired her acting. She concluded her friendly note by asking if the woman would be kind enough to pay the empress a visit in the palace.

Frau Schratt, flattered, promptly did so, and Sisi made sure to invite Franz to join them in her sitting room on the afternoon the visit occurred. Seeing how tongue-tied and flushed her husband was throughout the forty-five-minute encounter, Sisi declared that the three of them would have to meet more often. Sisi returned the favor of Katharina's visit several weeks later by paying a call to the actress at her own home just outside of the capital.

"Why would you visit Katharina Schratt, when she's the emperor's favorite actress?" Larisch asked on the evening of that visit, her bloodhound-like ability to sniff out gossip unnerving Sisi anew. They were back in Sisi's bedroom, and Sisi was changing into her dressing gown, having declared her intention to dine in private and decline Franz's invitation to that night's state dinner. She looked at Larisch now, making certain to mask the distaste she felt toward the attendant.

"Oh, my husband only admires Frau Schratt's acting because *I* admire her so. I've told him that I want to make her my friend, and he, like an agreeable husband, will do the same." In truth, what Sisi was up to was far more complicated, but Larisch was the last person in whom she would ever have confided.

Yes, Sisi did want to make Katharina Schratt her friend. She, Sisi, could not be Franz's lover or daily companion. As many times as she had considered it, she simply could not bring herself around to the idea of being intimate with him — or being his daily comfort, as a wife was supposed to be. He didn't make her happy, and even more, she knew that she couldn't make *him* happy.

But she knew that Franz's patience with being alone had reached its expiry. His were thankless days, and he craved some sort of domestic normalcy at the end of each one. He longed for female intimacy, for a feminine touch in his life; he needed more than what quick trysts arranged for him by his ministers could provide. He was lonely; he wanted to give and receive affection, even if it was in his own puerile, stilted sort of way. But Sisi could not give him that. She couldn't stand the thought of staying, always, in Vienna. Living this tedious life and giving over her body like a broodmare with no purpose other than to produce more royal offspring. No, those days were over. She wanted to travel and explore the world and meet interesting people.

And yet, she knew what her absence and neglect meant. She knew that Franz, in not receiving love from his wife, couldn't help but to look elsewhere. He was lonely and vulnerable, and that filled Sisi with pity — and anxiety — if not anything akin to jealousy. She couldn't allow him to fall in love with another noblewoman at court. That was far too dangerous. If he fell in love with a powerful, aristocratic, rich woman, the lady would set herself up as Sisi's rival. She might even put dangerous ideas into his head about an annulment and a second marriage. More heirs, a son to replace the unstable Rudolf. Some of Franz's ministers, hostile as they were toward Sisi, might even take the other lady's side. There were plenty of courtiers who would prefer to have a more malleable and present empress — and plenty of willing, highborn ladies to step forward for the role. And the press, well, the Viennese press might very well take sides against Sisi, calling for her dismissal if another option was presented. Then what would happen to Sisi — and to Valerie?

No, if Franz was not getting what he needed from his wife, and if it was inevitable that he would seek to fill her absence in some other way, Sisi knew that he needed to find himself in love with a woman who would pose no threat to her or her daughter. A woman who would give Franz some domestic comfort, allowing Sisi to retain her freedom, while not supplanting her at court.

And that was why Katharina Schratt was perfect. She was in every way Sisi's opposite.

541

Where Sisi was statuesque and regal, Frau Schratt was plump and soft, even a bit homely. Where Sisi was noble, Frau Schratt was common born, an actress — she could never be queen. Sisi was complicated and sensitive and restless; Frau Schratt was simple and gregarious and easygoing. And the fact that Frau Schratt was still married, even if estranged, was yet another boon. Never would Franz and Katharina allow themselves to entertain the idea of marrying when it would mean the severance of two previous marriage vows.

The months passed. Sisi invited Katharina Schratt for ever more frequent visits to the palace. Often, Sisi would find herself pulled from her rooms on some absolutely urgent errand, leaving her husband behind with the unaccompanied lady visitor. She'd exit with a kind word: "Please, Kathi, make yourself comfortable. Help yourself to anything of mine that you'd like. Stay, stay as long as you wish; I won't be back for hours."

As the three of them slipped into this odd yet somehow harmonious trio, Sisi became more convinced than ever that Frau Schratt might very well be the key to Franz's happiness, and to her own freedom. She'd be able to keep her independence and continue to take adventures, while no longer feeling guilt or fear at the thought of leaving her husband behind. It was not normal or conventional —

it was not something she would have *ever* thought herself capable of condoning — but then, not much about her life with Franz had been normal or conventional. Hadn't it always been about doing what they needed to do in order for Franz to get his job done?

And it worked, Sisi's plan, because by the following summer, Franz released his wife once more, giving her his wholehearted blessing to escape the city and travel throughout Bavaria for the warmest months of the year. "You're certain you don't mind?" Sisi asked several days before her scheduled departure.

"My dear wife, I learned long ago that I might just as soon try to keep a cork from popping out of a champagne bottle as try to keep you at this court." Franz said it as a joke, and from the merry flicker in his light eyes, Sisi sensed a newfound ease about him. They understood one another and had each, once more, granted the other their freedom.

"Very well, Franz. Thank you. And please give Kathi my regards when you see her this afternoon," Sisi said, smiling so that her husband knew that she meant it.

Valerie, seeing how much happier her father had grown in the recent months, had even agreed to travel with Sisi, and so June found mother, daughter, and the rest of the empress's small household in the Bavarian town of Feldafing, in a rented villa near the shores of Lake Starnberg. The location was near enough to both Possi and Neuschwanstein for Sisi to make day trips to them. And yet, as the weeks went on, Sisi found herself reluctant to visit Ludwig, always making some excuse as to why she couldn't get away just yet. They wrote almost daily — Sisi knew from his notes that Ludwig was feuding via letters and telegrams with his outraged ministers in Munich.

Dearest Sisi,

The abuse continues, my dear cousin! It's grown so intolerable of late that I've threatened to disband the parliament and rule alone from Neuschwanstein. As I told you, I cannot allow them to interfere with my sacred mission, nor can I continue in this charade that those so-called ministers are any more competent than a band of suited apes.

Pray for me, on my mountaintop. Dear cousin, my sea gull, send wishes to your eagle! When we align ourselves with the divine, of course the rest of the ugly world can't understand, can't help but be threatened and hostile. They whisper vile things about me, but I hold firm to my sacred purpose. I won't let them shackle me! I shall not let the apes tell me, the rightful king, how to rule! I need not explain myself! I remain strong of spirit, even if these wearying feuds have driven me to feel feeble in body.

I remain your devoted and faithful servant, your cousin,

Ludwig

Before she could pen a response, Sisi read the day's news reports, where several columns discussed the king's quarrel with Munich. Ludwig's government was now threatening to forcibly depose their monarch and give the crown to a relative of his. The nickname "Mad King Ludwig" was no longer a slander that people whispered in private — it had become an accepted and oft-used alias. Sisi sighed, glancing back and forth between her cousin's tortured words and the journals' sensational updates. "Poor Ludwig is besieged," she said. *As much by himself as by his ministers,* she thought.

She really ought to visit, Sisi told herself, her feelings toward Ludwig filling her with an indecipherable jumble of guilt and discomfort and anxiety. Perhaps she could be the one to speak reason to her cousin? But then, a voice always cautioned her in reply — was it Franz's voice? Or Andrássy's? Or the voice of Marie Festetics's steady rationalism? Perhaps it was the voice of her own better judgment, exercising caution on her own behalf but also Valerie's. *It's not our place,* the voice said. *We cannot save Ludwig, not when*

545

he himself sees no need of saving. And so, Sisi put the papers away, hoping that tomorrow's news might finally cast a ray of hopeful light over the ghastly situation.

★   ★   ★

Sisi returned to her villa from mass with Valerie on the afternoon of Whitsunday. It was a mild summer day, the Bavarian air as clean and clear as the sparkling waters of Lake Starnberg that spread out before them. Sisi and Valerie had just sat down to dinner when Baron Nopcsa entered the dining room uninvited, his face pulled tight in concern, a telegram visible in his trembling hands.

Sisi lowered her fork slowly to her plate, drawing a fortifying breath before asking: "Has Rudolf had another accident?"

"No, Your Grace."

That surprised her. "Then, it's Franz?"

"Empress, it's your cousin King Ludwig of Bavaria."

"Ludwig?" Sisi waved the aide forward, took the telegram in her hand, and read it quickly. "Ludwig, deposed?" She looked to the aide questioningly, hoping he might make sense of the news.

"Empress, his ministers in Munich have consulted expert physicians who have declared the King of Bavaria unfit to rule. It was unanimous."

"On what grounds?"

"They say that he is unfit because . . . well . . ."

"Baron, please, let's have it."

"They've declared him mad."

"Mad King Ludwig," Sisi said, repeating the title under her breath, the nickname that she'd known of for years. And yet, that these threats of removal had come to pass, and so suddenly — it startled her. "It's a major deed to unseat the rightful king," she thought aloud, "when he's not done any true damage to the kingdom. Certainly, he has spent beyond his means, but they might simply rein him in. Kings have continued to rule for far longer, doing far more damage. It's not as though Ludwig is starting wars or torturing his subjects. . . ."

"Empress, he declared his intention to disband parliament, removing all of his ministers. In response his ministers in Munich have voted, and it was universal: they've declared him unfit to rule, and he's been officially deposed."

Sisi's head was awhirl. "For how long?"

"Majesty, he's not been suspended. He's been *deposed*. This is permanent. Ludwig shall no longer be King of Bavaria."

Sisi propped her elbows on the table, letting the telegram slip from her grip. "So . . . what is to become of him?"

"He has been taken from Neuschwanstein

to a lodging at Berg, where his ministers have sent a team of doctors to examine him. They've asked him to remain there, in Berg Castle, while these doctors provide him with consultation and treatment."

"Poor thing. I should invite him here instead of Berg. He must need company."

"They've . . . asked him to remain there, for the time being."

"Asked him to remain there?"

"Ordered him . . . I suppose you might say."

"So they've placed him under house arrest," Sisi said, her frame stiffening. "Well, then, at the very least, I must go and visit him. Today. Have them ready the carriage."

"Madame . . . I'm afraid that would be . . ." Baron Nopcsa stammered, "not only highly inadvisable, but also impossible."

Sisi raised an eyebrow, demanding further explanation.

"There are guards there, Your Majesty. As much for King Lud — *Ludwig's* own safety as for the safety of others."

"What do you mean, Baron?"

"They fear that he, or those loyal to him, might try to stage an armed resistance to his deposition. Might try to raise up an army and reinstate him as king."

Sisi scowled, thinking aloud now: "That in and of itself is madness. Ludwig may be eccentric, but he's the furthest thing from violent. Why, he wouldn't know the first thing about how to lead an army."

Baron Nopcsa shifted on his feet. "Your Majesty knows the king best, of course. Let us hope that the doctors, upon visiting with him, see it as you see it and rule that it's all been a big misunderstanding."

"God grant that it happen that way," Sisi concurred, looking down at the table, feeling helpless to assist her cousin. Perhaps she could write to Franz and seek his counsel on whether anything might be done from Vienna. "And . . . who will rule in his place?"

"Well." The baron shifted from one foot to the other. "As his brother, Prince Otto, is legally mad and already living in confinement . . . the crown cannot pass to him."

"No," Sisi said, her throat going dry as parchment.

"The ministers have invited Ludwig's uncle, Luitpold, to serve as regent of Bavaria."

Sisi nodded, feeling slightly faint. *What a mess,* she thought. For Bavaria. For Ludwig. For her entire family. Oh, who had ever said that to be royal was to be fortunate? "That's all . . . thank you, Baron." Her secretary bowed and left the room. Sisi turned back to the table, noting how her appetite had gone.

She walked outside and stood in solitary stillness, staring out over the sunlit expanse of Lake Starnberg. The days were at their longest this time of year, with the sun not falling from its high perch until after nine. Sisi remained out there, frozen, as the sky faded from clear blue to a swirl of soft pinks and oranges. Finally, velvety night crept in. Still, she gazed out over the lake, powerless in her anguish for her troubled cousin. Somewhere in the near distance, just kilometers away from her own shore, Ludwig sat in his palatial prison at Berg. House arrest for the king who had given the world its finest castles and most beloved operas. Well, at least he was in one of his favorite places on earth, Sisi thought. And yet, even that place must have felt like hell for him, so alone and hemmed in by guards who had once been loyal to him. And poor sensitive Ludwig, as innocent and guileless as a child — what must he make of all of this?

"Oh, Ludwig!" Sisi exclaimed, crying out into the desolate night. She thought of a line from her favorite play, Shakespeare's *A Midsummer Night's Dream: "O, then, what graces in my love do dwell, That he hath turn'd a heaven unto a hell."* In his palaces, Ludwig had built the closest things man could achieve to celestial dwellings. But now he was destined to stay in one of them, forever, as a prisoner — watching as his heaven turned to hell. Was he truly mad? Ah, but then, in Shakespeare, the mad ones were always the most sensible ones. *Look at the world's most respected leaders,* she thought — *the kaiser of Germany, Queen Victoria of England, Franz Joseph, too. Isn't it madness that they, with all the power they could ever desire, willingly live imprisoned as they do?* Shackled by protocol and etiquette and petitions and centuries-old traditions. Ludwig didn't care for all that. Ludwig eschewed sycophantic ministers and bureaucrats and antiquated, meaningless traditions. Ludwig used his wealth and his power to bring beauty into the world. So who was to say that Ludwig wasn't the only one among them who *wasn't* mad?

How she wished she could go to him, to provide some small comfort for the sweet golden boy who had never known a mother's love, who had never enjoyed a loving embrace from a proud papa. To tell him that she understood — that he, like her, was a wild bird who couldn't help but go a bit mad within the cages that were constantly imposed over him. How she wished Ludwig could hear her crying out to him from across the lake, could feel her spirit aching for him on the nearby shore, her heart breaking with his and for him. Poor Ludwig. What would become of him, now that the entire world believed that he was too mad for it?

Sisi found no comfort in sleep that night, her mind remaining across the waters, on the opposite shore with her cousin. Dawn ushered in yet another glorious summer day, and Sisi rose as soon as the sun had begun to streak the sky with its first wisps of lilac and rose. That morning Sisi picked fresh handfuls of jasmine from her own gardens and sent the bouquet to her cousin, hoping it would provide Ludwig with some small comfort to know that she was thinking of him.

Baron Nopcsa bid her good morning with the news that the doctors who had declared Ludwig mad had done so from Munich, without ever examining the king in person. "Never examined him in person? So then this is farcical!" Sisi gasped, angry but somewhat relieved at the news. "Such a medical ruling carries no weight, surely. Poor Ludwig was set up by his ministers because he threatened to disband them."

What a vile thing a crown was, she thought. When did it ever lead to the happiness that its pursuers sought? All it provided was misery and an ever-growing list of rivals and enemies.

"The doctors are with him now, at Berg," the baron continued. "We shall see what they say, when they have examined him in person."

Sisi felt the tendrils of hope spreading through her now; perhaps all was not lost, after all. Perhaps this could be undone. Surely these doctors would be charmed by Ludwig. Ludwig would know that he needed to win them over, wouldn't he? Oh, she hoped he would!

Late morning brought with it more news from Ludwig's bizarre house party in Berg. "Empress, if I may enter?" Baron Nopcsa asked.

Sisi was walking into luncheon with Valerie. "Yes, come in. Tell me, what news? Have these more legitimate doctors reversed the opinion of that sham declaration in Munich?"

"He . . . they . . . well." The baron waffled a moment, stammering, before his entire frame slackened. Sisi noticed how his face went unnaturally pale as he said, "I regret to inform you, Madame, that His Majesty King Ludwig of Bavaria . . . is dead."

Sisi fell into her chair, more collapsing than intentionally sitting. It took several minutes before she could form the words, as simple as they were: "Ludwig, dead?"

Baron Nopcsa crossed himself. "Yes, Your Majesty."

"Dead? But, how?"

Again the aide crossed himself. "By his own hand, it would appear."

"Suicide?" Sisi breathed the word, her eyes going round in horror.

"And not just that," the baron said, his face grim. "There's more terrible news."

"What could be worse? How could there possibly be anything worse to add?"

"It seems as though, last night, shortly

before sunset . . ."

"Just as I was standing out at the lake, longing to see him," Sisi said, the veins in her neck pulsing and throbbing with frantic blood. "Longing to commune with him . . ."

"Ludwig asked his physician to take a walk with him. Away from the castle, down to the lake. They set out. The doctor, relieved as he was to see Ludwig's lifted mood, declined the company of any guards. They were found, hours later, in the lake. Both men. Ludwig appears to have taken his own life. But, before doing that, he seems to have taken the doctor's life as well. The doctor was found beside the king, upside down in the shallows of the lake, his face and throat bruised from strangling."

A murder *and* a suicide? Sisi clutched the table now, looking, aghast, at Valerie's pale, terrified features, wishing that her daughter had never heard such a report. Wishing that her pure, innocent child had never had to learn of the depths of miserable, horrifying humanity.

XIV

Geneva, Switzerland
September 1898
The two ladies step from the hotel out onto the street, and he knows immediately that it's the empress. She's the thin one in black, the lady clutching the parasol and walking with that intangible, inexplicable manner of authority. He's glad that it's just the two women — glad that her well-known habit of slipping her guards has led to this opportunity for him. His chance for *the Great Deed.*

Bright morning sunlight pours down on the boardwalk, and she blinks, wearing the skittish look of a hunted animal. Which she is, of course; not only by him, by everyone. All her life she's been stalked and pursued, ripped apart and pieced back together, taking on whatever identity the people needed to foist onto her. The way she clutches that parasol now, he suspects it's more for her protection from people's eyes and words than to fend off the autumn sun. That parasol might pose a problem for him.

The empress sets off at a brisk pace, speaking to the female attendant beside her as she hugs the side of the avenue. She speaks with the easy, innate self-assurance of one who knows that she's being listened to, one who has been assured that her words matter. What must it be like, he wonders, to be so certain that one's words matter? To speak and know that someone will listen, someone will care? Even respond?

She makes her way along the quay toward the boardwalk. He doesn't know why, but he finds her parasol to be almost blinding, a splash of white against an otherwise entirely black ensemble. She wears a high-necked jacket and long black skirt, a black cap atop her dark hair. That hair — so famous that even he has read about it — dark and thick and laced with errant bits of silver. She looks more suited for a funeral than a leisure cruise. He sniggers to himself, a throaty, sinister sound. It *will* be a funeral, before too long.

CHAPTER 14

Hofburg Palace, Vienna
December 1888

All of Vienna was in a state of anticipatory agitation, no one more so than Master Johann Strauss. The composer had taken to stomping the halls of the Hofburg, his arms keeping time with the melody in his head, his ink-black eyes flickering with the fury stoked by the waltz that danced, nearly completed, in his mind. He scowled at anyone who dared to address him, quipping that he was sounding out the final notes of what would surely be his greatest masterpiece yet.

It was to be called "Emperor Waltz," the piece to commemorate forty years of Franz Joseph's reign, and Master Strauss would debut it to the world in Vienna. How this musical genius would be able to capture the essence of a man as stoic and impenetrable as Franz Joseph, nobody knew, least of all the woman who had been married to him for three and a half decades.

Outside the weather turned raw. The city's stately chestnuts and sycamores shivered, their boughs plucked bald by winter's chilly grip, as the first snowflakes of winter fell. Pedestrians, merchants, hausfraus, and students piled on woolen scarves and mittens as they skidded across the ice-slicked Stephansplatz, St. Stephen's Square. The neo-Gothic and neo-Renaissance façades of Vienna's grand buildings sat dusted by a thin covering of white, appearing even more than usual like frosted cakes and puffs of pastry.

Sisi longed for the freedom to venture out into the streets beyond the palace walls, where the air was redolent with the aroma of roasted chestnuts and the sound of tinkling sleigh bells. She longed to wander the streets of the capital incognita; to laugh in delight at the children who begged their mothers for florin coins to buy gingerbread biscuits; to smile at the mothers who combed the Christkindl Market outside the Rathaus, the town hall, in search of noel treats. To wink at the young male students who wooed their lovers over steaming coffees and pots of molten chocolate topped with cream. But such simple pleasures were not possible for her in Vienna — there was no opportunity for aimless wandering and observing when one had a face as universally recognizable as hers.

Inside the palace, Sisi and Valerie sat down with the immediate family for the weekly private dinner in the imperial apartments. The great halls and corridors of the Hofburg were quiet that night, as the court prepared for the festivities scheduled to occur the following evening, when Master Strauss would finally debut his new waltz.

"He shall call it 'Hand in Hand,' I've learned, rather than 'Emperor Waltz.' " Franz, as usual, even in family settings, was the first to speak, and he did so now as he picked apart a *Semmelknödel,* a bread dumpling.

" 'Hand in Hand,' " Sisi repeated, having been unaware that Master Strauss had changed the name of his composition. "Does he refer to you and me?"

"Perhaps he refers to Rudolf and me," Stéphanie said, her spoon poised above her red goulash. Rudolf snorted into his wine cup. Sisi kept her eyes on her husband, not looking toward Stéphanie or Rudolf.

"Neither, in fact," Franz answered. "Master Strauss refers to me and . . . Germany's kaiser." His tone, uncharacteristically, betrayed his raw annoyance at the fact that a waltz initially dedicated exclusively to him was now being shared with a fellow emperor.

"Quite the shrewd diplomat, that Master Strauss," Sisi said to her husband.

"Indeed."

"I think I shall keep to the original title and call it the 'Emperor Waltz,' " Sisi said.

"Whatever you call it, I think we shall all

enjoy it very much," Franz said, wiping at his thick beard with a napkin, the tenor of formal, well-trained dispassion returning to his voice. "With this piece, Strauss aims to prove that he, the son, has finally overtaken his father's legacy. And to knock Liszt and Bruckner out of the way and establish himself, once and for all, as the best."

"The best?" Rudolf spoke for the first time, and Sisi looked toward her son. Only thirty years old, and with a build and bone structure that should have made him devastatingly handsome, Rudy already had a face that gave the impression of having been roughly used by life. His sallow complexion lacked any of the glow of youth. His eyes appeared bloodshot and red-rimmed from lack of sleep — or God knew what else. He wore a hard expression as he spoke to his father now, his mocking tone like an invitation to argue. "Some would say Wagner has already won himself that title."

Wagner. The mention of that man — her cousin's friend, the beneficiary of Ludwig's maddening generosity — stoked a familiar sadness in Sisi. A melancholy that refused to be buried.

Rudolf continued: "And Wagner is giving your Strauss quite a match, with his *Ring Cycle* going on this season in the Vienna Court Opera."

"Rudolf, why must you slouch so over the

table?" Franz might have appeared perfectly calm if not for the trace of scarlet that colored his cheeks beneath his beard. "Have you no respect for the ladies present?"

"Oh, I'm sorry. Is this better?" Rudolf asked, his voice sour as he sat up with rigid formality in his seat, his posture exaggeratedly stiff. Much like his father's.

"Yes, in fact, it is," Franz said, ignoring the mockery evident in his son's mannerisms. "Thank you. And anyway, he's hardly *my* Strauss. The man's achievements stand on their own."

"He's your court's composer."

"Yes, well, whatever the case is, their little competitive game is our empire's gain," Franz said, as if he didn't wish to engage his son further on the topic. "And one thing is for certain: when Master Strauss picks up his bow, the whole of Europe waltzes. I think we could all use a bit of that."

It was true; they did need a bit of music, both within the imperial family quarters and across the whole capital. Though it was a merry season, a time to celebrate the Savior's birth and the beginning of the New Year, a hum of noticeable unrest pulsed all around them. Certainly it was nothing so severe as in London, where an unnamed menace known as Jack the Ripper was haunting the city, murdering young women, mutilating their corpses in ways that defied the imagination.

Though it had no Jack the Ripper stalking its streets, Vienna, too, ailed. It was the wealthiest city in Europe, and yet, it also happened to have the highest number of suicides. The asylums were packed beyond occupancy with diseased minds and feeble bodies. The rush of young students hurling themselves into the Danube was almost an epidemic. How could one city possess such promise and simultaneously suffer from such utter despair?

And then there was the private, more personal malaise from which Sisi suffered. She now wore black most days; she was in mourning over the recent death of her father, as well as the abrupt and shocking death of Ludwig. Even as time went on, the loss of her cousin remained with her, persisting as a deep and unsettling ache that she found difficult to bear. She, like so many of his bereft and loyal subjects across Bavaria, simply could not accept the public medical ruling that Ludwig had committed suicide. It made no sense, not when witnesses had come forward to say that he had been found in shallow water. Were they really meant to believe that Ludwig, an unusually tall man and an able swimmer, had drowned himself in such a way? Or was she destined to live with this uncertainty — hearing conflicting witness accounts and conspiracy theories that seemed far more plausible than the quick and polished autopsy report — without ever understanding the final days and hours of her tortured cousin's life?

But the largest cause of Sisi's anxiety, the most malignant source of the disquiet in her family's apartments, was Rudolf. The strained relationship between father and son had taken a sharp dive toward even shakier ground when, just recently, Rudolf had nearly shot his father while the two men were out hunting together. All involved had labeled the near-miss as nothing more than an unfortunate accident. Rudolf, despite how often he wielded rifles and pistols, despite the pride he took in his massive collection of firearms, had never been a particularly good shot or successful hunter, lacking both the patience and the steadiness of his skilled father. Even Franz Joseph himself had declared it a meaningless mishap. However, whether it was acquiescence to his ministers' overly cautious advice or a decision made on his own, Franz Joseph had started having his secret police follow his son from that moment on. How they could be labeled "secret" police, Sisi didn't understand, for the whole court seemed to know within days that this tail had been put on the crown prince — including the crown prince himself. This did very little to rehabilitate the unraveling trust between father and son.

In response, Rudolf had struck back with his own very thinly veiled insult: he had begun penning "anonymous" editorials in one of Vienna's newspapers, the *Neues Wiener Tagblatt,* containing harshly worded critiques of his father. In his articles, he painted "the emperor" as willfully blind to the troubles of his empire. An antiquated, irrelevant old man who stood stubbornly obdurate against progress and liberalism. Rudolf never signed the articles that he wrote — but his close friendship with the newspaper's editor in chief was enough of a clue to everyone at court. And though no one in the Hofburg ever mentioned these printed attacks, everyone, including Franz, saw them.

Yes, there was no denying it — the imperial family most definitely needed a jolt of merriment. A bit of diversion to mitigate the tensions that simmered under the surface of forced familial cordiality. Perhaps Master Strauss's music could do the trick. He was, after all, known as the best.

And so, on that early December evening when Master Strauss was to debut his new piece, Sisi was determined to foster an air of lively celebration, both in her own rooms and within her family circle. She took her time dressing, selecting a gown of lush amethyst brocade. She adorned herself with the matching jewels and had her hair woven with peacock feathers, so that she would look sufficiently opulent against the gilded backdrop of the great hall.

The performance was to take place in Vienna's Musikverein, the capital's grandest concert hall and home to the philharmonic. As the imperial family entered, the crowded space erupted in applause. The royal guards fanned out around them, forming a protective cocoon. Overhead the chandeliers twinkled with hundreds of candles, their light shimmering off of the gold-gilt walls and balconied boxes. As sumptuous as this setting was, the clothes of the Viennese themselves proved equally arresting; the figures who turned now to survey the imperial family were a fanfare of jewel-colored gowns, glossy pearls, priceless heirloom diamonds, and elaborate coifs.

Sisi flashed a shy, timid smile as she felt the familiar barrage of hundreds of inquisitive, probing eyes turning on her. Tomorrow, every newspaper in Vienna would report on every detail of her dress, her hair, even her facial expressions. Beside her, Valerie seemed less fazed by the crowd, chattering excitedly as she looked around the hall. "This is just lovely! Look at the size of the ensemble. I bet Salvator would love this. Perhaps he shall come next time."

Sisi turned to her daughter now, momentarily forgetting the crowds in her surprise at the remark. It was surprising in that it was so wholly uncharacteristic for Valerie to say such a thing. Salvator? Their distant Habsburg relative? The young Italian army officer who had spent the past summer visiting them in Bad Ischl? Sisi hadn't noticed any particular attraction on the part of her daughter to the dark-haired, reserved archduke. Then again, Sisi hadn't really looked, had she? It had never really crossed her mind to look, had never seemed plausible that Valerie would take note of a young man, since she never had before. But then, she *was* twenty. It was natural that Valerie would have begun to notice men. And Salvator was handsome, Sisi supposed. But had Valerie really been taken with her shy, quiet cousin? The realization seeped through Sisi now that there might actually be much about her favorite daughter that she, the mother, didn't know. All of this and more raced through her mind in several moments of surprised, confused, slightly panicky reflection. But when she answered her daughter, she managed to keep her tone calm. "Salvator, my darling girl?"

Valerie nodded, a highly atypical flush coloring her pale cheeks. "Yes, Cousin Franz Salvator. I told him that we were attending Master Strauss's debut tonight. He said that he'd very much enjoy something like this. Perhaps he will come next time."

"You write to your cousin Salvator, my darling?"

"Yes."

"Since when?"

566

"Since the summer. Mamma, why do you look at me like that? Am I not allowed to write to . . . ?"

"It's just that . . . well, I never knew, that's all."

And then, sensible Valerie shrugged, answering: "You never asked."

It was true. Sisi *hadn't* ever asked. Had barely ever even raised the topic of courtship or love with her daughter. Perhaps a part of her — a very selfish part, she conceded — had been hoping that Valerie would never want those things, would never leave her mother's side for the home of a husband. And then, as if skimming the thoughts directly from her mother's mind, Valerie said, an edge of defiance to her voice, "I'm not fifteen, Mamma. I am nearly twenty-one. And I am not being *sold.* I would be willingly entering into matrimony. Surely you might modulate your feelings on the institution if you saw how different the circumstances were?"

Sisi fell speechless now. Her daughter was responding to something that Sisi had said, recently, about her own marriage. Perhaps it had been the only time she had really discussed the topic with her daughter, but Valerie had clearly listened, for her words now echoed Sisi's own previous confession: *Marriage is a ridiculous institution. Why, when I think of myself, sold as a child of fifteen, and taking an oath I did not understand . . .*

Valerie's features softened now, and she offered a gentle smile as she and Sisi took their seats beside each other. "Mamma, you'll be all right. I won't be dead; I'll just be married."

Sisi swallowed, a cold lump of understanding settling in her belly. Her daughter — her wise, practical, sensible daughter — was preparing her. She was telling Sisi that it would happen, that it was inevitable. She, Valerie, the only true, constant love of Sisi's life, had fallen in love with a man and would be leaving home eventually. Confusion and surprise shifted into outright panic.

"Mamma?"

Sisi blinked. "Yes, dear?"

"You're as pale as a ghost. Are you going to faint?"

Sisi shook her head, feeling as though the amethysts that lined her throat might choke her.

"Mamma?" Valerie put her hand on her mother's. "You *will* be all right, won't you? You knew that this would happen someday, surely?"

Sisi shut her eyes for a moment, fending off dizziness. If only she could remove this corset, this too-heavy necklace around her neck. Oh, what must all of the spectators be thinking, watching her swoon like this?

"Mother, I'm terribly frightened — you look ill."

"Sisi, are you ill?" Franz interjected now, lowering himself into the seat on Sisi's other side.

Sisi drew in a long, slow inhale, forcing herself to master this tempest of emotions. "I'm fine." She opened her eyes, waving a hand to dismiss Franz's concern as she turned to face her daughter. "Of course. I shall be so delighted if you tell me that . . . if you wish to be married." A fragile, noncommittal smile, but she managed one just the same. "Of course, my darling."

Valerie cocked her head to the side, like a dubious elder eyeing a fibbing child. "Are you telling me the truth, Mamma?"

"Of course, Valerie, my darling one. I shall be happy . . . as long as you are happy." Sisi supposed that, in the end, that would be the truth. She loved Valerie so much that, at the core of everything, the girl's happiness trumped anything else. Even if it would break her own heart to lose her daughter's daily company. She forced another smile, this one more determined. "And, well, it will be good."

Valerie pressed her lips together, still suspicious.

"It *will* be, Valerie dear. It will give me time to pour my heart into my new building project."

"Oh, Mamma." Valerie widened her eyes now. "You're not *really* going to move to a new villa in Corfu, are you? I thought that your Greek building project was just another one of your fantastical daydreams. You don't *really* want to move that far away?"

Sisi considered the question but was quickly distracted, as just then Master Strauss strode out before the orchestra, and the crowded hall erupted into uproarious applause. The composer bowed his tall frame several times toward the imperial family before acknowledging the rest of the audience, and the assembly fell silent. Though she'd seen him hundreds of times before, Sisi studied the musician now with great interest. He appeared windswept and feral, his hair disheveled, his mustache even more unruly than Sisi had ever seen it. As if laboring over this piece had, in some ways, been a divine struggle, like Jacob wrestling in the arms of God.

Turning back to the orchestra now, Master Strauss lifted his violin bow, his favorite tool for conducting. One last moment of anticipatory silence pulsed throughout the hall, and then, the "Emperor Waltz" began.

Sisi shut her eyes to listen, allowing herself to be pulled in by the swell of music. It began gently, the opening measures of violin and flute unfurling in a soft, delicate melody in triple meter. That was right, Sisi thought, remembering back to so many years ago, to the garden in Bad Ischl. Franz, for her, *had* begun as delicate and gentle, his eyes holding her in a pale glow of Alpine moonlight. As tender a young lover as there had ever been, as soft a supplicant as any young girl could have hoped for.

As Strauss led the orchestra onward, the brass and drums became more prominent. The volume mounted and so, too, did the potency behind the music, a latent energy giving way to a full eruption of loud, beautiful, overwhelming sound. The winds yielded their warbles and trills, their whimsy swallowed up into a steady, stately march. Sisi was overcome. She felt goosebumps rise to the surface of her flesh, recognizing that Master Strauss, truly the genius they all declared him to be, had succeeded in doing something she never would have thought possible; she felt Franz in every note.

The music built and crescendoed with a triumphant swell of brass and drums and violins, all the divergent threads coming together to form a perfect whole. Strauss united them all, making a rich harmony, just as Franz had woven all of his lands and people into his improbable empire. And then, unexpectedly, the proud, stately melody modulated back to the soft, languid sweep of violins and winds. Strauss, his bow keeping the three-quarter time with feverish energy, his hair flying away from his face, led the musicians back and forth between these different threads of lovely and delicate, strong and regal. It happened seamlessly. The mood of the audience rose and fell as the notes carried them along on this unexpected journey, its course so surprising and delightful that Sisi felt she might laugh and weep simultaneously.

She marveled at how Strauss said so much with these notes and these instruments. It was Franz. It was his empire. This waltz was the music of the softly falling snow on the regal new buildings of the Ringstrasse. It was the spring tulips covering the lawns and arcades in front of Schönbrunn Palace. It was the indomitable, majestic peaks of the Alps, the red-cheeked goatherds plucking wild edelweiss from the summits. It was the spirited laughter of the Viennese students, wooing and debating in the beer gardens and cafés. It was the stately blue Danube, it was the cathedrals, it was the mountain chalets, and it was the ancient villages sprung up around church bell towers and brooks and streams. It was all of it, and it was all Franz Joseph.

At the end, after a final, exultant burst of brass and drums and strings, Strauss returned to softness. The waltz became so slow and quiet that it felt almost fragile, and Sisi leaned forward to make sure that she did not miss a single note.

When at last the instruments fell silent, the final notes rippling across the stunned assembly, Sisi glanced to her side to see how the man embodied by this masterpiece responded. There sat the emperor, as still as stone. Entranced. Sisi stared at him in wonder. She never saw Franz moved like this, not since the death of his mother. Before that, the only other times had been when they had lost their darling first baby and when he had waited for her, a nervous bridegroom, at the front of the church aisle. Johann Strauss truly was a genius, a master who had achieved the impossible — he had drawn tears to Emperor Franz Joseph's eyes.

★　★　★

Back at the Hofburg, the members of the royal family climbed the private marble Emperor's Stairway and bid one another good night as they scattered, yawning, toward their respective apartments. At the top of the stairs, Franz, however, lingered a moment longer than usual. Sisi paused, looking at him. Clearly still moved, he puffed up his cheeks and let out a long, audible exhale. She watched him recover the equanimity that had fractured in the concert hall. And then, with his features rearranged and pressed smooth once more, he spoke to her: "Well, Sisi, now that that is over, we look to our next celebration. Christmas. And your birthday."

Sisi sighed, slipping her hands out of her

gloves. Her head ached from the weight of her upswept hair pulling against her scalp, and she longed for her bedchamber. It had been a night fraught with emotions — first with Valerie's revelation, then with the moving ode to a husband for whom she felt so many warring feelings. She longed for privacy in which to ponder and sort through it all.

"We will celebrate with a family dinner on Christmas Eve," Franz said now, completely poised once more.

"Must we celebrate my birthday?"

"Why should we not?"

Sisi thought about this. "Another year older? I don't celebrate the fact that time is tightening its grip on me." *Pulling Valerie away from me,* she thought. *Draining me of my vigor and my beauty.* But she didn't voice these last thoughts.

"But another year wiser, too," Franz offered good-naturedly.

Sisi smiled at him. "Come now, my husband, we both know that that is not true." They began walking toward the family apartments on the Hofburg's Amalia wing now, side by side, the others far enough ahead that they remained in private conversation. "So tell me, did you enjoy your waltz, Emperor?"

"I did. Immensely."

"I thought it set you to music so very accurately."

"Did you? How so?"

"It was all that you are, Franz. Stately. Dignified. Balanced. Inspiring."

Franz thought about this, speaking only after a long pause. "Thank you."

Sisi recalled the melody, humming to herself. She looked forward to hearing it again.

"You know, if you were a song, Sisi . . ." Franz paused his steps.

Sisi turned to face him. "Yes?"

Candlelight flickered overhead and from the gilded sconces all around them, giving his light eyes a brilliant, almost sad sort of glow. "You wouldn't be brass or drums or the fanfare of trumpets."

Sisi lowered her gaze. "No, I suppose I wouldn't be." What would her song sound like? she wondered. Franz took up that unspoken question, his voice gentler than she'd heard it in years. "You, Sisi, would be . . ." He tossed his head back, thinking a moment before he looked at her once more. "The soft trill of the flute, mingling with lark and morning birdsong." He swallowed, continuing: "The gentle pluck of the harp beside a stone-lapping brook."

Sisi noticed with surprise how her face flushed with warmth, how her eyes began to sting with the threat of tears. For Franz, sensible Franz, to be moved to poetry . . . Johann Strauss must have truly stirred something deep within him. Franz went on now: "You would be the most delicate of violins in a garden, bathed in moonlight, the sweet scent of jasmine perfuming the evening air."

"Franz —" She looked down as she noticed how he took her hand in his, giving her fingers a quick squeeze.

"You, to me, Sisi, are the most perfect piece of art I have ever beheld."

★ ★ ★

The family gathered on Christmas Eve, the night of Sisi's birthday, in her personal drawing room. A hearty fire warmed the space as Marie Festetics and Ida put the final trimming on a stately fir tree, its fragrant boughs hanging heavy with candles and garlands. Sisi stood in a rich gown of midnight blue, her long waves pulled loosely back, greeting her family members with a smile. "Come in, come in. Don't you see how cozy Marie and Ida . . . and Larisch . . . have made my rooms?"

Rudolf's mood seemed uncharacteristically bright as he was announced at Sisi's door, Stéphanie at his side and his little Elisabeth, nicknamed Erzsi after the Hungarian pronunciation, in his arms. "Merry Christmas, and happy birthday, Mother!" He looked fresh faced and relaxed, his chestnut hair combed neatly, the hint of a rare smile turning up his lips.

"Thank you, Rudy dear," Sisi said, allowing her son to kiss her cheek. "Stéphanie, please come in." She offered her daughter-in-law a smile before leaning in to nuzzle her little granddaughter. "Wait until you see what Grandmother has for you, my little Erzsi."

"What did we teach you to say now, Erzsi?" Rudy said, practically beaming at his little girl.

"Happy birthday, Grandmother," the little girl mumbled, before applauding her own success. All around her, the adults broke out into laudatory laughter.

"Why, thank you, my dear little one," Sisi said. "Do you see my *Tannenbaum* in the corner? Go and see the Christmas tree all decorated!"

Valerie arrived next, nearly bursting through the door. "Happy birthday, Mamma."

"Valerie, my darling, hello." Sisi embraced her daughter. "Darling, are you warm? Do you have a fever?"

The girl's cheeks bore a rosy flush, as if heated by embers smoldering inside her belly. "No, I'm well." She avoided her mother's eye contact, waved off the palm Sisi tried to press to her forehead, and continued farther into the room. "Hello, Rudolf, Stéphanie. Erzsi-lamb!"

If Rudolf appeared unusually chipper and

Valerie unusually flustered, Franz appeared also entirely unlike himself. He didn't smile as he entered Sisi's room, his arrival announced by the servant and his own agitated, heavy footsteps. Kathi Schratt was away, visiting her own family for the Christmas holiday — Franz always grew more irritable the longer his *friend* was away from him.

"Merry Christmas, Franz." Sisi tried to lift his spirits now, greeting her husband with a smile and a glass of champagne as the rest of the family assembled around the tree. Rudy was showing Erzsi the garlands as Stéphanie and Valerie chatted with Larisch and Marie Festetics and Ida.

"Happy birthday, Sisi." Franz was, as always, starched and impeccably well groomed in his cavalry officer's uniform, but his frown betrayed some inner disarray he couldn't completely mask. Perhaps it was even deeper than simply missing Kathi. Was there some concern of the state that weighed on him? Sisi wondered. Or had some quarrel occurred between father and son, the cause of which she was not aware?

"Come now, you must have your gifts, Mother." Rudy interrupted her thoughts, holding forth a large parcel wrapped in red tissue paper and ribbon. He put the heavy package in Sisi's hands, his face animated and boyish, almost bashful. "This is something I've been so eager to share with you."

"Why, thank you, Rudy dear," Sisi said, looking from her son to the gift he handed to her. "It's heavy."

"It took me months to locate this."

"Oh? Well, you've certainly piqued my interest." Sisi made to tear the paper.

"Wait!" Valerie stepped forward, throwing a look from her brother to her mother. "Sorry! Before gifts, there's something I must tell you all."

Sisi felt her stomach flip over on itself. Whatever it was, whatever Valerie's news, it was clearly the cause of the girl's agitated mood, the reason for her blushing cheeks. "What is it, Valerie?" Sisi asked, putting the parcel down on the nearby table, its contents entirely forgotten.

Valerie shifted from one foot to the other, looking from her mother to her father. "I don't know how to say it. Oh, I suppose I should just be out with it — Salvator and I are going to marry!"

Silence filled the room now but for the pop of a decomposing log within the white porcelain stove. "Salvator?" Sisi lowered herself into the nearest chair. "You and Salvator are engaged to be married?"

"He's asked for my hand, and I've accepted."

Sisi looked from Valerie to Franz. Her husband was as stunned by the news as she was, if his wide, unblinking eyes were any indication. How different things were these days, Sisi thought. Why, her own engagement had been the business of almost everyone *but* herself. Sisi hadn't even known of her own engagement until after all the parents, government ministers, ambassadors, priests — even the *pope* — had discussed and considered and approved of the terms. And now here was Valerie, telling her parents how it would be.

"Salvator, our cousin?" Rudolf's face crumpled in disbelief. "You wish to marry *him*? An insignificant Tuscan?"

Stéphanie sniggered beside Rudolf.

"Yes," Valerie said, her tone defiant as she stared at her brother. "I wish to marry him."

"But he's in the army. In Italy," Sisi said.

"So I shall move there to be with him," Valerie replied, shrugging. "What is it? It's not as though I'm the first young lady to ever be married. Why do you all look as if I've told you I plan to move to America?"

"Well . . ." Franz spoke for the first time since the news, clearing his throat. "This calls for a celebration."

"I would say so, even if you all look as though I've just died, rather than told you I'm in love."

"Ida, some champagne, if you would?" Franz nodded.

Several bottles were popped, and Franz made a toast to his daughter's happiness and health, but the assembly had taken a decided turn away from the previously festive ambiance. Only Erzsi was impervious to the shift in mood, and she now stepped toward her grandmother and tugged on her skirts. Sisi looked down at the girl. "Yes, my darling?"

"There," Erzsi said, pointing at the parcel that Sisi had yet to unwrap. "Papa's present to you. Open!"

"She wants to play with the ribbon," Stéphanie explained.

"Well, then I had better open it," Sisi said, her voice breathless even as she tried to sound enthusiastic. The truth was, she now could not care about Rudy's gift or any of the other presents. Not now, not when she had just learned that Valerie had accepted a proposal for marriage and would be leaving. Moving far away. And how soon, Sisi didn't know.

Sisi took the heavy parcel in her hands and tore at the paper, rending it apart in two quick motions. There in her hands sat a pile of aged leather books. She stared at them, taking several moments to form any response. "Books," she said finally, her voice flat. "How lovely. Thank you, Rudolf."

"Not just any books, Mamma," Rudolf said, setting down his flute of champagne and approaching his mother's side. "Look here." He pointed at the cover of the top book.

"Heinrich Heine," Sisi read aloud, nodding.

"They are original letters, Mamma, written by Heine himself. Personal letters he wrote to relatives all over the globe. I know how you venerate Heine. I've had my agents tracking these down for months. And here" — Rudy riffled through the pile — "is a collection called *The Austro-Hungarian Monarchy in Word and Picture.*"

Sisi nodded, absorbing perhaps half of what her son said.

When she offered no reply, Rudolf crossed his arms in front of his chest, staring at her. After a moment, his voice entirely deflated, he said, "This is priceless material, Mother."

Sisi blinked, trying to muster some enthusiasm to match her son's. On any other day, she knew she would have agreed with Rudolf — this *was* indeed priceless material. And clearly not easily found or procured. She should have been ecstatic to possess such a rare memento from her favorite writer. She would have been moved to tears at her son's show of love and thoughtfulness. And yet, what did a collection of letters matter when her most cherished child was leaving her? "Thank you, Rudolf." She smiled thinly, placing the books down on the table. "I shall look forward to reading them."

Rudolf continued to stare at her, his expression shifting like the sky when a gray cloud glides over it to darken resplendent, bright sunshine. "I thought you adored Heine," he said, more under his breath than aloud. And with that he turned, picked up his champagne glass, and crossed the room to demand a refill.

The remainder of the gifts were given and opened. Franz was no longer alone in his surliness, now that Rudolf had retreated to the corner, speaking only to Larisch, and in tones so low that no one else could make out his words. At one point, the girl giggled loudly as Rudolf leaned close to pinch the bare flesh of her arm, and Sisi noticed Franz's troubled look as he observed the exchange. Sisi took little pleasure in giving Erzsi the garden furniture set she had had commissioned, nor did she take much notice when she unveiled the drawing that Stéphanie presented to her, a mediocre rendering that her daughter-in-law had made of the ocean.

They moved into Sisi's private dining room for the Christmas Eve dinner. Liveried footmen brought in an endless procession of platters, depositing them on the full table as a cluster of the imperial musicians struck up a melody in the corner. At the table, the Christmas feast made a dazzling tableau. The white porcelain dishes shone, their golden edges etched with the crest of the Habsburg double-headed eagle. Gilded bronze centerpieces twinkled beneath piles of fruit and sweetmeats, and playful little putti held up candelabras that cast an ethereal glow over the lavish spread. The chefs had prepared goose liver pâté and breaded perch and Franz's favorite boiled beef, *Tafelspitz*, heaped with apples and horseradish. Next came *rindfleisch* fillet and schnitzel and potato noodles and *Salzburger Nockerln* dumplings. Franz directed the platters around the table, the dishes growing more aromatic as the diners sliced into them. The sound of their cutlery mingled with the sweet notes of the violins, but no one at the table spoke.

Eventually it was Rudolf who broke the silence, after he'd availed himself of half a dozen flutes of champagne. "There is a new young doctor here in town. I've had the chance to read some of his early writings — simply fascinating, his advances in science," Rudolf said, wiping his thin mustache with a napkin. "Dr. Sigmund Freud is his name. Are you familiar with his work?" His eyes went first to his father.

"I am not," Franz answered, his attention more focused on cutting into the fillet on his plate than his son's inquiry.

"You ought to look into it, Father. He has some interesting theories." Rudolf took a long draw from his wineglass. "Interesting what he says about fathers and their sons."

"Hmm." Franz's reply sounded more like a grunt than an actual expression of interest; there was nothing in that sound to encourage further conversation from his son.

Just then Erzsi stood up on her chair and leaned over the table, reaching her hands toward the flames of the nearest candelabrum. An instant before the damage was done, Marie Festetics snatched the little girl away, pulling her back into her chair. Sisi looked at Stéphanie, who giggled as if she hadn't noticed the near disaster.

Rudolf tried once more to draw his father into discussion. "Additionally, Dr. Freud has some interesting theories on melancholy. He refers to it as depression. He believes it's an actual physical malady, rather than a choice or a matter of the mood. He advocates a cocaine cure for those who —"

"That's nonsense," Franz growled, looking up now, his fork and knife suspended over his plate. Sisi and Valerie exchanged a look — they'd seen this scene play out dozens of times before, on any number of topics. Sisi glanced down at her plate, feeling her appetite recede.

"What is nonsense, Father? That people might suffer from prolonged periods of deep melancholy, against which they are not able to rise up?"

"That, yes. It's called fortitude. We all face tragedy — that's life. Through strength of character, and adherence to the performance of one's duty, and faith in the Almighty, well, one simply must not *let* oneself become so self-indulgent as to succumb to melancholy and all that. But —"

"It's not nonsense, Father. It's very real. It's not a choice one makes."

"No, but I refer more to the idea of giving patients cocaine as part of a cure."

"Have you tried it, Father?"

"Tried what?"

"Cocaine."

"No, but I don't need to try cocaine to know that it's rubbish. How a person could put a substance such as that into his body and expect —"

"You really ought to try something before you launch into such a vehement criticism," Rudolf said, his lips curling up into a mocking smile. "Otherwise, how can you defend yourself from someone who might say you are being ignorant?"

Erzsi, who was poking at her plate with her fingers, scowling after having been thwarted in her effort to grab the candles, interjected: "Grandmother?"

Sisi turned to the child, grateful for a diversion in the conversation. "Yes, darling?"

"Mother tells me that nobody at court cares for you, and that you don't care for anyone but yourself and Auntie Valerie."

Sisi's mouth fell open as her gaze slid from her granddaughter to her daughter-in-law. Stéphanie flew out of her chair in an instant, lurching toward her daughter and scooping her up into her arms, pressing the girl's face to her own breast so that any additional words might be muffled. "Bedtime for you, lamb." With that, Stéphanie nearly ran across the room, holding tight to her protesting, kicking child. Rudolf took a long sip from his drink, not acknowledging his departing wife or daughter.

"You're not going to see your wife out, or wish your daughter a Merry Christmas?" Franz asked, eyeing his son with thinly veiled disdain.

"Say what you will about Dr. Freud . . ." Rudolf turned toward his father, ignoring the question. "Even if you won't acknowledge the advances *he* makes, you must admit, Father, that we must modernize in the field of science, as well as a whole host of other areas."

Franz turned back to his plate, taking a long time to chew his next bite before he asked: "Such as?"

"Everything," Rudolf said, placing his silverware down to raise his hands. "Science, education, our treatment of the mentally ill, our antiquated aristocratic class system, our inequitable tax structure." Rudolf ticked the topics off on his gloved fingers as he spoke.

"Rudolf, son." Franz lifted his palm, and Rudolf, surprisingly, fell quiet. "Go to that window and look out on my capital city."

"I know what Vienna looks like. I don't need to look out the window to see it,"

Rudolf said, his jaw fixing in a tight line.

"Good. Then you know that I have modernized Vienna in such ways as to make us the envy of all other capitals in Europe. Look at the Ringstrasse. And when you are there, stop in at any number of the theaters or opera houses or performance halls, and listen to the world's best musicians, performing songs composed right here in my city."

"The arts, the arts, the arts," Rudolf said, waving his hands. "Fine, so you've paid for some splendid buildings and commissioned some nice operas. But what about our future? What good will some pretty paintings do if we don't encourage people to care about more than just such decadent pleasures?"

"Interesting that you now take such a strong stance against decadence." Franz threw a pointed glance at his son's empty wineglass. "You, with your cocaine cures and your gambling debts and your alcohol to palliate your . . . *melancholy.*"

Sisi squirmed in her chair as Rudolf absorbed the barb, his cheeks flushing a deep scarlet. "Go to London, Father. Go to Paris. Go to New York. Those cities look to the future! Those cities look ahead to progress. They belong to the aspiring middle classes — the shopkeepers, the students, the merchants. There, people want to be *modern!*"

"I think that's enough. . . ." Sisi said, but Franz raised a gloved hand, silencing her.

He spoke now, his clear eyes fixed squarely on his son. "You know my personal motto, Rudolf?" Franz's tone remained unnervingly calm even as Rudolf's voice had grown louder.

Rudolf didn't answer, so Franz said it. *"Ich weiss nicht ändern."*

"I do not change," Rudolf repeated, his lips pressed close together.

"Precisely," said Franz, nodding at his son. "I hold strong. I keep order. And *that* has been what has held this empire together. I've never been one to go in for fads."

"Fads?" Rudolf threw his hands up. "Father, the world is changing, whether you like it or not. You may sit at the helm of an empire with a glorious past, but if you so single-mindedly refuse to look ahead to the future —"

"You may lecture me, Rudolf, *after* you've spent forty years laboring to hold a fractious empire together. After you've crushed rebellions and restored peace and held on to that peace. Once you've ushered in an unprecedented era of prosperity and growth and amity. Once you've stared down your own mortality on a field of battle or in the face of an assassin's blade. Until then . . . well, until then, stick to your rifles and cocaine cures and salons, and leave the governing to me." Franz put his fork down with a clatter, signifying that he was done. So, too, was everyone else.

589

■ ■ ■ ■

Valerie lingered in Sisi's rooms longer than anyone else, waiting for the others to retire. "I want a word alone with you, Mamma."

"Yes, dear?" Dinner had been dreadful; Sisi couldn't remember the last time she felt so weary. And tomorrow would be a day full of state celebrations and mass and feasting. The family, as much as they all dreaded it, would be forced to spend the entire Christmas Day in one another's company, smiling as though there was so much for which to rejoice.

Valerie fidgeted before her. "I wanted to be sure that . . . well, that you were telling me the truth before, when you said that you were all right with my news."

Sisi lifted a hand and traced a finger along her daughter's cheek. "My darling, it's as I've always said: as long as you are happy, I am happy."

"Really?"

"Really."

Valerie smiled now, relief breaking across her features. "Good. Well, I *am* happy, Mamma. So very happy."

"Then I am, as well." Sisi saw Valerie out, walking her as far as the doorway into the corridor. There, to her shock, she discovered a figure huddled outside her door. "Rudolf? Heavens, you startled me. What . . . is everything all right?"

Rudolf turned when they spotted him, nodding quickly. His eyes were bloodshot and red rimmed, as if he'd been weeping.

Sisi put a hand to her breast. "What is the matter, Rudolf?"

He didn't answer his mother. Instead, turning to his sister, he leaned forward, pulling her into an abrupt, rough hug. "Congratulations on your engagement, Valerie," he gasped out. "I'm sorry that I derided Salvator before." Valerie caught Sisi's eye over her brother's shoulder, her eyebrows arching upward in startled confusion. But Rudolf turned and then, as abruptly as he had done with his sister, he collapsed toward his mother, wrapping her in his embrace. "Happy birthday, Mamma. I love you so."

Sisi heard how he fought back sobs as he said it. "Why, thank you, dear," Sisi said, patting her son's back. He really felt quite thin beneath his officer's uniform, almost frail.

He choked out his next words. "Mother, I hope you were made happy by receiving —"

"Indeed, I was very happy to receive Valerie's news."

"— the Heine gift I gave you."

At that Rudolf pulled away, his lower lip falling open, but no other words came out. Sisi realized her error too late, and she groaned inwardly as she saw disappointment pull sharply on Rudolf's already troubled features. He threw his shoulders back, tugging down on the hem of his jacket as he nodded, looking once more at each of the women. And then, turning on his heels, he took off down the corridor, his figure receding deeper into shadow until he appeared to be nothing more than a spectral apparition, not entirely grounded in this world, but not at peace enough to leave it, either.

Sisi's mind stayed with Rudolf as she completed her evening toilette. As Marie Festetics helped her into her sleeping gown, she recounted the story of the odd exchange in the hallway, omitting only the part about ignoring his gift. Marie listened silently, the ruts in her worn brow deepening as she considered Rudy's behavior.

Wrapped now in her heavy nightclothes, Sisi crossed the room to the window and pressed her forehead up against the cold, frost-tinged pane. It was nearly midnight. Outside, snow fell across the capital as bundled churchgoers hurried to midnight mass, the bells of St. Stephen's Cathedral pealing out a summons in the night. Inside millions of homes across her kingdom, parents were tucking giddy children into cozy beds, their minds awhirl with the feasts and celebrations and treats promised for the next day. Sisi remembered what that had felt like — snuggling into bed beside Helene, whispering about what they hoped to find upon waking on Christmas morning. And yet, from where she stood now, Sisi found it hard to summon any of that joy or excitement. "Marie?" The breath steamed out with her words, clouding the window before her. She wiped it with her hand.

"Yes, Empress?" Marie Festetics spoke quietly, stepping toward Sisi's bed. "Your Majesty will catch cold there. Come away from that window."

Sisi turned and walked toward her. "Do you think I've failed Rudolf?"

Marie Festetics frowned as she considered the question. "Failed the crown prince, Your Majesty?"

Sisi climbed into bed and burrowed into the sheets, Marie having already warmed them with bricks from beside the porcelain stove. Sisi yawned. "Your silence would seem to say so."

"You're tired, Empress. Perhaps we can discuss this another time. Certainly Christmas Eve is no time for such sad thoughts."

"So then, you do. You think I've failed Rudolf."

Marie Festetics fidgeted beside the bed, looking toward the chamber door as if she longed to flee through it. Eventually, she turned back to Sisi, her tone mournful. "Not failed him, Empress. But . . . I believe that . . . perhaps you have been more like a beautiful apparition to him than a mother."

Sisi stared at her attendant, unsure of her meaning. Weariness pulled on Sisi's body, but her mind spun. "What do you mean by that?"

Marie Festetics exhaled audibly. "You've been to him like a fairy. You come in, and then you go, and then you come back, and then you're gone again. Leaving, always, before you might do any of your much-needed magic."

Sisi collapsed into the soft goose down of her mattress, staring up at the bed hangings as she thought these words over. Perhaps Marie was right; perhaps that *was* how it had been. And perhaps the only thing that might save them all now was a bit of magic.

XV

We live in a slow, rotten time. Who knows how much longer it will last. Each passing year makes me older, less keen and fit. . . . And this eternal living-in-preparation, this eternal waiting for great times of reform, weakens one's best powers.

— *CROWN PRINCE RUDOLF OF AUSTRIA-HUNGARY*

CHAPTER 15

Vienna
January 1889
The New Year was only days old, the good luck punch only just sipped and the social season only just under way, and yet its high point was already upon Vienna. Outside the Hofburg, the weather had turned unseasonably mild. Rather than snow, a blanket of balmy, thick fog hovered over the capital, drawing residents away from their hearths and into the streets to enjoy this rare respite from winter's icy clutches.

The crowds on the café terraces and inside the restaurants and dance halls all discussed one topic: opening night of the new Court Theater building. The entire city teemed with anticipatory predictions and chatter. Newspapers across the continent were already heralding the new Court Theater, known to the Viennese as the Burgtheater, as the finest performance hall in any European capital. Every blue-blooded aristocrat, bourgeois businessman, and aspiring artist sought a ticket for opening night, hoping to be in the crowd along with the imperial family and, still more, to win the right to brag about such elect status in the days prior to this inaugural performance. Those fortunate enough to have secured seasonal boxes already seemed to walk the streets with their chins angled slightly upward, their eyes twinkling with the irrefutable surety of their own superiority.

A young artist in his twenties, a man by the name of Gustav Klimt, had been commissioned for the remodeling of the theater's interior. Franz Joseph had hired Klimt for a sweeping mural that would be called *The Chariot of Thespis,* depicting the first actor from ancient Greece. As Klimt's deadline loomed, bookies and theater-goers across the city placed bets as to whether the artist's paint would dry in time, and the papers reported that the young Klimt was now spending both day and night strapped to the ceiling, color dripping into his hair and speckling his face as he raced to complete his imperial commission.

For a city that relished gossip the way Vienna did, there was much to discuss when it came to the upcoming opening night, and the capital's residents took up the task with admirable gusto. They debated the appropriate wardrobe choices for the attendees, the selection of shows to be put on that season, opinions on the design of the new interior, as well as the roster of actors selected for the various roles. And yet, one matter alone consumed the vast majority of all discussions that January; one morsel of gossip proved particularly ubiquitous at dinner parties and at high-society salons, on the Burgplatz and in the beer gardens off of the Ringstrasse. It had nothing to do with Gustav Klimt's mural, or with the theater's neo-Renaissance façade hiding under the scaffolding, waiting to be unveiled. It was not the controversy over the odd new buzz of thousands of electric lights that would illuminate the hall's interior, nor was it the topic of the sumptuously dressed audience members. It wasn't even the fact that the emperor's "friend," Katharina Schratt, would be performing for both emperor *and* empress on opening night. No, all of Vienna was eager for opening night at the new Court Theater for one reason: everyone hoped to catch a glimpse of the lady who now occupied center stage in Crown Prince Rudolf's life.

While the actors and actresses would take their places for their performances, one lady alone would be the true star in the city's most salacious drama that evening. Baroness Mary Vetsera, the journals reported, had taken a parterre box in the theater for the opening night performance. She could afford it, being a member of the nouveau riche, even though she wasn't an accepted constituent of the old aristocracy.

The capital's entire population, it seemed, had gathered outside of the building by midday on the date that the Court Theater's doors were scheduled to open; even those not fortunate enough to have secured tickets of entry still showed up to witness the show that would be performed *outside* the doors. Men and women alike had been reading about the pretty socialite for months. Her name filled the capital's fashion and society columns while at the same time her famous figure was apparently filling the crown prince's notoriously restless arms.

By early evening the crowd on the sidewalks had swollen to the thousands, and guards were called in to place barricades outside the theater and manage the throngs. Mounted police officers shouted out for order, determined not to allow the mob to disturb or in any way inconvenience the procession of gilded carriages that was expected or the noble cargo that would soon step out of them. The scaffolding had only just been removed, revealing the new façade for the first time, and as sunlight faded, thousands of electric lights popped to attention, illuminating the glorious neo-Renaissance exterior.

The carriages began to roll up to the theater just before six o'clock. Each arrival whipped the crowds into a further frenzy of gossiping and elbowing and neck craning. Sisi and Franz and the rest of the imperial family, their journey from the adjacent Hofburg to the Burgtheater only minutes long, traveled by an incognito coach that dropped them outside a private side entrance. From there they were whisked through an exclusive passageway that fed right into a private lobby, reserved only for the emperor, his family, and their attendants. There, undetected and unbothered, they made their way to the imperial box.

If their journey had been a well-guarded secret, their entrance into the imperial box attracted the notice of the entire theater. The audience members, busy a moment ago with exchanging greetings and stealing appraising glances at one another's wardrobe selections, turned in unison when their host and hostess arrived. Thousands of necks stretched as hands broke into applause and lips cried out shouts of support and greeting.

"Emperor Franz Joseph!"

"Empress Elisabeth!"

"Crown Prince Rudolf!"

Sisi stood between Rudolf, who was looking incredibly handsome in his infantry officer's uniform, and Franz, clad in his red-and-white cavalry attire. She wore a snug-fitting gown of gold brocade trimmed in crystal and lace. Franz, Rudolf, and Stéphanie offered waves to the crowd as Sisi, Valerie, and Larisch crossed the box and took their seats with demure smiles and nods.

The electric lights that had replaced flickering candles bathed the room in an unnatural brightness, making snooping and spying that much easier. As Sisi settled into her place, she noted how Rudolf raised his theater binoculars and fixed his gaze to the lower left side of the theater. There, in a parterre box, sat two impeccably well-dressed women. One appeared older — an attractive lady of middle age — and Sisi recognized her wide, smiling face as vaguely familiar. But it was the second, younger woman who drew Sisi's attention now. She sat in a gown of white tulle, her plunging neckline ornamented by her ample feminine curves as well as a thick choker of diamonds. A headpiece of diamonds — appearing almost like a crown, Sisi noted — glittered in her thick black hair. She tossed her head back now in laughter, either unaware of or disinterested in both the crown prince's and the empress's observation. But it wasn't just the two of them, Sisi noticed, who were staring at this dark young beauty — everyone else in the theater was doing the same. Most of the men even mimicked the crown prince in angling their theater binoculars toward her.

"Larisch?" Sisi pulled her gaze from the distant box. "Isn't Mary Vetsera the middle-aged woman in that box down there to the left? The unsavory woman who hosts salons in her mansion on Salesianergasse?" For once Sisi was happy to have the gossipy Larisch beside her, to clear up her confusion.

Her attendant leaned close now to answer. "You're not far off, Empress. The Baroness *Helene* Vetsera is down there, and you've met her. She is the middle-aged widow known for her . . . *hospitality* . . . with the gentlemen of Vienna. But *Mary* Vetsera sits beside her. Mary is her daughter."

Sisi's chest seized as she looked back toward the two women, the younger one sheathed in tight-fitting white tulle, her thickly lashed eyes darting about the theater, as if brazenly meeting — even inviting — all of the stares that so hungrily admired her curves. "Her daughter?" Sisi repeated.

Larisch nodded.

Sisi spoke low so that Stéphanie and Rudolf, seated on the other side of the box, wouldn't hear. "The woman with whom Rudy professes to be in love . . . is that pretty girl there in white? The daughter?"

"Yes, the younger one."

Sisi stared at the distant box, understanding now the cause of the girl's dark-eyed self-importance and preening. "How old is she, this Mary Vetsera?"

"I believe she's eighteen, Your Majesty."

Younger than Valerie, by years. And a social climber of the nouveau-riche class rather than a lady of noble birth. But neither of those facts was nearly as troubling as the fact that Rudolf was already known to have had romantic liaisons with the mother and now professed to be in love with the daughter. And perhaps most bizarre of all was that Mary Vetsera sat beside that same mother, the older woman looking like a proud Pandarus, all too willing to offer her girl up for the pleasure of the married crown prince and the scrutiny of their ruthless aristocratic society.

Sisi shut her eyes, her head suddenly dizzy, made so not by the droning buzz of the electric lights or the explosive riot of hundreds of bright dresses and jewels. When she opened her eyes a moment later, blinking them back into focus, Sisi noticed that the girl, Mary Vetsera, sat with an unashamed smile, her gaze pointed squarely at Rudolf where he sat between his ashen wife and his tight-jawed father.

"My goodness," Sisi said, taking Larisch's hand in her own. "The girl seems, rather than to shrink from the gossip and notoriety, to blossom from it!"

"Oh, yes, Empress. Neither the little baroness nor her mother is new to gossip or social intrigue. They seem, rather, to court it. In fact, the only thing they seem to chase harder than the companionship of wealthy men is scandal."

"I would imagine that the two often come in tandem," Sisi said, throwing a discomfited glance at her son. She noted, with dismay, that his eyes returned Mary Vetsera's brazen stare.

As the rest of the crowd filed in, filling the last few empty seats, the musicians began to tune up. Sisi turned away from Mary Vetsera and gazed at the glittering splendor all around her, at the immaculate dresses and tuxedos adorning the nobles and nouveaux riches, at the theatergoers who seemed far more concerned with the intrigue and wanton dramas in which they and their neighbors participated than with the art that was to unfold on the stage. Sisi couldn't help but think — as her eyes feasted on the decadent scene — of a banquet of splendid fruit. A bouquet of fresh-clipped roses. Even a bottle of a vintner's finest wine. Here sat Vienna's — perhaps even Europe's — wealthiest men and most refined ladies. This was the choicest arrangement of the capital's prized harvest. This, here, was the pinnacle of society gathered in the city's most luxurious setting. Years of progress in the arts and of architectural advances and of human sophistication had all led to this moment and this gathering. Franz presided over what was surely a golden age, Sisi reflected.

And yet, if nature was their guide, what could they expect to come next? How did it go in nature? In nature, beauty matured, growing ever more lovely. Flowers bloomed; fruit ripened. Then what? If they had, here, achieved the perfection of ripeness, what was to follow? Ripeness itself was a state of fleeting and precarious fragility; fruit and wine and flowers, once aged to perfection, began their inevitable decline. Fruit spoiled, turning bruised and sodden. Flowers shriveled, their pleasing aromas becoming the breath of noxious decay. Wine turned, its taste suddenly becoming that of sour vinegar.

Where, then, was Vienna? Was Vienna teetering on some fleeting, ephemeral brink? Was the entire empire hovering in that fragile moment — beautiful and ripe and glorious, yet about to become overripe and spoiled? Did the attainment of perfection always lead to inevitable decline? If so, would Sisi see it in her lifetime? Would her children? Her grandchildren? She wondered who would pay the price for such splendor and decadence and frivolous abandon; just who would be standing ready when the forces of inevitability came to collect?

But her troubling reverie was cut short as, all around her, the electric lights dimmed in a perfectly orchestrated instant. The conductor took his place in the pit to the sound of applause, and as he raised his hands, the musicians readied their instruments. And then, the final curtain of the night lifted, and the eyes turned from Sisi and Franz and Rudolf and Mary Vetsera to the actual performers in the hall.

★ ★ ★

The opening of the Court Theater was declared an unmitigated success. The next day's papers applauded Franz Joseph as a visionary for remaking such a significant theater, applauded the performers for their skills, applauded Master Klimt for his artistry. And yet, inside the Hofburg, the mood was uneasy.

Sisi sat in her study following breakfast, perusing the news journals. The lead story was, unsurprisingly, a meticulous account of the Burgtheater's opening night. She read the description of her own clothing and complexion, as well as the dissection of Valerie's and Stéphanie's appearances. Right after that came the ode to Mary Vetsera's beauty. Sisi growled and turned to the next story.

That report was of an entirely different quality: Sisi read the grisly recounting of a murder-suicide in which a young student had taken the life of his lover before plunging into the frigid waters of the Danube. The worst thing about the article was the reporter's reminder that such an event was hardly uncommon; all that fall and winter, reports such as this one had filled the papers. Vienna's businessmen, students, artists, and

606

workers were hurling themselves into the river in startling numbers, turning the capital's proud blue waterway — the inspiration for Strauss's waltzes and artists' brushes — into a grisly thoroughfare of corpses and terror.

Beneath the horrific article detailing the student's murder-suicide was an editorial responding to the story. In it the reporter addressed what he labeled "a general air of discontent, a breath of melancholy brushed through our society. The rich do not enjoy their surfeit. The poor can bear their misery less than ever."

Sisi put the *Neue Freie Presse* aside, frowning. This sense of malaise, this "air of discontent" — it was not an uneasiness that plagued only the commoners and bourgeoisie. It festered inside the palace as well. That fact was made all the more clear when Sisi received an unusual midday note from Franz. It was an invitation, a request from the emperor that Sisi join him for a private audience at lunch.

Sisi studied the note, frowning, as she considered the summons. Franz liked to work at his desk during lunch; she'd learned that fact all too harshly as a lonely young bride. It was his routine, and Franz kept meticulously to his routine, had done so for decades. That he wanted — no, needed — her companionship in the middle of the day made Sisi uneasy.

Franz filled the first half of luncheon enumerating to Sisi his many foreign policy difficulties. Germany's ailing emperor had died, passing his absolute power on to his son. Wilhelm was, by all accounts, a bellicose young man, and he planned to make an upcoming official visit to Vienna. "And worst of all," Franz said, making quick work of his luncheon, "the young German emperor, younger than Rudolf, will expect to be honored as an old friend and cherished ally while in town."

Sisi groaned inwardly. So that visit would be a tedious few days.

Franz continued with his list of woes. Russia's tsar, an important supporter, was in increasingly poor health, and the question was whether his son — a spoiled, timid boy by the name of Nicholas, whose household was reported to be full of charlatans — would be able to maintain his father's vast empire. "Russia is sick from the inside. Her people are starving, and there are radical groups trying every day to stir up discontent. They're crying out for the rights of the shackled worker . . . the overthrow of all monarchies. The only thing keeping that powder keg from exploding is the absolute power of the tsar. If the Romanovs lose the reins, we could lose Russia. And an unstable Russia would be a disaster for us, indeed, a disaster for all of Europe." Franz's facial expression darkened at the thought.

But Sisi suspected that there was even more to this lunch invitation than this list of troubles festering beyond Franz's borders. And she was correct. As the final plates were cleared before dessert, Franz turned to the topic of his ongoing difficulty with his own son and heir. "I've just learned that Rudolf" — Franz wiped at his mouth with an agitated motion — "the crown prince . . . has reached out to the Vatican in pursuit of a papal dissolution of his marriage."

Sisi's mouth fell open. "He has? Did you know . . . Did you know that he intended to do so?"

Franz shook his head. "He did it without my permission."

Though it was a matter of family delicacy and dynastic significance, Rudolf had written to Rome without telling anyone, begging Pope Leo for an annulment of his union with Stéphanie. The unspoken implication of this was, of course, that he intended to make his new mistress, Mary Vetsera, his wife.

"God help us all if she is already pregnant," Sisi said, looking uninterestedly at the plate of dessert pastries now deposited before her. Would Rudolf dare? Would he have the audacity to jilt his wedded wife, the daughter of a king? To turn his baptized daughter, Erzsi, into a bastard?

Franz's voice was low as he said, "The pope, God bless him, rather than responding directly to Rudolf, forwarded the request on to me, expressing his confusion at having been written to about the matter. He will not consider it without my response, of course."

Sisi nodded, her mind spinning to make sense of it all. This latest bit of mischief came just days after a distraught Viennese man had arrived at the Hofburg gates with a petition to speak to the emperor. The man was inconsolable, and soon enough Franz Joseph shared his distress when he heard how the crown prince had jumped a horse over the funeral procession of this man's beloved wife. "If you could have seen that poor man, Sisi, when he came to tell me of his heartbreak. Of my son's shameful, insensitive behavior," Franz said now, tossing his napkin down on the table, too disgusted to continue with his dessert. "That Rudolf used that dead woman's coffin as an obstacle in his horse race through the capital . . ."

Sisi shut her eyes, and Franz stopped speaking, knowing that Sisi understood the depths of his own discontent. They sat opposite each other in silence, Franz cupping his chin in his hands, a rare lapse in his ordinarily impeccable posture. After a moment, Franz sighed. "And this is just the latest incident in a pattern of increasingly bad behavior."

"What shall we do, Franz?"

"What *can* we do?"

"Perhaps an annulment wouldn't be the worst thing," Sisi reasoned aloud. "He and Stéphanie have never been happy."

"*Happy?* One does not annul the union made with and before God just because one is un*happy,* Sisi. Why, we both know perfectly well that there was no impediment to the match, no sound reason why it should be annulled. No, I will not embarrass Stéphanie in front of the whole world, and provoke Belgium — and the Almighty — just to appease my reckless son."

Sisi thought about this, rubbing the bridge of her nose in an attempt to soothe the headache that ripped across her brow. "I don't understand where . . . or when . . . he . . ."

Franz let out an audible exhale. "And I know that he abuses opium. Claims he uses it to treat his back pain after the fall from that horse. But he takes it daily now, mixing it with his champagne and cognac."

Sisi's stomach turned on itself, a bramble of knots, as she realized just how far past any possible paternal intervention her son was. That Rudolf was a man now somehow, beyond the grip of either Sisi or Franz Joseph. And that the last time they, father and mother, had spoken this honestly about their troubled boy had been when she had insisted that his sadistic tutor be dismissed. Had they really gone this long without speaking, openly and frankly, about raising their son? Sisi seethed with anger now — anger at herself, anger at Franz. Anger at the woman, long dead, who had raised her little boy and had set him on his tragic course toward mistrust and anger and nervousness.

Franz sat before her in wordless, frowning rumination. That he was being so reckless with his time — sitting at the luncheon table even though he was no longer eating — showed the depths of his alarm. There were papers to be reviewed and signed, ministers to be heard. And yet, they sat there, man and wife, in an uneasy silence, both of them thinking of their son.

Franz broke the quiet, his words coming out with a deflated but resolved exhale. "Well, only one thing to do. We shall do what we've always done, I suppose."

Sisi lifted her wineglass and drained its contents before asking: "What is that?"

"What did I tell you on our wedding day? *Repräsentazions-pflicht.*"

"Keeping up the front," Sisi said, repeating the court dictum.

Franz answered with nothing more than a grim nod before rising from the table. Lunch was over.

★ ★ ★

The capital's printing presses hummed hot and black all winter, churning out new reports each day on the crown prince's infatuation with the charismatic little baroness. Odd, Sisi thought, as she read the articles; one would not have guessed that Rudolf was a man "aglow with love" from the way he behaved inside the Hofburg. As January progressed, the weather turned back toward the frigid, and a curtain of iron-gray clouds rolled over the city. Rudolf's demeanor inside the palace remained as dark as ever.

On the last weekend of the month, Franz Joseph hosted a grand dinner. The reception was in honor of Germany's new young Kaiser Wilhelm, whose visit to Vienna was considered by imperial family members to be a substantial part of why Rudolf was so irritable. The following night the imperial family was expected at the German embassy, where yet another dinner was slated in Kaiser Wilhelm's honor. Sisi attended along with Franz, Rudolf, and Stéphanie. Though it was in their city, custom dictated that both Franz and Rudolf were to wear the German military uniform in honor of their visiting guest.

It was a raw night of icy wind and the threat of snow. Inside the German embassy, hundreds of close-packed bodies generated some heat, but the mood was far from warm. Court and government officials from both Berlin and Vienna shuffled in, an uneasy and forced cordiality enveloping their stilted interactions. Kaiser Wilhelm, an unsmiling young man, had brought with him what appeared to be a small army of attendants and aides. Rudolf stood by without saying much, allowing Franz, Sisi, and his wife to greet the guests. Only late in the evening did his eyes take on any sort of glimmer — when Baroness Helene Vetsera was announced, along with her daughter, Mary.

Sisi felt the Vetseras approach — making their way through the receiving line — as one feels an illness slowly overtaking one's body. By the time Mary Vetsera stood before her, Sisi fought hard to keep her hands from trembling. Her voice cool, she bid the lady welcome with a noncommittal nod of her chin as the two Vetseras curtsied before her. Franz did the same. As Mary and her mother slid to the place right in front of Rudolf, Sisi's eyes followed them.

"Long time no see." Mary beamed at Rudolf, showing none of the requisite humility that was due to Austria-Hungary's crown prince, and all the more so from a presumptuous girl of the nouveau-riche class. Mary did look beautiful, Sisi admitted to herself begrudgingly. Her cheeks shone warm; her body was sheathed in a gown of soft blue with lemon-yellow detailing that fell perfectly over each one of her soft, well-shaped curves.

"Baroness Vetsera." Rudolf offered his first smile of the evening. Beside Rudolf, Stéphanie's pinched face seemed to match the drab color of her ash-gray gown. Though she had dressed as elaborately as Mary Vetsera, Stéphanie looked frumpy and dull by comparison, with even the flowers in her hair seeming to wilt as she beheld her husband's mistress.

Mary, who had no choice but to pass Stéphanie right after passing Rudolf, did not offer a second curtsy, did not offer any recognition of the crown princess, but instead slid her eyes back to the man whose side she'd just left, flashing one more smile at her lover before walking right past his jilted wife. Everyone in the crowded hall seemed to take in a collective gasp — everyone but the crown prince, his lover, and his lover's mother. Sisi looked to her daughter-in-law, whose eyes had widened to two impossibly round orbs. And then, a moment later, Stéphanie recalled herself. She shut her mouth, collected her stunned features, and turned to her father-in-law. With a tone of entirely unnatural cheer, she asked: "Father, when shall we have some dancing?"

Toasts were made by Franz and Germany's ambassador. Waltzes were danced. Franz, ever dutiful, was nevertheless eager to be gone, eager to be out of the German uniform and out of the presence of the self-satisfied young German kaiser. Rudolf's mood turned back toward the sour as soon as Mary and her mother left the party — perhaps with some instructions as to where Mary was to meet Rudy later that night, Sisi thought. Stéphanie put on a valiant show all night, chattering and laughing with an almost frenzied determination to appear merry, but when it was finally time to return to the Hofburg, Sisi did not know who among their small party was most relieved to be leaving.

As the horses carried them the short distance across the city, the mood inside the carriage was as cold as the frigid outdoor air. "What an unbearable burden," Rudolf grumbled, practically ripping the German coat as he yanked it off.

"I thought you looked handsome in it," Stéphanie said.

Rudolf grunted dismissively as Franz looked out the window, not acknowledging his son's complaint. This had the effect of making Rudolf's next words just a bit louder, just a bit more agitated: "I don't know how you do it, Father."

Now Franz turned, his pale eyes catching a sliver of light from a passing streetlamp. "How I do what? Act as a gracious host?"

Rudolf smirked, a short laugh escaping his tight-pressed lips.

"No, you wouldn't, would you, Rudolf? You

wouldn't understand how I do anything that involves duty or graciousness."

"Graciousness? That's how you saw yourself — as a gracious host?" Rudolf's words were heavy with mockery. "More like playing puppet before that buffoon. This uniform . . . his self-important ministers . . . Mark my words, Father; an alliance with that man, with Germany, will only get us into trouble. It will only lead to war. A great big war."

"Don't be foolish, Rudolf," Franz said. Sisi sensed the silent fury just barely contained by her husband's Herculean self-control; she could almost feel the pulse of rage lurking behind his measured words. "I've forged the alliance with Germany to *avoid* a war."

"But with them as a friend, we will be drawn into war."

Franz laughed — a joyless, exasperated laugh, the way one vents frustration with a small, uncomprehending child. "No one would dare. With Austria-Hungary and Germany and Russia united?"

"Russia is ripe for trouble within. The tsar abuses his people, and they will rise up to overthrow him. I know it, and you know it."

Franz shrugged dismissively. "Foolish talk from a foolish boy. You know nothing of what it is to lead an empire."

"No, I don't. Because you never allow me to learn. You hold everything to yourself, make everything so secret. Except your secret police, who follow me in absolutely no secrecy."

"When you start to act like you are worthy of the job, I shall reward you by involving you."

"Worthy? What does worth have to do with it when you rule by *divine right*? Aren't you *God's chosen vessel,* sir?"

"Your mockery is only further proof to me that you are still only a boy. Would that you carried yourself like Wilhelm. Say what you will about his arrogance or self-importance; at least he holds himself like a ruler."

"Wilhelm is younger than me! And yet he has the crown. He has a purpose. As for me? All I do is wait and wait. I can't bear it. Each passing day, each passing year, is like —"

"You are not worthy to be my successor!" Franz roared. This, at last, served to silence Rudolf, whose cheeks blanched an unnatural shade of white. Through the shadows of the dimly lit carriage, Sisi saw how fatigue had carved deep semicircles under her son's eyes, yet his gaze was smoldering. Weary but alert, a hunted animal's.

A hum of tension buzzed inside the otherwise silent coach as the horses pulled them through the palace gates. "We're back," Sisi said, breaking the standoff, stepping forward as the coach door opened. She had never imagined — had never thought it possible — to feel so relieved to return to the Hofburg.

The next day, a Monday, Sisi kept to herself, exhausted by the weekend of the kaiser's parties and even more exhausted by her family's ongoing discord. She knew that Rudolf intended to go hunting with some male members of his household at the lodge at Mayerling in the Vienna Woods. He left without saying goodbye to either of his parents, but Sisi watched his party leave through her frost-tinged windows. *Good,* she thought, *let him take some time away from his father, some time to clear his head with the cold air and outdoor sport.*

The next evening was the night of their weekly family dinner in Franz's private rooms. When Sisi and Valerie arrived, they found Stéphanie pale and Franz fuming. Rudolf had just sent his father a telegram excusing himself from the family gathering, claiming that a cold prevented him from traveling back from Mayerling Lodge. The meal was a quick, quiet affair. Franz alone was permitted to initiate conversation, but he did not. As a result, no one spoke.

Later that night, after completing her evening prayers in her bedroom, Sisi undressed for bed. "Marie?"

"Yes, Empress?" Marie Festetics looked up from where she crouched, picking up the bricks that she had placed before the porcelain stove. She carried them now to the empress's bed and began to warm the sheets.

"Rudolf seems to be slipping further from our grip," Sisi thought aloud.

Marie frowned; she did not need to offer words for Sisi to know what she thought.

"You think I should speak with him, don't you?"

Marie stood up from her position leaning over the bed and walked slowly toward Sisi. "Empress, I've long thought that the crown prince yearns for his mother. He may look like a grown man, but inside, he is still just the frightened, timid boy."

"You are right," Sisi said, sighing. As she climbed into bed, fighting back a yawn, she made her decision. "Tomorrow. When he returns from Mayerling, I will speak to Rudolf. I might even speak to Stéphanie, as well." Now she leaned back into the warmed pillows, feeling relief at having her hair undone, her body free of the tight corset. She guessed that sleep might come easily for her that night, without its usual resistance. But just then, a thought occurred to her. "Where is Larisch? I have not seen her all day."

Marie's scowl was visible in the glow given off by the candle she held. "She said she had to go into the city . . . had to see to some *errands*." It was clear that Marie did not approve of Larisch's activity, whatever activity it was.

■ ■ ■ ■

Sisi awoke Wednesday to the familiar ache in her rheumatic limbs. She completed her prayers before ordering her daily bath. She took her time moving through her morning toilette. She grazed on a breakfast of tea and toast before welcoming her Greek tutor into her rooms in the late morning.

Just before eleven, while she was in the final minutes of her lesson, a knock sounded on Sisi's door. *That's odd,* she thought. Baron Nopcsa and her ladies guarded her privacy ferociously — and the footmen always turned away petitioners who came uninvited or without appointment. Kathi Schratt was expected to visit with her and Franz later that day, but surely she would not have come this early.

Just then Ida burst into the room, her mouth open as if she were choking on words she couldn't stand to utter. Baron Nopcsa swept in right behind her. "What is the meaning of this?" Sisi gasped, rising, still clutching her Greek book in her hands. She was entirely unused to such abrupt interruptions. "I have not invited either of you in here." But when she saw the baron's pale face, her irritation vanished, replaced by a sensation of thick dread. "What . . . what is it?"

"Your son, the Crown Prince Rudolf . . ."

the baron began.

"Yes, what about Rudy? He's at Mayerling, at the hunting lodge with his gentlemen."

"He was at Mayerling hunting, indeed. But not with his gentlemen. With the lady."

Sisi blinked, suppressing the groan that formed in the back of her throat. "What do I care about his female company?"

"Your Grace." Baron Nopcsa swallowed, as if the words could not make their way past his lips.

The Greek book slipped from Sisi's hands, falling to the floor. "What? What is it, Baron?"

"The Crown Prince and Mary Vetsera . . ."

"Yes, what of them?"

"They are both dead."

★ ★ ★

OUR CROWN PRINCE IS DEAD!

The black ink crawled spiderlike across the front page of every newspaper in Austria-Hungary as, around the capital, everything went dark. Black banners were unfurled, draping the windows of the Hofburg, every façade on the Ringstrasse, and the city's churches. Black garb enshrouded the people who shuffled, heads down, through the quiet streets.

Outside the palace the crowds wept and prayed, this gathering entirely different from

622

that of thirty years earlier, when they had descended upon the outer gates of the Hofburg to dance and celebrate. When Sisi, a young mother, had held her newborn Rudy to her breast, infatuated with him and reveling in the merriment outside her bedroom windows that heralded his birth. Now she drew the shades of that same bedroom, closing out the light and the sight of the mourners, inviting in nothing but black.

Blackest of all was the news that came the following day. While all around the capital and the empire the initial reports swirled, inside the palace, Sisi and Franz Joseph slowly came to understand the cause of their son's death. Rudolf's sudden demise was not the result of some hunting accident or attack by a mad Slavic separatist, as initially supposed. It was not a case of poisoning at the hands of a court enemy or vengeful servant. It was not an assault by a jilted husband, hoping to avenge himself on the lascivious prince. It was not due to a heart attack or a fatal mixing of the prince's medications. It wasn't even, as some reports indicated, a result of the infatuated Mary Vetsera murdering her royal lover, as Sisi had come to believe.

No, the truth was worse than all of that. Worse than what the worst report had suggested. Their deaths were the result of a suicide pact — a ghoulish contract initiated and acted out by Rudolf himself. Rudolf, so long denied authority and respect by his father and his father's court, had exerted his authority over the one person who had told him that he was her god. As the crown prince of the city known as "the suicide capital of the world," Rudolf had staged one ultimate and irreversible act of defiance. In shooting his willing lover and then shooting himself, he had found himself, at last, to be brave and powerful. And he had finally gotten his father's attention.

Rudolf had left a letter to his mother, apologizing for not being a better son. He had left another note for Valerie, urging her and her fiancé to leave Austria. But most telling of all was the fact that he had left no letter for his father, Emperor Franz Joseph.

The blows kept coming, arriving at the Hofburg like storm-fueled waves assaulting the shore. The following day, the distressed and confused Baroness Helene Vetsera arrived at the gates of the Hofburg, begging for information. Her daughter had been missing for days, and she'd had no word from her. The last she knew was that the girl had gone out with a female friend to do some shopping. This friend, a confidante of the crown prince's, had been planning to take Mary with her to see the prince, and together the lovers were to travel to Mayerling Lodge. Baroness Vetsera lingered in the palace, weeping and begging for admission to Sisi's rooms. Pleading for any information the palace might share with her of her daughter's whereabouts.

Meanwhile, on the other side of her doors, Sisi received more terrible news: palace aides and doctors had completed their search of the crown prince's rooms and clothing, including the clothing he had worn on the fateful night of his suicide. Found in the prince's uniform pocket was a letter from the lady who had served as go-between for Mary Vetsera and Rudolf — the lady who had facilitated their meeting and their trip out to Mayerling to enact their morbid plot. The name of that lady: Countess Marie Larisch.

This last bit of news, on top of the previous days' shocks and discoveries, sent Sisi into a state of near paralysis. Someone carried her to bed — Marie? Ida? — where she lay, her head splitting with pain and her thoughts clawing their way through her mind in quick, unrelenting succession. She, Sisi, was to blame! She had brought Larisch into this household. She, the mother who had given Rudolf his sensitive and moody disposition, had refrained from speaking to her son about his dangerous behavior. She had denied how deep the troubles ran, always taking refuge behind her own personal unhappiness. In so many ways, she had aided this horrific and ghastly turn of events. It was her fault — she might as well have fired the gun that killed her only son!

Both Valerie and Franz agreed that Sisi was in no state to attend the funeral. It promised to be a draining and very public event, attended by heads of state from across Europe, as well as the thousands of commoners who had descended upon the capital. Instead, Sisi spent the day of the funeral in bed, covers pulled tight over her, bedroom shades drawn. Even with the windows shut and the daylight blocked, Sisi could hear the doleful drums as, outside, the funeral procession glided past. Franz, dutiful Franz, was out there, marching with his son's coffin. Shouldering his burden, playing his imperial part. As the parade moved on and eerie silence settled in its place, Sisi was left alone once more with her own thoughts. Her own inescapable realization that she, more so than anyone, could have saved her son. And yet, she hadn't.

Late that night, after all the mourners had scattered, Franz Joseph returned to the Hofburg. As he shut himself into his room to grieve in private, Sisi dressed. She covered herself in black, pulling a thick veil over her face, and she slipped out a side door of the palace. There, under cover of the dark wintry night and her mourning attire, she made her way on foot, anonymously, to the nearby Capuchin Crypt where Rudolf's body rested. *Odd,* she thought, her body numb to the frigid air and bitter midnight wind. *I finally find a way to slip out of the palace to walk the city incognita.*

Sisi knocked outside the gates of the ancient monastery. Overhead the church tower clamored abruptly, the bells beginning their twelve peals. A cloaked figure emerged from the far door, the aged man's face registering shock at the black-garbed figure that lurked at his gates, like a haunting midnight apparition.

"Good evening, Father."

The priest approached hesitantly. "May I help you, Madame?"

"Please, Father, won't you let me in to visit the tomb of the crown prince?" Sisi felt that even the utterance of these words sapped so much of her strength that she might collapse. She clutched the rusted iron gate for support.

The priest looked up at the bell tower, still chiming overhead, as if to confirm the midnight hour. "The crown prince? But . . . but you come so very late. And who are you, Madame?"

"I am his mother. And you are correct; I'm so very late, entirely too late."

XVI

She lies motionlesss in bed, detecting a soft
gurgling sound, like the trickle of water. Surely
she is dreaming, because she is indoors, in her
bedroom, where no brook can reach her. And
yet, water seeps in now through the crack under
her door. The stream of water picks up until it is
no longer a trickle but a flood, pouring in
through the sides of her door and her windows.
Does she dream? She sits up, horrified, as she
stares out the windows, glimpsing the moon
shining in through the water. But this is no
ordinary moon: it shines as bright as the midday sun, and the room is suddenly bathed in a
cool, otherworldly glow.

"Irma!" she calls out, terrified. The flow of
water has stopped, but the door opens slowly,
creaking and groaning, sloshing the water about
on the parquet floor. Irma would have rushed
in, would have come running at the sound of
her mistress's terror. But this isn't Irma who
stands before her in the blinding moonlight.
"Ludwig?" She says the name with a mixture of

shock and incredulity. "Ludwig? It can't be you. Can it?"

Ludwig stands unresponsive, his entire figure soaking wet, his clothing and hair heavy with moisture.

"Ludwig! Why are you so wet?"

Now he answers, his voice calm. "I've come from the lake."

She feels her skin ripple with goosebumps. Surely she is dreaming. But why is it that she cannot force herself to wake, as she always does during her other nightmares? "The lake? But . . . you're dead."

Ludwig stares directly at her, his light eyes illuminated by the sunlike moon. "Dead, but not yet free."

She dreams — surely she dreams. "Not free?" she repeats. "Why not free?"

"Because . . . my fate is tied to others."

She shivers under the bedcovers, saying nothing.

"Soon you will join me," Ludwig continues, still standing in the doorway, "and we shall be free, and we will be together."

"Join you?"

"Yes." He nods, his damp hair matted to his handsome, youthful face.

"Join you . . . where?"

Ludwig turns, stepping back through the door. If he isn't real, if he isn't really here, why do his boots thump on the floor, disrupting the puddles of water? Before leaving, Ludwig pauses, turning back to Sisi as he hovers at the threshold. "In paradise. It won't be much longer now."

CHAPTER 16

Gödöllő Palace, Hungary
Spring 1889
Grief stalked Sisi, following her to Gödöllő, turning the place of so much earlier joy into a haunted, uninhabitable perdition. The glimpse of new crocuses pushing their way through the frozen earth reminded her that life continued on, even though her son was gone. She recalled how she had once delighted in springtime in Hungary — the smell of acacia, the vivid hues of the river, the stables and meadows lined with tulips — but even those memories now caused her raw and red-rimmed eyes to sting with fresh tears. This was, after all, the country that had loved and been most dearly loved by Rudolf. They loved him because of his relationship to her, Sisi. They loved him for his physical and emotional resemblance to her. The memory of that love now curdled into heartbroken grief, overwhelming her, carrying with it the noxious medley of reminder and rebuke.

Nowhere would she ever be safe from memory. And thus, from self-rebuke.

Nor was she safe from the reports being written back in Vienna. Vicious stories claiming that the empress, driven mad with grief, kept to her rooms; descriptions of her cradling a pillow in her lap, cooing and speaking to it as if it were her baby boy, the crown prince. As the public learned the truth of Rudolf's suicide — a truth that Franz's ministers had frantically tried to conceal — the newspapers churned out reports and commentaries on Sisi's connection to the Wittelsbach madness, a genetic taint that had steadily and patiently seeped its way across the family's borders, poisoning even the steady and sensible Habsburgs, as surely as a plague. Always the blame was on her, Sisi; never did the writers concede that Franz, a Habsburg, was also 50 percent Wittelsbach. That his mother, Archduchess Sophie — the most sensible of them all — had passed her Wittelsbach blood to her son. No, it was always Sisi's diseased heritage; the taint of madness was always *her* parental contribution and birthright. The Wittelsbach madness, they all suspected — the scourge that had first taken her father, then her cousin Ludwig, and now Rudolf — would surely take her next.

Back in Vienna, Franz, who sought his familiar and tested form of therapy by burying himself in his work, made a valiant effort to refute these reports. He even addressed parliament directly, disavowing the rumors that his wife now added to his sorrow and burden with her own unstable behavior. And yet, the slanders continued to slide off of the printing presses and into the hands of voracious readers across the continent and, indeed, as far away as America.

"I should just give myself up to madness, to make them all happy rather than make them liars," Sisi said one morning in early spring, looking over the papers as her breakfast turned cold on the table before her. "Well, at least all of those people who have always hated me so much can take satisfaction in the fact that my son shall never sit on the Habsburg throne." With that, she propped her elbows on the table and wept.

Into this state of melancholy came, at last, some welcome news, like a spear of sunlight piercing the walls of a black cloud. Andrássy wrote. He had heard that she was in Hungary, and he wished, after all this time, to visit her. She told him that his visit would be most welcome.

Sisi received Andrássy in her private rooms. Though she stood to welcome him, she felt her legs tremble at actually beholding her guest. Here he was, after all this time apart, after so much life had been lived, and lost, in his absence.

"Hello, Sisi." He hovered in her doorway, looking tenuously at her, as if he felt a shyness that he'd never before displayed, even in the earliest days of their acquaintance.

"Andrássy, hello. Please come in." She watched him enter, taking in his appearance. She noted how his hair, once so thick and dark, now fell limp and white around his face. His eyes, once like black velvet, appeared sunken, the skin creeping in on them from all sides. Andrássy had become an old man, Sisi realized, with a pang of fresh sadness.

But of course he had, she reasoned, chiding herself for such nostalgia. It had been years, decades, since they had been young idealists, falling in love with each other and the idea of Hungarian autonomy. And yet, to behold him so changed, to see how drastically this present version of the man disagreed with the version of him that she held in her mind — it was staggering.

"Thank you for coming," Sisi said, her voice slightly breathless. If he looked so ragged and weary to her, how must she appear to him? And suddenly, for the first time in she didn't know how long, she felt a blush warm her cheeks, a sensation he had always pulled from her, but one she hadn't experienced in what felt like an eternity.

"Sisi." He smiled at her now, and she saw the faintest glimmer in his eyes, like the last flames of a fading fire.

"It's good to see you, Andrássy. You look very well."

He lifted a finger, wagging it at her. "You've never been good at lying. You've never been able to hide your thoughts."

She couldn't help but laugh now. "Not from you, at least. Please, sit."

He did so, willingly, but she noticed how he winced, grabbing his lower stomach as he settled into the chair.

"Can I order us some tea?" she asked.

He shook his head, so she ordered just a cup of tea for herself. "Then if not tea, how about something else? Champagne? Perhaps even we have cause to celebrate; it's not every day I have my old friend back with me after all this time."

"I wish I could, but it causes me such terrible pain to drink." He grimaced at the thought. "I won't subject you to that."

"Are you ill?"

"Yes. My physician calls it a cancer." Andrássy pointed toward his lower abdominals.

"Is it . . . is it serious?"

"They do not know. They don't know much about it. So, I suppose, as with all unanswerable questions, only time shall reveal the truth."

She nodded, sipping her tea as a silence spread between them. Andrássy and illness were two things that had never mingled together in her mind, two threads of clashing

635

colors that could never be woven into the same braid. Andrássy, to her, was strength, perpetual and unfailing strength. And yet, even he now failed.

His next words pulled Sisi from her reverie. "I can't tell you how devastated I was — we all were — to hear the news."

She shifted in her chair as she felt her eyes begin to sting. Taking a sip of tea, she fought off the threat of fresh tears.

"We all loved him here."

"I know," Sisi said, lowering her teacup. "Thank you."

But he leaned forward, continuing: "I hope you don't blame yourself. No mother should ever have to see . . . It was not something —"

She lifted a hand, silently begging him to stop. Knowing that she would not be able to fend off the grief that was surging through her if he went on. "I know, Andrássy. He was . . . Rudy was . . . a troubled man." It was all she could manage.

Andrássy ran his hands through his limp white hair, and Sisi fought hard, clutching and clawing her way out of the suffocating haze of despair that lurked all around her. She looked back at Andrássy and forced her thoughts to land elsewhere, on anything other than the memory of Rudy. She focused on the man before her, forced herself to remember the thick waves of brown that had once flown wildly around his animated features.

When he spoke next, she heard a trace of his old passion. "I could flay the people who have dared to write anything about you. They won't leave you in peace, even now?"

At this, she felt less raw. It was easier to talk about her own anger — that had hardened and scabbed over after all of these years — than it was to speak of the fresh and aching pain of Rudy's recent death.

"I don't know how you do it, Sisi. How you weather it." Andrássy's fingers rapped absently on the low table between them. "The things they say about you. I just wish that I could correct the record. That I could tell them all about you — about the version of you that *I* know."

Sisi saw him wince and realized that his words, the passion behind them, caused him pain deep in his ailing gut. She smiled sadly. "Thank you, Andrássy."

"Sometimes I feel as if . . ." he began. "When I read those awful, untrue reports . . . I feel as if I'm the only person in this world who truly knows you."

That was true. Or, at least, there was a part of her that only he knew. She looked down at her teacup, nodding.

"How is the new fellow? Your nephew?"

"Archduke Franz Ferdinand?"

Andrássy nodded in reply.

Sisi replaced her teacup in the saucer. "He's a perfectly predictable Austrian bureaucrat.

Overbred, overly concerned with his own heritage and the tradition of the office he now prepares for. He makes Franz look imaginative and flexible."

Andrássy whistled out a long, slow note. "And so that is how it will go. . . ."

Sisi's eyes probed his as she asked: "What do you mean?"

"We've got the rigid and bellicose Wilhelm on the throne in Germany. And we now lose our one hope, our crown prince who would have modernized . . . moved toward England as opposed to Germany."

Sisi groaned inwardly as Andrássy continued, his mind inflamed by politics, the other former love of his life. "Rudolf has been replaced by an unimaginative, rigid hardliner," Andrássy said. "I always knew that Europe as we knew it would guarantee its own collapse with these insane hereditary monarchies."

"Franz is a good emperor," Sisi said.

"A great emperor. But his era will soon be over. And we need someone young and modern. We needed Rudolf. Rudolf, who was to be good, because he was yours."

Sisi brought her hands to her face and gave in to the weeping that would no longer be stanched.

"Fool that I am, I'm so sorry." Andrássy reached forward, putting a hand on her leg. "Oh God, how could I have been so insensitive? Please, forgive me. You know me; I never could quite moderate myself when I got on the topic of politics. Or on the topic of your merits, for that matter." He pulled a handkerchief from his pocket and dabbed at her cheeks. She let him do so, her eyes holding his. Eventually, he spoke. "Please excuse me and my depressing talk. There *is* after all some good news."

Sisi took the handkerchief he held forward, clutching it in her hands, certain that she would need it again. "There is?"

"Yes." Andrássy nodded. "Why, I read that Valerie is engaged."

"Oh, that news. Yes, to her Salvator."

"Are you not happy about it?"

Sisi sighed. "I suppose I'm just not happy about much of anything these days. But Salvator is a good man. And Valerie loves him. I'm happy that she will marry for love, not as some Habsburg bargaining tool. Only, the poor girl has had to put her hopes for a wedding on hold, given . . . all of this. It'll be next summer."

"Will you please give her my best? Tell her I wish her well" — he flashed a restrained smile — "though I know she won't want to hear it. I know that Valerie never cared much for me."

Sisi looked at Andrássy now, returning the handkerchief to his hands, allowing her palm to rest in his as she said, "Only because she knew that, apart from her, you were the person in this world whom I loved most."

* * *

News reached Sisi months later that Count Andrássy had died of bladder cancer. The man whose loss Sisi had mourned so many years ago was now irretrievably gone, and the permanance of it hit Sisi like the stab of a knife. That devastating news from Hungary had followed shortly after the first anniversary of Rudolf's death. And then, three months later, Sisi traveled to Possi to make her final farewell to her beloved sister Néné.

As she left Néné's bedside, feeling weak and utterly depleted, Sisi whispered to Marie Festetics: "Death is to be my constant companion, until it becomes my master. Can't I just give myself over now, and save us both the prolonged struggle?"

It was on the heels of these blows that Sisi traveled to Bad Ischl for her daughter's wedding. Franz, conceding to the requests of his wife and daughter, eschewed protocol and allowed Valerie to have the private wedding she longed for, rather than a state event. Instead of the capital's Augustinerkirche, Valerie chose the modest local church at Bad Ischl for the marriage. It was not attended by foreign ambassadors and magnates but by family members and commoners of the congregation. The imperial florists were not enlisted, but instead Sisi and Valerie picked wild Alpine roses and edelweiss to adorn the altar. Sisi and Valerie rode in an open carriage rather than a gold-gilt coach, arriving to the town square where young girls danced around maypoles and old women showered the bride and her parents with flower petals.

Inside the small country church, Sisi and her family looked on as Valerie made her vows to Salvator. "She looks lovely," Gisela whispered, shuffling her smallest child on her hip. "And so happy."

"Yes," Sisi said, nodding. She glanced from one daughter to the other. Neither of her girls was beautiful. But they were both happy. *And better off, not being beautiful,* Sisi thought; they were lucky in their plain, unremarkable looks. Beauty was not a gift to covet. Beauty had been bestowed on her in heaps, but it had brought her no joy. It had allowed for no peace. She considered the beautiful women she had known — theirs had been the most tragic of the stories. Herself, to be sure. And Empress Eugénie. Marie Larisch. Mary Vetsera. Even Sophie-Charlotte's life had been made more tumultuous by her lovely charms. As Sisi stood at the front of the church, watching her youngest daughter wed, she couldn't help but think: how might her life have been different had she been born with Néné's plain looks instead of her own?

641

Sisi helped Valerie out of her wedding gown and into her traveling wardrobe, and saw her off with the rest of the family at the train platform in Bad Ischl. The couple was to travel for a time as newlyweds before settling in at Lichtenegg, where Salvator was stationed in the army. Valerie would make a home there with her new family, Sisi realized, forcing herself to smile and wave, even as, inside, she longed to weep. She felt the departure of Valerie as a great loss, yet another farewell and cause to mourn. But she had done her work as a mother, hadn't she? She'd loved and raised her child, protecting her from the pain that lurked around a court childhood. She'd taught Valerie to trust and to love, and she'd given her away to the man she had chosen for herself. Wasn't that, in itself, cause for great celebration? Yes, it was, Sisi avowed, standing still as the train slipped from sight, trailed only by its thin braid of smoke, a dark column curling upward toward the vast Alpine sky.

Where, now, would Sisi call home? Bad Ischl reminded her too much of her youth, of her summers with Franz as a happy young bride. And now the place felt far too large and quiet, made all the more so by Valerie's absence. Hungary was haunted by Andrássy. By the victories of her earlier days and the defeats that had followed. The Hofburg and Schönbrunn carried more ghosts than she

642

cared to name. She needed a place untouched by Rudolf or Andrássy, by Néné or her parents. A place even untouched by Valerie and Franz. But could such a place be found? To seek it out, Sisi knew, she would need to travel farther than on any other voyage she had ever undertaken. And this realization, this promise of a new adventure kindled some latent, eager flame from deep within her, its sparks not yet ready to burn out.

XVII

A man who has been through bitter experiences
and traveled far enjoys even his sufferings after
a time.

— *HOMER,* The Odyssey,
ONE OF SISI'S FAVORITE EPICS

CHAPTER 17

Achilleion Palace, Corfu
Spring 1894
Passenger cruises and cargo-filled ocean liners would pass at erratic intervals, belching up columns of steam and sounding their low, melancholy horns as they slid across the horizon. Otherwise, for the most part, Sisi stared out at a vast panorama of sapphire-blue sea, untouched and uninterrupted by human activity. At her villa on the Greek island of Corfu, Sisi had finally attained that which she had professed to search for her whole adult life: Peace. Solitude. Quiet. Here, in her sprawling, sunlit estate, she had set herself apart from all other human life, and she could go days without seeing or being seen by the outside world. Here the sound that filled her days, pulling her from her solitary reverie, was the whisper of a salty breeze as it slid through the grove of olive trees. The soft trill of a swallow as it hopped along the hanging vines of bougainvillea. The

clip of an unseen gardener's shears as he trimmed her fragrant orange and lemon trees. The shrill caw of the gulls as they soared along the craggy cliffs and out over the shimmering Ionian Sea.

Even the voices to which Sisi had grown so accustomed had fallen silent; her household had all but retired. Marie Festetics and Ida Ferenczy and Baron Nopcsa had, at last, declared themselves unable to continue with Sisi on her endless travels. In their places were two newcomers: a young Hungarian countess named Irma Sztáray as her attendant, and a young gentleman named Frederick Barker who served as her secretary.

Valerie, Sisi's onetime constant companion, visited now only in letters. Valerie, who had settled into domestic life with an ease that astounded her mother, wrote happily of her home and her husband, of the babies she had in quick succession following her wedding. First came a daughter, Elisabeth, who was now a little toddler. And then Valerie had borne two sons in a row, Franz Karl and Hubert Salvator. This full and rich family life of Valerie's, Sisi knew, was the reason that her own dream would never come true. Her dream that if she built a magnificent villa here in Corfu, where the days were filled with continual sunshine and the vast, glistening aqua blue, Valerie and her new husband would follow her here. Here, with Valerie and her brood beside her, Sisi might finally settle down. But Valerie had not come.

This place, which Sisi had dubbed the Achilleion in homage to her beloved Homer, did at first bring her some measure of peace. Her hours unfolded in a pleasant, tranquil rhythm here. When her back pain allowed, she spent her days hiking in the cliffs with Irma. Afterward she'd bathe in the marble and gold tubs that poured warm seawater over her, massaging oil into her tender joints. She'd use seaweed wraps to keep her skin soft and supple. She'd oversee the landscaping of the new cliffside garden that featured a marble bust and monument to her beloved poet Heine. And she'd study ancient Greek, taking lessons with a solicitous, short young Greek man named Constantine Christomanos.

Everything at the Achilleion had been conceived and constructed according to Sisi's exact wishes and tastes. Franz had indulged her every whim, even negotiating with the Greek government when there were disputes over developing the land. Anxious for his restless wife to, at last, have a place where she might find contentment, where he might know where to find her, Franz had acquiesced on everything, even the millions that Sisi had needed for the construction. Even though Franz would have preferred his wife's home to be within his vast empire and not in a distant country, he had supported the building project. He had fought his imperial budget masters, had bucked the Viennese gossip and press to sign off on the fabrication of special new china and glass and silver services, all emblazoned with Sisi's new, personally designed crest of dolphins. He had indulged her fancy for electrical wiring that had required its own new power station. He had approved the designs of the hanging gardens and the colonnades and even the fruit bowls that lit up with electrical bulbs as if by a fairy's magic. And yet, as the work had come to an end, as the workmen had carved out their final designs and prepared to pack up their tools, as the Achilleion had neared completion and Sisi's chores around the grounds had diminished, she had felt the familiar itch of restlessness setting in.

Now that the massive project was done — what would she do all day? She wasn't an old woman, not by many years. She wasn't yet sixty. Though her body had aches, it still hummed with a child's vigor. Her figure retained its svelte, youthful proportions, preserved by decades of exercise and an assiduous diet. She could not fathom an old age of sitting still, waiting for her body to slowly and willingly yield to the humiliating, debilitating crawl of time. She longed to stay busy, to stay diverted, to travel. To see interesting and beautiful sights. She longed for interesting company to pull her thoughts out of boredom and melancholy.

But who would provide that company? Franz would never retire from his duties, would never leave his capital, especially not now that he had found some measure of domestic peace with Kathi as his daily companion. Andrássy was gone. So were her parents, and Néné, and Ludwig, and Rudy. She'd even read a passing announcement in an English newspaper that the famed sportsman Captain "Bay" Middleton had died. He'd fallen from a horse in a fatal accident, leaving his wife, Charlotte Middleton, a widow. Sisi had spent that afternoon in bed daydreaming, remembering the English shires and hillsides and the hunting seasons she'd spent, blissfully happy, beside Bay. She mourned him in private, surrounded by people who had never even known he existed. People who did not remember the handsome English sportsman in the scarlet coat, who couldn't understand the way he had sustained her in that happy, active season of her life. Bay, like everyone else, had come into her life with such promise and passion, and he, too, was gone.

And Valerie wouldn't come, not all the way to Corfu. The longer Sisi stayed at the Achilleion alone, the more assured she became of that fact. And though she had sought peace and solitude here, the marble walls of the empty villa now echoed loudly with her loneliness. The sprawling proportions only reminded her how bereft she was of companionship. She thought often of the Heine line "Where I am not, there lies happiness." She thought, too, of Shakespeare, who had so sagely observed: "What graces in my love do dwell, that he hath turn'd a heaven unto a hell." Now that she was left alone with nothing but her own thoughts, Sisi's paradise here in Corfu had become a sort of fruitless, solitary hell. She needed to leave.

Franz was furious — his measured words made that plain enough when he responded to her letter telling him that she planned to sell the Achilleion villa and resume her traveling. He outlined the difficulties he had undertaken on her behalf, both with the Greek government and his own, while she had been overseeing the construction and decorating. He reminded her of the millions he had spent on the palace. He closed his letter by lamenting: "I had cherished a vain hope that, after you had built with so much pleasure and zest, you would remain quietly in the place that is your own creation. Now, however, that has come to nothing, and you will go on traveling and roaming the world."

And he was correct, for that was what she intended to do. The next few seasons saw Sisi on a rudderless journey, without a set itinerary or destination. She explored the ancient lands around Cairo, winding her way incognita through ancient, mazy streets, intoxicated by the aroma of spices and sweet-flavored tobacco and leather, by the views of crumbling ruins interspersed with hectic, bustling city life. She traipsed along the Bay of Naples, stopping at the ruins of Pompeii beneath Mount Vesuvius, where she marveled at the frescoes from millennia past, still vivid in scarlet and ochre and purple and turquoise. She enjoyed the views and seaside mountains at Sorrento and Ravello, where one could sit for hours on a cliffside terrace, eating ice cream flavored by fresh lemons and listening to the cacophony of the birds that hopped through the surrounding olive trees. She visited Biarritz, the small French spa town tucked into the Pyrenees, where rocky islands jutted up from a sapphire sea and the salty air licked her skin and cleansed her lungs.

On these journeys she would write to Franz, always ending her letters by saying that she hoped her next journey would be her longest one yet, that she longed to cross the vast Atlantic to explore that expansive and untamed country America, or set sail for the far reaches of the South Pacific. Franz would write back, always detailing his mundane schedule in Vienna, updating her on Erzsi and Gisela and Valerie and her growing number of children. Always he expressed his wish that Sisi might come home or, at the very least, consider spending a summer with him in Bad Ischl. He never encouraged, or even responded to, her wish to go to America or Asia.

Winter brought Sisi and Irma to southern France, to the Maritime Alps resort town of Cap-Martin. During her first week there, Irma came back from an errand in a state of excitement, giddily reporting to Sisi that Empress Eugénie was also in Cap-Martin for the winter, staying in a nearby hotel.

"You mean *former* Empress Eugénie?" Sisi said, remembering the woman who had been deposed in the brutal war with Germany.

"That's right," Irma agreed. "Napoleon's widow and the former empress of France. Perhaps Your Majesty would like to pay a visit?"

Sisi thought about this for a while, eventually nodding. "I think that sounds like a good idea. Why don't we go pay our respects to old Eugénie?"

And thus began Sisi's brief, unlikely friendship with her former rival. Together the two royal women spent afternoons strolling along the quay, looking out over the azure waters of the Mediterranean as they spoke wistfully of their pasts. Eugénie still paid close attention to politics, especially the politics of her former empire of France. Sisi — who cared less for politics these days than ever before — tried to arouse in Eugénie a passion for

652

poetry and philosophy. She'd quote from Heine and Shakespeare and Goethe, but Eugénie never seemed to share her excitement. The one topic to which both women happily and willingly turned was horseback riding, the shared passion of their lost youths.

"Can you imagine if either of us tried to get on a horse these days?" Eugénie sighed, sitting beside Sisi on a seaside bench. Eugénie, unlike Sisi, had thickened with age and grew tired after even the shortest of walks.

Sisi laughed, thinking of it. Her rheumatism had made riding impossible so many years ago, even after the loss of Bay had made it a less desirable pastime. Nevertheless, to remember her former skill and agility, to compare her stories with those of Eugénie — it provided a momentary respite from her otherwise gloomy thoughts. Before long, Sisi came to look forward to her daily walks with the deposed empress, finding in her a most pleasant and agreeable companion.

But even these simple pleasures were not to last, for grief always haunted Sisi, following her across the globe with the relentlessness of a shadow. This time, heartache came to her in the form of a telegram from Paris. In it, Sisi read the news that her youngest sister, the beautiful Sophie-Charlotte, the girl who would have been Ludwig's bride, had died in a calamitous fire in Paris.

The following summer found Sisi returning to Bad Ischl. It was to be a two-week stay for the imperial family, a reunion for Franz and Sisi before they were to return to the capital for the busy state celebrations of the upcoming golden jubilee. That autumn Franz would mark his fiftieth year on the throne. Fifty years of relative peace, prosperity, order, and progress — no small feat for a man whose fellow emperors had been toppled and replaced all around him.

Valerie arrived at Bad Ischl with Salvator and her brood of wild, lively children. Sisi delighted at being in her daughter's company once more, and the two of them often set off together for long walks into the fields and mountains, exploring nature as they had during so many summers before. One afternoon, as they paused atop a summit to take a rest, Valerie turned to her mother. "Are you happy to be here, in Bad Ischl, Mamma?"

Sisi smiled at her girl, taking Valerie's hand in her own. "Of course I am, my dear. I'm always happy to be wherever you are."

But Valerie's face remained serious, her features drawn tight in thought.

Sisi asked: "And you, my dear, are *you* happy to be here?"

Valerie remained quiet for a moment, weighing her words deliberately before she answered. "Of course I'm happy to see you and Papa. It's simply that . . ."

"Yes? What is it?"

"I had forgotten . . . how unnatural it all is," Valerie confessed. "How constrained everything must be. Life with Salvator is so sweet. And comfortable. Here, any chance for spontaneous pleasure is stamped out by our fossilized and suffocating protocol."

Sisi turned from her daughter and looked out over the view, surprised at Valerie's observation. If anything, Bad Ischl was where the imperial family was *relaxed,* where Franz allowed a slight reprieve from all of the protocol. And yet Valerie was finding this brief stay with her parents to be overwrought with procedures and rules? Sisi managed a faint, knowing smile. "Perhaps now you understand, Valerie, why I struggled as I did. Why I sought my chances to get away."

Valerie nodded. After a pause she asked: "Was it Grandmamma Sophie who instituted all of this? Prevented Papa from ever knowing simple, unforced intimacies?"

Sisi crossed her arms, considering the question. Of course the answer was yes. Sophie had instilled these rigid procedures in the court — rules to which her son still hewed, ever the obedient and faithful child. And yet, Sophie hadn't done it out of cruelty. She'd done it because it had been what she had thought best. What was proper and respectable. What was expected of the Habsburg family. Sisi sighed, simply saying, "I am glad that you are happy, Valerie. That's all that matters now, that you married for love."

"I am happy, Mamma."

"Then I succeeded as a mother." Her daughter was happy. And for those two weeks, she, Sisi, would force herself to feel happy as well.

This lasted until the following morning, when she awoke in her bed to a gnawing sensation crawling over her skin. Sisi peeled back the covers, looked down, and gasped in horror when she saw the terrible rash that streaked her body. She screamed and Irma came running into the bedchamber. "Your Majesty? What is it?"

"Fetch the doctor, Irma, at once!"

Dr. Widerhofer arrived and examined Sisi's splotchy red skin. He was confused by the condition and by its sudden appearance, but he declared that the empress was too ill to travel to the capital and participate in Franz's golden jubilee. Instead, she would need to travel to the western German spa town of Bad Nauheim for an intensive cure.

"But . . . I can't go to Bad Nauheim," Sisi protested. "I'm to go with the emperor back to Vienna."

"I'm afraid that is impossible, Madame," the doctor replied, unwavering. "This rash will only grow worse the longer Your Majesty neglects it. And the only place I know of where the physicians might be up to the task of treating Your Majesty is that facility."

"Will it . . . will it spread?" Sisi asked, shuddering.

"It will if Your Majesty does not treat it. And it may even spread to others, as well."

Sisi despaired at this doubly disappointing diagnosis — both for the news of her serious illness and her inability to join Franz for his jubilee. Unlike all the times she had pleaded or exaggerated sickness to get out of her official duties, this time she truly longed to participate, to be with Franz. To celebrate her husband and his admirable life as a servant to his people. Instead, she would send him back to the capital alone. Franz took the news with his usual stoicism, insisting that Sisi should do whatever she must in order to heal, while Sisi wept.

★ ★ ★

Sisi lay motionless in bed that night, detecting a soft gurgling sound, like the trickle of water. Surely she was dreaming, because she was indoors, in her bedroom in Bad Ischl, where no brook could reach her. And yet, water seeped in through the crack under her bedroom door. The stream of water picked up until it was no longer a trickle but a flood, pouring in through the sides of her door and her windows. Did she dream? Sisi sat up, horrified, as she stared out the windows, glimpsing the moon shining in through the water. But this was no ordinary moon: it shone as bright as the midday sun, and the room was suddenly bathed in a cool, otherworldly glow.

"Irma!" Sisi called out, terrified. The flow of water had stopped, but the door opened slowly, creaking and groaning as it did, sloshing the water about on the parquet floor. Irma would have rushed in, would have come running at the sound of her mistress's terror. But this wasn't Irma who stood before her in the blinding moonlight. "Ludwig?" Sisi said the name with a mixture of shock and incredulity. "Ludwig? It can't be you. Can it?"

Ludwig stood unresponsive, his entire figure soaking wet, his clothing and hair heavy with moisture.

"Ludwig! Why are you so wet?"

Now he spoke, his voice calm. "I've come from the lake."

She felt her skin crawling with goosebumps. Surely she was dreaming — but how come she couldn't force herself to wake, as she always did during her other nightmares? "The lake? But . . . you're dead."

Ludwig stared directly at her, his light eyes illuminated by the sunlike moon. "Dead, but not yet free."

She dreamed — surely she dreamed. "Not free?" Sisi repeated. "Why not free?"

"Because . . . my fate is tied to two others. One was the woman who burned. I know that she loved me, and so I waited for her to join me."

"The woman who burned." Sisi felt how her heart raced, as if trying to hurl itself from her breast. "Sophie-Charlotte, my sister. Burned in the fire in Paris."

Ludwig nodded.

"And . . . the other?"

"The other is you, Sisi."

She shivered under the bedcovers, saying nothing.

"As soon as you join us," Ludwig continued, still standing in the doorway, "the three of us shall be free, and we will be together."

"Join you?"

"Yes." He nodded, his damp hair matted to his handsome, youthful face.

"Join you . . . where?"

"In paradise." With that, Ludwig turned, stepping back through the door. If he wasn't real, if he wasn't really here, why did his boots thump on the floor, disrupting the puddles of water? Before leaving, Ludwig paused, turning back to Sisi as he hovered at the threshold. "It won't be much longer now."

★　★　★

Franz appeared as if he might weep, but he clung to his seasoned and well-trained fortitude as he said goodbye to his wife on the Bad Ischl train platform. "Farewell, my darling Sisi. You be safe, and take care of yourself."

Sisi clung to Franz, wanting to tell him about her dream of Ludwig. About Ludwig's strange and terrifying prophecy. But Franz would never care to hear such a foolish ghost story. Franz, sensible, unflappable Franz, was the furthest a person could be from superstitious. He would laugh it off, telling her it was just her overactive imagination. He might even make her feel better for a brief moment, might convince her that Ludwig's visit to her dreams did in fact mean nothing. But she didn't want that assurance from Franz, because for some reason she couldn't explain, Sisi felt more inclined to believe Ludwig's midnight predictions than Franz's reasonable daylight skepticism.

"Telegram when you arrive safely, to let me know you're settled, will you?" Franz said.

Sisi nodded. "Yes, I will."

"And please, do whatever is asked of you by the doctors. Yes?"

She smiled, sensing the depth of his concern in these gentle but urgent requests. "I am terribly sorry that I won't be with you in Vienna for the jubilee."

He shrugged. "It matters little, in comparison to your health."

She stared him squarely in the eyes. "Franz,

you are a good emperor."

He fidgeted, as if uncomfortable with the compliment. "Why, thank you. And you are a good empress."

She shook her head. "No, not as good as I should have been. Not like you. You are a good emperor, and a good man, and a good father, and a good and patient husband. I . . . I thank you."

He bowed his head a moment, overcome. All around them, the porters hustled about, loading her trunks and nodding at Irma's orders for readying the train carriage. The conductor blew a whistle as the train's engines rumbled in anticipation of the coming journey.

But amid all of that, the two of them stood motionless, indifferent to the activity around them, their eyes locked on each other before their imminent separation. Eventually, after a long silence, Franz lifted his hand and pressed it tenderly to her forehead, as if he were giving a blessing. And then, his voice soft, he said, "May God keep you, my darling Sisi."

★　★　★

The city came into sharper view as the steamer glided across the calm, crystalline waters of Lake Geneva. All around them, the Swiss countryside was in the throes of glorious autumn — the hills laced with gold and

661

amber and copper, a dusting of snow covering the jagged peaks of the nearby Alps.

Sisi couldn't help but marvel at the view surrounding her, at the raw and untamed beauty of this lakeside city. She couldn't believe that her husband and the others had written to her with such terrible things to say about Geneva: That it was a nest swarming with criminal and anarchist activity. That she was mad to travel there without her full household, refusing her attendants and an escort of police. As she looked at the view now — at the stony church steeples; at the famous and newly built Jet d'Eau, a fountain that spewed water impossibly high; at the orderly buildings tucked in between the lake and the mountains — Geneva appeared an idyllic location. Sisi was all the more glad now that she had disregarded their alarms and warnings and had kept her plans to visit; she and Irma would be perfectly safe here.

Irma had booked their rooms at the lakeside Hôtel Beau Rivage, under the alias of Countess Hohenembs. Sisi was traveling incognita and light, having brought with her only one lady-in-waiting and a few trunks. Much to Franz's dismay and his ministers' disapproval, she had refused even to alert the Swiss police of her visit to their city. If she did, they would insist on trailing her, and her alias would be compromised, the whole town alerted to her presence. She'd have no peace or privacy, which was exactly what she needed on this few days' respite from her tedious health cure.

As the steamer brought them closer to the landing berth, Sisi looked out over the deck, blinking against the soft September sunlight. Nearby, a little boy bounced a ball, unaware of his imperial company and that he might have disrupted her with his noisy laughter and play. But Sisi didn't mind his commotion, didn't find that the racket he created caused one of her familiar headaches. She felt good today — cheerful and optimistic. She even smiled at the boy, thinking he must be about the same age as Valerie's little Hubert.

She turned back to the letter in her hand, finishing off the last of Franz's words. She found, as she read, that she missed her husband. She longed for him in a way that she hadn't in . . . she couldn't recall how long. Franz missed her, too, as was evident in his writing. He told her about how, recently, while outside the palace, he had looked up at the window to her bedroom and had felt a great stab of sadness, longing as he did for his wife's return. He closed the letter now with a line of particular tenderness: *I commend you to God, my beloved angel.*

Sisi's eyes stung as she read and reread her husband's closing line. A tear slid down her cheek, landing on her smiling lips. She looked

663

up from the letter, glancing out over the mountains, allowing the gentle autumn breeze to dry her tear. She turned to her lady-in-waiting, who sat beside her on the deck. "Irma?"

"Yes, Empress Elis— er, Countess Hohen-embs?"

"I miss Franz."

Irma nodded, perhaps unsure of how best to respond to such a declaration. Marie Festetics and Ida would have burst into unadulterated smiles, perhaps even clapping their hands — so long had they hoped to hear those words from Sisi. Marie would have turned the boat around right then and there to chart a direct course back to Vienna. But Sisi and Irma didn't have that well-worn intimacy yet, that mutual understanding that came out of years of companionship and required only looks but not words.

"I must get well," Sisi said, sighing. "I must get well, and quickly. I must return to Franz."

Now Irma's features creased into a gentle smile. "And you shall, Emp— Countess. You are stronger every day. You shall be home to the emperor in no time."

Sisi nodded, standing from her seat as the ship touched softly against the landing dock. "Home." Where was home? She didn't know. All she knew was that, suddenly, she longed for her husband. "Yes, I shall be well in no time."

■ ■ ■ ■

That afternoon, once settled into their suite at the hotel, Sisi and Irma joined the Baroness Rothschild at her family's château just outside of the city for luncheon. The beautiful autumn weather continued, and so did Sisi's buoyant mood. The baroness was an old friend, and Sisi felt happy not only in her company but also in the picturesque surroundings.

The baroness served a delicious meal of chicken in a soft pastry shell with champagne. As dessert was served, a Hungarian ice cream, the hostess offered a toast to Sisi. "Empress Elisabeth, I see that Switzerland suits you."

Sisi nodded her thanks, taking a small sip of the cold champagne.

The baroness frowned thoughtfully now, her aged, aristocratic features crumpling as she said, "But traveling incognita, eschewing your escort of guards and attendants, need not mean that you forfeit all comfort and luxury as well." The old woman leaned close, as if she were a coconspirator. "I would gladly offer you our yacht to take you on to your next destination."

"You are kind, Baroness Rothschild," Sisi said, shaking her head. "But I am happy to take the public steamer."

"Where do you go from here?" the woman asked, picking delicately at the scoop of ice cream before her.

"To Montreux," Sisi answered.

"Then please, allow me to lend you our yacht. It's not far, just up the lake to the east."

"As you yourself say, it's not far. I am already booked on the steamer tomorrow. I am quite taken care of, Baroness."

The baroness cocked an incredulous eyebrow, not convinced. "But people might *bother* you."

Sisi smiled now. "That's precisely why I travel incognita — I look like any other old woman."

The hostess placed her spoon down and folded her hands demurely on the table before her. "I don't like the idea of anyone simply being permitted to approach you, Empress. Especially not here, not lately, when we've had quite an unpleasant spike in criminal mischief."

"You sound like my husband, the emperor. He begged me to avoid Geneva unless I agreed to a police escort."

"And yet you declined?" The baroness's mouth fell open now, displaying her shock that Sisi had disregarded the emperor's request.

"I'm tired of all sorts of escorts. I wish only to be left alone."

■ ■ ■ ■

Sisi returned to the city following the luncheon. She passed the afternoon walking around the Vieille Ville, the oldest quarter of the city, where she bought chocolates and sweets for her grandchildren. It wasn't until past dark that she returned to the hotel, where she ordered a light supper to her room and prepared for bed. "Leave those open, Irma," Sisi said, as she slipped out of her heavy dressing robe to climb into bed.

"The curtains?"

"Yes, leave them open. It's a full moon. I love sleeping in moonlight."

"But . . . Empress . . ." Irma turned back to the window. Beneath them, the city bustled with life in the warm evening. Fishermen and captains laughed and hollered on the lakeside quay, while traffic clamored noisily over the nearby Pont du Mont-Blanc, carrying couples to dinner, and students to bistros and bars, and international businessmen to their townhouses and hotels.

Irma, still looking out over the scene, seemed reluctant to walk away from the window. "But the city knows you are here, Empress. I think you ought to close the curtains."

"How could they know I'm here?" Sisi asked, yawning.

Irma sighed as, from beneath them on the street, loud laughter traveled in through Sisi's opened window. "Your alias lasted all but a few hours, Empress. It's in all the papers. Someone always whispers."

"Well, I won't let their whispers prevent me from a pleasant night's sleep. The lake and the mountain air do me good."

The next morning Sisi ate breakfast in her room. Irma had been correct, for when the solicitous hotel manager appeared with the morning newspapers, Sisi saw her name and image plastered across the front of the Swiss journals.

EMPRESS ELISABETH IS HERE!

FAMED AUSTRIAN EMPRESS VISITS GENEVA!

EMPRESS ELISABETH HONORS HÔTEL BEAU RIVAGE WITH A VISIT!

"Looks like I'm getting out just in time," Sisi muttered under her breath. The hotel manager certainly looked very pleased with himself as he smiled, asking Sisi if there was anything else he might do for her in her final few hours at the hotel. The way he said her alias, "Countess Hohenembs," Sisi felt as if he fancied himself on the inside of some small and intimate conspiracy.

"No, I am fine, thank you," Sisi said, and the man left.

As Sisi stretched out her morning toilette, Irma finished packing the trunks and sent the hotel's porters ahead to the dock with the luggage. Sisi took her time pinning her thick hair back into a low bun, not eager to board the ship and begin her journey back to the spa town where she was to finish taking the cure. She longed for her aching joints to be healed, for the rash that still covered much of her skin to go away — and she hated that it all kept her from Franz.

Finally, after Irma's repeated warnings that they would miss their ship — "Public ships don't wait for anyone, and since Your Majesty declined the offer of Baroness Rothschild's private yacht . . ." — Sisi began to dress. She selected a skirt and high-necked jacket of black silk, making sure to tuck Franz's most recent note into her pocket. She patted the fold of her skirt where the letter rested. Once she was aboard the steamer, she'd pen her reply to him. She already knew how she would open it: *Franz, I'll be home to you soon. . . .*

Then, because the newspapers had confirmed to her what Irma had said last night — that the city knew of her presence at this hotel — Sisi picked up a fan in one hand and a parasol in the other. Both common enough ladies' accoutrements, but also helpful tools with which she might subtly shield herself from followers and onlookers. Sisi glanced once more in the full-length mirror, nodding in approval at her tidy reflection. With that, she left the hotel room.

If the hotel staff hadn't already alerted the town to her presence, their send-off now surely would do so. The entire staff, it seemed, stood lined up with the manager at the front doorway of the building. They bowed in unison as Sisi walked toward the sunlit street.

"Countess Hohenembs!" The hotel manager stepped forward with a bow and a flourish of his wrist. "We hope Your Grace enjoyed the stay at the Hôtel Beau Rivage. We do sincerely wish you the safest of travels, and we humbly hope that we might have the pleasure of serving Your Grace again in the future."

"Thank you." Sisi smiled, nodding as she walked past the many staring faces. "It was lovely. Thank you all."

As she and Irma stepped out onto the bright street, she paused, opening her parasol wide. "We must hurry, Empress," Irma said, quietly. "We are late. We might miss the ship."

"It's close, right up there. I can see the ship," Sisi said. And she was grateful for it. If anyone had wandered over to the hotel to catch a glimpse of her, they wouldn't have much time to spot her in the very short walk.

As she and Irma hurried along the quay, Sisi held the white parasol close, blocking herself from the view of curious passersby, but also obscuring her vision of everything save for what lay right in front of her. Voices called out now from across the street as a small crowd of curious onlookers guessed her identity, and Sisi registered the sound of her name being shouted. She tensed, clutching her parasol tighter. Irma, right beside her, would guide her where she needed to go.

Because of her shielded vision, Sisi didn't see the short, thick man approach. Didn't sense his nearness until he struck her unexpectedly, landing a rough fist against her breast. The force of the man's blow caught her completely unaware, knocking her off balance and sending her falling backward. The world spun as Sisi noticed how her hair, long and thick as it was, and pinned in a low bun, softened her fall when her head hit the ground. She blinked. All around her now was a flurry of disorderly activity. A face she recognized, belonging to a porter from the hotel, leaned over her. "Are you hurt, Madame?"

Irma was muttering in Hungarian. "How could he? The scoundrel knocked right into Her Majesty! Was he not looking where he walked?"

Sisi allowed the porter to help her to her

671

feet, where, standing, she straightened her hat and patted down her skirt.

"We will find him, I promise you, Madame," the hotel manager said, standing nearby, his eyes scouring the street in the direction in which the man had continued his brisk stride. Then, turning back to Sisi, he asked, "But did he hurt you, Empress?"

Sisi glanced down over herself, then out at the street. The small crowd that had gathered on the quay was growing louder, now that they had something truly worthwhile to watch. She turned from the onlookers back toward the manager. "Hurt? No, I don't think so. Just a bit startled." It was true. The fall hadn't been bad, though her chest ached where the man had struck her with his fist. That would resolve itself shortly.

"Will Your Majesty come back to the hotel and rest a moment?" the manager suggested. "Perhaps take a glass of wine to calm your nerves?"

Just then the steamer blared its long, ground-shaking horn. "No, thank you. I'd like to make it to the ship," Sisi said, patting her skirt once more. "I'm fine, really." She looked at Irma, who nodded, appearing to agree with the plan to catch the ship before its departure. "Let's go, Irma."

"As you wish, Empress."

"Thank you," Sisi said, nodding farewell to the small group that had come to her aid.

The two ladies walked on, but Sisi found herself increasingly short of breath. As she stepped onto the gangway that would lead her up to the ship, her inhales grew ever more difficult. She made it to the lower deck just as the sailors hoisted the plank and gave the orders to push off.

"What did he want anyway?" Sisi asked, clutching her abdomen now as her breath lurched in and out in ragged, uneven gasps.

"The hotel manager?" Irma asked, keeping close to Sisi as they wove their way through the thin crowd along the deck's railing. "I think he wanted you to come back to the hotel to rest a moment."

"No, the other one," Sisi said, looking around for a powder room where she might loosen her corset and recover her breath. "That horrid man who struck me. Did he want money? Or perhaps he wanted to take my watch from me?"

Irma put a gloved hand on Sisi's arm, distress suddenly visible on the attendant's features. "Empress, you are pale."

Sisi forgot her labored breathing now as she watched her vision recede, the ship's deck and her lady's concerned face dissolving into a faded blur before her eyes. "Irma, give me your arm. Quickly. I think I might faint."

Sisi was half aware as Irma practically caught her and hauled her weak body to the upper deck. "Air, we must get you fresh air!"

Irma gasped as Sisi shut her eyes and slipped into unconsciousness.

She roused to the taste of something sweet, and her vision returned with a view of Irma overhead, pressing a rag soaked in sugary water to her lips. She was flat on her back, she realized, on the ship's upper deck. Behind Irma, more faces hovered against the backdrop of the clear autumn sky. "What is it?" Sisi asked, trying to sit up, but finding she didn't have the strength to do so.

Someone was fumbling with her bodice, saying, "Let her have more air! Let her breathe!" Ordinarily she would have protested against being undressed like this by a stranger, but she appreciated his efforts to remove her tight bodice now, because she did feel as though she could not breathe.

Irma turned to a man in a cap, surely the ship's captain, and said, "Please turn the ship around. We must return to the city. She needs a doctor."

"Turn around? We cannot turn around." The captain scoffed, his heavily lined brow pressed in frustration. "We've got more than one hundred paying customers aboard this ship who expect to be taken to Montreux! We don't turn around every time some old lady gets a bit queasy out on the water."

Irma stood up tall now, her body going rigid with indignation as she barked at the man. "This is not 'some old lady,' sir, and I'll thank you to show the proper respect, as you are in the company of the Empress Elisabeth of Austria-Hungary, and Her Majesty needs to see a doctor at once!"

Sisi's blouse was now fully unbuttoned. Irma, turning her attention back in Sisi's direction, gasped. "There's blood!" Irma said, her face blanching. "Blood, right there on her shift! That man didn't strike her with his fist — it was a blade. He's stabbed the empress!"

All the faces leaned in close now, examining Sisi and gasping out an indistinguishable chorus of horrified exclamations. Sisi shut her eyes, and once more, everything went black.

When she awoke, she was back in her hotel room in the Beau Rivage, lying in bed while a man in a doctor's uniform huddled next to another man, this one dressed like a priest. They spoke in soft, inaudible whispers, unaware that she had awoken. She could have opened her lips to address them, but the effort seemed too great, so she kept her mouth shut, deciding instead to spend the last bit of her strength on finding the paper in her pocket. Franz's most recent note to her. The last words he had ever written to her flashed before her blurry eyes: *I commend you to God, my beloved angel.*

The rustling of the letter must have caught the attention of the two men, for they turned to the bed in time to see Sisi drop the paper and close her eyes, forcing out a heavy, labored exhale. One of them — Sisi wasn't certain whether it was the man concerned with her body or the man concerned with her soul — said, "My God, she is lovely. But it looks like she is smiling."

And Sisi was certain that indeed she *was* smiling, because as she shut her eyes, she found herself leaving that hotel room and entering someplace else, someplace where she felt overcome with a sudden and inexplicable joy. She looked back, once, weighing whether to return to the hotel room, but the idea held absolutely no appeal. No, she longed to see this new place. The difficulty of her breathing — the anvil on her lungs from a moment ago — suddenly lifted. Her blurred vision became instantly clear, revealing to Sisi a place far lovelier than her hotel room in Geneva. Far lovelier than even the most glorious hall in Schönbrunn or the most breathtaking vista atop the Alps. Where she was, precisely, Sisi could not be certain, but she knew, somehow, that she was not alone. And then she saw why. Rudolf stood before her, smiling, his face free of care. His body light and youthful, his once-bloodshot eyes now sparkling like molten amber. Rudolf, as she had never before seen him. He was Rudolf, not broken, but whole. And there, beside him, was little Sophie, the auburn-haired cherub, her first beloved girl, taken from her far too young. Little Sophie greeted her now, little Sophie, not sick, but strong. And there was Andrássy, who glided toward her, his hands lifted in welcome, his dark eyes alight and alive. Andrássy, not tormented, but at peace. Then she saw Sophie, her mother-in-law. The old woman was restored to the strength and vigor of her youth — and she opened her arms wide in an embrace as she beamed at Sisi, her smile emptied of judgment and full of grace. And there was Ludwig, glorious, joyful Ludwig, his beautiful face no longer haunted. Sisi wished to laugh in delight, so she did. And as she did so, she saw that there, too, stood her mother. Mamma, free from worry. Beside her was Papa, no longer in pain or causing pain to others. With them stood Néné and Sophie-Charlotte, Sisi's beautiful sisters, their strong, healthy bodies seeming to glisten with a vivid, ineffable light.

As Sisi looked around now at the faces of so many of the people she loved, she noted that Franz Joseph and Valerie and Marie Festetics and Ida and Gisela weren't there yet. And yet, in that moment, Sisi did not long for them. No, there was no way to long for anyone or anything, not in this place; this place was too full of love for one to feel any lack. Instead, Sisi smiled, thinking of the others, wishing them peace in the time that remained for them, the time in which they had to endure, before at last they, too, would be able to join her here, in this place where one might lay down one's burdens and live in the light of grace.

Franz will come to her; she knows that. And when he does, she will help him to put down all of the cares that he has carried, so valiantly, all of these years. And together, they will take off on horseback and race through green fields and hillsides without ever growing tired. They will stop at crystalline streams, not because they thirst, but to taste the sweet water and to marvel at the reflections of the two happy, youthful faces that smile back at them from the tranquil pools of healing water.

All around Sisi now, love ebbs and expands, a vast, limitless sea. And Sisi feels it, for the first time, as whole. For the first time, it is hers to trust in and accept. There are no conditions on this love, no reasons why she cannot believe in it. Nothing that she does now will ever cause this love to forsake her. It doesn't come from her or from other broken people; it's nothing she has earned, yet she is invited to share in its perfection, and she knows, somehow, that it will never cease.

She, once so troubled by her brokenness, so plagued by her imperfections in the face of all those who expected perfection from her, she is, at last, free to taste all of the joy that comes from pure, perfect love. No more seeking, fleeing, weeping. She recalls, vaguely, that at one time there was something she felt and that it was called pain. But like a wisp of a cloud, that recollection slides away; she could no more tell you what pain feels like than she could grip a cloud in her hands.

Now someone else takes her hand. Someone she has never met before, yet someone who, somehow, she has always known. Or rather, he has always known her. As he smiles at her, lifting his hands to embrace her, all she feels is wholeness. Grace and mercy wash over her, making her more perfect than any earthly beautification ritual she might ever have imagined. The love of the people who stand before her, as vast and rich as it is, pales in comparison to the perfect love that enfolds all of them now. She is home. Her wandering has, at last, come to an end. She is, at last, free.

EPILOGUE

Vienna
September 10, 1898

Emperor Franz Joseph sits at his desk, staring at the massive portrait of his wife. Remembering the day, decades earlier, when she gifted him with this masterpiece. Oh, how he longs to see the beloved face that inspired this favorite painting of his. The real face that puts even this most cherished artistic rendering to shame. Soon now, he tells himself. He's detected a shift in her these past few months. He's sensed — fervently hoped — that his wife might be willing, at last, to return to him. That she might have finally forgiven him for the pain of their early years together. Even just the thought, the hope of her return, causes his aged heart to speed up within his breast. She's always done that to him — his heart has never quite grown accustomed to her, has never stopped racing at the thought or sight of her.

A knock on the door. He groans. He's

reluctant to be pulled from these pleasant musings on his Sisi's beauty; he's unwilling to return to the ugly business of governing right at this moment. But, as he's done so many thousands of times before, he yields to his duty. He puts Sisi aside so that he can turn back to the cares of his empire. "Yes, what is it?"

"Your Majesty — a telegram." An aide's pale face peeks tentatively around the emperor's door. "From Geneva."

"Geneva?" Franz sits up rigid at his desk. "Sisi." He waves the man forward. They have been writing letters every single day. Why would she send a telegram, unless it was a matter of immediate urgency? He feels his whole body tense beneath the stiff confines of his heavy uniform as he looks down at the telegram.

HER MAJESTY THE EMPRESS HAS PASSED AWAY.

Franz Joseph stares at the paper in disbelief. That is it? That is all? Can it be? All happiness — his very life — blotted out with just seven words on a piece of trembling paper. Sisi, dead? His heart stalls in his chest as his eyes fly once more to the portrait, where she smiles at him, her cheeks colored with her painfully enticing blush, her incomparable chestnut hair cascading over the perfect curve of her bare shoulder. How could she be dead? Franz Joseph lets out a low, guttural groan, tossing his head back to look up at the ceiling where, behind the gold gilding, a God who proves more incomprehensible than ever hides. It cannot be. Sisi dead?

"Is nothing to be spared me?" He raises his hands, as if he would reach into the heavens to bring her back to him. To rend her from death's grip. But his power is suddenly rendered farcical. His is a power of this earth, and not even he — Emperor Franz Joseph — can do such a thing, not unless the Almighty wills it.

As he weeps, his aides and ministers look on, aghast. None of them can hold back tears now, either; they've never seen Emperor Franz Joseph forget his ironclad self-control, and yet, here he sobs. He cries so hard that they fear he might choke, his whole body racked with convulsions of grief. The aides swear that, amid his sobs, they hear the emperor groan out the words: "No one will ever know how much I loved her."

★   ★   ★

Emperor Franz Joseph weathers this blow as he has weathered so many blows before it. Days later, he receives the corpse of his murdered wife, the Empress Elisabeth, and oversees arrangements for her state funeral and interment at the Imperial Crypt at Vienna's Capuchin Church. The Habsburgs' "Fairy Queen" makes one final tour along the capital's grand boulevards, this time amid none of the cheer or splendor with which the crowds, as thick as ever, once heralded her passage. As Sisi is laid to rest beside Rudolf, near the space that the emperor knows he'll someday fill, Vienna lowers its flags to half-mast. Black banners are draped over homes, churches, and public buildings. In Budapest and across Hungary, the people sink into a deep and collective melancholy as they mourn the loss of their queen, the most beloved Habsburg to ever sit on their hilltop throne.

Franz Joseph goes on to rule another eighteen years. He ushers in a new century while maintaining the old traditions and ways of life so assiduously defended in his first fifty years of rule. He maintains his staunch allegiance to Germany, but his friendship with Russia falters.

Sixteen years after his wife's murder, when his nephew and heir Archduke Franz Ferdinand is assassinated by the anarchist Gavrilo Princip in Sarajevo, Franz Joseph declares war on Serbia. His ally Germany follows suit by declaring war on Serbia's ally Russia. Russia's allies France and England enter the conflict, and the First World War begins. This war proves to be the most devastating conflict the world has yet witnessed, costing more than sixteen million lives and plunging Europe into decades of economic depression. The scars of this Great War create catastrophic conditions across the globe that give rise to radical social movements, unrest, brutal dictatorships, and eventually the Second World War.

Emperor Franz Joseph, who dies at age eighty-six, does not survive the First World War. Neither does his Habsburg Empire.

AUTHOR'S NOTE ON HISTORY

What an experience this was, diving into the imagined world of an enchanting, elusive, and mercurial empress, one who happens to be beloved the world over. Add to that the company Sisi kept: a dynamic and captivating cast that included the stoic, devoted, and indefatigable emperor; an idealistic and passionate Hungarian count; a tragic, willful, and drug-addicted crown prince; and a tortured dreamer who reigned from atop his Bavarian cliffs amid otherworldly splendor. And that doesn't even begin to touch on the cast of supporting characters.

I've said it so often as a writer of historical fiction: one truly cannot make this stuff up. One need search no further than the pages of history to find the most extraordinary, most inspiring, most delicious and dramatic story material out of which to mold a narrative. With Sisi and her Habsburg world, I felt that that was the case one hundred times over.

Writing this book was an incredibly humbling experience, for many reasons, but particularly because these characters and the events unfolding around them felt so very *big*. This was the stuff of epic: World War I and Strauss waltzes and Disneyesque castles and the golden age of imperial Vienna and an empress who raced horses and grew her legendary hair to the floor — this was a fairy tale meets a Shakespearean tragedy meets a family soap opera meets an international saga.

What cannot be overstated amid all of this drama and grandeur is the impact that these individuals had not only during their own time periods but on the entire course of history. All history books on the Habsburgs should come with the disclaimer "Handle with care." This is heavy, significant, and astonishing material. And it actually happened!

Not one of us can truly know what any of these moments must have felt like, for Sisi or for any of the other characters involved. For over a century now, meticulous and expert (and copious) historians have studied these individuals and events and have stitched together a complex and multipronged narrative, culled from the innumerable sources and perspectives made available throughout the years — letters, diaries, eyewitness accounts, newspaper reports, government documents, and more.

As a writer of historical fiction, it's my great good fortune to be the beneficiary of all of this research and work. The blueprint is there; this history and these individuals become the rich and colorful threads with which to weave my story. With the historical facts and figures as the inspiriting wind at my back, I've charted one imagined course through this material, offering one fictionalized view of how it might have looked and felt to inhabit these scenes. How it might have felt to walk through these rooms with Sisi and experience these moments, scenes simultaneously so grand and so poignantly intimate.

Sisi was an individual who loomed larger than life. Even during her own time, the beloved and controversial empress inspired mythology and legend. Printers spilled incalculable amounts of ink chronicling her comings and goings, her very real trials and her overblown scandals. Crowds turned out by the thousands merely to catch a glimpse of her. Women aspired to dress and fashion their hair à la Sisi. She is one of the rare titans to pass through this world as a relatable and sympathetic mortal while also landing a place alongside the select few whose fates have been forever immortalized in the pantheon of the brightest, most undefinable immortals. How lucky are we, then, as devotees of historical fiction, to get to spend hundreds of pages with her! I could not have asked for a more fascinating, more intriguing, more beguiling leading lady to look to for inspiration.

As this is a work of historical fiction, and as Sisi was a figure who inspired tales of both fact and fable, there were times when, for the purposes of plot and pacing, I fictionalized historical details, utilizing the creative license that is afforded to us lucky novelists. Each instance was the result of much deliberation. Determining when and how to take the liberty that the fiction label allows is probably the biggest challenge for me as a writer of historical fiction and one that I must negotiate anew with each topic and novel and scene I tackle.

That said, I would have been foolish not to rely heavily on the historical facts in building this narrative of Sisi and her incredible life among the Habsburgs. All of the raw material to produce (what I *hope* is) a most compelling novel is already right there in the history books.

Take the character of Crown Prince Rudolf as an example. There, the history constitutes a tragic and true story of a lost soul and a grisly family disaster. Yes, Sisi did in fact intervene when she learned of her young son's abuse by the sadistic military tutor, Count Leopold Gondrecourt. All of the horrifying methods I mention in the novel — Gondrecourt's efforts to "strengthen" the crown prince's "delicate constitution" — were plucked from the history, and so, too, was the wording of Sisi's ultimatum to Franz Joseph: "Gondrecourt goes, or I go." Franz Joseph and Archduchess Sophie saw Gondrecourt's measures as necessary and appropriate, but when Sisi learned from palace aides and staffers about the harsh methods being employed and the boy's resulting health crisis, she intervened and did in fact replace Gondrecourt with Colonel Joseph Latour.

The most troubling moments pertaining to Rudolf throughout this novel are true. He did shoot the wildcat from the zoo in cold blood. Rudolf did fire at and narrowly miss his father while the men were out hunting. Details of the crown prince's opium and alcohol abuse, as well as his notorious philandering, come directly from the historical accounts. So, too, do the details regarding the tension that simmered between father and son, made so much worse by Rudolf printing harsh criticisms of his father in the newspaper. Franz Joseph did have his secret police trail his heir, and he was reported to have erupted at his son at times, apparently overheard by others in the palace as shouting, "You are not worthy to be my successor!" When Rudolf took his own life and the life of his lover Mary Vetsera, he left suicide notes for his mother and sister but not his father.

Also troubling — as well as incredibly frustrating and confounding — was Sisi's apparent refusal to get involved when it became clear just how disturbed her son truly was. After intervening in the young Rudolf's early educational crisis, the empress appears to have remained alarmingly aloof on future matters relating to the prince. She also had virtually no intimate relationship with her elder daughter, Gisela. Whether it was the result of a belief in her own ineffectiveness, a lingering wound from her mother-in-law's initial seizure of the children, her selfishness, her depression, or something else, I cannot know, but I found this aspect of Sisi's character tragic and frustrating. She saw the unhappiness of Rudolf's marriage to Stéphanie, and while she had no shortage of criticisms for her son's bride — some of her statements on that topic in the novel are exact quotes — Sisi never tried to help either of them. She maintained that, unlike her mother-in-law, she would not interfere in their domestic sphere. The heartrending irony of this is that Sisi, more similar to Rudolf than any of the other Habsburgs in her sensitive nature and highly complicated temperament, was perhaps the one person who could have understood, and might have helped, her lost son.

Unfortunately, the scene involving Sisi's callous disregard for Rudolf's gift of Heine letters on her birthday is plucked directly from the history. That night, Sisi was so consumed by the news of her beloved Valerie's engagement to Archduke Franz Salvator that she barely acknowledged her son's extremely thoughtful gesture. Rudolf did in fact break into tears that night, the last Christmas Eve he would spend on this earth.

Marie Larisch's character is hewn directly from the history. Loyal and longtime attendants Ida Ferenczy and Marie Festetics disliked the young woman and bemoaned her presence in the empress's household — a mistrust that would prove tragically prescient when it was discovered that Countess Larisch served as the go-between for Rudolf and Mary Vetsera in their ill-fated trip out to Mayerling to enact their suicide pact. Details of that horrid event are drawn directly from the sources. So, too, are the circumstances after the crown prince's death, such as the initial confusion over what exactly had happened, the efforts by the palace to conceal the news that it had in fact been a suicide, and the proliferation of slanderous reports of Sisi as a deranged mother cradling a pillow and cooing to it as if it were a baby. While Sisi was too bereft to join Valerie and Franz Joseph at the crown prince's state funeral, she did make a solitary midnight pilgrimage to the Imperial Crypt to visit his tomb, as outlined in this novel. And Franz Joseph did stand by his wife, giving her his staunch support when the press and the court criticized the empress during those dark days of mourning.

Sisi was never the same after Rudolf died; in a life filled with much sorrow, this was the blow from which the empress never fully recovered. The son whose troubles Sisi had so often avoided in life became a ghost who remained with her until her own tragic death. I can't help but wonder: How might history have been different if Rudolf had been a more functional and effective member of the Habsburg regime? If he had enjoyed harmonious relationships with his parents and grown into his role in the family? He, who advocated for closeness to England rather than Germany and spoke out for enhanced freedoms and modern reforms and a more liberal society — could he have influenced his father's later politics? Might he have helped avert the Great War, saving millions of lives and preventing global catastrophe? We'll never know, but regardless, we can weep over the dreadful tragedy and the utter waste of it all. I certainly shed many tears over Rudolf and his family and all of the unnecessary and excessive pain.

On the topic of tortured souls, a brief word on the character of King Ludwig of Bavaria is now in order. The details pertaining to Ludwig's castle Neuschwanstein are pulled directly from fact, and I have used many quotes from the king relating to his relation-ship with Richard Wagner, his feuds with his government ministers, his abortive engagement to Sophie-Charlotte, and his thoughts on life, beauty, kingship, and art. Sisi's first trip to Neuschwanstein in this novel is not based on one actual visit made at that exact moment, but Sisi did visit her cousin at his various magnificent castles on multiple occasions. She did find herself caught between her beloved cousin and her jilted younger sister. She did see herself as a sort of kindred spirit to the "Mad King," and she did struggle greatly around the time of his deposition and mysterious death — an event that to this day inspires conspiracy theorists and independent investigations. Sisi believed of her cousin, as she does in this novel, that Ludwig's problem was that he was "not mad enough to be locked up, but too mad to manage comfortably in the world." And reports allege that Sisi did also describe a bizarre dream in which Ludwig appeared to her, soaking wet, in the middle of the night just months before her death, prophesying that she would soon be joining him and another woman (whose description sounded a lot like Sisi's little sister Sophie-Charlotte) in paradise.

With regards to the fractious, troubled relationship between Sisi and her mother-in-law, it is true that Archduchess Sophie interfered in her son's marriage and took the lead in raising Sisi's three older children. Sophie, much more than Sisi, presided over all aspects of life at the Habsburg Court as if she in fact were the rightful empress and matriarch of the family. Sisi's journals and letters make very plain the fact that she saw Sophie as one of the — if not the — primary antagonists in her marriage and family and life at court. But it's also true that Sisi mourned the death of her mother-in-law intensely and spent Sophie's final days keeping a bedside vigil (as she does in this novel) beside the dying woman. I could not help but ask myself: After so much strife and animosity, what softened Sisi's heart toward the old woman in the final hours? Did Sisi realize that there were in fact two sides to this tragic relationship and that perhaps her mother-in-law had had her own worthy motivations for behaving the way she did? And even though this is a novel told from Sisi's perspective, didn't Archduchess Sophie deserve to have her final say, as well?

Those questions gave me the idea to have Sisi come upon Sophie's diary and learn a bit about her rival's intimate thoughts and feelings. The archduchess did in fact fall ill while in the midst of writing at her desk. The quotes I incorporate in Sophie's death scene are plucked directly from the fascinating pages of the woman's diary, as is the intriguing detail that the pages pertaining to Sisi were the pages most marked up and faded in her mother-in-law's journal. Discovering that fact made my heart lurch, and softened me toward the older woman. I don't know if Sisi ever learned these things her mother-in-law thought and wrote about her, but I needed my readers to know this other side of the story. And the fact that Sisi did such a complete about-face, holding a bedside vigil to the point of exhausted collapse, means that she must have known that the archduchess was not simply the evil meddler that Sisi had proclaimed her to be for so much of her life.

Reading the archduchess's moving words about her son and her daughter-in-law certainly made Sophie a more complex and human figure for me. With her final breaths, she expressed her love for her son and her hopes that he'd fulfill his duty, and I was happy to see that she passed away surrounded by both the devoted Franz Joseph and Sisi. That said, though Sisi showed genuine grief at the archduchess's death, she was met at the time (as she is in this novel) with vicious press reports and gossip, stories outlining the empress's selfishness and ineptitude and painfully cataloguing her longtime feud with her more worthy, more capable Habsburg mother-in-law. Any goodwill that might have been Sisi's after she showed such affection at the deathbed was quickly forgotten, and what was remembered was how hostile the relationship had always been.

And Sophie's death wasn't the only time when Sisi found herself lambasted by the Austrian press. The article "The Strange Woman," included in this novel, is taken directly from the papers, as was the anniversary article stating that "twenty-five years that should have been spent in home-making have instead been spent in horseback riding." Count Bellegarde was an outspoken and unapologetic critic of the empress's, as were the powerful adjutants Count Grünne and Count Crenneville.

Sisi did experience moments of unpopularity with the people, as well, often as a result of her frequent and expensive travels away from her husband and her court. The irony of it is this: the more her peers criticized Sisi, say, for traveling, the less inclined she was to remain in Vienna amid (what she perceived to be) a hostile court. An extremely sensitive individual, Sisi, once she suspected even the slightest censure, would hasten to see disapproval and antagonism everywhere, even when it wasn't there. So, criticisms of her travels usually led to further travels. Commentary on her inadequacy as a mother led to further estrangement from her children. Critiques of her vanity prompted her to take further refuge in the familiarity and comfort of her beauty regimens. One could certainly argue that this was a most dysfunctional case of chicken and egg playing out on an imperial stage.

Some of the lighter, more entertaining moments — scenes that seem so outlandish that they must certainly be fiction or, at the very least, embellished — were in fact drawn directly from the history. For instance, in the chapter involving Vienna's World Exposition, the colorful details of the shah's visit come directly from the historical accounts. So, too, do the stories such as the Prince of Wales throwing a chair through the window at the ball, the German empress earning the nickname of "Foghorn," the Russians demanding such intense protocol, and so on. And it was during the World Exposition that Sisi's interest in English fox hunts was first roused, though this was from conversation with the Prince of Wales, not Princess Victoria.

Which brings us to Sisi's time in Great Britain and the blustery, roguish sportsman in the scarlet jacket, Captain Bay Middleton. Bay's critical statements to Lord Spencer before Sisi's arrival to England are direct quotes. So, too, are the facts of his quick change of heart upon beholding Sisi in all of her beauty and equestrian skill. Their chemistry was instantaneous and undeniable. Details of Sisi's rented estates, her hunting experiences, her falls from the mount, the steeplechase, and Bay's prolonged engagement to Charlotte Baird are all taken from history.

The facts of Bay's visit to Hungary, his rivalry with Esterházy, and his raucously disastrous outing to Budapest are also based on the true events, even the tidbit about his being robbed by a prostitute. So, too, are the details about Sisi's tense relationship and visits with Queen Victoria, as well as the controversy generated by Sisi's affection for Ireland and the inadvertent offenses she caused by thinking she could travel incognita. Even the fact that she arrived at Queen Victoria's castle too early, requiring the disgruntled matriarch to leave a church service, is pulled from the history.

I sprinkled in as many amusing historical tidbits as I could, simply because they were so abundant in the record and, I hope, so interesting and informative for readers. The special and top secret "Imperial Fold" of the napkin actually existed — and it was in fact a guarded state secret passed down orally to only several living people at any given time. Clearly, this was a matter of the utmost importance! Details of the rules dictating meal etiquette, such as Franz deciding who might speak, who might serve from which dish and when, and so on, were true as well. The details of Strauss's music and Klimt's artwork and the architecture near and around the Ringstrasse all come directly from the rich and vibrant history. So does the fact that the kaiser of Germany reportedly declared that he couldn't stare at Sisi too long without his passions becoming too inflamed.

And what of our confounding, chimerical, elusive leading lady herself? Sisi was in fact as intelligent, well educated, moody, charming, intrepid, and complex as one would think. She loved and could recite from memory Shakespeare and Heine and ancient Greek epics. Her toilette and dress rituals were as elaborate as I describe them to be; it took hours to wash and style her floor-length hair. The extreme measures to which she went to preserve her legendary beauty are also historically accurate. Sisi was fiercely concerned with her weight and maintaining her youthful physique. She ate sparingly, exercised vigorously, and laced her corset so tightly that when you look at her dresses today, it's staggering to see her dimensions — even after four children.

Sisi was nearly paralyzed with fear over the thought of aging or losing her famously good looks, and she approached her physical self-preservation with the gusto of a scientist seeking a magical anti-aging elixir. I loved walking her former rooms in the Hofburg and in Schönbrunn and seeing her handwritten recipes for different homemade tinctures to nourish her skin and tame her plentiful waves. Perhaps my two favorite boudoir secrets of Sisi's are the facts that she (1) slept with raw veal on her face to fend off wrinkles and (2) hooked a string from her hair to the ceiling to relieve the weight of her copious coif.

In addition to horseback riding, her beauty regimens, and her studies, traveling became one of Sisi's obsessions and favorite diversions. Later in life, Sisi became so manic in her drive to escape and to seek entertainment and to travel that I couldn't possibly include all of the places she actually visited. The book would have turned from a novel into a travel guide, and our heads would be spinning at the itinerant existence she maintained. She traveled everywhere from Amsterdam to Cairo to the most far-flung Greek islands. The details of her sprawling Achilleion villa at Corfu are historically accurate, and so are Franz Joseph's frustrations when Sisi abandoned her new Greek palace so shortly after its completion.

While Sisi was gone on her frequent travels, Katharina Schratt, "the friend," kept Franz Joseph happy by his imperial hearth. As bizarre as it may seem, I have related the circumstances surrounding this three-way relationship as I found them in the history. Franz Joseph first came to admire Katharina Schratt when she played Kate in *The Taming of the Shrew*. Frau Schratt then in fact came to the *Kaiserbund* meeting in Moravia to perform. The Russian tsar became smitten with the young actress, giving her gifts as he does in this novel, and Franz Joseph became visibly jealous. Sisi, detecting her husband's interest, realized that Frau Schratt could be the answer to her and Franz Joseph's marital impasse. Sisi then actively cultivated a relationship with Frau Schratt, making it perfectly clear to both her husband and the actress that Katharina was welcome in their home and in their familial circle. The Katharina Schratt relationship was probably an even bigger deal in real life than I made it in my novel. "The friend" soon had a villa at Bad Ischl adjoining the emperor's Kaiservilla, and Franz Joseph would visit her each morning when he was there. While historians debate whether or not their liaisons had a physical component, what cannot be disputed is the committed, long-term relationship that the two enjoyed, and the deep love they openly expressed toward each other. And the fact that Sisi never displayed even the slightest jealousy over Frau Schratt's daily presence in her husband's life. In fact, it seemed to improve the harmony of the imperial marriage; Franz Joseph's letters to Katharina Schratt burst with declarations of his affection for the actress while also waxing poetic about his unwavering love for his beautiful and elusive wife. As I said — one cannot make this stuff up.

As we marched closer to the tragic day of September 10, 1898, I found myself growing more and more despondent for Sisi and

Franz Joseph. I've outlined the schedule and circumstances of Sisi's last days in Switzerland much as they occurred. She did in fact visit the Countess Rothschild and decline the countess's offer of a private yacht. She did decline a security detail, in spite of repeated warnings that Geneva was rampant with criminal and anarchist activity. It is suspected that someone at or near the Hôtel Beau Rivage leaked the news of Sisi's visit, because the city learned of her presence there in spite of the alias she used. Luigi Luccheni, who had come to town to assassinate France's Duke of Orléans, changed his plans and fixed his blade on Austria-Hungary's empress. Remarkably, Sisi's thick hair did soften her fall, and neither she nor anyone who saw the strike realized that a tiny blade had been stuck into her breast. She and Irma continued onward and boarded the steamer, and Sisi did remark, as she does in the novel, that perhaps the man had been trying to steal her watch. It wasn't until she collapsed on the boat that anyone realized she was bleeding and had been the victim of a stabbing that would soon prove fatal.

In this novel filled with both heartbreak and joy, perhaps nothing moved me more than finding the tenderly prophetic words of Franz Joseph's final note to Sisi: "I commend you to God, my beloved angel." I relayed Franz's grief-stricken reaction to his wife's murder with historical accuracy, because really, it lacked for nothing by way of heartrending and moving detail. The emperor found out about Sisi's death via telegram while working in his study, surrounded by portraits of the woman whom he adored. In spite of it all, Franz Joseph had never stopped worshipping at the altar of Sisi. And now, after all of their separation and heartache, the stoic leader showed unprecedented anguish at learning that the wife he'd longed for and missed for all those years would never return home to him. He railed against God and did in fact demand, "Is nothing to be spared me in this world?" while also murmuring through his tears, "No one will ever know the love we had for one another."

With tears in my own eyes, I sought to conclude the book with some measure of peace and hope, confident that Sisi was at last reunited with those she had loved and lost. Our heroine finally found rest in an afterlife for which she had always hoped and prayed, and, at last, she and Franz Joseph are finally joined together in the perfect harmony that so long evaded them in life.

A NOTE ON SOURCES

Writing this book was an exquisite and life-altering journey for me, and one that involved many literal journeys. I traveled from Budapest to Gödöllő; from Vienna's Schönbrunn and Hofburg palaces to the hills of Salzburg; from Munich to Madeira and beyond. Retracing Sisi's footsteps was the most inspiring way to enter into her world and imagine it as it might have been. I savored so many moments, such as walking up the aisle of her wedding church, looking out her bedroom window over her daily panorama, studying her glimmering dining table and her writing desk, and imagining her seated before her vanity bureau.

I'm so grateful to the countless and remarkable historians and curators and researchers who have kept the imperial residences so well preserved and who honor these deceased Habsburg icons by allowing us to see their world as they themselves inhabited it. So, too, do I owe a debt of gratitude to all those scholars who have labored over countless newspapers, journals, letters, and eyewitness accounts, those who have translated and distilled and breathed life into Sisi's original thoughts and words and experiences.

The scholarly work on Sisi and the Habsburgs is boundless and rich and worth exploring. In addition to my trips to the imperial residences and my conversations with historians there, I relied exclusively on nonfiction accounts, all of which came with extensive bibliographies and source references. I thank these talented historians for making my job one of pure delight and inspiring discovery. While this list is by no means exhaustive, readers who are interested in learning more about this extraordinary empress's life might enjoy any of the following:

A Nervous Splendor: Vienna 1888–1889 by Frederic Morton

Empress Elisabeth of Austria 1837–1898 by Renate Hofbauer

Fin-de-Siècle Vienna: Politics and Culture by Carl E. Schorske

Franz Joseph and Elisabeth: The Last Great Monarchs of Austria-Hungary by Karen Owens

The Fall of the House of Habsburg by Edward Crankshaw

The Habsburg Monarchy, 1809–1918 by A. J. P. Taylor

The Lonely Empress: Elizabeth of Austria by Joan Haslip

The Reluctant Empress: A Biography of Empress Elisabeth of Austria by Brigitte Hamann

The Sporting Empress: The Story of Elizabeth of Austria and Bay Middleton by John Welcome

The Swan King: Ludwig II of Bavaria by Christopher McIntosh

Twilight of the Habsburgs: The Life and Times of Emperor Francis Joseph by Alan Palmer

ACKNOWLEDGMENTS

While writing is typically a solitary venture, the process of actually turning that *writing* into a *book* is anything but. I am so thankful to the many people who helped bring *Sisi* to life.

Special thanks go to my literary agent Lacy Lynch and the team at Dupree Miller & Associates; my editor, Kara Cesare, as well as Susan Kamil, Avideh Bashirrad, Leigh Marchant, Sally Marvin, Nina Arazoza, Allyson Pearl, Gina Centrello, Loren Noveck, and the entire team at The Dial Press and Random House; Lindsay Mullen, Katie Nuckolls, Alyssa Conrardy, and the whole Prosper Strategies crew; and to Beth Adams, Jonathan Merkh, Carolyn Reidy, and everyone at Simon & Schuster/Howard Books, I thank you for beginning this journey with me and continuing to be invaluable partners.

To the numberless historians, curators, translators, and biographers who have excavated Sisi from history and have allowed her to come to life in my imagination: my words will never be sufficient to express how deep my gratitude runs.

And of course to my parents, my siblings, my in-laws, my treasured friends: each one of you has supported and encouraged, nourishing not only my passion for Sisi but for life and for writing and telling stories.

And to my husband, best friend, and cocreator, Dave: you inspire me every single day. I could not imagine life's journey without you beside me.

ABOUT THE AUTHOR

Allison Pataki is the author of the bestselling novels *The Traitor's Wife* and *The Accidental Empress.* The daughter of former New York State governor George E. Pataki, she was inspired to write about Sisi thanks to her family's deep roots in the former Habsburg Empire of Austria-Hungary. Pataki is the cofounder of the nonprofit organization ReConnect Hungary. She graduated cum laude from Yale University with a major in English and is a regular contributor to *The Huffington Post,* as well as a member of the Historical Novel Society. She lives in Chicago with her husband and their daughter.

allisonpataki.com
Facebook.com/AllisonPatakiPage
@AllisonPataki